International Conference on Applied Computing 2022 and WWW/Internet 2022

AA005032

Lisbon, Portugal
8-10 November 2022

ISBN: 978-1-7138-6379-3

Printed from e-media with permission by:

Curran Associates, Inc.
57 Morehouse Lane
Red Hook, NY 12571

Some format issues inherent in the e-media version may also appear in this print version.

Printed with permission by Curran Associates, Inc. (2023)

For permission requests, please contact International Association for Development of the Information Society (IADIS) at the address below.

International Association for Development of the Information Society (IADIS)
Rua Sao Sebastiao Da Pedreira
No. 100, 30, 1050-209
Lisbon, Portugal

Phone: 351 21 3151373
Fax: 351 21 3151244

secretariat@iadis.org

Additional copies of this publication are available from:

Curran Associates, Inc.
57 Morehouse Lane
Red Hook, NY 12571 USA
Phone: 845-758-0400
Fax: 845-758-2633
Email: curran@proceedings.com
Web: www.proceedings.com

TABLE OF CONTENTS

FULL PAPERS

PROSPECTS FOR THE IMPLEMENTATION OF HEURISTIC ALGORITHMS FROM THE EVOLUTIONARY COMPUTING AS NEW EXPERIMENTAL APPROACHES IN SYNTHETIC BIOLOGY: IN SILICO TESTS 3
Alexander Spirov, Ekaterina Myasnikova

DEEP LEARNING APPROACH TO CLASSIFYING SOLAR RADIO BURSTS 13
Herman le Roux, Günther Richard Drevin, Roelf Du Toit Strauss, Petrus Johannes Steyn

TORUS-CONNECTED TOROIDS: AN INTERCONNECTION NETWORK FOR MASSIVELY PARALLEL SYSTEMS 21
Antoine Bossard

MULTIPLE INHERITANCE MECHANISMS IN LOGIC OBJECTS APPROACH BASED ON A MULTIPLE SPECIALISATION OF OBJECTS 29
Macaire Ngomo

SUNSPOT DETECTION USING DEEP LEARNING TECHNIQUES 39
Pieter Swanepoel, Günther Richard Drevin, Roelf Du Toit Strauss, Petrus Johannes Steyn

FIRST SYCL IMPLEMENTATION OF THE THREE-DIMENSIONAL SUBSURFACE XCA-FLOW CELLULAR AUTOMATON AND PERFORMANCE COMPARISON AGAINST CUDA 47
Donato D'Ambrosio, Giovanni Terremoto, Alessio De Rango, Luca Furnari, Alfonso Senatore, Giuseppe Mendicino

ENHANCED FEATURE EXTRACTION USING OPTIMAL WHITENING AND STACKED AUTOENCODERSArchana Mathur, Akarsha Paralkar, P.J.S.A. Kumar 55

IDENTIFYING AND CHARACTERIZING CONCEPTS IN UNSTRUCTURED TEXTS USING AUTOMATIC ANNOTATION 63
Tiago Fraga, Orlando Belo, Anabela Barros

GAMIFIED VR SIMULATION IN NURSING EDUCATION: HOW TO GENERATE VALUE WITH VR IN NURSING EDUCATION 71
Roger Seiler, Ruben Straumann, Christian Weber, Andreas Block

ONTOLOGY MODEL FOR SMART OPEN LEARNING ENVIRONMENT BASED ON COPUTATIONAL THINKING 79
Bènène Fradi, Lilia Cheniti-Belcadhi

VR IN NURSING EDUCATION- HIGH-FIDELITY VS LOW-FIDELITY IMPLEMENTATIONS 87

EVALUATION OF DATA OPTIMAL STORAGE SYSTEM IN HYBRID CLOUD 95
Miho Imazaki, Satoshi Kaneko, Norihisa Komoda, Takenao Ohkawa

E-MONEY SECURITY DILEMMA: ADVANCED CYBERSECURITY MECHANISMS AND LEGACY MOBILE PAYMENTS IN SUB-SAHARAN AFRICA 103
Fabrice Neza, Anthony Joseph, Mary Joseph

SUPERVISED LEARNING BASED APPROACH FOR TURBOFAN ENGINES FAILURE PROGNOSIS WITHIN THE BELIEF FUNCTION FRAMEWORK 115
Rachid Hamza, Safa Ben Ayed

SUNSPOT DETECTION AND TRACKING USING IMAGE PROCESSING TECHNIQUES 123
Ruben du Toit, Gunther Richard Drevin and Roelf Du Toit Strauss

HIDROUFF DENSITY CALCULATOR: AN OPEN-SOURCE SOFTWARE FOR PREDICTING DENSITY OF COMPLEX MIXTURES USING PENG-ROBINSON EQUATION OF STATE 131
Valesca Moura de Sousa, Felipe Pereira de Moura, Mateus Pereira de Sousa, Rogério Fernandes Lacerda, Fernanda G. O. Passos

DESIGN AND IMPLEMENTATION OF A CHATBOT AS A TOOL TO ASSIST A HELPDESK TEAM 139
Diogo Pinto Ribeiro, Ana Anjo, Pedro Rangel Henriques

HMEDASYS: HOME MEDICATION INTAKE ALERT SYSTEM 148
Jardson Rodrigues, Christophe Soares, Pedro Sobral, Rui S. Moreira and José M. Torres

FROM PRACTICE TO SCIENCE: SOCIAL REACTIONS CAUSED BY CONVERSATIONAL AGENTS—A LITERATURE REVIEW FOR RESEARCHERS AND PRACTITIONERS 156
Sophie Hundertmark, Hans-Georg Fill, Edy Portmann

A STEP CLOSER TO UNDERSTANDING IMPLEMENTATION OF BUSINESS INTELLIGENCE IN THE ORGANIZATIONAL OPERATIONS: A SYSTEMATIC LITERATURE REVIEW 165
Ljerka Luic, Neva Babic, Ante Roncevic

MULTIVARIANT ANALYSIS IN VIDEO AD MARKETING CAMPAIGNS FOR WEB TRAFFIC QUALITY OPTIMIZATION 173
Marta López, Fernando Perales

CLASSIFICATION OF FINANCIAL MARKETS INFLUENCERS ON TWITTER 181
Inês Almeida, André Sabino

SHORT PAPERS

COVID19: INTELLIGENT CHATBOT AND FINANCIAL AID APPLICATION 191
Kenza Douifir, Naoual Chaouni Benabdellah, Ali Idri

ENHANCING TYPE SYSTEMS WITH FIRST-CLASS PATTERNS 196
Lutz Hamel, Timothy Colaneri, Oliver McLaughlin

INTELLIGENT SEMANTIC BASED FRAMEWORK FOR PERSONALIZED REHABILITATION TO CHILDREN WITH CEREBRAL PALSY 201
Rahma Haouas Zahwanie, Lilia Cheniti-Belcadhi and Saoussen Layouni

EXCHANGING PERSONAL DATA THROUGH BLOCKCHAIN TECHNOLOGY TO FULFIL INCREASING PRIVACY NEEDS 207
Petrus J. Roos and Henri E. van Rensburg

PROMOTING CYBERSECURITY AWARENESS UTILIZING A "BUILD YOUR OWN ADVENTURE" SERIOUS GAME 212
Christo Croucamp, Gunther Drevin, and Dirk Snyman

USE OF YOLOV5 OBJECT DETECTION ALGORITHMS FOR INSECT DETECTION 217
Lino Oliveira, Margarida Victoriano, Adilia Alves and José Pereira

STATE-OF-THE-ART ANALYSIS OF ARTIFICIAL INTELLIGENCE APPROACHES IN THE MARITIME INDUSTRY 222
Christos Kontzinos, Ioanna Kanellou, Vasilis Michalakopoulos, Spiros Mouzakitis, Giannis Tsapelas, Panagiotis Kapsalis, Giorgos Kormpakis and Dimitris Askounis

ESTABLISHING CYBERSECURITY AWARENESS OF TECHNICAL SECURITY MEASURES THROUGH A SERIOUS GAME 227
Jaden Harding, Dirk Snyman,, Gunther Drevin

A QUALITATIVE STUDY ON THE PERCEIVED DRIVERS OF THE DIGITAL DIVIDE IN A DEVELOPING COUNTRY 232
Ayanda Magida, Brian Armstrong

A PROOF OF CONCEPT: CYBERSECURITY LEARNING CONTENT IN LTI BASED, EDUCATIONAL SYSTEMS 237
Ehm Kannegieser, Sergius Dyck, Daniel Atorf

A CASE STUDY FOR ANALYSIS AND PREDICTION IN LEARNING USING A PEER LEARNING SYSTEM 241
Adelina Aleksieva-Petrova, Milen Petrov

CO-CREATING ICT SOLUTIONS TO AID MIGRANT INTEGRATION: LESSONS LEARNED FROM THE H2020 MIICT PROJECT 247
Karen Latricia Hough, Babak Akhgar

THE LEGAL UNCERTAINTY ASPECT OF THE REGULATORY APPROACH REGARDING ONLINE CONTENT MODERATION 253
Eduardo Helfer de Farias, Gabriel Rached

EXPLORING CLOUD COMPUTING PREVALENCE FOR COMPETITIVE ADVANTAGE IN ONLINE PUBLICATION PLATFORMS 257
Tendani J. Lavhengwa

REFLECTIONS

INFORMATION SYSTEMS INFRASTRUCTURE DEVELOPMENT – ROAD AHEAD 265
Seppo J. Sirkemaa

AI ADOPTION IN HEALTHCARE: TRUST AND PRIVACY CONCERNS 269
Mousa Albashrawi

FULL PAPERS

PROSPECTS FOR THE IMPLEMENTATION OF HEURISTIC ALGORITHMS FROM THE EVOLUTIONARY COMPUTING AS NEW EXPERIMENTAL APPROACHES IN SYNTHETIC BIOLOGY: IN SILICO TESTS

Alexander Spirov[1] and Ekaterina Myasnikova[2]
[1]*The Institute of Scientific Information for Social Sciences RAS, Moscow, Russia*
[2]*Peter the Great St. Petersburg Polytechnic University, St. Petersburg, Russia*

ABSTRACT

In vitro evolution ("evolution in a test tube", directed evolution) is a modern technology used in bioengineering that mimics the process of natural selection to direct proteins or nucleic acids to acquire a specific function. One of the most promising directions in the development of modern technologies for the evolution of macromolecules in vitro is the use of microdroplet devices based on the principles of microfluidics. A significant increase in the efficiency and cost reduction of in vitro evolution approaches can be achieved through the development and analysis of new heuristic evolutionary algorithms. This goal is achieved by numerical tests on computer models of real molecular genetic experiments (in silico experiments). This work was inspired by our recent key observation that many heuristic evolutionary algorithms can be associated with new engineering solutions for the modules of such microfluidic devices. Here, we have proposed and simulated new approaches to in vitro evolution with the prospect of their implementation in experimental microfluidic setups. In this report, we have demonstrated in our in silico experiments that some algorithms that have proven themselves in evolutionary computing turn out to be significantly more efficient than those algorithms that model the routine approaches of modern microdroplet microfluidics. Prospects for the implementation of such promising algorithms in new experimental approaches are discussed.

KEYWORDS

Evolutionary Algorithms, Computational Biology, Selection Techniques, Hill-Climbing, Biomolecular Experiments in Silico, Algorithms Implementation in Bioengineering

1. INTRODUCTION

In vitro evolution ("evolution in a test tube", directed evolution) is a modern bioengineering technology that mimics the process of natural selection in directing proteins or nucleic acids to acquire a desired function (Darmostuk et al., 2015; Vorobyeva et al., 2018; Komarova, Kuznetsov, 2019). One of the most promising directions in the development of modern technologies for the in vitro evolution of macromolecules is the use of microdroplet devices based on the microfluidics principles (Griffiths, Tawfik, 2006; Paegel, Joyce, 2010). A significant increase in the efficiency and cost reduction of in vitro evolution approaches can be achieved through the development and analysis of new heuristic evolutionary algorithms.

Design of any new modern technology should begin with a numerical study of its promising engineering solutions (i.e. Komarova & Kuznetsov, 2019; Voigt et al., 2002), and this is the goal of our article. This approach can significantly increase the efficiency of very, very expensive and resource-intensive experiments.

1.1 Basics and Perspectives of in Vitro Evolution

Macromolecular devices (molecular devices) of modern synthetic biology are able to highly selectively identify (and specifically bind) various target molecules in order to perform certain functions (e.g. Famulok et al., 2007; Trausch, Batey, 2015). For example, they can test a certain chemical agent in the environment and trigger the fluorescence, thereby quantitatively indicating the presence of the agent in the environment (environmental applications). Another example from biomedicine: such devices can highly-specifically recognize and bind to the specific targets on the surface of certain cancer cells specifically killing them and only them. Molecular devices are synthesized from nucleic acids (DNA and RNA) and proteins.

Molecular devices are typically synthesized experimentally by methods of directed evolution (in vitro evolution; reviewed in Spirov, Myasnikova, 2022a; Spirov, Myasnikova, 2022b). In this approach, an initial "population" is formed from macromolecules, usually of a given length, completely or partially randomized in sequence. Then molecules with a certain (desired) function are selected. The best molecules are copied (the rest are discarded) with mutations being introduced in copies, thereby restoring the population size. In the population of daughter individuals, the best ones are again selected for the desired function, and they again multiply with mutations. Such cycles are repeated until the desired fully functional molecular device is achieved.

Despite the perceived promise of in vitro evolution applications, experimenters are only at the beginning of the road to developing robust, efficient, and cost-effective methods for obtaining desired or required molecular devices.

1.2 Microfluidics for in Vitro Evolution

Experimental microdroplet microfluidics approaches to the directed evolution of biological macromolecules (nucleic acids and proteins) have been extensively developed over the past couple of decades (see, for example, Trausch and Batey, 2015; Price and Paegel, 2016). The fundamental novelty of microdroplet microfluidics methods is that evolutionary search and key experimental procedures are carried out at the level of individual sequences – each sequence in its own microdroplet (e.g. Griffiths, Tawfik, 2006; Paegel, Joyce, 2010; Ryckelynck et al., 2015).

On the other hand, microdroplet microfluidics has its limitations. It is costly and resource intensive and typically manipulates sequence libraries several orders of magnitude less than older approaches. This range of problems brings to the fore the search and testing of new approaches that have the potential of making evolutionary search more efficient (Spirov, Myasnikova, 2022a; Spirov and Myasnikova, 2022b).

1.3 Numerical Analysis of New Prospective Approaches (in Silico Experiments)

Many experimental researchers in the field of in vitro evolution systematically emphasize the importance and promise of preliminary numerical tests of the problems that experimenters have to solve (e.g. Voigt et al., 2002; Komarova & Kuznetsov, 2019; Spirov, Myasnikova, 2022a; Spirov, Myasnikova, 2022b). So, in silico tests should precede costly and resource-intensive real experiments, determining the choice of specific methods, the choice of parameters, as well as an assessment of the chances of success.

1.3.1 Transfer of Algorithms from the Evolutionary Computing

It is important that the field of evolutionary computations is a source of those methods and algorithms that could be used as numerical models of new experimental approaches in microdroplet microfluidics (Spirov, Myasnikova, 2022a; Spirov, Myasnikova, 2022b).

This approach is a clear example of the interdisciplinarity synergy, where the development of biotechnology is impossible without computational support, which, in turn, would not be feasible without the vast experience accumulated in the field of EC in computer science. Moreover, evolutionary algorithms were originally developed as a computational implementation of the evolutionary processes occurring in nature, while nowadays there is an increasing back transfer of ideas from computational theory to synthetic biology and biotechnology. It is this reverse transfer of algorithms from computer science to biology that we are going to implement (O'Hagan, Knowles, Kell, 2012; Eremeev, Spirov, 2021; Myasnikova, Spirov, 2021; Spirov, Myasnikova, 2022a; Spirov, Myasnikova, 2022b).

Our purpose is to study the effectiveness of a number of techniques and algorithms that are developed, well-researched, and well-proven in the field of EC by large-scale numerical experiments. Accordingly, these techniques and algorithms could have prospects for being implemented in experimental approaches to the in vitro evolution of biological macromolecules.

2. NEW ALGORITHMS WITH PROSPECTS FOR IMPLEMENTATION

As noted above, a clear advantage of microdroplet microfluidics is that it provides the possibility to manipulate individual molecules. This is despite the fact that today's standard microfluidics procedures in in vitro evolution are very primitive and, with rare exceptions, have not been even comparable with evolutionary computational approaches. Below we will briefly review those algorithms that may be promising for their implementation in experimental biology.

2.1 Selection in Evolutionary Computing

In EC, a number of selection techniques defining the proportion of individuals transferred from the parent population to the child one has been widely studied on standard tests and on real-life problems (Holland, 1975; Goldberg, 1989). The most well-known of these techniques are listed in Table 1.

Table 1. The best-known selection schemes in EC

Selection in evolutionary computing
Proportionate selection (roulette method). The probability for an individual to be selected is proportional to its fitness value (the value of objective function). **Tournament selection**. Initially, a given number of individuals is randomly selected (usually two), and then we pick an individual with the best fitness value. **Rank selection**. The selection probability depends on the place in the list of individuals, sorted by the fitness value. **Uniform rank selection** is a random choice. **Sigma truncation**. The fitness function is linearly transformed and scaled by its standard deviation in the parent population to prevent the premature convergence of evolutionary search.

Moreover, more general breeding strategies (we will use this term) have been widely researched and applied. Selection strategies determine whether the original individuals from the parent population are transferred to the daughter one and according to what rules. We will specifically focus on the elitism strategy.

The elitist strategy is to protect the best individuals in subsequent iterations. In a classical genetic algorithm, the fittest individuals do not always go on to the next generation. An elitist strategy is used to prevent the loss of such an individual. This individual is guaranteed to be included in the new population.

In general, the routine functioning scheme of the microfluidic device for in vitro evolution resembles the evolutionary algorithm (μ,λ) from EC. This selection method will be described in detail below. More complex procedures and algorithms (with rare exceptions) have not been considered in experimental biology.

2.2 Hill-Climbing Algorithms

Among hill-climbing algorithms, a simple random-mutation hill-climbing (RMHC) turned out to be one of the most effective for a number of benchmark problems as well as those of real-life (Mitchell, 1998).

2.2.1 The Random-Mutation Hill-Climbing (RMHC) Algorithm

This algorithm, proposed back in the early 90s, can be interpreted as a simplified version of the annealing method (namely, the Metropolis method at zero temperature) (Forrest, Mitchell, 1993; Mitchell, 1998). The procedure is aimed at maximization of objective (fitness) function and includes the following steps:

1. Choose a sequence of a given length at random.
2. Mutate each sequence position with the given probability.
3. If mutation results in an equal or higher fitness, then the current sequence is re-placed by the mutated one.
4. Go to step 2.
5. Repeat 2-4 until the optimal value of the fitness function is reached. Return the cur-rent sequence.

We note here that despite it is easy to implement a simple hill-climber on a computer, its experimental implementation using microdroplet microfluidics seems to be very cumbersome and inefficient. However, microfluidics may enable the implementation of parallel versions of hill-climbing algorithms.

2.2.2 Parallel Version of RMHC

In the parallel version, we simultaneously run N (up to several hundred) RMHC processes in parallel (with the same population size in each RMHC). At the same time, as soon as a more efficient solution is found in any of the populations, this finding is immediately copied to all the rest populations. It is in this sense that we consider each of these hundreds of RMHC procedures to be (semi-)autonomous: they are parallel and independent until one of the RMHC procedures finds a better solution.

2.3 Crossover Algorithms

In EC, crossover (recombination) has always been given great importance, so it is quite common to expect that these procedures are critical to evolutionary search and typically should enhance the role of mutations (see Holland, 1975). Therefore, in this article, we also systematically test the role of crossover in evolutionary search for our test problems.

It should also be noted that in experimental biology there are also very high expectations regarding the role of the crossover in in vitro evolution (Stemmer, 1994; Voigt et al., 2002).

3. NUMERICAL ANALYSIS OF NEW PROSPECTIVE APPROACHES (IN SILICO EXPERIMENTS)

In this section, we numerically explore those new evolutionary search schemes inspired by known EC heuristic algorithms that could be performed by new microfluidic devices.

For our numerical studies, we offer our original benchmark tests inspired by real-life problems of in vitro evolution.

3.1 New Real-Life Problems Require New Benchmark Tests

For this project, we have developed a new version of our test problems as a modification and extension of our original BioRS fitness functions (formulated in our publications Myasnikova, Spirov, 2021; Spirov, Myasnikova, 2022a).

3.1.1 Test Problem with Several Local Extrema

At first step, we generalize a single-domain (instead of multi-domain) version of BioRS (Myasnikova, Spirov, 2021; Spirov, Myasnikova, 2022a), which is based on the consensus of a specific aptamer to adenosine and some of its derivatives, known as the Sasanfar-Szostak aptamer (Sassanfar and Szostak, 1993). To make the problem realistic enough for this project (to get as close as possible to real life problems), we modify the search space in the following way. In addition to the Sasanfar-Szostak target consensus, the algorithm is able to find one (or several) other consensuses with sufficiently high levels of fitness. They represent local extrema in sequence space, but are not the goal of our numerical evolutionary experiments. The presence of several (or even many) local extrema, where the evolutionary search tends to get stuck, is a well-known problem in EC. This problem is also recognized when analyzing the results of real molecular biological experiments on the evolution of macromolecules in vitro. Specifically, in the case of aptamer sequences to adenosine and close sequences, many sequences have been obtained and characterized, differing not only in minor substitutions (and/or insertions, deletions, indels), but also qualitatively different (reviewed in Spirov, Myasnikova, 2022a).

As in the case of the Royal Road functions (Forrest, Mitchell, 1993; Mitchell, 1998), the fitness function is given by a series of sequences in the four-letter alphabet of nucleic acids. As a global extremum, we are looking for a consensus with five uniquely defined positions (out of 26 in total), nine two-valued positions, and three complementary pairs (the remaining six positions are arbitrary). At the same time, it is precisely due to the two-valued positions that the growth of the fitness level is ensured: one of the two values in each case gives an additional increase (delta) when approaching the consensus. Details are shown in Figure 1.

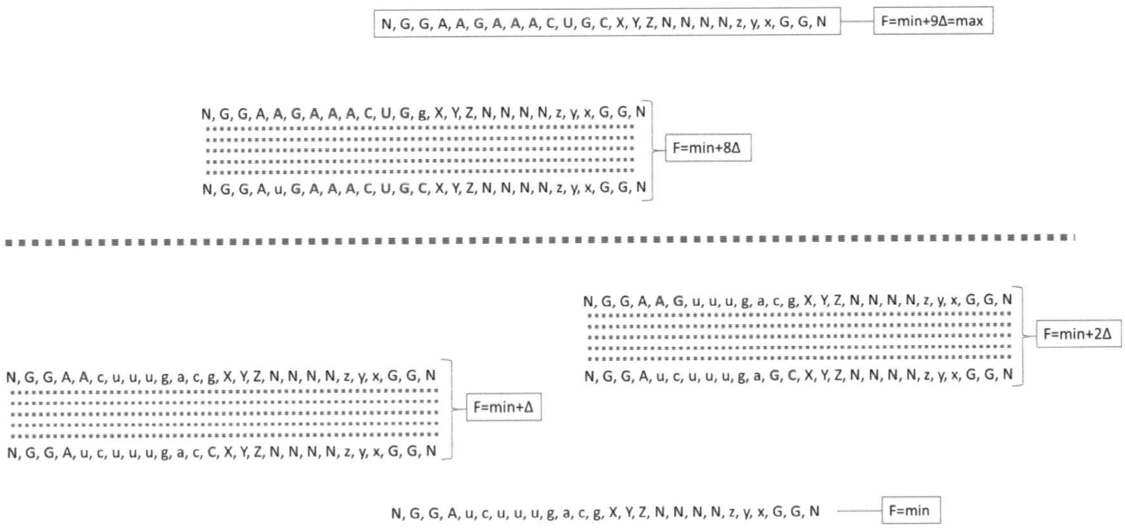

Figure 1. A family of sequences (26 characters long) in the RNA alphabet (A,T,G,U) that have a non-zero fitness level in our test problem. The family naturally breaks down into 10 groups. This is the lowest fitness sequence (Fitness=min), then eight groups with fitness levels from F=min+Δ to F=min+8Δ, and, finally, the sequence (consensus sequence) with the maximum fitness F=min+9Δ. N is arbitrary letter; X-x, Y-y, Z-z are complementary pairs. See text for further details

Further, local extrema (one or more) are characterized by only two complementary pairs, which provides a slightly higher efficiency of finding them compared to the consensus of the global extremum. Additionally, by definition, the global extremum consensus has a slightly higher level of (maximum) fitness (see Figure 1).

In arbitrary units of our tests, the finding of the minimally required Sasanfar-Szostak aptamer sequence yields 100 units (minimal fitness; Figure 1). Finding each preferred position from a set of nine two-valued positions yields an increment of delta each time ($\Delta = 8$). So, the global maximum has a fitness of 172. For local maxima, formally similar, we set $\Delta = 4$, so that one local extremum ends up with a fitness of 140 and another one of 136. All of our tests below are done on this particular version of our problem.

3.2 (μ,λ) Selection as Control in Numerical Experiments

Literature analysis in the field of in vitro evolution by means of microdroplet microfluidics leads us to the conclusion that selection above a certain fitness threshold level used as a control is sufficient formalization of a routine real experiment (compare Oh, Lee, McKay, 2011; Lee et al., 2011; Spirov, Myasnikova, 2022a). Typically, this threshold is quite low. In this case, the selected parental individuals are copied so as to achieve the required size of the child population. In copying a parent into the daughter population point mutations are introduced into the parent sequence. This is in line with experimental techniques used in in vitro evolution. Typically, this is the multiplication of nucleic acid molecules by an error-prone PCR (Lee et al., 2011; Spirov, Myasnikova, 2022a). At the same time, in the first approximation, it is reasonable to assume that all selected individuals are copied in the same proportion (they give approximately, on average, the same number of descendants to the daughter population, regardless of their fitness level). Further, the process of multiplying of a selected part of individuals by error-prone polymerase chain reaction (until a given population size is restored) can rather be interpreted as selection without elitism, because multiple copying of an original parental molecule is likely to result in mutating all copies of the original parental sequence.

Therefore, in the EC paradigm, the closest thing to real microfluidic experiments on in vitro evolution will be the (μ,λ) selection scheme without elitism. Three parameters of control tests are critical in terms of performance: mutation rate, μ/λ threshold (stringency of selection), and population size. It is essential that the efficiency depends on all three parameters, and when any of them changes, the rest must be selected for the highest search efficiency.

3.2.1 Effect of Mutation Rate in Control Tests

The level of mutagenesis is certainly one of the key factors both in EC and in vitro evolution. As it turned out, for our test problem, efficiency is the most sensitive to the mutation rate, while search speed is less dependent. As the mutation rate increases, the efficiency rapidly increases, reaching a maximum at Mmut=7, and then decreases. At the mutation rate Mmut=7, the efficiency reaches 68%. The speed of evolutionary search is gradually decreasing. The result is presented in Table 2.

Table 2. The efficiency of evolutionary search grows rapidly with the increase in the mutation rate, and then rapidly decreases; while the rate of evolutionary search decreases with increasing mutation rate (averaged over 400 runs; population size 4000, μ/λ 0.25)

Mmut	Average	StDev	Efficacy
3	197794.11	98192.81	47
5	193524.76	87847.11	58.25
7	206645.05	86566.50	68.25
9	229069.70	83337.71	60.25
11	273755.92	77253.41	32

Accordingly, based on the results of Table 2, we will take MMut=7 in subsequent tests (unless otherwise specified).

3.2.2 Effect of Parameter μ/λ Value (Proportion of Parent Population) in Control Tests

The μ/λ parameter is the key to this selection scheme and it determines the rigorousness of the selection. The search efficiency is also quite sensitive to the μ/λ parameter, comparable to the sensitivity to the mutation rate. The results are shown in Table 3.

Table 3. Effect of parameter μ/λ value on the evolutionary search (averaged over 400 runs)

Quote (μ/λ)	Average	StDev	Efficacy
5	149739.55	102762.22	70.5
10	145510.05	98499.62	66.5
25	206645.05	86566.50	68.25
40	212066	57795.55	2.5

We will typically use $\mu/\lambda = 25$ in subsequent tests for this problem (unless otherwise noted). We take such a fairly high quota in order to avoid strict selection (it can be seen from the table that with a lower quota (5 - 10%), evolutionary search is better for this our control).

3.2.3 Effect of Population Size in Control Tests

We have found out that a population of a few thousand individuals is already sufficient for a successful evolutionary search for our test problems. The results of the runs are shown in Table 4. It can be seen that in the range of 1 - 6 thousand, the efficiency is kept at about 70%. while the search rate increases with the population size.

Table 4. Effect of the population size on the evolutionary search (averaged over 400 runs)

Popul	Average	StDev	Efficacy
1000	181957.71	126089.09	71.25
2000	188256.92	114757.72	67.75
4000	206645.05	86566.50	68.25
6000	265339.69	107695.56	69.5

We will usually use Popul-4000 in subsequent tests for this problem (unless otherwise noted).

Thus, in the series of runs, we eventually established the ranks of the values of the main parameters at which our tests in control are sufficiently effective to be able to perform a large series of various runs in a reasonable time on a workstation (usually several hours on a DELL Precision M6700). It is with these controls that we will compare all other numerical experiments (with different selection schemes).

3.3 Sigma Truncation vs (μ,λ) Selection (without Crossover)

Sigma truncation (Table 1) refers to selection schemes aimed at preventing premature search convergence to local extrema. In general, it can be interpreted as one of the extreme variants of proportional selection, when individuals with greater fitness leave more offspring. But unlike proportional selection, with sigma truncation, even the most successful parents leave no more than few (usually, two) offspring.

Our tests have shown that sigma selection for our test problem compared to (μ,λ) control speeds up evolutionary search. The speed almost doubles (from 207k to 117k), but the efficiency decreases slightly (from 68 to 64%), as Table 5 illustrates.

Table 5. Sigma selection speeds up the evolutionary search but does not increase its efficiency (averaged over 400 runs)

Mmut	Average	StDev	Efficacy
5	129941,727272727	100482,81351216	55
7	130137,358974359	100002,344373163	58,5
9	128855,558951965	103550,825865692	57,25
11	117341,53125	107049,314391733	64
13	109978,368	99123,6004949845	62,5

This result is somewhat discouraging, if we take into account how much attention in the theory and practice of EC is paid to the problems of premature convergence of solutions and methods to avoid this. And it is sigma-truncation that is considered effective for overcoming such search difficulties. Below we will see that for these purposes it is also necessary to add a crossover to the sigma truncation.

3.4 Tournament Selection Is Ineffective in Our Tests

Our tests have shown that for our problem (and in the parameter ranges considered in this publication), tournament selection is practically inefficient. We tested tournament teams of 2 and 4 individuals, intermediate parent population sizes (obtained as a result of tournament selection) from 10 to 35%, and mutation rates from 1 to 22.

3.5 Parallel RMHC Is the Best

The simple RMHC algorithm classified as (1+1)EA (discussed above) turns out to be one of the most efficient and fastest algorithms for a number of real life and test problems. In the tests with our benchmark problems, we also made sure of the impressive efficiency of the parallel version of this algorithm.

This version of the parallel RMHC with explicit parallelization into many (partially) autonomous (1+1)EA processes (as described above) shows both a clear evolutionary search acceleration (from 207k to 110 k) and an increase in search efficiency (from 68% to 86%), when parallelized into several hundred (semi) autonomous processes. These results are illustrated in Table 6.

Table 6. Parallel version of RMHC is faster and more efficient than standard (μ,λ) for our test problem in the series of tests with the increase of (semi)autonomous processes (averaged over 400 runs)

PopNmb	Average	StDev	Efficacy
100	112857.36	104658.83	64.5
200	113591.66	99321.62	84
400	124260.46	106594.49	86
600	110720.93	99237.41	86

Thus, the parallel RMHC turns out to be the fastest and most efficient evolutionary search procedure for our test problems. Therefore, we are ready to recommend it in the first place for implementation in real microfluidic devices (see the section 4).

3.6 Elitism Improves the (μ,λ) Selection

Elitism is applicable to all selection schemes discussed in this publication. As we will see, in several cases it demonstrates its efficiency for our test problems.

So, elitism for (μ,λ) selection increases both the speed of evolutionary search and efficiency. The speed increases by about one and a half times (162k versus 207k), while the efficiency increases from 68% to 77%, as illustrated by Table 7.

Table 7. Elitism in the (μ,λ) selection increases both the speed of evolutionary search and its efficiency (averaged over 400 runs)

QuotElit	Average	StDev	Efficacy
20	161095.66	83746.31	71.25
25	162164.10	86163.91	77
50	152675.13	74108.08	70.25
75	148118.99	63452.31	56

The fact that elitism supports a simple (μ,λ) selection scheme suggests that this technique should be implemented in in vitro evolution. In other words, it is possible to propose procedures for transferring the best part of the parent population to the child population into the schemes of real biological experiments. The implementation of elitism in the approaches of real microfluidic experiments requires some modifications of the experimental schemes (and/or microfluidic device), and we will discuss this in the section 4.

3.7 Crossover Enhances Evolutionary Search

As might be expected from the structure of our benchmark test (obvious three-modality of the search space), the crossover enhances evolutionary search.

3.7.1 Crossover in (μ,λ) Selection

For our test problem with (μ,λ) selection, we used a scheme for selecting both parents from a quota of μ best individuals for the crossover. Our tests have shown that a standard single-point crossover improves the evolutionary search efficiency of our problem from 68% to 81%. The results are shown in Table 8. At the same time, the search speed for the runs with the best efficiencies does not practically change as compared to the control.

Table 8. Single-point crossover significantly increases the efficiency of evolutionary search in (μ,λ) selection but insufficiently increases the speed (averaged over 400 runs)

Cross(%%)	Average	StDev	Efficacy
0.5	211447.36	138562.66	80.5
1.0	195252.07	131229.29	80.75
2.5	221347.47	154077.49	80.75
5.0	200784.56	125076.15	78.5

Thus, even the simplest single-point crossover with a simple selection scheme (μ,λ) reliably increases the selection efficiency. Thus, our tests confirm well-known expectations about the role of crossover in the performance of evolutionary search. We made sure that the crossover increases the chances of a "jump" from a local maximum to a global one. Therefore, we are ready to strongly recommend that the experimental procedures of in vitro evolution techniques be supplemented with real experimental crossover methods (along with the point mutation procedures routinely used there).

3.7.2 Crossover in Sigma Truncation Selection

As we have seen, the single-point crossover favors evolutionary search in the case of sigma truncation. Efficiency increases from 68% to 78%, speed also increases slightly (158k vs 201k) as shown in Table 9.

Table 9. Single-point crossover in sigma selection significantly increases the efficiency of evolutionary search for our benchmark-test and increases the speed (averaged over 400 runs)

Cross(%%)	Average	StDev	Efficacy
0.1	158158.63	149907.30	77.75
5.0	177701.15	164113.85	73
10.0	189025.01	167849.72	67

Thus, as might be expected, the crossover improves the efficiency and speed of the search in sigma selection. However, for our tests, sigma selection does not end up being better (or not much better) than (μ,λ) selection if the mutation procedure is supplemented by a crossover in both cases (compare Table 8 and Table 9).

4. CONCLUSIONS

Our tests with various selection schemes from section "Selection Procedures in Evolutionary Computing" showed that, at least for our test problem, only hill-climbing turned out to be better than control runs. Elitism can also positively influence selection. The role of the crossover is also very significant.

A microfluidic modular device with new modules with new features, briefly discussed above, would allow the implementation of a whole series of heuristic algorithms, at least some of which demonstrate in numerical experiments reproducible efficiency in comparison with routine schemes of microfluidic devices for in vitro evolution.

In addition to the promising heuristic algorithms that we have considered in this paper, there are many more algorithms that are promising for implementation in in vitro evolutionary approaches.

Among these techniques there will be various modifications of genetic algorithms, probabilistic models, methods of multi-objective optimization (e.g. Mühlenbein & Mahnig, 2001; O'Hagan, Knowles, Kell, 2012; Verma et al., 2013).

At last, it is natural to expect that the next generation algorithms which were for a long time intentionally developed for various optimization problems, may prove to be significantly more efficient than standard GAs. Accordingly, their implementation in experimental procedures of in vitro evolution can be very effective and significantly resource-saving. It is in this direction that we plan the further research.

ACKNOWLEDGEMENT

The study is supported by the Russian Science Foundation grant 22-18-00383.

REFERENCES

Darmostuk, M. et al, (2015). Current approaches in SELEX: An update to aptamer selection technology. Biotechnol Adv., Vol. 33, Issue 6, Part 2, pp. 1141-1161.

Eremeev, A.V. and Spirov, A.V., (2021). Modeling SELEX for regulatory regions using Royal Road and Royal Staircase fitness functions. Biosystems, Vol. 200, pp. 104312.

Famulok, M. et al, (2007). Functional Aptamers and Aptazymes in Biotechnology, Diagnostics, and Therapy. Chemical Reviews, Vol. 107, No. 9, pp. 3715–3743.

Forrest, S. and Mitchell, M., (1993). Relative building-block fitness and the building block hypothesis, In D. Whit-ley (ed.), Foundations of Genetic Algorithms, Vol. 2: pp. 109-126, San Mateo, CA Morgan Kaufmann.

Goldberg, D.E., (1989). Genetic Algorithms in Search, Optimization and Machine Learning. Reading, MA: Addison-Wesley.

Griffiths, A.D. and Tawfik, D.S., (2006). Miniaturising the laboratory in emulsion droplets. Trends Biotechnol., Vol. 24, No. 9, pp. 395-402.

Griffiths, A.D. and Tawfik, D.S., (2006). Miniaturising the laboratory in emulsion droplets. Trends Biotechnol. Vol. 24, No. 9, pp. 395-402.

Holland, J.H., (1975). Adaptation in Natural and Artificial Systems. Ann Arbor, MI: University of Michigan Press.

Komarova, N. and Kuznetsov, A., (2019). Inside the Black Box: What Makes SELEX Better? Molecules, Vol. 24, No 19, pp. 3598.

Lee, Y.G. et al, (2011). Investigating vesicular selection: A selection operator in in vitro evolution. Applied Soft Computing, Vol. 11, Issue 8, pp. 5528 – 5550.

Mitchell, M., (1998). An Introduction to Genetic Algorithms. Cambridge, Massachusetts: MIT Press.

Myasnikova, E. and Spirov, A., (2021). Extensions of Royal Road Functions for Use in SELEX in silico. Proceedings of 17th International Asian School-Seminar Optimization Problems of Complex Systems (OPCS), pp. 60-64.

Mühlenbein, H. and Mahnig, T., (2001). Evolutionary Algorithms: From Recombination to Search Distributions. In: Kallel L., Naudts B., Rogers A. (eds) Theoretical Aspects of Evolutionary Computing. Natural Computing Series, Springer, Berlin, Heidelberg.

O'Hagan, S. et al, (2012). Exploiting Genomic Knowledge in Optimising Molecular Breeding Programmes: Algorithms from Evolutionary Computing. PLoS ONE, 7, No. 11, pp. e48862.

Oh, I.S. et al, (2011). Simulating chemical evolution. Proceedings of 2011 IEEE Congress of Evolutionary Computation, New Orleans, LA, pp. 2717–2724.

Paegel, B.M. and Joyce G.F., (2010). Microfluidic compartmentalized directed evolution. Chem Biol., Vol. 17, No. 7, pp. 717-724.

Price, A.K. and Paegel, B.M., (2016). Discovery in Droplets. Anal Chem., Vol. 88, No. 1, pp. 339-53.

Sassanfar, M. and Szostak, J.W., (1993). An RNA motif that binds ATP. Nature, Vol. 364, pp. 550–553.

Stemmer, W.P., (1994). Rapid evolution of a protein in vitro by DNA shuffling. Nature, Vol. 370, pp. 389-391.

Spirov, A. and Myasnikova, E., (2022a). Heuristic algorithms in Evolutionary Computation and modular organization of biological macromolecules: applications to in vitro evolution. PLoS ONE, Vol. 17, No. 1, pp. e0260497.

Spirov, A and Myasnikova, E., (2022b). Problem of Domain/Building Block Preservation in the Evolution of Biological Macromolecules and Evolutionary Computation, IEEE/ACM Trans Comput Biol Bioinform., doi: 10.1109/TCBB.2022.3175908.

Trausch, J.J. and Batey, R.T., (2015). Design of modular "plug-and-play" expression platforms derived from natural riboswitches for engineering novel genetically encodable RNA regulatory devices. Methods Enzymol, Vol. 550, pp. 41-71.

Verma, D. et al, (2019). Pareto Optimization of Combinatorial Mutagenesis Libraries, IEEE/ACM Trans Comput Biol Bioinform., Vol. 16, No. 4, pp. 1143-1153.

Voigt, C.A. et al, (2002). Protein building blocks preserved by recombination. Nature Structural Biology, Vol. 9, pp. 553-558.

Vorobyeva, M.A. et al, (2018). Key Aspects of Nucleic Acid Library Design for in Vitro Selection. Int J Mol Sci., Vol. 19, No. 2, pp. 470.

DEEP LEARNING APPROACH TO CLASSIFYING SOLAR RADIO BURSTS

Herman le Roux, Günther Richard Drevin, Roelf Du Toit Strauss and Petrus Johannes Steyn
North-West University Potchefstroom, South Africa

ABSTRACT

Solar radio bursts have a profound effect on the environment and the technological infrastructure of society. Due to the effects that solar radio bursts have, it is important to be able to correctly classify them in an efficient and timely manner. Recently, there has been great success in object classifying by using convolutional neural networks. Therefore, this paper attempts to classify type II, and type III solar radio bursts, and spectrograms containing no bursts, using a convolutional neural network. An in-depth study was conducted to understand the nature of type II and type III bursts and how convolutional neural networks can be implemented to classify these bursts. Data samples, in the form of FITS files, were collected from the e-Callisto network and processed into images. A convolutional neural network was created with the Python packages TensorFlow and Keras. This model was then trained and tested using the only raw data collected from the e-Callisto network. While the model was not able to reach a very high accuracy the paper shows that such a model can make correct predictions.

KEYWORDS

Solar Radio Bursts, Space Weather, Deep learning, Convolutional Neural Networks

1. INTRODUCTION

Solar radio bursts have the potential to greatly affect our wireless networks on Earth as well as our near-space environment, where a lot of space exploration and missions occur. Solar radio bursts cause problems for cell phone towers and in some cases cause worldwide GPS navigation outages (Gary, 2011). Research shows that more than a billion devices are currently connected to the Internet of Things (Pahlavan and Krishnamurthy, 2020). This should cause great concern when one considers that a large enough burst can cause radio blackouts and severely damage wireless networks. Currently, the classification of solar radio bursts at e-Callisto is done manually. Christiaan Monstein, a retired Senior Radio Engineer working at IRSOL, creates event lists that contain information regarding which stations recorded different types of solar radio bursts and at what times, from the e-Callisto network. As one could imagine, it is quite a tedious task, as evidenced by the lack of radio burst lists on the e-Callisto website from 2012 to 2019 due to a lack of manpower. Solar radio bursts are very complex events and have very specific characteristics. In the following literature review, the necessary background information regarding the origin and causes of solar radio bursts will be discussed. To be able to create a neural network to make predictions, it is necessary to understand the different types of solar radio bursts as well as how they are observed using spectrometers. First, the magnetic Sun is described (1.1) followed by solar radio bursts (1.2).

1.1 The Magnetic Sun

In our solar system the Sun, a burning plasma ball of hydrogen and helium, is the main source of energy and space weather events. Most of the energy the Sun emits is electromagnetic radiation. The magnetic structure of the Sun's photosphere is constantly changing. The Sun's magnetic field varies in magnetic activity. Due to high magnetic activity, concentrations of strong magnetic fields will occur called sunspots (Hanslmeier, 2020). The solar cycle is an 11-year periodic variation in the number of sunspots that can be observed on the surface of the Sun. Due to the Sun's highly conductive plasma, a process called magnetic reconnection occurs regularly. Magnetic reconnection is the result of magnetic field lines in the plasma breaking and reattaching, causing magnetic energy to be converted into the heating and acceleration of particles (Hanslmeier, 2020).

Magnetic reconnection is a process that occurs when magnetic field lines stretch, wrap or twist building up tension and eventually breaking their current connection and reconnecting to a polar opposite magnetic field line close by (Hesse and Cassak, 2020). After these field lines reconnect, they straighten out which results in the release of energy in the surrounding region and in the case of the Sun; plasma is usually released as well (Hesse and Cassak, 2020). Magnetic reconnection also occurs in situations where magnetic fields change direction, which happens on the Sun quite often (Hesse and Cassak, 2020). This process is the reason for most explosive bursts of energy on the Sun, such as solar flares and coronal mass ejections (CMEs) (Hanslmeier, 2020).

1.2 Solar Radio Bursts

Events caused by magnetic reconnection such as solar flares and coronal mass ejections (CMEs) cause an increase in emissions in EUV (extreme ultraviolet)-, X-ray, gamma-ray, and radio waves from the Sun's already continuous spectrum (Bothmer *et al.*, 2007). These solar radio bursts (SRBs) are observable using spectrometers and are usually either classified as Type II and Type III although there are five types of solar bursts which include: Type I, Type II, Type III, Type IV and Type V (Liu *et al.*, 2018). We will mainly focus on Type II and Type III solar radio bursts in this paper.

1.2.1 Type II Bursts

Type II solar radio bursts occur after the maximum phase of flares which is commonly about 5-20 min after the start of the solar flare (Wild *et al.*, 1963). It is accepted that these bursts originate in plasma waves (Wild *et al.*, 1963). The outward movement at supersonic speeds suggests type II bursts are related to magnetohydrodynamic shocks (Wild *et al.*, 1963). Strong shocks and shock-accelerated particles in the solar corona cause coronal mass ejections, which are events that are also highly associated with type II bursts (Cane and Stone, 1984). Coronal mass ejections are caused by magnetic reconnection which releases accelerated thermal electrons and plasma when they escape the reconnection site (Kou *et al.*, 2020). The starting frequency of the meter wavelength type II burst, as seen in Figure 2, ranges from 70-100 MHz (Wild *et al.*, 1963; Cane and Stone, 1984).

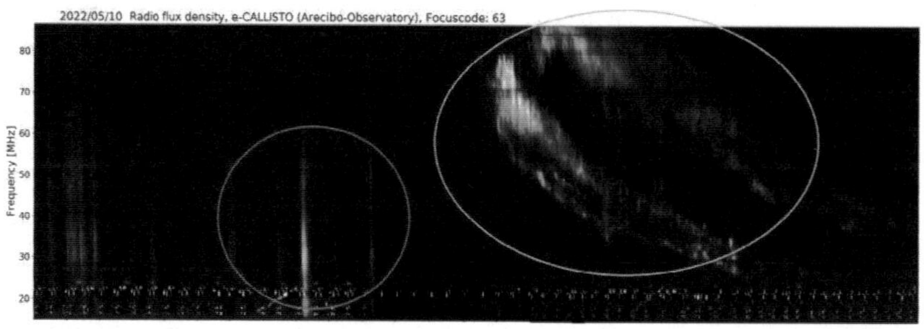

Figure 1. Type III and II solar radio bursts observed in Arecibo, Puerto Rico

1.2.2 Type III Bursts

Type III solar radio bursts individually last for approximately 10 seconds, yet they often appear to cluster in a group of ±10 as seen in Figure 1 (Wild *et al.*, 1963). These bursts are strongly associated with the occurrenceof solar flares and usually occur at the start of these flares (Wild *et al.*, 1963). These solar flares are the sudden intense events in the solar atmosphere that enhances electromagnetic radiation and accelerate electrons (Kou *et al.*, 2020). Type III solar radio bursts drift at a rate of 2 to 16 MHz per second (Ndacyayisenga *et al.*, 2021). The starting frequency for these meter wavelength bursts is 5 to 600 MHz (Wild *et al.*, 1963).

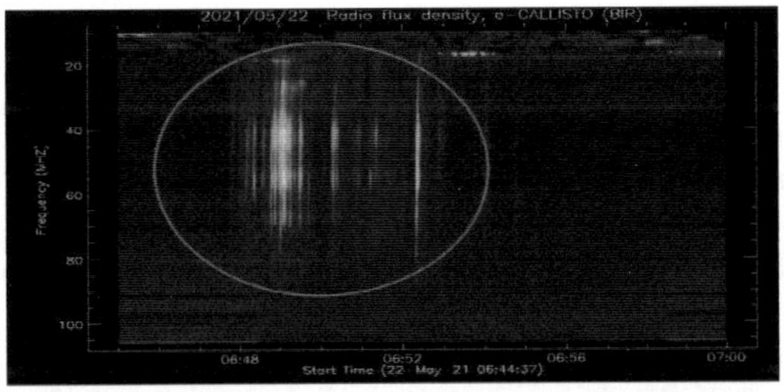

Figure 2. Type III solar radio bursts observed in Bir, Ireland

1.2.3 Summary of the Literature Review Regarding Solar Radio Bursts

The events produced through solar activity, including solar flares and coronal mass ejections, are products of the intense magnetic activity that is present on the surface of the Sun due to sunspots and the chaotic nature of the Sun's magnetic field lines. Solar radio bursts are spikes in radio waves caused by magnetic activity and within them lies the main cause of solar radio burst-related disturbances in our communication systems. The ability to forecast space weather events caused by these solar radio bursts is important due to these effects. When comparing Figure 1 and Figure 2 we can visually discern between the slower drifting type II and the faster drifting type III bursts.

2. CREATING THE DATASET

The e-CALLISTO network is a combination of all the data provided by CALLISTO instruments that are set up around the world. The spectrograms of solar bursts made by these instruments are plotted and stored as frequency over time graphs in FITS (Flexible Image Transport System) files, as seen in Figures 1 and 2. These stations are set up in a wide varietyof different ways but all of them provide the data with Coordinated Universal Time (UTC) timestamps. Data samples from January 2021 to August 2022 collected by the e-CALLISTO network were downloaded using thewebsite scraping library Beautifulsoup. These files were downloaded as compressed files and extracted to FITS files. The files were sorted into folders for type II and type III bursts as well as empty spectrograms using the labelled events list in the form of text files Christian Monstein provides. The FITS files were then divided randomly into training-, validation-, and test sets with the corresponding ratios of 0.7, 0.2 and 0.1. Due to type III bursts occurring more often than type II bursts stratified sampling was used to reduce empty- and type III samples to minimize the effect of data bias. While further refinement of data samples could have been done byensuring that the images recorded at different frequencies, due to different installations of the spectrometers, which can be observed at the end of file names e.g., HUMAIN_20220415_080000_**59,** ALASKA- HAARP_20220710_001500_**62** it was purposefully avoided in an attempt to ensure that the model would be able to predict raw data as is from any e-Callisto spectrometer. The final training set made use of 4690 samples,2088 of which being empty spectrograms. There are 1305 type II burst samples and 1297 type III bursts.

3. DEEP NEURAL NETWORKS

To create neural networks that make it possible to automate tasks, we need to understand how neural networks work. Deep neural networks (DNN) are a subset of machine learning and a tool that makes use of algorithms based on the human mind called artificial neural networks (Trask, 2019). One of the 5 types of neural networks is feedforward neural networks (FNN) (Shrestha and Mahmood, 2019). Convolutional neural networks (CNN) are implementations of FNNs and are considered responsible for the biggest leaps in our current understanding and implementations of feature detection and image classification (Shrestha and Mahmood, 2019; O'Mahony *et al.*, 2019). In this section, we discuss convolutional neural networks (3.1) followed by the Performance of convolutional neural networks on Solar radio bursts (3.2).

3.1 Convolutional Neural Networks

CNN is a popular and preferred neural network architecture for computer vision and is based on the visual cortex systems of humans (Shrestha and Mahmood, 2019). CNNs make use of kernels, also called filters, to detect edges and objects in images by spatially convolving through an entire image (O'Mahony *et al*., 2019). The CNN then uses the dot product of the kernel and the area of the original image to calculate the probability of the existence of that feature (O'Mahony *et al*., 2019).

3.1.1 Convolutional Layers

Starting at the top left of an input matrix the convolutional kernels (frequently 2x2 or 3x3) traverse through input data and calculate the product of the numbers at the same location in the input and the overlapping kernel (Wu, 2017). By adding these products together, we obtain a single value (Wu, 2017). This process is repeated for each possible input value until the bottom right is reached. Different types of kernels and biased operators can be added to the equations to highlight specific objects in images (Wu, 2017).

3.1.2 Pooling Layers

Pooling layers are layers inserted between convolutional layers to achieve sub-sampling which reduces the amount of memory used by the CNN and also speeds up the training process (Shrestha and Mahmood, 2019). Average pooling and max pooling are the two most used techniques (Yu *et al*., 2014). Average pooling is when the pooling operator maps a sub-region to its average and max pooling is when the pooling operator maps the subregion to the maximum value (Wu, 2017).

3.1.3 Fully Connected Layer

The fully connected layer then takes the input from feature extraction and pooling layers and uses weights to predict which labels to assign to the input images (Shrestha and Mahmood, 2019). By using activation functions, the output of the convolution layers can be summed with a bias term to facilitate the learning of these weights (O'Mahony *et al*., 2019). Rectified Linear unit (ReLu) is a commonly used activation function in CNNs due to its results in the field of image recognition (O'Mahony *et al*., 2019). ReLU's main goal is to make CNN more nonlinear (Wu, 2017). We want the mapping from CNNs input to its output to be very nonlinear because the semantic information in a picture is a highly nonlinear mapping of pixel values in the input (Wu, 2017). By using the functions' ability to activate features it is very useful when attempting to recognize complex patterns and objects in images (Wu, 2017). ReLU is also useful in stochastic gradient descent learning due to the function not suffering from the vanishing gradient problem (Wu, 2017). Therefore, the gradients of the activated features are easily back-propagated (Wu, 2017). Backpropagation is a popular learning rule and it is commonly used in supervised learning tasks (Werbos, 1990). Backpropagation is used in these supervised learning tasks for pattern recognition and fault diagnosis and simply put if we increase the weights and the error increases, we lower the weights and vice versa until we reach an error as close to zero as possible (Werbos, 1990).

3.2 Performance of Convolutional Neural Networks on Solar Radio Bursts

In the last few years, a few studies have implemented neural networks to classify or detect bursts. Some have used generated data and others have implemented LTSM models. No study could be found that specifically attempts to classify different types of bursts with raw data and rather focused on being able to detect bursts in images. Results from previous studies will be discussed in 3.2.1, and 3.2.2 followed by a summary in 3.2.3.

3.2.1 University of Alcalá

The first study that will be discussed was conducted by the space research group at the University of Alcalá (Mario F.R. *et al*, 2022). The goal of the paper was to create a neural network that automizes the recognition of solar radio bursts. This paper also makes use of data provided by the e-Callisto network and the burst lists provided by Christian Monstein. Their model was tested and trained with an initial dataset with images from the Glasgow observatory of events recorded from May 22 and May 24 in 2021 (Mario F.R. *et al*, 2022). The model had a true positive rate of 84% and provides some alternative to manually identifying the bursts (Mario F.R. *et al*, 2022). While this is a positive trajectory for detecting bursts in a dataset it does not address the problem of differentiating between different types of bursts.

3.2.2 Laboratory for Electromagnetic Detection (LEAD), Institute of Space Sciences, Shandong University, Weihai, Shandong, China

This second study, published in 2022, was done at Shandong University and focused on creating a model that could quickly and automatically classify data between bursts and non-bursts (Guo J.C. *et al.*, 2022). Their model achieved an average classification accuracy of 98.73% (Guo J.C. *et al.*, 2022). Their paper also compares the performance of their model to previous research conducted relating to the same topic. It is clear that their paper greatly improves from an early model with a 67.4% true positive rate, with regards to burst detection, to 99.9% (Guo J.C. *et al.*, 2022). This study does not address the problem of differentiating between different types of bursts as well.

3.2.3 Summary of Literature Regarding Previously Created Neural Networks

Type II and type III solar radio bursts are a danger to modern networking infrastructures and being able to automatically detect and classify them are important efforts as they will add to astronomical research. When one considers the papers published and publicly available data on the e-Callisto website is clear that there exists a large corpus of data which is mostly manually labelled. Convolutional neural networks are a very prominent implementation of machine learning in computer vision, object detection and image classification and have been used with success by various papers for bursts identification.

4. PROCESSING THE DATA AND THE STRUCTURE OF THE NEURAL NETWORK

After the FITS files were sorted into the training-, validation- and test sets, several pre-processing steps occurred. In the following section the various techniques that were applied to each of the FITS files as well as the layers of the convolutional neural network created using the available Python libraries will be described.

4.1 Converting FITS Files to Images

A python library called radiospectra was used to import the FITS files. The frequencies were linearized and background noise subtraction was applied using the matplotlib library. The resulting graph was then plotted without the X and Y axis labels as shown in Figure 3. The plot function applied a Vmin equal to 5 to normalize the colour map gnist_ncar which makes use of 128 distinguishable colours on the graph. The imageswere then processed into grey images using a function from the pillow library that only stores the luminance of a pixel, effectively greyscaling the image. This was done to simplify the input shape to 1 channel of grey scale values ranging from 0-255 and avoid having 3 channels (Red, Green, Blue) as part of our input shape The image was then cropped to contain only the data which resulted in an output image of the size 324x357 pixels. Only the data was cropped from the graph because it is unnecessary to train the model with input featureslike the title of the observation and the intensity-colour scale. These images were used to train the model.

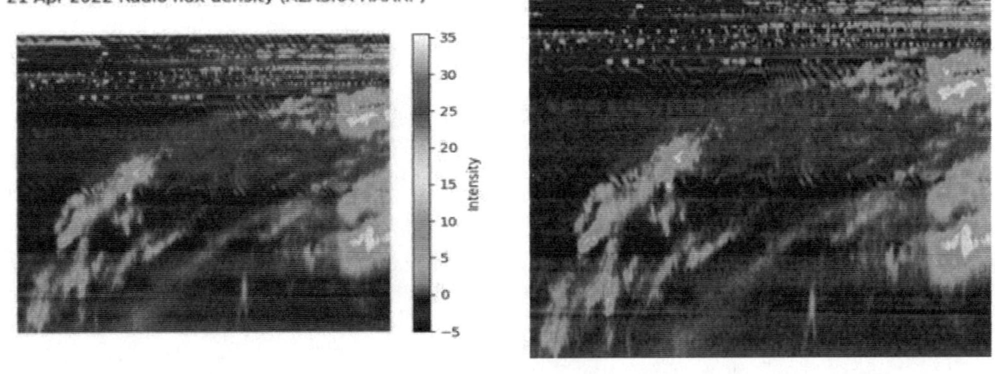

Figure 3. Displaying what the FITS files look like pre- and post-processing for a type II solar radio burst from the Haarp-Alaska observatory

4.2 The Structure of the Model

The TensorFlow flow_from_directory method was employed to load the data and fit the model. Due to the complexity of the images several convolutional layers were added to extract the necessary features to identify a type II and type III solar radio burst. Max pooling was applied to reduce the resulting output shapes. Four dropout layers were also added to prevent overfitting in the training set. The ReLu activation function was used in all the convolutional layers and the output was normalized using the SoftMax activation function.
Finally, the model was compiled using the sparse categorical cross entropy loss function and the adam optimizer function. The structure of the model is as follows:

Table 1. Structure of the convolutional neural network

Type of Layer	Kernel size	Trainable parameters	Output shape
Input	N/A	N/A	(324,357,1)
Convolution2D	(3,3)	160	(322,355,16)
Maxpooling2D	(2,2)	0	(161,177,16)
Convolution2D	(2,2)	1040	(160,176,16)
Maxpooling2D	(2,2)	0	(80,88,16)
Convolution2D	(3,3)	4640	(78,86,32)
Maxpooling2D	(2,2)	0	(39,43,32)
Dropout (0.5)	N/A	0	(39,43,32)
Convolution2D	(3,3)	9248	(37,41,32)
Maxpooling2D	(2,2)	0	(18,20,32)
Dropout (0.5)	N/A	0	(18,20,32)
Convolution2D	(3,3)	18496	(16,18,64)
Maxpooling2D	(2,2)	0	(8,9,64)
Dropout (0.5)	N/A	0	(8,9,64)
Flatten	N/A	0	(4608)
Full connection	N/A	4719616	(1024)
Dropout (0.5)	N/A	0	(1024)
Output (Softmax)	N/A	3075	(3)

5. EXPERIMENTAL RESULTS

The evaluation criterion (5.1.1) will be discussed followed by the results (5.1.2) and a discussion of the results (5.1.3).

5.1 Evaluation Criterion

Given that we need to create a confusion matrix for multiple classes we will need to create a multiclass confusion matrix to assess the experimental result. The true positive rate (TPR) is calculated as follows:

$$TPR=\frac{TP}{TP+TFN} \times 100\% \qquad (1)$$

where TP denotes a correctly classed positive sample (true positive), and TFN denotes the total incorrectly classified positive samples. In general, a larger TPR value for a particular type of sample indicates a higher likelihood of this type's successful identification. The overall accuracy will be given as:

$$Accuracy= \sum TP / \sum \text{Samples per class} \qquad (2)$$

The precision for each class is determined as the TP of the class divided by the number of actual samples forthe class. The recall is calculated as the TP of the class divided by the number of samples predicted as that class.

5.2 Results

The model received a total number of 674 labelled samples for training with 299 being empty spectrograms, 188 being Type II solar radio bursts and 187 being Type III solar radio bursts the following confusion matrix was created:

Table 2. Multiple class confusion matrix detailing the results

	Predicted Empty Spectrograms	Predicted Type II bursts	Predicted Type III bursts	Recall
Empty spectrograms	270	12	17	90,30%
Type II bursts	27	113	48	60,10%
Type III bursts	24	34	129	68,98%
Precision	84,11%	71,06%	66,49%	

The diagonal indicates the true positive result for each class e.g., Type II bursts and Predicted Type II bursts intersect with a value of 113 indicating that the number of true positives for the class Type II bursts is 113. The overall accuracy of the model is 75,96%, the average recall is 73,13%, and the average precision is 73,89%. The recall is the number of samples correctly predicted as the class it was indicated as, and precisionis the number of samples correctly predicted from all the samples that were predicted as that class.

5.3 Discussion

The total number of samples containing bursts from the dataset was 20814 of which 18947 samples were type III solar radio bursts. The recall for type II solar radio bursts was 60,10% and the recall for type III solar radio bursts was 68,98%. Due to the number of type III bursts not being fully utilized to train the model in anattempt to minimize the data bias one could argue that the type III bursts recall could have been improved upon. The model struggled to correctly identify type III solar radio bursts and the model struggled even moreto identify type II solar radio bursts, but as can be seen in Figure 4, there exist samples in the testing set that have features that appear to be of type III solar radio bursts. The lack of type II burst data samples is prescribed to the fact that it is a rarer occurrence than that of a type III solar radio burst. This, accompanied bythe fact that some testing samples and training samples could be considered contaminated with type III solar radio bursts and other radio noise, is the reason for the lack of performance when considering the type II solarradio burst recall. The model performed well when predicting empty spectrograms with a recall rate of 90,30% but this can also be improved by using the entire corpus of data that accounts for empty spectrogramswhich in February of 2021 accounted for up to 89000 samples for the month. The average precision is 73,88% which indicates that, on average, the model predicted the true positives for a specifically correctly 73,88% of the time. This is encouraging when one considers that as 2022 progresses into a more active part of the solar cycle and more samples will be able to be collected and added to the training set. Further steps can be taken to improve the accuracy by filtering the data set such that type II and type III samples are extremely clear for human perception but this will rarely be the case and models should be focused on learning the features of the solar radio bursts despite massive amounts of noise of different causes.

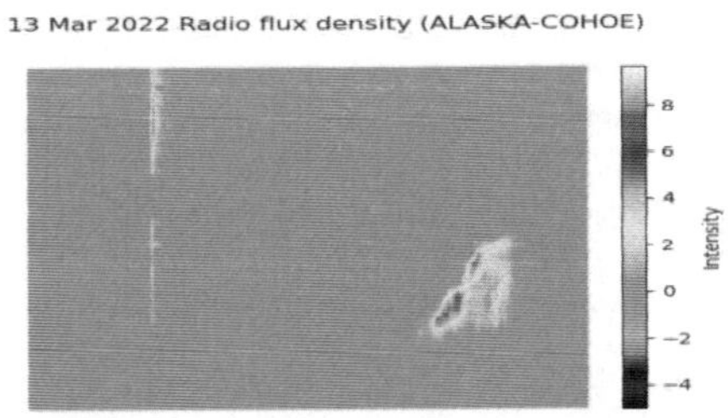

Figure 4. A type II solar radio burst from the test set was predicted as a type III solar radio burst

6. SUMMARY AND CONCLUSION

This paper is the first attempt at utilizing convolutional neural networks to automatically classify type II and type III solar radio bursts using a dataset constructed out of data downloaded between 2021 and 2022. A literature study was conducted to understand the nature of solar radio bursts, focusing on type II and type III solar radio bursts. Thereafter a literature study was conducted to understand convolutional neural networks and how the layers are utilized in terms of processing images and detecting features. A dataset was created using data collected from the e-Callisto website and event lists compiled by Christian Monstein. The data set was used to train a convolutional neural network created using the python libraries TensorFlow and Keras. The results of the model's prediction were given and discussed. The preliminary results have not shown a high accuracy but feature research is promising regarding the models' ability to identify the features of solar radio bursts.

ACKNOWLEDGEMENT

The Institute for Data Science FHNW Brugg/Windisch, Switzerland is acknowledged for making the data publicly available as data from different years were used. Christian Monstein is also acknowledged for compiling the event lists that were used to create the dataset.

REFERENCES

Bothmer, V., Zhukov, A., and Daglis, I. (2007). *The Sun as the prime source of space weather*, pages 31–102. Springer.

Cane, H. and Stone, R. (1984). Type II solar radio bursts, interplanetary shocks, and energetic particle events.
The Astrophysical Journal, 282:339–344.

Gary, D. E. (2011). Solar radio burst effects on wireless systems. In 2011 IEEE I*nternational Symposium on Electromagnetic Compatibility*, pages 661–664.

Guo J.C., Yan F-B, Wan G, Hu X-J, Wang S. 2022. A deep learning method for the recognition of solar radioburstspectrum. PeerJ Comput. Sci. 8:e855 DOI 10.7717/peerj-cs.855

Hanslmeier, A. (2020). *The Chaotic Solar Cycle*. Springer Singapore.

Hesse, M. and Cassak, P. A. (2020). Magnetic reconnection in the space sciences: Past, present, and future.
Journal of Geophysical Research: Space Physics, 125(2).

Kou, Y. K., Jing, Z. C., Cheng, X., Pan, W. Q., Liu, Y., Li, C., and Ding, M. D. (2020). What determines solar flares producing interplanetary type III radio bursts? *The Astrophysical Journal*, 898(1): L24.

Liu, H., Chen, Y., Cho, K., Feng, S., Vasanth, V., Koval, A., Du, G., Wu, Z., and Li,C. (2018). A solarstationary type IV radio burst and its radiation mechanism. *Solar Physics*, 293(4).

Mario F.R., Javier B.G., Manuel P.M. and Monstein C., Automatic detection of e-Callisto solar radio bursts by Deep Neural Networks, *2022 3rd URSI Atlantic and Asia Pacific Radio Science Meeting (AT-AP-RASC)*, 2022, pp. 1-4, DOI: 10.23919/AT-AP-RASC54737.2022.9814298.

Ndacyayisenga, T., Uwamahoro, J., Sasikumar Raja, K., and Monstein, C. (2021). A statistical study of solarradio type III bursts and space weather implication. *Advances in Space Research*, 67(4):1425–1435.

O'Mahony, N., Campbell, S., Carvalho, A., Harapanahalli, S., Hernandez, G. V., Krpalkova, L., Riordan, D.,and Walsh, J. (2019). Deep learning vs. traditional computer vision. In *Science and information conference*, pages 128–144. Springer.

Pahlavan, K. and Krishnamurthy, P. (2020). Evolution and impact of wi-fi technology and applications: Ahistorical perspective. *International Journal of Wireless Information Networks*, 28(1):3–19.

Shrestha, A. and Mahmood, A. (2019). Review of deep learning algorithms and architectures. *IEEE* Access,7:53040–53065.

Trask, A. W. (2019). *Grokking deep learning*. Manning.

Werbos, P. J. (1990). Backpropagation through time: what it does and how to do it. *Proceedings of the IEEE*,78(10): 1550–1560.

Wild, J. P., Smerd, S. F., and Weiss, A. A. (1963). Solar bursts. *Annual Review of Astronomy andAstrophysics*, 1(1): 291–366.

Wu, J. (2017). Introduction to convolutional neural networks. *National Key Lab for Novel SoftwareTechnology*. Nanjing University. China, 5(23):495.

Yu, D., Wang, H., Chen, P., and Wei, Z. (2014). Mixed pooling for convolutional neural networks. In *RoughSets and Knowledge Technology*, pages 364–375.

TORUS-CONNECTED TOROIDS: AN INTERCONNECTION NETWORK FOR MASSIVELY PARALLEL SYSTEMS

Antoine Bossard
Graduate School of Science, Kanagawa University
Tsuchiya 2946, Hiratsuka, Kanagawa, 259-1293 Japan
ORCID: 0000-0001-9381-9346

ABSTRACT

Modern supercomputers are massively parallel systems which include hundreds of thousands of compute nodes. To maximise performance, connection of these nodes is critical. To this end, torus-based interconnection networks have proven popular. For instance, the world no. 1 supercomputer as of May 2022, the Fujitsu Fugaku machine, is based on the torus topology. On the other hand, the network dimension of such torus-based devices is kept rather low, for instance three for the Fujitsu Fugaku supercomputer. So, in order to connect the numerous compute nodes with such a conventional approach, the arity of the torus is increased, which is at the cost of a greater diameter. Additional layers can also be introduced, thus inducing hierarchical interconnection networks (HIN). In this paper, we describe a novel topology for the interconnection network of massively parallel systems: torus-connected toroids. The merit of this network compared to existing topologies is that while retaining the popular torus structure, it smartly combines it with another layer, toroids, to reduce the diameter of the network. The proposal is formally evaluated and compared to conventional approaches to show its advantages.

KEYWORDS

Interconnect, Dependability, Supercomputer, High-Performance, Routing, Topology

1. INTRODUCTION

The TOP500 ranking lists the fastest supercomputers in the world. From these data, it can be noticed that the torus topology has been very popular as interconnection network of such massively parallel systems. For example, the world no. 1 supercomputer as of May 2022, the Fujitsu Fugaku machine (TOP500, 2021), is based on the torus topology. Several other, high-profile machines, such as the Fujitsu K – formerly world no. 1 –, and the IBM BlueGene/Q – rated the "Greenest Supercomputer in the World" in 2010's (IBM; Scogland et al., 2013) – are based on the torus topology (Ajima et al., 2009, 2018; Chen et al., 2011).

Besides, hierarchical interconnection networks (HIN) have also proven popular as they enable to reduce the network diameter, and thus cost (Bossard and Kaneko, 2015b,c). This is the case, for instance, of the Tofu interconnection network used by the previously mentioned Fujitsu supercomputers: Tofu combines a 3-dimensional torus on the higher level with a 3-dimensional (2, 3)-ary torus on the lower level (Ajima et al., 2009). We say that the higher level connects meta-nodes. A low degree and a low diameter are two properties which are now critical considering the huge number of compute nodes included by modern supercomputers: several machines in the top ten of the TOP500 world rankings have already passed the million-node barrier.

Recognising these two trends of the supercomputing industry – tori and HINs –, and aiming at further reducing the network degree and diameter compared to, say, Tofu, we describe in this paper the torus-connected toroids network (TCT) for the interconnect topology of massively parallel systems. Designing a hierarchical interconnection network which connects meta-nodes according to an n-dimensional torus requires for routing algorithm simplicity that each meta-node consist of $2n$ nodes. A first attempt was made with the torus-connected cycles (TCC) topology (Bossard and Kaneko, 2015a), itself inspired by older works such as the well known cube-connected cycles (CCC) topology (Preparata and Vuillemin, 1981). One issue of the TCC topology is that since meta-nodes are structured according to the ring topology, the diameter of the network rapidly increases as the network dimension is raised. With this TCT proposal, because meta-nodes include more nodes than those of Tofu and TCC, the network arity need not be as high as in the case of TCC to connect numerous compute nodes.

2. TOROIDS

Meta-nodes in a TCT are structured according to what we call toroids. The definition and properties of a toroid are given in this section.

2.1 Definition

Definition 1. *The node set V of an n-toroid has $2n$ nodes ($n \geq 1$): considering the Cartesian product $P = \{0,1\} \times \{0,1\} \times \{0,1,\dots,\lfloor (n-1)/2 \rfloor\}$, we have $V = P$ when n is even and $V = P \setminus \{(1,0,(n-1)/2),(1,1,(n-1)/2)\}$ otherwise. Two nodes $u = (u_x,u_y,u_z)$ and $v = (v_x,v_y,v_z)$ of V are adjacent if and only if one of the following conditions holds:*

- $u_x = v_x \wedge u_z = v_z$
- $u_y = v_y \wedge u_z = v_z$
- $u_x = v_x \wedge u_y = v_y \wedge u_z = v_z \pm 1 \bmod \lceil n/2 \rceil$
- $n\ odd \wedge u_y = v_y \wedge u_x \neq v_x \wedge u_z = v_z \pm 1 \bmod (n+1)/2 \wedge (u_z = (n-1)/2 \vee v_z = (n-1)/2)$

where $\wedge$ and $\vee$ denote the logical conjunction and disjunction, respectively.

As a remark, when n is even, an n-toroid is isomorphic to a $(2,2,n/2)$-torus, and when n is odd to a $(2,2,(n+1)/2)$-torus with the two edges $\{(0,0,(n-1)/2),(1,0,(n-1)/2)\}$ and $\{(0,1,(n-1)/2),(1,1,(n-1)/2)\}$ contracted (Diestel, 2016). Sample drawings of n-toroids are given in Figure 1.

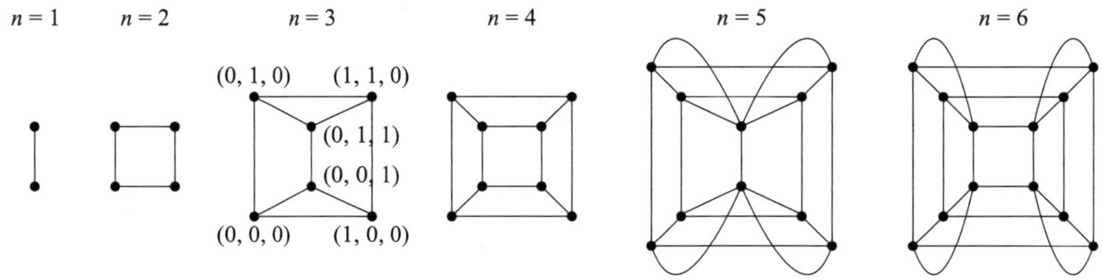

Figure 1. Sample drawings of n-toroids ($1 \leq n \leq 6$)

For the sake of simplicity, the three dimensions of a toroid are called X, Y and Z and respectively correspond to the coordinates u_x, u_y and u_z of node $u = (u_x,u_y,u_z)$. Furthermore, when $n \geq 5$, the edges that connect a node of Z coordinate 0 and one of Z coordinate $\lfloor (n-1)/2 \rfloor$ are called wrap-around edges.

2.2 Topological Properties

From Definition 1, we directly have that an n-toroid has degree four when n is even. When n is odd, the minimum degree is four and the maximum degree is five. Precisely, the $2n-2$ nodes (x,y,z) with $0 \leq x,y \leq 1$ and $0 \leq z < (n-1)/2$ have degree four and the two nodes $(0,y,z)$ with $0 \leq y \leq 1$ and $z = (n-1)/2$ have degree five.

The diameter of a toroid is discussed next.

Theorem 1. *The diameter $\tau(n)$ of an n-toroid is as follows:*

$$\tau(n) = \begin{cases} \lfloor n/4 \rfloor + 2 & when\ n\ is\ even \\ \lfloor (n-1)/4 \rfloor + 2 & when\ n\ is\ odd \end{cases}$$

Proof. We first consider the case n is even. Without considering wrap-around edges, the maximal distance on the Z dimension is $n/2$. Considering wrap-around edges, the maximal distance on the Z dimension is $\lfloor n/4 \rfloor$.

The maximal distance on the X dimension is 1, and 1 as well on the Y dimension. Therefore, the maximal distance in an n-toroid when n is even is $\lfloor n/4 \rfloor + 2$.

Next, we consider the case n is odd. Without considering wrap-around edges, the maximal distance on the Z dimension is $(n-1)/2$. Considering wrap-around edges but not the two nodes $(0, y, z)$ with $0 \leq y \leq 1$ and $z = (n-1)/2$, that is considering a $(2, 2, (n-1)/2)$-torus, the maximal distance on the Z dimension is $\lfloor (n-1)/4 \rfloor$. Finally, at most two edges are required to either move on both the X and Y dimensions, or to both reach a node of Z coordinate $(n-1)/2$ and move on the Y dimension (there is no move possible on the X dimension from or to a node of Z coordinate $(n-1)/2$). Therefore, the maximal distance in an n-toroid when n is odd is $\lfloor (n-1)/4 \rfloor + 2$.

2.3 Shortest-Path Routing

In this section, we describe and evaluate a shortest-path routing algorithm in a toroid. This routing method is detailed with pseudo-code in Algorithms 1 (two utility functions) and 2 (the main function). In the pseudo-code, a left-pointing arrow (←) is the assignment operator whereas a right-pointing one (→) denotes path concatenation (between two paths, between one path and one node or between two nodes).

Function route-xy(a, b)
  Input: two coordinates of either the X or Y dimension
  Output: a sequence of coordinates on the corresponding dimension
  if $a = b$ **then return** a **else return** $a \to b$;

Function route-z(n, a, b)
  Input: n and two coordinates of the Z dimension
  Output: a sequence of coordinates on the Z dimension
  if $a > b$ **then return** reverse(route-z(n, b, a));
  else
    $c \leftarrow a$; $p \leftarrow a$;
    while $c \neq b$ **do**
      if n even **then**
        if $b - a \geq \lceil n/4 \rceil$ **then** $c \leftarrow c - 1 \bmod n/2$ **else** $c \leftarrow c + 1 \bmod n/2$;
      else
        if $b - a \geq \lceil (n+1)/4 \rceil$ **then** $c \leftarrow c - 1 \bmod (n+1)/2$ **else** $c \leftarrow c + 1 \bmod (n+1)/2$;
      $p \leftarrow (p \to c)$;
    return p;

Algorithm 1. Functions for routing on one single dimension in an n-toroid

Function toroid-spr(n, u, v)
  Input: n, a source node $u = (u_x, u_y, u_z)$ and a destination node $v = (v_x, v_y, v_z)$
  Output: a shortest path from u to v
  if n even **then**
    $p_x \leftarrow$ map($\lambda: x \mapsto (x, u_y, u_z)$, route-xy($u_x$, v_x));
    $p_y \leftarrow$ map($\lambda: y \mapsto (v_x, y, u_z)$, route-xy($u_y$, v_y));
    $p_z \leftarrow$ map($\lambda: z \mapsto (v_x, v_y, z)$, route-z($u_z$, v_z));
    return $p_x \to p_y \to p_z$;
  else // n odd
    if $u_x = v_x = 0$ **then**
      $p_y \leftarrow$ map($\lambda: y \mapsto (v_x, y, u_z)$, route-xy($u_y$, v_y));
      $p_z \leftarrow$ map($\lambda: z \mapsto (v_x, v_y, z)$, route-z($u_z$, v_z));
      return $p_y \to p_z$;
    else if $u_x = v_x = 1$ **then**
      $p_y \leftarrow$ map($\lambda: y \mapsto (v_x, y, u_z)$, route-xy($u_y$, v_y));

$p_z \leftarrow$ map(λ: $z \mapsto$ **if** $z = (n-1)/2$ **then** $(0, v_y, z)$ **else** (v_x, v_y, z), route-z(u_z, v_z));
return $p_y \rightarrow p_z$;
else if $u_x = 1$ **then** // $u_x \neq v_x \wedge u_x = 1$
$crossed \leftarrow$ false; $p_z \leftarrow \emptyset$;
foreach z **in** route-z(u_z, v_z) **do**
if $crossed \vee z = (n-1)/2$ **then** $p_z \leftarrow (p_z \rightarrow (0, u_y, z))$; $crossed \leftarrow$ true;
else $p_z \leftarrow (p_z \rightarrow (u_x, u_y, z))$;
$(c_x, c_y, c_z) \leftarrow$ last(p_z);
$p_x \leftarrow$ map(λ: $x \mapsto (x, u_y, v_z)$, route-xy(c_x, v_x));
$p_y \leftarrow$ map(λ: $y \mapsto (v_x, y, v_z)$, route-xy(u_y, v_y));
return $p_z \rightarrow p_x \rightarrow p_y$;
else // $u_x \neq v_x \wedge u_x = 0$
return reverse(toroid-spr(n, v, u));

Algorithm 2. Shortest-path routing in an n-toroid

We next empirically confirm the maximum length and investigate the average length of a path produced by this shortest-path routing algorithm in a toroid. To this end, we have implemented the algorithm and conducted a computer experiment as follows: for $2 \leq n \leq 8$, the computer program solves 1000 random problem instances, that is, repeatedly generates randomly a source node and a destination node and calculates the path between them. For each such value of n, the maximum path length and the average path length are calculated from the 1000 selected paths. The obtained results are illustrated in Figure 2, with the standard deviation shown for the average path length. In addition, the theoretically established diameter is plotted for reference.

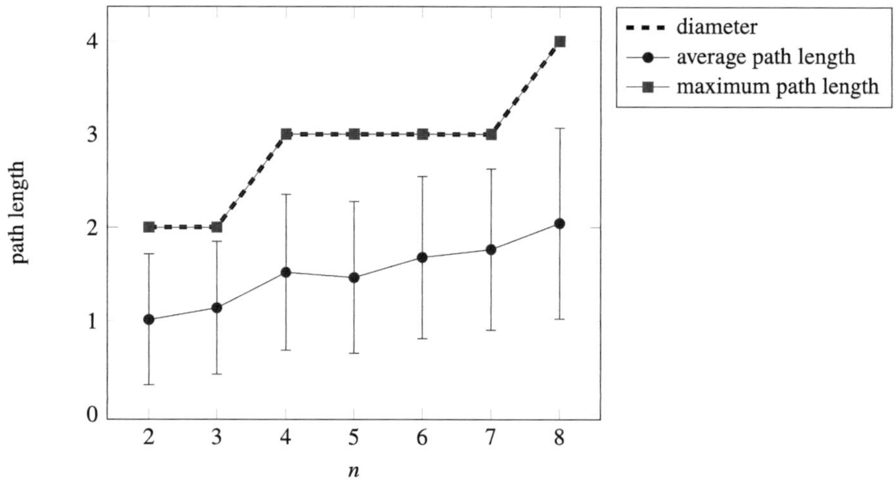

Figure 2. Experimental results of the empirical evaluation of the described shortest-path routing algorithm in an n-toroid. The maximum length and the average length of a selected path has been measured (the formally established diameter is also plotted for reference)

It can be observed from these results that the measured maximum path length confirms the formally established diameter: a selected path is of length at most $\lfloor n/4 \rfloor + 2$ when n is even and $\lfloor (n-1)/4 \rfloor + 2$ otherwise. Because the length of some paths is equal to the diameter, there were problem instances whose randomly selected source and destination nodes were diagonally opposed nodes.

3. TORUS-CONNECTED TOROIDS

3.1 Definition

Definition 2. *An* n*-dimensional* k*-ary torus-connected toroids network, denoted as* $\mathrm{TCT}(n,k)$*, consists of* k^n *toroids. Two nodes* $u = (u_0, u_1, \ldots, u_{n-1}, (u_x, u_y, u_z))$ *and* $v = (v_0, v_1, \ldots, v_{n-1}, (v_x, v_y, v_z))$ *are adjacent if and only if one of the following two conditions holds:*

- $\forall i, 0 \leq i \leq n-1, u_i = v_i \wedge \tau_n((u_x, u_y, u_z), (v_x, v_y, v_z))$
- $\exists j, \forall i, 0 \leq i, j \leq n-1, i \neq j, u_i = v_i \wedge v_j = u_j \pm 1 \bmod k \wedge u_x = v_x \wedge u_y = v_y + 1 \bmod 2 \wedge u_z = v_z$

where the predicate $\tau_n(a,b)$ *is satisfied when* a *and* b *are adjacent nodes in an* n*-toroid (see Definition 1).*

The above first condition induces internal edges, and the second one external edges. Part of a $\mathrm{TCT}(3,3)$ is illustrated in Figure 3: for the sake of clarity, only the nodes of one single value of the third dimension are illustrated. From Definition 2, the minimum degree of a TCT is thus five and the maximum degree six.

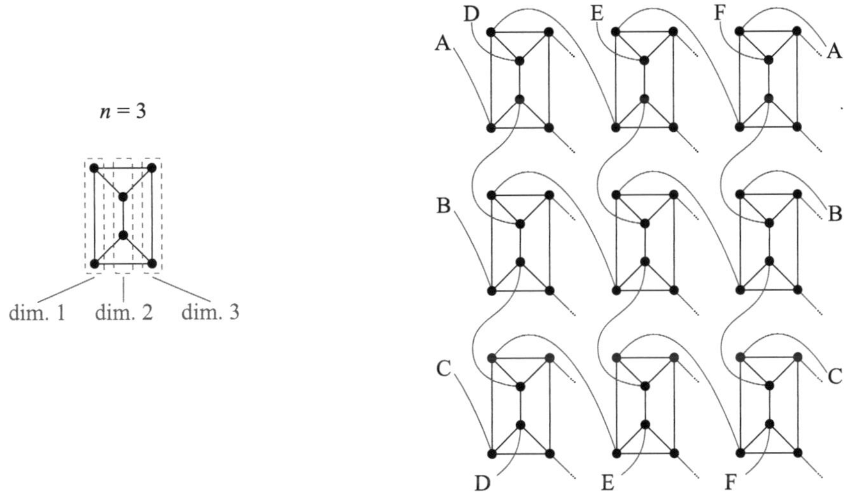

Figure 3. Connection scheme of TCT meta-nodes (left). Sample drawing of a 3-dimensional 3-ary TCT (right); only the nodes of one single value of the third dimension are illustrated though

3.2 Simple Routing

A simple routing algorithm in a TCT between a source node and a destination node can be simply derived as follows. Compared to the toroid routing algorithm described in Section 2, this algorithm is rather straightforward and its description here is thus less detailed. We assume that $k \geq 3$ to omit additional, verbose details for the special cases $k = 1$ and $k = 2$, these two cases being impractical considering the numerous nodes which have to be interconnected.

First, a path of meta-nodes is selected with a dimension-order routing algorithm in a torus (Duato et al., 2003) between the meta-node that includes the source node and the meta-node that includes the destination node. Let this path be $p: m_0 \to m_1 \to \cdots \to m_l$; it is recalled that m_0 includes the source node and m_l the destination node.

Second, apply the shortest-path routing algorithm in a toroid as described in Section 2 to find a path inside m_0 between the source node and the unique node u_0' that is adjacent to a node $u_1 \in m_1$. Inside m_i $(1 \leq i \leq l-1)$, apply the same toroid routing algorithm to select a path between u_i and u_i' where u_i is adjacent to a node $u_{i-1}' \in m_{i-1}$ and u_i' to a node $u_{i+1} \in m_{i+1}$. Apply the same toroid routing algorithm to select a path inside m_l between u_l and the destination node, where u_l is adjacent to a node $u_{l-1}' \in m_{l-1}$.

It should be noted that it is not guaranteed with this routing algorithm that the selected path is shortest. The advantage of this algorithm is its simplicity. The maximum path length induced by this routing algorithm in a TCT is further analysed in the next section.

4. EVALUATION AND DISCUSSION

In this section, we formally and quantitatively compare the torus-connected toroids topology with the Tofu interconnection network used by the Fujitsu K and Fujitsu Fugaku supercomputers.

4.1 Comparison based on an Estimation of the Network Diameter

The topology of Tofu (Tofu 1 (Ajima et al., 2009), Tofu 2 (Ajima et al., 2014) and Tofu D (Ajima et al., 2018) indistinctly) consists of meta-nodes connected according to a three-dimensional torus. Each meta-node is in turn a (3, 2, 2)-torus, thus consisting of 12 nodes. Compared to Tofu, the node degree in a TCT is smaller: it is equal to 5 or 6 depending on the parity of the TCT dimension n, and is equal to 10 in the case of Tofu.

Besides, the network dimension n is fixed to 3 for the high-level layer of Tofu – the structure of its low-level layer is constant: it does not depend on any variable. So, in the case of Tofu, the arity is solely used to increase the network order, which, as a result, induces a high diameter. We give an estimation of the network diameter of Tofu and TCT based solely on their number of nodes (i.e. the network order) and on their dimension n ($n = 3$ in the case of Tofu) for the sake of simplicity. That is, the network arity k is induced by uniformly distributing nodes on each of all the network dimensions.

For Tofu, $3\sqrt[n]{N/12}/2 + 3 = 3\sqrt[3]{N/12}/2 + 3$ is an estimation of the network diameter based on N and n, with N the number of nodes: $N/12$ is the number of meta-nodes, that is, the number of (3, 2, 2)-tori which each make one node of the high-level layer of Tofu, thus multiplied by the number of dimensions, and the term 3 is for the internal edges required at either the source or destination meta-node – only one such internal routing is indeed needed in the case of Tofu.

For TCT, $n\sqrt[n]{N/(2n)} + 2\tau(n)$ is an estimation of the network diameter based on N and n, with N the number of nodes and where $\tau(n)$ is the diameter of a toroid of an n-dimensional TCT (i.e. of an n-toroid) as established in Section 2.2. $N/(2n)$ represents the number of toroids per dimension, thus multiplied by n to obtain the total number of toroids. The two τ here represent the maximum number of internal edges selected inside the toroid of the source node and inside that of the destination node. Hence, the diameter of a TCT will be smaller than that of Tofu as the network dimension n increases. The threshold value of the dimension n depends on the arity k: more details are given below. But even for small values of n, the degree of a TCT remains half (i.e. 5) or half plus one (i.e. 6) that of Tofu (i.e. 10).

4.2 Comparison based on the Maximum Path Length from Simple Routing

Next, we give a more detailed comparison with respect to this diameter issue. Concretely, we compare the maximum length of a path selected with a simple dimension-order (with support for torus wrap-around edges) routing algorithm in the case of Tofu and TCT. Such a simple routing algorithm has been described in Section 3.2 for the case of a TCT. The same idea can be applied to Tofu: the path selected in the high-level layer is made of external edges (i.e. edges between meta-nodes) and edges selected inside a meta-node are internal edges.

On the one hand, the case of a k-ary Tofu network.

Lemma 1. *A simple dimension-order (with support for torus wrap-around edges) routing algorithm applied in a k-ary Tofu network induces a maximum path length $m_u(k)$ as follows:*

$$m_u(k) = 3\left\lfloor\frac{k}{2}\right\rfloor + 3$$

Proof. From the Tofu topology definition, at most $\lfloor k/2 \rfloor$ external edges are required for each dimension of the high-level three-dimensional torus. There are three dimensions, so at most $3\lfloor k/2 \rfloor$ external edges are selected in total. Once again, the term 3 represents the maximum number of internal edges required inside the meta-node of either the source or destination node.

On the other hand, the case of an n-dimensional k-ary TCT network.

Theorem 2. *A simple dimension-order (with support for torus wrap-around edges) routing algorithm applied in an n-dimensional k-ary TCT network induces a maximum path length $m_c(n, k)$ as follows:*

$$m_c(n,k) = 2n \left\lfloor \frac{k}{2} \right\rfloor + 2\tau(n) + n - 2$$

Proof. At most $\lfloor k/2 \rfloor$ external edges are required on one single dimension. There are n dimensions, so in total at most $n\lfloor k/2 \rfloor$ external edges are selected. The number of internal edges is as follows: at most 2 internal edges inside a toroid at a dimension change, at most $\tau(n)$ for routing inside the toroid of the source node and inside that of the destination node and 1 internal edge for all the other toroids included in the selected path. There are at most $n - 1$ toroids inside which routing is needed for a dimension change. So, in total, at most $2(n-1) + 2\tau(n) + ((n\lfloor k/2 \rfloor + 1) - (n-1) - 2) = 2\tau(n) + n(\lfloor k/2 \rfloor + 1) - 2$ internal edges are selected.

Because it may still be difficult to identify the values of the TCT parameters n and k for which such maximum path length would be shorter than in the case of Tofu, sample values are next given. For a fair comparison, it is needed to consider a Tofu network and a TCT network of same or near same orders. On the one hand, Tofu consists of $N_t(k) = 12k^3$ nodes. On the other hand, TCT includes $N_c(n,k) = 2nk^n$ nodes.

So, for instance, with $n = 8$, $k = 3$, a TCT connects 104,976 nodes with the length of a longest path obtained with a simple dimension-order (with support for torus wrap-around edges) routing algorithm being 30. This is to be compared with the at most 82,308 nodes connected in the case of a k-ary Tofu ($k = 19$) with the same length of a longest path (i.e. 30). As another example, with a maximum path length of 36, Tofu can connect at most 146,004 nodes ($k = 23$), which is to be compared with the 1,180,980 nodes of a TCT with the same maximum path length ($n = 10$, $k = 3$). To connect at least the same number of nodes, Tofu needs a maximum path length of 72 (i.e. $k = 46$ or $k = 47$, inducing 1,168,032 and 1,245,876 nodes, respectively). It is recalled that modern supercomputers include a number of nodes which is in this order: for example, the Fujitsu Fugaku (it is based on Tofu D) embodies 7,630,848 compute nodes and the Sunway TaihuLight 10,649,600.

Therefore, considering the huge number of compute nodes included nowadays in supercomputers – in the order of several million – the torus-connected toroids topology supersedes the conventional approach both in term of network degree and network diameter, in other words its cost is lower (it is recalled that the network cost is defined as the network degree multiplied by the network diameter). Additional sample values are given in Table 1 to illustrate the trend discussed previously.

Table 1. A comparison of the network order and the maximum path length induced by a simple dimension-order (with support for torus wrap-around edges) routing algorithm in the case of the TCT and Tofu topologies (sample dimensions and arities)

Torus-connected toroids				Tofu		
n	k	Network order	Max. length	k	Network order	Max. length
3	5	750	17	3	324	6
3	7	2,058	23	4	768	9
4	5	5,000	24	10	12,000	18
5	5	31,250	29	20	96,000	33
6	4	49,152	34	30	324,000	48
6	5	187,500	34	40	768,000	63
7	4	229,376	39	50	1,500,000	78
7	5	1,093,750	39	60	2,592,000	93
8	4	1,048,576	46	70	4,116,000	108
8	5	6,250,000	46	80	6,144,000	123

5. CONCLUSIONS

As shown by the TOP500 world supercomputing rankings, the torus topology has proven very popular as interconnection network of massively parallel systems. Besides, the number of compute nodes included in such machines has now passed the million-node barrier, with several supercomputers in the top ten even having two or more million. To retain the computing performance high, it is critical to try to reduce the network degree and diameter. To this end, and recognizing both the torus topology and hierarchical interconnection network trends of the supercomputing industry, we have proposed in this paper the torus-connected toroids topology. After first formally establishing the degree and diameter of a meta-node (i.e. toroid) of a TCT network, conducting a validation experiment and giving the TCT formal definition, we have shown that compared to the Tofu interconnect of the Fujitsu K and Fugaku supercomputers – the latter being ranked no. 1 in the world as of May 2022 –, the TCT topology improves on both the degree and diameter issues.

Regarding future works, one objective is to conduct additional experiments to further investigate the performance of the proposal in average. In addition, the diameter of a torus-connected toroids network remains to be formally established. This is however a difficult problem, and an upper bound on the maximum path length as established in this paper is usually sufficient to prove the performance of the topology.

ACKNOWLEDGEMENT

This research was partly supported by a Grant-in-Aid for Scientific Research (C) of the Japan Society for the Promotion of Science under grant no. 19K11887.

REFERENCES

Ajima, Y. et al., 2009. Tofu: A 6D mesh/torus interconnect for exascale computers. *Computer*, Vol. 42, No. 11, pp. 36–40. doi: 10.1109/MC.2009.370.

Ajima, Y. et al., 2014. Tofu Interconnect 2: System-on-chip integration of high-performance interconnect. In *Proceedings of the 29th International Supercomputing Conference (ISC)*. Leipzig, Germany, June 22–26, Vol. 8488 of Lecture Notes in Computer Science, pp. 498–507. doi: 10.1007/978-3-319-07518-1_35.

Ajima, Y. et al., 2018. The Tofu Interconnect D. In *Proceedings of the IEEE International Conference on Cluster Computing (CLUSTER)*. Belfast, UK, 10–13 September, pp. 646–654. doi: 10.1109/CLUSTER.2018.00090.

Bossard, A. and Kaneko, K., 2015a. Torus-Connected Cycles: A simple and scalable topology for interconnection networks. *International Journal of Applied Mathematics and Computer Science*, Vol. 25, No. 4, pp. 723–735. doi: 10.1515/amcs-2015-0052.

Bossard, A. and Kaneko, K., 2015b. A routing algorithm solving the container problem in a hypercube with bit constraint. *International Journal of Networked and Distributed Computing*, Vol. 3, No. 4, pp. 202–213. doi: 10.2991/ijndc.2015.3.4.1.

Bossard, A. and Kaneko, K., 2015c. A node-to-set disjoint paths routing algorithm in Torus-Connected Cycles. *International Journal of Computers and Their Applications*, Vol. 22, No. 1, pp. 22–30.

Chen, D. et al., 2011. The IBM Blue Gene/Q interconnection network and message unit. In *Proceedings of the International Conference for High Performance Computing, Networking, Storage and Analysis (SC)*. Seattle, WA, USA, 12–18 November, pp. 1–10. doi: 10.1145/2063384.2063419.

Diestel, R., 2016. *Graph Theory*. Springer-Verlag, Heidelberg, Germany, fifth edition.

Duato, J. et al., 2003. *Interconnection Networks – An Engineering Approach*. Morgan Kaufmann, San Francisco, CA, USA, revised printing.

IBM. IBM100 – Icons of Progress – Blue Gene. https://www.ibm.com/ibm/history/ibm100/us/en/icons/bluegene/. Last accessed June 2022.

Preparata, F. P. and Vuillemin, J., 1981. The Cube-Connected Cycles: A versatile network for parallel computation. *Communications of the ACM*, Vol. 24, No. 5, pp. 300–309. doi: 10.1145/358645.358660.

Scogland, T. et al., 2013. The Green500 list: escapades to exascale. *Computer Science – Research and Development*, Vol. 28, pp. 109–117. doi: 10.1007/s00450-012-0212-6.

TOP500, 2021. Still waiting for exascale: Japan's Fugaku outperforms all competition once again. https://top500.org/news/still-waiting-exascale-japans-fugaku-outperforms-all-competition-once-again/. Last accessed June 2022.

MULTIPLE INHERITANCE MECHANISMS IN LOGIC OBJECTS APPROACH BASED ON A MULTIPLE SPECIALISATION OF OBJECTS

Macaire Ngomo
Laboratoire d'Analyse Numérique, d'Informatique et Applications (LANIA), Faculté des Sciences et Techniques (FST) de l'Université Marien NGOUABI, Brazzaville, République du Congo
CM IT CONSEIL – Département Ingénierie, Recherche, Innovation – 32 rue Milford Haven 10100 Romilly sur Seine, France
IMAGINE TECHNOLOGY, Département Ingénierie, Brazzaville, République du Congo

ABSTRACT

This study takes place within the framework of the representation of knowledge by objects and within the framework of our work on the marriage of logic and objects. On the one hand, object-oriented programming has proved to be appropriate for the construction of complex software systems. On the other hand, logic programming is distinguished by its declarative nature, integrated inference and well-defined semantic capabilities. In particular, inheritance is a refinement mechanism whose mode of application leaves a number of design choices. In the context of this marriage, we describe the semantics of multiple inheritance in a non-deterministic approach based on multiple specification of logical objects. We also describe the conceptual choices for integrating multiple inheritance made for the design of the OO-Prolog language (an object-oriented extension of the Prolog language respecting logical semantics).

KEYWORDS

Object-Oriented Logic Programming, Object-Oriented Representation, Multiple Inheritance, Multi-Point of View, Semantics of Multiple Inheritance

1. INTRODUCTION

Inheritance is a refinement mechanism whose mode of application leaves a number of design choices. In this article, we describe the semantics of inheritance (Cardelli, 1984) in a non-deterministic approach as well as the conceptual choices of integration of monotonous multiple inheritance made for the design of the OO-Prolog language (Ngomo, 1996) as well as its application to the dynamic classification by multiple specialisations of logical objects. Our work concerns the multiple and evolutionary representation of objects that supports reasoning by classification (Capponi & Chaillot, 1993; Dekker, 1993; Drews, 1993; Euzenat, 1993; Marino & al., 1990; Marino & al., 1990; Masini & al., 1989; Mac Gregor & Burstein, 1991; Mac Gregor & Brill, 1992; Napoli, 1992; Rechenmann, 1984). This representation must therefore allow a dynamic classification of logical objects and follow classificatory reasoning. The inheritance management model of the OO-Prolog language is based on the non-determinism of logic programming, on explicit naming and on the concept of full attribute naming which allows conflicts to be resolved before they arise. The OO-Prolog language adopts a dynamic inheritance for both attributes and methods.

2. INHERITANCE IN THE OBJECT-ORIENTED APPROACH

The paradigm of object-based programming, born with Smalltalk (Goldberg & Robson, 1987) at the end of the 1970s, gives a great power of expression, ease of maintenance and reusability superior to other paradigms: imperative, functional (example with LISP Steele, 1990; Sterling & Shapiro, 1990) or logical (example with PROLOG (Sterling & Shapiro, 1990), etc. However, it requires a greater capacity for abstraction than imperative or functional programming in order to choose the "objects" to be reified and to define inheritance and composition between classes in a meaningful and coherent way. The main dimensions of the object paradigm which are classification, inheritance which introduces the notions of generalisation and specialisation, encapsulation and polymorphism (generic functions) were brought together for the first time in Smalltalk 76 (Goldberg & Robson, 1987), although the ideas of class and instance, and inheritance had matured with SIMULA (Doma, 1988). Classes were seen as objects, created by metaclasses, in the object languages created above Lisp, then in Smalltalk 80 (Goldberg & Robson, 1987) and this vision was taken up again in Java where everything is an object, the elements of world representation, the elements of graphical interfaces, but also the elements of the language like functions, classes, events, errors and exceptions. Composition was later added as an autonomous dimension with UML and is present in modern languages such as Java.

2.1 Inheritance

Inheritance is a mechanism for sharing information by factoring members. When several classes have common characteristics, it is possible to create a more general classifier that groups together these structure (classes) or behaviour (interface) properties. Inheritance makes it possible to infer all the members of a class that are not explicitly given there. This mechanism of inference comes back to an algorithm for browsing the class graph according to a defined strategy. Multiple inheritance is an extension to the simple inheritance model where one class is allowed to have several parent classes in order to model multiple generalization. An object can be considered from several points of view. However, the use of multiple inheritance is not without its problems. For example, if the two base classes have attributes or methods with the same name, there are naming collisions that need to be resolved. If inheritance causes a conflict of methods, a conflict resolution strategy, i.e. a choice or combination procedure as in CLOS (Daniel & al., 1992; Keene, 1989) should be used. We will come back to this dimension to describe the conceptual choices of integration of multiple inheritance made for the design of the OO-Prolog language and the strategies for resolving inheritance conflicts.

2.2 Inheritance Semantics

Almost all object languages implement a notion of inheritance between classes. The principle is to specialize and factorize. However, inheritance is a refinement mechanism whose mode of application leaves a certain number of design choices. To do this, we are faced with two design choices: the semantics of inheritance [Cardelli, 1984] and the path strategy of the inheritance graph. In this section, we come back to this concept of inheritance in order to describe its semantics as well as the choices that were retained for the conception of the OO-Prolog language. The traditional definition of inheritance presupposes non-monotonous semantics in the composition of the different inherited classes. Several languages and models are based on this inheritance model. In these languages, the semantics of inheritance is non-monotonic. Generally, these languages use the same strategies as those of common object languages such as the linearization of the classes of the inheritance graph. Examples are ObjVProlog (Malenfant, 1990]) and Prolog++ (Moss, 1994). Others support multiple inheritance and offer no means of resolving conflicts (e.g. the systems of Kowalski (Kowalski, 1979a; Kowalski, 1979b) and Zaniolo (Zaniolo, 1984)). Gallaire (1986), Leonardi and Mello (1988) propose, in object-oriented logic programming, to replace non-monotonous semantics by monotonous semantics where, by backtracking, one would explore vertically all the definitions, from the subclasses to the superclasses. This approach is interesting from the point of view of first-order logic, which is monotonous in nature. However, it poses a major problem. Indeed, if inheritance is used to build on the basis of another class, which supports the idea of monotonous semantics, it is also used to differentiate behaviours. It often happens that an entity is modelled by a class, saying: my instances will be like those of such and such a class (inheritance) except for such and such behaviour (differentiation). This last interpretation therefore requires non-monotonous semantics. This necessity to have a way to reintroduce non-monotonous semantics of inheritance has led Gandilhon (1987) to propose a new form of cut to prevent the backtracking on definitions in inherited classes. He calls this cut "cut_inheritance". Monotonous semantics provides a solution from the point of view of first-order logic programming. However, OO-Prolog adopts non-monotonic inheritance semantics because it is more common in object-oriented programming languages. For the design of OO-Prolog, we have retained the non-monotonous semantics of inheritance for two main reasons:

- because the traditional definition of inheritance assumes non-monotonic semantics in the composition of the different inherited classes
- because it is the most common in object languages and is necessary in many cases to differentiate the behavior of objects.

3. TECHNIQUES FOR RESOLVING INHERITANCE CONFLICTS

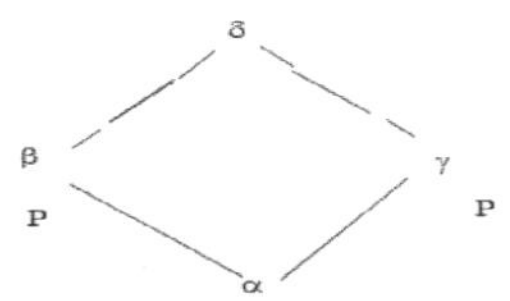

Figure 1. Primitive scene

Inhitance is a mechanism for both hierarchical and deductive information sharing, defined on a set of objects partially ordered by a specialisation relationship. Each of these classes has properties which are the object of inheritance. As a first approximation, these properties have values and a name (or selector). Multiple inheritance allows a more flexible modeling of an application by avoiding the multiplication of useless classes. On the other hand, this form of inheritance can introduce conflicts. The problem of conflicts falls within the general framework of Figure 1 taken from (Ducournau, 1993; Napoli & Ducournau, 1992).There is no universal technique for resolving these kinds of conflicts and there are a wide variety of techniques for resolving them. Different views on how to resolve them are often contradictory. In software engineering, the risks of error and confusion must be avoided at all costs: conflicts are generally prohibited because they are incompatible with a programming framework based on rigour and reliability. In artificial intelligence, multiple inheritance is a natural and indispensable principle for modelling real-world situations and entities. We describe below the common techniques (Booch, 1992; Bouché, 1994; Meyer, 1987; Meyer, 1990).

3.1 Conflict Resolution by Mistake

Error-based conflict resolution occurs when the semantics of the language consider the collision to be illegal and cause an error in compiling the inheriting subclass.

3.2 Conflict Resolution by Equivalence

We speak of conflict resolution by equivalence when the semantics of language consider the same name introduced by different classes as referring to the same field.

3.3 Conflict Resolution by Renaming

Conflict resolution by renaming occurs when the semantics of the language consider the same name introduced by different classes as referring to distinct fields, and thus duplicate the renamed components. The expressions "conflict resolution by duplication" and "conflict resolution by renaming" are synonymous. The Eiffel language uses this principle (Bouché, 1994; Meyer, 1987).

3.4 Conflict Resolution by Qualification

We speak of conflict resolution by qualification when the semantics of language require that all references to the selector fully qualify the source of its statement. In C++, for example, the attribute name includes the name of the overclass, so references to the name fully qualify the source of its declaration.

3.5 Conflict Resolution by Points of View

Here is an object-oriented description of the Computer with a technical and an accounting interpretation. In the example below, inheritance conflicts over the Duration and Priority attributes are handled by viewpoints in OBJLOG (Chouraqui & Dugerdil, 1988; Dugerdil, 1988; Dugerdil, 1991). Let us imagine the Computer class (see Figure 2). This class inherits the Accounting Service and Computer Workshop classes. The Accounting Service class will have a Lifetime attribute (depreciation period) and the Technical Service class will also have the Lifetime attribute (warranty period). When you want to access this attribute, you will have to specify by some means or other if you want to access its value from a "technical" or "accounting" point of view.

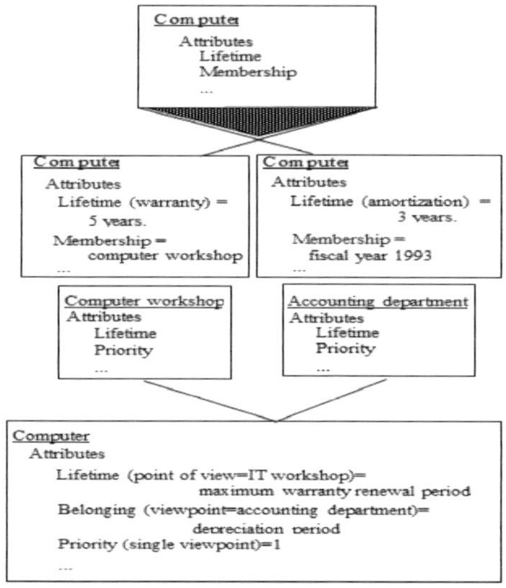

Figure 2. Points of view

"A point of view is an interpretation of all or part of the data of a class corresponding to an abstraction of the real world" (Bouché, 1994). A class may therefore have several points of view. The sum of these points of view will be called perspective. "A perspective is a composite class representing different interpretations (points of view) of the same abstraction of the real world" (Bouché, 1994). We will speak of conflict resolution by points of view when the semantics of the language use the modelling of perspective classes decomposed by the delimitation of points of view. This concept is fundamental in the problematic of knowledge representation (Vogel, 1988) where different types of knowledge do not have the same meaning in different domains of discourse. The OBJLOG language, for example, defines a mother class as a point of view for a daughter class. Unlike CLOS, which resolves possible conflicts by using a precedence list, OBJLOG enshrines the notion of point of view. The conflict resolution algorithm will reason by difference or equivalence of points of view.

3.6 Conflict Resolution by a Combination of Methods

The combination of methods aims, when sending a message, to combine the execution of different methods of the same object. These methods which have the same selector are in call conflict. This technique, used for example in the FLAVORS system, consists of labelling the methods in order to determine a certain sequence. In the KEE language, these labels aim at managing specialisation to avoid arbitrary masking of the methods code (overloading) or more generally conflicts in multiple inheritance (Bouché, 1994). In this case, a parameterization of the path of the inherited classes is given by the combination. This principle of method combination is at the basis of the generic functions introduced in the CLOS language (Daniel & al., 1992; Keene, 1989). We speak of conflict resolution by method combination when the semantics of the language use the notion of method labelling (daemon) to allow a certain chaining, moreover the combination provides a parameterisation of the path of the inherited classes.

3.7 The Path of the Inheritance Graph

In many languages, inheritance conflicts are resolved by defining an order in which outliers will be examined to find the property definition that will be used to respond to a message. Classically, this is equivalent to defining a total or partial order in the inheritance graph or in the sub graph whose source is the instantiation class of the object that receives the message. If the searched property is located at different places in the hierarchy, the first class found by the execution of the path algorithm will be selected; hence the importance of knowing the algorithm used during programming in order to predict the result. Here the direction of the graph will play a role in resolving the conflict since it will, to a certain extent, specify the priorities of the classes. Linear techniques have the major disadvantage of systematizing the treatment of each conflict, without taking into account the semantics of the properties involved. As Masini (Masini & al., 1989) points out, conflict resolution can only be reliable if it takes into account the knowledge related to the application. Systematically applying a default solution cannot therefore correctly resolve each case. The algorithms used in the graph must therefore be taken into account according to the nature of the problems to be solved (Bouché, 1994). Certain modes of conflict resolution prevent this arbitrary choice, dictated by the chronology of class specialization.

4. INHERITANCE MECHANISMS IN ORIENTED-OBJECT LOGIC APPROACH

The OO-Prolog is one of the many hybrid languages resulting from work on the integration of object-oriented programming paradigms and logic programming paradigms (Ait-Kaci & Podelski, 1991; Ait-Kaci & Podelski, 1993; Andreoli & Pareschi, 1992; Bowen & Weinberg, 1985; Chen & Warren, 1988; Conery, 1988; Gandriau, 1987; Davison, 1993; Ishikawa & Tokoro, 1987; Ishikawa & Jungclaus, 1993; Malenfant, 1990; Moss, 1994; Ngomo, 1996; Mac Gregor & Burstein, 1991). It supports multiple inheritance with non-monotonic semantics. To resolve inheritance conflicts, we adopt a solution based on non-deterministic resolution, the notion of viewpoint and the concept of full attribute name. For many common object languages, a default graph traversal strategy is required. Linear strategies remain, for the moment at least, the best compromise (Masini & al., 1989). For some, they are currently the only acceptable techniques (Ducournau, 1993; Napoli & Ducournau, 1992). However, three reasons lead us to propose a non-linear, non-deterministic approach for object-oriented logic programming. Firstly, as Masini (Masini & al., 1989) points out, there is probably no universal, ideal linear strategy that is satisfactory in all cases. Secondly, linear techniques have the major drawback of systematising the treatment of each conflict, without taking into account the semantics of the data involved. Finally, the possibility offered by Prolog to explore, by backtracking, all possible alternatives, allows, in case of ambiguities, to consider an object with all its points of view (without any discrimination). OO-Prolog adopts a dynamic inheritance for both attributes and methods. However, attribute inheritance and method inheritance are treated differently.

4.1 Attribute Inheritance

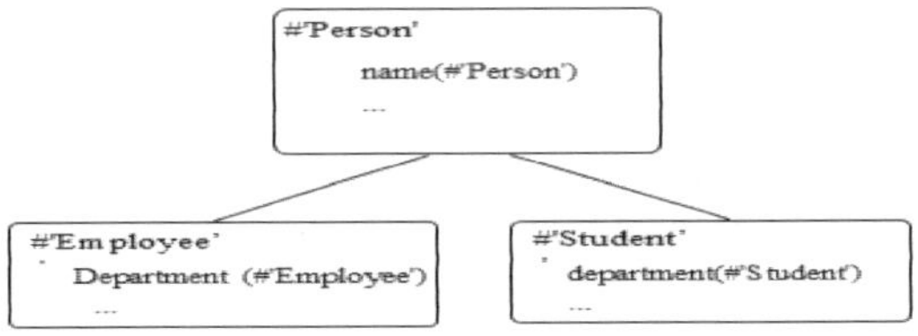

Figure 3. Full name of an attribute in OO-Prolog

For the choice of the inheritance model of the OBJLOG language, Dugerdil and Chouraki hypothesised that the conflicting attributes do not have the same semantics (Chouraqui & Dugerdil, 1988; Dugerdil, 1988; Dugerdil, 1991). We take up some of OBJLOG's ideas and retain this hypothesis in particular to provide the means to resolve name conflicts before they arise. In OO-Prolog, attribute name conflicts are resolved by the concept of full name (Escamilla, 1990). If an attribute is defined in a class, its full name is the term whose functor is equal to the attribute name and whose only argument is the definition class. This means that two attributes with the same name but not having the same origin (definition class) have different full names and are considered semantically different. This is the case here for the 'department' attributes defined in the classes #'Employee' and #'Student' (Figure 3). As we have already seen, an attribute is represented by a Prolog term of arity one. Its argument corresponds to the point of view that determines the interpretation of the attribute: <name>(<interpretation>). Each attribute inherited from an overclass therefore has a different interpretation from the others. A class then inherits all the attributes of its upgrades. Two attributes are homonymous if they have the same name and if the intersection of their labels is empty (for example, department(#'Employee') and department(#'Student') are homonymous). Conversely, two attributes are different if their names are different (for example, name(#'Person') and age(#'Person') are different). As in OBJLOG, we define a mother class as a point of view for a daughter class. Thus we can use the inheritance relation to introduce the notion of disjunctive interpretation of an attribute at the level of a class C, i.e. the set of interpretations of the attributes of the same name in the subgraph of C. It corresponds to the set noted {c1,...,cn}, where ci are classes, maximum lower bounds for this attribute at the level of class C.

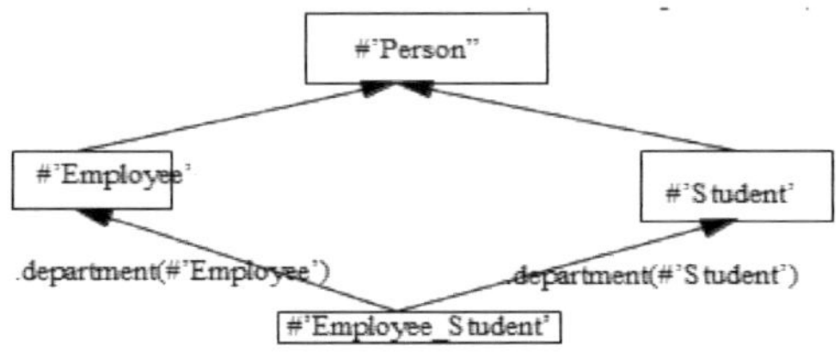

Figure 4. Interpretation of an attribute

In the context of Figure 4, the disjunctive interpretation of the 'department' attribute at class level #'Employee_Student' is {#'Employee',#'Student'}. The disjunctive interpretation of an attribute at the level of its definition class is the singleton composed of this same class. For example, the disjunctive interpretation of the department attribute at the class level #'Employee' is the singleton {#'Employee'}. Thus, when in a method call the interpretation of an attribute is a free variable, it is unified with each of the elements of the disjunctive interpretation of this attribute at the level of the current class. Let O therefore be an instance of the class #' Employee_Student ', having for study department "La Seine-Maritime" and for work department "La Haute-Seine". The processing of the following request is done as follows:

- first find the disjunctive interpretation of the "department" attribute at the level of the current class, here Employee _Student: {#' Employee',#'Student'},
- using backtracking, instantiate the variable Int with each of the elements of this set and calculate the value of the attribute corresponding to each interpretation.

One of its subclasses can be specified as in the following example. In this case, the value of the attribute is calculated in the same way, considering as the disjunctive interpretation of this attribute at the level of the subclass specified when calling the method.

4.2 The Inheritance of Methods

In this section we discuss one aspect of inheritance which is the inheritance of behaviour. We are in the most general case, that of multiple inheritance. Behaviour inheritance is a synthesis of the consequences of the inheritance relation at the level of methods; it describes the evolution of the behaviour of classes through user-defined inheritance links. In OO-Prolog, method inheritance is also dynamic but managed differently by three complementary strategies which can be combined dynamically.

4.3 The Non-Deterministic Strategy

In order to consider an object with all its points of view, OO-Prolog uses a partial order with backtracking in the case of remaining ambiguities. By default, sending a message activates all methods in conflict, taking advantage of the backtracking performed by the Prolog interpreter in his exhaustive search for solutions to a query.

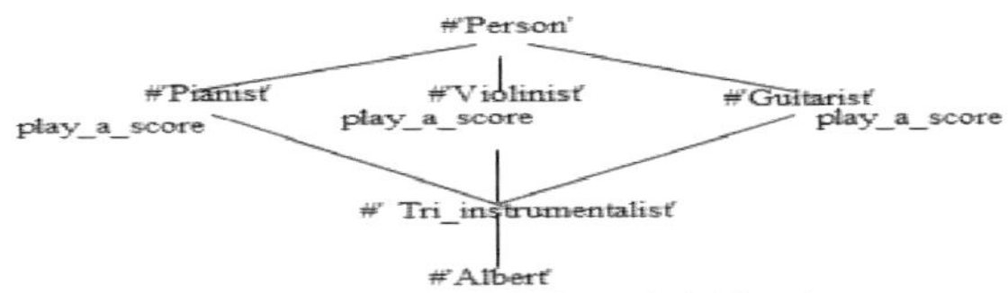

Figure 5. Points of view of #'Albert'

For example, in figure 5, #'Albert' designates an instance of the class #'Tri-instrumentalist' which itself inherits three classes: Pianist, #'Violinist', #'Guitarist'. In each of these classes the method play_a_score is defined. If Albert is asked to play a score by sending him the following message "#'Albert' <- play_a_score", which instrument will use #'Albert' to play his score? In a linear approach in which classes are given priority, Albert will consider the class with the highest priority and therefore use the instrument corresponding to that class by default. For example, in CLOS it will be the Pianist class. In OO-Prolog, this message is transformed into or logical on the maximum lower bounds of this method at the level of the class #'Tri-instrumentalist' ({#'Pianist', #'Violinist', #'Guitarist'}). This prevents an arbitrary choice dictated by the chronology of class specialisation and thus prevents the object from being questioned from all points of view (or in all its aspects). We can multiply examples of this kind. In the context of Figure 6, sending the message department(D) to the object #'Paul' is equivalent to #'Paul' as #'Employee' or #'Paul' as #'Student'. Thus, by default, OO-Prolog does not deal with method inheritance conflicts. Sending a message activates all the conflicting methods, taking advantage of the feedback provided by the Prolog interpreter in his exhaustive search for solutions to a query. Thus, while in the monotonous approach, backtracking is used to introduce monotonous inheritance semantics (Figure 7), we use it here to avoid introducing a horizontal order between classes. This makes it possible to consider an object with all its points of view, without any discrimination. In classical approaches, a choice is made, with no possibility of going back. In OO-Prolog, backtracking allows the application of all conflicting methods (Figure 8).

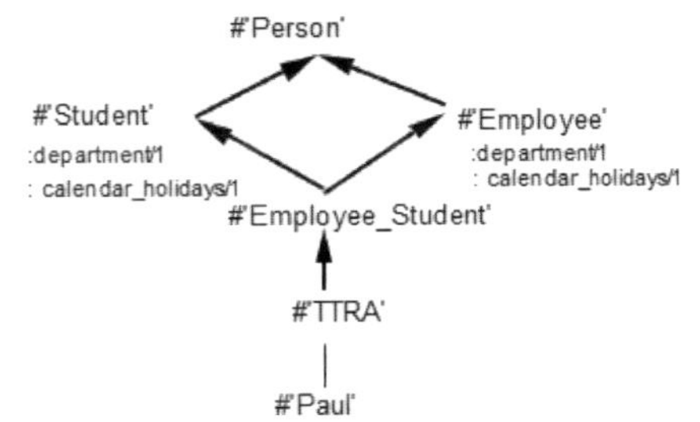

Figure 6. Student and Employee: which department/1 instance O uses at the TTRA level?

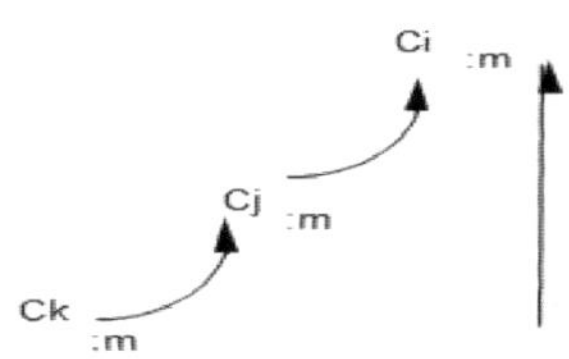

Figure 7. Vertical backtracking

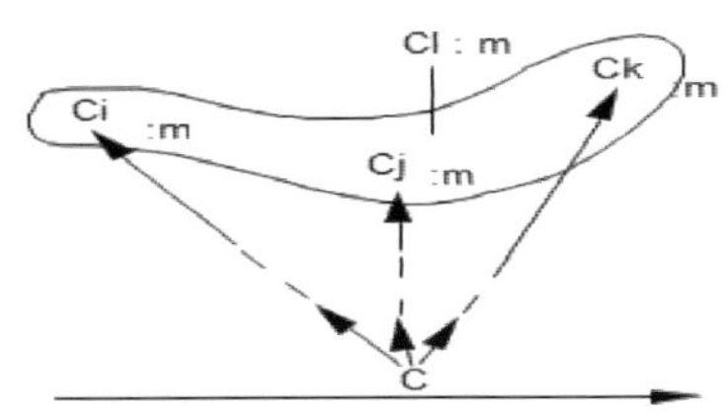

Figure 8. Horizontal backtracking

By default, the general rule is therefore that sending a message triggers all possible methods, taking advantage of the feedback provided by the Prolog interpreter. For example, in the context of Figure 6, sending the message department(D) to the object #'Paul' of the TTRA class is equivalent to or logical and is dealt with by exploring conflicting classes by backtracking. This strategy is in our opinion more general than a classical non-monotonous linear strategy such as Pclos, P1, etc. in that any solution obtained using such a linear strategy can also be a solution of this approach. For example, in the context of Figure 6, P1 and Pclos consider the class #'Student' as having a higher priority than the class #'Employee'. The object will therefore respond to the department(D) message as a student and eventually return to its study department.

4.3.1 Linear Strategy

A message of the form "O <-- Message" is processed using a predefined linear extension algorithm. Linear strategies are to be taken into account according to the nature of the problems to be solved. They do not always give the same result. The user must therefore be given the possibility to introduce his own strategies or to use several existing strategies (Pclos, P1, Pflavors, etc.). The solution currently adopted in OO-Prolog consists in making available to the programmer several path strategies that he can use according to his needs. By default it is the inversion or P1 route strategy that will be considered by the system. A simplified version of the inversion algorithm consists in removing the nodes from the graph in the order of stacking the deep path first, without masking the nodes already visited: the result therefore contains several occurrences of certain nodes. The resulting list is then browsed in reverse, removing as it goes along the elements already encountered at least once. In this way, only the last occurrence of each element in the initial list is kept in the final list.

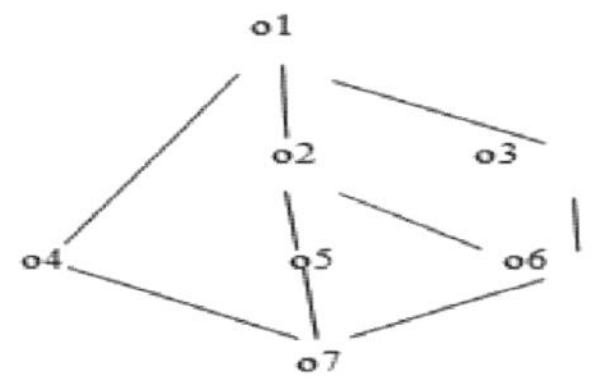

Figure 9. Example of an inheritance graph

Let us consider the graph in Figure 9 and calculate the priority list of o7 using this algorithm. The list provided by the depth path first is as follows: o7, o4, o1, o5, o2, o1, o6, o2, o1, o3, o1. The priority list obtained after removing duplicates is as follows: o7, o4, o5, o6, o2, o3, o1. The definition of a linear strategy is done by defining the predicate lookup (Class,Precedence,LookupName) where Class is the class at which the graph starts and Precedence is the precedence list of the Class class. The LookupName parameter is the name of the strategy. Thus, it is possible to define several independent linear strategies and to use them all in the same application. The primitive set_lookup then dynamically sets the strategy to be used: set_lookup(S), S being the strategy to be set. For example, if the user defines the strategy of CLOS, to fix it, just execute the goal : set_lookup(pclos). The primitive get_lookup(S) unifies variable S with the name of the current strategy. This assignment is temporary and defeated by backtracking.

4.3.2 The Explicit Designation

It consists in explicitly designating a class to which a method belongs. It is a tool made available to the user and allowing him/her to have greater control over the inheritance mechanism. By explicitly designating the class of origin of a property, it is thus possible to make certain choices "by hand", thanks to a horizontal masking of the other classes. A designation may be incomplete. This is the case when the designated class is not the one in which the property is defined, but one of its superclasses. In this case, the basic strategy will be used, starting from the designated class. The explicit designation is introduced by the ":"/2 operator:

<(<object> <- (<class>):<message>

Still in the context of Figure 6, the application allows you to consider the object O, a direct instance of the class #'Employee_Student', as a direct instance of the class #'Employee' and to hide horizontally the department/1 method defined in the class #'Student'.

(a) Explicit multiple designation

In OO-Prolog, the explicit designation can be multiple, i.e. several classes can be designated. Although the designated classes are considered in this order, it is not of great importance since, regardless of the order given, the result is the same. Thus, we can also write:

?- D <- ([#'Swimming_Bird', #'Flying_Bird']) :mode(Mode).

(b) Explicit designation and masking

When a class is explicitly designated, a control mechanism makes it possible to check that the principle of vertical masking is respected.

(c) Designation and path of the inheritance graph

It is also a means of reducing the complexity of the methods in the inheritance graph, since it consists of making a jump to the designated class and consequently reducing the method search graph.

5. CONCLUSION AND PERSPECTIVES

We have described a new model for handling multiple inheritance and its application in the context of object-oriented logic programming. The logic approach has many advantages over traditional methods. It brings a lot of flexibility on the handling of inheritance. Our method of handling inheritance avoids an arbitrary choice dictated by the system. It is even possible to combine different strategies depending on the problem to be treated. This vision of inheritance allows us to implement more easily classification mechanisms based on multiple specialization. Such mechanisms combined with the delay mechanism allow to freeze all the classification constraints and to trigger them only when the missing data are available.

REFERENCES

Ait-Kaci & Podelski, (1991) Ait-Kaci, H. & Podelski, A. "Towards a Meaning of LIFE". Proc. of the Thirsd Int'l Conf. on Programming Language Implementation and Logic Programming, Lectures Notes in Comp. Sciences, Passaü, Aug. 1991.

Ait-Kaci & Podelski, (1993) Ait-Kaci, H. & Podelski, A. "Towards a Meaning of LIFE". Journal of Logic Programming, 16:195-234, 1993.

Andreoli & Pareschi, (1992) Andreoli J.M., Pareschi R., "Linear objects: A logic framework for open system programming", In A. Voronkov, editor, Inter. Conference on Logic Programming and Automated Reasoning LPAR'92, pp 448 450, St. Petersburg, Russia, July 1992.

Daniel & al., (1992) Daniel G. Bobrow, Linda G. DeMichiel, Richard P. Gabriel, Sonya E.Keene, Gregor Kiczales and David A. Moon. "Common Lisp Object System specification", ACM SIGPLAN Notices, 1988

Booch, (1992) Booch G. "Object Oriented Design with applications" The Benjamin/Cummings Publishing Company, Inc., Redwood City, California, 1992.

Bouché, (1994) Bouché M., "La démarche objet. Concepts et outils.", AFNOR, 1994.

Bowen & Weinberg, (1985) Bowen, K.A. et Weinberg, T. A Meta Level Extension of Prolog, IEEE Inttl Symp. on Logic Prog. 'B5 (1985), pp.48 53.

Cardelli, (1984) Cardelli L., A semantics of Multiple Inheritance, LNCS, vol.137, Springer-Verlag, pp.51-67, 1984.

[Capponi & Chaillot, (1993) Capponi C., Chaillot M., Construction incrémentale d'une base de classes correcte du point de vue des types, Actes Journée Acquisition-Validation-Apprentissage, Saint-Raphael, 1993.

Chouraqui & Dugerdil, (1988) Chouraqui E., Dugerdil Ph., Conflict olving in a Frame-like Multiple Inheritance System, ECAI, Munich, pp.226-232, 1988.

Chen & Warren, (1988) Chen W. and Warren D. S.. Objects as intensions. In Logic Programming: Proc. 5th Int'l Conf. and Symp., Seattle, WA, USA, 15 19 Aug 1988, pages 404 19. The MIT Press, Cambridge, MA, 1988.

Conery, (1988) Conery J., Logical Objects. Proc. of the Fifth Int'l Conf. on Logic Prog. , p.p. '20-443, 1988.

Davison, (1993) Davison, A. "A Survey of Logic Programming-based Object Oriented Languages". In Research Directions in Concurrent Object-Oriented Programmaing. The MIT Press, Cambridge, MA, 1993.

Dekker, (1993) Dekker L., « Frome : représentation multiple et classification d'objets avec points de vue », Thèse de doctorat en Sciences appliquées, Sous la direction de Gérard Comyn. Soutenue en 1994, à Lille 1.

Doma, (1988) Doma, A. "Object-Prolog: Dynamic Object-Oriented Representation of Knowledge". In T. Henson, editor, SCS Multiconference on Artificial Intelligence and Simulation: The Diversity of Applications, pages 83-88, San Diego, CA, Feb. 1988.

Drews, (1993) Drews O. M.. Raisonnement classificatoire dans une représentation à objets multi-points devue. Interface homme-machine [cs.HC]. Université Joseph-Fourier - Grenoble I, 1993. Français. tel-00005133

Ducournau, (1993) Ducournau R., Héritages et représentations, Mémoire, Diplôme d'Habilitation à diriger des recherches, spécialité : Informatique, Université Montpellier II, 1993.

Dugerdil, (1988) Dugerdil P., Contribution à l'étude de la représentation des connaissances fondée sur les objets. Le langage OBJLOG. Thèse de l'Université d'Aix-Marseille II, 1988.

Dugerdil, (1991) Dugerdil P., Inheritance Mechanisms in the OBJLOG language : Multiple Selective and Multiple Vertical with Points of View in Inheritance Hierarchies in Knowledge Representation, M.Lenzerini, D.Nardi and M.Simi (éd.), John Wiley & Sons Ltd., pp.245-256, 1991.

Escamilla, (1990) Escamilla J., JEAN P., Relationships in an Object Knowledge Representation Model, Proceedings IEEE. 2nd Conference on Tools for Artificial Intelligence, Washington D.C. USA, pp.632-638, 1990.

Euzenat, (1993) Euzenat J., Classification dans les représentations par objets : produits de systèmes classificatoires, Rapport interne, Equipe SHERPA, INRIA, 1993.

Gallaire, (1986) [Gallaire, 1986] Gallaire, H. "Merging Objects and Logic Programming: Relational Semantics, Performance and Standarization". In Proc. AAAI'86, pp.754-758, Philadelphia, Pensylrania, 1986.

Gandilhon, (1987) Gandilhon T. "Proposition d'une extension objet minimale pour Prolog.", Actes du séminaire de Programmation logique, Trégastel (mai 1987), pp. 483-506.

Gandriau, (1987) Gandriau, M. "CIEL: classes et instances en logique". Thèse de Doctorat, ENSEEIHT 1988, 151p.

Goldberg & Robson, (1987) Goldberg, A. and Robson, D. "Smalltalk-80: The language and its implementation". Addison-Wesley, 1983.

Ishikawa & Tokoro, (1987) Ishikawa, Y. et Tokoro, M. Orient84/K: An ObJect Orlented Concurrent Programming Language for Knowledge Representation, Object Oriented Concurrent Programming (1987), W 159 198.

Ishikawa & Jungclaus, (1993) Ishikawa, Y. R. Jungclaus. Logic Based Modeling of Dynamic Object Systems. PhD thesis, Technical University Braunschweig, Germany, 1993.

Keene, (1989) Sonja E. Keene, "Object-Oriented Programming in Common Lisp : a Programmer's Guide to CLOS", Addison-Wesley, 1989.

Kowalski, (1979a) Kowalski, R. "Algorithm = Logic + Control", Comm. ACM 22, 7 (1979), 424-436.

Kowalski, (1979b) Kowalski, R. "Logic for problem solving". North-Holland, Amsterdam, 1979.

Leonardi & Mello, (1988) Leonardi L. and Mello P., "Combining logic- and object-oriented programming language paradigms", in Proceedings of the Twenty-First Annual Hawaii International Conference on System Sciences. Volume II: Software track, Kailua-Kona, HI, USA, 1988 pp.376-385. doi: 10.1109/HICSS.1988.11828

Malenfant, (1990) Malenfant, J. "Conception et Implantation d'un langage de programmation intégrant trois paradigmes: la programmation logique, la programmation par objets et la programmation répartie". Thèse de PhD, Univ. de Montréal, Mars 1990.

Marino & al., (1990) Mariño O., Rechenmann F., Uvietta P. Multiple perspectives and classification mechanism in object-oriented representation, 9th ECAI, pp.425-430, Stockholm 1990.

Marino & al., (1990) Marino O., Classification d'objets composites dans un système de représentation de connaissances multi-points de vue, RFIA'91, Lyon-Villeurbanne, pp. 233-242, 1991.

Masini & al., (1989) Masini G., Napoli A. Colnet D. Leonard D., Tombre K., Les langages à objets. Interedition, Paris, 1989.

Mac Gregor & Burstein, (1991) Mac Gregor R.M., Burstein M.H. Using a Description Classifier to Enhance Knowledge Representation, IEEE Expert Intelligent Systems and Applications, juin, 1991.

Mac Gregor & Brill, (1992) Mac Gregor R.M., Brill D., Recognition Algorithms for the LOOM Classifier, AAAI, San José, CA, juillet, pp.774-779, 1992.

Meyer, (1987) Meyer B."Eiffel: Programming for reusability and extendibility", ACM SIGPLAN Notices, 22(2):85-94, 1987.

Meyer, (1990) Meyer B. "Conception et programmation par objets, pour le génie logiciel de qualité", InterEditions, Paris 1990.

Moss, (1994) Moss C., "Prolog++: The Power of Object-Oriented and Logic Programming", Addison-Wesley, 1994.

Napoli, 1992 Napoli A., « Représentations à objets et raisonnement par classification en intelligence artificielle », Thèse de doctorat en Informatique. Soutenue en 1992, au CRIN - Centre de Recherche en Informatique de Nancy, France.

Napoli & Ducournau, (1992) Napoli A., Ducournau R., Subsumption in Object-Based Representations,Proceedings ERCIM Workshop on theoretical and practical aspects of knowledge representation, (rapport ERCIM 92-W001) pp1-9, Pisa (IT), 1992.

Ngomo, (1996) Ngomo M. "Intégration de la programmation logique et de la programmation par objets : étude, conception et implantation". Thèse de Doctorat d'Informatique, Université de Rouen - INSA Rouen, Décembre 1996.

Vogel, (1988) Vogel C., Génie Cognitif, Collection Sciences cognitives, MASSON, PAris, pp.97 1988.

Steele, (1990) Steele G. L. "Common Lisp : the language" second edition, Digital Press, 1990.

Sterling & Shapiro, (1990) Sterling, L. et Shapiro, E. "L'Art de Prolog". MASSON 1990.

Zaniolo, (1984) Zaniolo, C. "Object-Oriented Programming in Prolog". In Proc. of the IEEE Internatial Symposium on Logic Programming, pp. 265-270, Atlantic City, New Jersey, 1984.

Rechenmann, (1984) Rechenmann F., Bensaid A. et Granier D., SHIRKA: des systèmes experts centrés-objet. Actes 4ièmes journées internationales sur les systèmes-experts et leurs applications, actes polycopiés, Avignon, FR, 1984.

SUNSPOT DETECTION USING DEEP LEARNING TECHNIQUES

Pieter Swanepoel, Günther Richard Drevin, Roelf Du Toit Strauss and Petrus Johannes Steyn
North-West University Potchefstroom, South Africa

ABSTRACT

Accurate and automated monitoring of space weather has become increasingly important in our modern-day world, due to the reliance on critical infrastructure such as wireless communication, power grids, satellite communication, and aviation systems. Solar events such as solar flares and coronal mass ejections can disrupt or damage these system and sunspots are used as markers to determine solar activity through a manual process, thus automated detection and tracking of sunspots form part of the prediction of solar events and prediction of space weather. In this paper the use of deep learning techniques for automated sunspot detection will be investigated.

KEYWORDS

Sunspots, Space Weather, Deep Learning, Object Detection

1. INTRODUCTION

Sunspots are dark regions characterized by a dark core called the umbra and a filamentary outer layer named the penumbra that appears in the photosphere of the Sun which starts at the surface and extends about 500km and can be observed in the visible parts of the continuous radiation spectrum. sunspots appear darker due to the difference in temperature compared to the surrounding photosphere. Umbral diameters may vary from 10^4 km to 20^4 km (Wilkinson, 2012). Penumbral diameters vary between 10^4 km and 15^4 km. Sunspots start out as small dark spots referred to as pores, whereas only certain pores develop into full Sunspot regions. These regions may then grow larger and darker and even break away to form groups of sunspots. Sunspots are, a phenomenon due to the buildup of magnetic field pressure in the core of the Sun. Due to the pressure then becoming larger than that of the outer layers, the spot starts rising to the outer layers and becomes visible on the surface. The plasma processes that cause the phenomena is due to the dense hot plasma that is confined within the tangled magnetic fields that are rising from the interior part of the Sun, and these phenomena contain large amounts of free magnetic energy which is thought of as the main source of transient phenomena. Re-configurations of these magnetic fields may be accompanied by clouds of plasma that are ejected into interplanetary space, also referred to as a coronal mass ejection. When these eruptions occur at smaller scale, electrons are released that can collide with denser matter at the surface of the Sun which produces a burst of electromagnetic radiation which is particularly noticeable in the EUV and X-ray wavelengths called solar flares (Hanslmeier, 2004). As the Sun rotates these sunspots or sunspot groups travel along the Sun from east to west and may shear and change shape. One theory suggests sunspots are formed by the convergence of magnetic elements and pores which need a driving force. This force is theorized to be the individual fragments that form sunspots and are part of a larger flux tube in the convection zone as opposed to a coalescence of smaller flux tubes (Solanki, 2003). Sunspots not only have visual characteristics, but the magnetic structure of a Sunspot can also provide information regarding the solar magnetic field of the Sun. The polarity of a Sunspot is directly related to the solar cycle, where 22 years is a full cycle. This is due to the polarity of the Sun that changes with every 11 years (Wilkinson, 2012). Sunspot numbers were found to vary according to a 11-year cycle, whereas the relative Sunspot number goes through a maximum and minimum known as the solar maximum and the solar minimum (Solanki, 2003). As a rule, it is regarded that the Sunspot cycle is closely related to the magnetic structure of the Sun, due to how Sunspot numbers vary as the magnetic structure of the Sun changes. At the beginning of a solar cycle, most sunspots will form at 25 degrees north or south of the solar equator, whereas, later in the cycle, they will form closer to the equator. This formation of sunspots only in those regions and latitudes indicate that they are only forming in activity belts of the Sun. Because sunspots are only in very active regions leads to the understanding that sunspots are the heart of the active regions with a great deal of magnetic activity surrounding the sunspot (Solanki, 2003). Figure 1 shows there exists a clear correlation between solar events and the number of sunspots on the solar surface. When the Sunspot cycle goes through a maximum, there is a peak in solar events.

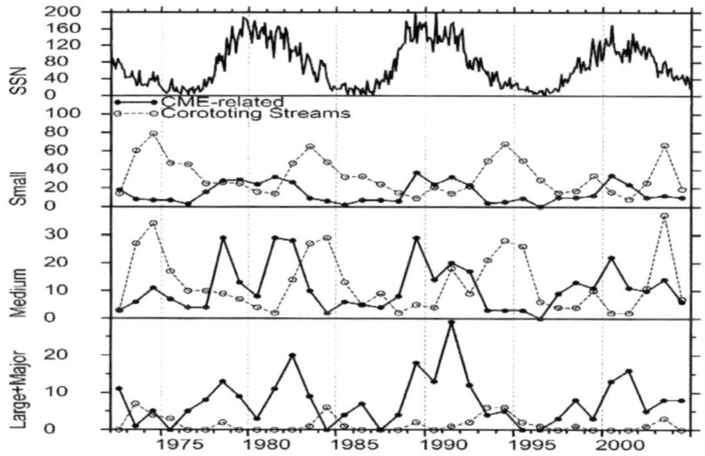

Figure 1. Sunspot numbers with associated small, medium, and large solar events

Solar events occur in multiple stages and start with the emission of energetic X-ray photons which is more commonly called a solar flare and affects various systems and processes. Following the X-ray flash, there is a release of solar energetic particles which then propagate into interplanetary Space (Hanslmeier, 2004, Hapgood, 2017). This is then followed by a coronal mass ejection which is a continuous release of particles and solar plasma but is much slower and takes longer to reach Earth (Hanslmeier, 2004). Solar flares and coronal mass ejections both contribute to space weather and influence Earth in very different ways. In general, there are two types of solar flares: the first type is a simple loop flares which is not usually associated with coronal mass ejections due to the flare being very small, usually brightens up, and remains unchanged because it only consists of a single magnetic flux tube. The other type of flare, referred to as a two-ribbon flare, is generally associated with major class types and can be much more dramatic with a longer duration, which is associated with coronal mass ejections. The flux of high energy particles produced by two ribbon flares enhances solar wind, which compresses the magnetosphere and increases the magnetic field near the surface of the earth (Hanslmeier, 2004). Once the solar wind plasma enters the magnetosphere it is stored in the tail of the magnetosphere and can cause a re-connection event which releases an explosion of stored energy that causes what is known as a sub-storm. Major solar events can create a sudden large influx of energy into the magnetosphere which can then set off an ensemble of sub-storm, termed geomagnetic storms (Hapgood, 2017). Being aware of solar events, will allow for proper mitigation plans to be in place, and avoid the consequences of these events. This can be achieved through automated monitoring and notifications systems, to allow proper measures to be in place. The primary aim of this study is to train and test state of the art object detection models to detect and monitor sunspots. Related Research surrounding event detection using images alongside text-based reports have been performed to classify events with an 88% accuracy (Fang, 2019). This was done using a convolutional neural network. Similar areas of study include brain metastases detection due to the appearance being like the blob structure of sunspots. This study used SSD for metastases with an 84% accuracy (Zhou, 2019). Other Studies include Condition classification using a CNN and a support vector machine that achieved a 99% accuracy (Channabasava & Biabl, 2022).

2. METHOD

The Data set used to train the models consists of 815 images of which the training data was separated into 570 for training, 164 for validation and 82 for testing. The images were obtained from the Royal Observatory of Belgium, with their corresponding arch drawings on which manual sunspot identification was done. These arch drawings were used in the labeling as the ground truth source. To further enhance the dataset and have more training data the initial 570 training images underwent a series of pre-processing steps to not only enhance, but also augment the images. The enhancement was needed as some images are very partially obscured when there are clouds in the sky. The images span across the start of 2008 to 2019, of which there are images which were taken that had no sunspots which were discarded. Object detection models from different areas were implemented falling into either single stage or two stage detection, which have various tradeoffs regarding speed and accuracy under different circumstances. The models trained for this paper were faster RCNN, YOLO (You Only Look Once), SSD (Single Shot Detector), and EfficientDet using a NVIDIA V100. Thus, comparing which of the object detection models have the best precision in detecting sunspots on white light images.

2.1 Regional Proposal (Two Stage) vs Regression Classification (One Stage)

High level overview of two stage and one stage detection:

- Region proposal is a two-step process which was designed to extract regions of interest and was inspired partially by the attentional mechanism of the human brain (Zhao, 2019). This mechanism functions by scanning the entire scenario coarsely, and then focuses on the regions that are of interest. a convolutional neural network is used as a backbone to extract features, which allows predictions of bounding boxes directly from locations of the topmost feature map after obtaining the relevant confidences of the underlying objects (Zhao, 2019).
- The regression classification detection framework is based on global regression classification, which maps straight from the pixels to bounding box coordinates and class probabilities. Single stage detectors were adapted and designed to use deep neural networks with regression final layers instead of soft-max activations as the final layers which is capable of generating object binary masks (Zhao, 2019). The final step is to draw the bounding boxes from the masks, by re scaling the masks to the input image and estimating the coordinates.

2.2 Training Process

High level overview of modelling and training:

1. Build a config and training pipeline file in framework format
2. Process and format data into correct format for the model
3. Iterate with training at different batch sizes and number of epochs
4. Adjust hyper parameters
5. Train the model until no meaningful precision increase occurs without overfitting
6. Test and validate the model against the testing images
7. Change the model back bone and or architecture
8. Iterate the process again.

2.3 Faster RCNN (Two Stage)

The Faster RCNN model was trained using Detectron 2, TensorFlow 2 and PyTorch. All the frameworks use different training formats and input formats, and this was done to note if there is any meaningful difference between a model between the frameworks. Different backbones were also used throughout training to establish if a deeper backbone that has more training parameters would yield better precision or only add more training time and yield no increase in average precision.

Overview of Faster RCNN training process:

- The region proposal network receives an image of the sun as input from a convolutional feature extractor which outputs a feature map

- The feature map is then fed into the region proposal network which applies a sliding window protocol with a small network.
- The sliding window will then map the features to a lower dimensional or more recognizable feature.
- The lower dimensional features are then fed into two sibling fully connected layers which are a box-regression layer and a box-classification layer to perform detection and classification.

Figure 2 illustrates a detection by one of the Faster RCNN models, specifically showing the capability of the model to detect sunspots that are just going out of sight on the outer edge of the solar limb.

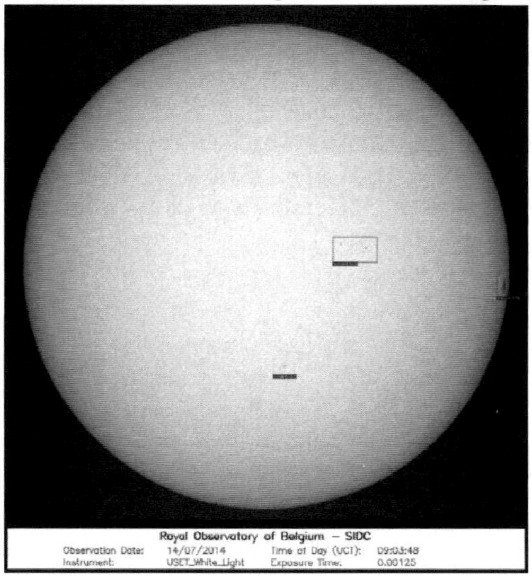

Figure 2. Faster RCNN sunspot detection

2.4 YOLO

The YOLO model was trained using PyTorch and TensorFlow 2, as Detectron 2 does not support any YOLO architectures. Different formats of data structures were used for the two frameworks and all the architectures of yolo available including the darknet architecture were trained and iterated with using different hyperparameters and architectures.

Overview of YOLO training process:

- The input image is divided into a grid, where if an object falls into the center of a grid cell that cell is responsible for detecting that object.
- These grid cells each predict several bounding boxes and confidence scores for the corresponding boxes, which are then used to evaluate the intersection over union using the ground truth
- If a box does indeed contain a object that value will be assigned to the box or zero otherwise.
- Each of the grid cells have corresponding bounding boxes with predictions, labelled and the confidence where the center is of the box, which are relative to the bounds of the grid cell.
- The height and the width are predicted relative to the whole image.
- Confidence is predicted using the ground truth box and the intersection over union between the predicted and ground truth box.
- Each of the grid cells also predicts several conditional class probabilities. Only one set of class probabilities is produced per grid cell regardless of the number of bounding boxes.
- When the test occurs the conditional class probabilities and the individual box confidence predictions are multiplied, which produces a class -specific confidence for each of the classes appearing in the box and how well the box is situated around the object.

Figure 3 illustrates sunspot detection precision from the YOLO model on an image where a sunspot is just going around the solar limb

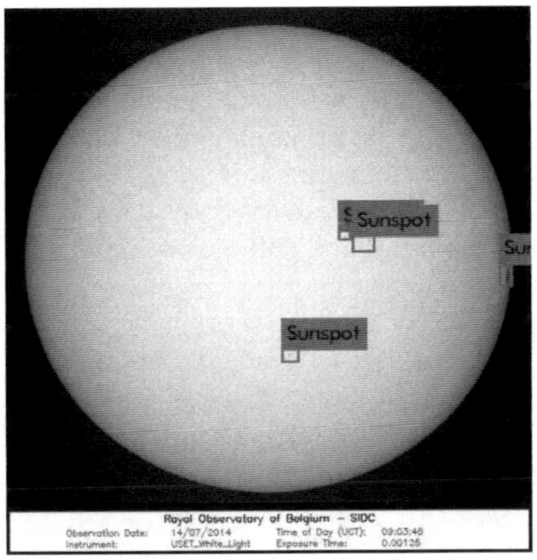

Figure 3. YOLO Sunspot detection

2.5 SSD

The Single Shot Detector was trained using TensorFlow 1.5 because TensorFlow 2 does not have a SSD available yet, and also Detectron 2 where mobile friendly versions were also trained to establish if lighter smaller models meant for less powerful hardware could detect sunspots. Due to the Single Shot Detector being on TensorFlow 1.5 older versions of CUDA and cuDNN had to be used alongside older version of NVIDIA drivers. The different architectures and versions of the SSD were trained.

Overview of SSD training process:

- The input image is used to predict category scores and box offsets for a fixed set of default bounding boxes that are of different scales and aspect ratios
- A set of default anchors then aid in helping to discretize the output space with the various scales of and aspect ratios of the anchor boxes
- These various predictions of the different feature maps are then fused
- This is followed by a non-max suppression step to produce the final output decisions, whereas the early layers are based on high quality classifier networks for good feature extraction

Figure 4 illustrates sunspot detections on a Single Shot Detector using the same image as in 2.2.

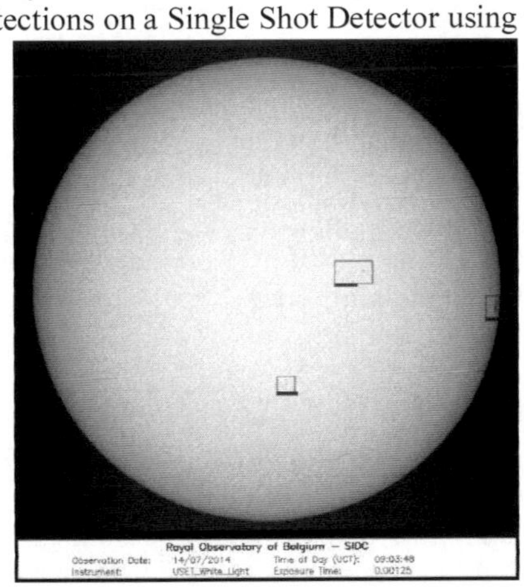

Figure 4 SSD sunspot detection

2.6 EfficientDet

EfficientDet was trained using PyTorch and TensorFlow 2, the model has only a single version and does not have different backbones, but the different versions of the model are the same architecture just with differ scales applied across the backbone, image resolution and feature fusion neck. The models go from d0 to d7 getting bigger as you go up from d0. Only d0 to d3 were trained as the model is very memory intensive and requires multi-graphics processing unit set ups to train all the way to d7.

Overview of EfficientDet training process:

- Extract irregular features from the backbone network.
- Fusion occurs in a bidirectional neural network where features are fused for each layer in the backbone using bidirectional cross scale connections repeatedly and fast normalized fusion
- Perform class and box prediction on fused features with a box regression and classification layer.

Figure 5 illustrates detection of sunspots on a group of sunspots and where some sunspots are just moving over the solar limb.

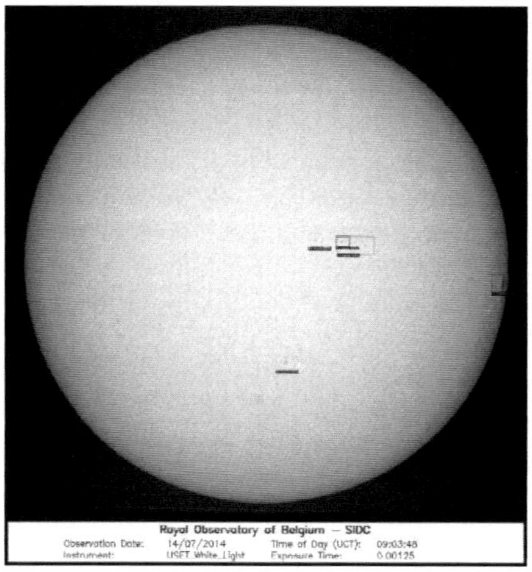

Figure 5. EfficientDet sunspot detection

3. RESULTS

These models were trained and tested using different architectures, different backbones, hyper parameters and frameworks. Models were also trained with and without the augmented data set to establish if the augmentations and enhancements were improving average precision. The results will now be discussed.

3.1 Faster RCNN

The average precision achieved by the Faster RCNN model varied between all the different backbones and hyper parameters. The best performing model achieved an 82.5 % mean average precision, whereas the rest of the Faster RCNN models varied between 79 – 81. The best performing model did not detect any false positives and was very good at picking up sunspots around the solar limbs that were either going out of sight or coming into sight. Sunspots appear in groups also and all the Faster RCNN models were able to contextually learn this, and none of the sunspot pair were seen as two individual sunspots. The Faster RCNN model is very good at sunspot detection and proved very accurate also.

3.2 YOLO

The YOLO models proved that single stage detection techniques can keep up in terms of accuracy with two stage detectors and the best model achieved an 81% accuracy, where no false positives were picked up and the model was very good at detecting sunspots around the solar limbs. However, the yolo models struggled to see a sunspot pair and sunspot group as a single sunspot. This problem was present on all YOLO models except the best performing one and a version which uses a transformer backbone. The YOLO models, however, are very efficient at detection and, are very fast when processing an image for detection.

3.3 SSD

The SDD models performed worse when the backbone network is small, and although this works well in scenarios where objects are large in images, sunspots vary from very large to very small. This is due to the way the SSD approach uses fixed anchors at every layer of the backbone and when the network is small the features are limited. However, when the SSD is used with a large and deep backbone network, the precision increases as the anchor boxes become more. The best mean average precision achieved was 79.6% and the model had no false positives and only one sunspot that was missed. This can be alleviated with more data as the sunspot missed was a very large sunspot and these were very few in the data set.

3.4 EfficientDet

The EfficientDet proved very difficult to train on a single graphics processing unit as the model is very memory intensive. Only d0 – d3 models were trained and between them no meaningful difference in mean average precision was apparent. The best accuracy achieved was 62%, and although the model did not have any false positives, there were overlapping bounding boxes where the model sees a sunspot group and each individual sunspot shown in figure 5. The model did also miss very small sunspots around the solar limbs, but the model has potential and is very efficient at processing an image for detection.

3.5 Results

Model	Backbone	AP %
EfficientDet d2	Bidirectional feature pyramid (Efficient-b2)	62
Faster-RCNN	ResNet-50 conv4 with conv5 as head	79
Faster-RCNN	ResNet-50 conv4 with conv5 as head	80
Faster-RCNN	ResNet-50 conv5 with conv5 dilations	81.6
Faster-RCNN	ResNet -50 and Feature pyramid	80
Faster-RCNN	ResNet-101 conv5 with conv5 dilations	81
Faster-RCNN	ResNext-101 and Feature Pyramid	82.5
Faster-RCNN	Resnet-152 v1	79.4
Faser-RCNN	Inception Resnet v2	80.4
SSD Retinanet	ResNet -50 and Feature pyramid	78.4
SSD Retinanet	ResNet -101 and Feature pyramid	79.6
Yolo v5	CSPDarknet-53	76.8
YoloS	Vision Transformer block	54.2
Yolo v4	CSPDarknet-53	79
Yolo v6	EfficientRep	75
Yolo v7	CSPDarkent-53 With new E-ELAN computation block	81
YoloX	DarkNet-53	80.6

4. CONCLUSION

The Faster RCNN model proved the most accurate at detecting sunspots on any area of the sun and did not have any false positives. Although the other models performed well and did also show very good accuracy the EfficientDet requires more processing power to be trained effectively. The two-stage detection method provides more finer grain detail to do detection as opposed to the single stage detectors which were designed for computational efficiency. The YOLO model showed very good performance on the best model and on the transformer backbone model, indicating that the newer changes to the architectures might be aiding in catching up to the fine grain details of the Faster RCNN backbones. The other model which shows much promise is the SSD as, the best performing model achieved great results, and when considering the SSD was designed for lower power hardware, it might be a good choice to run on satellites or ground based observatories. These models can also be enhanced at pore detection and on other image formats for other solar phenomena. Future work that can be derived from this study includes:

1. Sunspot classification
2. Sunspot real time counting
3. Continuous retraining as detection occurs
4. Space weather forecasting
5. Solar event prediction

REFERENCES

Channabasava, C and Biabl, B, 2022. Detection and classification of sunspots via deep convolutional neural network. *Global Transitions Proceedings*, Vol. 3, No. 1, pp 177-182.

Fang, Y *et al*, 2019. Deep Learning for automatic recognition of magnetic type in sunspot groups. *Advances in Astronomy*, Vol. 2019, pp 1-10.

Hapgood, M, 2017. *Space Weather.* IOP Publishing, Bristol, UK.

Hanslmeier, A, 2004. *The Sun and Space Weather.* Kluwer Academic Publishers, New York, USA.

Solanki, S, 2003. Sunspots: An overview. *In The Astronomy and Astrophysics Review*, Vol. 11, No. 2, pp 153-286.

Wilkinson, J, 2012. *New Eyes on the Sun.* Springer, New York, USA.

Zhao, Z *et al*, 2019. Object Detection with Deep Learning: A Review. *IEEE Transactions on Neural Networks and Learning Systems*, Vol. p, No. 2, pp 1-21.

Zhou, Z *et al*, 2020. Computer-aided detection of brain metastases in t1-weighted mri for stereoactic radiosurgery using deep learning. *Radiology*. Vol. 295, No. 2, pp 407-415.

FIRST SYCL IMPLEMENTATION OF THE THREE-DIMENSIONAL SUBSURFACE XCA-FLOW CELLULAR AUTOMATON AND PERFORMANCE COMPARISON AGAINST CUDA

Donato D'Ambrosio[1], Giovanni Terremoto[1], Alessio De Rango[2], Luca Furnari[2], Alfonso Senatore[2] and Giuseppe Mendicino[2]

[1]*Department of Mathematics and Computer Science, University of Calabria, Ponte Pietro Bucci, Cubo 30B, 87036 Rende, Italy*

[2]*Department of Environmental Engineering, University of Calabria, Ponte Pietro Bucci, Cubo 44A, 87036 Rende, Italy*

ABSTRACT

We present the results of a first SYCL vs CUDA performance assessment for the case of the three-dimensional XCA-Flow subsurface Extended Cellular Automata model. A grid domain of **100 x 100 x 50** cubic cells of 0.3 m side was considered, where two different heterogeneous hydraulic conductivity fields were imposed, resulting in different computational loads. For each conductivity field, a 10 days test case simulation with a constant infiltration rate over the central part of the upper domain's interface and no-flow condition at other boundaries was designed as a benchmark for performance assessment. The stencil-based kernels of the XCA-Flow model were implemented by considering the one-thread-one-cell thread-to-cell mapping and global memory accesses. A global reduction, needed by the algorithm at each computational step to find the minimum of a domain's state variable, exploited the device's on-chip local memory (shared memory in the CUDA nomenclature). The CUDA back-end featured SYCL compiler adopted was the Intel DPC++. The experiments were performed on an Nvidia Titan Xp GPU by considering different configurations of SYCL/CUDA thread blocks. Each simulation was re-executed four times by selecting the minimum elapsed time. As expected, the CUDA implementation performed slightly better. Nevertheless, SYCL provided satisfying results, with a limited mean gap of approximately 8%.

KEYWORDS

XCA-Flow 3D Subsurface Model, Extended Cellular Automata, SYCL vs CUDA, Performance Assessment

1. INTRODUCTION

In recent years, new shared memory data-parallel architectures and APIs were proposed. Hardware vendors like Nvidia, AMD, and Intel, offered GPUs (Graphics Processing Units) and many-core computing accelerators that rapidly arose as reference devices in the High-Performance Computing (HPC) field (Owens et al., 2007).

The Nvidia Compute Unified Device Architecture (CUDA), proposed in 2008, rapidly became mainstream (see, e.g., Blecic et al., 2013; Arca et al., 2015; D'Ambrosio et al., 2012; D'Ambrosio et al., 2013 for some examples of application) due to, among others, the higher performance/cost ratio of CUDA devices compared to the alternative CPU-based solutions, and the C-like CUDA single source CPU/GPU heterogeneous programming model that made it easy to port existing codes to the new architecture. The main CUDA drawback is portability, since CUDA applications can only run on Nvidia hardware.

Aiming at overcoming the CUDA portability issue, Khronos Group released the OpenCL (Open Computing Language) specifications in 2009 (Stone et al., 2010) as an open standard. OpenCL offered a programming model similar to CUDA, though targeting heterogeneous devices like CPUs, GPUs, and other accelerators (see, e.g., Du et al., 2012; Su and Keutzer, 2012; Cercos-Pita, 2015; Macri et al., 2015; Senatore et al., 2016; De Rango et al., 2019 for some examples of application). Alternative solutions to CUDA and OpenCL were also proposed like OpenACC (see, e.g., Wienke et al., 2012) and OpenMP (starting from the release 4.0 - see, e.g., De Rango et al., 2018).

One of the most recent and promising shared memory data-parallel technologies is SYCL, a set of specifications by Khronos Group defining a C++ compiler-embedded abstraction layer for data-parallel programming. Modern C++ is supported, and the single-source programming approach permits mixing host and device code in the same translation units. SYCL was initially based on OpenCL, but the last specifications allow for different back-ends, including CUDA (Reyes et al., 2020). The interest in SYCL has become very high and its adoption is growing (see, e.g., Shin et al., 2020; Goli et al., 2020; Christgau and Steinke, 2020; Reguly et al., 2021). Several supercomputers in the Top500 list support SYCL (Thoman et al., 2019).

In this paper, we performed a first comparative analysis to assess the performance of the CUDA back-end featured Intel DPC++ SYCL compiler with respect to the Nvidia nvcc CUDA compiler. To this end, we considered the Extended Cellular Automata class of computational models (von Neumann, 1966; Di Gregorio and Serra, 1999). Specifically, we selected the three-dimensional XCA-Flow subsurface hydrological model, already applied to real and synthetic case studies in previous works (De Rango et al., 2020a; De Rango et al., 2020b; De Rango et al., 2021a; De Rango et al., 2021b; Furnari et al., 2021). This paper considered two 10-day long simulations differing by the heterogeneous hydraulic conductivity parameters to have different infiltration behaviors and computational loads. The simulations are characterized by a $100 \times 100 \times 50$ grid domain with cubic cells of 0.3 m side, a constant infiltration rate over the central part of the upper domain's surface, and no-flow condition at other boundaries. SYCL and CUDA implementations of the XCA-Flow kernels only referred to GPU's global memory, even if a global reduction needed by the algorithm to find the minimum of a domain's state variable also exploited the on-chip local memory (shared memory in the CUDA nomenclature). The simulation experiments were performed on an Nvidia Titan Xp GPU.

The paper is organized as follows: Section 2 provides the theoretical foundations of the subsurface flow XCA-Flow model, together with details regarding computational aspects, while Section 3 describes the case-study simulations; Section 4 briefly characterizes the XCA-Flow kernels and presents the achieved computational results, while Section 5 eventually concludes the paper with a general discussion, by also outlining possible future developments.

2. THE XCA-FLOW HYDROLOGICAL MODEL

The XCA-Flow subsurface hydrological model is based on the direct discrete formulation of the Richards' equation as formalized by Mendicino et al. (2006). The Richards' equation, governing the subsurface water flow process, is a nonlinear degenerate elliptic-parabolic partial differential equation (List and Radu, 2016). It describes double-phases flow in porous media by combining the mass conservation equation with the Darcys' law, representing the momentum conservation equation. Considering the pressure head ψ as the dependent variable, the Richards' equation for an isotropic porous medium is written as (Celia et al., 1990):

$$(1) \quad C_c(\psi) = \frac{\partial \psi}{\partial t} - \nabla[K(\psi)\nabla\psi] - \frac{\partial K(\psi)}{\partial z} = 0$$

where the pressure head ψ [m] is related to the hydraulic head h [m] by the equation $\psi = h - z$, being z [m] the elevation, $C_c(\psi)$ *is* the specific retention capacity [m^{-1}], given by the relation $C_c(\psi) = \frac{d\theta}{dh}$, where in turns θ is the moisture content [$m^3\ m^{-3}$] and $K(\psi)$ is the hydraulic conductivity [$m\ s^{-1}$].

According to the Cellular Automata computational paradigm, XCA-Flow is a space-time discrete simulation model based on local transition rules of evolution, called kernels or elementary processes. The new cell's state depends on the current state of the cell itself (called central cell) and those of a limited set of adjacent cells. The central cell together with its adjacent cells forms the so-called neighborhood, whose geometrical pattern is referred to as stencil. In XCA-Flow, the three-dimensional von Neumann stencil is adopted, defined below in terms of relative coordinates with respect to the central cell, which belongs to its own neighborhood:

$$X = \{(0,0,0), (-1,0,0), (0,-1,0), (0,1,0), (1,0,0), (0,0,-1), (0,0,1)\}$$

The three computing kernels, $\sigma_\rho, \sigma_\beta$, and σ_τ, together with a global reduction used to assess the physical time corresponding to the XCA-Flow computational step, γ_t, are formally defined below.

- $\sigma_\rho: Q_h \times Q_{C_c} \rightarrow Q_h$ accounts for input rain, where Q_h and Q_{C_c} represent the sets of values for the hydraulic total head and specific retention capacity state variables, respectively. Specifically, if $h, C_c, r_{ir}, \Delta t$ and Δs^2 denote hydraulic head, specific retention capacity, rain intensity rate, time interval corresponding to an XCA-Flow transition step, and surface of the cell side, respectively, σ_ρ updates the hydraulic head within the cell as:

$$h' = h + \frac{r_{ir} \cdot \Delta t}{\Delta s^2 \cdot C_c}$$

- $\sigma_\beta: Q_h \rightarrow Q_h$ sets the boundary condition on the boundary cells that are not affected by rain. The Neumann boundary conditions, which fix the water flow to a constant value, for instance $h' = h$ represent a no flow condition; the Dirichlet boundary conditions, which fix the hydraulic head to a constant value, can be adopted.
- $\sigma_\tau: Q^{|X|} \rightarrow Q$, where Q and $|X|$ represent the set of all possible cell's states and the number of neighboring cells, respectively, corresponds to the discrete time explicit resolution of Eq. 1 and can be written as:

$$h_c' = h_c + \frac{\Delta t\left[\sum_{\alpha=1}^{6} \overline{K}_\alpha (h_\alpha - h_c)\ \right]}{\Delta s^2 C_c}$$

Here, $\overline{K}_\alpha$ is the average hydraulic conductivity between the current cell c and the cell in the α neighbor calculated using:

$$\overline{K}_\alpha = \frac{2\Delta s^3}{\frac{\Delta s^3}{K_\alpha} + \frac{\Delta s^3}{K_c}}$$

Also, the q_θ, q_K and q_{c_c} state variables are updated according to the constitutive equations between ψ, θ and K, as proposed by Mualem (1976) and Van Genuchten (1978).
Finally, the state variable $q_{conv} \in Q_{conv}$, is updated adopting the Courant-Friedrichs-Lewy condition to achieve numerical convergence:

$$\Delta t \leq \frac{\Delta s^2 C_c}{\sum_{\alpha=1}^{6} \overline{K}_\alpha}$$

- $\gamma_t : Q_{conv}^{|D|} \rightarrow \mathbb{R}$ evaluates a reduction over the Q_{conv} substate in order to evaluate the physical time corresponding to a state transition of the automaton. Specifically, if Δt denotes the time step size, we have:

$$\Delta t = \min_{\iota \in D} q_{conv_\iota}$$

The complete XCA-Flow model's formalization, here omitted for the sake of brevity, can be found in Furnari et al. (2021) - Appendix A.

3. THE TEST CASE SIMULATIONS

The XCA-Flow model was applied to three-dimensional heterogeneous test cases. Two different pseudo-random synthetic fields of saturated hydraulic conductivity, K_s, were generated through the application of simple kriging techniques with an exponential semivariogram model (Pebesma, 2004), as already done in Furnari et al. (2021). The field generation method required the assignment of both mean μ and variance σ^2 values of the K_s field. Due to the wide range of variability of such parameter, the logarithmic transform of the variable was used. A value of μ equal to -4.19 and σ^2 equal to 2.0 were imposed, used for generating the two K_s fields shown in Figure 1. Choosing $\sigma^2 = 2.0$, imposed a large variability in the hydrological soil properties.

Table 1. Hydrological parameters in the test case. θ_r is the residual moisture content, θ_s is the saturated moisture content, α and n are soil parameters used in the Van Genuchten model, ψ_0 is the continuity parameter to ensure the passage between unsaturated and saturated conditions (Paniconi et al., 1991), S_s is the specific storage

θ_r	θ_s	$\alpha(m^{-1})$	n	$\psi_0\ (m)$	$S_s(m^{-1})$
0.095	0.348	3.473	1.729	0.001	10^{-6}

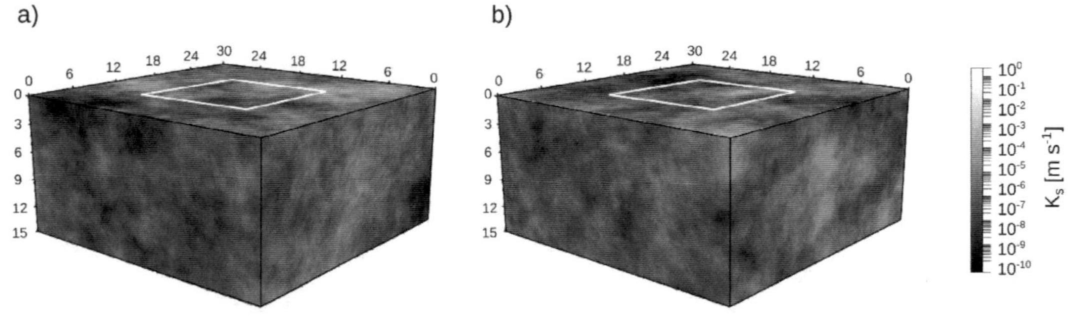

Figure 1. The three-dimensional computational domains used in a) test case simulation Sim_1, b) test case simulation Sim_2. Colors represent the saturated hydraulic conductivity K_s. The surface delimited by the white square on the top part of the domain is affected by infiltration of 0.02 md^{-1}. The domain extends 30 meters long and wide, with a depth of 15 meters, resulting in a grid of 100 × 100 × 50 with a cubic cells side of 0.3 m

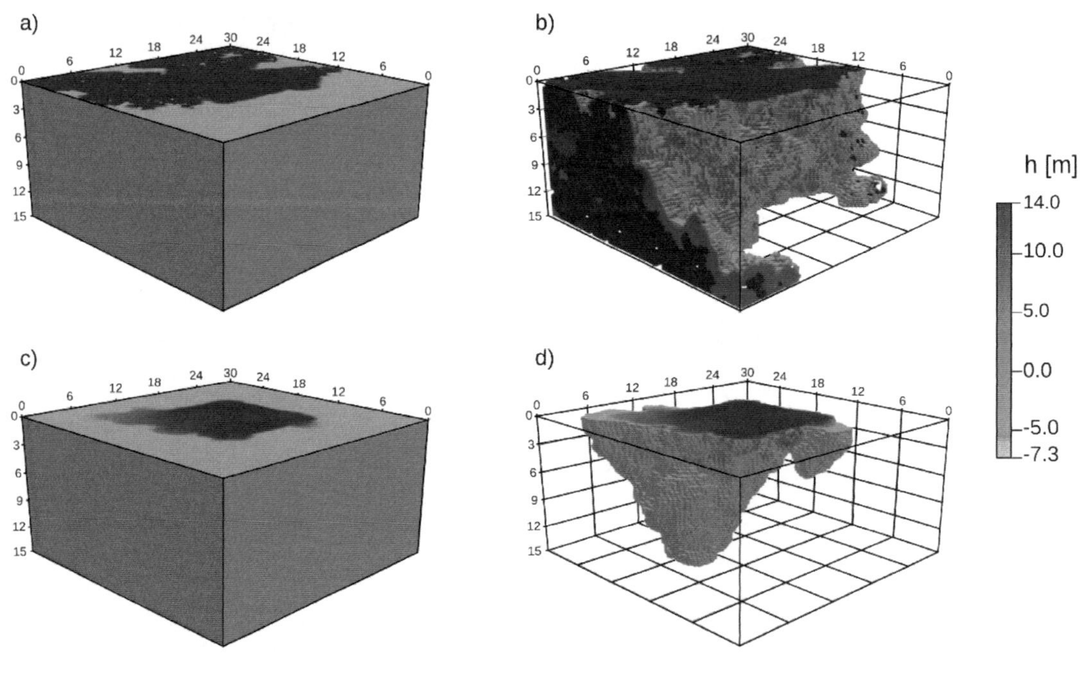

Figure 2. Three-dimensional simulation test cases: overview of the computational domains and wet front propagation. Colours represent hydraulic head values at the end of the simulations. a), b) refer to the test case simulation Sim_1; c), d), refer to the test case simulation Sim_2. In b) and d), hydraulic head values less than or equal to the initial total hydraulic head, namely -7.34 m, are not displayed. In particular, b) and d) highlight the effective wet front propagation

The space domain was composed of a parallelepiped 30 meters long and wide, with a depth of 15 meters. The mesh size was fixed to 0.3 m, generating 100 × 100 × 50 grid points. Neumann's no-flow conditions were set for all boundaries, except a constant infiltration rate of 0.02 md^{-1} interesting the central part of the upper border of the domain. Specifically, the infiltration affected a 12×12 m^2 square area located in the centre of the upper face of the domain, as shown in Figure 1. The experiments simulated a physical time of 10 days, with a constant initial total hydraulic head of -7.34 m. The resulting simulation is shown in Figure 2. The hydrological parameters are reported in Table 1.

4. KERNELS IMPLEMENTATION AND COMPUTATIONAL RESULTS

The XCA-Flow model is based on the three computational kernels and the global reduction described in Section 2., which are executed at each iteration of the simulation loop. In this first work, we considered a basic implementation of the computational kernels, with global memory accesses, and monolithic (one-thread/one-cell) thread-to-cell mapping. Conversely, the reduction kernel was implemented by applying a classical sequential addressing parallel reduction algorithm, whit local memory (shared memory in the CUDA nomenclature) usage (Kirk and Hwu, 2017).

As stated, we exploited an Nvidia Titan XP GPU for the experiments, which belongs to the Pascal architecture. The GPU is connected through the PCI express channel to a scientific workstation running Arch Linux. The adopted SYCL compiler was the Intel DPC++. In particular, we used the sycl llvm fork from Intel at https://github.com/intel/llvm, commit hash 68b089f. Nvcc version 11.6 was used to compile the CUDA code.

Regarding the experiments, we ran each test case simulation (see Figure 2) on eight different block configurations, ranging from 8x8x1 to 16x16x2 threads. Specifically, we repeated each experiment four times, by registering the fastest execution. The computational results, expressed in terms of simulation elapsed time, are shown in Figure 3 and Figure 4 for the test case simulations Sim_1 and Sim_2, respectively.

As expected, CUDA performed slightly better than SYCL for both the $Sim_1$and Sim_2 simulations. In the case of Sim_1, the best SYCL result was obtained in correspondence with the 16x16x2 block configuration, with a gap of 5.57% with respect to CUDA. On average, the SYCL gap was 8.2%, with a variance of 2.89%. Similar results were achieved for Sim_2. The best SYCL result was obtained in correspondence with the 16x16x2 block configuration, with a gap of 4.96%. On average, the SYCL gap was 7.63%, with a variance of 2.62%. Results are summarized in Table 2.

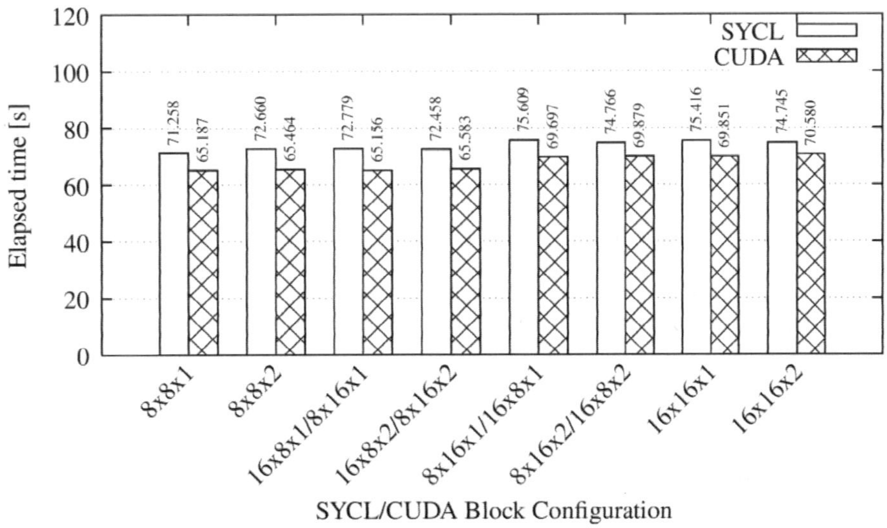

Figure 3. SYCL/CUDA elapsed times of the test case simulation Sim_1 (i.e., the one considering the K_s field in Figure 1a) executed on the Nvidia Titan Xp GPU with different thread block configurations. The exact elapsed time is reported on top of each bar. Statistics are reported in Table 2

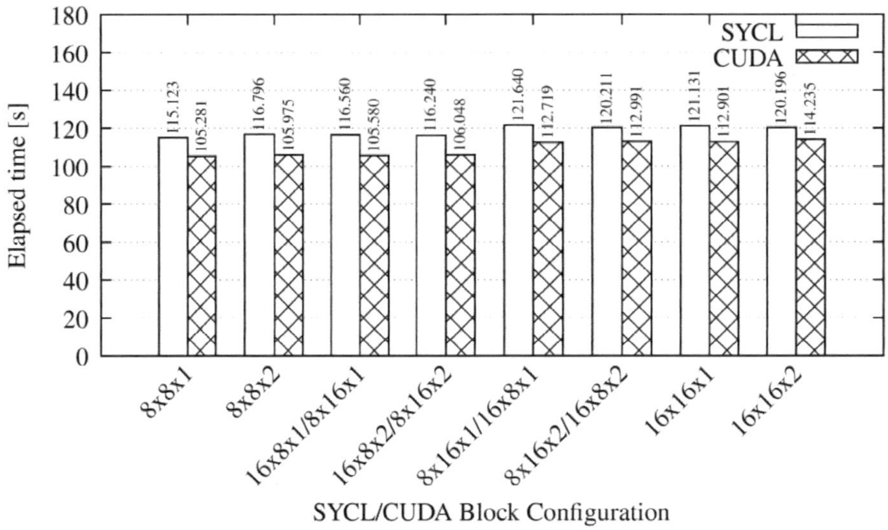

Figure 4. SYCL/CUDA elapsed times of the test case simulation Sim_2 (i.e., the one considering the K_s field in Figure 1b) executed on the Nvidia Titan Xp GPU with different thread block configurations. The exact elapsed time is reported on top of each bar. Statistics are reported in Table 2

Table 2. Comparison between SYCL and CUDA elapsed times of the two test case simulations expressed in terms of percentage gaps. Minimum, average, maximum and variance values are reported

Simulation	Minimum gap [%]	Average gap [%]	Maximum gap [%]	Variance gap [%]
Sim_1	5.57	8.20	10.47	2.89
Sim_2	4.96	7.63	9.42	2.62

5. CONCLUSION

In this work, we presented a first SYCL implementation of the XCA-Flow three-dimensional subsurface Cellular Automata model by assessing its computational performance on an Nvidia Titan Xp GPU compared to an equivalent CUDA implementation of the same model. The SYCL compiler used is the CUDA back-end featured Intel DPC++.

We considered two test case simulations characterized by different hydraulic conductivity fields, resulting in different computational loads for the GPU. We tested different thread block configurations by running each experiment four times and taking the minimum elapsed time. As expected, the CUDA implementation performed slightly better, with SYCL limiting the gap to approximately 8%. The minimum gap registered was approximately 5%, with a variance of less than 3%.

Considering that the CUDA back-end of DPC++ is still experimental, the achieved results can be regarded as satisfying. Nevertheless, better performance is expected with the successive revisions of the compiler.

Future developments will consider the XCA-Flow kernels characterization regarding operational intensity, which is needed to perform a comprehensive Roofline analysis (Williams et al., 2009; 38. Yang et al., 2020). This preliminary analysis will give us information about the kernels that could take advantage of local memory (shared memory in the CUDA nomenclature) tiled implementation. Therefore, a tiled implementation of these kernels will be developed. As a further development, a multi-GPU version of the XCA-Flow simulation model, with applications to extended domains, will be designed and implemented. In this phase, a load balancing algorithm (e.g., Giordano et al., 2021, Giordano et al., 2020) will be adapted and applied to the new multi-GPU context. All the above-cited developments will be implemented in SYCL and CUDA for comparison. Eventually, distributed MPI/SYCL and MPI/CUDA versions of XCA-flow will be developed. Even in this case, a load balancing algorithm will be adopted to distribute the simulation load to the involved computing resources evenly. The software developed in this study is available on request by writing to the first author.

REFERENCES

Arca, B., Ghisu, T., Trunfio, G., (2015). GPU-accelerated multi-objective optimization of fuel treatments for mitigating wildfire hazard. *In Journal of Computational Science*, Vol. 11, pp 258-268.

Blecic, I., Cecchini, A., Trunfio, G., (2013). Cellular automata simulation of urban dynamics through GPGPU. *In Journal of Supercomputing*, Vol. 65, No. 2, pp 614-629.

Celia, M.A., Bouloutas, E.T., Zarba, R.L., (1990). A general mass-conservative numerical solution for the unsaturated flow equation. *In Water Resources Research*, Vol. 26, No. 7, pp 1483-1496.

Cercos-Pita, J., (2015). AQUAgpusph, a new free 3D SPH solver accelerated with OpenCL. *In Computer Physics Communications*, Vol. 192, pp 295-312.

Christgau, S. and Steinke, T., (2020). Porting a Legacy CUDA Stencil Code to oneAPI. *International Parallel and Distributed Processing Symposium Workshops (IPDPSW).* New Orleans, USA., pp. 359-367.

D'Ambrosio, D., Filippone, G., Marocco, D., Rongo, R., Spataro, W., (2013). Efficient application of GPGPU for lava flow hazard mapping. *In Journal of Supercomputing*, Vol. 65, No. 2, pp 630-644.

D'Ambrosio, D., Filippone, G., Rongo, R., Spataro, W., Trunfio, G., (2012). Cellular Automata and GPGPU: An Application to Lava Flow Modeling. *In International Journal of Grid and High Performance Computing*, Vol. 4, No 3, pp 30-47.

De Rango, A., Furnari, L., Giordano, A., Senatore, A., D'Ambrosio, D., Spataro, W., Straface, S., Mendicino, G., (2021). OpenCAL system extension and application to the three-dimensional Richards equation for unsaturated flow. *In Computers and Mathematics with Applications*, Vol. 81, pp 133-158.

De Rango, A., Furnari, L., Senatore, A., D'Ambrosio, D., Straface, S., Mendicino, G., (2021). Massive simulations on GPGPUs of subsurface flow on heterogeneous soils. *29th Euromicro International Conference on Parallel, Distributed and Network-Based Processing (PDP)*, Valladolid, Spain, pp. 249-252.

De Rango, A., Napoli, P., D'Ambrosio, D., Spataro, W., Di Renzo, A., Di Maio, F., (2018). Structured Grid-Based Parallel Simulation of a Simple DEM Model on Heterogeneous Systems. *26th Euromicro International Conference on Parallel, Distributed and Network-based Processing (PDP)*, Cambridge, UK, pp. 588-595.

De Rango, A., Furnari, L., D'Ambrosio, D., Senatore, A., Straface, S., Mendicino, G., (2020). The quantization algorithm impact in hydrological applications: Preliminary results. *20th International Conference on Computational Science, ICCS 2020*, Amsterdam, The Netherlands, pp. 191-204.

De Rango, A., Furnari, L., Giordano, A., Senatore, A., D'Ambrosio, D., Straface, S., Mendicino, G., (2020). Preliminary model of saturated flow using cellular automata. *Numerical Computations: Theory and Algorithms*, Le Castella Village, Italy, pp. 256-268.

De Rango, A., Spataro, D., Spataro, W., D'Ambrosio, D., (2019). A first multi-GPU/multi-node implementation of the open computing abstraction layer. *In Journal of Computational Science*, Vol. 32, pp. 115-124.

Di Gregorio, S., Serra, R., (1999). An empirical method for modelling and simulating some complex macroscopic phenomena by cellular automata. *In Future Generation Computer Systems*, Vol. 16, pp. 259-271.

Du, P., Weber, R., Luszczek, P., Tomov, S., Peterson, G., Dongarra, J. (2012) From CUDA to OpenCL: Towards a performance-portable solution for multi-platform GPU programming. *In Parallel Computing*, Vol. 38, No. 8, pp. 391-407.

Furnari, L., Senatore, A., De Rango, A., De Biase, M., Straface, S., Mendicino, G., (2021). Asynchronous cellular automata subsurface flow simulations in two and three-dimensional heterogeneous soils. *In Advances in Water Resources*, Vol. 153, 103952.

Giordano, A., De Rango, A., Rongo, R., D'Ambrosio, D., Spataro, W., (2021). Dynamic Load Balancing in Parallel Execution of Cellular Automata. *In IEEE Transactions on Parallel and Distributed Systems*, Vol. 32, No. 2, pp. 470-484.

Giordano, A., De Rango, A., Rongo, R., D'Ambrosio, D., Spataro, W., (2020). A Dynamic Load Balancing Technique for Parallel Execution of Structured Grid Models. *Numerical Computations: Theory and Algorithms*, Le Castella Village, Italy, pp. 278-290.

Goli, M., Narasimhan, K., Reyes, R., Tracy, B., Soutar, D., Georgiev, S., Fomenko, E., Chereshnev, E., (2020). Towards Cross-Platform Performance Portability of DNN Models using SYCL. *IEEE/ACM International Workshop on Performance, Portability and Productivity in HPC (P3HPC)*, GA, USA, pp. 25-35.

Kirk, D.B., mei W. Hwu, W., (2017). Chapter 5 - Performance considerations. *Programming Massively Parallel Processors (Third Edition)*. Morgan Kaufmann Publishers, San Francisco, USA.

List, F., Radu, F.A., (2016). A study on iterative methods for solving Richards' equation. *In Computational Geosciences* Vol. 20, No. 2, pp. 341-353.

Macri, M., De Rango, A., Spataro, D., D'Ambrosio, D., Spataro, W., (2015). Efficient Lava Flows Simulations with OpenCL: A Preliminary Application for Civil Defence Purposes. *Proceedings of the 10th International Conference on P2P, Parallel, Grid, Cloud and Internet Computing, 3PGCIC*. Krakow, Poland, pp. 328-335.

Mendicino, G., Senatore, A., Spezzano, G., Straface, S., (2006). Three-dimensional unsaturated flow modeling using cellular automata. *In Water Resources Research*, Vol. 42, No. 11, pp. 2332-2335.

Mualem, Y., (1976). A new model for predicting the hydraulic conductivity of unsaturated porous media. *In Water Resources Research*, Vol. 12, No. 3, pp. 513-522.

von Neumann, J., (1966). *Theory of Self-Reproducing Automata*. University of Illinois Press, Champaign, IL, USA.

Owens, J., Luebke, D., Govindaraju, N., Harris, M., Kruger, J., Lefohn, A., Purcell, T., (2007). A survey of general-purpose computation on graphics hardware. *In Computer Graphics Forum*, Vol. 26, No. 1, pp. 80-113.

Paniconi, C., Aldama, A.A., Wood, E.F., (1991). Numerical evaluation of iterative and noniterative methods for the solution of the nonlinear Richards equation. *In Water Resources Research*, Vol. 27, No. 6, pp. 1147-1163.

Pebesma, E.J., (2004). Multivariable geostatistics in S: the gstat package. *Computers & Geosciences* 30(7), pp. 683-691.

Reguly, I., Owenson, A., Powell, A., Jarvis, S., Mudalige, G., (2021). Under the Hood of SYCL – An Initial Performance Analysis with An Unstructured-Mesh CFD Application. *36th International Conference, ISC High Performance 2021*, Virtual Event.

Reyes, R., Brown, G., Burns, R., Wong, M., (2020). Sycl 2020: More than meets the eye. *Proceedings of the International Workshop on OpenCL*, Association for Computing Machinery, New York, NY, USA.

Senatore, A., D'Ambrosio, D., De Rango, A., Rongo, R., Spataro, W., Straface, S., Mendicino, G., (2016). Accelerating a three-dimensional eco-hydrological cellular automaton on GPGPU with OpenCL. *AIP Conference Proceedings*, Vol. 1776, 080003.

Shin, W., Yoo, K.H., Baek, N., (2020). Large-Scale Data Computing Performance Comparisons on SYCL Heterogeneous Parallel Processing Layer Implementations. *In Applied Sciences* (Switzerland), Vol. 10, No. 5, 1656.

Stone, J., Gohara, D., Shi, G., (2010). OpenCL: A Parallel Programming Standard for Heterogeneous Computing Systems. *In Computing in Science and Engineering*, Vol. 12 No. 3, pp. 66-72.

Su, B.Y., Keutzer, K., (2012). clSpMV: A Cross-Platform OpenCL SpMV Framework on GPUs. *Proceedings of the 26th ACM international conference on Supercomputing*. Venice, Italy, pp. 353-364.

Thoman, P., Salzmann P., Cosenza, B., Fahringer T., (2019). Celerity: High-Level C++ for Accelerator Clusters. *Euro-Par 2019: Parallel Processing*, Göttingen, Germany, pp. 291-303.

Van Genuchten, M.T., (1978). Calculating the unsaturated hydraulic conductivity with a new closed-form analytical model. Researh Reprot - Water Resour. Program, Dep. of Civ. Eng., Princeton Univ., Princeton, NJ.

Wienke, S., Springer, P., Terboven, C., an Mey, D., (2012). OpenACC — First Experiences with Real-World Applications. *Euro-Par 2012 Parallel Processing*, Göttingen, Germany, pp. 859-870.

Williams, S., Waterman, A., Patterson, D., (2009). Roofline: An insightful visual performance model for multicore architectures. *Communications of the ACM*, Vol. 52, No. 4, pp. 65-76.

Yang, C., Kurth, T., Williams, S., (2020). Hierarchical Roofline analysis for GPUs: Accelerating performance optimization for the NERSC-9 Perlmutter system. *Concurrency and Computation: Practice and Experience*, Vol. 32, No. 20, e5547.

ENHANCED FEATURE EXTRACTION USING OPTIMAL WHITENING AND STACKED AUTOENCODERS

Archana Mathur, Akarsha Paralkar and Pramod Jain Saligrama Amendra Kumar
Nitte Meenakshi Institute of Technology, Yelahanka Bangalore-560064, India

ABSTRACT

There are multiple preprocessing techniques used across the globe to enhance classification performance. Researchers in the past have incorporated various methods to improve feature extractions from image and text dataset. Extracting optimized features is still a challenge in the current scenarios, not only because size of the data is humongous, but it also involves noisy components. In this manuscript, we have proposed a method to compute the most optimized features from datasets by first transforming the features into the optimal ZCA features which are later fed into a 2- layered Stacked Autoencoder (SA). The novelty of the manuscript lies in the idea of deriving optimal features by performing optimal whitening (instead of plain ZCA) which is followed by feature extraction via stacked autoencoders. The in-depth features learned from SA are then fed into a feed-forward neural network as a final step towards classification. We have experimented rigorously on 10 non-computer vision, 2 hyperspectral remote sensing data set, and 1 computer vision datasets and found that classification accuracy increases to 2-4% on an average across many datasets. Additionally, we have validated the feature extraction method across plain vanilla neural network architecture and found the performance to increase by at most 5% on a few datasets.

KEYWORDS

Machine Learning, Stacked Autoencoder, Zero Component Analysis, Optimal Whitening, Hyperspectral Remote Sensing Dataset

1. INTRODUCTION

Autoencoders is a deep learning architecture that can learn the most salient features of a dataset by first compressing the input into its latent representation and then decompressing them back to the original form. Basically, autoencoders are a family of neural networks that performs encoding and decoding of features by means of two separate, serially arranged units, known as encoder and decoder. The encoder constricts input to the network and decoder reconstructs the output back to original data. The hidden layer that is common for encoder and decoder (for single layer autoencoder) is responsible for generating the latent representation of data. Apparently, this is an unsupervised means of learning new data projections. Though there are multiple interesting applications of autoencoders from extracting latent features to dimensionality reduction, we have experimented to investigate the effect of pre-processing of input features in regards to generalization. In this manuscript, a 2-layered Stack autoencoder (SA) is built in Python to derive hidden features from data and later, these features are trained to perform classification using a classifier. A vanilla feed-forward neural network is used for classification that internally employs sigmoid activation function in hidden and output layer. Also, the network uses back propagation along with gradient descent optimizer to train the weights. The loss function employed is mean square error. Additionally, before feeding the input data to SA, we have whitened the data using optimal whitening transformation, W^o. We have shown that the optimal whitening for an input x can be obtained by finding an optimal variable z^o multiplied with $Cov\_x^{(-1/2)}$. While experimenting on different datasets, we have found the optimal z^o for each data by exhaustively searching over specified parameter values using grid search. Previously, researchers have used traditional Autoencoders for extracting features. In (Chen et al.,2016), Chen Xing Et.al. have fused the Denoising and Stacked Autoencoder to eliminate noise from the hyperspectral images. Our work is different from Chen Xing et.al. mainly because we focused on deriving optimal features by whitening transformation. Additionally, Chen Xing et.al. have used logistic regression classifier whereas we made use of neural network classifier for performance evaluation.

The remainder of the paper is organized as follows. We begin by detailing the problem statement and describing several challenges we need to solve in order to arrive at an acceptable solution. In Section 2, we briefly describe the related work done on the similar lines. Section 3 and section 4 illustrates the working of a SA and whitening transformations. The combined effect of whitening transformation on a stacked autoendoer is explored in section 5. Further, section 6 investigates on computing the optimal whitening transformation on a given dataset. Section 7 gives details about the extensive experimentation (done on 10 datasets and 2 hyper-spectral datasets) using 2 layered SAs with and without using optimal whitening. The outcome of all methods are shown and justified in Sections 9 along with their comparison.

2. LITERATURE REVIEW

Baldi (Baldi, 2012) in his work have built a framework to investigate the working of linear and non-linear Autoencoders. Boolean autoencoders are evaluated in Baldi's work which also demonstrates the critical parameters of these Autoencoders with respect to learning complexity, critical points, and their horizontal and vertical composability and similarity with the clustering algorithms. Vincent et.al. (Vincent et al., 2010) explored denoising autoencoders and expressed in their work how a denoising autoencoders can learn Gabor-like edge detectors from natural image patches and denoise a corrupted image patch thus enhancing the classification accuracy of an SVM classifier. Lei Le (Le, 2018) came up with the notion of a supervised autoencoders and showed empirically as well as theoretically that the architecture stacked across multiple hidden layers with different activation functions can improve generalizability of any network. In another interesting research by Abdulrahman Al-Abassi et al. (Al-Abassi et al., 2020) the authors have tackled the data balancing issue in an imbalance data in real power systems while trying to detect the cyber-attacks. A deep learning ensemble method is proposed by fetching samples from imbalance datasets and sending it to a stacked auto encoder and deriving multiple balanced representations of the data. Random forest classifier is applied on each of these representations and the final output of the classifier is fused to a vector that is utilised as the input to a second RF classifier, which serves as the final step in identifying the presence of attacks. The proposed method is tested on different levels of imbalance data. The reliability of this procedure is demonstrated through comparisons to several classifiers (Monta nez et al., 2018).

A 2-layered Stacked Sparse Autoencoder is efficiently used to classify MR slices for tumor detection (Amin et al., 2019). This paper employs a high pass filter image to emphasize the non-uniform field impact of the MR slices when combined with the input slices which are then subjected to a median filter. The edges of the input slices are highlighted and smoothed, which improves the quality of the produced slices. Following that, a 4-connected seed growth technique is applied depending on the intensity of these slices, and an appropriate threshold is used to cluster related pixels from the input slices. The segmented slices are then sent to the proposed two-layer stacked sparse autoencoder (SSAE) model. The authors have compared their method with eighteen other methods, such as CNN-based approaches, generative models, the random forest method, etc., and the findings manifest enhanced performance. In (Chen et al., 2016) Chen Xing Et.al. have fused the denoising and stacked autoencoders to extract the noise from hyperspectral images in their experiment. They used logistic regression to fine-tune their model. While training, the authors compared their performances by using two different activation functions ReLU and sigmoid. Another feature extraction techniques explored in (Hammouche et al. 2022) relies on fusing multiple feature extraction techniques from images for obtaining enhanced features. The authors used the popular Gabor filter bank along with Sparse autoencoders and later reduced the feature vector by employing PCA and LDA. Their approach is similar to our method but they had to rely on hand-crafted feature techniques for feature extraction.

Another series of research has been carried out on whitening transformation. Agnan Kessy et al. (Kessy et al., 2015) have deeply explored the different whitening mechanisms and came up with two critical methods - ZCA-cor whitening and PCA-cor whitening. They theoretically claimed that the optimal whitening can be obtained by whitening the variables that are maximally similar to the original. Integrating the outcomes from the above research findings, we propose the method of extracting optimal features by transforming feature space in to a new space derived from optimal whitening and feed the features into 2-layered SA before sending them for classification.

3. SUPERVISED LEARNING WITH UNSUPERVISED AUTOENCODERS

Autoencoders (AE) (Baldi, 2012), (Liu et al.,2018) are popularly known to be an unsupervised technique where the goal is to transform features into a new representation that predicts well.

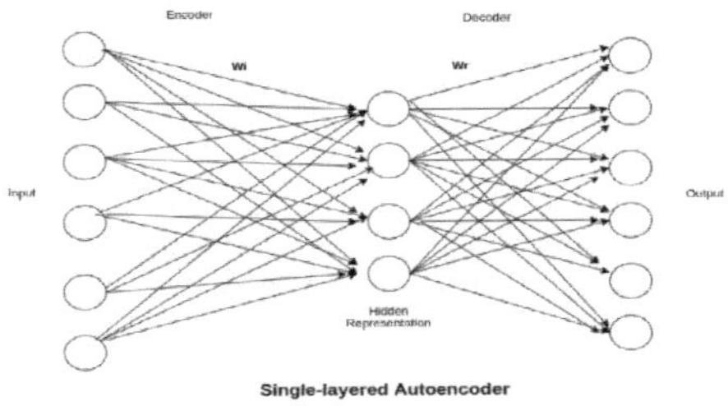

Figure 1. Autoencoder

Here we consider a supervised AE that learns a function on inputs $x \in \mathbb{R}^n$ to be able to predict the targets $y \in \mathbb{R}^m$. The AE is trained on a vector of inputs (x_i, y_i) where it extracts a representation of original features and transforms the features into the new representation. A supervised layer is added in the end for prediction. AE have been primarily used for representation learning but we have attempted to build a supervised AE by adding a supervision layer after AE learns hidden representation. Considering a single hidden layer AE network with d inputs, m outputs and p hidden neurons, L_r as reconstruction loss (Michelucci, 2022) and L_s as supervised loss (MSE in both cases). Let $\mathbb{W}_i \in \mathbb{R}^{dxp}$ be weights at input layer, $\mathbb{W}_r \in \mathbb{R}^{pxd}$ weights at reconstruction layer and $\mathbb{W}_s \in \mathbb{R}^{pxm}$ are weights at supervision layer. The total loss (during reconstruction and supervision) is

$$L_{total} = \frac{1}{Z}\sum_{i=1}^{Z} \left[L_r(\mathbb{W}_r\mathbb{W}_i x_i, x_i) + L_s(\mathbb{W}_s\mathbb{W}_i x_i, y_i)\right]$$

considering L2 loss

$$= \frac{1}{Z}\sum_{i=1}^{Z} \left[\|\mathbb{W}_r\mathbb{W}_i x_i - x_i\|^2 + \|\mathbb{W}_s\mathbb{W}_i x_i - y_i\|^2\right]$$

A greedy layer wise approach is used to construct the autoencoder that internally uses encoding and decoding to pretrain the connection weights. Once weights are trained, decoder is detached from the network and single forward pass of the original features onto the encoder generates latent features (h1) at hidden layer. The features are stored for deriving further layers of the whole architecture and encoder forms the first layer of the autoencoder (L1). The second layer is built by training another autoencoder that takes h1 as input, compresses it via encoder and reconstructs it at output layer. The network is trained by incorporating back propagation along with gradient descent. Once trained, the latent features h2, are obtained from the hidden layer. Repeating the step, decoder is removed from the network and encoder forms the second layer of autoencoder (L2). So, L1 and L2 forms the two layers of autoencoder and the concluding layer, L3, is a classifier that uses sigmoid activation function to train the output from L2 (h2) for performing classification. Thus, the 2-layered SA finds first-order features and second-order features ultimately use them for classification on a neural network.

4. WHITENING TRANSFORMATION

Assume that we have n dimensional data arranged as $[A]_{D\chi n}$. Σ_A is the covariance matrix of A given as $\Sigma_A = AA^T$ The eigen decomposition of covariance matrix Σ_A is given as $\Sigma_A = U\Lambda U^T$, where U and Λ consists of eigenvectors and eigenvalues of Σ_A respectively. Whitening is a process of transforming matrix A with nXn covariance matrix Σ_A into a new matrix C, as $C = WA$ of the same dimension with variance $\Sigma_C = I$, where I is the identity matrix. The whitening transformation requires a suitable matrix W and most popular choice of finding W is with Principal Component Analysis (PCA). For PCA, W is taken as $W = \Lambda^{-\frac{1}{2}}U^T$, where $\Lambda = \mathrm{diag}(\sigma_1, \ldots, \sigma_n)$ are the eigen values and $U = [u_1, \ldots, u_n]$ are the associated eigen vectors of Σ_A. Other ways of obtaining W are PCA-cor, Cholesky Whitening (Siarohin, 2019), (Dong M., 2009), Zero-phase Component Analysis (ZCA) and ZCA-cor. Cholesky whitening has $W = L^T$, where L is

Cholesky decomposition of $\Sigma^{-\frac{1}{2}}$. ZCA is another popular choice of whitening procedure, where $W^{ZCA} = \Sigma_A^{-\frac{1}{2}} = U\Lambda^{-\frac{1}{2}}U^T$.

While performing ZCA whitening, the matrix involves computing division by square root of eigen values (due to $\Lambda^{-\frac{1}{2}}$). If few eigen values are close to zero, then W^{ZCA} will return a very high value. To avoid his, a hyper-parameter ϵ is added to eigen values as a regularization step. Finally,

$$W^{ZCA} = U(\Lambda + \epsilon)^{-\frac{1}{2}}U^T$$

5. AUTOENCODER WITH SINGLE HIDDEN LAYER AND ZCA

Given the input vector $\mathbf{x} \in \mathbf{R}^n$, a single-layer autoencoder uses back-propagation to minimize MSE loss such that the reconstruction output $\mathbf{o_i} = \mathbf{x_i}$ (here, $\mathbf{o_i}$ is the reconstruction output vector for the input $\mathbf{x_i}$). Formally, the output can be written as,

$$\mathbf{o_i} = \boldsymbol{\sigma}(\mathbf{W_r^T}\boldsymbol{\sigma}(\mathbf{W_i x_i} + \mathbf{b}) + \mathbf{c})$$

where $\boldsymbol{\sigma}$ is the activation function (usually sigmoid), $\mathbf{W_r}$ is the reconstruction and $\mathbf{W_i}$ is the input weight-matrix. For any iteration i, ($\mathbf{i} \in \mathbf{R}$) when $\mathbf{W^{ZCA}}$ is applied to the input, the reconstructed output becomes,

$$\mathbf{o_i} = \boldsymbol{\sigma}(\mathbf{W_r^T}\boldsymbol{\sigma}(\mathbf{W^{ZCA}x_i} + \mathbf{b}) + \mathbf{c})$$

For the Z training examples, the reconstruction loss $\mathbf{L_r}$ is written as,

$$\mathbf{L_r} = \frac{\mathbf{1}}{\mathbf{Z}}\sum_{\mathbf{i=1}}^{\mathbf{Z}} \|\boldsymbol{\sigma}(\mathbf{W_r^T}\boldsymbol{\sigma}(\mathbf{W_i W^{ZCA} x_i} + \mathbf{b}) + \mathbf{c} - \mathbf{W^{ZCA}x_i})\|_2^2$$

Which is equal to,

$$\mathbf{L_r} = \frac{\mathbf{1}}{\mathbf{Z}}\sum_{\mathbf{i=1}}^{\mathbf{Z}} \left\|\boldsymbol{\sigma}\left(\mathbf{W_r^T}\boldsymbol{\sigma}\left(\mathbf{W_i U}(\boldsymbol{\Lambda} + \boldsymbol{\epsilon})^{-\frac{1}{2}}\mathbf{U^T x_i} + \mathbf{b}\right) + \mathbf{c} - \mathbf{U}(\boldsymbol{\Lambda} + \boldsymbol{\epsilon})^{-\frac{1}{2}}\mathbf{U^T x_i}\right)\right\|_2^2$$

6. OPTIMAL WHITENING TRANSFORMATION, W^o

Let $\mathbf{R^m}$ be the m dimensional space, $\mathbf{I_m}$ be the $\mathbf{mXm}$ identity matrix, $\mathbf{x} \in \mathbf{R^m}$ be a random vector, $\mathbf{Cov_x}$ be the covariance matrix. Using ZCA, we whiten the vector $\mathbf{x}$ using a transformation matrix W, such that $\mathbf{y} = \mathbf{Wx}$, where y is the whitened vector. We wish to propose and find $\mathbf{W^o}$ the optimal whitening transformation such that vector y is as close as possible to original vector x. Let $\mathbf{Cov_y} = \mathbf{z^2 I}$ be the covariance matrix for some $\mathbf{z} > \mathbf{0}$ such that $\mathbf{Cov_y} = \mathbf{WCov_x W^*}$, (*) adjoint of a transformation. We propose optimal whitening transformation to be the one that minimises the mean squared error Loss between x and y. For some $\boldsymbol{\delta}_{\mathrm{E}}$,

$$\boldsymbol{\delta}_{\mathrm{E}} = \sum_{\mathbf{i=1}}^{\mathbf{m}} \mathbf{E}(\mathbf{x_i} - \mathbf{y_i})^2$$

Now, lets define a Unitary transformation U such that, $\bar{\mathbf{x}} = \mathbf{Ux}, \bar{\mathbf{y}} = \mathbf{Uy}, \mathbf{Cov_y} = \mathbf{z^2 I}, \mathbf{Cov_{\bar{y}}} = \mathbf{z^2 I}$. Further, the eigen decomposition of $\mathbf{Cov_{\bar{y}}}$ is given by $\mathbf{Cov_{\bar{y}}} = \boldsymbol{VDV^*}$ Where d is a diagonal matrix and its $\boldsymbol{d_i}$ are its diagonal elements. The mean square error between $\bar{\boldsymbol{x}}$ And $\bar{\boldsymbol{y}}$,

$$\delta_E = \sum_{i=1}^{m} E(\bar{x}_i - \bar{y}_i)^2 \quad (1)$$

$$= \sum_{i=1}^{m} E(\bar{x}_i)^2 + \sum_{i=1}^{m} E(\bar{y}_i)^2 - 2\sum_{i=1}^{m} E(\bar{x}_i, \bar{y}_i) \quad (2)$$

Since we have chosen $\bar{x}_i = Vx$ and we know that $Cov_{\bar{x}} = VDV^*$ where D is a diagonal matrix with d_i as diagonal elements, we can write $\sum_{i=1}^{m} E(\bar{x}_i)^2 = d_i$. Further, it should be noted that $\bar{y}_i$ can be chosen proportional to $\bar{x}_i$

since $\bar{x}_i$ is uncorrelated. If $\bar{y}_i = \epsilon\bar{x}_i$ then $E(\bar{y}_i)^2 = \epsilon^2\bar{x}_i^2$. Assume that $\hat{y}_i$ is the optimal value of $\bar{y}_i$, then, by simple calculation $\hat{y}_i = \frac{\epsilon\bar{x}_i}{\sqrt{d_i}}$. Here, W and W^o are the optimal whitening transformation in original and new coordinate system, and $W = U^*W^oU$. W^o can be written as $zD^{-\frac{1}{2}}$. Thus

$$W^o = zD^{-\frac{1}{2}} = zVD^{-\frac{1}{2}}V^* = zCov_x^{-\frac{1}{2}}$$

We obtain the optimal value of z ($\boldsymbol{z^o}$) by minimizing equation 1 which computes $\boldsymbol{\delta_E}$, and later, we keep the value of $\boldsymbol{\bar{y}_i}$ as $\boldsymbol{\bar{y}_i} = \frac{z}{\sqrt{d_i}}\boldsymbol{\bar{x}_i}$ in equation 2. During experimentation, the various values of parameter z used in 13 datasets for finding optimal whitening transformation and subsequently enhanced features after zca are 0.1, 0.01, 1.0, 2.0. It is worth mentioning here that, every time the value of z is modulated, the original feature gets transformed into a different set of decorrelated features. More decorrelated the feature set is, better they are considered in terms of quality. Consequently, higher the quality of extracted features, better the classification accuracy of the classifier.

7. EXPERIMENTAL DETAILS

We experimented extensively on 10 datasets received from UCI Machine learning repository (Dua D. and Graff C., 2019) which includes Wine, Seeds, Car evaluation, Heart Disease, Wisconsin Breast Cancer, Sonar, Ionosphere, Haberman's survival, Census Income and Banknote Authentication. The experiment was also conducted on two hyperspectral image segmentation dataset - Satellite, Indian Pine - and a computer vision dataset - MNIST. The Satellite dataset comprises of 36 features each pertaining to a hyper spectral band of an image, 6435 samples and 6 classes in total. Training set is built using 80% of the samples and remaining is used for testing. 5 fold cross validation is performed on the training set, and later on, once the model is trained, it is sent for testing. This proces is followed on all the datasets. Similarly, Indian Pine dataset comprises of 10,392 samples, 16 classes and 200 features. 80% samples of each class is utilized in the training set and remainder forms the test set. The MNIST database of handwritten digits has 60,000 samples for training set and 10,000 for test set. The data has 784 input features and 10 classes. All the three datasets, along with the 10 popular machine learning datasets, were first whitened by using optimal whitening transformation (refer section 6 for details) and later used on autoencoders for deriving crucial features. Later, the features were fed on a vanilla feed-forward neural network for generalization. The accuracies obtained as a result of classification performed on the derived features are reported in table 1,2,3,4 and 5. The idea behind conducting the experiment is to investigate the effect of whitening transformation prior to feature extraction using SA. Additonally, we also focused on using the optimal parameter z, to enhance the quality of derived features and consequently on better classification accuracy. We performed the experiments in two stages. In the first state, all the datasets are fed on a SA for feature extraction which is followed by classification (note, the classifier in the last layer SA is neural network). In the second stage, optimal ZCA is applied on the datasets. The whitening optimality is achieved by searching the optimal z (i.e. varying the value of z till the loss was minimum).

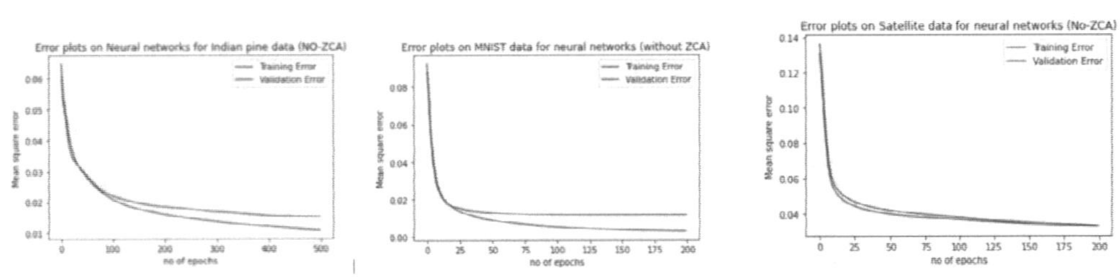

Figure 2. The error plot is run using learning rate of 0.05, 500 epochs and 50 hidden neurons, for the left figure and a learning rate of 0.01, 500 epochs and 57 hidden neurons for the middle figure, a learning rate of 0.015, 200 epocs and 25 hidden neurons for the right figure. Error plots on neural networks for different data without ZCA

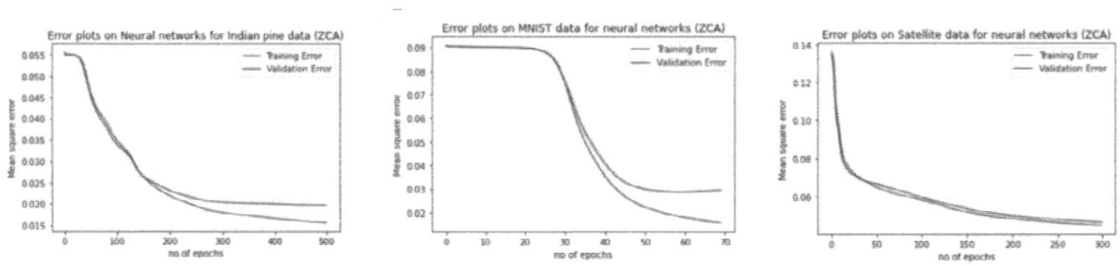

Figure 3. The error plot is run using run with a learning rate of 0.015, 200 epocs and 25 hidden neurons for the left figure and a learning rate of 0.05, 300 epocs and 25 hidden neurons for the middle figure and a learning rate of 0.3, 70 epocs and 25 hidden neurons for the right figure. These error plots are generated on neural networks for different data with ZCA

Different datasets pertaining to different z values are built and stored separately. For example, for Indian Pines, 3 whitened datasets were built, one with No-ZCA, second with ZCA (z =1.0) and third with ZCA (z =2.0). Similarly, for MNIST, four datasets were formed, one with No-ZCA, and remaining three with ZCA z=0.01, z=1.0, z=2.0.The accuracy, precision and recall is reported for each execution in each of the tables. During the experiment we observed that there is an increase in the accuracy when the classification is performed on datasets on which optimal ZCA is applied (refer tables 1,2 3,4 and 5). We also recorded that when z value is increased to 3.0, classification accuracy became stable and did not increase any further. Apparently, this is true for all datasets.

8. RESULTS AND DISCUSSION

Performance analysis of optimal ZCA on neural network and Stacked Autoencoder is as follows. Precision, Recall, and Accuracy is computed for these executions and recorded for every dataset. All the experiments are run for more than 100 epochs, and the learning rates used while experimenting are reported in the tables. Table 1 reports the performance indicators for the ten non-computer vision datasets experimented for plain neural network on normal and optimized (by using optimal ZCA) features. The optimal ZCA has increased the performance of 8 datasets out of 10, when compared against those which does not use the optimal features. Table 2 reflects the same performance parameters when the experiment is run on 2-layered SA. The optimized features obtained from optimal ZCA transformation as well as from the SA have increased performance on all the datasets. A set of observations, depicted in table 3, are the classification performance of autoencoder on Satellite dataset for two cases: one, when ZCA is not used and two, when ZCA is used. As already mentioned, it's a hyper-spectral image data of 36 features and 6 classes.

Table 1. Performance analysis of ZCA with Autoencoder. Precision, Recall, and Accuracy is indicated for every dataset

Performance comparison of neural networks with optimal ZCA on multiple data sets								
S. No	**Datasets**	**LR(epochs)**	**Neural Networks**			**Optimal ZCA + Neural Networks**		
			Accuracy	**Precision**	**Recall**	**Accuracy**	**Precision**	**Recall**
1.	Wine	0.1 (100)	0.97	0.95	0.96	**0.98**	0.97	0.98
2.	Seeds	0.08(100)	0.95	0.92	0.93	**0.97**	0.96	0.95
3.	Car Evaluation	0.1 (100)	0.95	0.92	0.80	**0.97**	0.88	0.88
4.	Heart	0.06(150)	0.96	0.81	0.81	0.82	0.83	0.82
5.	Cancer	0.1(100)	0.96	0.95	0.96	**0.97**	0.97	0.96
6.	Sonar	0.6(200)	0.83	0.81	0.84	0.77	0.78	0.78
7.	Ionosphere	0.8(200)	0.81	0.92	0.86	**0.85**	0.87	0.80
8.	Haberman	0.6(200)	0.76	0.68	0.62	**0.76**	0.70	0.57
9.	Census	0.05(150)	0.84	0.77	0.79	**0.83**	0.78	0.78
10.	Bank Note	0.015(150)	0.97	0.98	0.98	**0.98**	0.98	0.99

Table 2. Performance analysis of ZCA with Autoencoder. Precision, Recall, and Accuracy is indicated for every dataset

Performance comparison of SA with optimal ZCA on multiple data sets

S. No	**Datasets**	**LR(epochs)**	**SA**			**ZCA + Autoencoder**		
			Accuracy	**Precision**	**Recall**	**Accuracy**	**Precision**	**Recall**
1.	Wine	0.1 (100)	0.80	0.93	0.86	**0.82**	0.94	0.88
2.	Seeds	0.5 (200)	0.80	0.72	0.83	**0.83**	0.77	0.86
3.	Car Evaluation	0.01 (200)	0.71	0.57	0.62	**0.72**	0.59	0.64
4.	Heart	0.2 (200)	0.82	0.83	0.81	**0.85**	0.86	0.82
5.	Cancer	0.1 (300)	0.98	0.98	0.99	**0.99**	0.99	0.99
6.	Sonar	0.01 (200)	0.74	0.76	0.73	**0.74**	0.75	0.72
7.	Ionosphere	0.1 (200)	0.89	0.88	0.89	**0.90**	0.90	0.89
8.	Haberman	0.3 (200)	0.75	0.68	0.60	**0.77**	0.69	0.61
9.	Census	0.01 (200)	0.84	0.77	0.76	**0.84**	0.77	0.79
10.	Bank Note	0.02 (200)	0.92	0.92	0.92	**0.99**	0.98	0.99

It is evident from table 3, there is an increase in accuracy when classification is implemented on dataset with ZCA transformed features. The autoencoder is built using 2 hidden layers, with 19 and 11 hidden neurons in each layer. The output layer uses sigmoid to classify the samples.

Indian Pine data consist of 200 spectral bands at varying wavelengths captured for a scene that contains crops, forest and other natural vegetation. Autoencoder built for Indian Pine data has 150 neurons in first hidden layer and 70 neurons in second layer. The classifier uses a single layer of neurons equipped with sigmoid activation function. The performance is reflected in table 4. The classification results shown in table are obtained by using ZCA on MNIST dataset. The autoencoder used for MNIST takes 784 input features from dataset and derives 100 hidden features in its second layer and subsequently obtains 50 features in the third layer. The last layer works as classifier that deploys single layer of 10 neurons in its output (refer table 5 for results).

Table 3. With and without ZCA on NN/Autoencoders- Results of Satellite Data; comparing the performance across architeures. Model B does better than Model A (Exception seen for neural networks)

Satellite Dataset						
Model	Architecture	L_Rate	MSE	Accuracy	Precision	Recall
A	Neural Network	0.015	0.03261	0.952344	0.819713	0.8028324
B	Neural Network+ZCA(z=0.1)	0.05	0.04637	0.9066	0.76942	0.596353
A	Autoencoder	0.04	0.00186	0.949167	0.823213	0.815564
B	Autoencoder+ZCA(z= 3.0)	0.06	0.000765	**0.9505**	**0.861058**	**0.842283**

Table 4. With and without ZCA on Autoencoders - Results of INDIAN PINE Data. An increased accuracy is seen when performance is compared across with and without ZCA on the same architecture. Model B is better than Model A

Indian Pine Dataset						
Model	Architecture	LR (epochs)	MSE	Accuracy	Precision	Recall
A	Neural Network	0.05	0.02278	0.972034	0.900643	0.89535
B	Neural Network+ZCA(z=0.1)	0.1	0.01978	**0.978178**	**0.8903417**	**0.919872**
A	Autoencoder	0.006	0.01459	0.904549	0.522981	0.435787
B	Autoencoder+ZCA(z=2.0)	0.06	0.0033	**0.920565**	**0.590985**	**0.450903**

Table 5. With and without ZCA on NN/Autoencoders - Results of MNIST Data. An increased accuracy is seen when performance is compared across with and without ZCA on the same architecture. Model B is better than Model A

MNIST Dataset (NN/ SA)						
Model	Architecture	LR(epochs)	MSE	Accuracy	Precision	Recall
A	Neural Network	0.015	0.011466	0.9762	0.93053	0.93
B	Neural Network+ZCA(z=0.1)	0.3	0.029558	**0.9798**	**0.94083**	**0.9481**
A	Autoencoder	0.09	0.0006	0.9642	0.818528	0.814428
B	**Autoencoder+ZCA(z= 3.0)**	**0.09**	**0.00035**	**0.9808**	**0.899496**	**0.899025**

9. CONCLUSION

It is worthwhile to note that implementation of optimal ZCA as pre-processing tool for whitening the image data set, enhances the quality of derived features and as a result, facilitate a classifier to perform better generalization. Transparently, it is crucial to find out if the quality of derived features is improved after transformation of input features. A very popular method to investigate the quality of features is by computing correlation coefficient. However, computing the feature quality is left for the future work. We saw in our experiments that the accuracy, precision and recall on two out of four architectures (neural network without ZCA, neural network with optimal ZCA, SA without optimal ZCA and SA with ZCA) has increased by 2-4% on non-CV datasets while it increased by 7% for Banknote data (when used with SA, table 2). In satellite, Indain Pine and MNIST data, we witnessed an increase in accuracy by around 1-2%. However, it was evident from table 3 that the performance did not increase with the optimal features used in satellite data (just for neural networks). An investigation on this ambiguity is the scope of the future work.

ACKNOWLEDGEMENT

Archana Mathur would like to thank SERB for funding under the "Teachers Associate-ship for Research Excellence" scheme (SERB File Number: TAR/2021/000206) to carry this research.

REFERENCES

A. Al-Abassi , J. Sakhnini , & H. Karimipour , (2020), *Unsupervised stacked autoencoders for anomaly detection on smart cyber-physical grids* , 2020 IEEE International Conference on Systems, Man, and Cybernetics (SMC) (2020) 3123–3129.

A. M. N. Kessy , A. Lewin , & K. Strimmer , (2015), *Optimal whitening and decorrelation* . The American Statistician.

C. A. C. Montañez , P. Fergus , A. J. Hussain , & D. Al-Jumeily , 2018, *Analysis of extremely obese individuals using deep learning stacked autoencoders and genome-wide genetic data* , ArXiv abs/1804.06262.

Dong, M., (2009), An Approach for GPS Ambiguity Decorrelation Using Ordering and Cholesky Factorization. Journal of geomatics science and technology.

Dua, D. and Graff, C. (2019), UCI Machine Learning Repository [http://archive.ics.uci.edu/ml]. Irvine, CA: University of California, School of Information and Computer Science.

J. Amin , M. Sharif , N. Gul , M. Raza , M. A. Anjum , M. W. Nisar , & S. A. C. Bukhari , (2019), *Brain tumor detection by using stacked autoencoders in deep learning* , Journal of Medical Systems.

J. Liu , C. Li , W. Yang , (2018), *Supervised learning via unsupervised sparse autoencoder* , IEEE Access 6 73802–73814.

L. Le , Andrew Patterson, Martha White, (2018), *Supervised autoencoders: Improving generalization performance with unsupervised regularizers* ,NIPS'18: Proceedings of the 32nd International Conference on Neural Information Processing Systems.

P. Baldi , (2012), *Autoencoders, unsupervised learning, and deep architectures* , ICML Unsupervised and Transfer Learning.

P. Vincent , H. Larochelle , I. Lajoie , Y. Bengio , & P.-A. Manzagol , (2010), *Stacked Denoising Autoencoders: Learning Useful Representations in a Deep Network with a Local Denoising Criterion,* Journal of Machine Learning Research.

R. Hammouche , A. Attia , S. Akhrouf , & Z. Akhtar , (2022), *Gabor filter bank with deep autoencoder based face recognition system* , Expert Syst. Appl. 197 116743 .

Siarohin, A., Sangineto, E., & Sebe, N. ,(2019), Whitening and Coloring Batch Transform for GANs. ICLR.

X. Chen , L. Ma , X. Yang , (2016), *Stacked denoise autoencoder based feature extraction and classification for hyperspectral images* , J. Sensors 3632943:1–3632943:10 .

U. Michelucci , (2022), *An Introduction to Autoencoders.*

IDENTIFYING AND CHARACTERIZING CONCEPTS IN UNSTRUCTURED TEXTS USING AUTOMATIC ANNOTATION

Tiago Fraga[1], Orlando Belo[1] and Anabela Barros[2]
[1]*ALGORITMI Research Centre / LASI, School of Engineering, University of Minho, 4710-059 Braga, Portugal*
[2]*CEHUM, Centre for Humanistic Studies, University of Minho, 4710-059 Braga, Portugal*

ABSTRACT

Text annotation is an important and useful activity in semantic text analysis processes. The introduction of notes and marks in texts is one of the most common ways of valuing the content and revealing the semantics of a text, allowing its readers to have a more concrete idea of what is expressed in it. For a long time, text annotation processes were done manually often carried out in an *ad hoc* manner, without using a concrete method. It was a very time-consuming and labor-intensive process of different natures. Today, the great development of natural language processing, machine learning and mining text, promoted a strong emergence of applications in several domains. Text annotation was no exception. Through the combination of natural language processing and machine learning mechanisms, it is possible to develop systems that analyze texts, written in natural language, identifying words, creating contexts, and discovering and maintaining tags, their relationships and annotations, in an automatic way. In this paper, we present an automatic annotation system conceived and developed specifically for tagging the texts of the Book of Properties, a codex containing the inventory of the Archbishop's Table of Braga's properties (Portugal) in the 17th century. In addition to a general characterization of the system, we also describe the various stages of its annotation process with references taken from the Book of Properties.

KEYWORDS

Annotation Systems, Natural Language Processing, Machine Learning, Text Mining, Automatic Tagging, Data Analysis

1. INTRODUCTION

The area of semantic analysis of unstructured texts (Sinoara et al., 2017) has evolved a lot in recent years. The great emergence of tools and applications, particularly in the fields of text interpretation or content retrieval and extraction (Cornolti *et al.*, 2013) (Chu *et al.,* 2012) clearly proves this evolution. The increasing interest of researchers from various scientific domains, in knowledge contained in documents available in archives, libraries, databases, or in the Web, has promoted the development of much diversified solutions for the semantic analysis of these documents. Some of these solutions involve researching and application of text annotation techniques, structured or not, as a way of revealing and tagging, manually or automatically, textual elements with a particular semantic meaning. The need to make this annotation process more flexible, as well as to increase its speed and effectiveness, led to the development of systems to help the annotation of texts, both in initiatives that aimed at manual annotation and in other, more interesting and challenging ones, the use of automatic annotation systems.

A text annotation system (Moraes and Lima, 2008) is a mechanism capable of identifying concepts and relationships using a combination of text mining, natural language processing and machine learning techniques. In practice, this makes possible to develop text analysis systems — written in natural language — that are capable of (semi)automatically annotating sets of words, as well as their respective contexts of use, identifying concepts, characterizing them and establishing possible relationships. The extraction of concepts from texts is fundamental for any information retrieval process. However, it is difficult to perform, since obtaining annotated elements from a set of texts is a very complicated task. Automatic text annotation systems perform tagging tasks with a greater degree of speed and efficiency compared to conventional manual annotation processes. For cases involving a large volume of texts, manual annotation, even carried out by specialists with great experience, has become a task too expensive in time and resources (Cai and Hofmann, 2003). This is not acceptable, because it is very slow and inefficient, taking into account the operational and analysis requirements of current specialists and scholars.

In research and analysis of texts content, two of the most demanding tasks in annotation processes, especially when dealing with unstructured texts, written in natural language, it is usual to apply natural language processing and machine learning techniques. When properly combined, these techniques allow for preparing texts, identifying sets of relevant words, establishing research and relationship patterns, or discovering concepts and their relationships. All these elements are very useful for establishing definition tags for text contexts. Furthermore, these techniques eliminate, or at least mitigate, most of the disadvantages associated with the preparation and annotation of texts manually. However, the use of these techniques does not remove all manual tasks in the general annotation process, such as, for example, checking and validating tags, for adjusting parameters and improving the quality of the annotation process.

In this work, we present an automatic annotation system for unstructured texts, which we developed for tagging texts of a very singular document: the Book of Properties (Barros, 2019) (Barros, 2021). This manuscript of the 17th century contains the inventory of the properties of the Archbishop's Table of Braga (Portugal) in the beginning of that period. It describes in detail all the rustic and urban properties of several districts located mostly in the north of Portugal, as well as presents the rents and payments due to their lease. The annotation of this book is very important for identifying and highlighting particular elements (people names, place names, types of land, properties, degrees of kinship, etc.) and application contexts, for establish automatically maps of tag relationships to discover similar contents or the renewal of their definitions over time. Additionally, we will describe each of the processing stages of the system and illustrate some of the results achieved. The remaining part of this paper is structured as follows. Section 2 describes some related work in the area of text annotation, while section 3 exposes and describes the system we developed, and how it works in each execution stage. Finally, section 4 presents some conclusions and future work.

2. TEXT ANNOTATION

A text can be seen as a set of sentences that convey some kind of information to its readers. However, if there are no additional information elements, markings or notes throughout the text, its interpretation will differ more than expected between different readers. This means that a particular word or sentence can convey different ideas to different readers, especially in manuscript texts from past centuries. Text annotation (Gosal, 2015) is a task that adds value and specification to texts. It is possible to provide additional elements about the text, using a well-defined set of tags for helping readers in its interpretation. For example, when analyzing a conventional text, numerous punctuation marks are easily to found. They correspond to a set of marks, whose function is to help readers of that text in their reading and interpretation; however, these marks are quite different in old unpublished manuscripts. Tags also have this function, being defined according to the content of the texts. Usually, we call them as "content-oriented annotations" (Ferreira, 2011). The use of tags intends to indicate the presence of different types of elements in the text, such as people names, nicknames, place names, professions, or products, among many other information elements. The greater the presence of labels in a text, the greater the percentage of annotated text. Consequently, the easier it is the interpretation and understanding of the text. Text annotation is often performed in an *ad hoc* manner, which obviously does not reveal to the reader the true usefulness of this technique. However, when we done the annotation process methodically, and guided by the context and content of the text, highlighting its main ideas, the understanding of the texts increases significantly. Thus, text annotation can help readers to analyze their own ideas and thoughts, allowing them to have a direct and faster access to the most pertinent ideas and elements of a text (Lynch, 2021).

In recent years, a lot of work was made in the field of semantic analysis of unstructured texts, which has given rise to many applications, in areas so diverse as text interpretation or content retrieval and extraction. Perhaps the main reason for this development was the high number of documents available in companies, libraries, databases and websites. For this volume of data, manual annotation of texts is not feasible, as it becomes too exigent in terms of time and money, requires the involvement of specialized human resources and is not always carried out in a methodical and efficient way, which may cause errors and failures in annotation processes (Cai and Hofmann, 2003). For these reasons, many researchers have promoted the development processes of automatic annotation systems, as a viable way for a large part of the annotation problems in unstructured texts (Chu *et al.*, 2012). These initiatives quickly revealed a significant increase in the speed of execution of the annotation process and in the efficiency rate of recognition of textual elements of interest, in the identification and extraction of entities in texts, as well as dispensing with a large part of non-specialized human work. The development that has taken place in recent years in the areas of natural language processing, machine learning and text mining also contributed to this. The combination and use of tools from these areas makes possible to develop systems for analyzing structured or unstructured texts, written in natural language, taking note of words, contexts of use, concepts and their relationships. In some cases, they evolve as they do more and more annotation processes, that is, they have the ability to learn. We are, therefore, in another dimension of text annotation. However, they remain complex systems and difficult to implement (Finlayson and Erjavec, 2017). Despite these difficulties, the interest in automatic annotation systems by the research community increased significantly, according to the results observed in the applications that were being developed (Cornolti *et al.*, 2013). Today, we can say that the growth in the use of these tools and applications is remarkable. We can take as an example the area of big data systems, in which analysts of e-commerce sites or social networks use automatic annotation of website documents to establish, for example, user behavior patterns or discover trends in the purchase of goods and services. Regardless of the development context and application area, an automatic annotation system must work according to a robust annotation scheme, which clearly defines the annotation strategy and rules, as well as the different tags to use. This work must be carried out with the support of specialists in annotation and in the field of application of the texts. In addition, we need to select suitable computational tools for the annotation process, which allow for the recognition and division of words, identifying and classifying later concepts and their relationships. Several academic and business initiatives have made significant efforts in the development of automatic annotation systems and their application in areas of great interest. For example: the EXACT system (Chen *et al.*, 2019), developed at the University of Zhejiang, China, allows extracting entities from textual documents, through exploratory annotation operations that create attributes and associate them with tags; the Elketron system (Refinitiv, 2019), developed in an industrial context by Refinitiv, which has a concrete application in the areas of economics and financial markets; the Tagtop system (TagTop, 2022), which provides means for training a machine learning model for personalized annotation; or the UBIAI system (UBIAI, 2022), which is capable of performing Named Entity Recognition (NER) (Marrero *et al.*, 2013), relation extraction and document classification tasks. In addition to these examples, there are companies such as Uber, Apple or Microsoft using several types of annotation procedures to analyze their reputation in the field of social networks.

3. THE ANNOTATION SYSTEM

Usually, we develop an annotation system for very specific application domains, in order to facilitate the processes of interpretation and research the contents of texts. Although, we can do manually a text annotation process, its automation is highly desired, since, when possible, it simplifies the annotation process and drastically reduces its completion time, as already referred. Furthermore, when properly configured, it automatically establishes relationships that exist between discovered (and annotated) tags and the various textual elements that may be associated with them. The construction of an automatic annotation system requires the use of natural language processing mechanisms, commonly combined with machine learning mechanisms. This combination of technologies enables the development of systems capable of analyzing texts in natural language, with the ability to identify sets of words and create contexts of use, according to an established set of prerequisites, as well as discover and manage tags through techniques of word processing, more expeditiously and with a very high level of correction.

3.1 The Application Domain

Over the last few years, we have been developing a document management system (Barros et al., 2020) to accommodate the content of the Book of Properties, an impressive manuscript from the 17th century, which contains a detailed inventory of the rural and urban properties of the archbishops of Braga (Portugal). According to Barros (2021), the manuscript, having 1288 large pages, presents in detail and precision the inventoried properties of the Portuguese counties of Valença, Vila Real, Chaves and Braga, and also some properties in Porto and Santarém, in Portugal, and Galicia, in Spain. Due to the detail of this information, it is possible that researchers or readers of the Book of Properties, if they have roots in these locations, can find references or properties of their ancestors. The codex has a very impressive size, weight and binding, being handwrite in a very cultured and regular calligraphy, and presenting a detailed and extensive description of all the properties, rents and pensions of the Archbishop's Table of Braga. Only philologists, or researchers with experience in reading this type of documents, can read and interpret the information contained in the book. Other scholars, without this experience, may have difficulties in reading and handling the manuscript. In addition, the fact that the codex is not reproduced in digital format, and can only be consulted in person at the Braga District Archive, means that only one person can study it at a time. On the other hand, people far from the city have to travel to consult the book, which can sometimes lead to the abandonment of their study. With the increase in the number of researchers and due to the importance of the codex, the opportunity arose to store the contents of the manuscript, edited since 2015, in a digital format, overcoming all the difficulties for the study of the book mentioned. The document management system we implemented is a Web based application having the capacity to store, index and search the edited texts of the Book of Properties. It is a cross-platform system designed to run on the most relevant operating systems on the market. It is a client-server system, in which the backend received the native document management services, and the client sustain the user interaction and document loading and search services, running in conventional Web browsers. In practice, it is a web based application specially designed for the reception, processing and analysis of the texts contained in the Book of Properties, which has a set of specially created mechanisms for importing, cataloguing, modifying, removing, and analyzing texts stored in a document store.

3.2 The Annotation Mechanisms

In order to improve the research and analysis of texts of the document management system developed, as well as to reveal the various relationships between its various textual elements, a set of mechanisms, specifically oriented for annotating the document database, was incorporated into its structure. With the introduction of such mechanisms, the system received new means for incorporating tags into texts, which we consider relevant for the study of the Book of Properties, discovering and cataloguing anthroponyms, toponyms and microtoponyms, degrees of kinship, products, plants, properties and their location, etc. In this way, it was possible to maintain a base of tags indexing the most relevant information contained in the book. Furthermore, based on the tag specifications, the annotation mechanisms allow for analyzing the texts that are contained in the system and, similarly, suggesting a global annotation strategy for other tags, as well as generating a map of tag relationships that can be used to discover similar content. The quantity and diversity of the elements mentioned in the Book of Properties are surprising: all the names and surnames, nicknames, villages, professions, types of land and buildings, natural resources, cultures and ways of cultivation, among many others, are very important for the study and learning of geography, culture, agriculture, economy, architecture, religion and Portuguese language in the 17th century. The annotation of these elements expressively reveals their location in time and space, as well as their potential relationships, facilitating the study of the book and providing researchers, linguists, teachers and students with a valuable tool to reach and reinforce the knowledge about the codex.

When we made a detailed study of several existing automatic annotation systems – *e.g.* Benikova *et al.*, 2010), Ahmadi and Moradi (2015), Chen *et al.* (2019) or Dias *et al.* (2020) – we analyzed their most relevant models and features, as well as identified their functional architectures. In general, all these systems had very similar elements. Combining some of these models and their respective features, we sketched the working model of our automatic annotation system. Despite of its design having in mind its application to the Book of Properties, we consider that the system obtained is of widespread application, incorporating the most relevant functionalities that should be present in an automatic annotation system. The automatic annotation process we developed considers four working stages, namely: selection, tagging, validation and learning. Figure 1 presents an algorithm, in pseudo-code, which shows the most relevant operations performed by the system in each execution stage. In the next section, we will describe in detail each one of the mentioned stages.

```
def mainExecution():
   // 1.Selection
   text = selectAndReadText();
   // 2.Tagging
   tagsList = readTagsInfo();
   modernizationRules = readModernizationRules();
   textFormmated =
     formatText(modernizationRules, text);
   wordsList =
     applyTokenizationAndClassification(textFormmated);
   // 2.1 Automatic Tagging
   wordsCombination = calculateCombination(wordsList);
   for word in wordsCombination:
     for tag in tagList:
        dictionary = tag.getTermsDictionary()
        if word in dictionary:
           annotateWord(word, wordsList)
   // 2.1 Manual Tagging
   startConditionList = readStartConditions(tagList)
   stopConditionList = readStopConditions(tagList)
   for word in wordsList:
     if word in startConditionList:
       startPosition = word.getPosition()
       stopPosition = findStopWordInText(startPosition,
         wordsList, stopConditionList)
       annotateWordsBetweenStartAndStop(startPosition,
         stopPosition,wordsList)
   // 3. Valitation
   annotatedText = showText(wordsList)
   // 4.Learning
   saveAnnotatedText(annotatedText)
   updateDictionaries(annotatedText)
   updateIndex(annotatedText)
```

Figure 1. The annotation process in pseudo-code

3.2.1 Selecting Texts

This first stage (selection) is the simplest part of the system. Here, the system simply displays the texts that are available for annotation. When selected, texts are loaded into memory from a specific data collection in the system's document store. This step is not very demanding in terms of computational resources (memory and processor). Despite the large number of texts in the Book of Properties, each one of them, individually, does not have a large dimension, which makes the annotation process simple and fast.

3.2.2 Tagging Texts

During the tagging stage, the system performs five very distinct specific tasks on the text being processed, namely its classification, modernization, annotation using dictionaries (automatic tagging), annotation using NER (manual tagging) and, finally, aggregation. In the first task, classification, the system divides the words and aggregates them in a specific data structure, for using them later in other annotation tasks. This data structure receives the classification of words and stores the position of each of them in the text, as well as their homogenized form (in lowercase and without accents). The homogenized form is used throughout the dictionary search process, along with a logical value, which informs whether the word has already been annotated or not. The division and aggregation of the words in the text were implemented with the natural language processing tool LinguaKit (Gamallo and Garcia, 2017). This tool provided us mechanisms for diving text into words and making its morphological classification, so that it was possible to verify if a word would be a noun, an adjective, a verb, an adverb, etc. – the identification of these elements is essential in any annotation process. Then, the system performs some modernization of the orthography. As previously mentioned, the Book of Properties was written in classical Portuguese. The dictionaries of place names we used, for example, are in contemporary Portuguese, which imposes updating the spelling of the text. As most words do not follow current orthographic standards, and present multiple variants, or graphic forms, the detection of entities is difficult. To overcome this difficulty, we developed an automatic process for modernizing words, which works based on dictionaries and on a set of previously established lexical updating rules (Table 1). These rules match the classical patterns with the corresponding contemporary equivalents. The results of the word modernization process, the updated text and the data structure of the conversion dictionary, are stored in the system's document store, so that in all the time, whenever necessary, it will be possible to reverse the conversion (modernization) carried out and recover the original text. In Table 2 we can see an example of an original sentence extracted from a text (line 1) and the sentence that resulted from the modernization process (line 2).

Tagging using dictionaries is the third task of the annotation stage. Here, the system annotates entities from the word dictionaries referring to each of the tags that we want to use. For example, for tagging locations, it was necessary to create a specific dictionary – a gazetteer – with all locations in the Portuguese territory, with particular emphasis on the initial definition of annotation of locations, so that, in the future, we could apply the same or similar strategy to other types of tags. In this particular case, the dictionary was built from a specific dataset obtained from the Portuguese Public Administration Open Data portal (Dados.Gov, 2022), which disposes information about all districts, municipalities and parishes in Portugal. For the other types of tags established as essential, such as people names, types of land and houses, products, and others, we implemented similar processes.

Table 1. Some examples of spelling update rules

Classic	Modernized	Classic	Modernized
y	i	d'	de
ll	l	co'	com
uu	uv	q'	que
th	t	hu'	um
j [consonant]	l	nn	n
[vowel] u [vowel]	v	ee	e

Table 2. A modernized sentence from the Book of Properties

Original >	e	de	largo	pella	banda	do	sul	sessenta	e	quatro
Modernized >	e	de	largo	pela	banda	do	sul	sessenta	e	quatro

Finally, the system compares the words contained in the text with the terms registered in the tag dictionaries that are stored in the system and maintained over time. The comparison process used only words in lower case, without accents. With this strategy, it was possible to cover a greater number of cases, which was essential for increasing the level of accuracy and effectiveness of the tagging using dictionaries. Next, we have the tagging using NER task. In this task, the system identifies elements that are not present in the system dictionaries and to which no tag has been associated. The annotation performed in this task uses NER for identifying and recognizing entities in the text. As mentioned, the Book of Properties is a manuscript from the early of 17th century. As such, its texts contains references to names of people and places, lands or professions, which have changed over the years. The book also contains words that we do not use anymore, and thus automatically escape from the previous annotation process. For example, there are references to locations in the manuscript whose names and writing have simply changed. Cases like these are not present in the dictionaries. To handle them, we had to develop a process that was able to detect and record them properly, in a manual way. In this new process, we implemented a mechanism to verify the beginning and the end of class indicators. These words use to precede or belong to the term that we need to identify. For example, when processing words from the text, as soon as the system detects a start-of-class indicator it is quite likely that following words can be categorized by a specific tag. Once detected the starting point for a possible annotation, the system determines the different stopping points. When the system finds, for example, a determiner, a verb or an adjective, it defines a breakpoint. If a preposition was detected, the system checks the next word, which, if it belongs to the grammatical class of the stopping cases, determines the stop of the annotation of that case. Then, the system reuses the classification mechanism from the previous task, organizing the words in the text according to their morphological class. This allows for finding stopping cases contained in the texts and detect potential entities to annotate. At the end, we got an annotated text, having notes such as: "... e do nascente e sul com <name>Dona Maria </name> de semeadura" (in Portuguese). In this small example, the annotated name was identified based on the class start identifiers, which are the words that mark the beginning of the entity search, which in this case is "Dona". In turn, the stopping case is the preposition "de", which marks the end of the search. After identifying the referred limits, the system is able to identify the name "Dona Maria" and write it down correctly with the respective tag (<name>). After done the tagging tasks (automatic and manual), the system proceeds to the aggregation of annotated (and unannotated) words task. All the words were stored in a temporary JSON document, having a structure owning the attributes "word", "tag", "position", "annotated", "type" and "color". The "word" and "tag" attributes represent the form of the word, which may or may not contain a tag. For example, in an unannotated word, both attributes will have the same value. However, the same is no longer true for an annotated word. In this case, the "word" attribute will contain the word "surrounded" by the tag. As for the other attributes, they indicate, respectively, the position of the word in the text ("position"), whether or not the word is annotated ("annotated"), the type of tag used ("type") and the color that identify the tag in the text ("color").

3.2.3 Validating Tags

During the tag validation stage, the system verifies the annotation made in the previous stage, having user supervision. Based on the results of the previous stage, the system displays the tags defined and applied to the text. The user confirm the tags that have been defined, or cancel the validation process, which will cause the system to discard all the annotation work performed. The reviewing tasks do not require large computational resources. However, it obviously requires some work from system user. Additionally, the user can make new manual annotations or change one or more annotations of entities made previously. This process happens mainly when user wants to correct a tagging error or add new tags, in case of annotation failure.

3.2.4 Learning and Incorporating Tags

Learning is the last stage of the system. The first task of this step stores the text previously annotated in the system document store. Thus, any user will be able to view the annotated text, without having to perform any annotation task, in any access they make to the system. In a second task, the system updates the various tag indexes it has, identifying the occurrences of each of the tags in the texts. This task indicates the texts in which we can find references to relevant data elements, such as localities, professions, terrains, etc. Finally, the system updates tag dictionaries that it usually uses in the automatic annotation task. Updating dictionaries over time, after each annotation process carried out, we can say that the annotation system has some learning capabilities. This is because, during the annotation process, new entities can be discovered, from the manual annotation task or from annotations made by users in the validation state. As result, the system acquires and reflects appropriately in its storage structures that tagging actions, enriching the dictionaries and improving its own annotation process in future iterations. In Figure 2 we can see two tagging views for a (fragment of a) text: a) the annotated text, having the words annotated colored, and b) the text annotated, with the annotated words and their respective tags in sight. In this state of the annotation process, if necessary, it is possible to recover the original text. The system's document store maintains the various versions of the text created during annotation process.

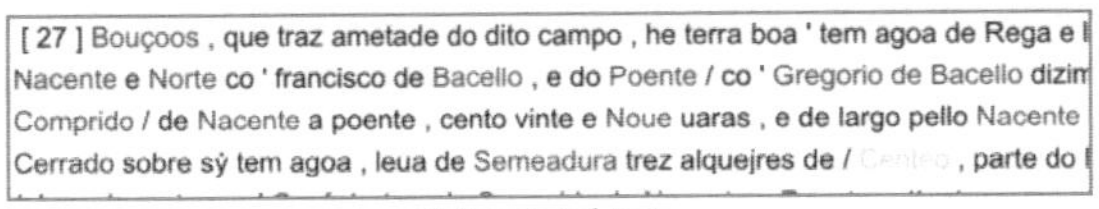

a) Annotated text

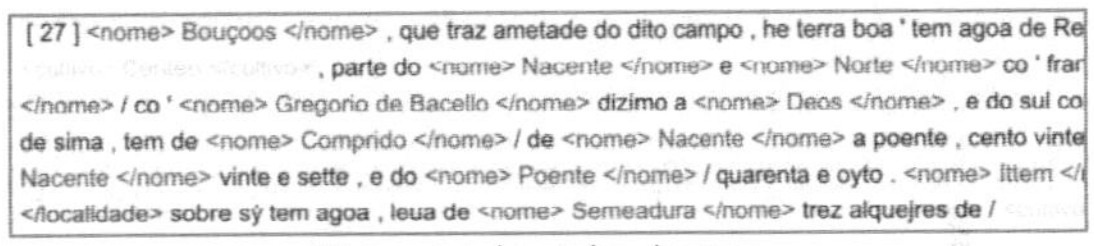

b) Annotated text showing tags

Figure 2. Two distinct views of a text fragment

4. CONCLUSIONS AND FUTURE WORK

In this paper, we presented an automatic annotation system specially designed and implemented for tagging the texts of the Book of Properties. The system provides a set of services for the automatic identification and annotation of various data elements referred in the book, such as names, locations, professions, terrains, as well as other elements with high historical interest of a large Portuguese territory. Such elements are very important to researchers, professors and students, for studying sociocultural, economic, architectural, agricultural, linguistic and religious aspects of the 17th century in the north of Portugal. At this point, we have available an operational version of the system, working as planned. However, as expected, the implementation system was not simple. It raised a very diverse range of challenges, ranging from modelling to tagging. It was difficult to integrate a supervised machine-learning module into the system, due to the lack of data for training the model we designed. Once the Book of the Properties was written in classical Portuguese, it was not feasible to use current texts in the training. In addition, the editing of this codex, from handwritten to digital form, is still in progress. It is a very time-consuming task, and at this moment the edition, already resulted in four books with more than two thousand pages. During the design and development phase of the system, the number of texts stored in the system was not large. Even so, we developed the bases for training and implementing the tagging system, obtaining a nice set of annotated texts. This allowed us to demonstrate the usability and utility of the system. As future work, we intend to increase significantly the number of texts in the system's document store (a task wich is recomended only when the last edition criteria will be definitelly fixed, after the completion of the codex edition, since it will affect all the text orthography), in order to improve the automatic annotation techniques, with new tagging services and learning mechanisms, increasing system robustness and performance. With this, we expect to open the use of the system to a selected community of researchers, professors, and students.

ACKNOWLEDGEMENT

This work has been supported by FCT – Fundação para a Ciência e Tecnologia within the R&D Units Project Scope: UIDB/00319/2020.

REFERENCES

Ahmadi, F., Moradi, M., 2015. A Hybrid Method for Persian Named Entity Recognition. 7th Conference on Information and Knowledge Technology, IKT 2015, May. DOI: 10.1109/IKT.2015.7288806.

Barros, A., 2019. Apontamentos lexicais sobre o Livro das Propriedades ou Tombo da Mitra Arquiepiscopal de Braga: designações de terras e outros aspectos das propriedades. In Estudos de linguística histórica: mudança e estandardização, Coimbra: Imprensa da Universidade de Coimbra, pp. 393-428.

Barros, A., 2021. A edição do Livro das Propriedades ou Tombo da Mitra Arquiepiscopal de Braga. In Os sete castelos. Congresso de Homenagem a D.Rodrigo de Moura Teles, Braga.

Barros, A., Belo, O., Gomes, J., Fraga, T., Martins, R., Carvalho, J.P., 2020. A Computational Instrument for Students Accessing and Exploring The Book of Properties of The Braga Archbishop's Table (17th Century), In Proceedings of 13th Annual International Conference of Education, Research and Innovation" (ICERI'2020), 9th-10th November.

Benikova, D., Yimam, S., Santhanam, P., Biemann, C., 2010. Germa-NER : Free Open German Named Entity Recognition Tool. 1(1):31–38.

Cai, L., Hofmann, T., 2003. Text Categorization by Boosting Automatically Extracted Concepts. In SIGIR '03 Proceedings of the 26th Annual International ACM SIGIR Conference on Research and Development in Information Retrieval, edited by ACM, 8. Toronto, Canada.

Chen, K., Feng, L., Chen, Q., Chen, G., Shou, L., 2019. EXACT: Attributed Entity Extraction by Annotating Texts. In ACM, editor, SIGIR'19 Proceedings of the 42nd International ACM SIGIR Conference on Research and Development in Information Retrieval, page 4, Paris, France. DOI: 10.1145/3331184.3331391.

Chu, B., Zahari, F., Lukose, D, 2012. Benchmarking T-ANNE: Text Annotation System. In ACM, editor, i-KNOW '12 Proceedings of the 12th International Conference on Knowledge Management and Knowledge Technologies, page 5, Graz, Austria. DOI: 10.1145/2362456.2362464.

Cornolti M., Ferragina, P., Ciaramita, M., 2013. A Framework for Benchmarking Entity-Annotation Systems. In WWW '13 Proceedings of the 22nd international conference on World Wide Web, page 11, Pisa, Italy. University of Pisa, Italy, ACM. DOI: 10.1145/2488388.2488411.

Dados.Gov, 2022, Portal de Dados Abertos da Administração Publica, Web Site [online] <https://dados.gov.pt/en/> [Accessed in 25 August 2022].

Dias, M., Boné, J., Ferreira, J., Ribeiro, R., Maia, R., 2020. Named entity recognition for sensitive data discovery in portuguese. Applied Sciences (Switzerland), 10(7). DOI: 10.3390/app10072303.

Finlayson, M., Erjavec, T., 2017. Overview of Annotation Creation: Processes and Tools, pages 167–191. 06 2017. DOI: 10.1007/978-94-024-0881-2 5.

Gamallo, P., Garcia, M., 2017. LinguaKit: uma ferramenta multilingue para a análise linguística e a extração de informação. Linguamática, 9(1), pages 19–28, jul. DOI:10.21814/lm.9.1.243.

Ferreira, L., 2011. Medical Information Extraction in European Portuguese. PhD Thesis, Universidade de Aveiro.

Gosal, G., 2015. A Survey on Semantic Annotation of Text. International Journal of Advanced Research in Computer Science and Software Engineering, Volume 5, Issue 9, September.

Lynch, E., 2021. Annotating Text Strategies That Will Enhance Close Reading, 2021. [online] < https://www.sadlier.com/school/ela-blog/teaching-annotation-to-students-grades-2-8-annotating-text-strategies-that-will-enhance-close-reading> [Accessed in 25 August 2022]

Marrero, M., Urbano, J., Sánchez-Cuadrado, S., Morato, J, Gómez-Berbís, J., 2013. Named Entity Recognition: Fallacies, challenges and opportunities, Computer Standards & Interfaces, Volume 35, Issue 5, Pages 482-489. DOI: 10.1016/j.csi.2012.09.004.

Moraes, S., Lima, V., 2008. Abordagem nao Supervisionada para Extração de Conceitos a partir de Textos. In ACM, editor, WebMedia'08 Companion Proceedings of the XIV Brazilian Symposium on Multimedia and the Web, page 5, Vila Velha, Espírito Santo, Brazil, DOI: 10.1145/1809980.1810066.

TagTop, 2022. The Text Annotation Tool to Train AI. [online] <https://www.tagtog.com/> [Accessed in 25 August 2022]

UBIAI, 2022, Transform Your Unstructured Data Into Intelligence. [online] <https://ubiai.tools/> [Accessed in 25 August 2022]

GAMIFIED VR SIMULATION IN NURSING EDUCATION: HOW TO GENERATE VALUE WITH VR IN NURSING EDUCATION

Roger Seiler, Ruben Straumann, Christian Weber and Andreas Block
Zurich University of Applied Science, St.-Georgen-Platz 2, P.O. Box, CH-8401 Winterthur, Switzerland

ABSTRACT

A shortage in nursing staff in Switzerland has reached a high level, and forecasts see the problem growing for the next years as there is a lack of candidates who are willing to sign up for nursing education programs. Prior research suggests that virtual reality (VR) can have positive effects on motivation, learning outcome, and trust. Therefore, we examine if VR in nursing education can help raise the attractiveness of education programs and help raise the number of people signing up for education programs which incorporate VR in their training and education.

KEYWORDS

VR, Nursing Education, Self-Efficacy, Customer Value, Customer Satisfaction, Customer Trust

1. INTRODUCTION

Virtual reality (VR) is a technology that is immersive and hence helps to keep students focused (Loureiro et al., 2021). Furthermore, gamification is also a concept that is emerging in the field of education (Loureiro et al., 2021) and simulators as well as serious games have already been adopted in the field of medical education (Jiang et al., 2022). Not only is gamification a very enjoyable way of learning (Charlier & De Fraine, 2013) but it also positively affects knowledge retention (Brom et al., 2011). Related to the branch of medicine just mentioned is the field of nursing, which is one area that may be aided by VR. The nursing profession in Switzerland is understaffed by 11,000 jobs (Kryeziu, 2022), and until 2028, a serious lack of qualified nursing personnel in Switzerland is forecasted (Merçay et al., 2021). This lack of personnel is, on the one hand, due to staff not transitioning to the labor market after graduating (Merçay et al., 2021) as high stress levels are a reason for staff leaving (Kryeziu, 2022). On the other hand, the scarcity stems from low graduation rates in nursing programs in which there is a high dropout rate that negatively affects the work force available for nursing jobs (Dolder & Grünig, 2016). The combination of high stress, inadequate qualified personnel, and high responsibility (e.g., devastating consequences for patients resulting from a wrong drug administration or wrong dosing) is challenging. Therefore, education in this field should use available technology, such as VR, to help to tackle these challenges by attracting and keeping students in the profession, for this technology has shown positive effects (e.g., knowledge retention) in the past (Brom et al., 2011). Therefore, this paper aims to address this issue by testing for the effects VR may have on students' self-efficacy, satisfaction, word-of-mouth (WOM), loyalty, and trust to enhance the attractiveness of nursing education.

2. LITERATURE REVIEW

Garzon et al.'s (2019) meta-analysis on augmented reality (AR) showed positive effects of augmenting reality (an e.g., a heads-up display (HUD) in automobiles or an alarm clock that projects the time on the bedroom ceiling) on learning experiences, learning motivation, and learning effectiveness. Additionally, positive effects of AR on academic success were reported by Batdi and Talan (2019). AR has mainly been researched in the context of cognitive achievements such as communication skills, engagement, and language learning (Reisoğlu et al., 2017). Potential benefits such as positive effects on learning outcomes (Merchant et al., 2014) as well as advantages of VR in education (Freina & Ott, 2015) can be identified. Additionally, Kavanagh et al. (2017) investigated application type as well as effects on motivation, and type of learning as well as hardware used was covered by Hamilton et al. (2021).

In customer management literature, positive effects of word of mouth (WOM) on purchase intentions have been reported (Babić Rosario et al., 2016). WOM could help acquire more nursing staff as this young target group tends to rely on online reviews or electronic word of mouth (eWOM; Erkan & Evans, 2016; Utz et al., 2012) as well as WOM. Furthermore, effects of VR on satisfaction were reported (Bryant et al., 2015; Jung et al., 2020) with higher satisfaction leading to positive WOM (Ladhari, 2007) or behavioral intentions such as promoting a product or experience (Trunfio et al., 2022). Thus, finding ways to improve satisfaction could help to acquire new nursing staff students. Furthermore, loyalty effects of satisfied students were reported in the education context as well (Munizu & Hamid, 2015).

In the specific context of public speaking and treating public speaking anxiety, positive effects of VR training were reported (Nazligul et al., 2017; Sakib et al., 2019; Yadav et al., 2020). These results are further confirmed by Reeves et al.'s (2021) meta-analysis and Daniels et al.'s (2020) systematic literature reviews. The roads to birth example where knowledge of anatomy is visualized with the help of this technology (Jones et al., 2019) is an example where VR is used to support learning.

Nevertheless, these advantages do not come without limitations such as barriers to using the technology including technical limitations, e.g. incompatible or missing cables, that pose an obstacle to using VR in higher education settings (Evans, 2019). Furthermore, the population (soldiers versus elderly people) or task type (cognitive, physical, or mixed) being trained can influence if VR/AR is an effective medium for training (Kaplan et al., 2021).

However, although prior research and meta-analyses have been conducted on AR and VR, the educational usefulness of the technology remains unclear (Radu, 2014). Furthermore, "Second Life" or quasi-experiments are very common in VR (Reisoğlu et al., 2017). Therefore, this paper closes this research gap by experimental means and extends the context of prior research to the nursing domain to check if VR is beneficial and valuable in this context.

VR training in medical education has been proven to have a positive effect on learning outcomes (Cohen et al., 2005). This finding is backed by a meta-analysis concluding that VR and AR have positive effects on motivation and learning success (Garzón et al., 2019) and can be applied in continuous education, for instance, in the form of edutainment (Fritz, 1997). Furthermore, VR training can be used to deliver speech training to children, who readily accept this form of training and who benefit as a result (Liu et al., 2017). The technologies also have limitations, however. Health and safety issues (Hicks, 2016), such as the risk of cybersickness (Meeri, 2019), are a possible obstacle in VR simulation and training.

Based on the literature mentioned, we conducted an extension of the systematic literature reviews and meta-analyses by analyzing further literature (see Table 1). We conducted a search with the keywords "nursing," "VR," "simulation," "virtual reality," "gamification," and "education." Out of 16 identified papers, eight were included as they were relevant to the research questions.

VR simulations are cost efficient and allow for delivering lectures or better training remotely (Aebersold et al., 2012). Furthermore, VR can contribute to the acquisition of knowledge, even though some studies find no difference compared to traditional methods of teaching (Chen et al., 2020), which contradicts previous research (e.g. Cohen et al. (2005)) as well as research found in this paper. Smith and Hamilton (2015) found positive effects of VR on students' learning performance as students benefitted from more time to practice and solve exercises in VR. Other studies such as that conducted by Dubovi et al. (2017) found that VR can be used to improve conceptual as well as procedural knowledge and hence close the gap between theory and practice in tertiary education.

Empirical evidence suggests that gamification works in an educational context, too (Hamari et al., 2014). In the content of nursing education, gamification can improve students' learning as well as motivate them (Castro & Gonçalves, 2018). Furthermore, gamification positively affected satisfaction, creativity, and perceived control with a significant impact on decision making and few negative effects (García-Viola et al., 2019).

However, the success of gamification depends on the domain or context to which it is applied, so Hamari et al. (2014) called for more rigor regarding methodology. The literature research conducted in this paper found an interculturally validated scale for measuring gamified learning experiences called GAMEX (Márquez-Hernández et al., 2019).

Although this is a rather general finding that can be applied to different VR applications and IT projects, it is worth mentioning because taking the needs of nursing students into account is important (Jeon et al., 2020). Specifically, a wide range of scenarios, capabilities, levels of difficulty, instant feedback, and simulations of emergency situations are needs that were specifically mentioned in Jones et al.'s (2019) study, and these requirements or needs may be taken into consideration when implementing VR applications in the field of nursing.

Table 1. Overview of literature extending existing meta-analysis and systematic literature reviews

Authors	Classification	n	Core findings
Aebersold et al. (2012), USA	VR experiment (crisis management)	51	- VR simulations are a cost-efficient form of training - Remote training without location on premise is possible
Castro and Gonçalves (2018), Brazil	Experiment in gamified VR learning environment	15	- Gamification can motivate students and improve their learning. - Gamification positively affects learning processes in the context of nursing education.
Chen et al. (2020), International	Meta-analysis of 12 studies on the effectiveness of VR	821	- VR can contribute to expanding students' knowledge but compared to traditional methods, no differences in learning outcomes could be identified.
Dubovi et al. (2017), Israel	Experiment with non-immersive desktop VR application	129	- Conceptual, procedural knowledge could be improved - Positive correlations were reported between feeling of presence and learning effect. - Gap between theory and practice in tertiary education was reduced.
García-Viola et al. (2019), Spain	Experiment on effects of gamification on decision making of nursing staff.	191	- Gamification positively affects satisfaction, creativity, perceived control, and further aspects. - No or few negative effects were reported. - A significant impact on decision making was found.
Jeon et al. (2020), Korea	Qualitative study (focus groups and interviews)	14	- Needs of nursing students should be considered when developing VR simulations. - A wide range of scenarios, capabilities, levels of difficulty, instant feedback, and simulation of emergency situations was mentioned.
Márquez-Hernández et al. (2019), Spain	Intercultural validation of the GAMEX scale	226	- GAMEX can measure the experiences during learning.
Smith and Hamilton (2015), USA	Experiment with immersive Unity VR application.	20	- Performance is improved by the VR simulation. - The VR simulation enables more time for exercises. - The VR simulation can be used to train capabilities used in clinics (e.g., catheter placement) - Research on VR simulation in a clinical context is insufficient.

The literature is not clear on exactly how VR can be beneficial (Smith & Hamilton, 2015) in the context of nursing education. Therefore, the research question is posed as follows:

RQ: How can VR provide value in the context of nursing education?

Furthermore, four sub-research questions regarding value and gamification from a student as well as an educational institution perspective are posed:

SRQ1: How can VR add value for students?

SRQ2: How can gamification add value for students?

SRQ3: How can VR add value from the perspective of the institution providing this education?

SRQ4: How can gamification add value from the perspective of the institution providing this education?

Regarding the education, the aspects of the educational provider that influence students' decisions in choosing an institution are relevant too. Therefore, the attractiveness of the educational program and the organization providing it in the eyes of customers or students is relevant. There are seven factors influencing this decision: image of the institution, influence of parents or friends and recommendations, quality of the education or service, costs and expenses, physical location, job perspectives, and offering of degrees the institution provides (Munizu & Hamid, 2015; Simões & Soares, 2010). Furthermore, word-of-mouth (WOM) is relevant (Chen, 2016) as this may lead to acquisition of further students, which is quite relevant to business schools and private tertiary education organizations alike. Also relevant is customer satisfaction since it can lead to WOM (Chen, 2016) and thus reduce acquisition costs.

As mentioned in Section 1, one of the reasons a shortage of staff in nursing exists is the high drop-out rate, so customer loyalty (in this case, continuing and finishing the education) and transitioning into the workforce are relevant constructs. Satisfaction correlates with loyalty in general (Bae et al., 2020; Casaló et al., 2008;

Curtis et al., 2011), and this holds true also for the nursing industry (Chen, 2016; Munizu & Hamid, 2015). Furthermore, customer loyalty, customer value, and customer trust are relevant as they tend to be linked with each other (Curtis et al., 2011; Mahaputra, 2017) and with satisfaction (Kim et al., 2009; Mahaputra, 2017).

A further concept that is linked to learning, motivation, and satisfaction is self-efficacy. It can positively affect motivation and the construct itself can be positively affected by achievements, experiences, observations, feedback, and psychological state (van Dinther et al., 2011). Furthermore, self-efficacy is an important indicator of students' success (Bartimote-Aufflick et al., 2016) which holds true for nursing students as well (Zengin et al., 2014) and can positively affect satisfaction (DeWitz & Walsh, 2002). Prior research suggests that VR can positively affect self-efficacy (Nissim & Weissblueth, 2017).

3. METHOD

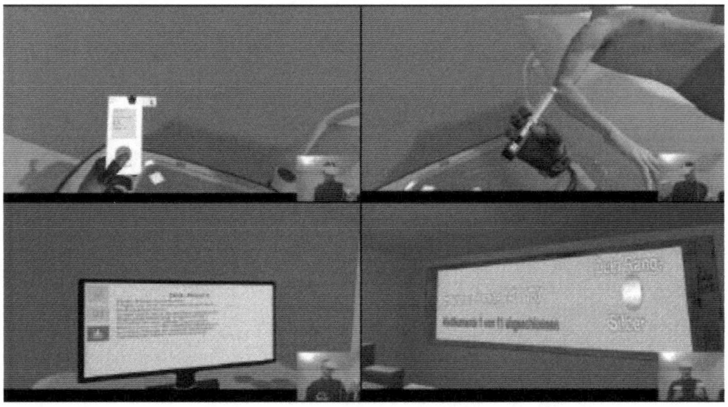

Figure 1. Screenshot of the prototype

An experiment is conducted to answer the research questions by inviting nursing students in their second and sixth terms to use a VR prototype (see Figure 1) and take a subsequent survey. The experiment was split into three phases. In the first phase, the students learned the controls of the VR application. In the second phase, they used the VR application in a learning mode. Finally, in the third phase, the students took the survey. The operationalization was implemented as follows: Age, gender, place of residence, education (current and previous), years of working experience, and hours of experience in VR were control variables. The constructs were measured by scales used in past research: psychometric skills (Stump et al., 2012), customer satisfaction (Elliott & Shin, 2002), customer loyalty and referral (Chen, 2016), hedonic and utilitarian customer value (Kim & Hall, 2019) and trust (Ghosh et al., 2001). Nineteen students in their second term participated in the experiment. They were randomly assigned to the treatment (VR application with gamification) and control (VR application without gamification) groups. A small incentive for participating was provided as participation in the experiment was optional. Participants filled out a questionnaire before using the VR application (baseline) and another one after the VR experience.

4. RESULTS, DISCUSSION, FURTHER RESEARCH, AND LIMITATIONS

The participants of this study were on average 21.53 years of age. Furthermore, they had an average of 1.79 years of working experience. The majority (79%) were female, were residents in urban regions (53%), and did not have any experience yet with VR (58%). First, a test on normal distribution was conducted (Shapiro-Wilk) and apart from the self-efficacy and referral, all of the variables followed a normal distribution. Therefore, parametric testing could be conducted with these two exceptions. Of the variables, only years of work experience had significantly higher levels in the control group than in the treatment group. All other control variables showed no significant group differences.

Hypotheses H1 to H3 (see Table 2) were tested by t-test and showed p values of .00, .07, and .73, respectively. Hypothesis H1a showed significant differences whereas H2a and H3a did not. Hypothesis H1b showed significant group differences with a p value of .00 whereas H2b and H3b did not with p values of .33 and .61, respectively. Hypotheses H4 to H10 were tested by regression analysis. All hypotheses, except H5 ($p = .45$), showed significant p values of .00 and hence could be accepted (see Table 2).

Table 2. Overview of hypothesis

Hypotheses	**Path**	***p* value**	**Result**
H1a	VR simulation → self-efficacy	.00	Accept
H1b	Gamification moderates (VR simulation → self-efficacy)	.00	Accept
H2a	VR simulation → customer satisfaction	.07	Reject
H2b	Gamification moderates (VR simulation → customer satisfaction)	.33	Reject
H3a	VR- simulation → customer value	.73	Reject
H3b	Gamification moderates (VR simulation → customer value)	.72	Reject
H4	Customer value → customer satisfaction	.00	Accept
H5	Self- efficacy → customer satisfaction	.45	Reject
H6	Customer satisfaction → customer loyalty	.00	Accept
H7	Customer satisfaction → WOM	.00	Accept
H8	Customer loyalty → WOM	.00	Accept
H9	Customer trust → customer value	.00	Accept
H10	Customer trust → customer loyalty	.00	Accept

The moderation effect was only significant for the gamification's moderating effect on the path VR simulation to self-efficacy. Therefore, gamification fostered VR effects neither on customer satisfaction nor on customer value. The VR simulation had significant effects on self-efficacy but affected neither customer satisfaction nor customer value directly. Furthermore, self-efficacy did not affect customer satisfaction.

However, customer satisfaction had a significant effect on customer loyalty and WOM. In turn, customer loyalty had a positive effect on WOM. Customer trust affected both customer value and customer loyalty. Not only did the VR simulation affect self-efficacy, an important and relevant concept of learning outcomes, but also gamification had positive effects on self-efficacy. This result matches that of past research on VR (e.g., Nissim & Weissblueth (2017); Hsiao (2021)) and traditional simulations (Nishisaki et al., 2007). Also, self-efficacy did not directly affect customer satisfaction; however, it is possible that indirect effects not modelled in this research, such as effects on trust and in turn on satisfaction, may play a role as self-efficacy may trigger emotions or affect cognitive as well as affective aspects of customer trust. The results also showed that customer satisfaction affected customer loyalty and WOM. Customer loyalty in turn affected WOM. Both customer value and customer loyalty were affected by customer trust. From a didactic point of view, the use of VR and gamification is beneficial regarding self-efficacy. With regard to the traditional customer-related aspects such as trust, customer satisfaction, customer value, and customer loyalty, the picture was less clear. Although the hypotheses were accepted and the customer-related constructs as well as beneficial customer behavior such as WOM held true in the context of nursing education, no direct link between VR and gamification and customer-related constructs could be reported. A further analysis and regression with utilitarian and hedonic customer value showed a clearer picture in favor of the hedonic customer value. Furthermore, a simple cross-table comparison suggested that VR positively affected the customer-related constructs as these results were higher in the post questionnaire than in the baseline one.

Therefore, further research may take a closer look at the customer-related constructs that account for direct and indirect effects. Additionally, adding further constructs which are more hedonically related such as the affective dimension of trust may further help shed light on the complex and presumable emotional affective effects of VR and gamification in a nursing education setting. As these results can be considered preliminary, further research may analyze larger or comparable sample sizes with structural equation modelling (SEM) like in the latest research of Hsiao (2021) on self-efficacy in order to test for further direct or indirect effects of VR and gamification on the constructs discussed in this paper.

Primary limitations of this study are the small sample size, the relatively young ages of the participants as they were from the second term in their education, and the gender bias towards female participants. A final aspect which deserves note, though, is that the number of years of working experience was significantly different between the two experimental groups. Nevertheless, since this study focused on the nursing profession, the results are interesting and relevant as the makeup of the profession is relatively young and primarily female. Hence, the study is relevant and applicable to the target group of nursing students.

5. CONCLUDING REMARKS

The results of this research suggest that adding VR simulations to nursing education curricula and training may help improve students' self- efficacy. Furthermore, traditional customer management constructs hold true in this branch, too. In education and elsewhere, customer satisfaction affects customer value. Happy students are more loyal and tend to give more positive WOM, which in turn can reduce the cost of acquiring new students which is important to business schools as well as private tertiary schools. Customer loyalty, too, positively affects WOM. The younger target group in this study tends to seek information online, so positive ratings and WOM are thus relevant and important. To this end, VR can help foster customer satisfaction, and with affective and emotional effects, this technology can enable customer behavior, such as WOM, that is beneficial to educational institutions. Furthermore, trust has been identified as highly relevant to business success in the past and even more so online, so trust positively affects customer value as well as loyalty, both aspects beneficial to the success of educational institutions.

REFERENCES

Aebersold, M., Tschannen, D., Bathish, M., (2012). Innovative Simulation Strategies in Education. Nursing Research and Practice 2012, 1–7. https://doi.org/10.1155/2012/765212

Babić Rosario, A., Sotgiu, F., De Valck, K., Bijmolt, T.H.A., 2016. The Effect of Electronic Word of Mouth on Sales: A Meta-Analytic Review of Platform, Product, and Metric Factors. Journal of Marketing Research 53, 297–318. https://doi.org/10.1509/jmr.14.0380

Bae, S., Jung, T.H., Moorhouse, N., Suh, M., Kwon, O., (2020). The Influence of Mixed Reality on Satisfaction and Brand Loyalty in Cultural Heritage Attractions: A Brand Equity Perspective. Sustainability 12, 2956. https://doi.org/10.3390/su12072956

Bartimote-Aufflick, K., Bridgeman, A., Walker, R., Sharma, M., Smith, L., (2016). The study, evaluation, and improvement of university student self-efficacy. Studies in Higher Education 41, 1918–1942. https://doi.org/10.1080/03075079.2014.999319

Brom, C., Preuss, M., Klement, D., (2011). Are educational computer micro-games engaging and effective for knowledge acquisition at high-schools? A quasi-experimental study. Computers & Education 57, 1971–1988. https://doi.org/10.1016/j.compedu.2011.04.007

Bryant, R., Miller, C.L., Henderson, D., (2015). Virtual Clinical Simulations in an Online Advanced Health Appraisal Course. Clinical Simulation in Nursing 11, 437–444. https://doi.org/10.1016/j.ecns.2015.08.002

Casaló, L.V., Flavián, C., Guinalíu, M., (2008). The role of satisfaction and website usability in developing customer loyalty and positive word-of-mouth in the e-banking services. International Journal of Bank Marketing 26, 399–417. https://doi.org/10.1108/02652320810902433

Castro, T.C., Gonçalves, L.S., (2018). The use of gamification to teach in the nursing field. Rev. Bras. Enferm. 71, 1038–1045. https://doi.org/10.1590/0034-7167-2017-0023

Charlier, N., De Fraine, B., (2013). Game-Based Learning as a Vehicle to Teach First Aid Content: A Randomized Experiment. Journal of School Health 83, 493–499. https://doi.org/10.1111/josh.12057

Chen, C.-T., (2016). The Investigation on Brand Image of University Education and Students' Word-of-Mouth Behavior. HES 6, 23. https://doi.org/10.5539/hes.v6n4p23

Chen, F.-Q., Leng, Y.-F., Ge, J.-F., Wang, D.-W., Li, C., Chen, B., Sun, Z.-L., (2020). Effectiveness of Virtual Reality in Nursing Education: Meta-Analysis. J Med Internet Res 22, e18290. https://doi.org/10.2196/18290

Cohen, C.J., Hay, R., Urquhart, A., Gauger, P., Andreatta, P., (2005). A Modular Interactive Virtual Surgical Training Environment, in: Interservice/Industry Training, Simulation, and Education Conference (I/ITSEC). pp. 2074–2086.

Curtis, T., Abratt, R., Rhoades, D., Dion, P., (2011). Customer Loyalty, Repurchase and Satisfaction: A Meta-Analytical Review. Journal of Consumer Satisfaction, Dissatisfaction and Complaining Behavior 24, 1–26.

DeWitz, S.J., Walsh, W.B., (2002). Self-Efficacy and College Student Satisfaction. Journal of Career Assessment 10, 315–326. https://doi.org/10.1177/10672702010003003

Dolder, P., Grünig, A., (2016). Nationaler Versorgungsbericht für die Gesundheitsberufe 2016. Nachwuchsbedarf und Massnahmen zur Personalsicherung auf nationaler Ebene. Bundesamt für Gesundheit, Schweizerische Konferenz der kantonalen Gesundheitsdirektorinnen und -direktoren & Nationale Dachorganisation der Arbeitswelt Gesundheit, Bern.

Dubovi, I., Levy, S.T., Dagan, E., (2017). Now I know how! The learning process of medication administration among nursing students with non-immersive desktop virtual reality simulation. Computers & Education 113, 16–27. https://doi.org/10.1016/j.compedu.2017.05.009

Elliott, K.M., Shin, D., (2002). Student Satisfaction: An alternative approach to assessing this important concept. Journal of Higher Education Policy and Management 24, 197–209. https://doi.org/10.1080/1360080022000013518

Erkan, I., Evans, C., (2016). The influence of eWOM in social media on consumers' purchase intentions: An extended approach to information adoption. Computers in Human Behavior 61, 47–55. https://doi.org/10.1016/j.chb.2016.03.003

Evans, L., (2019). Barriers to VR use in HE, in: Proceedings of the Virtual and Augmented Reality to Enhance Learning and Teaching in Higher Education Conference 2018. IM Publications Open LLP, pp. 3–13. https://doi.org/10.1255/vrar2018.ch2

Freina, L., Ott, M., (2015). A literature review on immersive virtual reality in education: state of the art and perspectives, in: The International Scientific Conference ELearning and Software for Education. pp. 10–1007.

Fritz, J., (1997). Edutainment - Neue Formen des Spielens und Lernens?

García-Viola, A., Garrido-Molina, J.M., Márquez-Hernández, V.V., Granados-Gámez, G., Aguilera-Manrique, G., Gutiérrez-Puertas, L., 2019. The Influence of Gamification on Decision Making in Nursing Students. J Nurs Educ 58, 718–722. https://doi.org/10.3928/01484834-20191120-07

Garzón, J., Pavón, J., Baldiris, S., (2019). Systematic review and meta-analysis of augmented reality in educational settings. Virtual Reality 23, 447–459. https://doi.org/10.1007/s10055-019-00379-9

Ghosh, A.K., Whipple, T.W., Bryan, G.A., (2001). Student Trust and Its Antecedents in Higher Education. The Journal of Higher Education 72, 322–340. https://doi.org/10.2307/2649334

Hamari, J., Koivisto, J., Sarsa, H., (2014). Does Gamification Work? – A Literature Review of Empirical Studies on Gamification, in: 2014 47th Hawaii International Conference on System Sciences. Presented at the 2014 47th Hawaii International Conference on System Sciences, pp. 3025–3034. https://doi.org/10.1109/HICSS.2014.377

Hamilton, D., McKechnie, J., Edgerton, E., Wilson, C., (2021). Immersive virtual reality as a pedagogical tool in education: a systematic literature review of quantitative learning outcomes and experimental design. J. Comput. Educ. 8, 1–32. https://doi.org/10.1007/s40692-020-00169-2

Hicks, P., (2016). The Pros And Cons Of Using Virtual Reality In The Classroom [WWW Document]. eLearning Industry. URL https://elearningindustry.com/pros-cons-using-virtual-reality-in-the-classroom (accessed 11.28.21).

Hsiao, S.C., (2021). Effects of the Application of Virtual Reality to Experiential Education on Self-Efficacy and Learning Motivation of Social Workers. Frontiers in Psychology 0. https://doi.org/10.3389/fpsyg.2021.770481

Jeon, J., Kim, J.H., Choi, E.H., (2020). Needs Assessment for a VR-Based Adult Nursing Simulation Training Program for Korean Nursing Students: A Qualitative Study Using Focus Group Interviews. IJERPH 17, 8880. https://doi.org/10.3390/ijerph17238880

Jiang, H., Vimalesvaran, S., Wang, J.K., Lim, K.B., Mogali, S.R., Car, L.T., (2022). Virtual Reality in Medical Students' Education: Scoping Review. JMIR Medical Education 8, e34860. https://doi.org/10.2196/34860

Jones, D., Siang See, Z., Billinghurst, M., Goodman, L., Fealy, S., (2019). Extended Reality for Midwifery Learning: MR VR Demonstration, in: The 17th International Conference on Virtual-Reality Continuum and Its Applications in Industry. Presented at the VRCAI '19: The 17th International Conference on Virtual-Reality Continuum and its Applications in Industry, ACM, Brisbane QLD Australia, pp. 1–2. https://doi.org/10.1145/3359997.3365739

Jung, T., Moorhouse, N., Shi, X., Amin, M.F., (2020). A Virtual Reality–Supported Intervention for Pulmonary Rehabilitation of Patients With Chronic Obstructive Pulmonary Disease: Mixed Methods Study. Journal of Medical Internet Research 22, e14178. https://doi.org/10.2196/14178

Kaplan, A.D., Cruit, J., Endsley, M., Beers, S.M., Sawyer, B.D., Hancock, P.A., (2021). The Effects of Virtual Reality, Augmented Reality, and Mixed Reality as Training Enhancement Methods: A Meta-Analysis. Hum Factors 63, 706–726. https://doi.org/10.1177/0018720820904229

Kavanagh, S., Reilly-Luxton, A., Wuensche, B., Plimmer, B., (2017). A systematic review of Virtual Reality in education. Themes in Science and Technology Education 10, 85–119.

Kim, D.J., Ferrin, D.L., Rao, H.R., (2009). Trust and Satisfaction, Two Stepping Stones for Successful E-Commerce Relationships: A Longitudinal Exploration. Information Systems Research 20, 237–257. https://doi.org/10.1287/isre.1080.0188

Kim, M.J., Hall, C.M., (2019). A hedonic motivation model in virtual reality tourism: Comparing visitors and non-visitors. International Journal of Information Management 46, 236–249. https://doi.org/10.1016/j.ijinfomgt.2018.11.016

Kryeziu, I., (2022). Pflegenotstand: Wie weiter? Careum. URL https://careum.ch/de/aktuell/pflegenotstand-schweiz (accessed 8.29.22).

Ladhari, R., (2007). The effect of consumption emotions on satisfaction and word-of-mouth communications. Psychology & Marketing 24, 1085–1108. https://doi.org/10.1002/mar.20195

Liu, D., Bhagat, K.K., Gao, Y., Chang, T.-W., Huang, R., (2017). The Potentials and Trends of Virtual Reality in Education, in: Liu, D., Dede, C., Huang, R., Richards, J. (Eds.), Virtual, Augmented, and Mixed Realities in Education. Springer Singapore, Singapore, pp. 105–130. https://doi.org/10.1007/978-981-10-5490-7_7

Loureiro, S.M.C., Bilro, R.G., Angelino, F.J. de A., (2021). Virtual reality and gamification in marketing higher education: a review and research agenda. SJME 25, 179–216. https://doi.org/10.1108/SJME-01-2020-0013

Mahaputra, R., (2017). The Influence of Trust and Customer Value to Customer Satisfaction on Bank BRI Branch Soetomo Jambi.

Márquez-Hernández, V.V., Garrido-Molina, J.M., Gutiérrez-Puertas, L., García-Viola, A., Aguilera-Manrique, G., Granados-Gámez, G., (2019). How to measure gamification experiences in nursing? Adaptation and validation of the Gameful Experience Scale [GAMEX]. Nurse Education Today 81, 34–38. https://doi.org/10.1016/j.nedt.2019.07.005

Meeri, K., (2019). Cybersickness: Why People Experience Motion Sickness During Virtual Reality [WWW Document]. Inside Science. URL https://www.insidescience.org/news/cybersickness-why-people-experience-motion-sickness-during-virtual-reality (accessed 11.28.21).

Merçay, C., Grünig, A., Dolder, P., (2021). Gesundheitspersonal in der Schweiz - Nationaler Versorgungsbericht 2021. Bestand, Bedarf, Angebot und Massnahmen zur Personalsicherung (No. Obsan Bericht 03/2021), Bestand, Bedarf, Angebot und Massnahmen zur Personalsicherung. Schweizerisches Gesundheitsobservatorium, Neuchâtel.

Merchant, Z., Goetz, E.T., Cifuentes, L., Keeney-Kennicutt, W., Davis, T.J., (2014). Effectiveness of virtual reality-based instruction on students' learning outcomes in K-12 and higher education: A meta-analysis. Computers & Education 70, 29–40. https://doi.org/10.1016/j.compedu.2013.07.033

Munizu, M., Hamid, N., (2015). Satisfaction and Loyalty Improvement Model on the Quality of Higher Education Services. JDM (Jurnal Dinamika Manajemen) 6. https://doi.org/10.15294/jdm.v6i1.4293

Nazligul, M.D., Yilmaz, M., Gulec, U., Gozcu, M.A., O'Connor, R.V., Clarke, P.M., (2017). Overcoming public speaking anxiety of software engineers using virtual reality exposure therapy, in: European Conference on Software Process Improvement. Springer, pp. 191–202.

Nishisaki, A., Keren, R., Nadkarni, V., (2007). Does Simulation Improve Patient Safety?: Self-Efficacy, Competence, Operational Performance, and Patient Safety. Anesthesiology Clinics 25, 225–236. https://doi.org/10.1016/j.anclin.2007.03.009

Nissim, Y., Weissblueth, E., (2017). Virtual Reality (VR) as a Source for Self-Efficacy in Teacher Training. IES 10, 52. https://doi.org/10.5539/ies.v10n8p52

Radu, I., (2014). Augmented reality in education: a meta-review and cross-media analysis. Personal and Ubiquitous Computing 18, 1533–1543. https://doi.org/10.1007/s00779-013-0747-y

Reisoğlu, I., Topu, B., Yılmaz, R., Karakuş Yılmaz, T., Göktaş, Y., (2017). 3D virtual learning environments in education: a meta-review. Asia Pacific Educ. Rev. 18, 81–100. https://doi.org/10.1007/s12564-016-9467-0

Sakib, M.N., Yadav, M., Chaspari, T., Behzadan, A.H., (2019). Coupling virtual reality and physiological markers to improve public speaking performance, in: 19th International Conference on Construction Applications of Virtual Reality (CONVR2019), Bangkok, Thailand. pp. 171–180.

Simões, C., Soares, A.M., (2010). Applying to higher education: information sources and choice factors. Studies in Higher Education 35, 371–389. https://doi.org/10.1080/03075070903096490

Smith, P.C., Hamilton, B.K., (2015). The Effects of Virtual Reality Simulation as a Teaching Strategy for Skills Preparation in Nursing Students. Clinical Simulation in Nursing 11, 52–58. https://doi.org/10.1016/j.ecns.2014.10.001

Stump, G.S., Husman, J., Brem, S.K., (2012). The Nursing Student Self-Efficacy Scale: Development Using Item Response Theory. Nursing Research 61, 149–158. https://doi.org/10.1097/NNR.0b013e318253a750

Trunfio, M., Jung, T., Campana, S., (2022). Mixed reality experiences in museums: Exploring the impact of functional elements of the devices on visitors' immersive experiences and post-experience behaviours. Information & Management 103698. https://doi.org/10.1016/j.im.2022.103698

Utz, S., Kerkhof, P., Bos, J.V. den, (2012). Consumers rule: How consumer reviews influence perceived trustworthiness of online stores. Electronic Commerce Research and Applications 11, 49–58. https://doi.org/10.1016/j.elerap.2011.07.010

van Dinther, M., Dochy, F., Segers, M., (2011). Factors affecting students' self-efficacy in higher education. Educational Research Review 6, 95–108. https://doi.org/10.1016/j.edurev.2010.10.003

Yadav, M., Sakib, M.N., Nirjhar, E.H., Feng, K., Behzadan, A., Chaspari, T., (2020). Exploring individual differences of public speaking anxiety in real-life and virtual presentations. IEEE Transactions on Affective Computing 1–1. https://doi.org/10.1109/TAFFC.2020.3048299

Zengin, N., Pınar, R., Akinci, A.C., Yildiz, H., (2014). Psychometric properties of the self-efficacy for clinical evaluation scale in Turkish nursing students. J Clin Nurs 23, 976–984. https://doi.org/10.1111/jocn.12257

ONTOLOGY MODEL FOR SMART OPEN LEARNING ENVIRONMENT BASED ON COPUTATIONAL THINKING

Bènène Fradi and Lilia Cheniti-Belcadhi
PRINCE Research Group, ISITCom, University of Sousse, Tunisia

ABSTRACT

Due to the rapid development of innovative technologies, current digital society faces challenges for changing the environment. Constructing and applying Smart Learning Environments (SLEs) has emerged for supporting knowledge representation and learning content creation. In this paper, we focus on Smart Open Learning Environment (SOLE) that provide adaptive self-regulate learning based on Computational Thinking (CT). This contribution describes the progress of a pedagogical scenario promoted by Open Learner Model (OLM) to enhance CT through a SOLE that aims to support the learning process and to provide Adaptive Self-Regulated Learning.

In this paper, we present our work, which takes advantage of different technologies such as ontology, Learning Analytic for a SOLE in order to be better managed and to offer more flexibility and comfort. Subsequently, we describe a learning scenario through SOLE and we propose a model for it that describes the interaction of its components. Then we propose different ontological models for the semantic of SOLE and we detail OLM ontology. We aim to deliver open content, which is adapted to specific learner context, profile, progress and CT's Level in the learning process.

KEYWORDS

Smart Open Learning Environment, Computational Thinking, Ontology, OLM, Open Education Resource, Adaptive Self-Regulated Learning

1. INTRODUCTION

The daily evolution of the world and our current digital society faces challenges for changing the environment and the rapid development of modern technologies. One of the major relevant fields is Learning Environment that has been advanced in many different ways. As mobile technology continues to evolve, learning environments are emerging that have the potential to revolutionize the approach and approach to the learning process. Designing and constructing Smart Learning Environments (SLEs) has emerged for supporting knowledge representation and learning content creation. Smart learning can be described as a technology-based learning model that dynamically recognizes and acts on learners' individual circumstances, backgrounds, learning needs and styles, and the state of their learning process (Molina-Carmona, R. et al 2019). In this context, SOLE have surfaced. Our objective is to provide adaptive open learning based on Computational Thinking (CT). We need flexibility and interoperability to provide learners with different resources to suit their contexts, needs and preferences (Harchay, A. et al. 2012 ICCIT). The goal of the smart Open learning environment will be the development of Adaptive Self-Regulated Learning (ASRL) and CT's skill. It aims to improve the quality of learning and the qualities of the learner and his CT's competencies throughout the learning period and to enable a learner to learn more concretely, more efficiently, more flexibly and more comfortably at any time and any place.

We also propose to examine learning outcomes and skill level of learner toward open assessments. For that, we propose to promote SOLE with Open Learner Model (OLM), which will be an important tool to deploy Adaptive Self-Regulated Learning (ASRL). OLM will be used for helping learners visualize their current knowledge or their skill levels in various ways. Open Learner Models have proven their efficiency in facilitating the follow of learner's skill level and profile and then to produce an adaptive Self-Regulated Learning using Open Education Resources (OER). Learners differ in their skills, needs and profiles that should be considered in the design of the learning process (Harchay, A. et al. 2014). We need to track learners when learning and to gather more data from learning contexts and environments. These collected data are being analyzed to give actionable insights for an adaptive self-regulated Learning. In order to meet the needs of learners, it is necessary to include an assessment process; to analyze and transfer distributed knowledge in a smart environment to share the same meaning, relate to different domains, and make decisions at the right time (Samia, Z. et al. 2018). Adaptive content engine provides learners with personalized learning paths and learning content based on their profile (Chen, W. 2019). To reflect the knowledge proposed by a SOLE, learning materials should be designed. For that, we propose to take advantage of innovative technological solutions such as ontologies and Learning Analytic (LA).

The objective of our research work is to propose ontological models for SOLE promoted by CT and that provide ASRL. In this paper, we introduce the use of ontologies and LA to promote the learning process. Further, we use the ontology to model the semantics of SOLE. It will be used for facilitating information integration and knowledge sharing. To do this, we will first detail our pedagogical scenario for a learning process in a SOLE based on Computational thinking and we propose a model for it. Thus, we propose different models to implement the semantics of our framework of SOLE based on Computational Thinking; hence, we propose an ontology for Open learner model. Finally, we give a conclusion, and outlook of future work.

2. ONTOLOGY AND SMART LEARNING ANALYTIC FOR SOLE

For our proposed SOLE, an interesting characteristic is to provide an ASRL that takes care of the learners' preferences, CT's skill level, learning style and needs. For that, we propose the use of learning analytics that has proven its importance in education since its inception (Rezgui, K. et al. 2014). It makes the learning process easier, comfortable, and more convenient by visualizing data about the learning process. LA involves the measure, the collect, the analyze and the report of contextual learner data to understand and optimize learning and learning environments (Siemens, G. (2012). To better visualize learners' information such as knowledge, skill level motivation and performance, OLM is used. It can be considered as a specific type of LA. Learning analytics is considered as an important component in SLE. It contributes as a data-driven approach; it helps to provide complex data available to better help learners to understand, to optimize and to interpret aspects of their learning process. It provides OLM with information about learning traces for learners, the current state of the learner and learning process and activity data of the learners. Combining learning analytics with an open learner model helps to make learning analytics visualizations more meaningful for the learning process, and experiences with big data and visual analytics can advance OLM with today's data-rich, evidence-based online learning opportunities (Bull, S et al. 2016). LA has the ability to contribute to smart learning and to improve learning experiences and outcomes.

Along with this, the learning process should not be limited on time or location. The learner can learn when he wants. Whenever and wherever an opportunity is available, the learning process can take place. This opportunistic learning process needs ubiquitous learner support such as technical support and feedback (Rezgui, K. et al. 2014). For that, we propose the use of Smart learning analytics (SLA) which is considered as a variant of LA and it concerns data on how students learn. Smart LA is dedicated to improving learning by tracking learner competencies in as many learning activities as possible and providing tailored feedback to facilitate context-aware learning. It facilitates self-regulation, allowing learners to visualize their individual learning progress and design a study plan for themselves (Rezgui, K. et al. 2014).

Such as SOLE is built around OLM in order to deliver ASRL, we propose the use of Smart LA to improve learning experiences. This combination appears to be essential, aiming to enhance students' self-reflection through easily perceptible visual representations, enable adaptive self-directed learning, increase user motivation, and even facilitate collaboration. Smart LA will promote OLM, and as a result, SOLE will be able to better sense, infer, anticipate and promote Adaptive Self-Regulated Learning.

Furthermore, semantic web tools such as ontology and knowledge representation, resource semantic annotation, knowledge argumentation, and services are also widely used by educators to improve the quality of education (Melesko, J. et al 2018).

The use of ontology in the area of Education has shown encouraging results. In a SLE, the use of SLA for the evaluation of the learner's performance and the monitoring of learner's state of knowledge can be enhanced by the use of Ontologies. The ability to conceptualize a taxonomy of learning goal motivate the use of ontology (Costa, L. et al. 2018). Besides, many elements such as competencies and competency-related groupings of competencies, e-portfolios, CT skill, learning style and preferences are essential elements of Open Learner

Model for adaptive learning and personalization in technology-based learning. However, in order to be handled by humans and software tools, OLM should be represented by an ontology (Paquette, G. et al. 2021). The use of ontologies provides the ability to infer learner knowledge from the information provided and allows for reuse and scalability in different learning contexts (Costa, L. et al. 2018). Ontologies enable the understanding of the structure of the presented information. Ontologies can not only be used as learning tools, but can also be used to assess learners' abilities (Melesko, J. et al 2018). For that, we propose the coordination between ontologies and SLA to evaluate learning process, learners' outcomes and performances. The use of ontologies can enhance the semantic organization of learning content; also, it can provide an adaptive learning process.

3. LEARNING PROCESS SCENARIO

3.1 Scenario Description

In this section, we describe a scenario relevant to the learning process in higher education. It is related to our work to design and develop a conceptual framework for the Smart Open Learning Environment (SOLE), driven by Self-Regulated Learning to improve CT. The learning process happens when the learner is ready to learn in the ideal format and adaptable way. Our scenario describe the learning process in a SOLE promoted by OLM to deliver Adaptive Self-Regulated Learning considering the learner information and his CT skill level, OER and Open Assessment. The interaction between these elements will improve the quality of learning and the qualities of the learner, his competencies and his CT's skills.

A prerequisite for the start of our learning process is the presence of learners with smart devices. In the first step, the learner accesses the platform, if he is not registered, he must register. Otherwise, our system will start following learner who will be closely tracked across all activities in the system. The learning process begin by the planning. The learner will choose SRL Tools, which refers to SRL Strategies, define his competencies goal and manage his information. Then he is free to choose between accessing his OLM or accessing the first suggested course selection which is CT.

Through OLM, the learner can visualize his skills and knowledge in different ways, participate in the reflection, decision-making, and design of his personal learning.

The second step is the preparation for the learning process. In order to access the first available course CT, it is necessary to assess his initial knowledge to determine his CT skill level. CT's competency levels, combined with other feature such as learning style, preferences and competencies, is used for suggested CT's content courses or other courses and related Assessment that are more appropriate to the learner's abilities.

The third step is to start the learning. The learner can choose and organize his Course and Assessment from the recommended Course and Assessment. In addition, he is able to choose Social Tools for his learning.

All information related to the learner such as initial knowledge, preferences, learning style, collected data from tracking, evaluation result, CT's skill, level and feedback will be analyzed using Learning Analytics approaches, then appropriate Strategies which refers to a particular learner and the specificities of his learning can be defined.

The step number four, is to reflect about his learning Process. The learner access to his OLM to reflect about his learning, and the needed regulation of his goals and planning.

At this level, the learner return to the first step and can changes his planning, the selected SRL Tools and his goals according to the reflection made in the latest step.

3.2 Learning Scenario Analysis

The goal of this study is to enhance learner Computational Thinking by providing a new Smart Open Learning Environment through the adaptation of Self-Regulated Learning based on Open Learner Model, CT and OER. Since our scenario is proposed for SOLE, we need to study and define the principal characteristics of smart open environment. Also, we focus on the objectives for the application of Open Learner Models in higher education to enhance CT in the context of self-regulated learning, the characteristics of Open Learner Models and how these have been associated to different phases and areas of self-regulated learning and how Open Learner Models promote self-regulated learning in different areas and phases in order to reach Adaptation self-regulated learning. In order to acquire and enhance CT competencies our Self-regulated learning approach will deliver the most appropriate content and resource depending on the context. So, it is necessary to study the concept of context and its different features. Similarly, We propose to regulate our learning process through our OLM, than to deliver resource and content adapted to the context, and in conformity with the OLM (CT skill level, preference, style...) and the SRL strategies. For that we need the use of a set of technologies, such as semantic web and web services, for the development of a framework relative to our scenario.

3.3 Learning Scenario Model

In this section, we detail the scenario model, as shown in Figure 1, representing a learning activity in a SOLE. In order to manage appropriately learning scenario, different entity and dispositive need to coordinate to deliver Adaptive SRL. Scenario model is useful to describe learning process in SOLE in diverse context and for different domain. Our Scenario model define the entities that are needed for the success of the learning process and describe interaction between them. It aims to promote learner to be an active learner who is able to decide and to take decision about his learning process. The proposed scenario model aims to provide SRL tools to assist learner in conducting Adaptive SRL through the four phases of SRL when considering OLM. Self-assessing, CT's skill level, learning performance, learning preference, competencies are considered for defining SRL strategies.

The scenario model consider the four phases of SRL such as defined by Zimmerman (Panadero, E. 2017), which are the "self-evaluation and monitoring", the "setting of goal" and the "planning of strategies", the "implementation of strategy" and the "monitoring of planning "and finally "the monitoring of outcome".

Our scenario model for Adaptive SRL process is based on principal module. The learner, as an active learner in the learning process, is in the heart of our scenario model and interact with the other module "OLM", "SRL Tools", "Domain", "Context", "Course", "Assessment", "SRL Strategy", and "Social Tools",

In a "Context", a learner manages "OLM" which is related to a "Domain". Through OLM learner can visualize and manage many features such as 'profile', 'Preference', 'CT skill', 'Competencies', 'Assessment Portfolio' and 'Feedback'.

In addition, Learner applies "SRL Tools" that refers to "SRL Strategy". For "SRL Strategy" we propose cognitive, Metacognitive, Resource management and Assessment Management. Learning activity recommendation is an interesting feature in the learning process, for that Resource management and Assessment Management are used for recommending appropriated OER and Open Assessment. In our scenario model we suggest that the definition and the planning of SRL strategies depends on the analyze of information delivered by OLM such as CT skill level, learning Style, preferences...Similarly, the goals related to CT and competencies are managed and regulated considering the defined SRL Strategies and its associate phase.

Furthermore, a learner have the opportunity to choose his course and assessment related to it. Course and Assessment are delivered from recommended OER and Open Assessment that are proposed according to SRL strategy.

The learner have the ability to use a set Social Tools during his learning Process. Our Learning scenario model for self-regulated learning enhances learner CT's skill level, competencies, performance and promote the learner in thinking about his Learning process. The learner interact actively with the SOLE and focus on the acquisition of knowledge and competencies as well as the planning, the reflection and the monitoring of his learning process. The learner is involved into the learning process, make important decision and became self-directed.

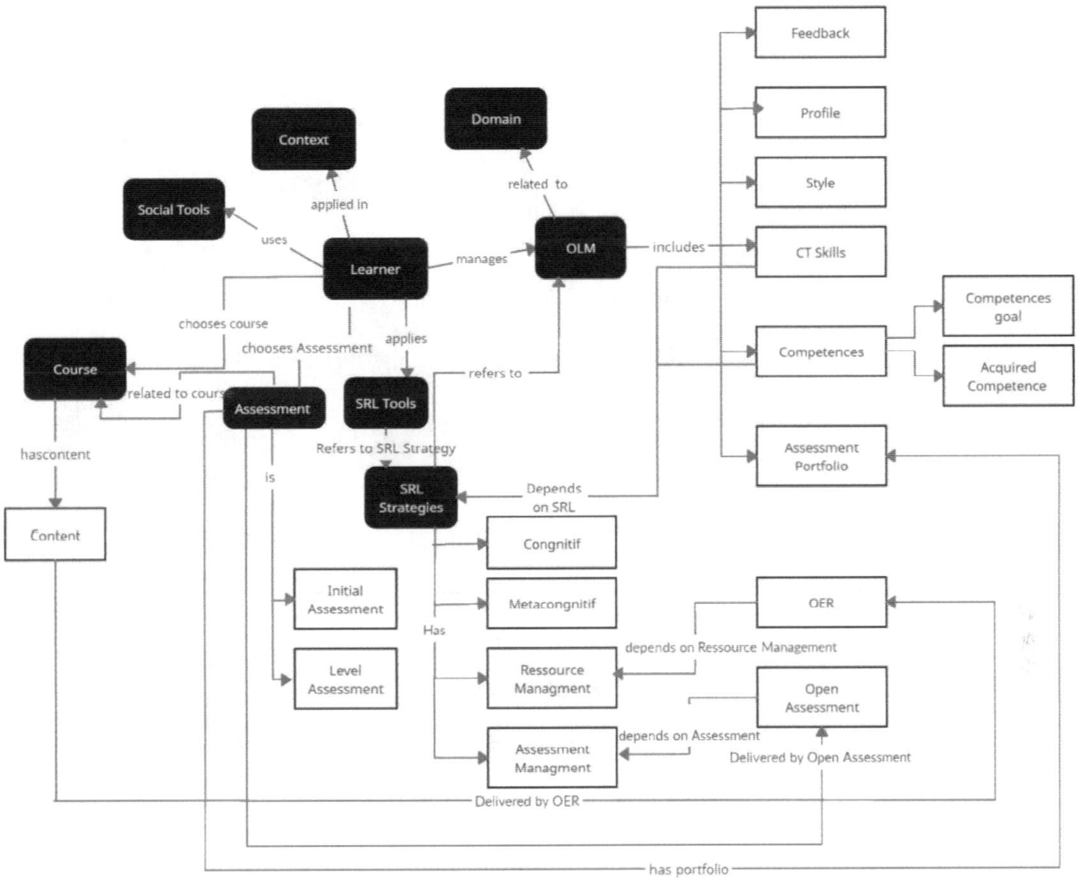

Figure 1. Elements Learning Scenario Model

4. ONTOLOGICAL MODELS FOR SOLE FRAMEWORK

4.1 Proposed Models for SOLE

For the development of framework for SOLE, we need to use a set of technologies such as Semantic Web to ensure greater flexibility and interoperability in providing learners with different resources tailored to their context, needs and preferences (Harchay, A. et al. 2012 ICCIT).

Our objective is to propose an ontological model for our framework for SOLE in order to deliver ASRL. For the design of model related to proposed pedagogical scenario, we need to consider the formal models and criteria involved in adaptive hypermedia systems that form the basis of most adaptive learning systems (Aroyo, L. et al. 2006).

In our work, we suggest different models that will be described by ontologies in order to implement the semantics of our framework. Ontology is one of the most practical that enable the representation of data and enable to represent and interchange semantic (Harchay, A. et al. (2012).

Indeed, we consider a SOLE as an open system that needs to coordinate different model in order to provide ASRL. Thus, to implement the semantic of SOLE we suggest using the design of a set of ontological models for delivering adaptive and personalized resources to each learner. For that, we refer to adaptive hypermedia systems that consider five models to present the knowledge driving the adaptation process (Aroyo, L. et al. 2006). The set of proposed models in (Kravčík, M. et al. 2006) are the domain model, the user model, the context model, the activity model and the adaptation models.

In our work, we propose a set of models for SOLE framework as shown in figure 2 open learner model, Context model, Domain model, SRL model, Resources model, Scenario model and CT model.

- Open learner model: the adaptation and self-regulation of content through the learning process should be done according to the learner profile, needs, competencies and CT skill level. Thus, open learner model identify the learner and represents his characteristics such as his profile, competencies, CT skill level, performances, preferences, and goal.
- Context model: it refers to the context in which the learning take place, it describe the circumstances and "the environment characteristics" in which the learning process occurs (Kravčík, M. et al. 2006) such as spatial and temporal dimensions. Complementing the user model
- Domain model: it aims to conceptualize the design of adaptive and self-regulated hypermedia application and to specify what to provide, adapt and regulate (Kravčík, M. et al. 2006). It defines a set of concepts and their relationship in order to create the knowledge base for learning domain.
- SRL model: it describes the semantics of self-regulation. It consider four dimensions: processes, materials, adaptation strategies and self-regulation strategies.
- Resources model: it enables the identification of different resources needed for the learning process and provides a common scheme for describing the indexing structure of the resources delivered from OER.
- Scenario model: it describe the progress of self-regulated learning process through SOLE in order to deliver adaptive content and resources from OER.
- CT model : it provides CT information for a learner and describe the progress of acquired CT's skill level.

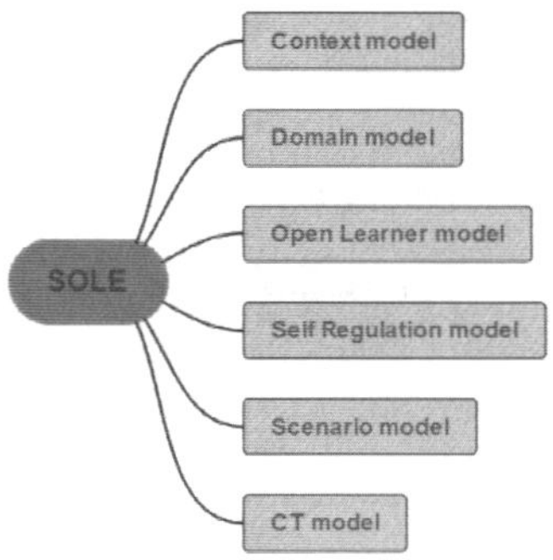

Figure 2. SOLE models

4.2 Open Learner Model Ontology

Ontology becomes a key technology for representing conceptual knowledge and performing semantic search in documents (Samia, Z. et al. 2018). In SOLE, the learning process uses information that is really large and complex as an information for the everyday work to receive and retrieve it. SOLE that uses advanced technologies needs to coordinate different tools and features.

Adaptive Self-Regulated Learning in a SOLE should be based on the learner profile, CT's skill level, preferences, competencies and needs. In order to deliver ASRL, SOLE considers a collection of a set of concepts from different models such as the OLM model, the SRL model, context model, the domain model, etc. These concepts interact and collaborate to provide the most appropriate learning process. The combination and coordination of the different models enables Adaptive Self-Regulated Learning.

In this section, we propose an OLM ontology as shown in Figure 3 that details the information about the learner, his knowledge and his learning process details.

For our OLM ontology, we have used other ontologies such as:

- IMS/LIP Information Management System Learning Information Package: Specification for describing personal and professional information of learner, it enable to stored learner's information (Oneto, L. et al. 2009).
- SIOC ontology for specifying social communities and their relationships Blogs, and wikis.
- FOAF ontology focuses on the relationship between users and their communities.

- PAPI Learner specification (Rezgui, K. et al. 2014). Designed to support the storage, retrieval, search and exchange of learner data between different systems.

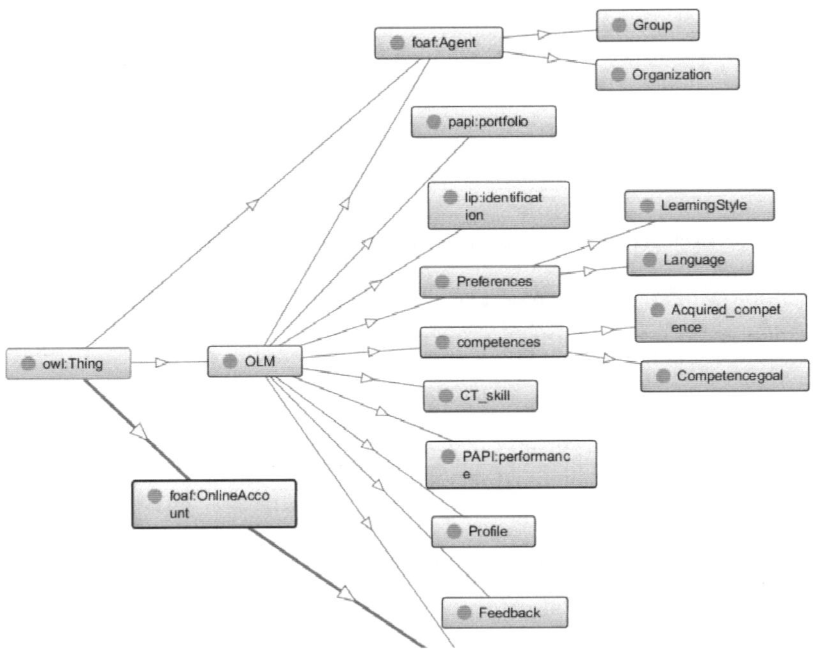

Figure 3. OLM Ontology

Our OLM Ontology includes the following elements:

- CT-skill: it refers to the learner's CT skill level.
- Competencies: it refers to the competencies goal and to the acquired competencies.
- Performance: it describes the measured performance such as certification and experience.
- Profile: it defines the learner's profile such his knowledge and discipline.
- Agent: it refers to FOAF ontology, we suggest the use of its sub class 'Group' and Organization.
- Identification: it refers to (IMS LIP) and it enables to identify a learner using identifier, name, email address, diploma.
- Portfolio: it represents a collection of learners' works, or references to them for verification of his achievements and abilities.
- Feedback: it describes learner responses to their learning experiences, interactions with groups, and the complexity and usefulness of learning materials.
- Preferences: it describes the learner's preferences, language, his preferred learning style and his interest.

5. CONCLUSION

In this paper, we are interested in developing a framework for SOLE based on Ct. we proposed the use of technologies for supporting the Learning Process. Technologies such as Learning Analytics and ontology are used to promote our SOLE. We have first presented the proposed technologies and the benefits of their use for our proposed SOLE. Then, we have proposed a Learning process scenario through SOLE. We have proposed a description for our scenario and for the different features involved in this scenario. Subsequently we suggest a Learning Scenario Model that show the interaction and collaboration between the proposed fields in order to deliver Adaptive Self-Regulated Learning.

Thereafter, we proposed different ontological models to promote Then, we propose an ontological model for the OLM. The Smart Open Learning Environment (SOLE) has as goal the improvement of the quality of learners' learning and their CT skill level throughout the learning period. It aims to enable learners to learn in a more specific, efficient, flexible and comfortable way.

Regarding our further work, we will develop the necessary ontologies for the proposed models for SOLE. We also envision implementing and collaborating on proposed technologies in a framework. In fact, this framework will allow us to provide adaptive self-regulated learning to promote learner on his learning process and to enhance his CT skill level.

REFERENCES

Aroyo, L. et al. (2006). Interoperability in personalized adaptive learning. *Journal of Educational Technology & Society*, 9(2), 4-18. (Aroyo, L. et al. 2006)

Bull, S., & Kay, J. (2016). SMILI☺: A framework for interfaces to learning data in open learner models, learning analytics and related fields. *International Journal of Artificial Intelligence in Education*, 26(1), 293-331.

Costa, L. et al. (2018, October). Evaluation of academic performance based on learning analytics and ontology: a systematic mapping study. *In 2018 IEEE Frontiers in Education Conference (FIE)* (pp. 1-5). IEEE.

Chen, W. (2019). Knowledge-aware learning analytics for smart learning.

Harchay, A. et al. (2014). A Context-Aware Framework to Provide Personalized Mobile Assessment. IxD&A,23,82-97.

Harchay, A. et al. (2012, June). A model driven infrastructure for context-awareness mobile assessment personalization. *In 2012 IEEE 11th International Conference on Trust, Security and Privacy in Computing and Communications (pp. 1676-1683).* IEEE.

Harchay, A. et al. (2012, June). Towards a formal description of mobile personalized assessment. *In 2012 International Conference on Communications and Information Technology (ICCIT)* (pp. 270-275). IEEE.

Kravčík, M., & Gašević, D. (2006, August). Adaptive hypermedia for the semantic web. *In Proceedings of the joint international workshop on Adaptivity, personalization & the Semantic Web* (pp. 3-10).

Kinshuk ,Vivekanandan Kumar Advancing learning through smart learning analytics: a review of case studies 2017.

Melesko, J., & Kurilovas, E. (2018, June). Semantic technologies in e-learning: learning analytics and artificial neural networks in personalised learning systems. *In Proceedings of the 8th International Conference on Web Intelligence, Mining and Semantics* (pp. 1-7).

Molina-Carmona, R., & Villagrá-Arnedo, C. (2019, October). Advances in smart learning. In Proceedings of the *Seventh International Conference on Technological Ecosystems for Enhancing Multiculturality* (pp. 649-652). Panadero, E. (2017). A review of self-regulated learning: Six models and four directions for research. *Frontiers in psychology*, 422.

Oneto, L. et al. (2009) Conversion models between GRAPPLE and LMSs.

Paquette, G. et al. (2021). A new competency ontology for learning environments personalization. *Smart Learning Environments*, 8(1), 1-23.

Rezgui, K. et al. (2014). An Ontology-based Profile for Learner Representation in Learning Networks. *International Journal of Emerging Technologies in Learning,* 9(3).

Siemens, G. (2012, April). Learning analytics: envisioning a research discipline and a domain of practice. *In Proceedings of the 2nd international conference on learning analytics and knowledge* (pp. 4-8).

Samia, Z. et al. (2018, October). Multi-agent systems and ontology for supporting management system in smart school. *In 2018 3rd International Conference on Pattern Analysis and Intelligent Systems (PAIS)* (pp. 1-8). IEEE.

VR IN NURSING EDUCATION - HIGH-FIDELITY VS LOW-FIDELITY IMPLEMENTATIONS

Roger Seiler, Benjamin Lemcke and Andreas Block
Zurich University of Applied Sciences, St. Georgen- Platz 2, P.O. Box, 8401 Winterthur, Switzerland

ABSTRACT

With nursing personnel in short supply, innovative approaches to teaching such as the use of virtual reality (VR) can be one way to attract more students to this field. The beneficial effects of VR in terms of customer motivation, satisfaction, and loyalty suggest that the application of VR application is also feasible in learning settings. However, the implementation of VR software can be expensive. This paper compares a high-interaction fidelity approach (complex and costly implementation) and a low-fidelity approach (a simple and less costly prototype). An experiment with nursing students was conducted to compare the two approaches regarding their effect on self-efficacy, perceived ease of use, perceived usefulness, trust, and intention to use. No relevant or significant differences between high- vs low-interaction fidelity implementation were found. Therefore, we recommend low-fidelity approaches to VR use in delivering basic nursing education as they are easier and less costly to implement without having a negative effect on other relevant constructs.

KEYWORDS

Virtual reality (VR), Nursing Education, High Fidelity, Low Fidelity, Technology Acceptance Model (TAM), Trust

1. INTRODUCTION

In 2020, 153,000 people worked as nursing staff in Switzerland (BFS, 2020). However, there is a nursing staff shortage, and fewer and fewer people are prepared to study, and stay in, nursing. A serious shortage of qualified personnel in Switzerland is forecasted by 2028 (Merçay et al., 2021) while, on a global scale, 5.7 million additional nurses will be needed by 2030 (World Health Organization, 2020). To make matters worse, many graduates, that changed their mind about the profession due to hands on experience gained during their studies, do not transition to the labour market (Merçay et al., 2021), graduation rates are low, and dropout rates high (Dolder and Grünig, 2016).

This paper addresses the issue by offering an approach to enhancing the value of nursing education. Using virtual reality (VR) applications may boost the appeal of nursing programmes and presumably can help to attract and retain more personnel in their profession because VR tends to foster emotions and especially as intrinsic motivation to use VR is high among students (Makransky and Lilleholt, 2018).

Furthermore, VR can also foster intrinsic motivation (Makransky and Lilleholt, 2018) and satisfaction with the education program (Hudson et al., 2019; Makransky and Lilleholt, 2018). The effects are even stronger if a form of delight accompanies satisfaction (Ahrholdt et al., 2016), and VR can be a delightful experience as empirical evidence shows (Potter et al., 2016). In a study on virtual environments (VE), interaction with and immersion in VR also had positive effects on loyalty (Hudson et al., 2019). The element of satisfaction is an important one as 33 percent of nursing staff admitted to being somewhat or completely exhausted in a Swiss study on work-related stress (SECO, 2010). Finally, according to customer management theory, satisfaction is linked to loyalty (Schirmer et al., 2018). It is therefore likely that VR may contribute towards reducing the current nurse shortage.

This paper adds to the existing knowledge of how to implement VR applications in the context of nursing education. In particular, the experiment we conducted sheds light on whether high- or low-interaction fidelity is to be preferred in the context of nursing education. A high interaction fidelity for opening a windows is going through each and every step of opening a window (e.g. approaching the window, unlocking it and eventually opening it and stepping away from the window just opened. A low interaction fidelity example of opening the window could be implemented by just point and clicking on the window and the window is opened with one click. The detailed individual steps needed in between are skipped. In the following, an overview of existing literature on the topic is given.

2. LITERATURE REVIEW

VR has proven to be an effective learning tool. It can provide multisensory stimulation (Chavez and Bayona, 2018), and it can improve social and creative skills (Papanastasiou et al., 2019) as well as memory. The positive effects of VR on learning extend to medical training and education (Cohen et al., 2005). In addition, VR training can be cost effective (Aebersold et al., 2012) and improve both procedural knowledge (Dubovi et al., 2017) and performance (Smith and Hamilton, 2015).

Jones et al. (2019) reported positive effects of VR in training midwives. There are prototypes and concepts for visualizing anatomy (Izard and Méndez, 2016), the emergency training of team leaders of advanced life support (ALS) teams (Moore et al., 2019), and the training of ergonomic transfer of patients (Dürr et al., 2021).

Some studies have found that VR contributes to a higher degree to the acquisition of knowledge than traditional methods but not to learning performance (Chen et al., 2020). There are also caveats and pitfalls to using VR in educational settings, for example in tertiary education. According to Evans (2019), these include: 1) the materiality of VR headsets and cables, 2) interfaces and issues with haptics, 3) the 'language of VR' to communicate the benefits of VR, 4) cybersickness and gender issues in VR use, and the 5) cost of VR.

Self-efficacy (SE), a term coined by Bandura (1982), refers to trust in one's own skills – an important concept in the context of human motivation and behaviour (Nissim and Weissblueth, 2017). Self-efficacy has a positive effect on motivation (van Dinther et al., 2011), learning outcomes (Renganayagalu et al., 2019), and, ultimately, students' performance (Bartimote-Aufflick et al., 2016). This also holds true in the context of nursing education (Zengin et al., 2014).

Research has suggested that VR can have a positive effect on self-efficacy (Nissim and Weissblueth, 2017). There is also a link between display fidelity (Buttussi and Chittaro, 2018; McMahan, 2011), simulation fidelity (Renganayagalu et al., 2019), interaction fidelity (McMahan et al., 2012), and self-efficacy. Interaction fidelity (IF) is essential as well as important concept in the context of learning as immersion and interaction are necessary in order for VR to have a positive effect on learning in terms of learning outcomes, realistic experience, and fostering intrinsic motivation (Chavez and Bayona, 2018).

VR can be seen as technologically sophisticated way of delivering educational content. Whenever technology and users interact, the technology acceptance model (TAM) proposed by (Davis, 1989) can be used, according to which, perceived usefulness (PU), perceived ease of use (PEOU), and intention to use (ITU) play a role in users' acceptance of technology (Davis, 1985).

When users interact with technology, they become more experienced and develop trust. Research on online shopping has identified a link between trust and the TAM (Gefen et al., 2003) and extended it to VR, which resulted in the VR hardware acceptance model (VR HAM) (Manis and Choi, 2019). However, there is still little research on the TAM and VR in general, let alone on the specific context of nursing staff education. We choose to use this model, however, as it allows us to compare past and more recent research findings and their results. The concept of trust is included because it is relevant to business success (Batsaikhan, 2017) and making purchasing decisions (Hajli et al., 2017).

Although there is research on the effects of VR on self-efficacy, there is a research gap regarding interaction fidelity. Buttussi and Chittaro (2018) focussed entirely on the degrees of freedom as interaction fidelity and in their call for further research suggested taking a closer look at the procedural knowledge gain. Furthermore, Renganayagalu et al. (2019) clearly pointed out that rudimentary VR knowledge of their participants was a limitation and hence complex, high fidelity interaction may be too complicated for novice users.

In our research, IF was modelled as an independent variable and Hypothesis 1 (an overview of the hypotheses and results is given in Table 3) The hypothesis that IF positively influences SE is derived. McMahan et al. (2012) reported a positive effect of interaction fidelity on the usability of the application. Hypothesis 2, therefore, states that IF positively affects PEOU. In line with the TAM, Hypothesis 3 states that IF positively affects PU. No direct effect of IF on trust was found in the existing literature. Nevertheless, simulation fidelity (McMahan et al., 2012) affects PU and PEOU affects trust (Gefen et al., 2003). Hypothesis 4 states that IF positively affects trust. Hypotheses 5 to 9 are derived from the TAM. As mentioned above, they are listed in in Table 3 for the sake of completeness and to test if the TAM holds true in a nursing educational context.

Based on these considerations, the research question is as follows: *How should a VR application be implemented in a nursing education context in order to provide value to students and education institutions?* There are also four subordinate research questions: *What role does interaction fidelity play (SRQ1)? How does interaction fidelity affect technology acceptance (SRQ2)? How is self-efficacy affected (SRQ3)? How is trust affected (SRQ4)?*

3. METHOD

Our research using the model of sequential mixed-methods-research (Halcomb and Hickman, 2015) containing a qualitative as well as subsequent quantitative part consists of three phases,: 1) expectations and requirements (focus group consisting of seven nursing students), 2) development of the VR prototype, and 3) experiment with the VR prototype (nine students in the treatment group and nine in the control group).

The prototype was developed in Unity (see Figure 1) for the Oculus quest HMD. The treatment group had the high-interaction fidelity version of the VR application, whereas the control group tested the low-interaction fidelity version. The Unity packages XR Plugin Management (V. 4.2.0) and OpenXR Plugin (V. 1.3.1) were used in the prototype. Furthermore, assets from the unity asset store (realistic hands, hospital patient character, hospital room, hospital modular building, props and characters, surgical instruments – hospital props), from cgtrader (IV blood bag dropper stand low-poly 3D model), and from Sketchfab (AZ vaccine vial) were used to implement the scenario. The sound files used (confirm jingle, confirmation downward, wrong, completed, crowd noise light 3_1night) in the prototype are from freesound.org. All sounds were normalised to -1.0 dB in the open-source software Audacity.

Figure 1. Screenshot of the prototype in Unity

The operationalization was implemented as follows: Age, working experience in years, and gender composed the demographic variables (own items). Furthermore, the main constructs of this project were derived from existing literature and validated scales. These were self-efficacy (Riggs et al., 1994), PEOU (Kolitz, 2008), PU (Kolitz, 2008), and trust (Chao, 2019) (see Table 1).

Table 1. Overview of operationalisation

Construct	Variable name (scale)	Authors
Demographic	Age in years (interval) Working experience in years (interval) Gender, postcode, hours spent in VR (nominal)	own item
Self-efficacy	7 items (5-point Likert)	(Riggs et al., 1994)
Perceived ease of use	3 items (5-point Likert)	(Kolitz, 2008)
Perceived usefulness	4 items (5-point Likert)	(Kolitz, 2008)
Trust	5 items (5-point Likert)	(Chao, 2019)

The experiment was conducted in three stages. 1) Participants signed a letter of acceptance confirming that they were taking part voluntarily. 2) They completed a first questionnaire followed by a short instructional video before putting on the Oculus head-mounted display (HMD). A quick check was conducted to ensure that the HMD fitted correctly, and the VR application could be seen clearly. 3) After completing the steps in the VR scenario, participants filled out a second questionnaire. The survey consisted of paper-and-pencil questionnaires, and the software used for analysis was IBM SPSS Statistic 28.0.1.1.

The first phase (focus groups) showed that there is agreement regarding the importance of what activities should be trained using VR. It was generally felt that these should be processes.

In the second phase, a decision was made on what process activity should be implemented by comparing multiple scenarios regarding the value of a VR implementation as well as suitability for VR implementation.

It was found that a suitable scenario would be drawing medicine from a vial and subsequently injecting it into a patient. This scenario consists of the following steps: closing the window, disinfecting the work area, hand disinfection, putting on gloves, removing the cap of the infusion flask, turning the vial upside down 10 times, disinfecting the vial, removing the cap of the syringe, ventilating the vial, drawing the content of the vial into a syringe, injecting the content of the syringe into the infusion flask, disposing of the syringe, applying a sticker to the infusion flask, removing the gloves, docking the infusion flask to the infusion set. The construct "interaction fidelity" was calculated using a framework for interaction fidelity analysis (FIFA) as described in McMahan (2011) for all the activities listed. The calculated FIFA scores were 1.62 (low-interaction fidelity) and 2.79 (high-interaction fidelity).

The third phase involved exposing participants to one of the two (high- vs. low-interaction fidelity) VR scenarios before asking them to fill out the questionnaire.

Of the 18 participants 14 were female and four were male. Compared to the 84.7 percent of women in Switzerland's nursing workforce (Merçay et al., 2021), the 77 percent in this sample are only seven percent lower. The average age of participants was 21.61 ($M = 21.61$, $SD = 1.539$) and their average years of work experience were 1.89 ($M = 1.89$, $SD = 1.875$).

4. RESULTS, DISCUSSION, FURTHER RESEARCH, AND LIMITATIONS

A first look at the mean values shows that all constructs (SE, PEOU, PU, and trust) have higher mean values in the low-interaction fidelity and high-interaction fidelity versions than in the baseline questionnaire (see Table 2).

Before continuing further, the analysis reliability of the constructs was tested with Cronbach's Alpha. The reliability is as follows: self-efficacy ($\alpha = .770$), PEOU ($\alpha = .702$), PU ($\alpha = .433$), and trust ($\alpha = .743$) for the baseline questionnaire. The low score of PU may be due to the usefulness was not yet being clear before exposure to the VR application. The reliability of the second questionnaire is as follows: self-efficacy ($\alpha = .606$), PEOU ($\alpha = .924$), PU ($\alpha = .918$), and trust ($\alpha = .728$). If Item 5 ("I have all the necessary skills to do my job.") in the self-efficacy construct is removed, the reliability falls within the cut-off value proposed by Nunally (1978). The low score of Item 5 can be explained by the fact that participants were students and was, therefore, removed from further analysis.

A comparison of the high-interaction and low-interaction versions (after exposure to VR application) with the baseline (before exposure to the VR application) shows that, apart from trust, all construct means are higher for the low-interaction fidelity version.

Table 2. Comparison of pre- and post-VR-application exposure questionnaire

Construct	Baseline					Low-Interaction Fidelity					High-Interaction Fidelity				
	N	*Min*	*Max*	*MW*	*SD*	*N*	*Min*	*Max*	*MW*	*SD*	*N*	*Min*	*Max*	*MW*	*SD*
SE	18	2.00	3.89	3.19	.565	9	3.00	3.89	**3.57**	.383	9	1.78	3.67	**3.20**	.613
PEOU	18	2.67	4.33	3.69	.435	9	3.67	5.00	**4.44**	.553	9	3.33	5.00	**4.41**	.619
PU	18	3.00	4.67	3.84	.393	9	3.00	4.75	**4.00**	.696	9	3.25	4.75	**3.89**	.435
Trust	18	3.00	4.50	3.68	.491	9	3.00	4.25	**3.72**	.423	9	3.25	4.50	**3.89**	.377

To test for the effect that interaction fidelity has on the constructs. a Mann-Whitney-U test on high- vs. low-interaction fidelity was conducted as the sample size was rather small and normal distribution could not be assumed. The test had the following values for self-efficacy: $U(18) = 20.00$, $z = -1.82$, $p < .068$, for PEOU $U(18) = 40.00$, $z = -0.05$, $p < .962$, for PU $U(18) = 35.00$, $z = -.49$, $p < .622$, and for trust $U(18) = 48.00$, $z = .69$, .$p < .493$. None of the constructs show significant differences between high- and low-interaction fidelity.

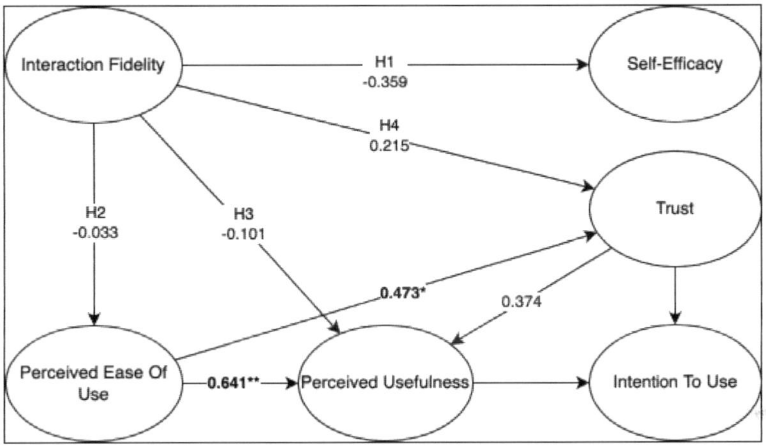

Figure 2. Conceptual model and correlation analysis (* p<.05, ** p<0.01 two-tailed)

The conceptual model containing the TAM was verified using correlation analysis (see Figure 2) and, therefore, all the hypotheses are tested (see Table 3). Significant correlations could be reported for H5 and H6 but not for H7. H8 and H9 were not tested as participants had to use the VR application and, hence, intention to use was not tested.

Table 3. Overview of Hypotheses 1 - 9

Hypothesis	Path	Result
H1	Interaction fidelity → Self-efficacy	Rejected
H2	Interaction fidelity → Perceived ease of use	Rejected
H3	Interaction fidelity → Perceived usefulness	Rejected
H4	Interaction fidelity → Trust	Rejected
H5	Perceived ease of use → Trust	Accepted
H6	Perceived ease of use → Perceived usefulness	Accepted
H7	Trust → Perceived usefulness	Rejected
H8	Trust → Intention to use	N.a. (compulsory use)
H9	Perceived usefulness → Intention to use	N.a. (compulsory use)

4.1 Further Research

In the future, researchers might take a closer look at subject loyalty and retention, which are not covered in this preliminary study of high- vs. low-interaction fidelity. Because trust is such a key concept in business and human behaviour and both in the low- and high-interaction fidelity scenarios, and because the mean values (see Table 2) of trust are higher than in the baseline questionnaire, further research may want to focus on the effects that trust has in VR applications in a nursing educational context.

4.2 Limitations

The sample size of our study was rather small, and the average age of our subjects was low because they were students. Gender is biased towards female participants, which is not a real issue given that 84.7 percent of nurses in Switzerland are female. Furthermore, participants asked more questions about the correct use of the VR application after completing the high-interaction fidelity scenario than the low-interaction fidelity scenario. Hence, participants have more trouble interacting with the high-interaction fidelity version and this potentially could have affected the results presented in this paper. The low-reliability score of some constructs must also be mentioned, but as this concerns the baseline questionnaire, it can be explained by participants not being able to answer the questions to PU as they had not yet been exposed to the VR application.

It should also be considered that, coincidentally, participants had another VR experience prior to taking part in this experiment. However, a comparison between high- and low-interaction fidelity is still feasible as the earlier VR experience was not related to this research focus.

Finally, the results presented in this paper hold true for first early-stage projects, early-stage proof-of-concepts and early-stage use cases as the students were not repeatedly exposed to the VR application. Hence, if VR applications are used over a longer period, such as in regular training sessions for a whole semester of study, the results may be different.

5. CONCLUDING REMARKS

The results of our preliminary study apply to activities with a process character (i.e., processes) as the example presented in this paper (injecting the content of a vial into an infusion flask and infusion set). Interaction fidelity does not have a significant direct effect on self-efficacy, perceived ease of use, perceived usefulness, or trust. This result leads to the recommendation that in a nursing education context, low-interaction fidelity implementation is sufficient for activities that have a sequential, process-like character. However, this may not hold true if the interaction with the VR application is prolonged, such as over a whole semester, and if students are repeatedly and regularly exposed to the VR application.

We recommend that educational institutions should take the initial steps towards introducing low-interaction fidelity VR to their nursing programmes, especially for activities with a process character. This is relevant as low-interaction VR applications are less costly to implement, easier to handle, and tend to require fewer explanations than high-interaction ones. In addition, a lower cognitive load imposed on students due to technical aspects leaves more cognitive power for learning and practice.

The (already widely accepted) TAM seems viable in the context of nursing education too. Perceived ease of use affects both perceived usefulness and trust. What is more, both trust and perceived usefulness can lead to word-of-mouth (WOM) dissemination. As a result of relying on online information and referrals (common among the target group, i.e., potential nursing students), WOM can lead to higher student numbers in nursing programmes, which, in turn, can lower acquisition costs.

Usability is a key aspect of VR applications. TAM is, therefore, relevant, in particular with regard to perceived ease of use and trust. This should be kept in mind when implementing low-interaction fidelity VR applications in nursing programmes. With its potential to cut costs and simplify teaching, low-interaction fidelity may leat to the neglection of usability. This is not advised as this may eliminate the potential benefits (for example higher learning performance, higher self-efficacy, higher learning, or higher motivation) VR applications can have.

REFERENCES

Aebersold, M., Tschannen, D., Bathish, M., (2012). Innovative Simulation Strategies in Education. Nurs. Res. Pract. 2012, 1–7. https://doi.org/10.1155/2012/765212

Ahrholdt, D.C., Gudergan, S.P., Ringle, C.M., (2016). What Drives Customer Loyalty? Nonlinear Effects of Customer Delight and Satisfaction on Loyalty and the Moderating Role of Service Experience, in: Campbell, C., Ma, J. (Jonathon) (Eds.), Looking Forward, Looking Back: Drawing on the Past to Shape the Future of Marketing, Developments in Marketing Science: Proceedings of the Academy of Marketing Science. Springer International Publishing, Cham, pp. 742–750. https://doi.org/10.1007/978-3-319-24184-5_181

Bandura, A., (1982). Self-efficacy mechanism in human agency. Am. Psychol. 37, 122–147. https://doi.org/10.1037/0003-066X.37.2.122

Bartimote-Aufflick, K., Bridgeman, A., Walker, R., Sharma, M., Smith, L., (2016). The study, evaluation, and improvement of university student self-efficacy. Stud. High. Educ. 41, 1918–1942. https://doi.org/10.1080/03075079.2014.999319

Batsaikhan, M., (2017). Trust, Trustworthiness, and Business Success: Lab and Field Findings from Entrepreneurs. Econ. Inq. 55, 368–382. https://doi.org/10.1111/ecin.12359

BFS, (2020). Beschäftigung und Berufe im Gesundheitsbereich [WWW Document]. Swiss Confed. URL https://www.bfs.admin.ch/bfs/de/home/statistiken/gesundheit/gesundheitswesen/beschaeftigung-berufe-gesundheitsbereich.html (accessed 9.23.22).

Buttussi, F., Chittaro, L., (2018). Effects of Different Types of Virtual Reality Display on Presence and Learning in a Safety Training Scenario. IEEE Trans. Vis. Comput. Graph. 24, 1063–1076. https://doi.org/10.1109/TVCG.2017.2653117

Chao, C.-M., (2019). Factors Determining the Behavioral Intention to Use Mobile Learning: An Application and Extension of the UTAUT Model. Front. Psychol. 10, 1652. https://doi.org/10.3389/fpsyg.2019.01652

Chavez, B., Bayona, S., (2018). Virtual Reality in the Learning Process, in: Rocha, Á., Adeli, H., Reis, L.P., Costanzo, S. (Eds.), Trends and Advances in Information Systems and Technologies, Advances in Intelligent Systems and Computing. Springer International Publishing, Cham, pp. 1345–1356. https://doi.org/10.1007/978-3-319-77712-2_129

Chen, F.-Q., Leng, Y.-F., Ge, J.-F., Wang, D.-W., Li, C., Chen, B., Sun, Z.-L., (2020). Effectiveness of Virtual Reality in Nursing Education: Meta-Analysis. J. Med. Internet Res. 22, e18290. https://doi.org/10.2196/18290

Cohen, C.J., Hay, R., Urquhart, A., Gauger, P., Andreatta, P., (2005). A Modular Interactive Virtual Surgical Training Environment, in: Interservice/Industry Training, Simulation, and Education Conference (I/ITSEC). pp. 2074–2086.

Davis, F.D., (1989). Perceived Usefulness, Perceived Ease of Use, and User Acceptance of Information Technology. MIS Q. 13, 318–340.

Davis, F.D., (1985). A technology acceptance model for empirically testing new end-user information systems.

Dolder, P., Grünig, A., (2016). Nationaler Versorgungsbericht für die Gesundheitsberufe 2016. Nachwuchsbedarf und Massnahmen zur Personalsicherung auf nationaler Ebene. Bundesamt für Gesundheit, Schweizerische Konferenz der kantonalen Gesundheitsdirektorinnen und -direktoren & Nationale Dachorganisation der Arbeitswelt Gesundheit, Bern.

Dubovi, I., Levy, S.T., Dagan, E., (2017). Now I know how! The learning process of medication administration among nursing students with non-immersive desktop virtual reality simulation. Comput. Educ. 113, 16–27. https://doi.org/10.1016/j.compedu.2017.05.009

Dürr, M., Schweitzer, D., Reiterer, H., (2021). ViTT: Towards a Virtual Reality System that Supports the Learning of Ergonomic Patient Transfers, in: The Adjunct Publication of the 34th Annual ACM Symposium on User Interface Software and Technology. Presented at the UIST '21: The 34th Annual ACM Symposium on User Interface Software and Technology, ACM, Virtual Event USA, pp. 78–82. https://doi.org/10.1145/3474349.3480234

Evans, L., (2019). Barriers to VR use in HE, in: Proceedings of the Virtual and Augmented Reality to Enhance Learning and Teaching in Higher Education Conference 2018. IM Publications Open LLP, pp. 3–13. https://doi.org/10.1255/vrar2018.ch2

Gefen, D., Karahanna, E., Straub, D.W., (2003). Trust and TAM in Online Shopping: An Integrated Model. MIS Q. 27, 51–90. https://doi.org/10.2307/30036519

Hajli, N., Sims, J., Zadeh, A.H., Richard, M.-O., (2017). A social commerce investigation of the role of trust in a social networking site on purchase intentions. J. Bus. Res. 71, 133–141. https://doi.org/10.1016/j.jbusres.2016.10.004

Halcomb, E., Hickman, L., (2015). Mixed methods research. Nurs. Stand. 29, 41–47. https://doi.org/10.7748/ns.29.32.41.e8858

Hudson, S., Matson-Barkat, S., Pallamin, N., Jegou, G., 2019. With or without you? Interaction and immersion in a virtual reality T experience. J. Bus. Res. 100, 10.

Izard, S.G., Méndez, J.A.J., (2016). Virtual reality medical training system, in: Proceedings of the Fourth International Conference on Technological Ecosystems for Enhancing Multiculturality. Presented at the TEEM'16: 4th International Conference on Technological Ecosystems for Enhancing Multiculturality, ACM, Salamanca Spain, pp. 479–485. https://doi.org/10.1145/3012430.3012560

Jones, D., Siang See, Z., Billinghurst, M., Goodman, L., Fealy, S., (2019). Extended Reality for Midwifery Learning: MR VR Demonstration, in: The 17th International Conference on Virtual-Reality Continuum and Its Applications in Industry. Presented at the VRCAI '19: The 17th International Conference on Virtual-Reality Continuum and its Applications in Industry, ACM, Brisbane QLD Australia, pp. 1–2. https://doi.org/10.1145/3359997.3365739

Kolitz, K., (2008). Systemdesign im Market-Engineering - Experimente zu Teilnehmerverhalten und Technologieakzeptanz. Universitätsverlag Karlsruhe, Karlsruhe.

Makransky, G., Lilleholt, L., (2018). A structural equation modeling investigation of the emotional value of immersive virtual reality in education. Educ. Technol. Res. Dev. 66, 1141–1164. https://doi.org/10.1007/s11423-018-9581-2

Manis, K.T., Choi, D., (2019). The virtual reality hardware acceptance model (VR-HAM): Extending and individuating the technology acceptance model (TAM) for virtual reality hardware. J. Bus. Res. 100, 503–513. https://doi.org/10.1016/j.jbusres.2018.10.021

McMahan, R.P., (2011). Exploring the Effects of Higher-Fidelity Display and Interaction for Virtual Reality Games. Virginia Polytechnic Institute and State University, Blacksburg, VA.

McMahan, R.P., Bowman, D.A., Zielinski, D.J., Brady, R.B., (2012). Evaluating Display Fidelity and Interaction Fidelity in a Virtual Reality Game. IEEE Trans. Vis. Comput. Graph. 18, 626–633. https://doi.org/10.1109/TVCG.2012.43

Merçay, C., Grünig, A., Dolder, P., (2021). Gesundheitspersonal in der Schweiz - Nationaler Versorgungsbericht 2021. Bestand, Bedarf, Angebot und Massnahmen zur Personalsicherung (No. Obsan Bericht 03/2021), Bestand, Bedarf, Angebot und Massnahmen zur Personalsicherung. Schweizerisches Gesundheitsobservatorium, Neuchâtel.

Moore, N., Yoo, S., Ahmadpour, N., Tommy, R., Brown, M., Poronnik, P., (2019). ALS-SimVR: Advanced Life Support Virtual Reality Training Application, in: 25th ACM Symposium on Virtual Reality Software and Technology. Presented at the VRST '19: 25th ACM Symposium on Virtual Reality Software and Technology, ACM, Parramatta NSW Australia, pp. 1–2. https://doi.org/10.1145/3359996.3365051

Nissim, Y., Weissblueth, E., (2017). Virtual Reality (VR) as a Source for Self-Efficacy in Teacher Training. Int. Educ. Stud. 10, 52. https://doi.org/10.5539/ies.v10n8p52

Nunally, J., 1978. Psychometric theory. McGraw-Hill, New York.

Papanastasiou, G., Drigas, A., Skianis, C., Lytras, M., Papanastasiou, E., (2019). Virtual and augmented reality effects on K-12, higher and tertiary education students' twenty-first century skills. Virtual Real. 23, 425–436. https://doi.org/10.1007/s10055-018-0363-2

Potter, L.E., Carter, L., Coghlan, A., (2016). Virtual reality and nature based tourism: an opportunity for operators and visitors, in: Proceedings of the 28th Australian Conference on Computer-Human Interaction, OzCHI '16. Association for Computing Machinery, New York, NY, USA, pp. 652–654. https://doi.org/10.1145/3010915.3011854

Renganayagalu, S.K., Mallam, S., Nazir, S., Ernstsen, J., Haavardtun, P., (2019). Impact of Simulation Fidelity on Student Self-efficacy and Perceived Skill Development in Maritime Training. TransNav Int. J. Mar. Navig. Saf. Sea Transp. 13, 663–669. https://doi.org/10.12716/1001.13.03.25

Riggs, M.L., Warka, J., Babasa, B., Betancourt, R., Hooker, S., (1994). Development and Validation of Self-Efficacy and Outcome Expectancy Scales for Job-Related Applications. Educ. Psychol. Meas. 54, 793–802. https://doi.org/10.1177/0013164494054003026

Schirmer, N., Ringle, C.M., Gudergan, S.P., Feistel, M.S.G., (2018). The link between customer satisfaction and loyalty: the moderating role of customer characteristics. J. Strateg. Mark. 26, 298–317. https://doi.org/10.1080/0965254X.2016.1240214

SECO, S. für W., (2010). Stressstudie 2010: Stress bei Schweizer Erwerbstätigen - Zusammenhänge zwischen Arbeitsbedingungen, Personenmerkmalen, Befinden und Gesundheit [WWW Document]. URL https://www.seco.admin.ch/seco/de/home/Publikationen_Dienstleistungen/Publikationen_und_Formulare/Arbeit/Arbeitsbedingungen/Studien_und_Berichte/stressstudie-2010--stress-bei-schweizer-erwerbstaetigen---zusamm.html (accessed 11.23.21).

Smith, P.C., Hamilton, B.K., (2015). The Effects of Virtual Reality Simulation as a Teaching Strategy for Skills Preparation in Nursing Students. Clin. Simul. Nurs. 11, 52–58. https://doi.org/10.1016/j.ecns.2014.10.001

van Dinther, M., Dochy, F., Segers, M., (2011). Factors affecting students' self-efficacy in higher education. Educ. Res. Rev. 6, 95–108. https://doi.org/10.1016/j.edurev.2010.10.003

World Health Organization, (2020). State of the world's nursing 2020: investing in education, jobs and leadership. World Health Organization, Geneva.

Zengin, N., Pınar, R., Akinci, A.C., Yildiz, H., (2014). Psychometric properties of the self-efficacy for clinical evaluation scale in Turkish nursing students. J. Clin. Nurs. 23, 976–984. https://doi.org/10.1111/jocn.12257

EVALUATION OF DATA OPTIMAL STORAGE SYSTEM IN HYBRID CLOUD

Miho Imazaki[1,3], Satoshi Kaneko[1], Norihisa Komoda[2] and Takenao Ohkawa[3]
[1]*Research & Development Group, Hitachi, Ltd., Yokohama, Japan*
[2]*Corporate Adviser, Code Solution K.K,.Osaka, Japan*
[3]*Graduate School of System Informatics, Kobe University, Kobe, Japan*

ABSTRACT

A hybrid cloud is a mix of compute systems, storage systems and services consisting of on-premises systems, private clouds and public clouds for satisfying requirements such as security and performance. In the case of hybrid cloud configuration where data are in on-premises storage systems and compute systems is in public clouds, data should be transferred to the public cloud when a read/write command is issued by compute systems. Thus, long data transfer time is a problem since the on-premises systems and public clouds are connected by the internet. One possible solution is to create an additional cache area inside the compute system; however, it is not clear how effective it is. In this paper, we verify the effect of the data cache by creating the hybrid cloud environment with/without the cache area and measuring input/output latency. We created the measurement environment in the hybrid cloud with dm-cache technology and set up the assumed workload of TPC Benchmark™ E with the write-through mode. The average latency with the cache area reduces by up to 79% compared to without the cache area, and we confirm the effect of installing cache areas in this environment.

KEYWORDS

Hybrid Cloud, Storage System, Public Cloud, Data Cache

1. INTRODUCTION

The demand for IT infrastructure flexibility increases the number of companies using the public cloud which is defended as computing services. The public cloud infrastructures are managed by a third-party provider and shared with multiple users over the internet. However, some users require high performance and have sensitive data whose they want to keep in their own data centers to manage where are stored. This environment type is called a on-premises system. And there is another case that some users need a dedicated system environment for a higher level of security with flexible operations like a public cloud's ones. For these users, a private cloud is offered, and it is built in on-premises systems or public clouds by users, therefore users should be managed private cloud by themselves. As a mentioned above, each system has its own characteristics, and one of the popular IT environments is using a mix of on-premises system and public clouds, which is called a hybrid cloud (Weinman, 2016) (Shibambu, 2022). A development and test (dev/test) are one of popular use cases for the hybrid cloud. This is because users can keep the data in the production environment of secure and high-performance on-premises systems while create and delete the dev/test environment easily with public cloud services. For the demand of using modern applications/computing services with the public cloud in the dev/test however the transferring only the minimum required data to the public cloud securely, one of hybrid cloud architectures is that a storage system volume in the physical data center's on-premises system is attached to a virtual machine (VM) created in the public cloud.

In this dev/test environment, the data in the physical data center should be transferred to the public cloud as needed. The physical data center is connected to the public cloud through the internet. Public cloud vendors offer high-speed internet services; however, this has limitations in reducing latency compared to internal networks. Thus, the problem in this environment is that it takes too long time to complete the data transfer before starting the dev/test.

To solve this problem, reducing the amount of data transfer and appropriate data placement in storage systems are important. There are some methods to do this, a data cache and a data tiering (Arteaga et al, 2016)

(Zhang et al, 2010). The data cache method is that creating a data cache area in the public cloud and storing accessed data in it. And the data tiering method is that setting up a device in the public cloud and storing the high frequency access data in it. However, it isn't clear how much each method can reduce the amount of data transfer. There are related studies: creating and measuring a cache area in a computing system on a public cloud (Park et al, 2020); creating cache servers among cloud block storage devices (Zhang et al, 2020). However, they assume only public cloud configurations and does not consider hybrid cloud configurations. Therefore, we choose the data cache method and measure and evaluate the improvement of data caching technology in the hybrid cloud.

The rest of this paper organized as follows. Section 2 describes the data cache method in a public cloud. We describe the measurement environment to show the effect of the data cache method in Section 3, and the measurement result in Section 4. Finally, Section 5 concludes the paper.

2. DATA CACHE METHOD IN PUBLIC CLOUD

We consider the dev/test environment that the data are in the physical data center and the VM as compute is in the public cloud. In this environment, there are 2 major issues: it takes a long time to transfer the data from the physical data center before starting a dev/test; the cost of public cloud storage system is too expensive to store the all dev/test data. Therefore, the key point to solve them is reducing the amount of data transfer between the on-premises system and the public cloud. To reduce it, the dev/test application in the public cloud directly need to access to the dev/test data in the on-premises system. However, this causes high access latency from the dev/test application to the dev/test data.

One of the solutions to this is that the part of dev/test data, which are frequently accessed from the dev/test application, are stored in the VM's data cache area. The compute system where the dev/test application runs already has a virtual dynamic rando-access memory (DRAM) as a data cache area. However, the size of DRAM in a public cloud is not large enough and its cost is relatively high if you want to read/write large amount of data.

To solve this, you can use a virtual volatile storage volume in a public cloud as a data cache area. Figure 1 shows the overview of this solution. In this case, the dev/test data are not necessary to copy to public cloud before setting up a dev/test environment. When a dev/test application starts to run on the VM, it accesses to dev/test data in the on-premises, and they are stored in the cache area on VM. After a certain period, only dev/test data with high access frequency are stored in the cache area, and dev/test data transferring between the on-premises and the public cloud hardly occurs if the cache area size is appropriate.

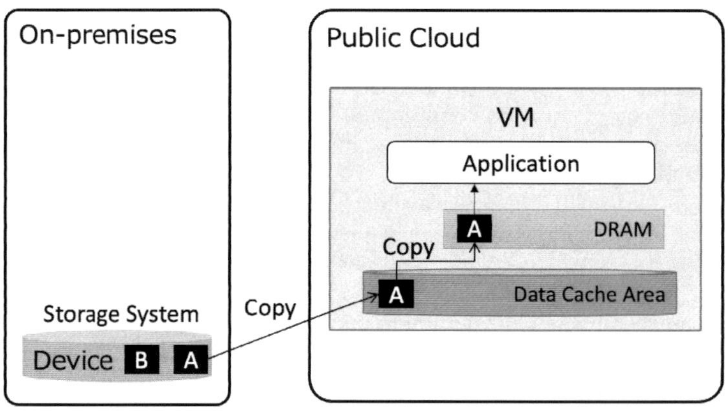

Figure 1. Caching data in a public cloud

We describe read and write processes in this configuration. A data cache program checks if there is the target data in the VM's DRAM when the application issues a read data request. If the answer is no, the program checks if the data is stored in the data cache area. If the data are not stored in it, the program commands the data copy from the on-premises storage system to the data cache area in the VM, then copies it to the DRAM. And the application reads the target data from the DRAM. After that, it can be read from the DRAM or the data cache area through the public cloud internal network when the same data are read from the application, resulting in a shorter response to the application. While about the write process, there are 2 modes: a write-through mode and a write-back mode (Jouppi, 1993). The write-though mode is that the target data are written into the DRAM first then written into both the data cache area and the on-premises storage system at the same time. While the write-back mode is that the target data are written into the DRAM first then write into the data cache area. And the data are written to the on-premises storage system asynchronously with the process described above. In this mode, the data cache program can send a write completion message to the application immediately after writing to the data cache area. Thus, the write process response is shortened. However, there is a possibility to lose track of how much data were written if an error occurs in the VM before the data is transferred to the on-premises storage system. While in the write-through mode, the possibility of data loss is lower than in the write-back mode since the application receives the write completion message is complete. However, the write process response in the write-through mode is longer than in the write-back mode.

There is the case of no free space in the data cache area due to the read/write process, since the capacity of the data cache area is limited. In this case, if data have not yet been written to the on-premises storage system, the data are transferred to it and then deleted from the data cache area. Alternatively, read data with low access frequency is deleted from the data cache area.

This data cache method is theoretically valid to reduce the data transfer between on-premises system and public clouds. However, it's not clear that how effective this method is.

3. MEASUREMENT OF DATA CACHE EFFECT

3.1 Evaluated Environment

To be clear the effectiveness of the data cache method, we consider the verification environment which is shown in Fig 2. We prepare Hitachi Virtual Storage Platform G370 as the on-premises storage system which is a block storage and stores the data in the data center, and the Amazon Web Service Elastic Computing (AWS EC2) with an instance store volume as the compute in the public cloud (Hitachi Vantara, 2018) (Amazon Web Service, 2022a). An instance store provides temporary block-level storage which is a volatile memory (Amazon Web Service, 2022a). The storage system and the compute instance relate to AWS Direct Connect 10 Gbps, which is the AWS high-speed private network service (Amazon Web Service, 2022b). The protocol is iSCSI. We use the instance store volume as the cache area and set a data cache function with a dm-cache (Thornber, 2015). The dm-cache is a component of the Linux kernel's device mapper and improves performance of a block device by dynamically migrating some of its data to a faster and smaller device. When the AWS EC2 needs to access to the data in the on-premises storage system, the data is copied to the instance store volume.

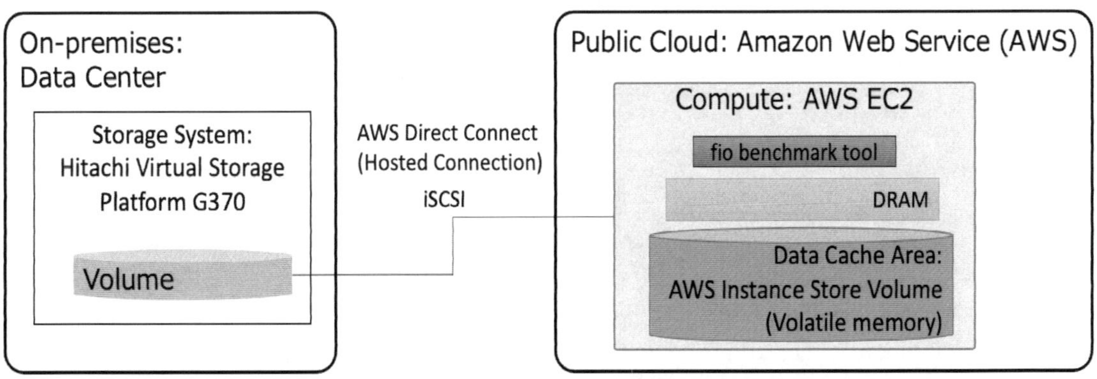

Figure 2. Caching data in public cloud

Figure 3 shows a detail of the cache architecture. The cache area is managed in units of chunks which are data aggregates. The cache pool is consisted with the cache area and the cache area meta data.

When the read command is committed from the AWS EC2 to the on-premises storage system, the dm-cache algorithm judges whether the target data are stored in the cache pool. In the case of the data are stored in it, the data are read from the cache pool through the DRAM and the AWS EC2 doesn't need to access to the on-premises storage system. Other than that, the data should be read from the on-premises storage system to the cache area with the chunk included with the target data and the only target data are read from the cache area through the DRAM.

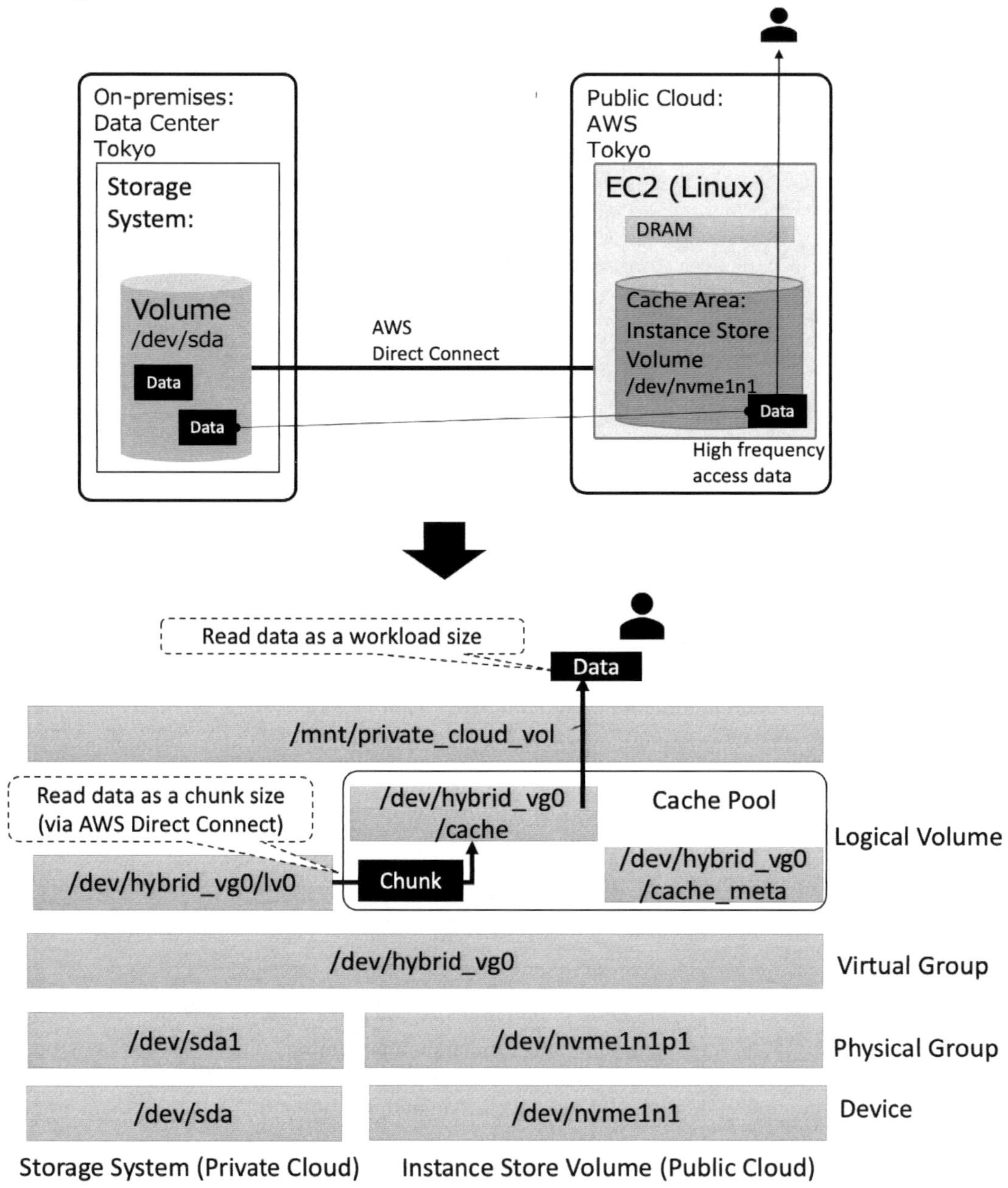

Figure 3. Cache area architecture

In this dm-cache environment, we set up the write-through mode which is that data is written to the on-premises storage system without the cache area when a write command is issued. The reason for choosing it is that the data with the write back mode may be broken when the system has an error before the data are transferred to the on-premises storage system.

3.2 Workload and Measurement Condition

The workload in this environment is based on TPC Benchmark™ E (Transaction Processing Performance Council, 2015). TPC Benchmark™ E is an on-line transaction processing benchmark. It models the activity of brokerage firm that must manage customer accounts, execute customer trade orders, and be responsible for the interactions of customers with financial markets. And The TPC Benchmark™ E Input/Output (IO) request breakdown for data devices is clear in the related research (Chen, 2011). Therefore, in this study, we set up the issuing IO set as shown in Table 1 and this IO is issued to the device using fio benchmark which is the tool spawn a number of threads or processes doing a particular type of IO action as specified by a user (Axboe, 2022).

Table 1. I/O patterns

I/O pattern	Data size [kByte]	Event probability [%]
Random Read	8.0	90.0
Random Write	8.0	10.0

Table 2 shows other measuring conditions in this study. We select 3 types of cache chunk size to confirm the effect of different chunk sizes. The number of chunks decreases as the chunk size increases since the cache area size is fixed.

Table 2. Measurement

Item	Detail
I/O access range	5 GBytes
Measurement time	6 minutes
AWS EC2 type	r5d.xlarge (Instance Store: 150 GBytes)
Cache area size	150 GBytes
Cache chunk size	32 kBytes, 128 kBytes, 160 kBytes
Volume size in the on-premises storage system	170 GBytes

4. MEASUREMENT RESULTS

We measured IO latencies in this cache environment and compared the differences between the ones with/without cache area.

Figure 4 shows the result of single I/O average latency in the random read/write mix. The latency with the cache area and 160 kBytes chunk reduced by maximum 79% compared to without the cache area. Following this result, we confirmed that there is an effect of data caching in this workload. However, in the case with the cache area, a chunk read occurred from the storage system in the on-premises system for the first I/O. Therefore, the latency reduction effect with the cache area at the first time was low.

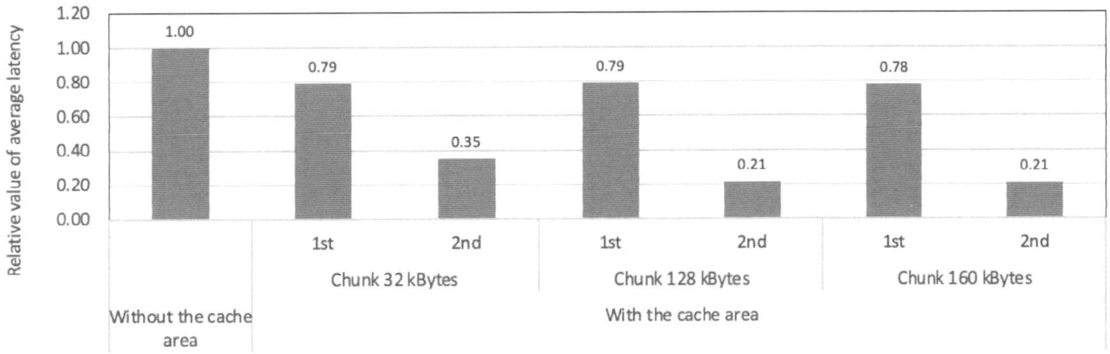

Figure 4. Single I/O latency: random read / write mix

We evaluated the latency reduction effect for each random read and random write in the measurement result Figure 4 shows. Figure 5 shows the result of single I/O average latency in the random read. In the case with the cache area, a chunk read always occurred in the first I/O access. Therefore, the maximum latency, especially for large chunk sizes, tended to be higher than without the cache area. We thought that the larger the chunk size is, the higher the maximum latency is. However, the first measurement showed that the 160 kBytes chunk had a lower maximum latency than the 128 kBytes chunk in this workload. We consider that this was because the data to be accessed was already stored in the cache area in more cases with the 160 kBytes chunk than with the 128 kBytes chunk due to the access locality of this workload.

We also thought that the second measurement would have less latency than the first one, since the most of chunk copies were already done. However, the second maximum latency was 17% higher than the first maximum latency in the case of 32 kBytes chunk. We believe that this is because of the access locality of this workload.

Even with the cache area, the average latency was reduced by more than 26% in the first measurement and by more than 79% in the second measurement compared to the case without the cache area. This means large latency didn't occur frequently. Therefore, the effect of using the cache area is confirmed.

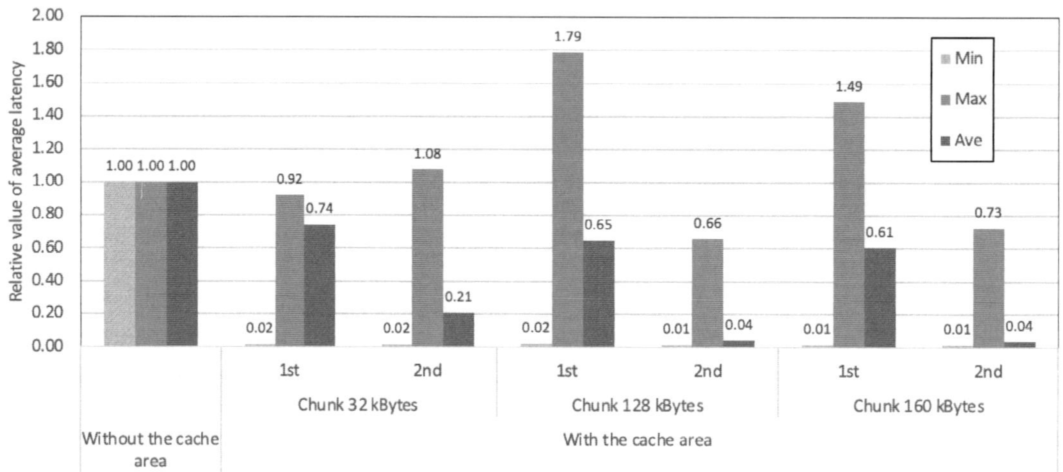

Figure 5. Single IO latency: random read

Figure 6 shows the result of single I/O average latency in the random write. We measured them with the write though mode. However, the larger the chunk size is, the higher the maximum latency is. We think this is because some write operations are disturbed by reading chunks in the case with the cache area. In the second measurement, the average latency was the same with and without the cache area since the number of reading chunks was reduced. Thus, we can confirm the effect of the cache area in this workload. However, there may be a risk that it leads to particularly poor write performance if the chunk size is not set up appropriately for a workload and operation time.

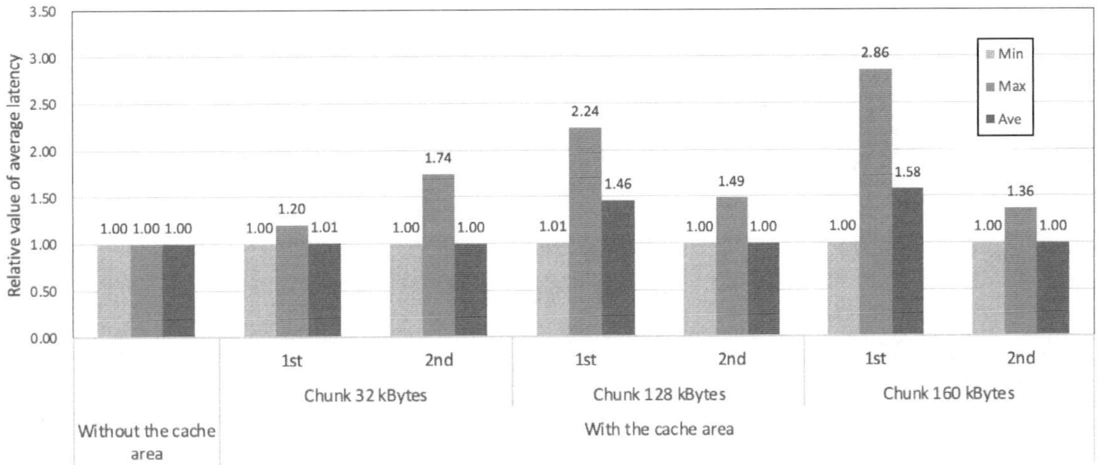

Figure 6. Single IO latency: random write

5. CONCLUSION

We verified the effect of data caching, which is one of the methods for reducing the amount of data transfer between the on-premises system and the public cloud, in the hybrid cloud environment where the compute system and the storage system were located separately. We created the measurement environment in the hybrid cloud with the dm-cache technology and set up the assumed workload of TPC Benchmark^{TM} E with the write-through mode. And it is confirmed that the average latency with the cache area reduced by maximum 79% compared to without the cache area. The latency increased when transferring chunks occurred, thus having the cache area increased the difference between maximum and minimum latencies. However, when comparing the average latencies with/without the cache area, it is considered that setting up the cache area is effective for the workload verified this evaluation. In addition, we found that setting up an appropriate chunk size is important especially in write-through mode to prevent write latency degradation, as data access characteristics change as workload change.

REFERENCES

Amazon Web Service, Inc., (2022a). *Amazon Elastic Compute Cloud User Guide for Linux Instance*, Available at: https://docs.aws.amazon.com/AWSEC2/latest/UserGuide/concepts.html (Accessed: 2 September 2022).

Amazon Web Service, Inc., (2022b). *AWS Direct Connect User Guide,* Available at: https://docs.aws.amazon.com/directconnect/latest/UserGuide/Welcome.html (Accessed: 2 September 2022).

Arteaga, D. et al, (2016). CloudCache: On-demand Flash Cache Management for Cloud Computing. *Proceedings of the 14th USENIX Conference on File and Storage Technologies (FAST '16)*, Santa Clara, USA, pp. 355-369.

Axboe, J., (2022). fio-Flexible I/O tester rev.3.30, Available at: https://fio.readthedocs.io/en/latest/fio_doc.html (Accessed: 2 September 2022).

Chen, S., (2011). TPC-E vs. TPC-C: Characterizing the new TPC-E benchmark via an I/O comparison study. *ACM Sigmod Record*, 39(3), pp. 5-10.

Hitachi Vantara Corporation, (2018). *VSP G350 and G370 Hardware – Hitachi Vantara Knowledge*, Available at: https://knowledge.hitachivantara.com/Documents/Storage/VSP_G130_GF350_GF370_GF700_GF900/88-07-0x/About_Your_System/VSP_G350_G370_Hardware (Accessed: 2 September 2022).

Jouppi, N.P., (1993). Cache write policies and performance. *ACM SIGARCH Computer Architecture News*, 21(2), pp. 191-201.

Park, H. et al, (2020). More IOPS for Less Exploiting Burstable Storage in Public Clouds. *Proceedings of 12th USENIX Workshop on Hot Topics in Cloud Computing (HotCloud 20)*, online.

Shibambu, A., (2022). Migration of government records from on-premises to cloud computing storage in South Africa. *South African Journal of Libraries and Information Science*, 88(1), pp.1-11.

Thornber, J. et al, (2015). Linux kernel documentation: Documentation/device-mapper/cache.txt, Available at: https://www.kernel.org/doc/Documentation/device-mapper/cache.txt (Accessed: 2 September 2022)

Transaction Processing Performance Council, (2015). *TPC BENCHMARKTM E Standard Specification version 1.14.0*, Available at: https://www.tpc.org/tpc_documents_current_versions/pdf/tpc-e_v1.14.0.pdf (Accessed: 2 September 2022).

Weinman, J., (2016). Hybrid cloud economics. *IEEE Cloud Computing, 3(1)*, pp. 18-22.

Zhang, G. et al, (2010). Adaptive Data Migration in Multi-tiered Storage Based Cloud Environment. *Proceedings of 2010 IEEE 3rd International Conference on Cloud Computing*, Miami, USA, pp. 148-155.

Zhang, Y. et al, (2020). OSCA: An Online-Model Based Cache Allocation Scheme in Cloud Block Storage Systems. *Proceedings of 2022 USENIX Annual Technical Conference (USENIX ATC 20)*, online, pp. 785-798.

E-MONEY SECURITY DILEMMA: ADVANCED CYBERSECURITY MECHANISMS AND LEGACY MOBILE PAYMENTS IN SUB-SAHARAN AFRICA

Fabrice Neza[1], Anthony Joseph[2] and Mary Joseph[3]
[1]*Mastercard, Inc., New York, New York, USA*
[2]*Pace University, New York, New York, USA*
[3]*Herbert Lehman College, City University of New York, Bronx, New York, USA*

ABSTRACT

Mobile Network Operators (MNO) infrastructures are expanding in many Sub-Saharan African (SSA) countries that are increasingly adopting mobile payment services. The adopted model is outdated and not compliant with today's more secure, dynamic, and application-driven environments. Unstructured Supplementary Services Data (USSD) legacy technology is widely deployed in SSA countries due to several factors including compatibility with handsets, user experience, cost, and ease of deployment for the MNOs. A survey reveals that USSD is used by approximately 65-75% of the population for mobile payments. The MNOs infrastructure was developed for connectivity, rather than security, making the e-money ecosystem prone to cyber-attacks. End-to-end encryption (E2EE) is one of the recommended cybersecurity solution mechanisms. This research shows that tokenization with identity based encryption techniques is a suitable model to secure financial transactions over USSD as it provides an end-to-end encrypted path when combined with Internet Protocol Security (IPSec) and Transport Layer Security (TLS) while lessening changes to the technology itself and the underlying network. This implementation introduces additional cost for maintenance and management, and therefore, the governments need to adopt market-friendly laws, regulations, and policies to develop employable skills and facilitate MNOs' return on investment.

KEYWORDS

Cybersecurity, E-payment Services, USSD, Tokenization, Identity Based Encryption

1. INTRODUCTION

In 2021, 90% of individuals in developed countries were online compared to only 19% of individuals in the least developed countries of the world (ITU, 2021). By the end of 2021, there were more than 4.3 billion mobile internet subscribers (63% of the world's population), and the mobile broadband covered 95% of the world's population (Bahia & Delaporte, 2022). However, this adoption was not evenly distributed: Europe had the highest rate of Internet usage whereas Africa had the lowest rate. Moreover, Sub-Saharan Africa (SSA) had the very lowest mobile internet adoption rate and usage of any region; it has almost half the world's population not covered by mobile broadband networks and its broadband (3G and 4G) connections only exceeded 2G in 2019 (Wyrzykowski, 2020).

Africa's young population is a potential asset for a relatively high growth in Internet usage and its economy (ITU, 2021; Wan, 2022). Chironga et al (2018) ranked Africa second among the world's largest banking markets for growth and profitability, but Africa's growth and profitability are mainly concentrated in five countries, two of which are in SSA: Nigeria and South Africa (Cook, 2019). Because of the increasing adoption of mobile electronic payment (epayment), Mobile Network Operator (MNO) infrastructures are expanding in many SSA countries. This expansion was driven, in part, by the very low availability of bank branches and the improved availability, reliability, and security of electronic channels (Srinivas & Wadhwani, 2019). The two epayment services that have emerged are MNOs' mobile money transfer and banking institutions' mobile banking system (offered through MNOs infrastructures). The SSA region is the current epicenter of mobile money activities in the world with an estimated 70% of the 2021 global total transactions (Onyango, 2022). While mobile money started as a simple payment service in many SSA countries, it evolved into a platform that allows MNOs to compete in the digital financial services. According to Pazarbasioglu et al (2020), mobile wallets outnumber bank accounts and mobile payment platforms' financial services include credit and savings accounts. Aramé et al (2022) reported on the GSMA's 2021 Global Adoption Survey that 44% of mobile money providers' financial products include savings, insurance or credits.

Most large scale mobile financial services in SSA rely on the Unstructured Supplementary Services Data (USSD), as the key solution for a faster and more economical technology to support mobile money platforms. Though USSD is not the only communication service available for mobile payments, it is estimated that over 90% of mobile money transactions in SSA are driven by USSD (GSMA, 2018). The other options include the Short Messaging Service (SMS), Subscriber Identity Module (SIM) Toolkit (STK), and mobile Internet (Butler et al., 2020). USSD is a session based communication protocol used by the Global System for Mobile (GSM) that is almost seven times faster than SMS. Its operations are simple, do not require access to the Internet access or the user's SIM card and it can be used on basic mobile phones, feature phones, and on smartphones. Most MNOs agree that USSD may be the best available option for SSA's low-income customers because of the security, user experience, compatibility with handsets, real-time interactivity, cost, and ease of deployment (Mosweunyane et al., 2014). The World Bank projected that Africa will house 90% of the world's very poor by 2030 if the current trend of rising extreme poverty continues (Wadhwa, 2018).

Mobile financial services over USSD can be risky if proper cybersecurity measures are not put in place because the USSD packets are transmitted in clear text over the out-of-band signaling channel of the Global System for Mobile (GSM) communications standard (Heine, 1999). While GSM information networks are most secure and immune to destruction when they are most distributed and decentralized, they are also most vulnerable to interception and unauthorized access (Weichbroth & Łysik, 2020). USSD deployments are most vulnerable to interception at the air interface where the consumer mobile phones and MNOs wirelessly interconnect. Whereas developed countries have dropped the use of USSD-like designs in favor of the end-to-end encryption (E2EE) concept, the current mobile network model in SSA countries for financial services is outdated and not compliant with the recommended more secure, dynamic, and application-driven environments. This inherent risk will likely lead to more security breaches as increasingly mobile phones become the effective delivery channels for financial services to poor people and those living in rural and remote areas without proper financial service infrastructures. Moreover, it is typical that in cases of frauds the consumers are the ones who bear the cost, not the providers.

This paper will mainly focus on basic and feature phones because they continue to account for the majority of the African mobile phone market due to their relative affordability and durability, and until they are replaced by smartphones and customers can access the mobile money provider directly via the Internet, they will likely continue to use MNO's USSD platform for financial services (Silver & Johnson, 2018). The main objective of this paper is to develop a prototype that combines identity based encryption with tokenization techniques as a suitable model to secure financial transactions over USSD as it provides end-to-end encryption when combined with Internet Protocol Security (IPSec) and Transport Layer Security (TLS) while lessening changes to the technology itself and the underlying network.

2. BACKGROUND

2.1 Terminologies

Table 1

Acronym	Meaning	Acronym	Meaning
AuC	Authentication Center	**BSS**	Base Station Subsystem
BSC	Base Station Controller	**BTS**	Base Transceiver Station
EIR	Equipment Identity Register	**IMEI**	International Mobile Equipment Identities
MoMoAS	Mobile Money Application Server	**CLAE**	Certificate-Less Authenticated Encryption
HLR	Home Location Register	**IMSI**	International Mobile Subscriber Identity
MS	Mobile Station	**MSC**	Mobile Switching Center
NSS	Network SubSystem	**SIM**	Subscriber Identity Module
TMSI	Temporary Mobile Subscriber Identity	**VLR**	Visitor Location Register

Note: A complete list of acronyms can be found in Heine (1999).

2.2 GSM Architecture

GSM developed in the 1980s, deployed in the early 1990s, is perhaps one of the most successful telecommunications technologies of the last few decades (Scourias, 1996). A typical GSM architecture consists of a mobile station, base station system, and a network subsystem. A GSM mobile station (MS) has a Subscriber Identity Module (SIM) protected with a Personal Identification Number (PIN). Each GSM subscriber is identified through the International Mobile Subscriber Identity (IMSI). The MS stores the ciphering algorithm (A5) while the SIM stores the ciphering key generating algorithm (A8), authentication algorithm (A3), authentication key, and the IMSI (Heine, 1999). The base station subsystem (BSS) is where the mobile phone interfaces with the Base Transceiver Station (BTS) via the air interface. BTS houses the radio transceivers that define a cell and handle the radio-link protocols with MS (Heine, 1999). They are controlled by the Base Station Controller (BSC) for radio-channel setup, frequency hopping of calls, and constant monitoring of calls to determine a call handover from one BTS to another (Heine, 1999). Moreover, BSC connects MS via BTS to the Mobile Service Switching Center (MSC); MSC is a central component of the Network Switching Subsystem (NSS) that provides the set of database and control functionalities needed to handle a mobile subscriber (Heine, 1999). The MSC together with the Home Location Register (HLR), the Visitor Location Register (VLR), Equipment Identification Register (EIR), and the Authentication Center (AuC) constitute NSS (Heine, 1999). HLR contains the administrative information of each subscriber registered in a GSM network while VLR contains certain administrative information already in HLR required for call control and allocates the Temporary Mobile Subscriber Identity (TMSI) to support the subscriber identity confidentiality. EIR and AuC registers are databases used for authentication and security purposes.

Although GSM is a relatively secure public wireless standard, it has security weaknesses to which there are proposed solutions (Gardezi, 2006; Srinivas, 2001). Moreover, Srinivas (2001) argued that cellular communications systems are less secure than their wired counterparts and presented solutions to existing weaknesses while Pagliusi (2002) proposed a security model for GSM network architecture that uses the SIM as a security module to encrypt the user authentication on radio interface. Kune et al (2012) demonstrated how attacks against TMSI are possible; they proposed a shorter TMSI allocation time than the time delay between two calls.

2.3 USSD Architecture and Security

Modern mobile telecommunications networks, such as the GSM, allow the transfer of USSD messages between an application and a MS. The USSD session is initiated by either the MSC, HLR or VLR; the USSD initiation process is characterized by a mobile originated USSD transaction (MO-USSD) or a mobile terminated USSD transaction (MT-USSD) (Klinger, 2021). However, in this research the focus will be on the MS originated transactions. The USSD application can reside either in MSC, VLR, HLR or in an Internet Protocol (IP) network using an appropriate interface (ETSI, 1996). When an MS initiates USSD transactions not destined for applications in the MSC, VLR, or HLR in this hierarchical order, or when they are able to decode the service request but cannot support the required application, a USSD handler routes the message to the USSD gateway (USSD GW) using the Mobile Application Part (MAP) protocol (ETSI, 1996). The USSD GW then routes the message to the application server (AS) that handles the subscriber's request. The AS subsequently replies to the USSD GW that forwards the response to MS (ETSI, 1996). In an MS-initiated service request scenario, the session created between the network application and the MS is used for all information transfers until it ends. If the mobile-initiated USSD operation is unsuitable for the network, the service request would be rejected usually with a notification response to the MS (ETSI, 1996).

Because USSD rely on the legacy Signaling System 7 (SS7) protocol to provide MS the capacity to initiate a USSD operation during or outside a call, attacks utilizing the out-of-band signaling channel expose USSD to the same security issues found in GSM networks (Loughney et al., 2004). With the emergence of IP-based networks and broadband technology, IP Signaling Transport (SIGTRAN) was proposed to carry signaling messages over IP. However, it inherited SS7 signaling protocol's vulnerabilities that could allow an intruder to easily intercept the mobile network. Exploiting these vulnerabilities could result in confidential data leaks, financial loss to individual subscribers, or disruption of communication services. Butler et al (2020) identified both passive and active attacks as the two main types of attacks against digital financial services running over USSD on the GSM signaling channel. To lessen these attacks, ITU (Butler et al., 2020) recommended the use of standardized cryptographic libraries in all applications and end-to-end encryption with standardized protocols, including Transport Layer Security (TLS) v1.2 or higher for the communication between the USSD GW, the Mobile Money Application Server and other back-end services. This paper is about encrypting the data from the mobile user to the Mobile Money Application Server. Furthermore, RFC3788 (Loughney et al., 2004) stipulates that when a network using SIGTRAN protocols involves more than one party, end-to-end security should be the goal and recommends that IPsec or TLS be used to ensure confidentiality of user payload. Additionally, the Central Bank of Nigeria (2019), one major player in SSA's economy, requires "secure transmission of USSD signals between network operator & the USSD aggregators, and between the USSD aggregators & the bank."

While Public Key Cryptography (PKC) is mostly used in TLS certificates that are issued by reputed Certificate Authorities (CA) to provide the confidentiality, integrity, authentication, and non-repudiation required in the end-to-end encryption, the complexity of setting up and using a PKC in basic and feature phones environment could be expensive because it may require additional infrastructure and high computing power, and might not be suitable in processor or bandwidth limited environments. Similarly, the use of STK or java applications to secure USSD transactions adds overhead to the network and requires changes in the network and the mobile devices that may be too costly to customers. To achieve end-to-end encryption on an USSD channel using basic and feature phones, a form of PKC that utilizes some kind of identifier as the basis for the encryption mechanism and has the means to encrypt messages (or verify signatures) absent of any prior key distribution between the communicating entities would be more appropriate. This solution should be able to generate public keys locally and be as transparent to users as practicable.

To achieve the objective of end-to-end encryption in USSD-based financial transactions, this research paper combines two models in a prototype: identity-based encryption (IBE) and tokenization. The resulting model uses an improved Certificate-Less Authenticated Encryption (CLAE) method along with Tokenization, Internet Protocol Security (IPSec) and Transport Layer Security (TLS). The features incorporated in this model are a Token Server (TS), a Trusted Module (TM), a Database and a Hardware Security Module (HSM).

2.4 Identity Based Encryption and Tokenization

Identity Based Encryption (IBE) is a solution to the encryption key management problem; it can use an arbitrary string as a public key to enable secure data transfer without certificates. Protection is provided by a key server, Private Key Generator (PKG), (Islam et al., 2015) that controls the dynamic generation of private decryption keys that correspond to public identities. The IBE system design originated with Shamir (1985) and was refined by Boneh and Franklin (2001) after it was further developed by Fiat and Shamir (1986) and Feige et al (1988). Al-Riyami and Paterson (2003) combined IBE with conventional PKC to produce certificate-less PKC (CL-PKC). By separating authentication and authorization from private key generation through the key server, the CL-PKC framework simplifies operation and scaling. CL-PKC authenticates public keys without certificates but instead uses a trusted third party (TTP) that possesses a master key. There are similarities between CL-PKC and identity-based public key cryptography (ID-PKC) but unlike ID-PKC, CL-PKC can be viewed as a model for PKC because it does not have a key escrow property problem (Al-Riyami & Paterson, 2003).

The proposed model in this paper provides a certificate-less authenticated encryption (CLAE) method for sending an encrypted message over a network using identity-based encryption between a sender (MS) having a unique sender identity (idMS) formed by the combination of MSISDN and IMSI, and a recipient (Mobile Money Application Server) having a recipient identity string (idMoMoAS). Prior to encrypting a plaintext message (M) the MS verifies the plurality of public parameters (PK) from the trusted module (TM). During financial transactions, tokenization is used to substitute the actual mobile money account number with non-sensitive placeholders. Tokenization is especially practiced in the payments processing industry and the process involves protecting sensitive data by replacing them with an algorithmically generated number called a token that is by design unrelated to the actual data (Liu et al., 2020; Iwasokun et al., 2018).

2.5 Related Work

Most of the research on mobile payments over USSD security does not describe end-to-end encryption (E2EE) in depth. They focus on the security of the GSM network algorithms, ignoring the plaintext transmitted USSD packets (ETSI, 1996). Nonetheless, a significant number of papers discussed mobile phone communications security solutions using public key cryptography or third-party applications. Wu et al. (2011) proposed an integrated mobile payment framework based on 3G network and the SIM card ToolKit (STK). The research recommended a public key infrastructure to improve mobile payment security wherein the private key would be stored in the phones integrated circuits cards. Nyamtiga et al (2013) and Sekyere et al (2018) proposed a java application installed in the customer's phone to capture the security details, generate secure messages and send USSD commands over the GSM network. Wu & Tan (2009) used RSA-1024 asymmetric algorithm as well as AES and 3DES symmetric algorithms to provide "an end-to-end secure channel between server-side and mobile terminal" for SMS communication. Thomas and Panchami (2014) presented an encryption method that included EasySMS protocol, Blowfish encryption algorithm, and MD5 hashing algorithm for authentication, confidentiality, and integrity respectively to ensure very secure SMS message transfers between mobile users. Agwanyanjaba (2018) explored the challenges of using PIN as the only factor of authentication in USSD-based financial transactions and proposed the use of time bound USSD push augmented with biometric authentication to secure transactions. While evaluating the security challenges of Mobile Money, Castle et al (2016) focused on Android applications and presented a systematic threat model for the challenges associated with mobile money deployments in the developing world. Klinger (2021) proposes the use of a sufficiently powerful quantum computer to run quantum safe symmetric cyphers on simple Universal Integrated Circuit Cards (UICCs) to secure USSD transactions. Moreover, several other identity-based encryption solutions have been proposed to provide security in multiple mobile networks. Islam (2015) proposed the use of symmetric key and identity based techniques for encryption and key management to ensure secure and highly reliable end-to-end SMS communication over GSM networks. Boneh and Franklin (2001) developed a functional IBE scheme, "based on ciphertext security in the random oracle model," with a distributed PKG to disperse the location of the master key. Smith et al (2009) presented an identity-based key agreement system and its implementation for mobile telephony in GSM networks. Additionally, Kumar et al (2006) presented an identity-based cryptography (IBC) mutual authentication and key agreement approach for GSM networks. Unlike the work of this paper, they only used the IMSI number for the public identity key and the protocol security relies on an assumed secure channel to the HLR and VLR. In an extensive search of the research literature published on USSD security, no paper was found involving end-to-end encryption of the USSD sessions in the mobile payments transactions as recommended in different security standards. This paper's contribution is to provide a prototype E2EE that addresses this gap as well as the shortcomings of the existing USSD security in mobile payments.

3. REQUIREMENTS AND SPECIFICATIONS

In the survey conducted to support this study, more than 70% of the 110 SSA respondents stated that they fear their phone getting hacked or data communication intercepted as their biggest concern regarding mobile phone use for financial transactions. Over 70% of the respondents consider mobile money and mobile banking to be safe to very safe, yet these same respondents believe that people's personal information is not safe when using these services: 58% for mobile money and 55% for mobile banking. This apparent contradiction in the respondents' perceptions suggests that there is a general need for stronger security in mobile money and mobile banking services over USSD as the technology has proven to be the most accessible, economical, and practical way to remove traditional barriers to digital financial systems in SSA. According to Aramé et al (2022), mobile money transactions in 2021 were over US $1 trillion and registered mobile money accounts were 1.35 billion, exceeding the 2012 number by a factor of 10.

This research work uses the engineering approach to problem-solving where the problem is identified and the solution is pursued through design. It presents a prototype that ensures end-to-end security of data between the MNO subscriber and the digital financial application server whether located in the MNO infrastructure (mobile money) or in the external financial institution (mobile banking). The model uses an improved certificate-less authenticated encryption (CLAE) method along with Tokenization, Internet

Protocol Security (IPSec) and Transport Layer Security (TLS). The features incorporated in this model are a Token Server (TS), a Trusted Module (TM), a Database and a Hardware Security Module (HSM). The TM is configured for generating a plurality of public parameters and it may be a dedicated server or as part of distributed systems. In this case, it also includes additional software components for the TS. Other security mechanisms might be deployed on the TM hardware as deemed necessary (Malek, 2014).

Traditionally in the PKC, public keys are generated by a trusted center (certificate authority) guaranteeing that a public key belongs to a certain recipient. However, those public keys are not protected as they are exchanged over insecure channels and are prone to interception and tampering. In contrast, the CLAE scheme presented with this model, allows the sender (MS) to remove the need for public key certificates by using the identity of the recipient (idMoMoAS) and prior to encrypt the message, locally verify the public parameters of the TM to ensure they were not altered. This verification reduces the risk of an attacker equipped with an IMSI catcher who would replace the public parameters. Instead of using a predetermined parameter to generate the public/private key pair, the MS integrates the identity of the TM (idTM) as well as the identity of the recipient (idMoMoAS). The point of trust is established from the public identity of the TM (idTM) that can be a hostname or a fully qualified domain name. This provides greater flexibility to the proposed model in generating the encryption keys, as the MS can arbitrarily choose any identity of the TM (idTM) and can be assured that its selection will be enforced on the recipient (MoMoAS). Once the system is initialized, any entity in the system (MS or MoMoAS) can self-generate the public key of the other entity and encrypt the sensitive data by using the recipient's locally generated public key derived from the recipient's identity and the plurality of public parameters (PK) from the TM. Equipped with the public parameters, the MS is able to communicate with the MoMoAS independent of the TM over a secure channel by encrypting the message using the MoMoAS's public key (pubMoMoAS), which is generated locally by the MS using the public parameters obtained from TM and the MoMoAS identity string (idMoMoAS). Only the true recipient is then able to decrypt and retrieve the sensitive data using its private key known only to the recipient and derived from the TM (Islam et al., 2015; Malek, 2014).

In GSM network, every user is uniquely identified by the IMSI, a 15-digit number that is assigned to the mobile user by the MNO and is stored on SIM card. Since the IMSI is the SIM card identifier, if a new SIM card is issued it will have a new IMSI. If a SIM card is moved to a new phone, the IMSI moves with the card and doesn't stay with the phone. The Mobile Station International Subscriber Directory Number (MSISDN) is the telephone number with full international prefix used to send a text message or make a call (Heine, 1999). Unlike an IMSI, which is bound to a particular SIM card, MSISDNs can be transferred from phone to phone, and from SIM to SIM. While it might be tempting to use the MSISDNs alone as unique identifiers in mobile money transactions, problems arise when that number is recycled to a new user and that user inadvertently access the previous user's information. Moreover, because MSISDNs are usually public, using them to authenticate users in mobile money transactions as primary identifiers has made the number itself (MSISDN) vulnerable to malicious attacks. Hence, the proposed model will use the combination of MSISDN and IMSI as a unique identity of the MS (idMS) for the identity-based encryption. The key to authenticating the MS securely, reliably and quickly is to use the MSISDN and perform the verification using the SIM card's IMSI number. Identifying the MS based on a combination of MSISDN and IMSI is the strongest and least problematic solution for user identity as it removes the risk of account details being compromised when numbers are recycled, thus keeping users secure and protected. Through this combination, insider attacks will likely be detected as soon as the MS is checked in the HLR and AuC due to the MS identity (idMS) mismatch; the attacker MSISDN and IMSI combination will fail, hence the correct computation of the actual MS public key (pubMS) would fail too since it is derived from the MS identity (idMS). The distribution of the plurality of public parameters (PK), the identity of the financial application server (idMoMoAS), and the idTM can be integrated into the GSM lookup mechanism and carry the information over the SS7 protocol (Dryburgh & Hewett, 2003).

Since the lookup functionality to locate the HLR and the current location of the MS already exists in GSM networks, a flag can be attached to the request message, stating that the public parameters of the TM be sent piggybacked onto the response. A flag is suitable because the public parameters need to be queried only for the very first USSD session request from an MS. All subsequent sessions from the same MS to the MoMoAS do not need any further public parameter lookup. In operation, both the MS and MoMoAS need to communicate with the TM to obtain respective private keys (prvMS and prvMoMoAS) and a plurality of public parameters. However, the MS private key (prvMS) can be embedded on the SIM card similar to the individual subscriber authentication key (Ki) utilized as a secret key to authenticate the MS and the GSM operator that is never transmitted over the radio channel.

The introduction of the Hardware Security Module (HSM) in the design is to offload TS. The HSM stores encryption keys and serves as a secure network computer system of cryptographic operations: key generation, exchange, and encryption that essentially implements algorithms for encryption and hashing for different financial transactions over USSD. TS and TM implement additional logic on top of HSM whereby HSM gets the key generation request from TS through an application programming interface (API). TS receives the transacting MSISDN, and using the HSM capabilities, it encrypts the communication and generates the relative token. Subsequently, if MSISDN needs to be processed later, only the token is available, HSM would be unable to provide the requested data because it does not store all the necessary values. HSM only stores the encryption key; it does not store the token and the encrypted value. This is a critical security measure because in the event where HSM is compromised, it would be unable to provide any suitably meaningful data. In the rare case when an attacker might gain entry into HSM, the attacker would have difficulty matching the held keys with a particular transaction as HSM does not control the key; it is only used to encrypt each value at a given moment. In contrast, TS stores the encrypted values and tokens and keeps track of the encryption keys to be able to rotate them with time. It is able to decrypt any value from the token as it records the key-value relationship. In a real-time encrypted session initiated between MS and the USSD platform, tokenized data are sent back and forth when the service is invoked. The encrypted session remains open over a radio connection until the USSD service is completed, the user terminates the application, an incorrect option is entered from the menu, or a time-out happens. This minimizes the time an attacker would have to intercept and try to decode the random and encrypted token. Each allowable transaction is limited to a specific token. All Internet Protocol (IP) links between different nodes are encrypted. The interface between the MoMoAS, USSD GW and HLR or MSC over SS7 or SIGTRAN is protected using TLS (Loughney et al., 2004; Aramé et al., 2022). All SIGTRAN peers implementing TLS for the security solution authenticate as part of the TLS session establishment and TLS is used on all bi-directional streams; no directional streams are to be used (Loughney et al., 2004). With E2EE being the goal, IPSec and TLS are used to ensure confidentiality of the payload especially for external applications over the Internet. Edge devices (firewalls) are linked with IPSec because TLS only protects the payload. Thus, IPsec Encapsulating Security Payload (ESP) encrypts and protects the TLS payload information in the established tunnel.

4. PROTOTYPE IMPLEMENTATION AND DISCUSSION

The primary objective of this end-to-end encryption and tokenization security solution is to encrypt the communication so as to prevent eavesdropping and other security breaches from compromising the confidentiality, integrity, and availability of the exchanged data (Quentin et al., 2020). The prototype of the proposed model is represented in Fig. 1. Generic names are used instead of the actual terms (Figure 1) because different network generations introduce different names for each component. For instance, in GSM, cell towers are called "BTS", in Universal Mobile Telecommunications System (UMTS) they become "NodeB", in Long-Term Evolution (LTE) "eNodeB", and in 5G they are termed "gNB" (Gupta & Jha, 2015). Hence, the use of generic terms is more convenient and easier to follow and thereby making the model more applicable. As shown in Fig. 1, when the subscriber initiates a mobile money request (1) through a USSD code comprising an asterisk (*) and hash (#) keys along with a combination of digits (0 to 9), the MS recognizes the code format, and instead of initiating a call it invokes the use of the normal GSM encrypted signaling channel (USSD bearer) to communicate with the USSD infrastructure. The goal is sending an encrypted message by the MS having an identity string (idMS) derived from the combination of the MSISDN and IMSI to a recipient (MoMoAS) having an identity string (idMoMoAS) over a network using identity-based encryption. In this step the MS identifies the TM by idTM (i.e. "mcc.mnc.nameofTM" where MCC is Mobile country Code and MNC is Mobile Network Code). The exchange of the PK (associated with or generated by TM) between MS and TM occurs as part of the normal GSM parameters exchange (2) and are distributed by HLR (3) to the mobile user through the MSC/VLR. Among the flags returned by the HLR in (3) is the identity of the recipient (idMoMoAS). The idMoMoAS is only sent to SIM cards provisioned with mobile money services in HLR. The sender, MS, determines if it has a private key (prvMS), that can be burned directly onto the chip when the SIM is manufactured, and verifies the plurality of public parameters (PK) of the TM, received in (3). The verification process to ensure that the public parameters have not been modified relies on the properties of the PK and prvMS, the known idTM and the idMS (Malek, 2014). The MS then identifies the recipient (MoMoAS) to receive the plaintext message (M) by idMoMoAS received in

(3) from HLR through mobile money user profile provisioning. It is worth noting that idMoMoAS may be the MoMoAS full qualified domain name (FQDN) or hostname. MS generates the identity-based public key encryption of the MoMoAS (pubMoMoAS) using the PK and idMoMoAS (Malek, 2014). This approach allows generating pubMoMoAS locally for offline encryption and communication with TM is not required as a certificate issued by TM is not necessary to authenticate the pubMoMoAS. In this manner, MS is able to send M as an encrypted message to the MoMoAS without accessing the TM, as long as the MS has the required PK and its own prvMS. Furthermore, with the PK and its own prvMS, the MS is able to verify that the PK has not been compromised to ensure that only the MoMoAS having the prvMoMoAS will be able to decrypt C. The MS then encrypts the USSD message (M) as ciphertext (C) including the encrypted message, as well as extra information necessary for decrypting the message. Additional authentication information may also be appended to C (Malek, 2014). In (4), MS transmits the encrypted C to the MoMoAS and safely travels the unsecured GSM channel. An attacker who would intercept it, would require the MoMoAS private key (prvMoMoAS) and the PK of the TM to read the message (Ramadan et al., 2016).

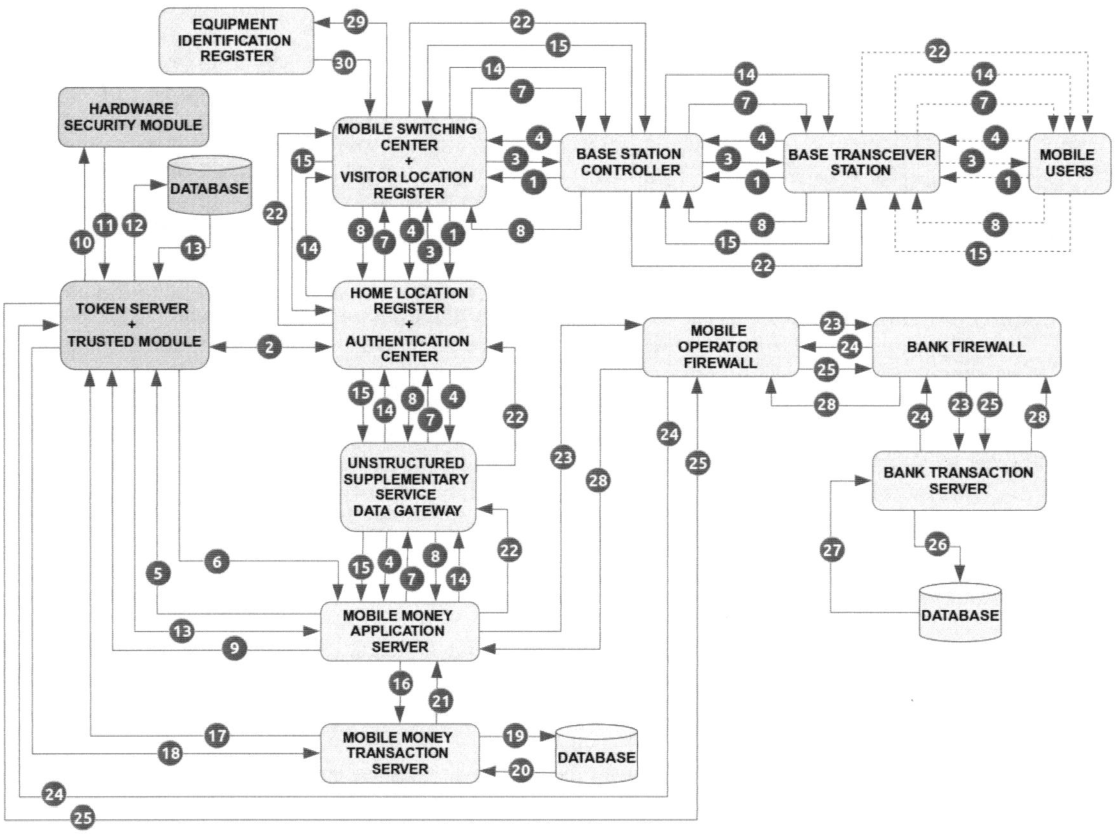

Figure 1. Encryption and tokenization scheme flow diagram

LEGEND
1. MS initiates the USSD session and identifies the trusted module (TM) by the TM identity string (IdTM)
2. Exchange of the plurality of public parameters (PK) between the trusted module (TM) and HLR
3. The PK associated with or generated by TM is distributed by the HLR to the mobile user through the MSC/VLR
4. The MS transmits the ciphertext (C) to the MoMoAS over the mobile network (BTS-BSC-MSC/VLR-HLR/AuC-USSD GW)
5 & 6. The MoMoAS retrieves the PK from TM and its own prvMoMoAS
7. MoMoAS generates pubMS, decrypts (C), and displays a menu at MS along with the request to submit the MoMoAN
8. The MoMoAN is submitted to the MoMoAS
9. The MoMoAS uses the TS's API to securely request a token related to the MoMoAN
10 & 11. The TS uses the HSM to create the token
12. The token, MoMoAN, and possibly the couple MSISDN-IMSI are stored in the token data store (database)
13. The TS securely returns the token to the MoMoAS
14. The token is sent back through USSD GW and HLR to MS where it is securely stored
15. The mobile user securely initiates the action to complete the transaction

16. The MoMoAS securely sends a request to the TrS
17. The TrS securely sends the token to the TS to retrieve the actual MoMoAN
18. The MoMoAN is securely returned to the TrS
19 & 20. The transaction information is securely sent to the Database to be validated and eventually completed
21. The transaction status is securely sent back to the MoMoAS
22. A notification status is sent back to MS through HLR with a flag to terminate the original USSD session
23. If the TrS is located outside the MNO network, the MoMoAS sends requests to the MtrS through an IPSec link
24. The MtrS securely initiates the request to the MNO's TS to retrieve the actual MoMoAN
25. The MoMoAN is securely returned to the MtrS
26 & 27. The transaction information is sent to the bank database to validate and complete the transaction
28. The transaction status is sent back to the MoMoAS and then to the mobile user via (22)
29 & 30. These flows are not relevant to the transactions undertaken between the MS and the MoMoAS.

Upon receipt of C, the MoMoAS determines whether it needs to get a prvMoMoAS from TM to decrypt C and retrieve M. If MoMoAS has not previously stored in memory its prvMoMoAS associated with the idTM, it authenticates itself with the TM to receive its own private key (prvMoMoAS) and the TM's public key (pubTM), as described in (5) and (6). At this time, the MoMoAS may also receive an updated set of PK from the TM. The MoMoAS verifies the sender of the message by inspecting C components, the MS public key (pubMS) generated locally from idMS and the idTM. Once the sender has been verified, the MoMoAS restores M and a menu requesting to submit the Mobile Money Account Number (MoMoAN) is displayed on the MS screen (7). When the mobile user submits this information to the MoMoAS (8), the MoMoAS processes the request and uses the TS's API to request a new token for the MoMoAN (9). The TS in its turn uses HSM (10 and 11) to create the token. HSM is only used to securely manage, process, and store cryptographic keys separately from sensitive data. The token, MoMoAN, and possibly the couple MSISDN-IMSI and the rest of the customer information are stored in the token database (12). The communication path between these back-end servers, MoMoAS, HSM and the TS is performed through TLS (Butler et al., 2020). The copy of the original MoMoAN is overwritten in MoMoAS so that it does not persist in memory and TS returns the token to the MoMoAS (13). In (14) and the token is sent back to the MS through USSD GW and HLR. This process is similar to the authentication scheme in GSM where the RAND is transmitted (via the BSC/BTS) to the mobile station (MS). The token will be used throughout the MNO/MMO's environments, instead of the real MoMoAN and it can't be extracted into anything valuable to fraudsters (Securosis, n.d.; PCI Security Standards Council, 2011). The mobile user performs a transaction in (15) and the MoMoAS sends a request to the Transaction Server (TrS) (16). The TrS sends the token to TS over TLS to retrieve the actual MoMoAN (17) and when TS receives the request, it validates the token using its copy of the token key and de-tokenizes it to obtain the original MoMoAN that is returned to the TrS (18). The transaction information is securely sent to the Database to be validated and eventually completed (19) and (20). The transaction status is sent back to the MoMoAS (21) and a notification status is sent back to MS through HLR with a flag to terminate the original USSD session (22). When the TrS is located outside the MNO network (mobile banking), steps 1-15 apply and MS uses the assigned token to transact with the Mobile Money Operator (MMO). To complete a transaction in this scenario, the mobile user initiates the action (15) and the MNO MoMoAS sends a request to the MMO Transaction Server (MTrS) over a secure connection, through the MNO firewall connected by IPSec to the bank firewall (23). When the MTrS receives the transaction request, it initiates the request to the MNO's TS over TLS to retrieve the actual MoMoAN (24). The communication between the two servers is encrypted by SSL/TLS certificates which are usually signed by trusted public Certificate Authorities (CAs). Another strategy is to issue self-signed SSL certificates and in this case, the certificate is self-signed with its own private key, instead of requesting it from a public or a private CA. If the certificate is generated on the MNO's TS it needs to be securely distributed to the MtrS and applied in its keystore. After the MNO's TS receives the request to retrieve the actual MoMoAN, it validates the token using its copy of the token key and de-tokenizes it to obtain the original MoMoAN which is returned to the MtrS over the secure link (25). The transaction information is sent to the bank database to validate and complete the transaction (26) and (27). The transaction status is sent back to the MoMoAS (28) and a notification status is sent back to the MS through HLR with a flag to terminate the original USSD session (22). Though the flow (29) and (30) are used in normal GSM phone hardware authentication, they are not relevant to the transactions being undertaken between the mobile user and the MoMoAS. For each transaction, a new token is generated and used only once and within a certain valid time period. If a token is used outside of these parameters, it is flagged as invalid to prevent the ability to replay past transaction requests (replay attack). In the replay attack scenario, the same transaction request is resent, and another transaction can be done with the same data.

USSD transactions are performed using an MS when a mobile money customer initiates requests via the mobile network and terminates at the mobile money application server that can be administered by the MNO or an independent technology vendor such as a bank. Despite USSD being a session-based technology providing relatively stronger security than SMS, it can still be breached because GSM encryption is only applied between the MS and the BTS but not across of the rest of the MNO's network where messages are transferred in plaintext. This research work proposes new technologies for end-to-end encryption of USSD-based financial transactions and demonstrates how these new technologies are integrated and applied into the existing USSD technology. The exchange of public parameters from the TM to the MS through HLR is compatible with that used to authenticate the mobile station (MS) on a GSM network. Moreover, the changes made within the network will not negatively impact it because the benefits of the added tokenization and security features are likely to outweigh the additional cost of the inclusion of the TM and TS subsystem. The proposed prototype model is adaptable. It is likely to be sustained over time because USSD is a device-independent technology that can even be used with smartphones and potentially in newer related devices.

5. CONCLUSION

This paper provided a solution that demonstrated how an improved CLAE scheme coupled with tokenization add a security layer to USSD-based financial services. The solution allows the sender and the recipient to securely communicate with each other with the sender verifying public parameters from a trusted third party and locally generate the recipient's public key derived from its identity prior to encrypting a plaintext message. This potentially low cost solution increases mobile payments security over USSD without having to make deep changes in the GSM network architecture. Future research will pursue simulation and testing of the proposed prototype. Other researchers are also encouraged to do the same so that the potential efficiency and cost effectiveness of the proposed CLAE with tokenization solution can be determined. However, governments will need to adopt market-friendly laws and regulations as well as link talents with adequate MNOs or financial institutions which need specific skillsets to fill the knowledge gap once the solution is deployed. Creating a supportive environment in the initial stages of this solution's implementation could help speed-up the return on investments for MNOs as investments will be needed to support changes in accommodating new equipment or issuing SIM cards supporting the solution. Governments might also need to define guidelines and policies to support the proposed solution including the creation of an environment that safeguards security and privacy, information standards, and a legal framework for citizen privacy enforcement. There are security standards which address advanced cybersecurity mechanisms that are already implemented in many SSA countries in a locally customized form such as the General Data Protection Regulation (GDPR), Control Objectives for Information and Related Technology (COBIT) and ISO 27001 (Yadav, 2019).

REFERENCES

Al-Riyami, S. and Paterson, K., (2003). Certificateless public key cryptography. *Advances in Cryptology - ASIACRYPT 2003: Springer Lecture Notes in Computer Science*, Vol. 2894, pp. 452-473.

Agwanyanjaba, W., (2018). Enhanced Mobile Banking Security: Implementing Transaction Authorization mechanism via USSD Push. University of Nairobi. http://erepository.uonbi.ac.ke/handle/11295/153184

Aramé et al., (2022). State of the Industry Report on Mobile Money 2022. GSMA. https://www.gsma.com/sotir/wp-content/uploads/2022/03/GSMA_State_of_the_Industry_2022_English.pdf

Bahia, K. and Delaporte, A., (2022). The State of Mobile Internet Connectivity 2022. *GSMA*. https://www.gsma.com/r/wp-content/uploads/2022/10/The-State-of-Mobile-Internet-Connectivity-Report-2022.pdf

Boneh, D. and Franklin, M., (2001). Identity based encryption from the Weil pairing. *Advances in Cryptology - Crypto' 2001: Springer Lecture Notes in Computer Science*, Vol. 2139, pp. 213-229.

Butler, K. et al., (2020). Security Testing for USSD and STK Based Digital Financial Services Applications. *ITU and The Financial Inclusion Global Initiative (FIGI)*. https://figi.itu.int/wp-content/uploads/2021/04/Security-testing-for-USSD-and-STK-based-Digital-Financial-Services-applications-1.pdf

Castle, S. et al., (2016). Let's Talk Money: Evaluating the Security Challenges of Mobile Money in the Developing World. 1-10. 10.1145/3001913.3001919

Central Bank of Nigeria, (2019). The Regulatory Framework for the Use of the Unstructured Supplementary Service Data (USSD) in the Nigerian Financial System. *CBN*. https://www.cbn.gov.ng/Out/2020/FMD/CBN%20Rule%20Book%20Volume%201.pdf

Chironga, M. et al., (2018). Roaring to Life: Growth and Innovation in African Retail Banking. https://www.mckinsey.com/~/media/mckinsey/industries/financial%20services/our%20insights/african%20retail%20bankings%20next%20growth%20frontier/roaring-to-life-growth-and-innovation-in-african-retail-banking-web-final.ashx

Cook, M., (2019). This Country Recently Became Africa's Largest Economy: Now it's Too Big for Businesses to Ignore. *Brink*. www.brinknews.com/this-country-recently-became-africas-largest-economy-now-its-too-big-for-businesses-to-ignore/

Dryburgh, L. and Hewett, J., (2003). *Signaling System No. 7: Protocol, Architecture, and Applications*. Cisco Press.

ETSI, 1996. GSM Technical Specification (GSM 09.02), Version 5.3.0. *European Telecommunications Standards Institute (ETSI)*. https://www.etsi.org/deliver/etsi_gts/09/0902/05.03.00_60/gsmts_0902v050300p.pdf

Feige, U. et al., 1988. Zero-knowledge proofs of identity. *Journal of Cryptology*, Vol. 1, pp. 77-94.

Fiat, A. and Shamir, A., (1986). How to prove yourself: Practical solutions to identification and signature problems. *Advances in Cryptology - Crypto' 86: Springer Lecture Notes in Computer Science*, Vol. 263, pp. 186-194.

Gardezi, A., 2006. Security in Wireless Cellular Networks. *WUSTL*. https://www.cse.wustl.edu/~jain/cse574-06/ftp/cellular_security/index.html

GSMA, (2018). State of the Mobile Money Industry in Sub-Saharan Africa. https://www.gsma.com/mobilefordevelopment/wp-content/uploads/2019/07/GSMA-Sub-Saharan-Africa-SOTIR-presentation.pdf

Gupta, A. and Jha, R., (2015). A Survey of 5G Network: Architecture and Emerging Technologies. *IEEE Access*, Vol. 3, pp. 1206-1232.

Hanouch, M. and Chen, G., (2015). Promoting Competition in Mobile Payments: The Role of USSD. https://documents.worldbank.org/en/publication/documents-reports/documentdetail/586781468127790413/promoting-competition-in-mobile-payments-the-role-of-ussd

Heine, G., (1999). *GSM Networks: Protocols, Terminology, and Implementation*. Boston, Mass: Artech House.

Islam, S. et al., (2015). Secure end-to-end SMS communication over GSM networks. *Proceedings of 12th International Bhurban Conference on Applied Sciences and Technology (IBCAST)*, pp. 286-292.

ITU, (2021). *Measuring Digital Development Facts and Measures, Development Sector*. Geneva: International Telecommunication Union. https://www.itu.int/en/ITU-D/Statistics/Documents/facts/FactsFigures2021.pdf

Iwasokun, G. et al., (2018). Encryption and Tokenization-Based System for Credit Card Information Security. *International Journal of Cyber-Security and Digital Forensics*, Vol. 7, pp. 283-293.

Klinger, A., (2021). Low resource requirement, quantum resistant, encryption of USSD messages for use in financial services. ITU. https://www.itu.int/dms_pub/itu-t/opb/tut/T-TUT-PROTO-2021-PDF-E.pdf

Kumar, P. et al., 2006. Mutual Authentication and Key Agreement for GSM. *Proceedings of the 2006 International Conference on Mobile Business*. https://ieeexplore.ieee.org/document/771073

Kune, D. et al., (2012). Location Leaks on the GSM Air Interface. https://www.researchgate.net/publication/267805153_Location_Leaks_on_the_GSM_Air_Interface

Liu, W. et al., (2020). Review of State of the Art: Secure Mobile Payment. *IEEE Access*, Vol. 8, pp. 13898-13914.

Loughney, J. et al., (2004). Security Considerations for Signaling Transport (SIGTRAN) Protocols. *IETF*. https://tools.ietf.org/html/rfc3788

Malek, B., (2014). Method and System for a Certificate-less Authenticated Encryption Scheme Using Identity Based Encryption, US Patent No. 8, pp. 694 771.

Mosweunyane, G. et al., (2014). Design of a USSD System for TB Contact Tracing. *Health Informatics*, Vol. 8, pp. 15-26.

Nyamtiga, B. et al., (2013). Security Perspectives for USSD versus SMS in Conducting Mobile Transactions: A Case Study of Tanzania. *International Journal of Technology Enhancements and Emerging Engineering Research*, Vol. 1, pp. 38-43.

Onyango, S., (2022). Africa accounts for 70% of the world's $1 trillion mobile money market. Quartz Africa. https://qz.com/africa/2161960/gsma-70-percent-of-the-worlds-1-trillion-mobile-money-market-is-in-africa/

Pagliusi, P., (2002). A Contemporary Foreword on GSM Security. *Infrastructure Security*, pp. 129-144.

Quentin, C., (2020). Towards a Triad for Data Privacy. 10.24251/HICSS.2020.535.

Scoping SIG & Tokenization Taskforce, August (2011). PCI Data Security Standard (PCI DSS) Information Supplement: PCI DSS Tokenization Guidelines, version 2. *Payment Card Industry (PCI) Security Standards Council*. https://www.pcisecuritystandards.org/documents/Tokenization_Guidelines_Info_Supplement.pdf

Pazarbasioglu et al., (2020). Digital Financial Services. World Bank. https://pubdocs.worldbank.org/en/230281588169110691/Digital-Financial-Services.pdf

Ramadan, M. et al., (2016). EEE-GSM: End-to-end encryption scheme over GSM system. *International Journal of Security and its Applications*, Vol. 10, pp. 229-240.

Scourias, J., (1996). Overview of GSM: The Global System for Mobile Communications. https://citeseerx.ist.psu.edu/viewdoc/download?doi=10.1.1.24.3034&rep=rep1&type=pdf

Securosis, (n.d.) Understanding and Selecting a Tokenization Solution. https://securosis.com/assets/library/reports/Securosis_Understanding_Tokenization_V.1_.0_.pdf

Sekyere, B. et al., (2018). Improving Electronic Banking in Ghana using USSD. *International Journal of Computer Applications*, Vol. 180, pp. 8-13.

Shamir, A., (1985). Identity-based cryptosystems and signature schemes. *Advances in Cryptology - Crypto' 84: Springer Lecture Notes in Computer Science*, Vol. 196, pp. 47-53.

Silver, L. and Johnson, C., (2018). Internet Connectivity Seen as Having Positive Impact on Life in Sub-Saharan Africa. *Pew Research Center's Global Attitudes Project*. https://www.pewresearch.org/global/2018/10/09/internet-connectivity-seen-as-having-positive-impact-on-life-in-sub-saharan-africa/

Smith, M. et al., (2009). Securing Mobile Phone Calls with Identity-Based Cryptography. *Proceedings of the Advances in Information Security and Assurance Third International Conference and Workshops*, pp. 210-222.

Srinivas, S., (2001). The GSM Standard (An Overview of its Security). *SANS Institute*. https://www.sans.org/reading-room/whitepapers/telephone/gsm-standard-an-overview-security-317

Srinivas, V. and Wadhwani, R., (2019). Recognizing the Value of Bank Branches in a Digital World. *Deloitte*. www2.deloitte.com/us/en/insights/industry/financial-services/bank-branch-transformation-digital-banking.html

Thomas, M. and Panchami, V., (2014). An encryption protocol for end-to-end secure transmission of SMS. *IEEE Transactions on Information Forensics and Security*, Vol. 9, pp. 1157-1168.

Wan, H., (2022). Increases in Africa's Older Population Will Outstrip Growth in Any Other World Region. United States Census Bureau. https://www.census.gov/library/stories/2022/04/why-study-aging-in-africa-region-with-worlds-youngest-population.html

Wadhwa, D., (2018). The Number of Extremely Poor People Continues to Rise in Sub-Saharan Africa. *World Bank*. https://blogs.worldbank.org/opendata/number-extremely-poor-people-continues-rise-sub-saharan-africa

Weichbroth P. and Łysik, L., (2020). Mobile Security: Threats and Best Practices. *Mobile Information Systems, 2020*, pp. 1-15.

Wu, H. et al., (2011). Mobile Payment Framework Based on 3G Network. *Proceedings of the Third International Symposium on Electronic Commerce and Security Workshops (ISECS '10)*, pp. 172-175.

Wu, S. and Tan, C., (2009). A High Security Framework for SMS. *Proceedings of the 2nd International Conference on BioMedical Engineering and Informatics (BMEI)*. https://ieeexplore.ieee.org/document/5305796

Wyrzykowski, R., (2020). Mobile connectivity in Sub-Saharan Africa: 4G and 3G Connections Overtake 2G for the First Time. *GSMA* https://www.gsma.com/mobilefordevelopment/blog/mobile-connectivity-in-sub-saharan-africa-4g-and-3g-connections-overtake-2g-for-the-first-time/

Yadav, N., (2019). ISO 27001 vs. COBIT: A Comparison. *Advisera*. https://advisera.com/27001academy/blog/2019/05/06/cobit-vs-iso-27001-how-much-do-they-differ/

SUPERVISED LEARNING BASED APPROACH FOR TURBOFAN ENGINES FAILURE PROGNOSIS WITHIN THE BELIEF FUNCTION FRAMEWORK

Rachid Hamza and Safa Ben Ayed
CESI-LINEACT. UR7527, Arras 62000, France

ABSTRACT

Recent developments in maintenance modeling, powered by data-driven approaches such as Machine Learning (ML), have enabled a wide range of applications. For example, industrial systems coming with a huge operating database make ML an ideal candidate for their predictive maintenance (PdM). PdM is the process of predicting malfunctions using data from equipment monitoring and process performance measurements. Indeed, PdM and ML have developed a very strong connection. However, it is not always easy or straightforward to perform effective predictive maintenance for several reasons such as imperfect data. Therefore, we aim, during this paper, to manage uncertainty and/or imprecision during learning, using an evidential supervised learning approach built on a powerful framework called the belief function theory. This research work is applied on NASA's C-MAPSS dataset for turbofan engines failure prognosis.

KEYWORDS

Predictive Maintenance, Machine Learning, Belief Function Theory, Uncertainty

1. INTRODUCTION

Today, a new revolution is emerging with "The Fourth Industrial Revolution", a term also known as "Industry 4.0". It is primarily merging automation with advanced manufacturing to reduce direct human effort and resources. The diffusion of new digital technologies using connected objects, the Internet of Things, cloud, and artificial intelligence have led to the development of a new concept of maintenance known worldwide under the name intelligent predictive maintenance for Industry 4.0. Nowadays, Prognostic and Health Management (PHM) systems are some of the main protagonists of the Industry revolution. PHM is a research area with multiple methodologies and functions as a decision support tool that aims at minimizing maintenance costs and predicting when a failure could occur by the assessment, prognosis, diagnosis, and health management of engineered systems. The core of PHM is failure prognostic. It refers specifically to the phase involved with predicting future behavior and the system's useful lifetime left in terms of the current operating state and the scheduling of required maintenance actions to maintain system health. This useful lifetime is often called the remaining useful life (RUL) and is defined as the length from the current time and operating state to the end of the useful life. The notice of pending equipment failure allows for sufficient lead time so that necessary decisions, personnel, equipment, and spare parts can be organized and deployed, thus minimizing equipment downtime and repair costs. By leveraging RUL estimation, industries, such as aerospace, maritime, and energy, can improve maintenance schedules to avoid catastrophic failures and, consequently, save lives and costs. The industry has also to assure that its asset utilization is optimum by guaranteeing timely, but not premature. Furthermore, this practice promotes sustainability as the use of spare parts is optimum and no useful life is wasted. There are different recent works that have been used in literature for predictive maintenance and reliability engineering. Some of these approaches are Markov chains (Tierney, 1996), Petri nets (Chaouiya, 2007), fault tree analysis (Lee, et al., 1985), and analytic hierarchy process (Vaidya & Kumar, 2006). In addition, quantitative methods have been proposed using heuristic methods (Kleining & Witt, 2001), simulation techniques (Rivera-Gómez, et al., 2020), and analytical methods (Angius, et al., 2018). Among approaches used for PdM, machine learning-based ones are considered to be the most suitable approaches because they can handle high-dimensional problems that consist of hundreds or thousands of variables such as voltages, flows, and currents (Susto, et al., 2014). There exist two main categories of machine learning-based techniques for PdM. The first one is supervised approaches where the failure information exists in the dataset. The second one is unsupervised approaches, where there is only process information, and no failure-related information exists. KNN generally depends on unsupervised learning procedures where distances between classes in the neighborhood play an important role in PHM. However, most often, the data are imperfect and uncertain. Indeed, the source providing the information may be insecure or prone to making mistakes or giving intentionally incorrect information. To tackle this problem, there are several theories that can be used such as probability theory, fuzzy set theory (Zadeh, et al., 1996), possibility theory (Dubois & Prade, 1995), and belief function theory (Dempster, 1967; Shafer, 1976). In this paper, we will manage this uncertainty within the framework of the belief function theory, which has been applied in different fields (Ben Ayed, et al, 2022). For it, the paper is organized as follows: Section 2 gives an overview of the basic concepts regarding the belief function theory. Section 3 gives an overview of the data analysis, including the approach used in the experimental verification to analyze the residuals. Section 4 gives the experimental results on the real use case where the evidential machine learning based approach for PdM has been implemented and tested.

2. THE BELIEF FUNCTION THEORY: BASIC CONCEPTS

The belief functions theory, also known by the evidence theory or the Dempster-Shafer theory (Dempster, 1967; Shafer, 1976), is an ideal tool for modeling uncertainty and imprecision. This theory has been interpreted differently using several models such as the Transferable Belief Model (TBM) (Smets, 1998). Consider a set Ω called the frame of discernment, containing the elementary and exclusive hypotheses of a given problem. The key point of this theory is the basic belief assignment (*bba*) which is noted $m: 2^{\Omega} \rightarrow [0,1]$ as a belief function that satisfies the following normalization condition:

$$\sum_{X \subseteq \Omega} m(X) = 1$$

A bba allows for the assignment of elementary beliefs on different combinations of hypotheses. The uncertainty about a hypothesis $A \subseteq \Omega$ is modeled by the value of the bba: the higher the bba is (close to 1), the more confidence there is in A. However, if the value of bba is low (close to 0), it means that few pieces of evidence support A. The hypothesis A is called focal element if $m(A) > 0$. Other belief functions can be defined such as the *credibility function (Bel)* and the *plausibility function (Pl)*. They are defined, respectively, as follows:

$$Bel(A) = \sum_{\emptyset \neq B \subseteq A} m(B) \text{ and } Pl(A) = \sum_{A \cap B \neq \emptyset} m(B).$$

Given m_1 and m_2 deux *bbas* on Ω induced from two independent sources of information. They could be combined to yield a new bba m_{12} using, for instance, the Dempster's rule of combination which is identified by the orthogonal sum $\oplus$ and is defined such that:

$$m_{12}(\emptyset) = (m_1 \oplus m_2)(\emptyset) = 0$$

and

$$m_{12}(A) = (m1 \oplus m_2)(A) = \frac{\sum_{B,C \subseteq \Omega; B \cap C = A} m_1(B).m_2(C)}{1-\kappa} \quad with\, A \subseteq \Omega; A \neq \emptyset$$

where κ presents the conflict degree and is defined such as: $\kappa = \sum_{B \cap C = \emptyset} m_1(B).m_2(C)$

Finally, to make a decision within the belief function theory, several solutions have been proposed. For instance, the Pignistic Probability (*BetP)*, which is offered by Smet's TBM model (Smets, 1998), is considered as a powerful way for decision making. To do, the event $\omega \in \Omega$ having the highest value of BetP, according to the following equation, will be selected:

$$BetP(\omega) = \sum_{\omega \in A} \frac{m(A)}{|A|} \quad \forall \omega \in \Omega$$

3. EVIDENTIAL KNN BASED APPROACH FOR TURBOFAN ENGINES FAILURE PROGNOSIS

This section presents a case study of the proposed method using NASA's C-MAPSS dataset for engine performance degradation tracking and RUL prediction. The dataset is generated from a C-MAPSS commercial turbofan engine simulator (Dean, et al., 2012). The role of prognostics is particularly important in the context of aircraft engine health condition assessment due to the high cost associated with in-flight malfunctions, maintenance-related delays and cancellations, increased fuel consumption, and especially, potential loss of human lives. The main contribution of this work is to build a RUL prediction model using an evidential KNN. The proposed RUL prediction process is shown in Figure 1, and the procedure in each step is detailed in the following subsections.

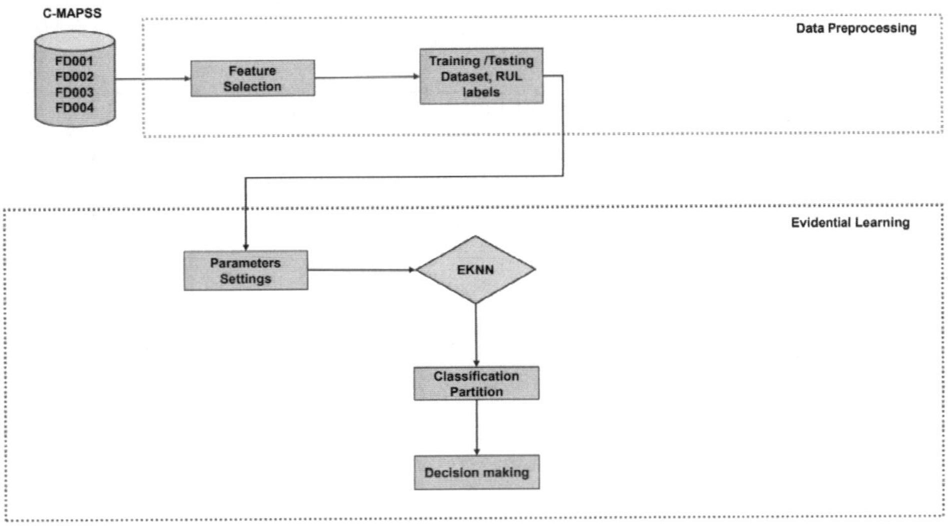

Figure 1. Flowchart of the proposed approach

3.1 Commercial Modular Areo Propulsion System

Prognostics estimates remaining useful component life. The remaining useful life estimates are in units of time. Commercial Modular Aero Propulsion System Simulation (C-MAPSS) (Abhinav, et al., 2008) datasets were generated to allow the development and benchmarking of various prognostic approaches. C-MAPSS is a tool for simulating a realistic large commercial turbofan engine. Figure 2 is a simplified diagram of the simulated turbojet engine showing the main components, such as the low-pressure compressor (LPC), the high-pressure compressor (HPC), the fan, and the combustor.

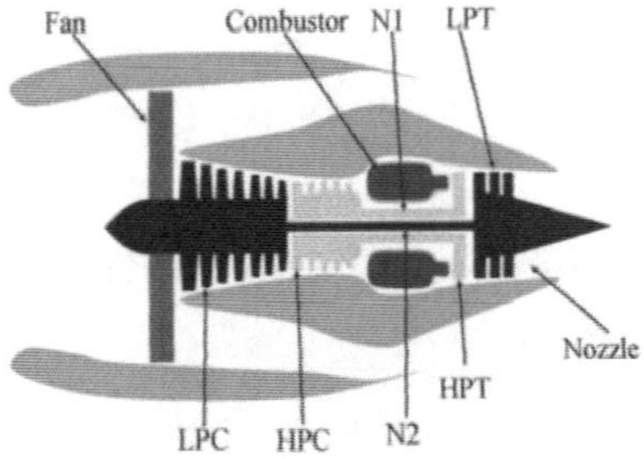

Figure 2. Simplified diagram of a simulated turbojet in C-MAPSS

The C-MAPSS datasets pose several challenges, in particular, management of high variability due to sensor noise, effects of operating conditions, and presence of multiple simultaneous fault modes are some factors that have a great impact on the generalization capabilities of prognostics algorithms. Four datasets have been generated which are called turbofan datasets and consist of training and test data. A learning instance represents the degradation of a turbojet engine seen by 21 sensors. At each operational cycle of an engine, one observation is logged in the form of a multivariate observation comprising the measurements of 21 sensors, three operational parameters, a timer feature, and the engine ID. The C-MAPSS data have been split into four sub-datasets (FD001, FD002, FD003, FD004). Each dataset can operate under different operating conditions and the system failure can be caused by two components: the turbine and the compressor. Thus, FD001 and FD003 operate under the same conditions although FD003 includes engines whose failure could be caused by either of the two mentioned components. Then, FD002 operates under 6 operating conditions as does FD004, while in FD004, as in FD003, the failure conditions cover both turbine and compressor failure as shown in Table 1.

Table 1. Information on the C-MAPSS dataset

Sub-Dataset names	**FD001**	**FD002**	**FD003**	**FD004**
Turbofan for train	100	260	100	249
Fault Modes	HPC	HPC	HPC, and Fan	HPC, and Fan
Operating condition	1	6	1	6

3.2 Data Pre-Processing

Pre-processing data is intended to transform the raw data into a format that is easier and more effective to use for future processing steps. For each subset, the 21 sensors record different data, and the data range between different sensors varies significantly. Feature Selection (FS) is the process of reducing the number of input variables when developing a predictive model, this step aims to select the best feature in the data set. FS helps understand the data, reduces computing needs, and improves performance. In fact, from analyzing the statistical properties of each feature, it was observed that not all sensor measurements provide useful information for RUL prediction. For example, the standard deviation of sensors 1, 5, 6, 10, 16, 18, and 19 is statistically insignificant in FD001, therefore, the variables will be excluded from the rest of the study. In addition, unprocessed data affected the performance of predicting the engine RUL, so it is essential to standardize the data. Data normalization is an essential step in data pre-processing. Normalization can improve the training time because all data used in training have the same scale, in the range of 0 and 1. For this purpose, the following formula is implemented, where X_{max} andX_{min} represent, respectively, the maximum and the minimum and values of each feature:

$$X_{\text{norm}} = \frac{X - X_{\min}}{X_{\max} - X_{\min}}$$

Before proceeding with a complicated task such as RUL estimation, a simpler task such as turbojet health classification can show the complexity of the problem. The first and last 50 cycles of each unit are considered healthy and faulty respectively. We have chosen to delimit the classes by 50 cycles to have balanced data between the three classes.

3.3 Evidential Learning on the C-MAPSS Dataset

In order to manage uncertainty during the supervised learning step of our proposal, we perform the Evidential k-Nearest Neighbor (EK-NN) (Denoeux, 1995) that is a pattern classification method based on the belief function theory. Contrary to the hard KNN classification method, EK-NN offers, as output, a credal classification of data instances, which presents a richer information content. According to EK-NN method, the frame of discernment Ω contains the set of N possible classes. In the frame of C-MAPSS dataset classification, we define Ω as the set containing three classes such as: $\Omega = \{C1, C2, C3\}$, with $C1, C2, C3$ referring, respectively, to "Normal", "Moderate degradation", "Near-to-failure degradation". The first and last 50 cycles of each unit are considered as a criterion for determining the engine's Near-to-failure degradation and Normal status, respectively.

Let X_i be the set of all the n objects within the C-MAPSS dataset, defined as $X_i = \{X_1, X_2, \ldots, X_n\}$, and X is a new object to be classified. Classifying X means assigning it to one class in Ω which is done through handling pieces of evidence to manage uncertainty regarding that assignment. We note, also, $N_K(X)$ as the ensemble of the K-Nearest Neighbors of X.

3.3.1 The EK-NN Method

Based on the selected training set of C-MAPSS dataset, the evidential k-NN method classifies every new instance X that should be assigned to one class of the selected neighbors modeled by $N_K(X)$. However, EK-NN models the knowledge regarding the assignment of each neighbor X_j to its class $C_q \in \Omega$ through a piece of evidence. For this reason, the cardinality of $N_K(X)$ identifies the number of bba functions to be handled, where each function supports a number of hypotheses towards the class of the object X to be classified. These pieces of evidence are built in function to the distance between X and every neighbor X_j (e.g., the euclidean distance). For every $X_j \in N_K(X)$, the knowledge that $L_j = C_q$ is seen as a piece of evidence that boosts our belief regarding the assigning of X to C_q. Since we cannot be totally certain towards this piece of evidence, the Dempster-Shafer formalism allows to model it by saying that only some part of our belief is committed to C_q. To do, EK-NN uses a function, called the simple support function, where the bba has only one focal element aside the frame of discernment Ω. It is, therefore, defined as follows:

$$m_{X,X_j}(\{C_q\}) = \alpha$$

$$m_{X,X_j}(\{\Omega\}) = 1 - \alpha$$

$$m_{X,X_j}(\{C\}) = 0 \qquad \forall C \in 2^{\Omega}\{\Omega, C_q\}$$

where α is defined in what follows in function to the euclidean distance between X and its neighbor X_j denoted by $d(X, X_j)$, a constant α_0 fixed to 0.95, and a positive parameter γ_q assigned to each class C_q:

$$\alpha = \alpha_0 exp^{-(\gamma_q^2 \, \mathrm{d(X,Xj)}^2)}$$

Once the K different bbas are generated by the EK-NN, they will be combined using the Dempster's rule of combination such that:

$$m_X = m_{X,X_1} \oplus m_{X,X_2} \oplus \ldots \oplus m_{X,X_K}$$

3.3.2 The Credal Classification Partition and Decision Making

As a result of its strategy, EK-NN provides a credal classification partition that allows each object to be assigned, with a degree of belief, not only to all the classes but also to the total ignorance defined by Ω. In our context, this classification partition M presents an $n \times 4$ matrix; The rows of M are the instances in the C-MAPSS dataset and the columns refer respectively to $m_{X_j}(C1)$, $m_{X_j}(C2)$, $m_{X_j}(C3)$, and $m_{X_j}(\Omega)$, which makes the sum of all the columns' values, in every row, is equal to 1. To make decisions regarding the class of each object, we need to move on from the credal level to the pignistic level. To do so, the aforementioned pignistic probability method has been used.

4. EXPERIMENTAL ANALYSIS

In this article, the experiments are carried out on C-MAPSS data, which are assumed to be uncertain and imperfect. Classic RUL predictions do not take into account the uncertainty of the data, therefore the aim of this experimentation is to use evidential KNN to predict RUL and compare the performance with the existing machine learning models in the literature. For each prediction model, we obtain results from the RULs that we will compare to know the best model.

The evclass package in the R environment currently contains functions for the evidential K-nearest neighbor (EK-NN) rule (Denoeux, 1995; Zouhal, & Denoeux, 1998]). In contrast with classical statistical classifiers, evidential classifiers quantify the uncertainty of the classification using Dempster-Shafer mass functions. The main functions are *EkNNinit*, *EkNNfit*, and *EkNNval* for the initialization, training, and evaluation of the EK-NN classifier.

4.1 Parameters' Setting

The principle of the evidential K-nearest neighbor (EK-NN) classifier is explained in Section 3.3.1, and the optimization of the parameters of this model is presented in (Zouhal & Denoeux, 1998). Here, we focus on the practical application of this method using the functions implemented in *evclass* (Denoeux, 2017). The EK-NN classifier is implemented through three functions: *EkNNinit* for initialization, *EkNNfit* for training, and *EkNNval* for testing. Let us initialize the classifier with $K = 45$ neighbors. EkNNval classified instances in a test set using the EV-KNN classifier. EkNNval is used in the following form:

$$\text{EkNNval (xtrain, ytrain, } x \text{ tst , } K, ytst = y \text{ test, param } = EkNNfit)$$

The used parameters are:

- *Xtrain*: Matrix of size $ntrain \times d$, containing the values of the *d* attributes for the training data.
- *Ytrain*: Vector of class labels for the training data.
- *Xtst*: Matrix of size $ntst \times d$ x d, containing the values of the *d* attributes for the test data.
- *K*: Number of neighbors.
- *Ytest*: Vector of class labels for the test data.
- *Param*: Parameters, as returned by EkNNfit.

4.2 Evaluation Criteria

In this study, precision, recall, and F1 are used to evaluate the performance of the proposed model of RUL estimation. The confusion matrix is a cross table between the actual values and the predictions. Precision is the accuracy of positive predictions calculated by:

$$\text{Precision} = \frac{\text{TP}}{\text{TP} + \text{FP}}$$

where TP is True Positives and FP is False Positives.

Recall is the fraction of correctly identified positives calculated by:

$$\text{Recall} = \frac{\text{TP}}{\text{TP} + \text{FN}}$$

where FN is False Negatives.

F1 Score is a metric for comparing two classifiers. It is obtained by finding the harmonic mean of precision

$$\text{F1} = 2 * \frac{\text{Precision} * \text{Recall}}{\text{Precision} + \text{Recall}}$$

and recall.

The support is the number of occurrences of each class.

The confusion matrix for the dataset FD001 indicates that 299 instances of class *Near-to-failure degradation* status were correctly predicted on the support of 998, 206 were wrongly predicted as Moderate degradation status, while the class Normal turbofan engine has only 89 wrongly classified instances on the support of 1011. This appears reasonable considering the difference in the number of instances. It is expected that the classifier mistakes class Moderate degradation status for class *Near-to-failure degradation status* as the environmental measurements or both classes do not differ significantly.

4.3 Results and Discussion

Overall, the models achieved accurate results for the prediction of the RUL of aircraft engines in the testing set. Based on the three evaluation criteria, Tables 2, 3, 4 and 5 present the performance of the trained models on the testing set for the four aforementioned datasets.

Table 2. Obtained results in terms of Precision, Recall, F1, and Support for FD001

Average	**Precision**	**Recall**	**F1**	**Support**
KNN	0.70458	0.7	0.7022	4 127
EV-KNN	**0.70471**	0.7	0.**7031**	4 127

Table 3. Obtained results in terms of Precision, Recall, F1, and Support for FD003

Average	**Precision**	**Recall**	**F1**	**Support**
KNN	0.74406	**0.73**	0.**7369**	4 944
EV-KNN	**0.74459**	0.71	0.7268	4 944

Tables 2 and 3 show the classification results of KNN and EV-KNN, when applied on the FD001 and FD003 datasets. The number of predicted instances is 4127 and 4944, respectively. In addition, we note that results are somehow competitive, with some benefits offered by EV-KNN. For instance, the EV-KNN classifies positive classes more accurately with a precision of 0.7047 for FD001 and 0.74459 for FD003, while KNN follows closely but achieves higher recall and F1 score on FD003.

Table 4. Obtained results in terms of Precision, Recall, F1, and Support for FD002

Average	**Precision**	**Recall**	**F1**	**Support**
KNN	**0.70710**	0.7	0.7034	10 752
EV-KNN	0.70705	0.7	**0.7035**	10 752

Table 5. Obtained results in terms of Precision, Recall, F1, and Support for FD004

Average	**Precision**	**Recall**	**F1**	**Support**
KNN	**0.73506**	0.69	0.7118	12 250
EV-KNN	0.73497	**0.7**	**0.7146**	12 250

As mentioned in Tables 4 and 5, EV-KNN and KNN are applied to FD002 and FD004, which contain a higher number of observations. The number of predicted instances is 10752 for FD002 and 12 250 for FD004, which provides more instances to accurately evaluate the results. We observe that in a different operation condition than in FD001 and FD003, the EV-KNN did not manage to achieve higher precision values than KNN. This might be due to the more complex behavior of the sensor measurements.

Finally, we remark that results show that the evidential based predictions can provide better performance in predicting the RUL. It has a slightly better performance compared to the hard KNN. However, the precision does not significantly outperform the KNN model. The evidential approach showed higher performance on smaller datasets such as FD001 and FD003, whereas on FD002 and FD004, the task is more complex, and the prediction is affected by the dataset type. In all predictions, the performance of the models on FD003 outperforms their performance on the rest of the datasets.

5. CONCLUSION

This article has implemented a supervised learning-based approach for turbofan engines failure prognosis and described how to manage the uncertainty within this data to develop and test prognostic algorithms. An aerodynamic propulsion system simulator, C-MAPSS, was used in this study. With the assumption that the data are uncertain and imperfect, the use of the evidential KNN model seems more effective than the hard KNN model according to the carried out experiments. The evidential technique has the potential to deal with complex sensor readings, and therefore avoid poor decision-making, which can lead to devastating consequences. However, the prediction aspect requires improvement and careful feature engineering by looking at similarities across similar units and identifying faulty sensor readings. In future studies, the predictive models should be improved by investigating more complex machine learning techniques merged with evidential theories, on larger datasets of different aerospace engine reading scenarios.

REFERENCES

Abhinav, S., Member IEEE, Kai, G., Do, S., Member, IEEE, Neil. E, Member IEEE, (2008). Damage Propagation Modeling for Aircraft Engine Run-to-Failure Simulation.

Angius, A., Colledani, M., & Yemane, A. (2018). Impact of condition based maintenance policies on the service level of multi-stage manufacturing systems. Control. Eng. Pract.76, 65–78.

Ben Ayed, S., Elouedi, Z., & Lefevre, E. (2022). CIMMEP: constrained integrated method for CBR maintenance based on evidential policies. *Applied Intelligence*, *52*(6), 6939-6954.

Chaouiya, C. (2007). Petri net modelling of biological networks. Briefings in bioinformatics, 8(4), 210-219.

Dean, K. F., Jonathan, A. D., & Jonathan, S. L. (2012). User's guide for the commercial modular aero-propulsion system simulation (C-MAPSS). Tech. rep.

Dempster, A. P. (1967) Upper and lower probabilities induced by a multivalued mapping. The annals of mathematical statistics, 325-339.

Denoeux, T. (1995). K-nearest neighbor classification rule based on Dempster-Shafer theory. IEEE Trans. Syst. Man Cybern. 25(5), 804–813.

Denoeux, T. (2017). Evidential Distance-Based Classification.

Dubois, D., & Prade, H. (1995). Possibility theory as a basis for qualitative decision theory. In IJCAI (Vol. 95), 1924-1930.

Kleining, G., & Witt, H. (2001). Discovery as basic methodology of qualitative and quantitative research. In Forum Qualitative Sozialforschung/Forum: Qualitative Social Research (Vol. 2, No. 1).

Lee, W. S., Grosh, D. L., Tillman, F. A., & Lie, C. H. (1985). Fault tree analysis, methods, and applications: a review. IEEE transactions on reliability, 34(3), 194-203.

Rivera-Gómez, H., Gharbi, A., KennÉ, J.P., & Montaño-Arango, O. Corona-Armenta, J.R. Joint optimization of production and maintenance strategies considering a dynamic sampling strategy for a deteriorating system. Comput. Ind. Eng. 2020, 140, 106273.

Shafer, G. (1976). A mathematical theory of evidence. Vol. 1. Princeton: Princeton university press.

Smets, P. (1998). The transferable belief model for quantified belief representation. In Quantified Representation of Uncertainty and Imprecision, 267-301. Springer, Dordrecht.

Susto, G. A., Schirru, A., Pampuri, S., McLoone, S., & Beghi, A. (2014). Machine learning for predictive maintenance: A multiple classifier approach. IEEE Trans. Ind. Inform., 11, 812–820.

Tierney, L. (1996). Introduction to general state-space Markov chain theory. Markov chain Monte Carlo in practice, 59-74.

Vaidya, O. S., & Kumar, S. (2006). Analytic hierarchy process: An overview of applications. European Journal of operational research, 169(1), 1-29.

Zadeh, L. A., Klir, G. J., & Yuan, B. (1996). Fuzzy sets, fuzzy logic, and fuzzy systems: selected papers (Vol. 6). World Scientific.

Zouhal, L. M., & Denoeux, T. (1998). An evidence-theoretic k-NN rule with parameter optimization. IEEE Transactions on Systems, Man, and Cybernetics, Part C (Applications and Reviews), 28(2), 263-271.

SUNSPOT DETECTION AND TRACKING USING IMAGE PROCESSING TECHNIQUES

Ruben Du Toit, Günther Richard Drevin and Roelf Du Toit Strauss
North-West University, Potchefstroom, South Africa

ABSTRACT

Space weather forecasting has become increasingly important over the past five decades as we have become more dependent on technology. Systems such as wireless communication, railway signaling, high voltage power grids and satellites can all be interrupted by solar activity events.
The detection and tracking of sunspots as well as the prediction of solar eruptions forms a part of the attempt to predict space weather. To make predictions regarding the behaviour of a sunspot it is necessary to track and monitor its evolution over time.
In this paper the use of Image Processing techniques to detect and track sunspots will be investigated.

KEYWORDS

Sunspots, Solar Activity, Detection, Tracking, Space Weather

1. INTRODUCTION

Sunspots are dark areas located on the outermost layer of the Sun that emits the light we see from Earth (Curto et al., 2008). By studying the morphology of sunspots, it may be possible to forecast space weather events. Since the temperature of a sunspot is lower than the area surrounding the sunspot, it appears darker and therefore becomes visible. Small dark spots, called pores, form on the photosphere and either decay early in their lifecycle or develop into sunspots. As sunspots start to enlarge, small portions tend to break away from the original sunspot. When a sunspot becomes large enough it forms a double-ended group with opposite magnetic polarities on either side (Curto et al., 2008).

Areas where sunspots are located on are known as active regions, which often lead to solar flares and coronal mass ejections (CMEs). When significant changes at the photospere of the Sun occur, it implies that the overlying magnetic field that is undergoing rearrangement must be strong. This is presumably in the low corona and the energy transported by magnetic disturbances propagating through the chromosphere to the photosphere may be an important component in the flare chromosphere energization (Fletcher et al., 2011) Solar flares occur after the magnetic field topology is rearranged and the magnetic field lines start reconnecting, resulting in solar flares (Guarcello et al., 2019). When these flares occur, large amounts of energy that was stored in the magnetic field is released. These energies are deposited both locally at the point of reconnection and onto the underlying dense chromosphere at the loop footprints of the field lines that the electron beams move along. Solar flares are often followed by another solar event known as a CME. When solar flares occur at active regions, forms of radiation, such as X-rays and radio waves take about eight minutes to reach the Earth from the Sun. Stray X-rays can disrupt the ionosphere enough to disrupt radio communications. They are not usually dangerous to the Earth, rather they act as indicators of potential coronal mass ejections (Guarcello et al., 2019).

Coronal mass ejections are large eruptions of magnetic fields and plasma that are launched into the helio- sphere. These eruptions carry energized electrons which produce various sources of high-intensity plasma emissions (Carley et al., 2017). These storms can affect and damage not only satellites that provide wireless communication from space, but also ground based systems, such as railway signalling, high voltage power transmission grids and telecommunications cables (Colak and Qahwaji, 2007). These CMEs can take a few hours to a few days to reach the Earth (Colak and Qahwaji, 2007).

Communication and power systems are critical for modern society to function optimally. However, these systems are often interrupted by natural events, which are beyond the control of humankind (Colak and Qahwaji, 2007). An example of these natural events is solar activity. Space weather research has taken a major role in the prediction of solar activity, especially since these events are the cause of the interruptions of wireless communications systems, railway signalling, high voltage power transmission grids, telecommunications cables and satellites (Colak and Qahwaji, 2007). Space weather refers to the time-variable conditions in the space environment that could in the worst-case scenario, endanger human life or health by affecting ground-based or space-borne technological systems, according to Koskinen et al. (2001). Being aware of and possibly avoiding the consequences of space weather events are the most important social and economic aspects of space weather. This can be done by efficient warning and detection systems that allow for preventive measures to be taken (Koskinen et al., 2001). Several attempts at systems that can detect sunspots exist (Colak and Qahwaji, 2007). In this section, the background on important concepts and existing systems will be discussed to give insight into this study.

The primary aim of this study is to develop and test various image processing techniques for the detection and tracking of sunspots. The algorithms will be implemented in the programming language Python. Due to the slow rate which sunspots change and move, accuracy in each algorithm is the primary aim instead of how fast it can be executed.

This paper is based on the Master's dissertation of the first author (Du Toit, 2022).

Previous work done on the detection and tracking of sunspots include a system that uses automated detection, characterization and tracking of sunspots on continuum images done in a study by Goel and Mathew (2014). A second approach is an automated sunspot detection using morphological reconstruction and adaptive region growing techniques done by Yu et al. (2014). The last is a system that automatically detect sunspot activities using an advanced detection mode done by Manish et al. (2014). Most previous work made use of different data sets (time intervals) and mainly focussed on determining the number of sunspots on each image, comparing this with available sunspot numbers.

In this paper however, the first aim will be to identify the sunspots and verify the results visually. The main aim of the paper is the tracking of sunspots over a number of days. Once a given sunspot can be tracked its evolution over time can also be studied.

The different methods investigated will be discussed in Section 2 and the results obtained with these methods will be elaborated on in Section 3. Finally conclusions and further work will be discussed in Section 4.

2. METHOD

The data set that was used consists of 20 different dates of images in 4096x4096 resolution with some taken on the same day, but a few hours apart. Four images were taken in 2011, three images in 2012, six images in 2013, six images in 2014 and one image in 2015 that was used for implementing the algorithms on. The data set was downloaded from the National Aeronautics and Space Administration (NASA) website[1].

For the purpose of identifying sunspots, three object detection methods: Canny edge detection; template matching; and watershed segmentation were implemented and tested using images of the Sun. Finally, a novel object tracking algorithm for tracking sunspots was developed and tested on the same images.

2.1 Canny Edge Detection

A high-level overview of the steps for identifying sunspots by using the Canny algorithm is:

1. Identification of the sunspots by using the Canny algorithm of the OpenCV library to detect all the edges of sunspots on the images;
2. The merging of all the bounding boxes that were created from the detected edges. All the bounding boxes are tested to see if they are within a certain distance of pixels of each other. If the boxes are within the distance, a new large single bounding box is created that replaces all the small boxes.

[1] SDO — Solar Dynamics Observatory. https://sdo.gsfc.nasa.gov/

The new bounding box is created with the smallest top left coordinates and the largest bottom right coordinates. The top right corner is the ending x-coordinate and the starting y-coordinate. The bottom left corner is the starting x-coordinate but with the ending y-coordinate and the bottom right corner is the ending x and y-coordinate. By adding and comparing all the small boxes coordinates, the extreme coordinates for the corners are acquired and used for the new box; and

3. At this stage, the bounding boxes are not yet drawn on the continuum image, and the process to merge the small boxes is repeated until there are no more small boxes close enough for merging into the new larger boxes. Then the final boxes are drawn from the new larger boxes. All the boxes are then drawn onto the continuum image and the resulting image is then saved.

The process of the Canny edge detection method is illustrated in Figure 1 and the result of the method is shown in Figure 2.

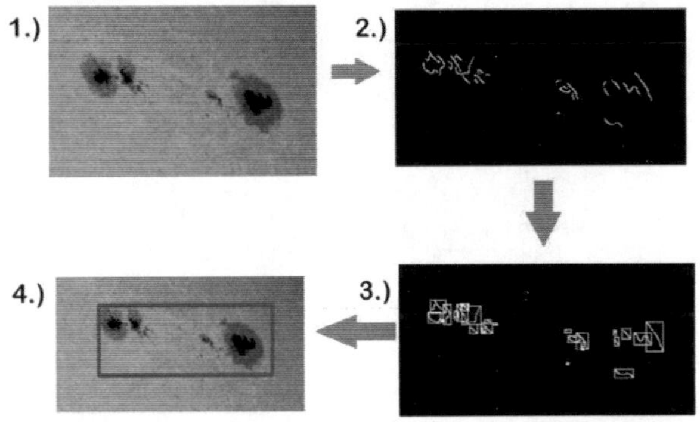

Figure 1. The process of the Canny algorithm

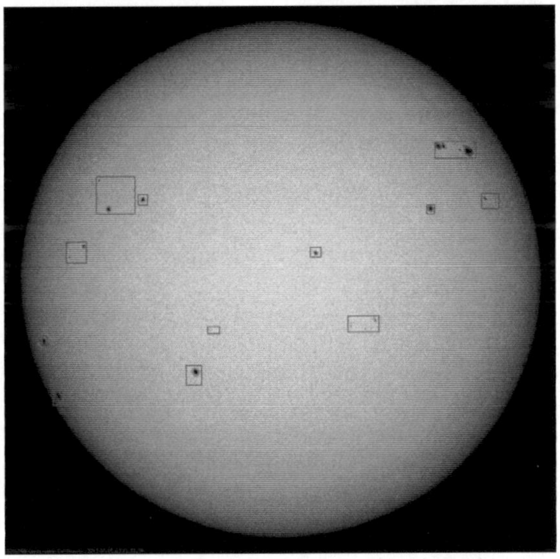

Figure 2. The result of the Canny method

2.2 Template Matching

An overview of the steps for identifying sunspots by using template matching is:

1. Identification of the sunspots by using the template matching algorithm of the OpenCV library to detect all the objects that resemble the templates of sunspots, on the images;

2. The same process to merge the boxes that were used for the Canny algorithm is also used here. The bounding boxes that will be merged were created from the resembling templates of sunspots that were detected; and

3. The bounding boxes are not yet drawn on the continuum image and step two is repeated until there are no more small boxes in merging distance, at which point the coordinates of the new larger boxes are also put through step two to get the final bounding boxes. All these boxes are then drawn on the image, which is subsequently stored to the file system.

A number of sunspots were extracted from images and used as templates for the template matching algorithm. These templates are shown in Figure 3.

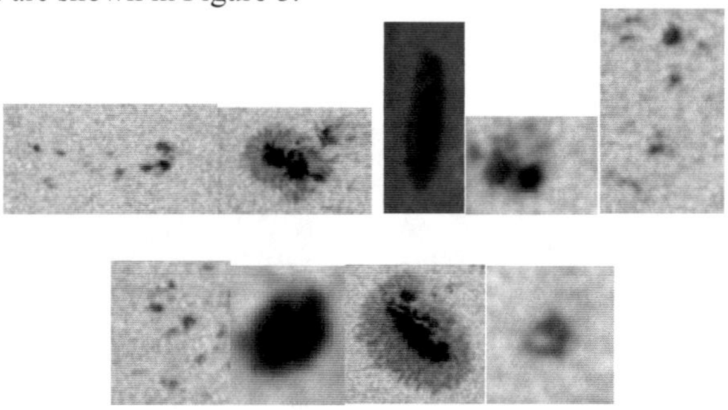

Figure 3. Templates used for template matching

2.3 Watershed

An overview of the steps for identifying sunspots by using watershed is:

1. The watershed algorithm uses the same implementation of the Canny algorithm for identifying sunspots;
2. The same merging that was done for both Canny and template matching is reused in the watershed algorithm;
3. Once the merging is done and the results of the Canny have been drawn on the image, the bounding boxes that were drawn are then extracted for watershed;
4. A default image of 2019-10-15 at 00:29 UT that contains no sunspots is subtracted from the extracted images. First, the same area of an extracted image is extracted from the default image and both are then blurred with a median blur. Both of the two extracted areas are subtracted and the result is saved. This is done for every extracted sunspot;
5. The subtracted image is then converted to binary with two different thresholds. The first threshold converts everything to white except that which is below the threshold; that is converted to black which is the umbra. The same principle is applied for identifying the penumbra where a threshold is applied to convert the penumbra area to black and the background to white; and
6. The subtracted penumbra and umbra images are then applied with the watershed algorithm. The penumbra is drawn with a red outline and the umbra with a green outline. The results of both images are then written on the original extracted image as well as on the original image. An extraction showing the process on a single sunspot and is shown in Figure 4.

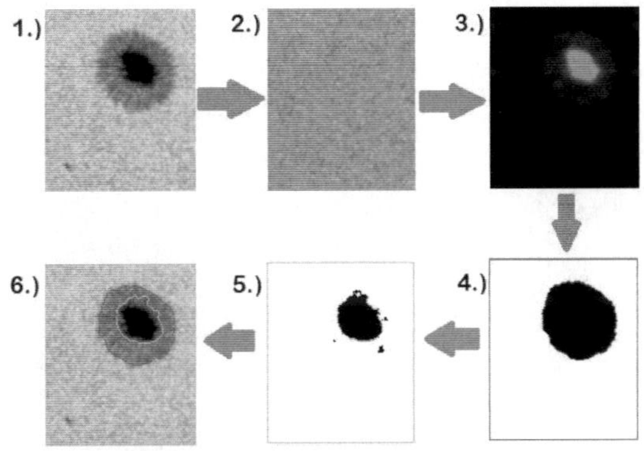

Figure 4. The result of watershed segmentation on a solar image

2.4 Algorithm for Tracking Sunspots

An overview of the steps for tracking sunspots is:

1. A starting image of the Sun is provided and sunspots are identified and bounding boxes are drawn using the steps discussed above;
2. The watershed algorithm is based on the results from the Canny algorithm that was implemented in the previous step. Thus, it uses the same implementation of the Canny algorithm for identifying the sunspots and merging the bounding boxes;
3. Assign an identification number to each of the bounding boxes;
4. Identify the sunspots on a second image, which will be used to compare to the starting image;
5. Calculate the time difference between images;
6. Determine the expected position of each of the sunspots identified on the starting image using the time elapsed multiplied by a predetermined coefficient. The coefficient is determined based on the range of the bounding box the starting x-coordinate is in.
7. Using this estimated position and a variance calculated using the time elapsed, find bounding boxes on the second image that are within range of estimated position +- variance.
8. The final step is to test if there are any bounding boxes close to the calculated distance from the starting image on the ending image. Depending on the time difference, the variance is also calculated to be larger for large time differences and the variance is less for smaller time differences between the images.

The process of tracking is illustrated in Figure 5 below. The starting image as well as the final image, 93 hours later, both show the sunspot group.

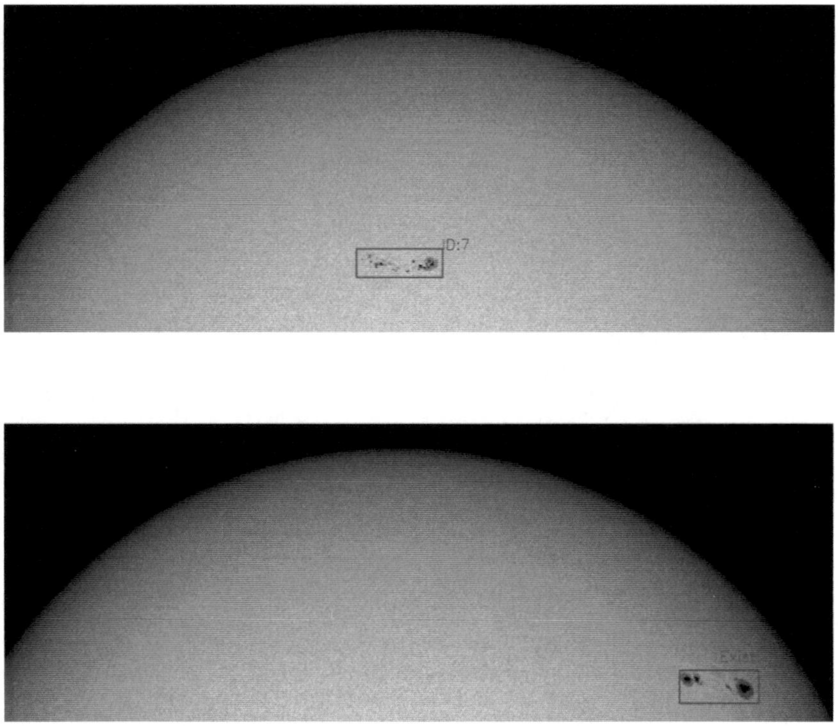

Figure 5. The result of the tracking algorithm. The top image that is the starting image for tracking with the date of 2013-01-01 starting at 06:00 UT. The bottom image is on 2013-01-05 at 03:00 UT in the morning. The bottom image is the result of tracking predicted at 93 hours later

3. RESULTS

The algorithms presented were tested on a number of solar images. These results of these tests will now be discussed.

Previous work done on sunspot detection was to produce a count of the number of sunspots on a given image. Furthermore, different time periods are used in different studies making it difficult to compare results with other studies. Also, the main aim of this study is the tracking of sunspots over a number of days. To be able to do this the sunspots first need to be identified and the success of these processes are therefore confirmed by visually comparing results with the images.

3.1 Canny Edge Detection

The results from the Canny algorithm proved to be accurate, in terms of detecting almost every sunspot as well as detecting a lot of pores on the Sun. A sunspot is counted when it has a clear penumbra as well as umbra area and a pore is classified as only small dark spots. When tested with an image that contains no sunspots, this algorithm does not detect any false positives on the image. From all the test images, 146 out of 153 sunspots were detected resulting in an error percentage of 5%. In only one case a false positive was detected and the sunspots that were missed were all on the edge of the Sun. The Canny method can be described as effective and accurate in detecting sunspots away from the limb.

3.2 Template Matching

The results from the template matching algorithm proved to be accurate, in terms of detecting almost every sunspot as well as detecting a lot of pores on the. A sunspot is counted when it has a clear penumbra as well as umbra area and pores are classified as small dark spots. Although, when tested with an image that contains no sunspots, this algorithm detects false positives that are not desired.

From all the test images, 144 out of 153 sunspots were detected resulting in an error percentage of 6%. In seven cases a false positive was detected and the sunspots that were missed were all on the edge of the Sun. The template matching method can be described as effective and accurate, but less accurate than the Canny method in detecting sunspots. The method was less sensitive in picking up small pores.

3.3 Watershed

For the purpose of being implemented on sunspots, the watershed algorithm was both sufficient and efficient. Additionally, it would be beneficial that more pores also be detected. This can be done by adjusting the threshold, but it was currently implemented in detecting the main focus of the images, which was the sunspots. The aim for this algorithm was satisfied with the results that were achieved.

3.4 Tracking

The tracking algorithm's results are given in Figures 5 and 6. It can be derived from the results below that the prediction of where the sunspots will be in the next image is highly accurate. It is important to note that this algorithm is based on the Canny algorithm's bounding boxes. Thus, if a sunspot is on the starting image but is not detected, and it is detected on the next image, it will be added as a new sunspot. Canny was chosen over template matching since it proved to more accurate and more stable in detecting true positives and not false positives such as template matching.

The only complex areas in this algorithm would be that if two sunspots are included in a single bounding box and in the next image the bounding box is split into two separate bounding boxes with the new box having a higher y-axis than predicted for. A close-up result of the algorithm's result is shown in Figure 2. An example of a single bounding box on the original image that is split into two bounding boxes on the next image, shows how the algorithm identifies both boxes with the same identification in Figure 6.

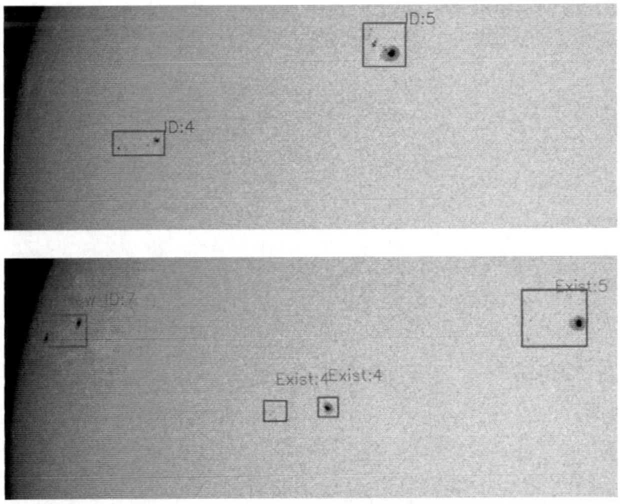

Figure 6. The result of the tracking algorithm where a bounding box is split into two boxes. The top image that is the starting image for tracking with the date of 2013-01-01 starting at 06:00 UT. The bottom image is on the 2013-01-02 at 21:00 UT in the evening. The bottom image is the result of tracking predicted at 39 hours later

4. CONCLUSIONS AND FUTURE WORK

The Canny algorithm proved to be the most accurate between it and template matching. Although, template matching drew the bounding boxes on separate sunspots where the Canny sometimes included both sunspots. The Canny algorithm also detected more pores than template matching making it much more sensitive to detecting not only the desired sunspots. When compared to using an image that contains no sunspots, the Canny method does not detect any false positives, whereas template matching detects false positives. The watershed algorithm performed efficient on large sunspots areas and the distinguishing between the umbra and penumbra was also efficient on the larger sunspots. Although, for better results between distinguishing the umbra and penumbra, pores and very small decaying sunspots that only has an umbra were not detected.

Tracking between a starting image and any following image also proved to be very accurate in predicting the position of the sunspots.

Future work that can be derived from this study includes:

1. The comparison against the accuracy for machine learning techniques in terms of identifying sunspots.
2. Investigation into algorithms that could help the prediction of CMEs could be incorporated or based on the results of this study.

REFERENCES

Colak, T. and Qahwaji, R., (2007). Automatic Sunspot Classification for Real-Time Forecasting of Solar Activities. *3rd International Conference on Recent Advances in Space Technologies*, Istanbul, Turkey, pp. 733– 738.

Curto, J. et al, (2008). Automatic Sunspots Detection on Full-Disk Solar Images using Mathematical Morphology. *Solar Physics*, Vol. 250, No. 2, pp 411–429.

Du Toit, R. (2022). Sunspot detection and tracking using image processing techniques. Master's thesis, North-West University, South Africa.

Fletcher, L. et al, (2011). An Observational Overview of Solar Flares. *Space Science Reviews*, Vol. 159, No. 1-4, pp 19–106.

Goel, S. and Mathew, S. K., (2014). Automated Detection, Characterization, and Tracking of Sunspots from SoHO/MDI Continuum Images. *Solar Physics*, Vol. 289, No. 4, pp 1413–1431.

Guarcello, M. G. et al, (2019). Simultaneous Kepler/K2 and XMM-Newton Observations of Superflares in the Pleiades. *Astronomy & Astrophysics*, Vol 622:A210.

Koskinen, H. et al, (2001). Space Weather Effects Catalogue. *ESA Space Weather Study (ESWS)*, Issue 2.2.

Manish, Tet al, (2014). Automatic Detection of Sunspot Activities using Advanced Detection Model. *IOSRJournal of Computer Engineering*, Vol. 16, No. 2, pp. 2278–8727.

Yu, L et al, (2014). Automated Sunspot Detection using Morphological Reconstruction and Adaptive Region Growing Techniques. *Proceedings of the 33rd Chinese Control Conference*, Nanjing, China, pp. 7168–7172.

HIDROUFF DENSITY CALCULATOR: AN OPEN-SOURCE SOFTWARE FOR PREDICTING DENSITY OF COMPLEX MIXTURES USING PENG-ROBINSON EQUATION OF STATE (PREOS)

Valesca Moura de Sousa[1], Felipe Pereira de Moura[2], Mateus Pereira de Sousa[3], Rogério Fernandes Lacerda[3] and Fernanda G. O. Passos[4]
[1]Institute of Computing, Universidade Federal Fluminense (UFF), Niterói, Brazil
[2]Institute of Chemistry, Universidade Federal Fluminense (UFF),Niterói, Brazil
[3]Engineering School, Universidade Federal Fluminense (UFF),Niterói, Brazil
[4]Engineering School, UFF, Niterói, Brazil / Atlântica - University Institution, Oeiras, Portugal

ABSTRACT

Commercial softwares dedicated to providing thermodynamic properties of complex mixtures in general have high-cost licenses and high computational cost, which makes its use limited for undergraduate students in remote classes or research tasks. Therefore, an open-source software was developed in Python, called HidroUFF Density Calculator, that is dedicated to predicting the density of complex mixtures using Peng-Robinson Equation of State (PREOS) as a resolution mechanism. Density was chosen for being one of the most requested thermodynamic properties. The proposed software was compared to a benchmark (UniSim Design), and its results were exactly equal or distant in less than 0.32%.

KEYWORDS

Density Calculator, Peng-Robinson Equation of State, PREOS, Thermodynamics Properties, Open Source Software

1. INTRODUCTION

The density of a fluid is a primary physical property for a wide range of engineering projects and studies. With this parameter, it is possible to obtain the volume that a fluid occupies, the weight contained in tanks, the pump sizing required, and the type of flow (Loria et al., 2009). In International System of units (SI), density is expressed in kg/m³, usually, in the oil and gas industry, the API (American Petroleum Institute) degree (API) is used, which expresses the specific gravity of the oil from the ratio between its density and the density of water, both at 60°F (American Society for testing and Materials, 2019).

For many real cases in engineering, mainly in offshore petroleum engineering, it is difficult and expensive to determine the density of certain fluids in their ambient conditions. Mainly due to the high pressure at which fluids are submitted, reaching over 200 atm. Therefore, several works in the literature have been dedicated to studying the *equations of state* for real fluids, which consider the interaction (pairwise, in a matrix calculation) between all the components of the mixture, and the compressibility factor Z (Borges, 2009). Among the main authors of versions for the *equations of state* for real fluids, we highlight Van der Waals with his proposition that starts the theme (1873), Redlich-Kwong (1949), Modification of Soave in Redlich-Kwong (1972) and Peng-Robinson (1976), widely used for hydrocarbons.

Solving these equations is not simple. Any modification in the working condition requires the observation of parameters tabulated in handbooks, matrix calculation between the n components of the mixture, calculations of accessory terms and, finally, the solution of a cubic equation. Currently, several commercial software dedicated to engineering already provide calculations for determination of specific mass and other more complex thermodynamic properties.

UniSim Design is a commercial-licensed software developed by Honeywell corporation which calculates physical, transport, separation, and reaction kinetics properties (Honeywell, 2018). However, the use of these commercial software is difficult for students, universities, and small companies due to the high price for acquiring these software licenses. This difficulty affects the teaching-learning relationship that will form future professionals in oil and petrochemical companies. In this context, it is necessary to produce low-cost and easy-to-use software.

This paper proposes an open-source software for calculating the density of complex mixtures using the Peng-Robinson equation of state, namely HidroUFF Density Calculator. We compare the density values with this software against those values gathered from the UniSim software, in order to validate our methodology. This work also analyzes the impact of using the software in classes of engineering courses, by means of being intuitive, easy-to-use and low-cost.

2. METHODOLOGY AND SOFTWARE DESCRIPTION

HidroUFF Density Calculator is an open source software under the GNU General Public License (GPL). The main feature of this application is the calculation of the density of gas mixtures, through the resolution of Peng Robinson's cubic equation of state (Peng and Robinson, 1976). PREOS is represented by Equation 1 as well as its terms in Equations 2, 3, 4, 5 and 6, where Z is the compressibility factor of the mixture, R is the universal constant of perfect gasses, and T is the working temperature.

For each substance in the calculator database, it is necessary to include three intrinsic terms: critical pressure (P_c), critical temperature (T_c), reduced temperature (T_R), obtained by T/T_c, and acentric factor (ω). For each pair of substances it is necessary to include an interaction parameter (k_{ij}). All these four parameters are taken from the National Institute of Standards and Technology (NIST) Online Handbook (NIST, 2022).

$$Z^3 - (1 - B) \cdot Z^2 + (A + 2 \cdot B - 3 \cdot B^2) \cdot Z - (A \cdot B - B^2 - B^3) = 0 \quad (1)$$

$$A = \frac{a \cdot \alpha \cdot P}{R^2 \cdot T^2} \quad (2)$$

$$B = \frac{b \cdot P}{R \cdot T} \quad (3)$$

$$a = \frac{0.45724 \cdot R^2 \cdot T^2}{Pc} \quad (4)$$

$$b = \frac{0.07780 \cdot R \cdot Tc}{Pc} \quad (5)$$

$$\alpha = (1 + (0.37464 + 1.54226 \cdot \omega - 0.26992 \cdot \omega^2)(1 - \sqrt{T_R}))^2 \quad (6)$$

2.1 Software Architecture

The software was developed in the Python programming language, chosen due its intuitive syntax. It is in growing use in universities and small companies and provides responsive libraries for specific steps. The proposed software uses its well-known libraries SimPy (Sympy Dev Team, 2021) — a process-based discrete event simulation framework — and Matplotlib (Matplotlib Dev Team, 2022) — a framework for static, animated, and interactive visualizations of data. PyQt5 library (PyPi, 2022) is used for the graphical user interface (GUI) with help of the tool Qt Designer (Qt Company, 2022), for designing and building GUI.

Figure 1 demonstrates the software architecture of the calculator's packages and modules. The packages are represented by the tree-larger rectangles. In blue, the modules that were implemented by the density calculator, and in yellow, the external modules (libraries). In green, the diagram shows the two CSV (Comma Separated Values) files – a database – that store the properties of substances added to the calculator.

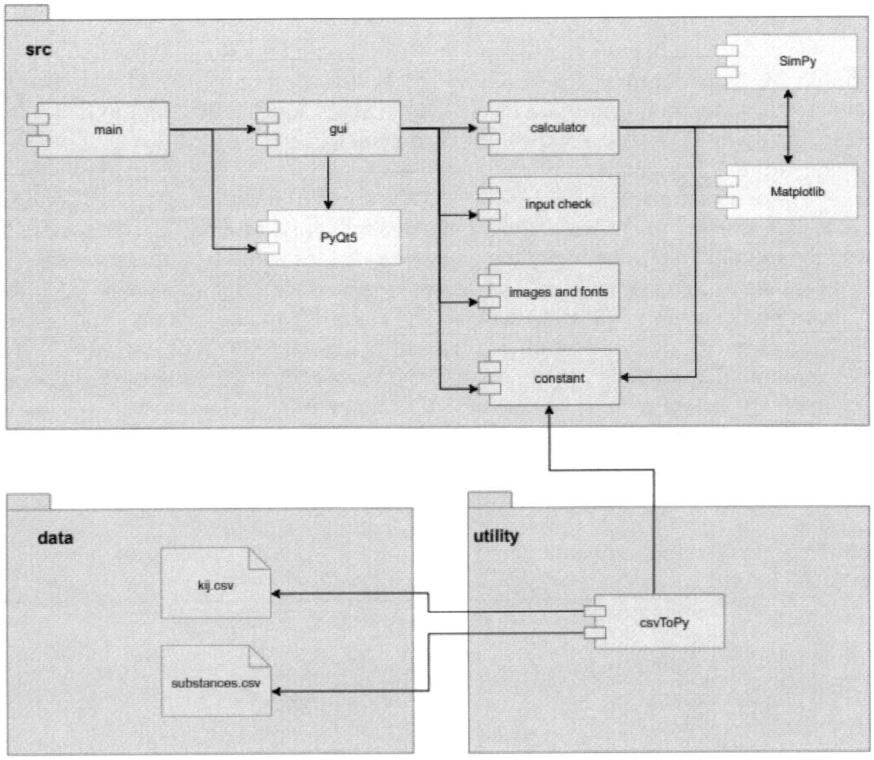

Figure 1. Software architecture representation

The src package stores the main code of the application and is composed of 6 modules: main, gui, calculator, constant, images and fonts and input check.

- **main:** this module used to launch the application through the PyQt5 and gui modules to build the graphical interface.
- **gui:** this module used for construction and user interaction with the graphical interface via PyQt5 and visual elements such as images and fonts. It is responsible for performing the data input, verifying them and passing them to the calculator module so that the necessary calculations are performed to display the result later.
- **calculator:** this module is responsible for performing density calculations by solving the PREOS equation and its terms defined in Equation 1. For this purpose, it receives the input data from the GUI module, that is informed by the user, and also the properties of the substances from the constant module. The SimPy module is used to help with density calculations and the Matplotlib module is used to generate the isotherm graphics.
- **constant:** this module contains the constants that store the values of the properties of substances that can be used by the program. This file is generated by the csvToPy utility from the files in data.
- **images and fonts:** this module stores the images and fonts used by the application in binary format.
- **input check:** this module contains the methods used to perform file and data input verification.

The data package stores input CSV files that contain the properties of the substances registered in the application, such as molar mass (g/mol), critical pressure (kPa), critical temperature (K) and acentric factor. Furthermore, it contains the values of the k_{ij} that represent the interaction parameters between each pair (i, j) of substances.

The utility package contains the utilities responsible for adding new substances to the application by transforming the files contained in data into a single file called constant.py in src for use by the application.

2.2 Software Functionalities

The diagram in Figure 2 demonstrates the flowchart (defined according to ANSI/ISO – American National Standards Institute/International Organization for Standardization) for the operations of the HidroUFF Density Calculator. Next paragraphs detail the workflow in this diagram.

When the software is initialized, the user can choose one of two options: 1) perform the calculation of density for a single pressure value (labeled *Yes*), or 2) for a range of pressure values (labeled *No*). According to this choice, the user must inform different input data. For both options, the user must specify the substances which compose the mixture, their respective molar fraction values and the temperature value with its scale degree (Fahrenheit, Celsius, or Kelvin). To inform the composition, the user clicks on the *Add* substance button, selects one of the available forms in the selection box, and enters the molar fraction value.

For option 1, the user may check *Single* choice. Then, the user types the pressure value, in atm. For option 2, the user must provide the initial and final pressure values and the steps between them. For this, the user needs to select the *Range* option and types these values, as exemplified in Figure 4b.

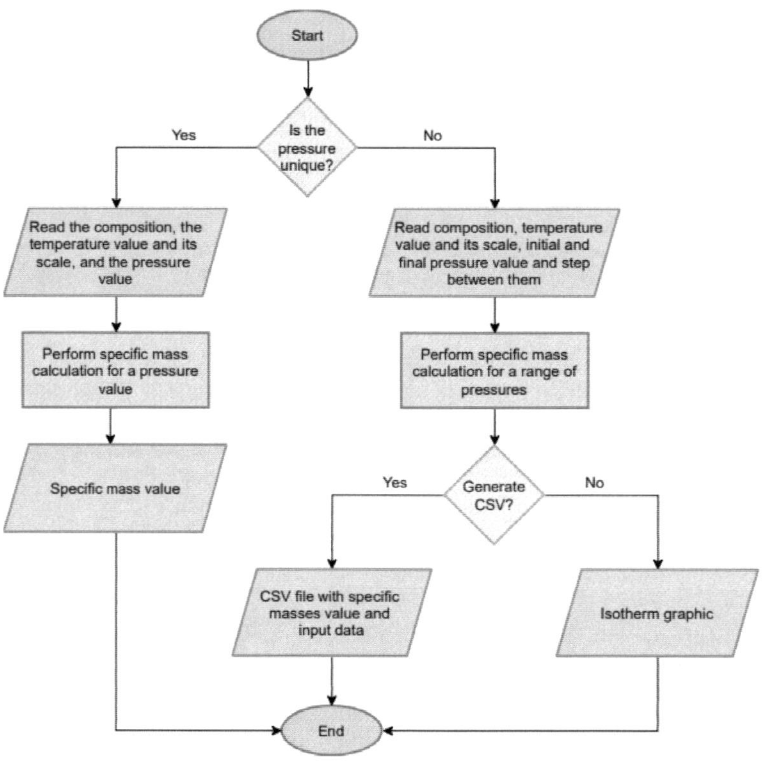

Figure 2. Software flowchart

For both options, the next step is to perform the density calculation using the PREOS (Equation 1). For option 1, the result of the density calculation is the specific mass and it is calculated only for the one pressure value. In this case, the workflow finishes here. For option 2, the user indicates the range of pressure values and the result is an isotherm graphic (density versus pressure). At this stage, in addition to data from the user interface, the software uses internal data that is stored in the constant module presented in Section 2.1. These data refer to the specific properties of the calculation for each substance.

After the density calculation, following the flowchart for option 2 in Figure 2, the user can choose to visualize the graphic in the tool by clicking on the button *Isotherm Graph*. This will generate and display an interactive graphic through the Matplotlib library, where the user can view, manipulate and save the graphic in various formats such as PNG, PDF, and SVG (see Figure 5 in Section 3). He/she also has the option to generate a CSV file by clicking on the button *Generate CSV*. Furthermore, the user can use his/her CSV file generated by the application as input and generate the isotherm graphic. This extra functionally is performed by clicking the first circular button in the upper right corner of the calculator interface and choosing the desired CSV file (see Figure 3 in Section 3). Focus on the software maintainability, new substances can be easily added to the calculator. A developer can change the data inside the files in package data (see Section 2.1), namely kij.csv and substances.csv. Molar mass (g/mol), critical pressure (KPa), critical temperature (K), acentric factor, and k_{ij} parameters for the desired substances are the editable values in the CSV tables. The csvToPy utility converts the CSV files into a suitable format to the Python language. As this data is sensitive to the software, we decided to keep these modifications at a development level.

2.3 Software Validation

For software validation, a hypothetical mixture (Mix A), composed of methane (40%), ethane (30%), and carbon dioxide (30%), has its density computed with the HidroUFF Density Calculator and UniSim Honeywell. The goal is to evaluate the differences between the values obtained by both softwares. UniSim is a commercial software already established in the market, and it is considered our baseline.

Table 1 shows the comparison results between the HidroUFF Density Calculator and UniSim software for Mix A in an isothermal condition at 4°C, varying the pressure from 1 atm to 300 atm. Table 3 shows the comparison results between the HidroUFF Density Calculator and UniSim software for Mix A in an isobaric condition in 200 atm, varying the temperature from 1°C to 300°C. The deviation of both result values, in the last column, is the main result of both tables. They show that HidroUFF Calculator presents results extremely close to the baseline UniSim. The magnitudes of 0.004% to 0.32% are characterized as a regular deviation due to the range of the calculations (precision of the numbers), and it does not indicate problems in our calculation.

Table 1. Comparison between the specific mass values, in kg/m³, obtained by the HidroUFF Density Calculator and by the commercial UniSim software for Mix A in isothermal condition (4°C)

Pressure (atm)	HidroUFF Calc. (kg/m³)	UniSim Honeywell (kg/m³)	Relative Deviation (%)
1	**1.27**	1.27	0
10	**13.34**	13.33	0.080
50	**91.57**	91.73	-0.170
100	**307.32**	308.30	-0.320
200	**464.12**	464.30	-0.040
300	**527.68**	527.70	-0.004

To evaluate programming errors and non-conformities in the software, exhaustive unit tests were performed, modifying input parameters: number of components, components, compositions, temperature, and pressure. It was verified that the software does not present non-conformities, being the calculator ready for utilization by potential users in academia.

For a qualitative validation of the software, the calculator was initially available to a small group of university professors, graduate, and postgraduate students. So that they could give their opinion on corrections and opportunities for improvement. With the preliminary use by professors and students, it was possible to observe from the reports of these users that the software was considered relevant, intuitive, easy to use, with low computational cost, and advantageous for being free.

3. ILLUSTRATIVE EXAMPLES

Screenshots of the HidroUFF Density Calculator user interface is displayed in Figure 3. In this window there is a circular button in the lower left corner that is responsible for switching among the three available languages: Portuguese (Pt), English (En) and Spanish (Es). In the upper right corner there are three buttons: the first one allows the user to load from his computer a CSV file (explained in Section 2.2) generated by the application so that its graph is displayed on the screen; the second button displays a help screen with application usage instructions; and the third button displays a screen with application development information such as developers and current version. In some fields, there is a small circular button that presents a tool-tip with information on how to fill in the field. In addition, there is a button labeled Clear fields used to clear all fields filled in at any time.

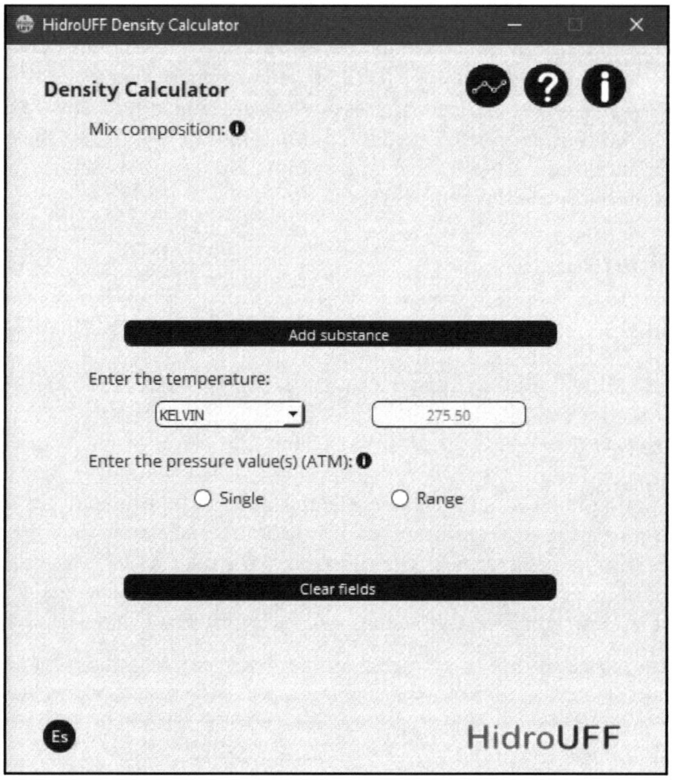

Figure 3. HidroUFF Density Calculator template

Still, in the main window of the software, the user can also add the chemical components, in the button *Add* substance and set the mixture composition. The temperature value and its scale (Fahrenheit, Celsius or Kelvin) is selected in the part labeled as "Enter the temperature". For density in a single point, the user must select *Single* and the window proceeds to Figure 4a, for just filling the pressure field, in atm. The result of the density appears immediately below the button *Calculate* when it is clicked. For density in a pressure interval, the user must select *Range* and the window proceeds to Figure 4b. Then, the user should fill the three fields: initial, final value and the step between them. In this case, the user can choose as output a file in CSV format or an isotherm graph (see Figure 5). All those functionalities were described in Section 2.2.

4. IMPACT

The results of densities obtained with the proposed software were compared to those found in literature and in benchmark. The values obtained for different mixtures had approximated the same values with very low deviation, in the order of 0.004% to 0.32%.

HidroUFF Density Calculator had a significant impact on the local academic community and has potential to be used in other universities and small companies. In preliminary validation with academic users (professors, researchers, undergraduate and graduate students), it was possible to observe from users reports that the software was considered relevant, intuitive, easy to use, with low computational cost and advantageous to be free, and it offers a Portuguese language option.

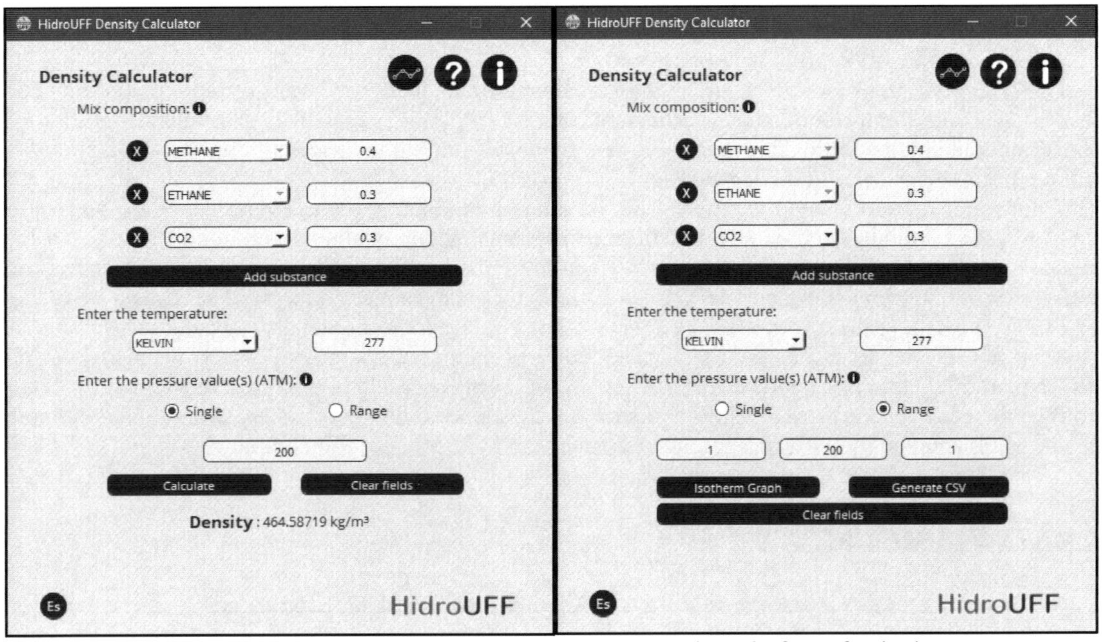

(a) For a single pressure. (b) In the form of an isotherm.

Figure 4. Demonstration of the two types of choice of presentation of results for the mixture A

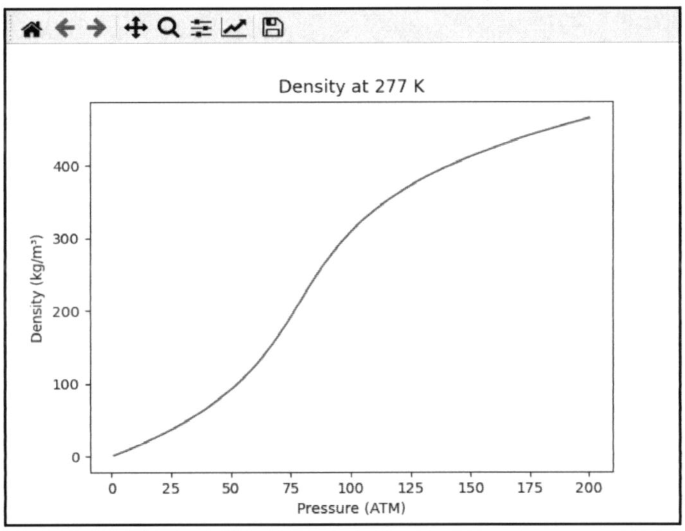

Figure 5. Isotherm (at 277 K) of the specific mass variation of the Mix A between 0 and 200 atm, in the software

The software, after its validation, was made publicly available (open source) in a GitHub repository and was published in the Zenodo platform repository (Sousa et. al., 2021). The professors of petroleum engineering and chemical engineering undergraduate courses of Universidade Federal Fluminense (UFF) started to disseminate the tool to their students as an alternative to a commercial software. In a future stage, it is intended to quantitatively evaluate the students opinion about the calculator through online surveys.

The use of the calculator by the academic community is even more interesting for the university dynamics, since classes are being taught remotely due to the COVID-19 pandemic. This makes it increasingly necessary to use free, intuitive, low computational cost, and low-cost software that students can use on their personal computers during lessons or remote tasks. Another impact consists in increasing the operational and economic competitiveness of start-up and small companies, which now have accessible software, avoiding costs with licenses and computer improvements.

5. CONCLUSION

HidroUFF Density Calculator allows predicting the density of complex mixtures of multi-components both with a single point (temperature and pressure) and with an interval, generating an isotherm. In addition, chemical substances not yet provided in the software's database can be easily added by a user, *e.g.* a professor, by filling in substance information in a well-known format CSV.

The software was successfully validated front benchmarks and had a positive response to the target user group (professors, graduate and undergraduate students), highlighting qualities such as free access and low computational cost. Currently, the calculator is being used by our research group in tasks of some projects with industry, and for students as support in classes such as thermodynamics, fluid mechanics, and petroleum engineering. We believe the software can be adopted at other universities and small companies.

In the future, our team intends to produce other software calculators of properties derived from thermodynamics, such as calculation of flash, viscosity and surface tension of mixtures. In addition, a web-application version of the density calculator was developed following the same design and is currently available to the community on the laboratory's website.

ACKNOWLEDGEMENT

We thank Petrobras for its support within the RAVES project and HidroUFF Laboratory.

REFERENCES

American Society for Testing and Materials, (2019). *Standard Test Method for API Gravity of Crude Petroleum and Petroleum Products (Hydrometer Method)*. ASTM D287 - 12B, Pennsylvania.

Borges, E. M. L, (2009). *Compressibility factors for natural gases by correlations and equations of state*. (Master 's thesis, Universidade do Estado do Rio de Janeiro). Available at: http://www.bdtd.uerj.br/handle/1/11927

Honeywell, (2018). Unisim Design version r.460.1, 2018.

Loria, H. et al., (2009). Prediction of Density and Viscosity of Bitumen Using the Peng–Robinson Equation of State. *Industrial & Engineering Chemistry Research*, v. 48, n. 22, p. 10129-10135.

Matplotlib Dev Team, (2022). Visualization with Python, https://matplotlib.org/, accessed: July, 2022.

NIST, (2022). Thermophysical properties of fluid systems, https://webbook.nist.gov/chemistry/fluid/, accessed: July, 2022.

Peng, D. Y., & Robinson, D. B., (1976). A new two-constant equation of state. *Industrial & Engineering Chemistry Fundamentals*, v. 15, n. 1, p. 59-64.

PyPi, (2022). Project PyQt5, https://pypi.org/project/PyQt5, accessed: July, 2022.

Qt Company, (2022). Qt designer manual, https://doc.qt.io/qt-5/qtdesigner-manual.html, accessed: July, 2022.

Reflich, O and Kwong, J. N., (1949). On the thermodynamics of solutions. V. An equation of state. Fugacities of gaseous solutions. *Chemical reviews*, v. 44, n. 1, p. 233-244.

Soave, G., (1972). Equilibrium constants from a modified Redlich-Kwong equation of state. *Chemical engineering science*, v . 27, n. 6, p. 1197-1203.

Sousa, V. M., Moura, F. P., Sousa, M. P., Passos, F. G. O., Lacerda, R. F. & Nascimento, E. A., (2021). HidroUFF Density Calculator: Version 1.3.0. Zenodo. https://doi.org/10.5281/zenodo.5719756.

Sympy Dev Team, (2021). Sympy, https://www.sympy.org/, accessed: July, 2022.

DESIGN AND IMPLEMENTATION OF A CHATBOT AS A TOOL TO ASSIST A HELPDESK TEAM

Diogo Pinto Ribeiro[1], Ana Anjo[2] and Pedro Rangel Henriques[1]
[1]Centro Algoritmi & Dep. de Informática, Universidade do Minho, Braga - Portugal
[2]VILT Group, Portugal

ABSTRACT

The existence of internal helpdesk teams is a common occurrence in companies nowadays, especially when considering the IT sector. These teams are an expensive resource and are only able to serve a limited number of users at a given moment, which evidences the importance of helpdesk teams operating as efficiently as possible. A common occurrence in the daily operations of these teams consists in the existence of a set of repeated tasks that could be automated through the usage of a chatbot capable of acting on behalf of helpdesk team members. By allowing a chatbot to perform some of these repeated actions, helpdesk teams are able to focus on other tasks, thus allowing to increase their productivity. Additionally, the usage of chatbots to assist a helpdesk team creates a highly available tool, capable of giving answers in a short time frame. In this paper, the design and implementation of such a tool is presented, including concepts and approaches related to chatbot development. As a result, a fully functional chatbot named Triton was produced, capable of helping employees of a consulting company with helpdesk-related problems and questions.

KEYWORDS

Chatbot, Helpdesk, Knowledge Bases, Conversational Agent, Rasa

1. INTRODUCTION

Nowadays, most companies that offer products or services have helpdesk teams available for different purposes. The existence of these teams is expensive and cannot guarantee that all users are served immediately or in a short time frame. One of the most common tasks of a helpdesk team consists in solving repetitive problems or replying to questions that have already been answered somewhere in the past. This takes up valuable staff time and could be solved with the existence of a chatbot. Other scenarios include cases where users need to access documentation pages, wasting time that helpdesk teams could be dedicating to other tasks. The process of searching for documentation could be done by a chatbot in an efficient and simple way. The existence of a chatbot allows users to get replies with a low response time compared to a human. Alongside low response times, a chatbot allows users to be more productive by automating certain tasks. Another advantage of a chatbot is its relatively low maintenance cost compared to a helpdesk team with the same level of availability and the fact that it allows the helpdesk team to focus on more important tasks.

The main motivation behind the development of a chatbot to assist the helpdesk team of a consulting company lies in the possibility of having an agent capable of integrating the helpdesk team and providing support to all employees, thereby freeing the helpdesk team to work on other tasks. Besides freeing the helpdesk team, another motivation for the implementation of a chatbot involves the possibility of employees getting faster and more straightforward answers to a set of common problems and questions.

The main goal of the implemented solution consists of having a fully functional chatbot capable of interacting with users by answering their questions with useful information regarding aspects such as company procedures or troubleshooting. To do so, it is expected for the chatbot to access the internal infrastructure of the company, including various knowledge bases in order to retrieve information. Some of the most relevant functionalities of the chatbot include the capability of searching information in wikis, getting links to open helpdesk tickets, or accessing troubleshooting pages.

In this paper, the implemented solution is presented, aiming to give a better understanding about the research and development process of a chatbot in an industry-focused setting.

The remainder of this paper is organized as follows. Concepts regarding chatbot development and related technologies are presented in Section 2. In Section 3, the architecture of the implemented solution is proposed. Section 4 explains the implementation details of Triton. It also discusses various problems faced during the development stage, along with their respective solutions. The Triton prototype so far implemented is presented in Section 5. Lastly, Section 6 ends this paper and discusses the state of the project, as well as future work.

2. STATE OF THE ART

A chatbot can be defined as an interface that allows users to interact with a software application using natural language. The main objective of a chatbot is to simulate a human conversation, and it can range from a simple Question & Answering System to a complex digital assistant. Chatbots may also be referred to as Bots, Conversational Agents, Chat Agents, or Conversational Interfaces (Shevat, 2017).

In this paper, text-based conversational interfaces are the main focus. This type of interface started to appear in the 1960s and 1970s in the form of Question Answering systems. The first systems to appear had a limited syntactic structure and rejected questions that were out of their scope, but decades later, with advances in research on topics such as AI and NLP, the capabilities of these systems evolved into tools that are used on a daily basis by all kinds of industries and millions of users (McTear, 2020). Chatbots are an example of text-based conversational interfaces and can be found on websites or applications such as WhatsApp or Slack.

According to Google Trends and as of May 2022, the term chatbot has a score (ranging from 0 to 100) of 78, having peaked in April of 2020. This is an excellent indicator of the popularity of chatbots alongside users. Looking at Figure 1, one can infer that chatbots are quite popular at the moment.

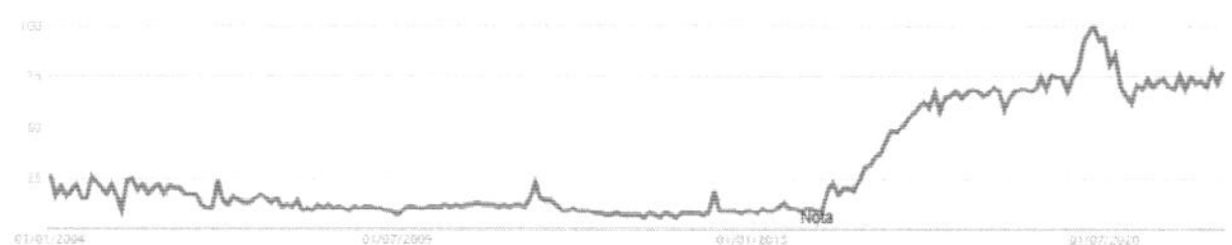

Figure 1. Google Trends result for the chatbot topic

According to research published on CNBC, by 2022, chatbots could help reduce business costs by more than $8 billion per year, being that the banking and healthcare industries are the ones that can benefit the most due to the high volumes of human interaction inherent to these businesses (Gilchrist, 2017). Even back in 2017, when this research was published and chatbots were still gaining some traction, the prediction of their impact on the industry was significant, which allows one to better understand the possibilities and magnitude of this kind of tool, and therefore, why it is interesting to be used to assist a helpdesk team.

Another interesting aspect regarding chatbots lies on the possibility of integrating them into existing messaging applications like Facebook Messenger or WhatsApp. Many of these messaging applications have millions of users worldwide, and in the case of WhatsApp, around 2 billion monthly active users according to Statista (2022). With these kinds of figures, an opportunity is presented for companies to reach their customers, using applications already installed on most of the user's mobile devices, instead of developing dedicated applications for chatbots. This would require additional development and deployment time, and there is no guarantee that users will be installing a dedicated application just to interact with a bot. Various companies have already taken advantage of this, having chatbots available on platforms such as Facebook Messenger. Some examples include Volkswagen and Domino's.

To build chatbots there are different tools available, being that some of the most known include Google Dialogflow (Google, 2022), Microsoft Bot Framework (Microsoft, 2022), Wit.ai (Wit.ai, 2022), IBM Watson (IBM, 2022), and Rasa (Rasa, 2022). Each tool has its strengths, but in this paper, the focus will be on Rasa given that this tool was chosen due to its open-source nature and the fact that it can easily be deployed in the company's infrastructure.

To evaluate the performance of a chatbot, different metrics may be collected. These can be grouped into different categories called perspectives such as the user experience perspective, the information retrieval perspective, the linguistic perspective, the technology perspective, and the business perspective (Peras, 2018). Different metrics were researched and are further explored in Section 5 as part of the evaluation process.

3. TRITON – ARCHITECTURE

The architecture of Triton is essentially composed by four components. The first of these components is the Conversational Agent. The Conversational Agent is the core of the proposed solution since it will contain all of the logic necessary to maintain conversations and execute actions. The Conversational Agent will need to communicate with at least three other components: an Input/Output Channel component, a component that allows interaction with the knowledge bases, and a component consisting in all Virtual Machines of the company's infrastructure. Ideally, there will be only one instance of the Conversational Agent for two reasons: the scale of the chatbot to be developed does not justify multiple instances of the Conversational Agent, and the limited resources available to build the bot only allow to build a centralized approach. Having a single instance of the Conversational Agent has some benefits like the lower cost to host the solution, and the simplification of the development process since concurrency problems will not be an issue. On the other hand, the main drawback of this approach consists in it being limited regarding the number of users that will be able to have conversations simultaneously.

As mentioned previously, the Input/Output Channel component is directly linked to the Conversational Agent and is used as the primary gateway between the user and the bot itself. Despite the Input/Output Channel not being directly part of the bot, it is the primary contact point for the user, and therefore has a huge importance regarding the perception of the bot by the users. With that in mind, the main focus will be to integrate the Conversational Agent with Google Chat given the fact that it has a user-friendly interface and allows for integration with bots through the available API.

The knowledge bases are another essential component in Triton's architecture. These knowledge bases contain information about various topics such as troubleshooting information or wiki pages.

The first of these knowledge bases is Zeus. Zeus is a platform that serves as a human resource management platform, project management platform, and knowledge base. Zeus allows employees to log in and register in their personal timesheet how many hours they have been working, register travel expenses, schedule vacations, signal if they are working from home, access information about different ongoing projects, and access information about topics such as troubleshooting, configurations, onboarding of new employees, or human resources questions. To access information about employees, Zeus interacts with an employee database hosting all employee data such as available holidays or working hours. The second knowledge base to be presented is Athena. Athena is built using Redmine and serves as a repository of different kinds of information regarding topics ranging from development guidelines to specific information about projects. The third and last knowledge base to be presented is Cognos. Cognos is built using a tool called Confluence which is developed by Atlassian and serves as a knowledge repository for the company. Cognos is an effort of centralizing information scattered across different platforms such as Zeus and Athena, with the main goal of helping employees access information in a streamlined and easy way. To access Cognos, employees use their credentials, just like with Zeus and Athena, and additionally, a VPN connection is required to access the platform. Logged users may create additional pages about new topics or add pages to existing ones. An interesting feature of Cognos consists in the availability of an API that allows one to search for content either by using a specific identifier or by using the Confluence Query Language.

The fourth and last component comprises the Virtual Machines present in the company's infrastructure. This component does not interact directly with the Conversational Agent, being that it is accessed indirectly by it, through knowledge bases with the target of accessing information.

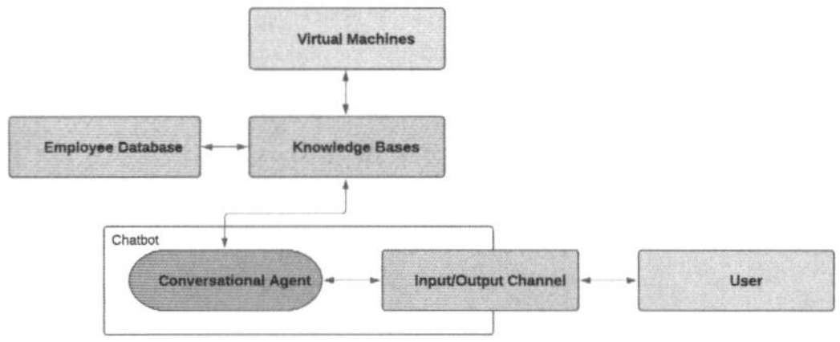

Figure 2. Triton high-level architecture

Figure 2 illustrates a high-level overview of Triton's architecture, including the interactions between the different components. This picture is an abstraction of the implemented solution, lacking any technical details to avoid unnecessary complications. Information about tools used and implementation details are presented in the following section.

4. TRITON – IMPLEMENTATION

To implement Triton, the tool of choice was Rasa (Rasa, 2022). This tool was chosen largely due to two reasons: allowing the deployment in the company's internal infrastructure and including an open-source component to develop the bot (Rasa Open Source). Additionally, Rasa includes an SDK that allows developers to write custom actions that can be triggered with certain user messages, being this a desirable trait for the problem at hand. These custom actions are executed by the Action Server, which will be the component of the bot responsible for interacting with the knowledge bases. As previously mentioned, the bot was integrated with Google Chat given that the company uses Google's suite of tools internally, and due to the fact that by integrating the boot in Google Chat, the bot gains support for both desktop and mobile interfaces. Triton's architecture is shown below in Figure 3, including the details regarding Rasa and the Google Chat integration.

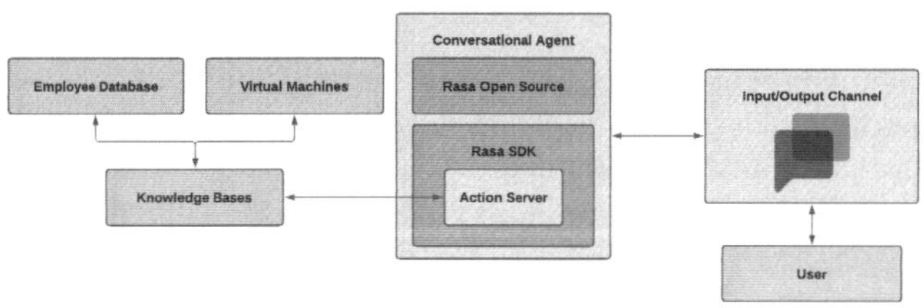

Figure 3. Detailed architecture

Before starting the implementation of the chatbot itself, a process of intent definition and gathering of respective utterances was undertaken. The result was a set of intents that the bot should be able to recognize and answer, being that for each intent, a set of approximately 10 utterances was gathered to train the bot's model. The process of gathering utterances was done using forms that collected data supplied by various employees that will become users in the future. This training data was used throughout the development stages of the bot and was tested at different moments to ensure that the model was behaving as expected.

4.1 Deployment and infrastructure

Regarding the deployment of the solution, there were three options available. The first option consisted in deploying the bot on the Google Cloud Platform, using the Compute Engine service. This service consists of customizable VMs that can be created in Google's infrastructure, and where one can deploy, for example, a chatbot built using Rasa. The second option consisted in deploying the solution in a machine present in VILT's own infrastructure. The third and last option consisted in deploying the bot in a cluster using Kubernetes.

After discussions with the engineering team, from the three options available, it was decided that deploying in the company's own infrastructure was the most adequate approach. By using an instance present in the infrastructure there is a higher degree of control regarding the access to information present in the instance, as well as allowing to save costs since there already exist machines waiting to be allocated to services. Besides the cost saving, deploying in the internal infrastructure may also grant some time savings, since it is easier to deploy the bot on a server, than in a Kubernetes Cluster. During the discussions, it was agreed that deploying the bot using Kubernetes would make sense if it was targeting a considerable number of users, which is not the case. Deploying in the GCP was also discarded since the costs to run the service would be significant.

Despite not using Kubernetes to deploy the solution, using containers is still a very valid proposition. By deploying the chatbot using Docker there are some inherent benefits such as performance compared to Virtual Machines and the portability that containers offer. By containerizing the application, it becomes very simple to deploy it in any other system, having the assurance that it will behave exactly in the same way. With that in mind, the deployment shall be done using Docker and Docker Compose.

Concerning the machine that will be used to deploy the bot, it is a remote Linux host with Ubuntu 20.04.3 LTS as its operating system. The machine has a Intel Xeon Gold 6138 processor, paired with 16GB of memory, and 20GB of storage.

4.2 Conversational Flows

The normal conversational flows are those the bot is trained to reply to, and that the bot is able to identify with a high confidence level. These scenarios may be considered the best-case scenarios when designing the bot since they are those that developers thought about and that match the training data with a higher classification confidence level.

The unsupported conversational flows are those which the bot is not trained to reply to or those which the bot attributes a low confidence level. If not handled properly, these scenarios may lead to a substandard experience for the user since the bot will either crash or will not reply to those specific conversations.

The conversations that the bot is not trained to reply to are designated as out-of-scope conversations. In these scenarios, the bot should reply to the users informing them that it is not able to handle that conversation. Despite being a simple solution, it is a very effective one for the problem at hand given that the bot that is being implemented is a Business Bot, implying that conversations should be concise, which is the case (Shevat, 2017).

There are also cases where the bot has a low classification confidence when predicting intents, in other words, the bot may not be sure if the message sent by the user matches a certain intent due to various reasons such as confusing message syntax or messages being too long or too short. Due to the frequency of these scenarios, it is important to control the outcome so that the user may have a more pleasant experience. This is done by implementing a fallback mechanism that either replies with a default message or tries to solve the existing ambiguity. To solve this ambiguity the bot may ask the user to rephrase the previous message. This is a very useful approach given that it is very likely that the user will rephrase the message sent in other words, thus helping the bot to classify the message with a higher confidence score.

Considering the tool being used to build the bot, there exists the possibility of activating an existing fallback mechanism and tuning some aspects of it. Rasa's fallback mechanism is triggered when a message sent by a user is below a predetermined classification confidence level. This minimum threshold is defined in a configuration file, and through testing, it was agreed that the best relation between the number of fallback situations and classification accuracy resulted in a minimum threshold of 0.9.

4.3 Action Server

The Action Server is a critical component of the solution being implemented given that it contains all the code that executes custom actions triggered by messages received from the users. The Action Server is implemented in Python and uses the SDK made available by Rasa.

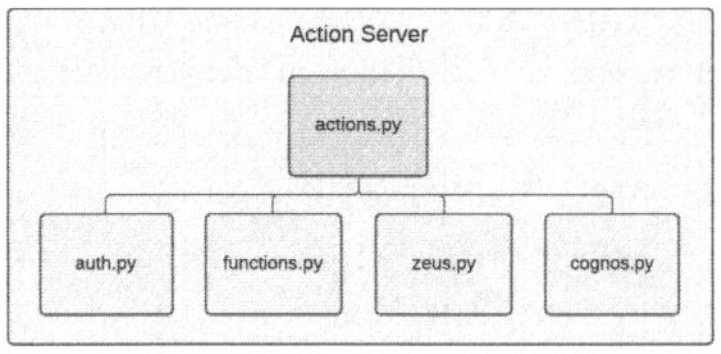

Figure 4. Action Server file structure

Figure 4 illustrates the file structure of the Action Server. The actions file includes the core of the Action Server, mainly all the structure of every available action. The auth file includes all functions related to the authentication process. The functions file consists of a small library of various functions needed to execute parts of different actions. The zeus file contains, as the name indicates, all the functions responsible for communicating with Zeus, similar to the cognos file which is responsible for all the functions related to searches on the Cognos wiki. The code isolation presented was chosen for maintainability reasons.

The implementation of the search capabilities in the knowledge bases followed two different approaches. The first approach consists in using a local Redis database to store data and generate search URLs for the missing information. The second approach uses the Confluence REST API to search for information. Regarding the first approach, after implementing an testing it, some issues were discovered, being that the most important was the necessity of constantly updating the database so that its content does not become obsolete. Given this issue, the second approach using the Confluence REST API was implemented. With the REST API, the consistency problems were solved, and the overall architecture of the solution became a lot simpler, as can be seen in Figure 5. Another interesting feature of the REST API lies in the usage of the Confluence Query Language used to search for information in Cognos. Regarding this approach, the search flow has between one and three steps. When the bot receives a keyword to search for, the first step will be to search by the resource labels. If a match is found, the result is sent to the user, otherwise, the chatbot proceeds with the following step, which consists of repeating the search using the title as a search parameter. As with the previous step, if a result is found, it is sent to the user, otherwise, the third and last step is executed. The last step consists in performing a query that searches for resources that include the given keywords in their page content. Just like before, if a result is found, it is returned to the user. In this specific case, if no result is found, a negative value is returned by the Cognos module in the Action Server, which is then translated into a specific message informing the user that no content was found.

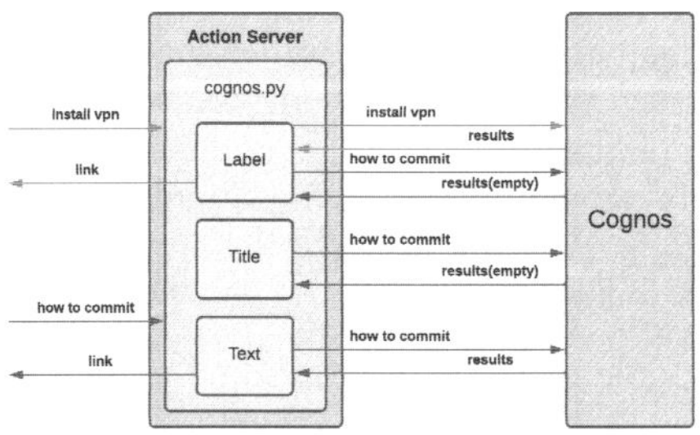

Figure 5. Cognos search flow

The security of the solution being developed was a major concern present in all decisions regarding the implementation of several functionalities, especially the ones interacting with Zeus. When interacting with these components, some prudence was needed regarding the approach that is used to implement the proposed requirements, given that some information should only be visible to specific users, and not all users should have the capability of executing the same set of actions. An example of this could be when a user wants to access information regarding a VM. Some VMs are only visible to a given set of users who have permission to do so. By allowing the bot to access information about VMs, this role authorization structure should be preserved.

Regarding the solution being developed, the first challenge that surfaced was related to the fact that by default, Rasa's implementation for the Google Chat channel identifies the users by their display name, which consists of the user's first and last name. This is a serious problem given that there may exist multiple users with the same display names, leading to a scenario where the chatbot is incapable of differentiating users. To solve this issue, the source code of the Google Chat channel was adapted to deliver the user's email as its identifier, instead of the display name. The email of a user is always unique given that it is built by joining the user's unique username, to the company domain, therefore solving the issue.

The ensuing challenge faced during the implementation of the chatbot was related to the authorization flow needed to access platforms like Zeus. When a user accesses Zeus, there is an assurance that the user only access resources to which it has access. Given that the bot will access resources on behalf of all users, it is important that the user permissions are preserved. To ensure this, the solution used consists in performing impersonation on top of the Zeus authentication workflow based on OAuth 2.0. To impersonate a user, the chatbot performs the steps described in Figure 6.

In this flow, the chatbot starts by requesting an access token to the Authorization Server, which is then used to make another request to translate a given username into a User ID present in the Authorization Server. With this User ID, the chatbot is able to request an impersonation token for that user to the Authorization Server. After obtaining the impersonation token, the chatbot is able to use this token the same way as a regular access token, impersonating a given user. In the scenario where a user tries to access a resource for which it does not have permissions, the Authorization Server will deny access to the resource returning an HTTP 403 status code. With this flow, the user permissions are preserved when the chatbot accesses Zeus, and therefore, the security concern is solved.

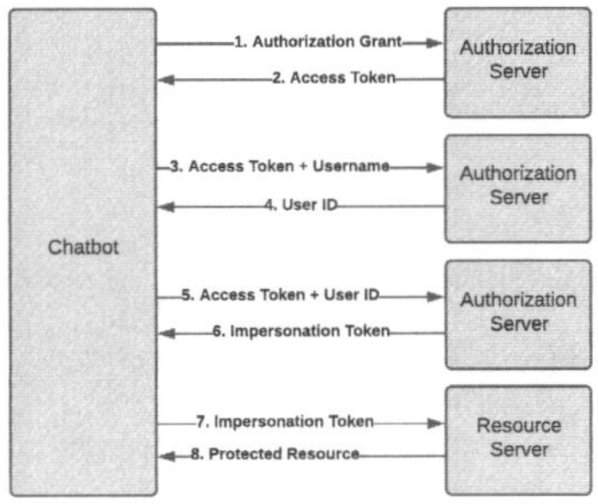

Figure 6. Impersonation flow

5. TRITON – TOOL OVERVIEW

The result of the implementation process is presented in this Section, including some examples of the most relevant functionalities. The first functionality to be shown is related to accessing the status of two different VMs, being that the impersonation flow is shown in action. This can be seen in Figure 7. The retrieval of information about a given VM is shown in Figure 8.

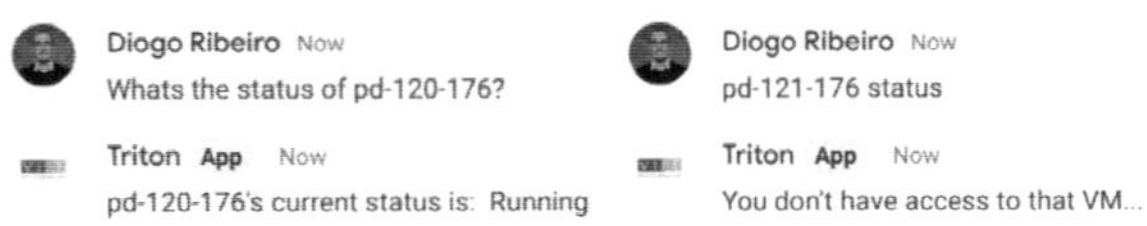

Figure 7. VM status examples

Figure 8. VM specifications example

Figure 9 illustrates the search capabilities of the chatbot in VILT's knowledge bases. In this case, two possible outcomes are shown: an outcome where the chatbot finds a match and returns it to the user, and an outcome where the chatbot is not capable of finding any matches, therefore, returning a message informing the user of the situation.

Figure 9. Search examples

The last two examples to be shown include a simple scenario where a user asks for a new VM, receiving a link with VM templates shown in Figure 10 and a scenario where a user expresses the same intent in two different ways as shown in Figure 11.

Figure 10. New VM ticket example

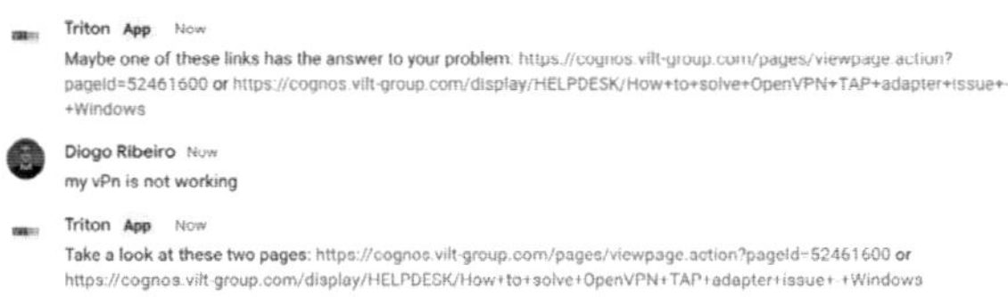

Figure 11. VPN troubleshooting examples

As part of the evaluation process of Triton, an experiment was conducted using a group of 9 employees at VILT with various roles inside the company. 78% of the enquired elements considered Triton's answers to be clear; 89% considered the conversational experience as pleasant. About 67% considered that the bot correctly classified all the messages sent. Overall, 78% of the enquired users considered that Triton was capable of answering their questions or solving their problems and did not need to contact the helpdesk team. Regarding the researched metrics, two were calculated: the Goal Completion Rate, which is around 90%, and the Fallback Rate, which is about 4%. These results are encouraging and show that overall, Triton is well received by the users which tested it and is capable of helping them.

6. CONCLUSION

In this paper, a chatbot named Triton was presented. Triton aims to assist a helpdesk team of a consulting company in helping employees with common problems. The implemented solution was built using Rasa and is integrated into Google Chat, being capable of fetching information from the company's various knowledge bases while preserving the user's security permissions. This implementation differs from other existing ones[1] given the strong customization present in the Action Server made to suit VILT's needs.

For the sake of space, it was not possible to include all research about various chatbot concepts and tools, as well as research related to the Action Server. Nevertheless, this research was included in a Master's dissertation about this topic (Ribeiro, 2022).

The developed chatbot is currently in the final testing stages with a restricted group of employees. This testing process reveals the actual behavior of the chatbot with real users and is helpful in finding errors and bugs. Some of the most interesting lessons learned with the development of this solution lie in the complexity of integrating a bot inside a company's infrastructure while preserving user permissions and without compromises.

---

[1] https://github.com/RasaHQ/helpdesk-assistant or https://github.com/ldulcic/customer-support-chatbot

Future work includes working on the chatbot's model so that it may handle a wider range of conversations, aiming to minimize the out-of-scope scenarios. Another direction for future work is the research for ways to overcome the limitation of only accessing information, making the bot also capable of executing actions, such as resetting VMs. Some aspects related to the security of the solution were considered in Subsection 4.3, while performance improvements are a topic to be studied in the future.

ACKNOWLEDGEMENT

This work has been supported by FCT – Fundação para a Ciência e Tecnologia within the R&D Units Project Scope: UIDB/00319/2020.

REFERENCES

Gilchrist, K., 2017. *Chatbots expected to cut business costs by $8 billion by 2022.* https://www.cnbc.com/2017/05/09/chatbots-expected-to-cut-business-costs-by-8-billion-by-2022.html

Google, 2022. *Dialogflow.* https://cloud.google.com/dialogflow

IBM, 2022. *IBM Watson.* https://www.ibm.com/watson

Mctear, M., 2020. *Conversational AI: Dialogue Systems, Conversational Agents, and Chatbots.* Morgan & Claypool, Sebastopol, USA.

Microsoft, 2022. *Microsoft Bot Framework.* https://dev.botframework.com/

Peras, D., 2018. Chatbot Evaluation Metrics: Review Paper. *36th International Scientific Conference*

on Economic and Social Development. Croatia, Zagreb, pp. 89-97.

Rasa, 2022. *Rasa.* https://rasa.com/

Ribeiro, D., 2022. *Chatbot for VILT's Helpdesk Team* (Master's thesis, University of Minho, Braga, Portugal). To Be Discussed

Shevat, A., 2017. *Designing Bots: Creating Conversational Experiences.* O'Reilly Media, San Rafael, USA.

Statista, 2022. *Most popular social networks worldwide as of January 2022, ranked by number of monthly active users.* https://www.statista.com/statistics/272014/global-social-networks-ranked-by-number-of-users/

Wit.ai, 2022. *Wit.ai.* https://wit.ai/

HMEDASYS: HOME MEDICATION INTAKE ALERT SYSTEM

Jardson Rodrigues[1], Christophe Soares[1,2], Pedro Sobral[1,2], Rui S. Moreira[1,2] and José M. Torres[1,2]
[1]ISUS Unit, Faculdade de Ciência e Tecnologia, Universidade Fernando Pessoa, Porto, Portugal,
[2]Artificial Intelligence and Computer Science Laboratory, LIACC, University of Porto, Porto, Portugal

ABSTRACT

The use of medication as treatment is often crucial to improve a patient's health. This process involves several factors, and often patients forgot to take their medicine. Thus, mechanisms that can contribute to therapy adherence are fundamental. The goal of this work has been the development of a real-time and automatic video object recognition system (HMEDASYS) to be used in the context of adherence and medication taking in-home care. The methodology followed has been to train a classifier model for medication pack recognition using Deep Learning. Combining and organizing data from previously annotated images, we retrained a neural network using the YoloV4-tiny Framework. In the experiments developed, two different classes of medicines were used for training and the system achieved a mAP of 98.33% on the test set. During the operation of HMEDASYS, the medication packs are real-time monitored using a video camera coupled with the developed system. In further 8 evaluation scenarios of the operation, only two errors were verified in a total of 16 medication packs to be identified.

KEYWORDS

Drug Recognition, Medicine Recognition, Deep-Learning, Computer Vision, YOLO

1. INTRODUCTION

Adherence to drug treatment is a very important factor for therapy to achieve the expected effect and result. This success includes not only taking medications at the prescribed times and days but also changing some habits (Lam & Fresco, 2015; Osterberg & Blaschke, 2005). Poor adherence to treatment can cause the progression of disease due to incorrect use of therapy. The more adherent the patient is, the better for his health (McDonnell & Jacobs, 2002; Mrosek et al., 2015). With the continuous evolution of technology, the use of Artificial Intelligence (AI) is becoming fundamental in daily tasks. Specifically, in the context of medication recognition, there is still a lack of low-cost, open source, solutions that can alert a patient with chronic or non-chronic diseases. This may assist the patient who takes multiple medications with remainders at a certain time based on the medication's schedule. Other solutions have been reported, but they require a large apparatus of equipment or are not fully autonomous.

This paper proposes a solution that consists of a system based on computer vision, using neural network architectures, with a low computational cost. We developed a software solution capable of assisting people to take their medication. The application works by monitoring the medication in real-time using a simple webcam. The problem addressed in this article consists of managing the schedules and taking medication. The most common problems identified are the discontinuation of treatment and the lack of professional monitoring, or the intrinsic complexity whenever the patients have to intake several medications many times a day. The use of cell phone reminders can help, but they cannot identify which medication has been taken. Therefore, a mechanism that incorporates the vision and identification of the medications on the table, time management, and identification of which medication needs to be taken, can considerably reduce the problems of low adherence. Our major contribution consisted of the creation of a prototype that allows the management of medication taking through computer vision using a low-cost system. The rest of the paper is organized as follows. Section 2 presents state-of-the-art as well as a collection of meaningful related works. The HMEDASYS system developed is presented in section 3 and describes the tools and techniques applied in this project. Section 4 presents an additional evaluation framework adopted and the results obtained. Finally, section 5 concludes this paper, also pointing to some directions in a near future.

2. RELATED WORK

In the first part of this section, some relevant medication take systems and solutions are mentioned and analyzed. The remainder of the section is reserved for the presentation of relevant computer vision, machine learning, and object recognition techniques and software libraries.

2.1 Medication Take Related Systems

One way to decrease medication-taking errors, especially for users without professional supervision, is the use of a medication-taking mechanism. This type of device can help with tasks that are prone to error. Several features are typical in these smart medication adherence products (MAP) as mentioned in (Aldeer et al., 2018; Faisal et al., 2021).

The PillStation system (Bear & Jain, 2011)provides a visualization of the pills that the patient must take over a certain period. The device uses the output of a camera, CCD image sensor, or similar sensor and image capture device focused on the interior space of a storage compartment of the device. An image capture device is positioned to capture an image of the interior space of each compartment, and a communication module transmits the captured image to a central monitoring station.

In (Wehba et al., 2014), the author designed a management system that includes multiple computers, including a medication management unit (MMU) the device is associated with a physician to place a medication order. The medication-by-management system is flexible and integrated to provide increased patient safety and caregiver productivity with a variety of hospital information (Wehba et al., 2014).

The eMar *(Electronic Medication Administration Record)* barcode technology incorporates various technologies into the nursing staff workflow to ensure that the medication is administered at the correct time and the correct dose and to the correct patient. In observations, in contexts without using eMar technology, there were 776 medication administration errors, a rate of 11.5% while in medical units using the technology 495 medication administration errors were observed, an error rate of 6.8%, which represents a 41.4% reduction. Medication administration errors out of schedule dropped from 3.1% to 1.6%, representing a 50.8 percent reduction (Poon et al., 2010).

A medication management system was proposed with a customized box for pills, a pill dispensing unit, software for automatic medication dispensing, and a recognition model for pills. A camera has been integrated into the system to acquire images of pills, which are transferred to the application for recognition of the *CNN Convolutional neural network*. Application software was developed for use with a smartphone with basic functions such as timing and counters. The dispensing of pills requires only the setting of their mixture during the initial parameter setting. The system can inform the taker when to take the medication, and according to the set parameters, the pills are dispensed separately. The need to compare with database images when using pill recognition resulted in a longer processing time (Tsai et al., 2020).

2.2 Object Recognition and Computer Vision

Computer vision has a wide variety of applications such as industrial, self-driving vehicles, surveillance, and others. It deals with varied areas such as computer interaction, image retrieval in digital libraries, medical image analysis, and rendering of synthetic scenes in computer graphics (Forsyth & Ponce, 2003). One of the most important areas is object detection in images or videos (Pop et al., 2017; Szeliski, 2022; Zou et al., 2019).

2.2.1 OpenCV Software Library

The *Open Source Computer Vision Library* (OpenCV) is a cross-platform, computer vision library. The library is written originally in *C* and *C++* and runs on multiple platforms, such as Windows, Linux, Android, macOS, FreeBSD, and OpenBSD, including embedded devices with CPUs based on ARM architecture. OpenCV is designed for computational efficiency and with a strong focus on real-time applications. One of the goals of OpenCV is to provide a simple computer vision infrastructure that helps people create very sophisticated vision applications. In some cases, high-level features in the library will be sufficient to solve complex computer vision problems (Bradski & Kaehler, 2008; Kaehler & Bradski, 2016).

2.2.2 YOLO and Darknet Software Framework

Darknet is a high-performance open-source framework for implementing neural networks and is used, for instance, to implement the object detector YOLO. Darknet is written in C and CUDA and can be integrated easily into CPUs and GPUs processing (Redmon, 2013). Advanced implementations of deep neural networks can be done using Darknet. These implementations include You Only Look Once (YOLO) for real-time visual object detection, ImageNet classification, and recurrent neural networks (RNN). Yolo or *You Only Look Once*, is an algorithm that detects and recognizes multiple objects in an image in real-time. Object detection in YOLOv4 is done as a regression problem and provides the probabilities of categories of the detected images. The architecture of YOLOv4 is composed of CSPDarknet53 as a backbone (Wang et al., 2020), an additional spatial pyramid pooling module, and a new backbone that can enhance the learning capability of CNN. The spatial pyramid pooling block is added to the CSPDarknet53 to increase the receptive field and separate the most significant context resources. Instead of pyramid networks of features for object detection used in YOLOv3, PANet is used as the method for aggregation and is mainly incorporated into the model to enhance the parameter segmentation process for different detector levels. Single-stage models (Bochkovskiy et al., 2020) allow multiple predictions on the same object in a single image, ambiguities are removed from these predictions and subsequently by a process called non-maximal suppression *NMS*, which only leaves the bounding box with higher probability and label for the object (Dazlee et al., 2022). The YOLOv4-tiny detector is proposed based on YOLOv4 to simplify the network structure and reduce parameters, which makes it suitable for development on mobile and embedded devices and improves real-time object detection (Jiang et al., 2020).

3. THE HMEDASYS SYSTEM

The HMEDASYS prototype described intends to contribute to the home healthcare area, providing the capability to detect and recognize medications and trigger alerts to users for medication intake. This system was trained to recognize a predefined number of different medications. In the experiments described in this document, the number of different medication packs trained to be recognized has been, NUM_MEDICATIONS = 2. One important requirement in development of the HMEDASYS was the possibility to use it on low-cost computer platforms, such as Raspberry Pi (Raspberry Pi Foundation, 2022).

The rest of this section presents an architectural overview of the HMEDASYS, the main elements that make up the system architecture for software implementation. The process of training the core model of the Visual Recognition module is also presented. Finally, an overview of the usage of HMEDASYS is described.

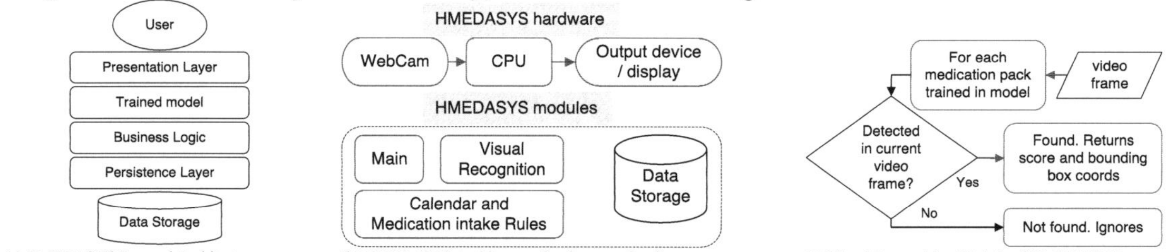

(a) HMEDASYS Layered Architecture (b) HMEDASYS Architecture: hardware and software (c) Visual Recognition Module of HMEDASYS

Figure 1. HMEDASYS Architecture

3.1 HMEDASYS Architecture

The HMEDASYS architecture can be organized through a set of software layers that aim to cover the major technical aspects relevant to its operation, as can be seen in Figure 1(a). The presentation layer, at the top, corresponds to the display of an interactive screen with the medicine intake and the alert messages. It is also possible to visualize in this layer the medicines that are being monitored. This presentation layer is detailed in section 3.3. In the Trained Model layer, it is done the recognition of the trained visual object types in the image frames that are acquired through the Webcam, corresponds, in a certain sense, to the Visual recognition Module. The description of the dataset and the process of model training are done in section 3.2. In the Business layer, calendar and medication intake rules are applied that consider three aspects: time information; the existence of the medications on the table or webcam visible surface; and the medical prescription for taking the medications. These rules are used to control the HMEDASYS alerts and outputs. In the Persistence layer, the storage of information on the recognized medications is saved in the Database along with medical prescription information. The implemented prototype offers a solution for monitoring and controlling the medication intake at home using a simple hardware setting (top of Figure 1 (b)). The central idea is to detect and recognize the medicine and to alert its taking to user, based on information stored in the local database. The HMEDASYS software modules are depicted in Figure 1 (b) bottom. The database (Data Storage) is used to store information about medication dose and hours of taking. During operation, the Visual Recognition module of HMEDASYS is constantly searching, in each video frame from the webcam, the occurrence of the trained medication packs in the model so is doing inference. If a visual object is detected with a confidence score greater than the predefined threshold (a default threshold of 0.25 has been used in the tests) then its bound box, label ID, and score are returned to the main module, see Figure 1 (c). One function of the Main module is to store, in a log file, the time intervals when each of the trained medications has been recognized in the viewpoint of the webcam, using the output of the Visual Recognition Module. This log file can be used by the Rule module to produce reports by the HMEDASYS system.

3.2 Dataset Creation and Model Training

For the training of the model, we created a dataset with labeled images of two sizes, 150×220 and 400×500, to improve the recognition and its invariance to image size. In the training stage, a total of 293 images were used: 205 images for training, 59 for validation, and 29 for testing. The relevant visual objects, the medication packs, were annotated as belonging to one of two possible classes (*NUM_MEDICATIONS = 2* as stated before). In Figure 2(a) it is possible to see a sample composed of 6 images of the used dataset, three of each class trained for the experiments. Each selected class represents a specific medication pack to be recognized by the model. In Figure 2(b) one relevant visual object is annotated using the LabelImg software (Tzutalin, 2015).

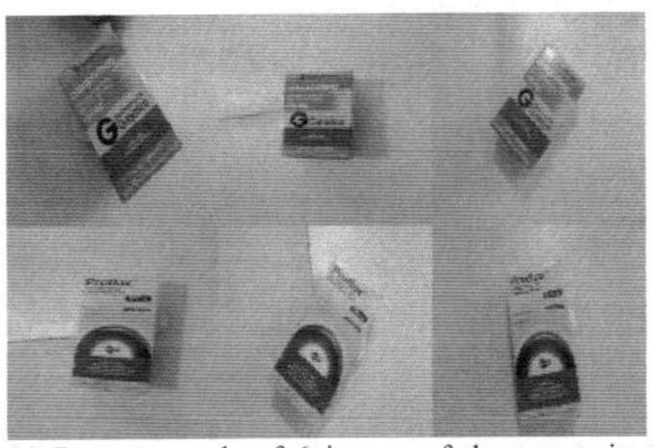

(a) Dataset sample of 6 images of the two trained classes: Class 1 (top row); class 2 (bottom row)

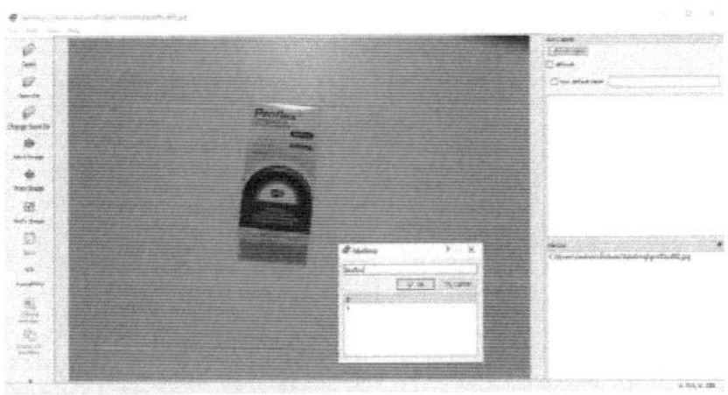

(b) Dataset annotation of ground truth using LabelImg

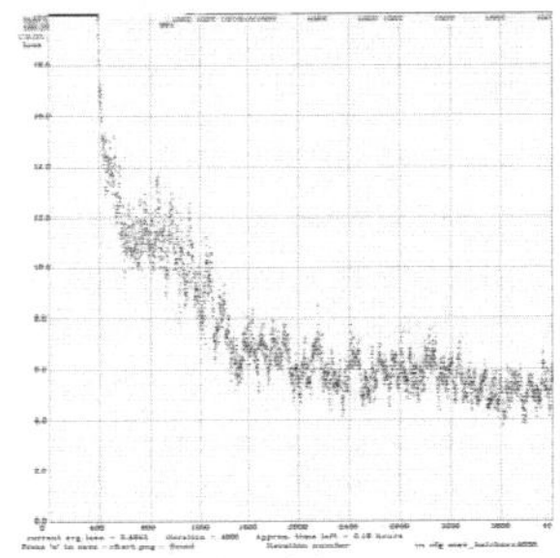

(c) Accuracy during training

Figure 2. Dataset creation and training

Using transfer learning, instead of training the model from scratch, allowed to use of the pre-trained YOLOv4-Tiny weights up to the first 29 convolutional layers. After a total of 4000 iterations, the model was trained for the detection and identification of the medicine. The accuracy graph can be seen in Figure 2(c). The mean Average Precision (mAP) obtained in the training was 98.33%.

3.3 Usage of HMEDASYS

3.3.1 User Profile

The typical user of HMEDASYS has diseases and takes several medications or goes through treatment so it is crucial to take the correct medication. This patient does not benefit from the presence of a healthcare professional and remains alone most of the day or night. In his house, he keeps all the medicines he needs on a table or a visible place. A Webcam is positioned over the medications. An alert is issued as a reminder to take the medication. When, for a short interval, the user removes the medication from the table, at the time of taking the medication, a dosing movement is counted, and the alert reminder until the next dose is deactivated.

3.3.2 Design and Usability

The HMEDASYS Medication Alert System graphical user interface (GUI) for the home user is composed of the main window divided into two panels. On the left panel, it is possible to visualize the medications recognized by the system and the webcam image. On the right panel, in the message and textual information area, it is possible to check the status information of the system, time of the day, and alerts triggered (Figure 3(a)). Two major behavior states were considered for HMEDASYS: i) behavior between medication intakes; ii) behavior at medication intake times.

HMEDASYS behavior between medication intakes

Considering all the medication packs previously trained, the system is constantly identifying and drawing a rectangle on the detected visual objects and comparing those with the database of prescribed medicines. On the right panel displays an Ok status message, the green color icon, in case everything all the prescribed medicines are visible, as can be seen in Figure 3(a). The system issues an alert if the prescribed medicine is not positioned adequately, informing the patient that a certain medicine is missing from the table. The system informs which medicine is missing (Figure 3(b)).

(a) Main Window of the HMEDASYS

(b) One Medication not identified

(c) All Medications Missing in scene

(d) Alert for the Medication Intake

(e) One Medication missing

Figure 3. One Medication not identified in the scene

In the cases where the system does not find any of the trained medicines in the scene being monitored, an alert is triggered along with the names of the medicines missing. Until the adjustment is made, the system will continue with the alert, as can be seen in Figure 3(c).

HMEDASYS behavior at medication intake times

The system always monitors the recognized medication packs, the current time, and the stored time of taking each of the prescribed medications. When it is time to take a particular medication, an alert is triggered with an image of a bell informing which medication needs to be taken, as shown in Figure 3(d). The medication intake alert remains on for a certain, configurable, period. During this period, the alert continues, with the bell being displayed until the moment the medication pack is removed from the scene. After the removal of the pack, the system changes the status to Medicine Missing, and informs the name of the medicine, suggesting that after taking the medicine it should be placed back on the table again to proceed with monitoring until the next medication intake time scheduled. After the removal of the medication, the system will identify that there is a certain missing medication that needs to be monitored, this is necessary for the monitoring to continue for the next scheduled time of medication taking for that patient (Figure 3(e)).

4. EVALUATION AND RESULTS

The experiments and evaluations performed are intended to verify the functionality and performance of the proposed system, as well as the representation of object recognition using machine learning. The prototype evaluated was developed using the Python language. The architecture selected for the recognition was Yolov4-Tiny, due to its lightness and ability to be deployed to other platforms, namely, low-cost single-board computers, such as a Raspberry Pi 4 (Raspberry Pi Foundation, 2022). Yet, in the experiments, the components selected for the tests of the Monitoring Module were the following: i) Image acquisition: USB 2.0 Webcam,

Logitech Quick Cam Pro 9000 with autofocus; ii) Computer: Intel I5 4590, 4th gen, 8GB RAM, 120GB SSD, OS Ubuntu 18.04.5 LTS and Nvidia Video Card with 2 GB RAM; iii) Display: 18.5" LCD monitor for interaction with the display and information system.

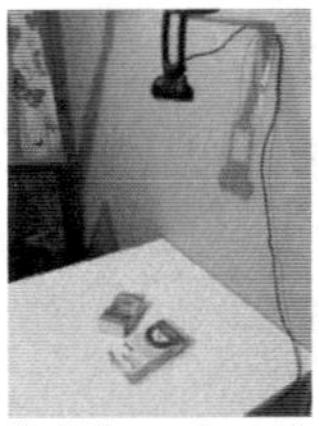

(i) Webcam Setup 1 (optical axis perpendicular to table plane, distance = 40cm)

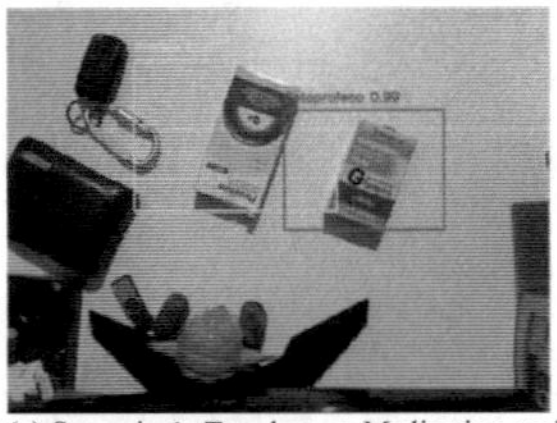

(a) Scenario 1: Two known Medication packs over the table (one of each trained class)

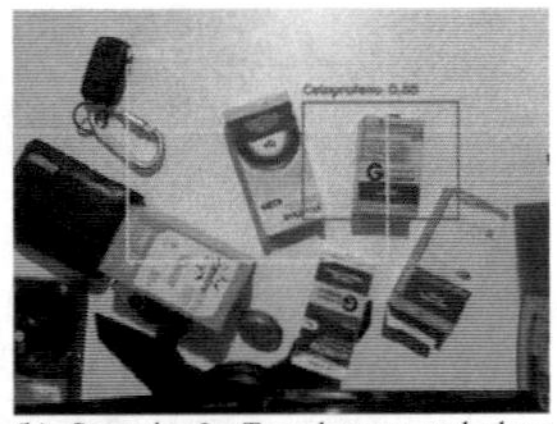

(b) Scenario 2: Two known and three unknown (untrained) medication packs over the table

(c) Scenario 3: Two known medications packs and low light conditions

(d) Scenario 4: Two known and three unknown (untrained) medication packs over the table and low light conditions

Figure 4. Evaluations Scenarios 1-4

4.1 Evaluation Setup

The system has been deployed only, with few resources and easy installation. The experiment consisted in choosing a suitable place for the installation and observing the height at which the camera needed to be fixed, to obtain a better field of view and with little distance from the objects of interest. A Webcam on the table, where the previously trained medication packs are, with a height of up to 40 centimeters, which is adequate for the system to work. This height value used during the experiments is like the one used during the dataset creation for the training stage. This setting can be observed in Figure 4(i) and Figure 5(ii) for the two camera orientations tested. The experiments described in this section were conducted indoors with the presence of natural and artificial light. The objective has been to test the recognition of the two trained visual objects among the objects left randomly over the table. One clear limitation of the approach tested in the experiments is its inability to recognize visual objects occluded or stacked, or only partially visible to the viewpoint of the camera. For that reason, we considered that all the medications are scattered randomly, but visible to the webcam.

4.2 Evaluations: Camera Optical Axis Perpendicular or 90° (Scenarios 1,2,3,4)

In the environment for this evaluation round, the webcam was positioned at a height of 40 centimeters above the medicines, as can be seen in Figure 4(a-d). The medicines are in the center of the image acquired by the webcam. Performed indoors, with artificial lighting, with a 9 W LED bulb, presenting only the trained medicines on the table, and in a second moment, other medicines were added.

4.3 Evaluation: Camera Optical Axis At 45° (Scenarios 5,6,7,8)

In this evaluation, the Webcam was positioned at a height of 40 centimeters above the medications, but, this time the Webcam was repositioned at a 45-degree angle. The medicines remain in the center of the image, but with a slight inclination. Performed indoors, with the same conditions as in the evaluation from section 4.2 as seen in Figure 5(ii). The trained medicines were positioned at first with few objects, then new medicines were added to simulate an environment with an increased level of difficulty in the recognition, see Figure 5(a-d).

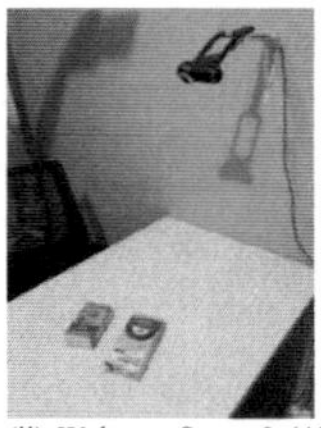

(ii) Webcam Setup 2 (45° angle between the optical axis and table plane, distance = 40cm)

(a) Scenario 5: same as 1 and webcam at 45- degree angle

(b) Scenario 6: same as 2 and webcam at 45- degree angle

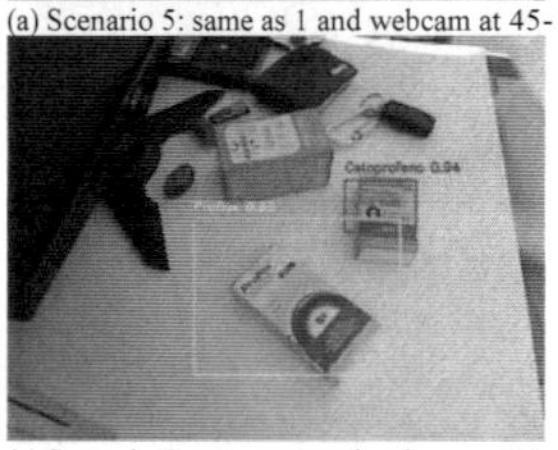

(c) Scenario 7: same as 3 and webcam at 45- degree angle

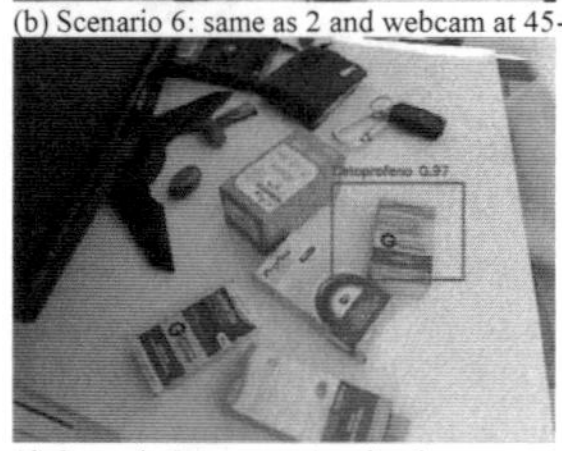

(d) Scenario 8: same as 4 and webcam at 45- degree angle

Figure 5. Evaluations Scenarios 5-8

4.4 Results

The visual recognition module of HMEDASYS was submitted to eight tests for recognizing medicines. Results can be seen in Table 1. Even with adverse situations, in the evaluation set performed in section 4.2, the system was able to recognize 100% of the medication packs trained. In the evaluation set from section 4.3, two failures were observed, one pack erroneously identified (scenario 6) and one pack that was not identified (scenario 8). In a certain sense the HMEDASYS system has a robust functionality that, in case the medication pack cannot be recognized, even if it is on the table, a *Missing Medication* warning is issued, along with the name of the medication as seen in Figure 3(b). In all cases, the alarm, according to the calendar, is triggered.

Table 1. Results of visual identification tests of the two trained Medication Packs

Scenario	Cam axis	Light	Packs over the table	Packs correctly identified	Packs erroneously identified	Error
1	90	normal	2	2	0	0
2	90	normal	5	2	0	0
3	90	low	2	2	0	0
4	90	low	5	2	0	0
5	45	normal	2	2	0	0
6	45	normal	5	2	1	1
7	45	low	2	2	0	0
8	45	low	5	1	0	1

5. CONCLUSIONS AND FUTURE WORK

This work presented HMEDASYS, a medication recognition system integrating an alert system that can be configured to attend to the medication intake of any patient. In the tested scenarios, failures occurred due to the webcam angle of 45 degrees and the low light conditions. These elements were not considered in the creation of the Dataset for the model training. In future work, we plan to enrich the training dataset to deal with more severe imaging conditions. Also, this problem can be reduced by using redundant sensor information, for instance, additional cameras. In future work, we are planning additional pretests using a Raspberry Pi as an edge device, real patients, and better models. Also, integration with Google calendar is an important identified feature as well as the generation of periodic reports for caregivers.

ACKNOWLEDGEMENT

This work was sponsored by Fundação Ensino e Cultura Fernando Pessoa (FECFP) and supported by Artificial Intelligence and Computer Science Laboratory, LIACC.

REFERENCES

Aldeer, M., Javanmard, M., & Martin, R. P. (2018). A review of medication adherence monitoring technologies. Applied System Innovation, 1(2), 14.

Bear, D. M., & Jain, Y. (2011). Medication dispenser with integrated monitoring system. Google Patents.

Bochkovskiy, A., Wang, C.-Y., & Liao, H.-Y. M. (2020). YOLOv4: Optimal Speed and Accuracy of Object Detection.

Bradski, G., & Kaehler, A. (2008). Learning OpenCV: Computer vision with the OpenCV library. "O'Reilly Media, Inc."

Dazlee, N. M. A. A., Khalil, S. A., Abdul-Rahman, S., & Mutalib, S. (2022). Object Detection for Autonomous Vehicles with Sensor-based Technology Using YOLO. International Journal of Intelligent Systems and Applications in Engineering, 10(1), 129–134.

Faisal, S., Ivo, J., & Patel, T. (2021). A review of features and characteristics of smart medication adherence products. Canadian Pharmacists Journal / Revue Des Pharmaciens Du Canada, 154(5), 312–323. https://doi.org/10.1177/17151635211034198

Forsyth, D. A., & Ponce, J. (2003). A modern approach. In Computer vision: a modern approach. Prentice-Hall.

Jiang, Z., Zhao, L., Li, S., & Jia, Y. (2020). Real-time object detection method based on improved YOLOv4-tiny. ArXiv Preprint ArXiv:2011.04244.

Kaehler, A., & Bradski, G. (2016). Learning OpenCV 3: computer vision in C++ with the OpenCV library. "O'Reilly Media, Inc."

Lam, W. Y., & Fresco, P. (2015). Medication adherence measures: an overview. BioMed Research International, 2015.

McDonnell, P. J., & Jacobs, M. R. (2002). Hospital admissions resulting from preventable adverse drug reactions. Annals of Pharmacotherapy, 36(9), 1331–1336.

Mrosek, R., Dehling, T., & Sunyaev, A. (2015). Taxonomy of health IT and medication adherence. Health Policy and Technology, 4(3), 215–224.

Osterberg, L., & Blaschke, T. (2005). Adherence to medication. New England Journal of Medicine, 353.

Poon, E. G., Keohane, C. A., Yoon, C. S., Ditmore, M., Bane, A., Levtzion-Korach, O., Moniz, T., Rothschild, J. M., Kachalia, A. B., Hayes, J., & others. (2010). Effect of bar-code technology on the safety of medication administration. New England Journal of Medicine, 362(18), 1698–1707.

Pop, C. M., Mogan, G.-L., & Boboc, R. G. (2017). Real-Time Object Detection and Recognition System Using OpenCV via SURF Algorithm in Emgu CV for Robotic Handling in Libraries. International Journal of Modeling and Optimization, 7(5).

Raspberry Pi Foundation. (2022). Raspberry Pi 4 Model B specifications.

Redmon, J. (2013). Darknet: Open Source Neural Networks in C.

Szeliski, R. (2022). Computer vision: algorithms and applications, Second Edition. Springer Cham. https://doi.org/10.1007/978-3-030-34372-9

Tsai, K.-L., Liau, B.-Y., Hung, Y.-M., Yu, G.-J., & Wang, Y.-C. (2020). Development of Smart Pillbox Using 3D Printing Technology and Convolutional Neural Network Image Recognition. Sensors and Materials, 32(5), 1907–1912.

Tzutalin. (2015). LabelImg: graphical image annotation tool for labeling object bounding boxes in images. In GitHub. Tzutalin.

Wang, C.-Y., Liao, H.-Y. M., Wu, Y.-H., Chen, P.-Y., Hsieh, J.-W., & Yeh, I.-H. (2020). CSPNet: A new backbone that can enhance the learning capability of CNN. Proceedings of the IEEE/CVF Conference on Computer Vision and Pattern Recognition Workshops, 390–391.

Wehba, S. R., Rinda, J. E., Trohimovich, B. M., & Pelletier, J. (2014). Medication administration and management system and method. Google Patents.

Zou, Z., Shi, Z., Guo, Y., & Ye, J. (2019). Object Detection in 20 Years: A Survey. arXiv. https://doi.org/10.48550/ARXIV.1905.05055

FROM PRACTICE TO SCIENCE: SOCIAL REACTIONS CAUSED BY CONVERSATIONAL AGENTS — A LITERATURE REVIEW FOR RESEARCHERS AND PRACTITIONERS

Sophie Hundertmark[1], Hans-Georg Fill[2] and Edy Portmann[2]
[1]*Lucerne University of Applied Sciences and Arts, 6343 Rotkreuz, Switzerland*
[2]*University of Fribourg 1700 Fribourg, Switzerland*

ABSTRACT

The number of publications focussing on the design of Conversational Agents (CA) has been continuously growing. However, from a research perspective, a review of the existing publications that visualizes both design elements and effects on user behavior is still missing but needed to reach an overall understanding of the connections and dependencies of researched design elements. From a company's perspective, practitioners are forced to first decide on certain design elements and then to optimize these according to their goals, due of the actual state of research. To close this gap, we conducted a systematic literature review and developed a conceptual model that links different design cues with social signals and social reactions. On the one hand our model helps researches to get a better understanding of the influence of several design cues of CAs. On the other hand, our model helps practitioners to design conversational agents according to their companies' goals.

KEYWORDS

Chatbots, Conversational Agents, Social Cues, Systematic Literature Review, Conversational AI

1. INTRODUCTION

Recently, influenced by the technological and scientific advances in the fields of artificial intelligence (AI) and by the growing acceptance of non-human communication partners, the number of companies using chatbots or conversational agents (CAs) to automate their customer touchpoints has grown (Maedche, 2019). In general, AI-based CAs have become a dominant service interface between providers and users (McLean, 2019). These CAs are designed with the intention of supporting users in their everyday lives as intelligent personal assistants (Di Prospero, 2017). Chatbots simulate human communication and can better take on human characteristics compared to other software-based programs (Dale, 2016) (Hilderbrand, 2021). To improve this type of communication technology, companies invest a large amount of effort in the technical development of CAs (Maedche, 2019). In parallel, an increasing number of scientists have focussed on the human perception of different chatbot design elements, also known as social cues and user interaction outcomes (Zierau, N. 2020). In the research fields of information systems (ISs) and human–computer interaction (HCI), the number of publications focussing on the design of CAs has been continuously growing. However, to our knowledge, there is no holistic scientific review or framework that considers chatbot design cues and user perceptions or behaviour outcomes and the relationship among them. From a research perspective, a review of the existing experiments and publications that visualises both design elements and effects on user behaviour and even uncovers the possible contradictions is still missing but needed to reach an overall understanding of the connections and dependencies of researched design elements. From a company's perspective, it is recommended to first define the goals of the chatbot before implementing specific design elements (Hilderbrand, 2021). However, because of the actual state of research, practitioners are forced to first decide on certain design elements and test them in daily businesses and then to optimise these according to their goals. We want to close the research gap and at the same time facilitate the work of practitioners. Therefore, we aim to answer the following research question:

How must conversational agents be designed to trigger certain user reactions and thus achieve the goals of the companies using conversational agents?

We start with information on the conceptual background of conversational agents and social reactions. Thereafter, a systematic literature review (SLR) informed by the work of Webster (2002) and vom Brocke et al. (2015) is conducted, and a taxonomy is developed, applied, and evaluated following Nickerson et al. (2013). Finally, based on the taxonomy we develop a model to show the dependencies between cues of CA, signals on the user's side and reactions on the user's side triggered by the CA.

2. CONCEPTUAL BACKGROUND

2.1 Chatbots and Conversational Agents

Chatbots or CAs are software-based systems that use natural language to simulate a human conversation (Bittner E, 2019). Using these chatbots, users can exchange information (Diederich S, 2019) or access data and services just by using natural language (Følstad A, 2019). Although the naming of these software-based systems is under constant discussion (e.g. CA, chatbot, chatterbot or digital assistant), the main purpose remains the same, that is, to have a non-human system chatting with a human to achieve some purpose (e.g. retrieval of information, use of a service) (Dale, 2016). The first chatbot, called ELIZA, was developed in 1966 by Joseph Weizenbaum as a text-based computer program that 'makes natural language conversation with a computer possible' (Weizenbaum, 1966). In the 1980s, text-based chatbots were extended by voice-based dialogue systems and embodied CAs (McTear, 2016).

2.2 Conversational Agents as Non-Human Social Actors

CAs using natural language can express human-like behaviour, which makes conversations feel like a chat with a real human (Gnewuch U. M., 2017). Nass et al. (1994) developed a paradigm called 'Computers Are Social Actors' (CASA) (Nass, 1994). According to this paradigm, users ignore the fact that the CA cannot have any human features during a conversation with a CA (Nass C. M., 2020). Rather, they direct their attention to the social cues applied by the chatbot to assign a social entity to it. This causes the users to attribute familiar stereotypes to chatbots and automatically apply social rules, expectations and scripts known from inter-personal communication when communicating with CAs (Nass C. M., 2020). Using social cues, chatbots can trigger responses from humans, regardless of how rudimentary those cues are (Moon, 2000).

2.3 Social Cues, Social Signals, and Social Reactions

This work is based on a construct of social cues, social signals, and social reactions according to Feine J. et al. (2019). In their research, they argue that a signal evolves from cues when they are created to have a communicative meaning, or the receiver attributes an informative meaning to them. Therefore, they defined a cue of a CA as any design feature of a chatbot salient to the user that presents a source of information (e.g. nodding) (Feine, 2019). This means that cues are antecedents of signals and comprise all the perceptible design features of a CA. Consequently, cues can evolve into a social signal through the attribution of socialness towards a CA (Smith, 2003). This attribution of a social signal is the result of the user's conscious or sub-conscious interpretation of the cues, which finally triggers a social reaction from the user (Nass C. M., 2020).

3. EXISTING RESEARCH

Analysing existing research reviews and classifications in the field of CAs, it seems that most of them focus on design cues to analyse their outcomes regarding users' feelings and behaviour. For instance, Zierau (2020) conducted an SLR aimed at developing a taxonomy that classifies CA characteristics into three major categories: functional, mechanical and human cues. Their work provides deeper insights into service designs with CAs and to support them in systematising and synthesising research on the effects of specific CA characteristics from a user experience perspective (Zierau, 2020). However, they did not distinguish between social signals and social cues. Feine et al. (2019) developed a taxonomy on social cues while structuring cues in four segments: verbal, visual, auditory and invisible. However, although their taxonomy is very detailed and considers many different social cues, there are no explanations for the consequences when applying certain design elements. Rapp et al. (2021) discussed the main factors influencing the interaction between humans and chatbots. However, they did not develop any framework or visualisation for their findings. Janssen et al. (2020) introduced a taxonomy of design elements for a domain-specific chatbot structure to differentiate and categorise domain-specific chatbots according to archetypal qualities that guide practitioners when making design-related decisions. Although they considered a huge number of design elements, they did not mention any dependencies between design elements and user behaviour.

In summary, to our knowledge, no review or taxonomy development established over the last few years has placed user behaviour first or analysed how it can be influenced using different CA design elements or social cues.

4. METHODOLOGY

A combination of different research methods was chosen to answer the research question. The work begins with a systematic literature review (SLR) according to Webster (2002) and vom Brocke et al. (2015). Based on the SLR, which is shown in Table 1, three taxonomies are then developed, using the methods based on Nickerson et al. (2013).

Table 1. Overview of the Systematic Literature Review (SLR)

Step	Research Approach	Outcome
1st Step	Keyword Research: Libraries: - IEEE Library - AIS Library - ACM Portal - Science Direct - Emerald	1893 papers in total: - ACM: 697 - AIS: 140 - Emerald: 12 - IEEE: 796 - Science Direct: 248
2nd Step	Results screening: Exclusion criterions are: - Research does not include an experiment neither and procedure of A-B testing - Research does not consider social cues and their effect on user`s reactions - Research that does not focus on text-based chatbots - Research that is not written in English language	49 papers in total: - ACM: 3 - AIS: 12 - Emerald: 1 - IEEE: 13 - Science Direct: 2
3rd Step	Additional search methods: - Backward search - Forward search - Snowballing approach	69 papers in total: - ACM: 4 - AIS: 21 - Emerald 1 - IEEE 20 - Science Direct 2

4.1 Phase 1: Literature Review

To find relevant literature as a basis for the analysis of the dependencies between social cues, social signals and social reactions, an SLR was conducted between March and May 2021. In their methodology, vom Brocke et al. (2015) suggest a definition of the scope to clarify and determine the basic features of a literature search before the actual work is conducted. Therefore, a sequential search process has been chosen. This means that the whole search process followed pre-defined steps. To reach a high level of transparency in this literature review, the main methodical search steps are described as follows.

Step 1 - Keyword search: Keyword search was performed on the relevant libraries for IS and HCI research: IEEE Library, AIS Library, ACM Portal, Science Direct and Emerald. To ensure that the right keywords and suitable libraries were used, knowledge exchange with other researchers from the field of chatbots and IS research was performed and their input was directly integrated. Finally, the focus was placed on the keywords 'conversational agent', 'chatbot' and 'chat bot'. All variations of the keywords (singular or plural, hyphenated or not hyphenated) used in the title or abstract were considered. Additionally, the search process focussed only on papers published in the last 10 years (2011 to May 2021).

Step 2 - Paper selection: All search results were screened according to pre-defined exclusion criteria. These exclusion criteria were as follows: the study does not include an experiment or a procedure for A-B testing, the study does not consider social cues and their effect on users' reactions, the study does not focus on text-based chatbots or the study is not written in English. Additionally, duplicates were removed. To find the dependencies among cues, signals and reactions, it is necessary to explore the causal connections between the three. However, not many methods suggest causality as conclusively as experiments do (Webster M. S., 2014). Experimental methods involve a systematic manipulation of independent variables while measuring the target behaviour to determine whether a relationship exists between the variables manipulated and behaviour (Sturmey, 2020). After this second step, a total of 49 papers were included in the literature research.

Step 3 - Additional research: With the papers selected from the previous step, backward and forward search were performed, and a snowball search approach was applied. Since most of the papers that remained after the previous step were published in the last one or two years, there was only a very small amount of literature that was added by the forward search. In sum, after the third step, 20 more research items were added.

Step 4 - Paper analysis: A total of 69 relevant papers were analysed in an iterative process. The main goal of this analysis was to obtain a list of master codes and master code descriptions. The relevant master codes focussed on the attributes of social cues, social signals and social reactions.

4.2 Phase 2: Taxonomy Development

In the fields of IS and HCI, the taxonomy development according to Nickerson et al. (2013) is widely used, therefore it was used as a basis for our taxonomy too. Nickerson et al. (2013) invented a step-by-step method for developing taxonomies while ensuring the completeness of the identified dimensions and characteristics of an object.

The first step is to focus on the taxonomy of social reactions, starting with defining the meta-characteristic as a basis for the classification of social reactions (Nickerson, 2013). It was decided to use any social reaction influenced by a CA as meta-characteristic. Next, in line with Nickerson et al. (2013), subjective and objective ending conditions that determine the termination of the taxonomy development process were defined:

1. At least one service cue is classified under every characteristic of every dimension.
2. No new dimension or characteristic has been added in the last iteration.
3. Every dimension and every characteristic in its dimension is unique and is not repeated.
4. Every known service cue is classified in the taxonomy.

In the iterative process of empirical-to-conceptual and conceptual-to-empirical approaches, a taxonomy of social reactions was developed. Second and third, two taxonomies for social signals and social cues were developed and social signals respectively cues were defined as meta-characteristics. Then, the same process as for social reactions was applied, and the same ending conditions were defined. Since it is possible to refer to the same paper analysis, development was restarted with the empirical-to-conceptual approach, followed by a combination of iterations of empirical-to-conceptual and conceptual-to-empirical approaches. An overview of all the papers considered and the taxonomies can be found in the appendix[1].

[1]https://drive.google.com/file/d/1dxzgsj-N0EodNlpbfHBVuxNBskwzAmO8/view?usp=sharing

4.3 Phase 3: Taxonomy Evaluation

After all the ending conditions were met, the iterative process of taxonomy development was complete (Nickerson, 2013). Over several iterations, three taxonomies were developed for social reactions, social signals, and social cues. According to Nickerson et al., (2013) to ensure that the new taxonomy is of a high quality, it should be assessed against the following five criteria: conciseness, robustness, comprehensibility, extendibility, and explanatory power. This study follows the procedure of Zierau (2020), who conducted semi-structured interviews with experts. Most of our experts were researchers from the relevant research field. Additionally, three practitioners were asked who are familiar with chatbots for more than three years. The following are the main points that were discussed during the interviews:

- Conciseness generally refers to the number of dimensions, which should cover the phenomenon sufficiently and at the same time should not overwhelm the reader (Zierau, 2020).
- Robustness means that, based on the dimensions and characteristics, it can be differentiated between objects of interest (Zierau, 2020).
- Comprehensiveness describes the ability of a taxonomy to classify all the objects of a phenomenon of interest (Zierau, 2020).
- Extendibility refers to the ability of a taxonomy to include new dimensions and characteristics (Zierau, 2020).
- Explanatory power refers to the ability of a taxonomy to highlight the inter-relationships between different elements and characteristics transparently and, thus, to uncover previously unknown aspects of a phenomenon (Zierau, 2020).

All in all, the expert interviews were highly positive, and most criteria were almost met. Those that were not met were adapted according to the experts' feedback.

4.4 Phase 4: Taxonomy Application

In the last step, all taxonomies were applied to analyse the selected literature, starting with analysing the dependencies between social reactions and social signals, followed by the analysis of social signals and their influence on social cues. The goal of this phase was to develop guidelines for practitioners and researchers on which social cues and signals must be created to trigger the desired social reactions with CAs. In the end, these guidelines will be visualised in a framework showing all the dependencies between the different factors. The results of this last phase can be found in the online appendix[1].

5. UNDERSTANDING THE TRIGGERS FOR SOCIAL REACTIONS

5.1 Combining the Taxonomies

During the taxonomy development, five independent categories of social reactions were found: satisfaction, trust, behaviour, sales and brand (connectivity)-related. For social signals, only four independent categories were found: utility, doubt, emotion and relationship-related. For social cues we defined the categories quality-related cues, language-oriented cues, cues influencing message intensity and cues explaining the chatbot itself, human-like cues, user-centred cues, cues dealing with failure and cues influencing the bot's character. Answering the research question, the dependencies between social reactions and social signals were first analyzed. Subsequently, the dependencies between social signals and social cues were evaluated. The previously defined taxonomies served as the basis for the analysis of the dependencies. In a third step, the dependencies between reactions, signals and cues were combined.

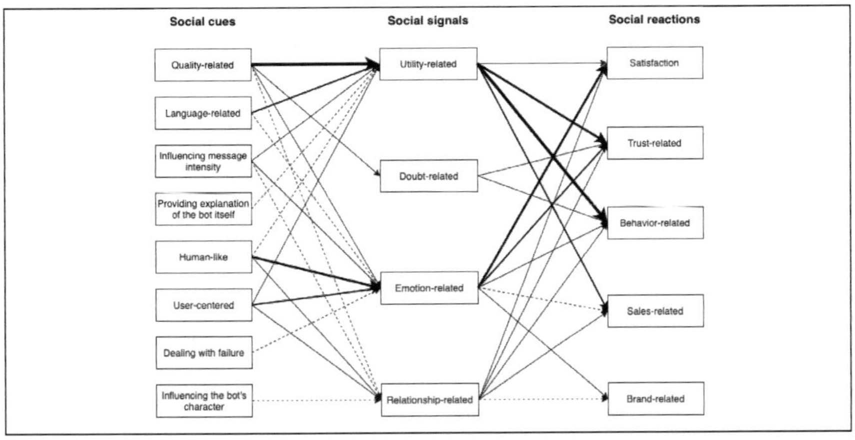

Figure 1. Conceptual model for cues, signals and reactions

Figure 1 shows the conceptual model that links social reactions, social signals and social cues. We see that the reaction satisfaction is mainly influenced by emotion-related signals. These are triggered mainly by human-like and user-centred cues. Trust-related and behaviour-related reactions are mainly triggered by quality-related cues, which cause utility-related signals. Sales-related reactions are consequences of utility-related signals and relationship-related signals. Whereas brand-related reactions are mainly triggered by human-like and user-centred cues.

5.2 Evaluation of the Model for Triggering the Desired Social Reactions

This model was built on the findings reached on social reactions, social signals and social cues and their dependencies. For a first validation of this model, four unstructured expert interviews with practitioners who already implement CAs in their companies were conducted. During the interviews, it was found that some companies do not consider social cues at all. They view CAs more as a software project, without considering the right design criteria. However, none of the interviewed persons rejected the model. Some connections were positively confirmed with practical examples, whereas other connections received at least positive approval from the interviewed people.

5.3 Applying the Model for Triggering the Desired Social Reactions

From a company's or practitioner's perspective, the model should be read from right to left. Each company first defines the goals that should be reached with the CA before defining the individual cues (Hilderbrand, 2021). In practice, companies and practitioners first decide which social reactions they want to trigger with the chatbot. Then, they decide which social signals must be evoked to trigger the defined social reactions, according to this model. After that, they find out which social cues their CA must integrate to trigger the needed social signals, according to the taxonomy. From a research perspective, the model may be read from left to right. Usually, research first focusses on specific social cues to analyse the consequences of applying these cues. It may then focus on the triggered social signals and their influence on social reactions.

6. DISCUSSION AND LIMITATIONS

Although this research followed well-established guidelines and relied on other reviews and taxonomy development processes in the fields of IS and HCI, there might be some limitations in our model, which we would like to discuss.

First, the defined search strategy might have missed relevant publications. As with any literature review, the identified and selected publications had an impact on the list of identified triggers and cues and on the developed model. If other literature sources are used and other reactions, signals and cues are considered, the model may change.

Second, although the SLR and taxonomy development are based on known methods in the fields of IS and HCI, namely, Webster (2002), vom Brocke et al. (2015) and Nickerson et al. (2013), the taxonomy development is still influenced by personal perceptions. To address this point, several expert interviews were conducted during the research process and feedback from other researchers was obtained on a regular basis. Consequently, the taxonomy and model were adjusted according to their feedback.

Third, the whole model with its analysed CA features has not been finalised. We believe that, because of technical advancements, more triggers and design elements may need to be added in the future. However, according to the results of the expert interviews, we assume that the model with its taxonomies provides a sufficient state-of-the-art tool for developing high-performance CAs.

7. CONCLUSION AND OUTLOOK

The research question can be answered with the framework that is developed in the course of this work. It should be emphasized that the model can be read from different perspectives, namely on the part of practitioners and researchers. Discussions with experts from companies that are already using chatbots or are at least planning to do so soon have shown that while the current framework is helpful in creating chatbots, further optimization is still needed. Discussions have shown that companies usually pursue several goals with their conversational agent. However, these are weighted differently. Thus, in the long run, it is difficult to apply the model exactly like this. Rather, a system must be developed that can also handle fuzzy values and that can consider the different weightings of the pursued goals. In the development of such a system, the discipline of fuzzy logic can be applied. Fuzzy systems can deal with fuzzy data and are therefore very well suited to form an ontology for the developed framework (Zadeh, 1988). Researchers who apply "fuzziness" not only classify cues, signals and reactions into fixed categories, but also take into account their position within the category (Zadeh, 1988). This would mean that the developed framework does not work exclusively with exact data or goals, but also with the different weighting or prioritization of the individual goals. In this case, reactions are defined as goals. Additionally, we must consider that the assignments between cues, signals, and reactions, only show the dependencies of the individual variables and assign a certain strength to these dependencies. The assignments in the model are therefore not always exact, but rather show which dependencies are stronger and which dependencies are weaker. All this leads to the idea to add a fuzzy system to the developed framework to make the framework applicable to conversational agents. Thus, future research should focus on the question "how fuzzy-logic can help to build a system that first considers individual companies goals which might be a mixture of several users reactions, and second considers various strength of the relationship between reactions, signals and cues". In the next steps we will develop a fuzzy cognitive map which will first consider the different relationships inside the framework itself. Afterwards, the fact that companies focus on more than one user reaction which are prioritised differently must be added to the new fuzzy system.

REFERENCES

Bittner E, O.-R. S. (2019). Where is the bot in our team? Toward a taxonomy of design option combinations for conversational agents in collaborative work. HICCS 52 proceedings. Maui, 284-293.

Brandtzaeg, P. F. (2018). Chatbots: changing user needs and motivations. . Interactions 25(5) https://doi.org/10.1145/3236669, 38-43.

Brendel, A. G. (2020). 'You are an Idiot!' - How Conversational Agent Communication Patterns Influence Frustration and Harassment. Proceedings of Americas Conference on Information Systems.

Bührke, J. B. (2020). Is Making Mistakes Human? On the Perception of Typing Errors in Chatbot Communication. Hawaii International Conference on System Sciences (HICCS), Kauai, Hawaii, USA.

Bührke, J., Brendel, A., Lichtenberg, S., Diederich, S., & Morana, S. (2021). Do you Feel a Connection? How the Human-like Design of Conversational Agents Influences Donation Behavior. Proceedings of the 16th International Conference on Wirtschaftsinformatik.

Chattaramana, V. K. (2019). Should AI-Based, conversational digital assistants employ social- or task- T oriented interaction style? A task-competency and reciprocity perspective for older adults. Computers in Human Behavior (90), 315-330.

Dale, R. (2016). "The return of the chatbots," Natural Language Engineering (22:5). 811–817.

Diederich S, B. A. (2019). Towards a taxonomy of platforms for conversational agent design. WI 2019 proceed- ings. Siegen, 1100-1114.

Diederich, S. B. (2019). Design for Fast Request Fulfillment or Natural Interaction? Insights from an Experiment with a Conversational Agent. Proceedings of the 27th European Conference on Information Systems (ECIS), Stockholm and Uppsala, Sweden, June 8-14.

Diederich, S. J.-M. (2019). Emulating Empathetic Behavior in Online Service Encounters with Sentiment-Adaptive Responses: Insights from an Experiment with a Conversational Agent. Proceedings of International Conference on Information Systems (ICIS), Munich, Germany.

Diederich, S. L. (2020). Not Human After All: Exploring The Impact of Response Failure on User Perception of Anthropomorphic Conversational Service Agents. Proceedings of European Conference on Information Systems (ECIS), Marrakech, Morocco.

Feine, J. G. (2019). Agents, A Taxonomy of Social Cues for Conversational. International Journal of Human-Computer Studies 132, 138-161.

Fogg, B. (2002). Computers as persuasive social actors. Persuasive Technology: Using Computers to Change What We Think and Do. Morgan Kaufmann Publishers, San Francisco, CA, USA, 89–120.

Fogg, B. N. (1997). How users reciprocate to computers. CHI '97 Extended Abstracts on Human Factors in Computing Systems. CHI '97 extended abstracts, Atlanta, Georgia. ACM, New York, NY, 331.

Følstad A, S. M. (2019). Different chatbots for different purposes: towards a typology of chatbots to understand interaction design. International conference on internet science proceedings. St. Petersburg, 145-156.

Følstad, A. a. (2014). "Chatbots and the New World of HCI". Interactions (24:4), 38-42.

Følstad, A. B. (2020). Users ' Experiences with Chatbots: Findings from a Questionnaire Study. Quality and User Experience, Springer International Publishing, 1–14.

Frommert, C. H. (2018). Using Chatbots to Assist Communication in Collaborative Networks (257-265). Springer.

Gnewuch, U. M. (2017). Towards designing cooperative and social conversational agents for customer service. Proceedings of the 38th International Conference on Information Systems (ICIS). AISel, Seoul.

Gnewuch, U. M. (2020). The Effect of Perceived Similarity in Dominance on Customer Self-Disclosure to Chatbots in Conversational Commerce. Proceedings of the 28th European Conference on Information Systems (ECIS 2020), Marrakech, Morocco.

Hilderbrand, C. H. (2021). A Strategy Framework to Boost Conversational AI Performance. Marketing Review St. Gallen 4 | 2021.

Janssen, A. P. (2020). Virtual Assistance in Any Context - A Taxonomy of Design Elements for Domain-Specific Chatbots . Bus Inf Syst Eng 62(3) https://doi.org/10.1007/s12599-020-00644-1, 211-225.

Maedche, A. L. (2019). AI-Based Digital Assistants. Business & Information Systems Engineering (61:4), 535– 544.

McLean, G. a.-F. (2019). Hey Alexa ... Examine the Variables Influencing the Use of Artificial Intelligent In-Home Voice Assistants. Computers in Human Behavior (99:April), 28– 37.

McTear, M. C. (2016). Conversational interfaces: Devices, wearables, virtual agents, and robots. In The Conversational Interface, 283-308.

Moon, Y. (2000). Intimate exchanges: using computers to elicit self-disclosure from con- sumers. J. Consum. Res. 26 (4), https://doi.org/10.1086/209566., 323-339.

Nass, C. M. (2020). Machines and mindlessness: social responses to computers. J. Soc. Issues 56(1), https://doi.org/10.1111/0022-4537.00153., 81-103.

Nass, C. S. (1994). Computers are social actors. Proceedings of the SIGCHI Conference on Human Factors in Computing Systems. New York, NY, USA. ACM,, 72-78.

Ng, M. K. (2020). Simulating the Effects of Social Presence on Trust, Privacy Concerns & Usage Intentions in Automated Bots for Finance. IEEE European Symposium on Security and Privacy Workshops (EuroS&PW).

Nickerson, R. C. (2013). A Method for Taxonomy Development and Its Application in Information Systems. European Journal of Information Systems, 336-259.

Smith, J. H. (2003). Animal Signals. Oxford University Press, Oxford, UK.

Sturmey, P. (2020). Functional Analysis in Clinical Treatment. https://doi.org/10.1016/C2015-0-05507-1: Elsevier Inc.

vom Brocke, J. S. (2015). Standing on the shoulders of giants: Challenges and recommendations of literature search in information systems research. Communications of the Association for Information Systems, 37, 205–224.

Webster, J. W. (2002). Analyzing the past to prepare for the future: Writing a literature review. MIS Quarterly, 26(2), 13–23.

Webster, M. S. (2014). Laboratory Experiments in the Social Sciences. https://doi.org/10.1016/C2011-0-07562-2: Elsevier Inc.

Weizenbaum, J. (1966). ELIZA - a computer program for the study of natural language communication between man and machine. Commun. Commun. ACM 9 (1), 36-45.

Zadeh, L. (1988). Fuzzy Logic. IEEE Computer, vol. 21, nr. 4, 83-93.

Zierau, N. T. (2020). The Anatomy of User Experience with Conversational Agents : A Taxonomy and Propositions of Service Clue. International Conference on Information Systems (ICIS), 1-17.

Zierau, N. V. (2020). A Review of the Empirical Literature on Conversational Agents and Future Research Directions. Forty-First International Conference on Information Systems, India.

A STEP CLOSER TO UNDERSTANDING IMPLEMENTATION OF BUSINESS INTELLIGENCE IN THE ORGANIZATIONAL OPERATIONS: A SYSTEMATIC LITERATURE REVIEW

Ljerka Luic, Neva Babic and Ante Roncevic
University North, Department of Economics, Jurja Krizanica 31b, 42000 Varazdin, Croatia

ABSTRACT

The development of business intelligence was marked by several key moments, in particular the development of the Internet and new technologies. The wide distribution of technology and the easier possibility to use it led to the finding of a solution for the tools used by organizations to be a good ratio of quality and invested financial resources, and the increase in digitalization give the opportunity for organization's business intelligence to involve more stakeholders. The purpose of this paper is to identify the prerequisites, importance and value of implementing business intelligence in the organizational operations. The analyzed sample is limited to the period from year 2020, given that this period noted the biggest changes in terms of technologies, and therefore transitions in the business of organizations. Based on a systematic literature review on two major scientific databases Web of Science and Scopus, there was found 2051 articles that were initially narrowed down to 65 papers connected to business intelligence directly and finally, to a total number of 10 relevant articles through a methodical approach, and which are connected to the topic of business intelligence in organizational context. Selected papers were analyzed using desk-based research method. This result represents a paper compilation of research results as cooperation of authors, achieved through the student-mentor relationship during the preparation of postgraduate specialist thesis. After conducting the research using text analysis technique, two main groups were determined based on subject of research: papers focused on organizational prerequisites and importance for the successful implementation of BI in the organization's operations and papers focused on the value of implementing BI in the organization's operations. From the analyzed papers, the conclusion is that a trend of studying business intelligence in organizations is visible, and it ranged from the study of organizational prerequisites for the successful implementation of BI during 2020 and the beginning of 2021 and moved towards the analysis of the value that BI has for organizations, mainly in 2021 and 2022.

KEYWORDS

Business Intelligence, Implementation, Innovation, Organizational Operations, Literature Review

1. INTRODUCTION

The term business intelligence (BI) is a ubiquitous and widely represented concept that can be viewed from different aspects, and thus there is no single definition of it. (Babic, 2022) The growth of companies and processes, and thus the amount of information and facts, has brought new challenges to the leaders of organizations in terms of processing this information and its successful management for the purpose of making strategic decisions and improving business processes. Precisely because of this, a new imperative was set before organizations - to become intelligent, which primarily meant making better decisions and being faster than the competition. For this purpose, and by means of data transformed into information and by deriving this information into intelligence, today it is possible to create collective organizational intelligence that enables insights into certain business processes and drawing conclusions based on which further business decisions are made. (Liautaud, Hammond, 2006:3) Today, business intelligence is viewed as "a technology-driven process for analyzing data and delivering actionable information that helps executives, managers and workers make informed business decisions." (Stedman, 2020) The concept of knowledge management is most often associated with the concept of business intelligence whereas business intelligence studies the hidden and relevant contexts in a large set of business and economic data, while knowledge management enables organizations to learn and understand based on their own experiences. (Ravlic, 2015) Business intelligence is a circular activity, with a cycle that has several fundamental phases. The business intelligence model as well as individual phases of the model direct the organization that uses business intelligence to move more easily between phases and determine the priorities and goals of each phase in order to fulfill the final goal of each such process, which is to obtain the necessary information for decision-making. (Javorović, Bilandžić, 2007:206-207) The development of business intelligence was marked by several key moments, and in particular the development of the Internet and new technologies contributed to this, which accelerated this process, i.e. enabled the processes and ideas behind the concept of business intelligence to take place smoothly, quickly and easily. (Heinze, 2014) The evolution of business intelligence has clearly shown that technology has successfully followed the demands imposed on it by the rapidly increasing amount of data and information, and it was necessary to organize it better and faster. (Chen et al. 2012) From everything above it can be concluded that in the coming period, an even greater increase in the development of business intelligence and the opportunities that the same provides is expected. (Costello, Rimol, 2021) For the purpose of a more detailed insight into the scientific perspective and research questions related to the concept of business intelligence and its role in the organizational context, below is a review of the literature on the mentioned topic using relevant scientific bases and a methodology adapted to everything mentioned. The focus of the research when creating the literature review was to determine the role, context and significance of the tools and concepts of business intelligence for the organization within which it is applied.

2. METHODOLOGY

The research analysis was carried out during June 2022 through the two largest citation databases, Web of Science and Scopus. The research is limited to the search of papers published between year 2020 and year 2022, and given the fact that this period records a significant development of information and communication technologies, which had to be followed by greater implementations of organizational changes in advance. At that time, business processes were experiencing the greatest transformations and were in the phase of the most intense changes. The term used in the search was: business intelligence. The criteria that were additionally set and according to which the research was further narrowed down were the following: only papers in English are included in the search and with regard to the scientific field, papers from the Social Sciences Citation Index (SSCI) category, and the papers from the field of social sciences in the Scopus database were observed.

After the given criteria, a total of 1,707 papers classified according to certain categories were found in the Web of Science database, of which the most papers were found in the Business category as shown in Figure 1.

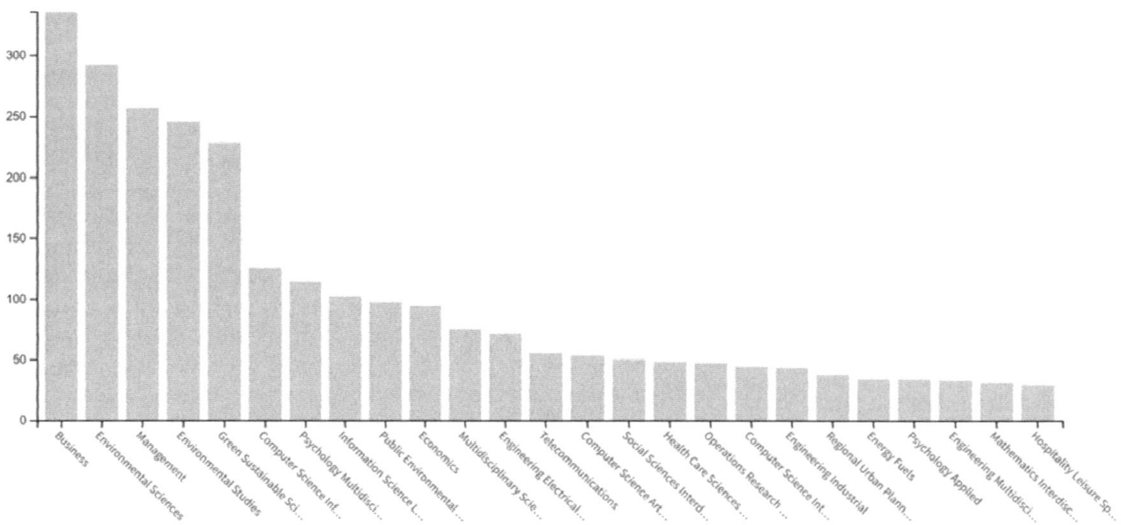

(Source: creation of the authors via the Web of Science database)

Figure 1. Display of the number of papers by individual categories within the search criteria

A total of 344 results were found in the Scopus database according to the given parameters, which is 38.3% of the total number of papers found within the mentioned parameters and at the same time the category that contains the largest number of papers about business intelligence as shown in Figure 2.

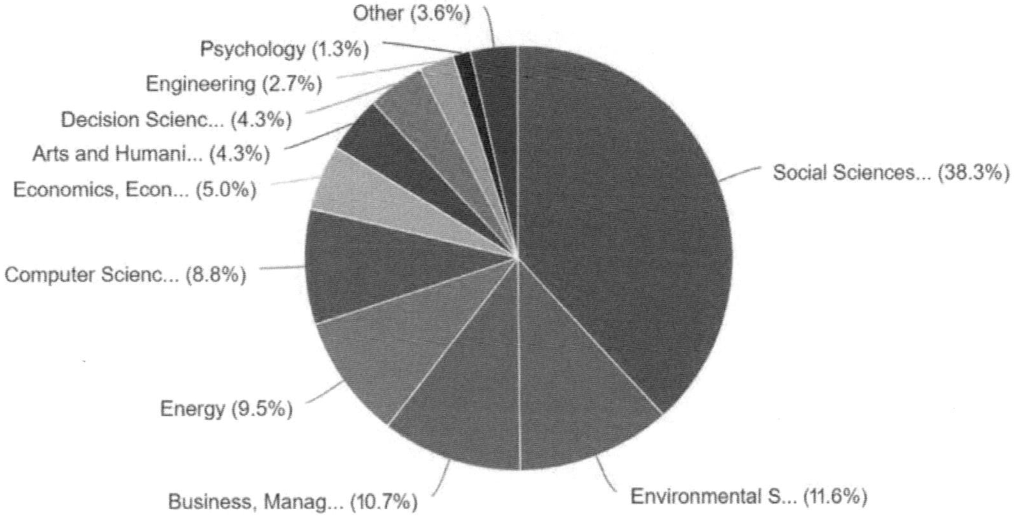

(Source: creation of the author via the Scopus database)

Figure 2. Presentation of papers according to the most frequently appearing categories

After reviewing the titles and abstracts of all papers in the Web of Science database, only papers containing the word business intelligence in the title or abstract were included in the further analysis. There was a total of 41 such papers, namely 16 papers from 2020, 19 papers from 2021 and 6 papers from 2022. One of the papers from 2021 was subsequently excluded from the research due to language barrier, so in 2021 there were 18 papers at the end, and a total of 40 papers classified by different categories within the searched term.

After reviewing the titles and summaries of all papers in the Scopus database, only papers that contained the word business intelligence in the title or were in some way related to the mentioned term were included in the further analysis. There was a total of 27 such papers, namely 6 papers from 2020, 11 papers from 2021 and 10 papers from 2022. One of the papers from 2021 and one from 2022 were subsequently excluded from further research due to limited access, leaving 10 in 2021, 9 in 2022, and a total of 25 papers classified by different categories.

Documents	Citations		<2020	2020	2021	2022	Subtotal	>2022	Total
		Total	0	2	36	32	70	0	70
Business intelligence: business evolution after industry 4.0	2021				7	5	12		12
Elucidating the determinants of business intelligence adopti...	2020			2	6	2	10		10
A business intelligence & analytics framework for clean ...	2021				4	5	9		9
IoT data visualization for business intelligence in corporat...	2022					7	7		7
A business intelligence framework for analyzing educational ...	2020				6	1	7		7

(Source: creation of the author via the Scopus database)

Figure 3. Presentation of the 5 most cited papers under the term business intelligence RESULTS

The next phase included the review of all remaining papers. After the analysis of a total of 65 papers, namely 40 papers from the scientific database Web of Science and 25 papers from the scientific database Scopus, 48 of them were excluded because they were related to a specific activity or industry or closely related to technology or a certain studied procedure, 1 paper was excluded because it was not available in full form, and a total of 6 papers were detected that were included in the analysis, and are in both databases. The final analysis was made on a total of 10 papers that are related to the topic of the concept of business intelligence in the organizational context. The mentioned papers were included in further processing in such a way that they were analyzed according to the following criteria and as furtherly shown in Table 1.

Table 1. A summary of the research according to the analyzed criteria (Source: creation of the author)

Authors	Year	Country	Target group	Research method	Research instruments
Bhatiasevi, V.; Naglis, M.	2020	Thailand	Small and medium enterprises in Bangkok, BI experts from various sectors	Quantitative and qualitative	Questionnaire, interview
Suša Vugec, D.; Bosilj Vukšić, V.; Pejić Bach, M.; Jaklić, J.; Indihar Štemberger M.	2020	Croatia and Slovenia	Top management and/or employees in charge of BI and BPM in Croatian and Slovenian organizations with more than 50 employees	Quantitative	Questionnaire
Chen,X.; Siau, K.	2020	USA	US company leaders using BI in their business	Quantitative	Questionnaire
Skyrius, R.; Valentukevičė, J.	2020	-	-	Desk-based research	Literature review/available research papers
Hortovanyi, L.; Szabo, R. Z.; Fuzes, P.	2021	Hungary	Fortune 500 company	Qualitative	Case study, semi-structured interview
Tavera Romero, C.A.; Ortiz, J.H.; Khalaf, O.I.; Ríos Prado, A.	2021	-	-	Desk-based research	Literature review
Huang, Z.; Savita, K.S.; Zhong-jie, J.	2021		Directors and experts of startup companies	Quantitative	Questionnaire
Paradza, D.; Daramola, O	2021	-	-	Desk-based research	Literature review
Darwiesh, A.; Alghamdi, M. I; El-Baz, A. H.; Elhoseny, M.	2022	-	-	Desk-based research	Literature review
Nazari, F.; Taghavi, S.S.; Valizadeh, E.	2022	Iran	Relevant experts and managers in 150 startup companies	Quantitative	Questionnaire

The conducted research generated articles that can be divided into 2 main groups: a) Research papers focused on organizational prerequisites and importance for the successful implementation of BI in the organization's operations; b) Research papers focused on the value of implementing BI in the organization's operations. Below is a summary of each previously described group.

2.1 Research Papers Focused on Organizational Prerequisites and Importance for the Successful Implementation of BI in the Organization's Operations

A total of 4 scientific papers from 2020 and 2021 were identified in the part of the research focused on organizational prerequisites and importance for the successful implementation of BI in the organization's operations. All the studies in this part were created with the aim of understanding the basic aspects of the organization's adaptation to the introduction of BI in business, two of which were conducted via a survey questionnaire on a sample of companies from Thailand and the USA, one was conducted as a case study on the example of Fortune 500 list of the most successful companies in the USA, while one study was conducted through a review of available literature sources on the mentioned topic. The authors of the first paper in the mentioned category (Bhatiasevi, Naglis, 2020) conducted quantitative and qualitative research using the scientific methods of questionnaires and interviews, and as an introduction, an overview of the literature on the topic of the paper was presented. The study proposed a comprehensive model that integrates the TOE framework with the BSC framework to identify the factors and degree of influence on BI adoption among SMEs in Thailand, as well as the factors and degree of influence on organizational performance. By testing hypotheses and factors that have an impact on the introduction of BI in business, it was determined that the factor with the highest degree of influence in the adoption of BI by Thai small and medium enterprises was precisely the support of the top management. Another study (Chen, Siau, 2020) was conducted using a questionnaire method that was sent to the leaders of companies in the USA that already use BI in their business. Research was conducted with the aim of assessing the impact of business analytics (BA) and business intelligence (BI), IT infrastructure flexibility and their interaction on organizational agility. The authors state that the mentioned study is one of the few empirical studies that investigate the importance of BA from the perspectives of its use, all with the aim of establishing that IT (information technology) and IS (information system) components can be key sources of organizational agility. Among other things, the importance of building a flexible IT infrastructure to improve organizational agility is determined. The third study (Skyrius, Valentukevičė, 2020) uses a literature review while simultaneously oriented to the agility of BI, information and organization, starting from the assumption that in ensuring organizational agility, information activities play a key role in orienting the environment towards important changes. The conclusion of the research by reviewing the available sources states that BI should play an important role in ensuring organizational agility and that the technological aspect of the introduction of BI technologies into business is much more prevalent and more often researched in relation to the human and managerial factor, i.e. the cultural aspect in the role of a means of information in construction agility competence of an organization. The last research in the mentioned category (Hortovanyi et al., 2021) presents the results of a longitudinal study on the path of a large corporation towards becoming an ambidextrous organization in the face of new technologies. The research was conducted through the principle of a case study on the example of an American Fortune 500 company using the semi-structured interview method with the aim of understanding the adaptation of business processes of large companies to market demands and changes. By exploring the interplay between top and middle management, the results show that business intelligence systems have enabled the company to pursue data-driven strategic renewal, automated and supporting rapid organizational learning.

2.2 Research Papers Focused on the Value of Implementing BI in the Organization's Operations

A total of 6 scientific papers from 2020, 2021 and 2022 were identified in the part of the research papers focused on the value of implementing BI in the organization's operations All the studies in this part were conducted with the aim of researching and questioning the value and positive aspects of the introduction of BI in the organization's operations, three of which were conducted through a survey questionnaire on a sample of companies from Croatia and Slovenia, i.e. directors, experts and relevant experts of startup companies, while the remaining three studies were conducted through a review of available literature sources on the mentioned topic. The authors of the first analyzed paper (Susa Vugec et al., 2020) conducted a questionnaire survey on organizations in Croatia and Slovenia with more than 50 employees in order to determine the compatibility of BI with Business Process Management, considering that the goal of both initiatives is to improve the performance of the organization. The research showed that business value can be generated through the use of common terminology and methodology as well as strong communication between BI and BPM experts, managers and teams. Also, the research showed the impact of BI on organizational performance, but also confirmed that BI and BPM initiatives must be coordinated in order to achieve business value. Another paper in this category (Tavera et al., 2021) analyzes the concept of Industry 4.0 as a set of technologies that organizations use to promote their innovative strategies and respond to rapid and dynamic market changes, and proposes the use of these technologies. Also, the paper talks about BI technologies and the ways in which they have had a positive impact on the organization. The research was conducted using the literature review method, and the results show that technologies serve as development pillars of companies because they support their decision-making process, forecasting and corporate economy. Also, it was shown that the support of effective leadership and training would make that development even better. The third paper (Huang et al., 2021) was created and written with the aim of assessing the impact of the BI concept on the financial performance of startup companies. Using the questionnaire method, directors and experts of startups were examined, and the statistical processing determined that the direct impact of BI technologies on financial performance is not clear, but the direct impact of BI technologies on innovation and online learning is obvious and clear, and that in turn contributes to better financial performance, which would could confirm the indirect influence of BI technologies on the financial performance of startup companies, where the mentioned technologies play an intermediary role in that process. The fourth paper (Paradza, Daramola, 2021) provides an overview of the literature on business intelligence and business value in organizations. As one of the main results of the research, the main critical factors for business value from the implementation of BI technologies are listed, namely: qualified human capital, BI infrastructure, data quality, BI application and its use/data, culture, alignment of BI with organizational goals and support top management, while the basic challenges relate to data quality and handling, data security and protection, as well as the lack of BI infrastructure and the lack of qualified human capital. The fifth paper in this category (Darwiesh et al., 2022) analyzes social networks and the importance of data on social networks to improve the competitiveness of companies in a post-pandemic world. As companies face numerous challenges after the pandemic, they are in great need to develop new methodologies and approaches. The research was carried out using the literature review method, and one of the main findings of the same is the proposed framework in which social networks and analysis of large databases are connected in order to establish BI systems. The sixth and last paper in this category (Nazari, et al., 2022) lists innovation, BI and knowledge management as important drivers of startup companies and tries to examine the impact of the BI concept on the mentioned companies using innovation and knowledge management as mediators in this process. Research was conducted on relevant experts and managers in 150 startup companies using the questionnaire method. The results of the research showed that business intelligence, innovation and knowledge management affect the performance of startup companies, and managers of startup companies are advised to take advantage of modern technologies in order to facilitate the process of innovation in their production process.

3. DISCUSSION

When talking about the concept of business intelligence, it is impossible to leave out the factor of organization as the key driver of all changes and processes. The readiness of the organization, especially the organization's leadership, as well as employee training and organizational culture, proved to be decisive factors in the successful implementation of the BI concept in business. In addition to technology, which is expected to be designed in such a way that it successfully meets all the needs of rapidly growing changes and the infrastructure required for this, the human factor is decisive in the creation of a successful BI system. Organizations at all levels should develop a culture of understanding the importance of such a concept and provide appropriate knowledge to their employees so that they are able to implement it in their work and use it in the correct way so that it contributes to the creation of business value. In this whole process, an important role is played by the leaders and management of the organization, who should be the initiators and leaders of such changes and serve as a kind of motivator for these changes to take place.

From the aspect of the value that BI brings to the organization, the conclusions are different, but they all point to one thing, which is that the value for the organization is multiple with the correct organization of the mentioned concept. It is particularly important to mention the development of technologies and rapid changes in the market, which prove that today BI is no longer a need of only large companies for the organization of their business processes, but is also an important component and aspect of the business of small organizations, especially startups. This importance has been separately analyzed through some scientific papers, and it has been confirmed that startup companies need to implement BI systems in their business for their survival and financial stability, because they are the initiators of great innovations as well as mediators in knowledge management, which today greatly increases the competitiveness of the organization on the market.

4. CONCLUSION

Due to the large number and quantity of sources on the topic of business intelligence, and especially business intelligence in the organization, the analyzed sample is limited to the period since the beginning of the pandemic, given that the period recorded the biggest changes in terms of technologies, and therefore transitions in the business of organizations. From the analyzed papers, a trend of study and analysis is visible, which ranged from the study of organizational prerequisites for the successful introduction of BI, which are mostly papers from 2020 and the beginning of 2021, and moved towards the analysis of the value that BI has for organizations, which papers and analyzes date mainly to 2021 and 2022. In those years, it was also possible to create literature reviews and analyze the specific impact of the mentioned concept. As the market has already changed and progressed a lot since then, and considering that some surveys carried out using the questionnaire method date back to earlier periods, from before the start of the pandemic, it would certainly be useful to review and repeat the same survey after some time in order to determine the increase in the number of such papers and analyze their direction of movement. Likewise, the literature review is focused only on business organizations, and it would be interesting to compare it with other types of organizations and their understanding of the BI concepts, methods and tools.

ACKNOWLEDGEMENT

The publication of this paper was possible by the funds of the University North, intended to support scientific research of the development project "a/AR-Learning: Active learning by applying augmented reality", for which the authors of this paper are extremely grateful.

REFERENCES

Babic, N., (2022). Identification of influence factors on the absorption of funds for science, research and innovation from European Union funds by application of business intelligence. Postgraduate specialist thesis, University North, Varazdin, Croatia

Bhatiasevi, V., Naglis, M., (2020). Elucidating the determinants of business intelligence adoption and organizational performance. *Information Development 2020*, Vol. 36(1), pp 78–96. https://doi.org/10.1177/0266666918811394

Chen, H., Chiang, R. H. L., & Storey, V. C., (2012). Business Intelligence and Analytics: From Big Data to Big Impact. *MIS Quarterly*, 36(4), pp 1165–1188. https://doi.org/10.2307/41703503

Chen, X., & Siau, K., (2020). Business Analytics/Business Intelligence and IT Infrastructure: Impact on Organizational Agility. *Journal of Organizational and End User Computing (JOEUC)*, 32(4), pp 138-161. http://doi.org/10.4018/JOEUC.2020100107

Costello, K., Rimol, M., (2021). Gartner Identifies the Top Strategic Technology Trends for 2022 [online]. *Gartner*. URL: https://www.gartner.com/en/newsroom/press-releases/2021-10-18-gartner-identifies-the-top-strategic-technology-trends-for-2022 (accessed: 22.6.2022.)

Darwiesh, A. et al., (2022). Social Media Big Data Analysis: Towards Enhancing Competitiveness of Firms in a Post-Pandemic World. *Hindawi Journal of Healthcare Engineering,* Volume 2022, Article ID 6967158, 14 pages. https://doi.org/10.1155/2022/6967158

Hortovanyi, L. et al., (2021). Extension of the strategic renewal journey framework: the changing role of middle management. *Technology in Society*, Vol. 65, p. 101540, https://doi.org/10.1016/j.techsoc.2021.101540

Huang, Z. et al., (2022). The Business Intelligence impact on the financial performance of start-ups. *Information Processing & Management,* Volume 59, Issue 1, January 2022, https://doi.org/10.1016/j.ipm.2021.102761

Javorović, B., Bilandzic, M., (2007). *Poslovne informacije i business intelligence*. Golden marketing – Tehnička knjiga, Zagreb, Croatia

Liataud, B., Hammond, M., (2006). *E-poslovna inteligencija*. Prudens Consilium, Zagreb, Croatia

Nazari, F. et al., (2022). An Investigation on the Impact of Business Intelligence over the Performance of Startup Companies according to Innovation and Knowledge Management as Mediators. *Hindawi Mathematical Problems in Engineering Volume 2022*, Article ID 3834696, 12 pages. https://doi.org/10.1155/2022/3834696

Paradza, D.; Daramola, O., (2021). Business Intelligence and Business Value In Organisations: A Systematic Literature Review. *Sustainability 2021*, 13, 11382. https://doi.org/10.3390/su132011382

Ravlic, D., (2015). From Information to Knowledge: Business Intelligence Usage and Perspectives. *Proceedings of the ENTRENOVA - ENTerprise REsearch InNOVAtion Conference*, Kotor, Montengero, 10-11 rujan 2015, pp 96-103

Skyrius R., & Valentukevičė J., (2020). Business Intelligence Agility, Informing Agility and Organizational Agility: Research Agenda. Information & Media, 90, pp 8-25. https://doi.org/10.15388/Im.2020.90.47

Stedman, C., (2020). business intelligence (BI). *TechTarget*. URL: https://www.techtarget.com/searchbusinessanalytics/definition/business-intelligence-BI (accessed: 22.6.2022.)

Susa Vugec, D. et al., (2020). Business intelligence and organizational performance: The role of alignment with business process management. *Business process management journal*, Vol. 26 No. 6, pp. 1709-1730. https://doi.org/10.1108/BPMJ-08-2019-0342

Tavera Romero, C.A. et al., (2021). Business Intelligence: Business Evolution after Industry 4.0. *Sustainability*, 2021, 13, 10026. https://doi.org/10.3390/su131810026

MULTIVARIANT ANALYSIS IN VIDEO AD MARKETING CAMPAIGNS FOR WEB TRAFFIC QUALITY OPTIMIZATION

Marta López and Fernando Perales
JOT INTERNET MEDIA España SL, General Ramírez de Madrid 8, 28020 Madrid, Spain

ABSTRACT

In digital marketing, performance can be used to determine which variables affect the quality of web traffic. There are different ways of collecting data, which allows us to enrich our data and gives us a lever to generate new ways of looking at and dealing with information. And yet, the large amount of data, the daily variation and the different level of granularity require dedicated data preparation. Our data will require prior preparation and cleaning, in order to be able to develop the multivariate and correlation analysis through the Cramer's V-diagram. Our objective, to analyze traffic quality, a parameter that is not only used by companies to verify the suitability of the audience concerned but is also directly related to the bandwidth awareness and profitability of video advertising campaigns. Analytical identification of the variables that most affect traffic quality can be used to optimize both marketing campaign structure and bidding strategy.

KEYWORDS

Video Ad Marketing, Quality Prediction, Data Preparation, Multi-Variant Analysis, Digital Marketing, Web Traffic

1. INTRODUCTION

During the last years, video marketing has been proved as a high-efficient media to engage the targeted audience at reasonable prices with good performance indicators (clicks and return of investment). These aspects motivates that the global video ad investment forecast predicts a continuous growth of 12% till 2025, reaching $148 B. This huge market means that enormous amount of web traffic, representing potential clients, will be redirected to the companies´ websites. However, based on the information reported by the video ad platforms in JOT video campaigns (Youtube), between 20-30% of this traffic comes from inauthentic users, mainly bots working through virtual protocol networks (VPNs) and programmed to spend the companies budget clicking in the ads with no post conversion, limiting marketing campaigns impact and reducing the return of investment by wasting companies' budget.

Due to this fact, in the market there exists several companies offering inauthentic traffic detection services:

• Click Cease: Offering a set of rules manually like time per session and clicks per time frame. Track conversions and post-click analysis. It is possible to define traffic filter rules at campaigns level and blacklist IP addresses and ranges limited up to 500.

• Click Guard: Enabling manual and automated filtering options based on the account level selected. It allows to manage the Google account based on the tracking template. The post click analysis is performed thanks to the ingestion of a tracking id.

• PPC (Pay Per Click) Protect: This service imports the tracking template, the blocking strategy is based on the traffic source. This service works at IP (Internet Protocol) number blocking.

There are also other solutions like ADEX, Traffic Guard and Traffic Cop that provide traffic monitoring, inauthentic traffic quantification and filtering and advanced analysis for sophisticated invalid traffic generation. However, none of them have access to historical data of the campaigns statistics so they need a long learning process to be able to define and implement reliable and robust traffic filters. In addition, some of them work on IP addresses which adds a GDPR related challenge to the development.

Considering this market status, the access to an already existing database describing the video web traffic (YouTube) of more than 12 websites during the last 6 months enables the development of unique the video ad traffic quality analysis, identifying which are the most relevant parameters conditioning the web traffic quality. This disposal also ensures that algorithms are trained, tested, and validated with real data, reaching the required insights quality and accuracy to be used in production conditions for decision making. The dataset generated compiles a set of 50 variables (combining performance indicators and descriptors as attributes).

At business level, by the multi-variant analysis for the identification of low quality traffic sources, it will be possible: (i) to increase the trust in video ad marketing as a reliable tool for business promotion, ensuring that all the users reaching companies' landing pages are real potential clients, so the marketing budget is fully spent in high quality audiences; and, (ii) the direct correlation of the video content to the user audience increase the user experience confidence, so the companies will get more and more interactions and visits through this media content.

Taking all the previous aspects into consideration, the goal of the paper is to answer the following questions:

- What are the main variables impacting the quality of the traffic?
- Is there any correlation among the variables used to describe the impact of the marketing campaigns?
- How can the traffic quality be predicted based on the analysis of historical data?

The paper is organized as follows. Section II presents the technical background related to multi-variant analysis and its relation to the quality prediction. In Section III, required work to generate the dataset is presented, covering data collection, key existing indicators and ETLs (Extraction, Transformation and Loading) needed to data merging. Section IV introduces the technical analysis is presented and the main results discussed. Finally, Section V highlights key conclusions and open issues for the future.

2. BACKGROUND

The easy and wide access to Digital Marketing (DM) services has allow the massive and periodic data collection of variables and indicators describing the performance of the marketing campaigns. This has pushed the marketing teams to approach data science as the only solution to process and analyze the vast amount of data available. Due to the large number of variables involved, one of the first goals is to understand their importance and correlation depending on the goals of the company, which allow the identification of the target parameter.

There are some references describing the different approaches for multivariant analysis (Black & Babin, 2019) and (Everitt & Hothorn, 2011) and specifically applied to marketing (Saura, 2021). They all state that in almost all the cases data preparation represents a significant bottleneck for marketing data processing, even conditioning the final quality of the results. For that reason, in our case the final data set used in the analysis has been specifically prepared, enabling both temporal analysis and correlations depending on the target variables: traffic quality (discrete variable) and conversion difference (continuous variable obtained by the difference in the reporting values for the same day with 7 days delay).

The final goal of this work is to generate a decision support system enabling the detection of inauthentic traffic sources based on real performance data analysis and predictive services, so the confidence and trust on the initial data must be maximized. For the generation of the predictive service, the temporal series of the variables must be considered. In Neusser (2016) and Hyndman and Khandakar (2008) the two conditions to develop this kind of services are defined:

1. availability of data about the past
2. assumption that past patterns will be replicated in the future

These two conditions are fully satisfied in our case, as data sets are collected daily from past months video marketing campaigns, also society interests shows periodic patterns depending on the seasonality and traffic quality can be described based on campaign indicators like the category and the keywords, which are 100% monitored.

The different stages of the process to develop the multivariant analysis are as follows[1,2]:

- *Objectives of the analysis*: This is the basis on which the technical work must be guided. The objective of the analysis is to determine whether there are correlations between the different variables that cannot be seen at first glance or by expert visualization and evaluate their influence on our target variables. The final goal is to understand how the quality of traffic to our ads can be improved to optimize the campaign results.

[1] http://www.est.uc3m.es/esp/nuevadocencia/getafe/estadistica/analisismultivariante/doc generica/archivos/metodos.pdf

[2] https://bookdown.org/chescosalgado/intro_r/tipos-y-estructuras-de-datos-en-r.html

Selection of data: As mentioned earlier, this is a crucial step. The right choice and quality of data determines to a large extent the satisfaction of the conclusions. It must be determined the time range studied, the sample size and the explanatory variables to be observed. Starting from the assumption of independence, it is analysed whether this is fulfilled.

Figure 1. Steps of the data analysis

Selection of the target variables: Representing the variables for which the analysis with show how the rest of the parameters affect. It can be one or several depending on the results obtained. In addition, data has been processed differently depending on its type. There are two types of target variable: (i) Quantitative variable (Composed of numerical values) and (ii) Qualitative variable (Composed of factors).

- *Data cleaning*: Prior to any type of analysis, the data must be cleaned to ensure that they are optimal. Among the cleaning tasks, a preliminary analysis is carried out, plotting the variables to see their distribution as well as their main statistics. This has allowed to decide how to transform the variables to select its correct typology. This analysis also provides information about the distributions of the different variables and their possible statistical transformations to create a predictive model. At the same time, the data cleaning also manages the outliers and missing values. Once this initial treatment is developed, the variables will be ready for use in a single dataset.
- *Analysis*: A treatment of correlations has been carried out, both between individual variables that are relevant to our study and between all the inputs. It has been carried out thanks to the correlation matrix (Cario & Nelson, 1997). In this way, it has been possible to analyze the interdependence and avoid multi-collinearity in future predictions. In this case it is a very useful step to see relationships that cannot have seen otherwise. It has been also seen how the inputs affect in order of importance on the target variables by means of the Cramer's V-plot (Isea, et al, n.d).
- *Conclusions*: This is the final step of our analysis. Based on all the data processed, infer the results and whether the hypothesis set out at the beginning has been fulfilled.

3. DATA MARK GENERATION

The most sensible part in any analytical project is the generation of the final dataset. The data included always impact in the results and insights strongly. Therefore, it must be as complete as possible. Also, the knowledge of the context and quality of the inputs support the decision of choosing the best data base to use.

In this case, several data sources have been used:

- *Google Ads*: Providing historical information about the impact statistics and investment of the campaigns, showing the cost information used to measure the profitability and the performance of ads.

• *Partner report*: Showing the economic results (revenue) together with the results of each advertisement once they have passed the corresponding traffic quality filters.

• *Intern information*: Containing internal information of the accounts, like identifiers enabling the data merging between different tables.

• *Partner traffic quality report*: Containing a critical part of our analysis, because shows the traffic quality of our ads grouped by a tag that allow distinct the different landings.

Both the definition of the problem and the knowledge of the project goals at technical and business level represent the adequate guidance for the analysis and predictions. If the data does not feed the predictive model with relevant inputs, the results will be surely poor and with low accuracy.

3.1 Collecting Video Ad Marketing Data

For this work, four different sources have been used to generate the data set. In this case, the data merge is successful because of the ad identifier, that allow us to analyze the information as disaggregated as possible. After the data merge, has been necessary the data preparation processes followed by the modelling part. These three steps will be the main points of the analysis. Data download has been automated through an API and collected in our SQL data base. Data access has been customized through SQL queries directly connected to excel, where four tabs corresponding to the four data sources are generated.

Within the excel framework, data has been transformed and merged using power query, which allows to have all the data updated and joined.

The specific technical details of each data source are the following:

- Google Ads: Providing cost information at the ad and day level. It also includes campaign and ad group names and ids. To do the data crossing with the other databases the *ad id* and *date* are used as they are unique identifiers.
- Partner report: Providing revenue information at the ad and day level. The data crossing is implemented with the ad id (at this case the name is "*type tag*") and the date. This report also includes the information of traffic quality per ad.
- Intern information: It is essential to the crossing because it relates *ad id* to *source tag* (provided by the partner includes all the landing pages of the same client) and accounts, campaigns, and ad information.
- Partner traffic quality report: This report is different than the others. In this case the data is grouped by source tag. For that reason, the report includes the information by country too, so it can be crossed with the rest of data sources.
- The final dataset (Figure 2) resulting from the data crosses. It includes 50 variables and allows us to begin with the multi variant analysis.

3.2 Campaign Statistics and Key Performance Indicators

With the aim of developing the most complete analysis possible, all the potential variables which we have access have been included. They describe: (i) the financial performance (Cost, revenue, Cost Per Click, Cost Per Acquisition, Revenue Per Click), (ii) date (day of the week, month, year, date), (iii) marketing account specifications (id, device, country, code, category, keyword, destiny, source tag) and (iv) performance indicators (clicks, impressions, conversion rate, conversions, traffic quality). These values are collected two times (initial and final), before and after Google traffic invalidation, and their differences are also analyzed.

Thanks to the disposal of this high-quality data, it is possible to carry out a wide catalogue of plots for visual inspection, like temporal representations, histograms, data exploratory for error detection and outliers and so on. This work is part of the data preparation rather than about the analysis for predictive modelling so no further details are included. The next figure contains the preliminary inspection of the dataset, that allows us to know the raw information of each variable. The first benefit of doing this type of representation is because the type of variable is quite clear to appreciate, and it give us feedback for the next steps. For example, some factor type variables (categorical) are wrongly coded as character. Others, such as day of the week, month, or year, can be changed to factor due to the low number of categories.

```
## tibble [237,409 x 50] (S3: tbl_df/tbl/data.frame)
##  $ Fecha                : POSIXct[1:237409], format: "2021-12-01" "2021-12-01" ...
##  $ Dia_sem              : chr [1:237409] "miércoles" "miércoles" "miércoles" "miércoles" ...
##  $ Dia                  : num [1:237409] 1 1 1 1 1 1 1 1 1 1 ...
##  $ Mes                  : num [1:237409] 12 12 12 12 12 12 12 12 12 12 ...
##  $ Año                  : num [1:237409] 2021 2021 2021 2021 2021 ...
##  $ Cuenta_id            : chr [1:237409] "1238797147" "1238797147" "1423963431" "1423963431" ...
##  $ Dispositivo_revenue : chr [1:237409] "Desktop" "Desktop" "Desktop" "Desktop" ...
##  $ Source_tag           : chr [1:237409] "cbs_d2s_xmlb_2236_answersite_gdn2" "cbs_d2s_xmlb_2236_answer
site_gdn2" "cbs_d2s_xmlb_2236_helpwire_gdn" "cbs_d2s_xmlb_2236_helpwire_gdn" ...
##  $ Source_tag_numero    : num [1:237409] 2 2 1 1 1 1 1 1 1 1 ...
##  $ Destino_codigo       : chr [1:237409] "ANS" "ANS" "HEL" "HEL" ...
##  $ Pais                 : chr [1:237409] "USA" "USA" "USA" "USA" ...
##  $ Pais_revenue         : chr [1:237409] "USA" "USA" "CAN" "USA" ...
##  $ Categoria            : chr [1:237409] "Insurance" "Insurance" "VideoMeeting" "VideoMeeting" ...
##  $ Keyword              : chr [1:237409] "insurify insurance quotes" "botox for tension headaches cove
red by insurance" "video meeting system" "video meeting system" ...
##  $ Coste_i              : num [1:237409] 0 0.629 1.979 1.979 1.197 ...
##  $ Coste_f              : num [1:237409] 0 0 0 0 0 ...
##  $ Cost_diff            : num [1:237409] 0 1 1 1 1 ...
##  $ Revenue              : num [1:237409] 2.202 0.479 0.607 7.126 0 ...
##  $ Profit_i             : num [1:237409] 2.2 -0.15 -1.37 5.15 -1.2 ...
##  $ Profit_f             : num [1:237409] 2.202 0.479 0.607 7.126 0 ...
##  $ ROAS_i               : num [1:237409] 2.202 -0.239 -0.693 2.601 -1 ...
##  $ ROAS_f               : num [1:237409] 2.202 0.479 0.607 7.126 0 ...
##  $ CPC_i                : num [1:237409] 0 0.629 1.979 0.165 0.599 ...
##  $ CPC_f                : num [1:237409] 0 0 0 0 0 ...
##  $ RPC                  : num [1:237409] 1.101 0.479 0.607 3.563 0 ...
##  $ CPA_JOT_i            : num [1:237409] 0 0.629 1.979 0.99 0 ...
##  $ CPA_JOT_f            : num [1:237409] 0 0 0 0 0 ...
##  $ CPA_G_i              : num [1:237409] 0 0 0 0 0 0 0 0 0 0 ...
##  $ CPA_G_f              : num [1:237409] 0 0 0 0 0 0 0 0 0 0 ...
##  $ CR_JOT_i             : num [1:237409] 0 1 0.5 1 0 0.5 0.2 1 0 0 ...
##  $ CR_JOT_f             : num [1:237409] 0 0 1 2 0 0 0.25 1.25 0 0 ...
##  $ CR_G_i               : num [1:237409] 0 0 0 0 0 0 0 0 0 0 ...
##  $ CR_G_f               : num [1:237409] 0 0 0 0 0 0 0 0 0 0 ...
##  $ Impresiones_i        : num [1:237409] 0 1 4 4 2 2 8 8 2 0 ...
##  $ Impresiones_f        : num [1:237409] 0 0 0 0 0 0 6 6 1 0 ...
##  $ Impressions_revenue : num [1:237409] 1 1 1 12 2 3 1 9 8 1 ...
##  $ Clicks_i             : num [1:237409] 0 1 2 2 2 2 5 5 0 0 ...
##  $ Clicks_f             : num [1:237409] 0 0 1 1 0 0 4 4 0 0 ...
##  $ Clicks_revenue       : num [1:237409] 1 1 1 12 2 3 1 9 8 1 ...
##  $ Conversiones_i       : num [1:237409] 0 0 0 0 0 0 0 0 0 0 ...
##  $ Conversiones_f       : num [1:237409] 0 0 0 0 0 0 0 0 0 0 ...
##  $ Conversiones_revenue: num [1:237409] 2 1 1 2 0 1 1 5 1 1 ...
##  $ Conv_diff_i          : num [1:237409] 2 1 1 2 0 1 1 5 1 1 ...
##  $ Conv_diff_f          : num [1:237409] 2 1 1 2 0 1 1 5 1 1 ...
##  $ Conv_diff_i_%        : num [1:237409] 2 1 1 2 0 1 1 5 1 1 ...
##  $ Conv_diff_f _%       : num [1:237409] 2 1 1 2 0 1 1 5 1 1 ...
##  $ Vistas_video_i       : num [1:237409] 0 1 5 5 2 2 6 6 1 0 ...
##  $ Vistas_video_f       : num [1:237409] 0 0 1 1 0 0 4 4 1 0 ...
##  $ TQ_TypeTag           : num [1:237409] 0 0 2.5 2.5 0 2 3 3 0.5 0 ...
##  $ TQ_SourceTag         : num [1:237409] 2 2 3 3 3 3 3 3 3 3 ...
```

Figure 2. Set of variables included in the dataset combining numeric and categorical variables

4. MULTIVARIANT ANALYSIS AND DISCUSSION

As mentioned previously, the goal of this analysis is to understand what variables affect more significantly the traffic quality in the video ad marketing campaigns. To do so, two target variables have been selected:

(i) *conversion difference*, which explains the invalidation of our ads and which we will consider the quantitative variable,

(ii) *TQ (traffic quality)* at source tag level, which gives us information about what value on a scale from 0 to 10 our source tag has. The rest of the variables are considered as explanatory or input variables.

Therefore, the first action implemented has been to correct the wrong data typologies. This allow us to plot the distribution of the variables where more information was obtained:

(i) In relation with the numerical variables, many of them show a right tail. It implies that they are skewed variables, with most of the data are clustered in the first values of the variable. Would be interesting to analyze if will be useful a transformation to normalize the data. The most common using transformations are logarithms, exponentials and roots, but exists models like h2o that do it automatically.

(ii) Another advantage is that potential groupings of the categorical variables are identified to make them more efficient, and if it helps us to improve our conclusions.

Given the fact that the data is classified by dates, it was convenient to consider whether there were temporal patterns. The best way to do this was to repeat the graphs of the distribution of variables, but this time adding the time factor. In our case it was proved that there is not much information in the input variables, however, the difference in conversions decreased over time. On the contrary, the score in the quality of traffic per source tag increased, confirming the importance of considering the temporal representation of the series.

Once implemented the initial inspection of the data, several transformations are carried out for the data cleaning, modifying the types of variables and transforming those that can be grouped. In our case, the traffic quality values has been transformed from numerical to categorical (Table 1), grouping them into a factor type with four categories (lowest, low, medium, high), so that it is easier to analyze them.

Table 1. Distribution of ad quality classification

Quality Classification	% of ads	TQ number range
Lowest	3.05	0
Low	86.93	1-3
Medium	7.39	4-7
High	0	8-10

The next step was the analysis of outliers (either very large or very small). The percentage of outliers per variable should be calculated to determine their potential impact and relevance in the data set. Based on the theory, if the result is less than or equal to 10% of the data, the outliers could be transformed to missing values, as they may be considered to have a low incidence. As seen in "*Table 2*", almost all the variables were below this threshold, so it is considered that they are not impacting the final results and can be transformed to missing values. In any case, before that, we will create a new variable to analyze the impact of the outliers, it will be called "Prop_missing" and it contains the provision of outliers.

Table 2. TOP-10 of variables with more outliers

Variable Name	% of Outliers
ROAS_i	10.38
ROAS_f	10.17
Impresiones_f	8.28
CPA_JOT_f	8.06
CPA_JOT_i	7.87
Impresiones_i	7.55
CPC_f	7.33
CPC_i	7.18
Revenue	6.17
Clicks_revenue	4.45

Finally, missing data were treated, so that if they exceed 50% of the data, the variable should be deleted as it would not yield any information. It is usual to impute missing data by the mean, median or both randomly, as they are then replaced by data that follow the same pattern. In our case the incidence was less than 10%, so we imputed randomly, eliminating any missing values.

Once our database was treated and free of significant outliers and missing values, the complete dataset was analyzed by means of a Cramer's V charts (Figure 3 and Figure 4). Cramer's V is a measure of the strength of association between two nominal variables based on chi-square, and Cramer's V chart returns in descending order the most significant variables in relation to the target variable. To increase the robustness and reliability of the results and as a quality control, two random variables have been added, so that any variable behind them is pure randomness and can be no relevant at all in the analysis.

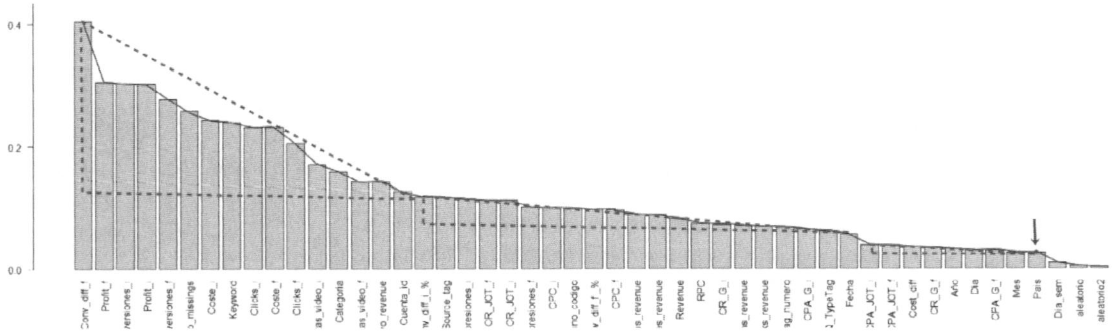

Figure 3. Importance of variables. Results of Cramer's V Plot - Conversion difference

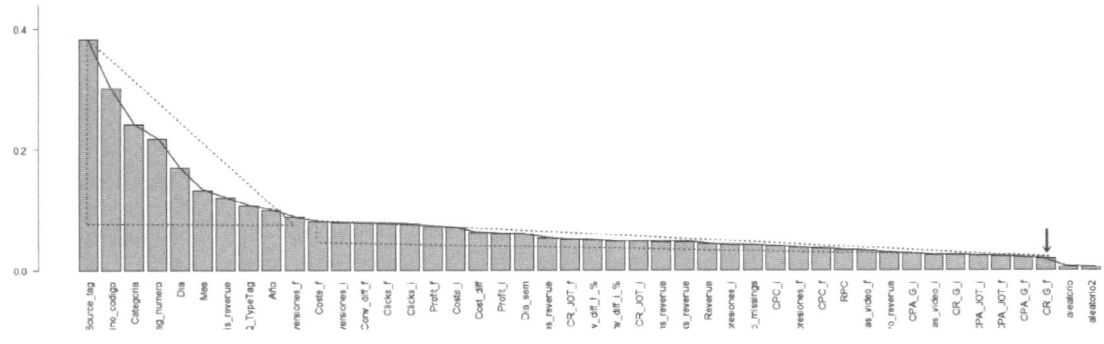

Figure 4. Importance of variables on TQ. Results of Cramer's V Plot - TQ by SourceTag

The first thing to notice is the different slopes founded in both graphs. The first and more pronounced belongs to the most relevant variables in relation to the target variable, the second one with more cushioned slope includes variables with less impact. The random variables allow to know what variables have random behaviour. Its last position implies a good sign of good choice of variables, because all of it are relevant for our target variables. Excepting one, "Dia_sem" that represent the day of the week has a similar behaviour as the random variables in Figure 3. In this case, we could remove it.

To answer the first main question, and ignoring the intrinsic relationships of digital marketing, what more relevant in this case, is that the category of the keyword used has quite a lot of weight on this adjustment in conversions. This means that there are keyword categories that show more invalidation than others. When analyzing the value assigned by the partner to the quality of the traffic (*Figure 4*), the category also plays an important role. This time the importance is higher, being the second. It is also remarkable that the day of the month also influences whether the traffic is better or worse considered. Based on business experience, it is also known that depending on the country the TQ is higher or lower. However, due to the differences in measurement between Google Ads and the partners' monetization feed, there are usually traffic leaks to other countries than the one targeted by the campaigns. This leakage also has some influence on traffic quality. The day is also important because Mondays usually have more records than other days, and it used to be the best day in revenue terms.

5. CONCLUSION

In short, thanks to this analysis, some unexpected relationships and variables impact on the conversions and TQ can be deduced that would have been impossible to identified otherwise. This type of analysis provides the basis for further knowledge and research into the predictive patterns resulting from it.

To answer the main second question about correlations, most of the explanatory variables in our model are calculated from other variables that we use as a basis. This means that the most likely, is that the variables are correlated with each other. This has been demonstrated by generating plots of influences and the correlation matrix. We found low to medium correlation between them, with the highest correlation being between initial clicks and initial cost measured on the Google Ads platform, with an 80% correlation. In fact, the biggest correlations we see are intrinsic to our business model.

Once the key parameters impacting the final quality of the traffic has been detected, next steps are now focused on the development of the algorithms enabling the prediction of the video ad marketing traffic quality, the main third question. Some objectives of the algorithms will be: (i) The reduction of inauthentic users will increase the trust in this digital media as channel to improve industry investment in video marketing, (ii) Video traffic authentication represents a new approach of optimizing the impact of the campaigns, reducing the dependencies in third parties, (iii) Development of video marketing campaigns decision support based on real user interactions, not being affected by the actions carried out by malicious bots and (iv) This project will deploy a new way to engage the real targeted audience and promote competitiveness in digital media content. All of them considering the existence of multicollinearity and that there may be external factors that we cannot handle or that we have not seen before. Therefore, it is important to have up-to-date information, digital marketing evolves day by day and we have to fluctuate with it.

Next steps are currently focused on the data standardization for model generation. There are a set of candidates that would perform better based on multilinear regression (LightGBM) for the conversion difference continuous variable and classification (Random Forest) for the categorical one, traffic quality.

ACKNOWLEDGEMENT

This work received partial funding from the European Commission Horizon 2020 AI4Media project (grant number 951911).

REFERENCES

Black, W., Babin, B.J. (2019). Multivariate Data Analysis: Its Approach, Evolution, and Impact. In: Babin, B., Sarstedt, M. (eds) The Great Facilitator. Springer, Cham. https://doi.org/10.1007/978-3-030-06031-2-16

Cario, M. C.& Nelson, B. L. (1997). Modeling and generating random vectors with arbitrary marginal distributions and correlation matrix (pp. 1-19). Technical Report, Department of Industrial Engineering and Management Sciences, Northwestern University, Evanston, Illinois.

Everitt, B., & Hothorn, T. (2011). An introduction to applied multivariate analysis with R. https://doi.org/10.1007/978-1-4419-9650-3.

Hyndman, R. J., & Khandakar, Y. (2008). Automatic time series forecasting: TheforecastPackage for*R*. *Journal of Statistical Software*, *27*(3). https://doi.org/10.18637/jss.v027.i03

Isea, R. et al. (n.d) Central University of Venezuela. Facultad de Humanidades y Educación. Retrieved from https://mariafatimadossantosestadistica1.files.wordpress.com/2018/06/coeficientes-v-de-cramer-y-c-de-pearson.pdf

Neusser, K. (2016). Time series econometrics. Springer Texts in Business and Economics. https://doi.org/10.1007/978-3-319-32862-1

Saura, J. R. (2021). Using data sciences in digital marketing: Framework, methods, and performance metrics. *Journal of Innovation & Knowledge*, *6*(2), 92-102. https://doi.org/10.1016/j.jik.2020.08.001

CLASSIFICATION OF FINANCIAL MARKETS INFLUENCERS ON TWITTER

Inês Almeida[1] and André Sabino[1,2]
[1]*Autónoma Techlab, Universidade Autónoma de Lisboa, Lisboa, Portugal*
[2]*IADE – Faculdade de Design, Tecnologia e Comunicação, Universidade Europeia, Lisboa, Portugal*

ABSTRACT

Information published by social network users can have an impact on the (virtual and physical) community, which supports the concept of influencer, which is a user generally focused on a set of interests (such as fashion, health, well-being, beauty, finances, etc.), whose opinion correlates with the behavior observed in a community of users who share those interests. The same concept of social network influencer may also be explored in the financial markets, considering user profiles whose expressed opinions align with the performance of a company's shares.
Several users interested in the stock exchange use Twitter as a platform to express their opinions on stocks. Considering that tweets express either a positive, negative, or neutral feeling about a stock, we present a model to describe the profile of an influencer, as well as analyze the correlation between their tweets and the performance of a stock.
Relying on a genetic algorithm to best describe an influencer's profile and selecting the best fit from a set of features, this study provides a comparison between sentiment analysis techniques, applied on social network content, produced by potential influencers. We present a study of several sentiment analyses approaches, namely using Support Vector Machines, Neural Networks, Naïve Bayes, and K-Nearest Neighbors. Results show that the method with the best performance is the Neural Network. This outcome is used as a parameter for analyzing an influencer's tweets.
Validation shows that, by integrating a genetic algorithm for influencer detection with a sentiment analysis technique based on Neuronal Networks, it is possible to identify users with social network content sentiment score correlated with variations in a share price, thus representing an information signal suitable to be used by prediction models.

KEYWORDS

Machine Learning, Sentiment Analysis, Financial Market Analysis

1. INTRODUCTION

Financial markets investment management involves constant assessment and decision making in a fast-pacing environment. Aside from official market data, there are several non-primary sources of information that may prove helpful when designing predictive models. Expert opinion is one of such sources, and it may be expressed through social networks, such as Twitter.

We propose to leverage user generated content on social media as a signal for financial markets behavior, by identifying correlations between the sentiment of a particular user's contributions about a company on the network (i.e., posts about the company) and the performance of the stock of that company.

We focus our study on Twitter, which enables its users to share information and opinions about almost anything (restricted by its terms of service). Posted messages are called tweets, and these may include references to other users (using the @ character, in the form of @UserName), eventually engaging them in conversation. Users may also forward a tweet from another user (i.e., a retweet), and include tags (using the # character, i.e., hashtags) in the tweet content (Drus and Khalid, 2019). Twitter also supports a special type of tag for stock market trading tickers, called cashtag, which prefixes the trading symbol with the $ character, such as $AAPL[1] for the Apple stock[2]. Each tweet has a maximum character limit, which currently is 280 characters, from 140 until 2017 (Gligorić et al., 2018).

[1] https://twitter.com/search?q=%24aapl
[2] https://www.nasdaq.com/market-activity/stocks/aapl

We define influence on a social network, such as Twitter, as the potential of a user's actions to cause actions from other users.

With the evolution of social networks, the concept of influencers is increasingly addressed. Leavitt, et al., focused on the analysis of influencer profiles on Twitter, concluding that the number of followers is not directly related to the number of retweets performed, i.e., there may be accounts with few followers, who's tweets have a high number of retweets. The study also found that an independent user may be more influential than a popularly known entity (Leavitt et al., 2009).

In another study, M. Cha, et al., analyzed the influence of Twitter users based on three measures: the number of followers; the number of retweets; and the number of mentions. The goal was to verify a user's ability to generate dialogues and actions (Cha et al., 2010). Aligning with the results from Leavitt, et al. (Leavitt et al., 2009), the study concludes that a large number of followers do not correlate with a high number of tweets. It was also found that influence is not acquired accidentally and usually requires a strategic effort from the user (e.g., by approaching a single topic per tweet). Furthermore, the authors conclude that users may be influencers over various topics (Cha et al., 2010).

E. Lahuerta-Otero and R. Cordero-Gutiérrez used a data mining tool, that combines graph theory with social influence theory, to investigate influencers on Twitter and discover common features between influencers. The study focused on 3 853 users who posted tweets about the automotive companies Toyota and Nissan. The authors concluded that influencers do not usually embed links in their posts, which usually have a low number of words and a high number of hashtags and mentions. It was also concluded that influencers have a high number of followers who themselves express their opinions. This research, instead of detecting influencers, analyzed the common properties of the tweets of users already identified by the community as influencers, aiming to characterize how influencers communicate with their users (Lahuerta-Otero and Cordero-Gutiérrez, 2016).

X.Zhang, H.Fuehres and P.Gloor forecasted financial market indicators, such as the Dow Jones Industrial Average (DJIA), NASDAQ and S&P 500 indexes using Twitter posts, which were collected for six months and labeled as "Positive" or "Negative" based on a selection of mood words (e.g., "fear" or "hope"). From these annotations, the authors computed a daily collective sentiment based on the number of occurrences of each mood word and report that when users express fear and concern in their tweets, indices such as DJIA, NASDAQ and S&P 500 register loss of value. The study also reports that users post more tweets when they feel positive, and when there is some uncertainty in the stock market, there is a tendency to express feelings such as fear or hope (Zhang et al., 2011).

Bollen, et al., studied the correlation between the collective sentiment measured from Twitter and behavior of the DJIA. The study filtered posts that matched a set of expressions the authors considered to state mood states, and characterized those posts according to 7 mood dimensions from two assessment tools: OpinionFinder (Wilson et al., 2005) and their own Google-Profile of Mood States (GPOMS). The study reported that at least one of those dimensions is able to forecast (i.e., reports a significate Granger causality) the DJIA index, namely, the "Calm" dimension measured by GPOMS. There was a large increase in prediction ability, reaching a success rate of 86.7%. The authors conclude that sentiment analysis of tweets enables automatic, fast, free and large-scale forecasting tools for financial market indices (Bollen et al., 2011).

Xu, et al., also studied potential correlations between sentiment analysis of tweets and the returns of the main global stock markets, based on the Multifractal Detrended Cross-Correlation Analysis (MF-DCCA) method). The study used the Daily Happiness Index[3] as proxy for the collective mood, and the analysis was carried out through the division between developed and underdeveloped countries, and report significant correlations between financial markets returns and tweets from a few developed countries (excluding South Korea and the United Kingdom, where no correlation was found), and if all developing countries considered. This correlation relationship is consistent over time in developed countries and fluctuates over time for developing countries. To a degree, these results confirm a dependence between sentiment and global financial markets (Xu et al., 2021).

These results support the hypothesis that there is a signal available on social networks which may be suitable to forecast financial markets. All works share a processing step where tweets are translated into a sentiment score, which we use to annotate tweets from a set of user profiles that are potential influencers.

The classification of social network profiles whose posts correlate with financial markets behavior has been studied by several authors. D. M. Limpo et al. presents a system for the identification and classification of users

[3] The index is built with data https://hedonometer.org/

whose content may correlate with a particular stock of the S&P 500 Financial Market Index. Most of the influencers found were entities/companies in the same sector of the stock in our study. The methodology yields better results than the recommendation service (Who-To-Follow) available at Twitter (Limpo, David M., 2016).

In a related effort, D. Sousa presents an opinion mining system for the S&P 500 Market Index stocks, which identifies the main characteristics of financial market influencers. The system uses a Naïve Bayes binary sentiment analysis algorithm (which classified the tweets as "positive" or "negative"), reporting accuracies of 72.16% and 75.45% over two distinct datasets, and a Genetic Algorithm to obtain optimal values for each parameter (i.e., characteristics such as account time, number of tweets, or number of followers) that defines an influencer (Sousa, 2017).

The goal of these studies was to propose, for each characteristic, the range of values suitable for an influencer. For example, if the "number of followers" characteristic has a range of values between 500 to 1000, then a user defined as influencer should have their number of followers within that range. Both studies concluded that influencers have a long-time account, are very active on Twitter in terms of published tweets and tend to use tweets to talk to other users.

J. Sacramento implemented a system for collecting, processing, and classifying tweets about a particular company to measure its impact on stock prices. Tweets from Facebook and American Airlines were analyzed. For Facebook, significative correlations of 0.39 in terms of stock volume and 0.42 for stock close price was found. For American Airlines, only the correlation in terms of stock volume (0.51) is significant (Sacramento, 2021).

2. METHODOLOGY

The system is composed of three modules, namely, data collection and processing, sentiment analysis, and influencer detection.

The data collection from Twitter includes tweet content and number of followers, among other useful information, which are preprocessed to filter out content that is not relevant for sentiment analysis. Financial data is collected from Yahoo Finance, namely, the date and adjusted closing price (see section 2.2).

All modules are developed in Python, mainly because it is supported by a rich ecosystem for machine learning.

2.1 Twitter Data Collection

Twitter information is collected with the snscrape[4] module, which enables filtering through Twitter's public API[5].

Posts about a company are filtered through the cashtag. The module also enables date filters, such as "until:2021-12-06 since:2021-11-24", which constrains the capture to a date interval, and user filters, such as "from TheTommRobinson", which constrains the capture to the posts of a given user. The module is only limited by the public Twitter API access policy and can retrieve all tweets from a given user since the creation of their account.

In this study, all collected tweets are in english and must contain a cashtag. Tweets with emojis are excluded to minimize errors in the sentiment analysis module.

Tweets are preprocessed in the extent that the following content is removed: Uniform Resource Locator (URLs); words with numbers; the cashtags; special characters, i.e., non-digits or letters.

Cashtags are removed because there is no value for sentiment analysis. Hashtags, however, are not deleted, since they potentially represent emotions, such as #happy. Note that the # symbol, being a special character, is removed. The same occurs with the $ character on cashtags. Both hashtags and cashtags are marked before the removal of the special characters, to avoid elimination by other criteria. Special characters and words with numbers are removed mainly because they are closely related with automatic spam tweets (Limpo, David M., 2016).

---

[4] https://pypi.org/project/snscrape/

[5] https://developer.twitter.com/en/docs/twitter-api

Finally, tweets are converted into lower case due to the application of the Naïve Bayes algorithm, which is case sensitive. Although it is not the only algorithm to be tested in this study, it is also evaluated.

2.2 Financial Data Collection and Stock Returns Calculation

For a particular historical record, the value of each stock is represented by the closing price and the adjusted closing price. The first represents the last gross price traded before the market closes, while the second represents the closing price of excluding the impact corporate actions that may affect it, namely, stock splits and dividends.

For example, on a dividend ex-date (i.e., the first day the stock is traded without the right to collect a particular dividend payment), the stock opening price discounts the dividend value which, and the end of the day, is accounted in the closing price. If the day trading session did not move the price of the stock, the closing price still records a loss in the same amount as the dividend. The adjusted closing price will discount the dividend value, more closely reflecting the effects of the actual trading session.

We use the yfinance[6] module to collected financial data from Yahoo Finance and analyze the adjusted closing price within a time interval of 1 month. The daily return of a stock is determined by

$$Return_i(Stock, d_i) = \frac{ClosingPrice_{adjusted}(Stock, d_i) - ClosingPrice_{adjusted}(Stock, d_{i-1})}{ClosingPrice_{adjusted}(Stock, d_i)} \quad (1)$$

where $Stock$ is the share under study, $\text{ClosingPrice}_{\text{adjusted}}$ is the adjusted closing price of a stock in a particular date, d_i the date of the calculation and d_{i-1} the previous date. The return of a share for a given day is obtained by the difference between the adjusted closing price values that day and the previous day, divided by the adjusted closing price of the previous day.

2.3 Sentiment Analysis

The sentiment analysis module combines combining machine learning with lexicon-based methods.

Most machine learning methods are supervised, which requires a training set, e.g., a set of Twitter posts labeled as "Positive", "Neutral" or "Negative". We use a lexicon-based approach to classify this training set.

The VADER (Valence Aware Dictionary for sEntiment Reasoning) Python module works from a set of previously annotated words (hence, lexicon-based) and provides a sentiment prediction for other texts and words.

According C.J. Hutto and E. Gilbert, VADER's performance stands out from comparable methods for text sentiment analysis on social networks. The VADER project reports correlation coefficient values (r = 0.881) as high as the values generated through human evaluation (r = 0.888). As for classification accuracy, the value produced considering the manual classification (F_1 = 0.84) is lower than the classification accuracy of VADER (F_1 = 0.96) (Hutto and Gilbert, 2014).

In our study, we calculate the sentiment of each tweet ("Positive", "Neutral" or "Negative"), as well as the number of positive and negative words using VADER with the following encoding: if a word's polarity, as determined by the VADER module, is equal to or greater than 0.05, the word is annotated as "Positive"; if the polarity is less than or equal to -0.05, it is annotated as "Negative"; if none of these conditions are met, the word is considered as "Neutral".

With an annotated training set, we consider the following machine learning methods: support vector machines (SVM); neural networks (NN); naïve bayes; k-nearest neighbors (kNN) (see Figure 1).

[6] https://pypi.org/project/yfinance/

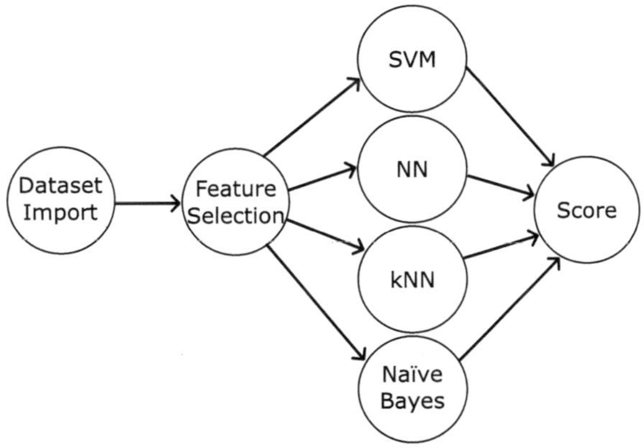

Figure 1. The workflow for sentiment analysis method comparison

SVM and NN rely on training sets of labeled data, which are used to build approximations of functions, optimized to label similar data points, i.e., given a set of features and a target, these methods work as non-linear function approximators.

An SVM builds the approximation function by maximizing separations between the training data points in their representation on expanded geometrical spaces (i.e., hyperplanes). The resulting model is defined by the actual functions.

In a NN, between the input layer (input features) and the output layer, there may be one or more non-linear layers, called hidden layers. Each neuron in the hidden layer transforms the values from the previous layer with a weighted linear sum, followed by a non-linear activation function. As a result, the output layer takes the values from the last hidden layer and transforms them into output values. The resulting model is defined by the set of training data points and their impact on the several neuron layers.

Naïve bayes and kNN are used as simpler base comparison models for SVM and NN.

2.4 Genetic Algorithm

We propose a genetic algorithm to determine which characteristics best define an influencer. This approach tries to select the best solution (i.e., a set of values for the collection of features used to describe an influencer) for a problem from a large set of candidates, through iterations where small changes are introduced into previous solution candidates. Ideally, these candidates evolve into an optimal solution.

The process iterates through generations of solutions, each based on combinations and modifications of the previous one. In each iteration, the most suitable solutions (or, *parents*) are selected according to a *fitness function score*.

Pairs of parents are combined to produce one or more *children* which contain a new set of values for each feature (i.e., *gene*). This combination is actually a crossover operation over the parents' genes, which is then submitted to a chance-based mutation process (Coley, 1999).

The algorithm terminates after a predetermined number of iterations, or when a *satisfactory* solution (see the fitness function, at equation 2) is found.

In the context of the genetic algorithm, an individual represents a set of users. For each feature, users are sorted in descending order according to the values they have for that feature, and each set is divided into several subsets (i.e., ranks). As an example, we consider the "number of followers" feature, where the first subset of users is composed of users with the most followers, and the last subset with the lowest number of followers. This process is repeated for the remaining characteristics under analysis. It is expected that the more users that are in each rank, the greater the range of values. On the other hand, high number of ranks implies that, for each rank, there is a small number of users, thus reducing the range of values.

In this study we focus on a total of 800 users, and consider 20 ranks, each composed of 40 users. Each rank is described by 5 genes (i.e., a *chromosome*), one for each characteristic to be analyzed.

The fitness function represented by equation (2) calculates the impact of tweets made on a given date for each user on a rank. This impact is calculated through the product of the tweet's polarity and the sum of the ACP gain during the 10 days preceding the tweet's publication. The goal is to find positive values, which means that the sentiment of the user's tweets was in line with the variation of the stock. Otherwise, if the value is negative, the user's prediction about the stock was not in line with its variation (Limpo, David M., 2016).

$$f(date) = \sum_{i=1}^{n} (\sum_{d=1}^{10} Return(Stock, tweet_i^{date} + d)) \times tweet_i^{polarity} \quad (2)$$

We set up a tournament selection method to choose between competing ranks is used for this process. n ranks are randomly selected for each tournament, in which the winner yields the best performance in the fitness function. In the study, we consider tournaments of three individuals, amounting to 10 tournaments overall, with 10 winning individuals. Winning ranks move on to the crossover phase.

The Tournament's outcome is a set of winning ranks designated as *parents*. In the crossover phase, *children* (which are also ranks) of each pair of randomly selected parents are formed by the junction of the genes of their parents. This junction if defined by two randomly selected cut-off points (double point crossover), yielding two children for each pair of parents.

In the first child, the genes between the cutoffs are copied from the first parent, with the remaining genes copied from the second parent. In the second child, the inverse occurs, that is, the genes between the cut-off points are copied from the second parent.

After the crossover process, the new population consists of parents and children, over which we apply a mutation process over the smallest number of genes in an individual, yielding a $\frac{1}{numOfGenes}$ rate (Limpo, David M., 2016), e.g., a 20% mutation rate for a set of 5 genes. This rate criterium is arbitrary, and a candidate for further studies.

3. VALIDATION

Our validation process was focused on Apple stock, which is traded with the AAPL ticker (cashtag $AAPL on Twitter). We collected tweets containing the $AAPL cashtag and respective users over 1 month, from January 12, 2022, to February 12, 2022.

We built a data collection script using the Python snscrape module. Along with the text of the tweet, the username and the date of publication of the tweet were also collected. We discarded all tweets with URLs, words with numbers, and/or emojis. This pre-processing helps with the elimination of content that does not contribute to sentiment analysis. Text was converted to lowercase. The final set of tweets has 13443 unique tweets, and 2668 unique usernames.

The study requires information about users, namely, the number of followers (followers), the total number of published tweets, the number of public lists the user is a member of, the ratio between the number of followers and number of friends of the user, and the age of the account since registration. This information will be used as characteristics for the detection of influencers through genetic algorithms and was collected using the Python tweepy module.

The tweepy module has a limitation in terms of the number of queries made to the Twitter API, so for the application of the Genetic Algorithm it will only be applied to a set of collected users. Which means that the total number of users selected for the analysis was 800.

We collected historical market data for the Apple stock between January 12, 2022, and February 12, 2022, which includes the adjusted close price (ACP), enable the calculation of the daily return (or *gain*) for the time interval (represented by equation (1)). Data was collected using the Python yfinance module, which gathers information from the Yahoo Finance platform.

The training set (7943 tweets) includes tweets that were published between January 12, 2022, and January 27, 2022. The test set (5500 tweets) includes tweets published between January 28, 2022, and February 12, 2022.

For each tweet, the polarity of each word was calculated and, consequently, the calculation of number of words with "Positive", "Negative" or "Neutral" sentiment in it, which is then aggregated into the polarity of the entire text. For a polarity value greater than or equal to 0.05, the word/text is classified as "Positive", whereas if a polarity value lower than or equal to -0.05 is obtained, the word/text is classified as "Negative". Otherwise, the word/text is "Neutral". The total number of tweets labeled as "Positive" was 3926, as "Negative" was 1472 and as "Neutral" was 2545.

Precision is the fraction of relevant instances. The best value is 1 and the worst value is 0. This measure is calculated as the quotient of the number of true positives and the sum of the number of true positives and false positives.

$$Precision = \frac{truepositives}{truepositives + falsepositives} \tag{3}$$

Recall is the fraction of relevant instances that were retrieved. Like precision, the range of values is between 0 and 1. This measure is calculated as the quotient of the number of true positives and the sum of the number of true positives and false negatives.

$$recall = \frac{truepositives}{truepositives + falsenegatives} \tag{4}$$

The F1 score can be seen as the harmonic mean of precision and recall measures. Like precision and recall, F1 score takes values between 0 and 1.

$$F_1 = 2 \times \frac{precision \times recall}{precision + recall} \tag{5}$$

We evaluate the performance of the several the sentiment analysis methods using the F1 score (combination between Precision and Recall) and report the following: 0.973 for K-Nearest Neighbors; 0.982 for Support Vector Machines; 0.988 for Naïve Bayes; and 0.999 for Neural Networks. Our results (which are comparable to Hutto and Gilbert (Hutto and Gilbert, 2014)), shows that Neural Networks are the most suitable approach for classifying the tweets.

After applying the genetic algorithm to the set of defined characteristics, it was possible to obtain the most appropriate rank, that is, the range of values, for each characteristic, that best defines an influencer. The evaluation yielded that the number of followers of an influencer user is between 1 842 and 3 073 followers. As for the number of tweets, these are between 62 698 and 1 726 179. In relation to public lists, an influencer user belongs to 9, 10 or 11. For the ratio between followers and friends this assumes a value between 0.26 and 0, 37. Finally, an influencer user has had a Twitter account for 3 or 4 years.

4. CONCLUSIONS

This paper presented a financial market influencer classification system relying on a genetic algorithm and hybrid sentiment analysis techniques, with a focus on Twitter. We concluded that Neural Networks are the best suited approach for sentiment analysis.

Our results show that such influencer is a user with a high number of tweets, with several followers greater than the number of friends, and a high number of followers. The user also belongs to several public lists, and it isn't a recent Twitter user.

Although our focus was on smaller observation windows, for future work, we propose that the high F1 we reported may be due to a lower number of tweets in the analysis and suggest studying the impact of larger observation windows.

We also plan to include the "verified" status of the profile, which may be relevant to refine our model.

ACKNOWLEDGEMENT

We acknowledge the support of Autónoma TechLab for supporting this work and providing a stimulating environment to carry out this research.

REFERENCES

Bollen, J., Mao, H., Zeng, X.-J., (2011). *Twitter mood predicts the stock market.* J. Comput. Sci. 2, 1–8. https://doi.org/10.1016/j.jocs.2010.12.007

Cha, M., Haddadi, H., Benevenuto, F., P. Gummadi, K., (2010). *Measuring User Influence in Twitter: The Million Follower Fallacy*, in: Proceedings of the Fourth International AAAI Conference on Weblogs and Social Media. Washington, D.C., USA, p. 8.

Coley, D.A., (1999). *Introduction to Genetic Algorithms for Scientists and Engineers*, Har/Dskt edition. ed. Wspc, Singapore ; River Edge, NJ.

Drus, Z., Khalid, H., (2019). *Sentiment Analysis in Social Media and Its Application: Systematic Literature Review.* Procedia Comput. Sci. 161, 707–714. https://doi.org/10.1016/j.procs.2019.11.174

Gligorić, K., Anderson, A., West, R., (2018). *How Constraints Affect Content: The Case of Twitter's Switch from 140 to 280 Characters*. Proc. Int. AAAI Conf. Web Soc. Media 12.

Hutto, C., Gilbert, E., (2014). *VADER: A Parsimonious Rule-Based Model for Sentiment Analysis of Social Media Text*, in: Proceedings of the International AAAI Conference on Web and Social Media. pp. 216–225.

Lahuerta-Otero, E., Cordero-Gutiérrez, R., (2016). *Looking for the perfect tweet. The use of data mining techniques to find influencers on twitter*. Comput. Hum. Behav. 64, 575–583. https://doi.org/10.1016/j.chb.2016.07.035

Leavitt, A., Burchard, E., Fisher, D., Gilbert, S., (2009). New approaches for analyzing influence on Twitter (No. 4), Web Ecology Project.

Limpo, David M., (2016). *Finding Influential Twitter Users for the Stock Market Optimized by Genetic Algorithm* (MSc Thesis). Universidade Técnica de Lisboa.

Sacramento, J., (2021). *Sentiment Analysis in the Stock Market Based on Twitter Data* (MSc Thesis). University Institute of Lisbon.

Sousa, D.J.M., (2017). *Using Naïve Bayes and Genetic Algorithms to Find Influential Twitter Users to Forecast the S&P 500* (MSc Thesis). Universidade Técnica de Lisboa.

Wilson, T., Hoffmann, P., Somasundaran, S., Kessler, J., Wiebe, J., Choi, Y., Cardie, C., Riloff, E., Patwardhan, S., (2005). *OpinionFinder: a system for subjectivity analysis, in: Proceedings of HLT/EMNLP on Interactive Demonstrations*, HLT-Demo '05. Association for Computational Linguistics, USA, pp. 34–35. https://doi.org/10.3115/1225733.1225751

Xu, K., Pang, Y., Han, J., (2021). *Dynamic Cross-Correlation between Online Sentiment and Stock Market Performance: A Global View.* Discrete Dyn. Nat. Soc. 2021, 1–11. https://doi.org/10.1155/2021/6674379

Zhang, X., Fuehres, H., Gloor, P.A., (2011). *Predicting Stock Market Indicators Through Twitter "I hope it is not as bad as I fear"*. Procedia - Soc. Behav. Sci. 26, 55–62. https://doi.org/10.1016/j.sbspro.2011.10.562

SHORT PAPERS

COVID19: INTELLIGENT CHATBOT AND FINANCIAL AID APPLICATION

Kenza Douifir, Naoual Chaouni Benabdellah and Ali Idri
Software Project Management Research Team, ENSIAS, Mohammed V University of Rabat, Morocco

ABSTRACT

Covid19 has devastated all continents causing disasters not only on the health sector but also at social, economic, and at political levels. The world is still trying to eradicate the virus. One of the measures taken is to inform citizens about the virus in order to avoid contamination as much as possible. Several people lost their jobs, and found themselves without any income. The whole world is confined, and the poor can no longer endure this critical situation. Financial assistance is therefore necessary in order to reduce the impact. This paper aims to propose an intelligent financial support application that computes the eligibility for a citizen to get a support during the pandemic; and to explain steps for chatbot using DialogFlow. The training realized using a machine learning algorithm was chosen after making a comparison between some other algorithms. Gradient Boosting Classifier algorithm was the accurate and most efficient for the application. It is possible to train the system again using other data set to make any adaptive results or computations.

KEYWORDS

K-Neighbors Classifier, Gaussian Naïve Bayes Classifier, Decision Tree Classifier, Logistic Regression Classifier, Chatbot, DialogFlow

1. INTRODUCTION

Unfortunately, the difficult sanitarium circumstances of Covid19 have taken world by storm. Some applications such as chatbots have been a real help to inform citizens on the virus and its impact on human health as how to prevent the virus. Besides, it can inform on the diagnosis in case of contamination to make a quick visit to the nearest medical service. In addition, they were used to broadcast the real time contaminations, deaths, and covers numbers' fluctuations. It helps them to stay up to date to ease the fear and guide them to the right habits or actions. Most of them have a relatively simple backend that looks up information by walking through a "decision tree" based on the users' input. Furthermore, the developed chatbot in this paper ought to facilitate the visualization and the displaying of any kind of documents related to Covid19. This can undoubtedly answer the frequently asked questions about the virus. Chatbots are widely used on the Internet by several services to simulate a conversation by voice or text exchange. The decision-making system to ensure some aid to COVID-19 crisis should be able to process the financial supports' requests. The decision is based on people in need information. It may be an acceptance or a refusal.

This paper is organized as follows: After the introduction in section 1, the section 2 cites several works that carried the financial supports measurements taken by several countries during the Covid19 pandemic and an overview of several studies conducted on developing chatbots. After that, section 3 defines the financial aid application and the different algorithms used to generate the most accurate decision making system. Section 4 explains the steps to develop the chatbot using google API Dialogflow. The summary and possible future works are discussed in section 5.

2. RELATED WORKS

2.1 Financial Support During Covid19: Overview

In (Kim,et al.,2021) authors presented the aid set up by USA under the name of CARES act (Coronavirus Aid, Relief, and Economic Security) to help people who have lost their jobs they minimized the number of consultations in clinics, and reduced the number of confrontations between sick patients and the medical staff. They want to expand the field of telemedicine, as a substitute for face to face consultations. Moreover, in (Poliak,and al.,2018) there are some programs related to the COVID pandemic. The main ones are: Public Health and Social Services Emergency Fund: $ 30 billion in grants dispersed to hospitals and physician practices, PPP and EIDL where small businesses can apply for loans. Authors in (Dennis, et al.,2020) examined the chaotic situation of American families and calculated whether they can continue to meet their typical monthly expenses with the cash assistance under the CARES act.

Many countries dealt with the crisis differently. In (Satiani, et al.,2020) authors showed the critical state of African countries in this pandemic. The large number of young Africans can be an advantage in order to minimize the harmful impact of the disease. Learning from previous pandemics and strengthening new partnerships were examples of measures taking by Africa. Authors in (Mehfooz, and al.,2021) presented the emergence of Covid19 and the EU's emergency response to this virus. The EU is committed to sourcing all necessary medical materials and promoting research into a potential vaccine or treatment. Authors in (Battineni, et al.,2021) gave an overview of the economic situation experienced by the world since the appearance of the virus in China in 2019. The government is obliged to offer financial assistance as an emergency for business and unemployed people.

2.2 Former Works on Chatbots During the Pandemic

Many works related to the development of chat bots during the pandemic was found in the literature. Some authors presented how they were developed, or made comparison studies between others existing in order to enhance their performance. There are others who sensed users' interests and opinions. They all have the objectives to support citizens, to guide them in preventing the contamination, to advise them in the nearest center for the Polymerase Chain Reaction known as PCR test, to fight hesitation to vaccines, and to inform them about the symptoms and treatments against the virus.

In order to recommend immediate measures when people are exposed to Covid19, some authors designed an intelligent chatbot for the diagnostic and providing the recommendations. Besides, a virtual assistant was presented to measure the infection severity and has the purpose to connect with registered doctors when symptoms become serious (Goniewicz, et al.,2020). Some chatbots have already been implemented in time of Covid19 such as LINE'S chatbot in Japan. It is the largest social communication application that counts 83 million active users. Based on its data collected over 431,106 individuals aged over 15 years until April 16, 2020 they noticed that hand washing and cough etiquette are quite widespread preventive actions, as about 90% of all age groups were practicing them (Mogaji,and al.2020). In (Höhn, et al.,2020) they focused on understanding how people respond to Covid19 screening chatbots. The test was conducted over 371 participants. They noticed that the chatbot's agent is less trustful than human as to make a correct diagnosis, to make the information private and specially answering users for their interest.

3. THE PROPOSED FINANCIAL AID APPLICATION

The application facilitates retrieving relevant information when requesting financial help. The user selects the request creation form in the menu. It is filled out; the information entered is processed by the automatic processing system. The treatment result is displayed and the user can see if his request for the financial aid has been accepted (Granted) or refused (Denied). In the case of acceptance, the user needs to attach the necessary supporting documents. On the other hand the administrator may validate the attached documents attached to the request. In the case there are missing or non-compliant documents the user is notified. He can display the list of pending requests. He can also consult the Pending requests and processes them. The proposed web application uses noSQL at the level of our database. The Fig.1 shows the Document Data Model used.

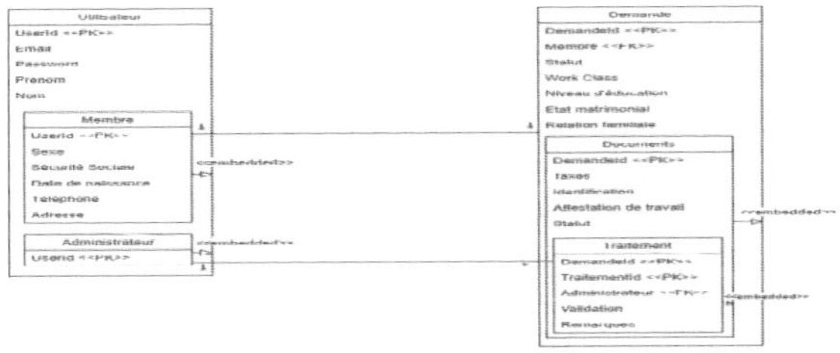

Figure 1. Document data Model

Three types of learning algorithms were applied for the training, instance-based algorithms, algorithms based on decision trees, and probabilistic algorithms, in addition to logistic regression specifically: K-neighbors classifier, Gaussian Naïve Bayes Classifier, KNN and Logistic regression Classifier algorithms. Table 1 presents a comparative table of the performances of each algorithm.

Table 1. Comparative table of algorithms used for the training

	Algorithm	Training accuracy	Precision	Recall	F1-score
Denied	Logistic	0.80	0.83	0.93	0.88
Granted	Regression		0.64	0.38	0.48
Denied	Gradient Boosting	0.84	0.87	0.93	0.90
Granted	Classifier		0.70	0.55	0.62
Denied	K-neighbors	0.82	0.87	0.90	0.88
Granted	Classifier		0.62	0.56	0.59
Denied	Gaussian Naïve	0.79	0.89	0.82	0.86
Granted	Bayes		0.54	0.69	0.60

In classification problem with unbalanced data, accuracy alone is not reliable in determining algorithm's performance for the dominant class that has high precision, the minority class has low precision. So the evaluation criteria used were f1-score, precision, and recall. F1-score represents the harmonic mean of the precision and recall value. The precision denotes the proportion of relevant data among all others offered. Whereas the recall is the proportion of relevant data proposed among all the other similar data. The type of algorithm that performs the best in this context is Gradient Boosting.

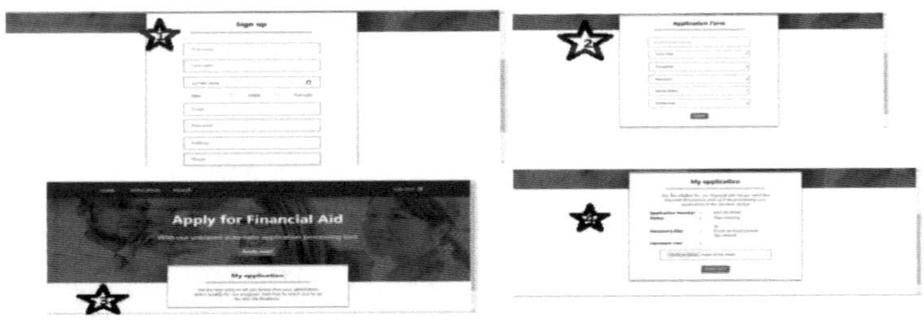

Figure 2. Some interfaces from the financial aid web application

After the training which is the process in the backend of the system. The interfaces of the application were developed to ease the use of citizens in need and to fill necessary information and documents for the financial support. There is a sign up before each request as it is shown in figure 2 first interface to the left. The form is to be filled as it is in the second interface to the top right of the figure 2. The status of the request is in interface 3. The fourth one of the figure 2 shows the answer in the case of an approved request, the member or the user is required to send supporting documents related to his request.

4. THE PROPOSED INTELLIGENT CHATBOT

The proposed chatbot is able to answer to users' questions related to Covid19. The user is able to visualize statistics of the contaminated, death and covered people from Covid19 worldwide relying on Google API. It is the natural language understanding platform offered by Google that facilitates the design and the integration of conversational user's interface in mobile applications and web applications. It can analyze several types of input. This includes text or audio input. It can also respond to customers in different ways, DialogFlow will be linked with the Python and Flask backend. Moreover, the user may receive a report that explains the preventive measures. In addition to that, he has access to interact with the intelligent agent as a Help Desk to answer his specific questions, to send the recent news asked for, announcements, images, and videos related to Covid19. Furthermore, all discussions are saved in the MongoDB database for future text mining analysis. Besides, during the realization of the chat-bot it was taken into consideration the quick responding, the reliability to avoid bugs, and the ergonomics user interface.

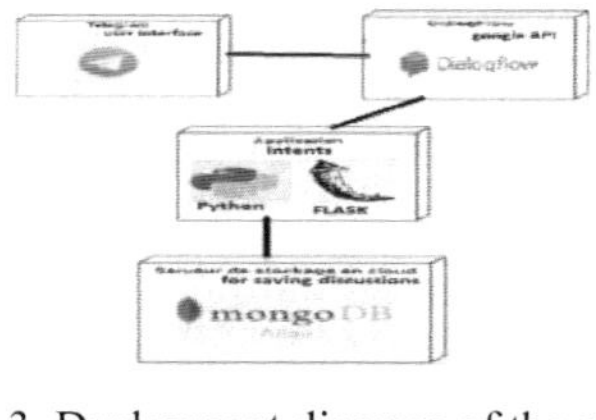

Figure 3. Deployment diagram of the chat-bot

The DialogFlow is an interface that uses Google's intelligence. Using its Cloud Natural Language API, it recognizes and understands sentences sent by users. Google look for the "intents" configured and takes the action in return programmed in the application. Intent is a messaging object that describes how to do something. It can be defined in one of two ways by providing the fulfillment for intent, or by requesting the fulfillment of intent by Google Assistant Intent is linked to one or more training phrases that were defined. It has contexts, training phrases, events, actions / parameters, and a response. Contexts represent the current state of the user's request. Their purpose is to allow the agent to transport information from intent to another. One context can be a context entry when it receives from the other intent if on the other hand it sends a message to another intent it is considered as an output context. By using combinations of the entry and the output contexts, users' conversations are controlled and saved in the dialog box. To make the connection with the data base, the creation of a cluster is necessary. The data base is configured by entering the Network address, and then it is possible to create the collections. That is made by copying the connection coordinates by clicking on connect and choosing the python language to connect the database to Python.

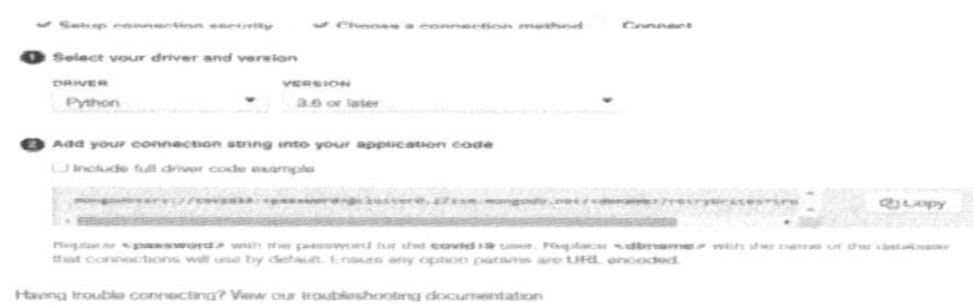

Figure 4. Establishing connexion in MangoDB

The application was deployed in Cloud Foundry. This allowed obtaining the URL link. This last was past into fulfillment web hook agent activation interface in dialog flow.

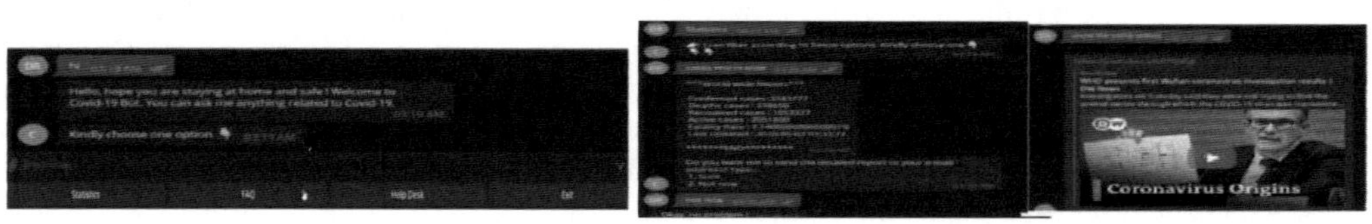

Figure 5. The interface of the chat bot integrated in telegram and answering questions and sending a video

5. DISCUSSION AND CONCLUSION

The financial aid application proposed integrates a decision making system based on data mining algorithms. The data used for the comparison of these algorithms were taken from an existent and public data set. Results might be better if the application is integrated for use and data gathered are processed as an entry to make training and reevaluating the chosen algorithm. As one of possible extension to this work is to experiment, after a certain period of the application's launching, reprocessing the comparisons for better results. However, including efficient classification algorithms in financial aid web applications is recommended for an accurate computation and right decision. A potential quality system evaluation of these applications can be considered as future work.

For the chatbot application, this paper explained in details the easy and the faithful way to create a chatbot using google API. It was developed to inform about Covid19 and it can also be used for other purposes and/or to communicate with citizens in other context. All conversations are saved in a data base for future analysis. Data text, the extraction of meaningful knowledge and finding a user pattern and/or understand the users' interests are possible to improve the chatbot. Both the proposed applications complement each other. They both serve the citizens and help them being well informed to be able to protect themselves and bring them the necessary formative or financial support. In addition, it should be noted that the applications have not been evaluated among citizens. In addition to the one described in this article, a new chat bot will be proposed and integrated into a learning management system as an extension of this work. The comparison process between both assists in determining the best methodology and type of bots. The effectiveness is measured in terms of the quality and time spent notifying students about new information and reminding them to take the next action in the learning platform.

REFERENCES

Battineni, G., Chintalapudi, N., & Amenta, F. (2020, June). AI chatbot design during an epidemic like the novel coronavirus. In *Healthcare* (Vol. 8, No. 2, p. 154). Multidisciplinary Digital Publishing Institute.

Dennis, A. R., Kim, A., Rahimi, M., & Ayabakan, S. (2020). User reactions to COVID-19 screening chatbots from reputable providers. *Journal of the American Medical Informatics Association*, *27*(11), 1727-1731.

Goniewicz, K., Khorram-Manesh, A., Hertelendy, A. J., Goniewicz, M., Naylor, K., & Burkle, F. M. (2020). Current response and management decisions of the European Union to the COVID-19 outbreak: a review. *Sustainability*, *12*(9), 3838.

Höhn, S., & Bongard-Blanchy, K. (2020, November). Heuristic evaluation of COVID-19 chatbots. In *International Workshop on Chatbot Research and Design* (pp. 131-144). Springer, Cham.

Kim, E., & Ko, K. (2021). Misalignment between coronavirus financial aid and public health policies: negative incentives for outpatient clinics in the United States. *Journal of Public Health Policy*, *42*(1), 160-166.

Mehfooz, F., Jha, S., Singh, S., Saini, S., & Sharma, N. (2021). Medical chatbot for novel COVID-19. In *ICT analysis and applications* (pp. 423-430). Springer, Singapore.

Mogaji, E. (2020). Financial vulnerability during a pandemic: insights for coronavirus disease (COVID-19). *Mogaji, E*, 57-63.

Poliak, A., Fleming, M., Costello, C., Murray, K. W., Yarmohammadi, M., Pandya, S., ... & Sedoc, J. (2020). Collecting verified COVID-19 question answer pairs.

Satiani, B., Zigrang, T. A., & Bailey-Wheaton, J. L. (2020). COVID-19 financial resources for physicians. *Journal of vascular surgery*, *72*(4), 1161-1165.

ENHANCING TYPE SYSTEMS WITH FIRST-CLASS PATTERNS

Lutz Hamel, Timothy Colaneri, and Oliver McLaughlin
Dept. of Computer Science & Statistics, University of Rhode Island
Kingston, Rhode Island, USA

ABSTRACT

It has been observed that patterns and in particular first-class patterns can be used to enhance the type systems of procedural languages, especially dynamically typed procedural languages. Here we describe some recent findings of our ongoing research on the impact of first-class patterns on the type system of our Asteroid programming language, a dynamically typed, multi-paradigm programming language that supports first-class patterns. First, we show that first-class patterns allow us to specify subtypes of data types providing a light-weight mechanism for type checking function domains amongst other things. Next, we introduce the idea of a pure constraint pattern which is a pattern that functions like a regular pattern but does not introduce any spurious bindings into the current scope. This is particularly useful for preventing non-linearities in formal function arguments when using first-class patterns. Finally, we demonstrate that first-class patterns can be used to define abstract base types enabling subtype polymorphism. This is particularly powerful in object-based languages like Asteroid that lack inheritance and therefore cannot rely on that mechanism to provide subtype-supertype relationships between user defined types.

KEYWORDS

Pattern Matching, First-Class Patterns, Type Systems, Programming Language Concepts and Design

1. INTRODUCTION

Pattern matching is a powerful programming paradigm which first appeared in applicative languages such as HOPE (Burstall, et al., 1980) in the 1970's and early 1980's to make data structure analysis and decomposition more declarative. It was adopted by functional languages such as Haskell (Peyton Jones, 2003) and ML (Milner et al., 1997) in the 1990's for similar reasons. First-class patterns were introduced into Haskell in the early 2000's (Tullsen, 2000), and were formally studied in the context of the lambda calculus later that decade (Jay & Kesner, D., 2009). First-class patterns do not increase the computational power of a programming language, but they do increase its expressiveness similar to the way higher-order programming with first-class functions increases the expressiveness of a programming language allowing for brand new ways of solving problems. Here we explore some aspects of this by using first-class patterns to enhance type systems. Today, almost all modern programming languages such as Python, Rust, and Swift incorporate some form of pattern matching.

It has been observed that patterns and in particular first-class patterns can be used to enhance the type systems of procedural languages, especially dynamically typed procedural languages such as Python and JavaScript, e.g. (Bloom & Hirzel, 2012; Kohn et al., 2020). Here we describe some recent findings of our ongoing research on the impact of first-class patterns on the type system of our Asteroid programming language (https://asteroid-lang.org), a dynamically typed, multi-paradigm programming language that supports first-class patterns. Our notion of first-class patterns as types is related to the ideas of first-class dynamic types developed in (Homer et al., 2019).

In this paper we show three applications of first-class patterns as types. First, we show that first-class patterns allow us to specify subtypes of data types providing a light-weight mechanism for type checking function domains amongst other things. Next, patterns can always be thought of as constraints in the sense that some functionality in a program is only invoked when a particular pattern is matched. This was precisely the idea behind the original design of patterns in functional programming languages. However, pattern matching, especially conditional pattern matching always introduces variable bindings into the current scope which might be undesirable due to name pollution of the current scope. Here we introduce our concept of "pure constraint pattern" where patterns behave like regular patterns but do not introduce variable bindings into the current scope. Finally, we demonstrate that first-class patterns can be used to define abstract base types (in the sense of abstract base classes) for both built-in as well as user defined types enabling subtype polymorphism. This is particularly powerful in object-based languages like Asteroid that lack inheritance and therefore cannot rely on that mechanism to provide subtype-supertype relationships between user defined types.

In terms of contributions, besides providing an implementation of these concepts in a working programming language, our ideas of pure constraint pattern and patterns as abstract base types seem to be novel.

2. FIRST-CLASS PATTERNS IN ASTEROID

In Asteroid, first-class patterns are introduced with the keyword 'pattern' and patterns themselves are first-class values that we can store in variables amongst other things and then reference them when we want to use them. Like so,

```
let p = pattern (x,y).
let *p = (1,2).
```

The first let statement assigns a *pattern value* to the variable p and on the left side of the second let statement we dereference the pattern stored in variable p and use it to match against the term (1,2) on the right side. The match introduces the bindings x → 1 and y → 2 into the current scope.

3. DEFINING SUBTYPES WITH PATTERNS

First-class patterns can be used to define subtypes of existing types in a program in a lightweight, dynamic fashion. For example, in Asteroid we can use a first-class pattern to define the natural numbers as a subtype of the integers as follows,

```
let Nat = pattern (x:%integer) if x >= 0.
```

The let statement defines a pattern Nat that, given a value x, checks if that value is of type integer and if its value is non-negative. We can now use this new pattern to restrict the values that can be assigned to a variable much like a type declaration would,

```
let v:*Nat = some_value.
```

This let statement will only succeed if the variable some_value has a value that is compatible with the pattern Nat. If the value is compatible with the pattern, then an appropriate binding of the variable v is inserted into the current scope. We can combine structural pattern matching and patterns that define data types to type check the domain of functions. Consider the factorial, which is only defined on non-negative integers,

```
-- define our subtypes of the integers as patterns
let Pos_Int = pattern (x:%integer) if x > 0.
let Neg_Int = pattern (x:%integer) if x < 0.

-- define function using structural decomposition on integers
function fact
    with 0 do
        return 1
    with n:*Pos_Int do
        return n * fact (n-1).
    with n:*Neg_Int do
        throw Error("undefined for "+n).
    end
```

Here we have a structural decomposition with three cases. The first case matches the constant 0 and returns the value 1. The second case matches the positive integers and performs the recursive factorial computation. Finally, the third case matches the negative integers and raises an exception since factorial is not defined over negative values. Notice that the first-class patterns in the latter two cases act like data types restricting the kinds of values that can be assigned to the formal argument n. The structural decomposition given here is not unlike the kind of structural decomposition one would see in functional languages with one major difference: here the patterns are values!

4. PURE CONSTRAINT PATTERNS

Patterns can always be thought of as constraints in the sense that some functionality in a program is only invoked when a particular pattern is matched. However, pattern matching, especially conditional pattern matching usually introduces variable bindings into the current scope which might be undesirable. Consider the code snippet based on our earlier pattern,

```
let Nat = pattern (x:%integer) if x >= 0.
let v:*Nat = 1.
```

When these two statements are executed, they will produce two bindings in the current scope: v → 1 and x → 1. The former is an intended binding due to the second let statement where we explicitly assign the value 1 to v. The latter is a spurious binding which is a side effect from evaluating the first-class pattern as part of the assignment in the second statement. Besides cluttering the name space these kinds of spurious bindings can be harmful because they might mask critical variables that are part of the core computation.

To prevent these spurious bindings Asteroid allows the user to turn any pattern into a "pure constraint pattern," that is, a pattern that does not introduce spurious bindings into the current scope. Pure constraint patterns are indicated with the '%[...]%' brackets. For instance, turning our Nat pattern into a pure constraint pattern gives us the program snippet,

```
let Nat = pattern %[(x:%integer) if x >= 0]%.
let v:*Nat = 1.
```

which will only produce a single binding in the current scope: v → 1. The evaluation of the variable x is now local to the pattern and that binding is not introduced into the current scope. One of the main applications of pure constraint patterns is the prevention of non-linear patterns in formal arguments of functions when employing first-class patterns. The following function uses the pure constraint pattern Nat we introduced above,

```
let Nat = pattern %[(x:%integer) if x >= 0]%.

function nat_add
    with (a:*Nat, b:*Nat) do
        return a+b.
    end
```

This function accepts two natural numbers and returns their sum. If we hadn't written the Nat pattern as a pure constraint pattern, then its repeated use in the formal argument of the function would introduce a non-linearity: the repeated instantiation of x in the argument pattern. Asteroid does not support non-linear patterns and therefore the program would be rejected. Turns out that even if Asteroid supported non-linear patterns, this program would not work due to the fact that non-linear patterns express constraints on the values bound to the repeated variables – in this case all repeated instances of x need to be bound to exactly the same value which means that nat_add would be limited to computations involving pairs such as (1,1), (2,2), etc.

5. DEFINING ABSTRACT BASE TYPES AS PATTERNS

An interesting application of first-class patterns is the definition of abstract base types enabling subtype polymorphism. The following Asteroid program demonstrates that,

```
load system io.

structure Circle with -- define the circle shape

   data radius.
```

```
   function print_shape
      with none do
         io @println ("circle: "+this @radius)
      end
end

structure Rectangle with -- define the rectangle shape

   data a.
   data b

   function print_shape
      with none do
         io @println ("rectangle: "+this @a+","+this @b).
      end
end

-- define abstract base type Shape with Circle and Rectangle as subtypes
let Shape = pattern %[x if (x is %Circle) or (x is %Rectangle)]%.

-- define function in terms of the abstract base type Shape
-- the argument of the function is restricted to values described by the pattern Shape
function print_any
   with s:*Shape do
      s @print_shape().
   end

-- the function print_any is subtype polymorphic
print_any(Circle(10)).
print_any(Rectangle(5,20)).
```

The program defines two shapes, Circle and Rectangle, together with some properties and a member function called print_shape, The member function does nothing else than write out what kind of shape object it belongs to and what the properties of this shape object are. Next, we define the abstract base type Shape as a first-class pattern. It is a pure constraint pattern that tests whether a given object is either a Circle or a Rectangle. In effect, this makes Circle and Rectangle subtypes of Shape. We then define a function called print_any whose argument is constrained to the abstract base type. If the passed-in object is of the correct type, then the function will call the member function print_shape on that object. If the passed in object does not belong to the Shape type hierarchy, then the program will flag an error. The last two lines of the program demonstrate that the print_any function is subtype polymorphic and will generate the following output,

```
circle: 10
rectangle: 5,20
```

We say that the pattern Shape represents an abstract type in that it functions as a type, but you are not able to instantiate any objects based on that type.

6. CONCLUSIONS AND FURTHER WORK

Here we provided a snapshot of ongoing research in the context of first-class patterns viewed as extensions to the type system of Asteroid. First, we showed that first-class patterns allow us to specify subtypes of data types. Next, we introduced the idea of pure constraint patterns which are patterns that function like regular patterns but do not introduce any spurious bindings into the current scope. Finally, we demonstrated that first-class patterns can be used to define abstract base types enabling subtype polymorphism.

One issue that we are concerned with when using first-class patterns is the loss of transparency during pattern matching. Consider pattern matching without the use of first-class patterns,

```
let (x,y) = (1,2).
```

It is clear that the value on the right is matched against the structure on the left with variable bindings $x \rightarrow 1$ and $y \rightarrow 2$. Now, if we replace the pattern with a first-class pattern the code becomes,

```
let p = pattern (x,y).
let *p = (1,2).
```

The second line is again a pattern match statement that matches the value on the right to the structure of the pattern. However, the binding of the variables is now somewhat obscured. In order to restore some of the declarative properties of pattern matching we propose the following,

```
let p = pattern %[(x,y)]%.
let *p bind [x,y] = (1,2).
```

Here the bind operator makes it explicit that pattern matching introduces bindings for the variables x and y in the current scope. The bind operator also allows you to rename bindings on the fly which is useful when a first-class pattern appears multiple times in a match statement,

```
let p = pattern %[(x,y)]%.
let (*p bind [x as a, y as b], *p bind [x as c, y as d]) = ((1,2), (3,4)).
```

The pattern on the left of the second line describes a pair of pairs and introduces bindings for variables a, b, c, and d. Of course, in this setting the mechanisms seems to be overkill because the patterns involved are so simple but keep in mind that first-class patterns can become complex as we demonstrated above with the idea of describing an abstract base type using a first-class pattern.

REFERENCES

Bloom, B. and Hirzel, M.J., 2012. Robust scripting via patterns. *ACM SIGPLAN Notices*, *48*(2), pp.29-40.

Burstall, R.M., MacQueen, D.B. and Sannella, D.T., 1980, August. HOPE: An experimental applicative language. In *Proceedings of the 1980 ACM conference on LISP and functional programming* (pp. 136-143).

Homer, M., Jones, T. and Noble, J., 2019, October. First-class dynamic types. In *Proceedings of the 15th ACM SIGPLAN International Symposium on Dynamic Languages* (pp. 1-14).

Jay, B. and Kesner, D., 2009. First-class patterns. *Journal of Functional Programming*, *19*(2), pp.191-225.

Kohn, T., van Rossum, G., Bucher II, G.B. and Levkivskyi, I., 2020, November. Dynamic pattern matching with Python. In *Proceedings of the 16th ACM SIGPLAN International Symposium on Dynamic Languages* (pp. 85-98).

Milner, R., Tofte, M., Harper, R. and MacQueen, D., 1997. *The definition of standard ML: revised*. MIT press.

Peyton Jones, S. ed., 2003. *Haskell 98 language and libraries: the revised report*. Cambridge University Press.

Tullsen, M., 2000, January. First Class Patterns? *In International Symposium on Practical Aspects of Declarative Languages* (pp. 1-15). Springer, Berlin, Heidelberg.

INTELLIGENT SEMANTIC BASED FRAMEWORK FOR PERSONALIZED REHABILITATION TO CHILDREN WITH CEREBRAL PALSY

Rahma Haouas Zahwanie[1], Lilia Cheniti-Belcadhi[1] and Saoussen Layouni[2]
[1]*Sousse University, ISITC, PRINCE Research Laboratory H-Sousse, Tunisia*
[2]*Sousse University, Department of Physical Medecine and Rehabiliation, Sahloul Hospital Medical Faculty Sousse, Tunisia*

ABSTRACT

Cerebral palsy (CP) is one of the most common developmental disorders. Technological development has allowed the transformation of the healthcare sector to provide more preventive services. This research proposes our intelligent decision support system" KineCP" that aims to assist a recommendation system based on Hybrid model and an intelligent system in which we proposed an ontology and we applied different SWRL rules to extract the inference and recommend solutions. These rules will be inferred for suggesting appropriate recommendations to the patient. The Framework could be used to help Children with Cerebral Palsy for personalized rehabilitation. The main idea is to help those children who attack CP to practice different home exercises under the supervision of parents.

KEYWORDS

Recommendation System, Intelligent System, Ontology, SWRL Rule, Cerebral Palsy, Personalized Rehabilitation

1. INTRODUCTION

The overall prevalence of cerebral palsy (CP) has remained at 1.96 per 1000 live births in recent years (Alabdulqader 2022), despite improvements in the survival rate of low-birth-weight infants. CP is the largest diagnostic group in pediatric rehabilitation. Children with CP feel limited in their social participation, independence, and self-efficacy because they are limited in their ability to perform daily activities. It is important to detect CP early so that treatment can begin as soon as possible and be as effective as possible. Therefore, developing Artificial Intelligence (AI) methods to detect cerebral palsy could significantly improve children's lives. Recent developments have shown encouraging results for cerebral palsy diagnostic purposes. In addition, AI combined with imaging technology can measure large data sets from video footage. It also makes it easier for medical professionals to share their insights into CP-related spontaneous movements and help them diagnose patients. In recent years, Expert Systems (ES) (Algehyne 2022), Case-Based Reasoning (CBR) (Huo 2022), and Ontology have become the basic techniques used to diagnose disorders. Ontology is an important tool for modeling knowledge in various areas of medicine, including diagnosis of disability and illness. This technology allows you to implement different types of interoperability and inference processes between different types of systems.

In this paper, we explore the technologies used in disability and disease symptoms, we study some examples that use intelligent frameworks, their strengths, and weaknesses. Then, based on these weaknesses, we propose several ontological models that support a coherent design of the data set related to rehabilitation. Finally, we present an implementation of our research where we highlight how the data can be recommended to patients and provide the necessary SWRL rules to describe the formal process of the intelligent framework.

2. RELATED WORK

This section discusses the research works related to intelligent framework and to Cerebral palsy. It also discusses papers describing intelligent chatbots used in medicine.

2.1 Representative Approaches based on Intelligent Framework for Healthcare

AI techniques can support healthcare professionals in a wide range of tasks. For theses, Sermet et al. proposed the creation of an informatory assistant for COVID-19 (chatbot) based on the Centers for Disease Control and Prevention (CDC) data in order to demonstrate the framework's usage (Sermet 2021). Essa et al. Proposed an efficient IFHDS approach using encryption algorithms in a distributed aspect among different cloud platforms to improves the performance of processing health data (Essa 2019). El-Sappagh et al. asserted two mature reasoning techniques (ontology&fuzzy logic) in a novel aspect to propose a Fuzzy Decision Support System for Diabetes Diagnosis (El-Sappagh 2018).

2.2 Representative Approaches to Examine Children with Cerebral Palsy

Cerebral Palsy (CP) is a neuro developmental confusion that envelop multiple neurological disorders that appear in minority or early childhood and persist through the lifespan of the individual (Pham 2021). CP is caused by abnormal brain development or damage to the developing brain and affects the ability of a person to control muscles. Symptoms of CP vary from person to person (Cooney 2021). People with severe CP may need to use special equipment to walk, may not be able to walk at all, and may require lifelong care. People with mild CP, on the other hand, may walk a little clumsy, but may not require special assistance. The exact symptoms can change over a person's life, but CP does not worsen over time.

Vengatesh et al. proposed to construct a computer vision-based communication system to monitor the kids (Vengatesh 2020). The intelligent agent based on computer vision is created to be built with the help of an OpenCV python library using a programming language and classifiers to recognize the image. It senses the movement of the youngsters through addressing the children's needs, pain, and emotions capturing the expressions on the face, body language, and through the webcam, the children's sign language is captured. However, we observe there are few emotions to be recognized in the current system, and the system's accuracy is minimal. Gong and Wu proposed an application of human-computer interaction technology in the field of cerebral palsy rehabilitation which is a is a robot auxiliary system that is needed as the output feedback system to feedback the recognition results and realize the interaction between human and robot(Gong 2021). Bionic robot hand is a kind of robot system which can make a variety of gestures with the same motion characteristics as human hand. It mainly realizes the control purpose through the internal control chip. Although, the robot assisted cerebral palsy rehabilitation training system based on action interaction, five kinds of limb actions are designed as action training schemes by applying action recognition, and the recognition results are fed back by the bionic robot hand system. Another approach proposed by Berdina et al. was to use a robot-assisted complexes with biofeedback for locomotor training of the upper and/or lower limbs that promote verticalization and the formation of direct motor stereotypies is now used in the rehabilitation of individuals with CP (Berdina 2017). The robot provides a transparent assistance by utilizing a low inertia motor and an impedance reduction control algorithm. This makes it possible to minimize discomfort by preventing unexpected resistance to the spontaneous movement of a patient with incomplete paraplegia. We observe for this system an absence of attention to the ontogenetic brain maturation principle and the development of the motor skills, and the gradual extinction of the primitive reflexes in children, very expensive.

So, we can result that the medical sector, and especially the physical and physiotherapy sector that deals with children affected by cerebral palsy, uses artificial intelligence in its various solutions to improve their health and help them to heal. In addition, semantic web technologies are presented as a method of data analysis that automates the creation of analytical models. These technologies consist of using machine learning models to search medical data and discover information to improve health outcomes and patient experiences. But none of these approaches uses Ontologies for data description and inferences. Besides all these environments do not use more than two of the three systems (intelligent system, recommendation system and personalization system). Based on their limitations and the above synthetic, we propose to build our solution for designing an intelligent framework for CP.

2.3 Research Example for Medical Chatbot

In the table below, we focus our study on some papers, that designed medical chatbot as an important system and especially we are interested in the technology used.

Table 1. Different technologies for medical chatbot

Approaches	Technologies
Chatbot for medical treatment using NLTK Lib	Natural Language Toolkit (NLTK)
Intelligent healthbot for transforming healthcare	Natural Language Processing (NLP), ML
Conception and realization of a chatbotsystem to support psychological and medical procedures	Support Vector Machine (SVM)
A personalized medical assistant chatbot: MediBot	Recurrent Neural Network (RNN), NLP
Automated medical chatbot	NLP and Classification

3. INTELLIGENT CP SYSTEM ARCHITECTURE

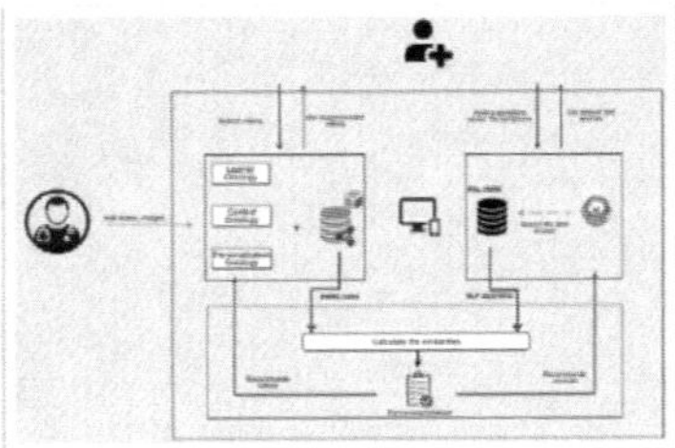

Figure 1. Proposed functional for intelligent kinecp

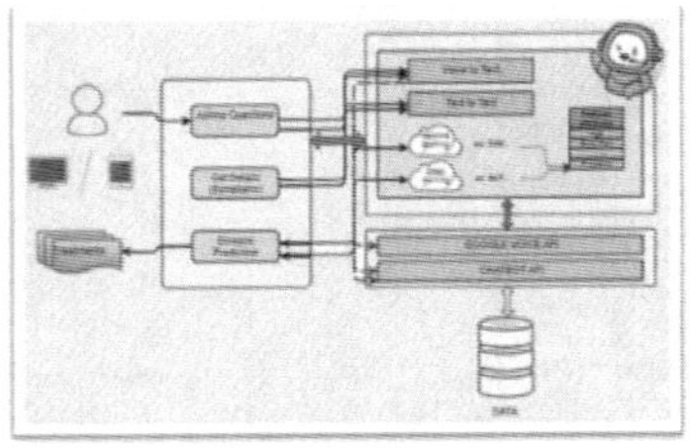

Figure 2. Hierachy of KineCP chatbot functionalities

Our CP intelligent Framework needs the services of an Apache Web server (figure 1). To do this, the client sends a SOAP request to the server in the form of an HTTPs message. The web service interprets the contents of the request and ensures that the service performs an action: Our system is composed of 3 ontologies which are: Learner ontology (contains the required knowledge about the user's preferences.), Context ontology (describe the structure of our system) and finally the Personalization ontology (present the concepts constituting medicine physical). A filter is performed via the ontologies and the representative nature of the concepts. It allows users to select the concepts presented in the ontologies and have a representativeness above a certain level. Thus, it allows the structural index to be built by associating the page in question with the ontologies concepts it contains. To obtain inference rules within the semantic web, we have used SWRL rules which are editing using the SWRLTab features. It ensures the processing of knowledge in the ontology supporting the command. The system uses a recommendation system by calculating the similarity of keywords in the data. After execution, the web service formulates a response and sends it back to the client, again using SOAP and HTTPs. The response is interpreted and the information is passed to the software where it is processed. To summarize, our system is composed of 4 main layers:

- **Presentation Layer:** provides information to users (patient and/or systems) and handles patient requests.
- **Application layer:** is responsible for executing system tasks, including authorization control.
- **Domain layer:** is accountable for mapping the problem domain.
- **Infrastructure layer:** is responsible for the technical issues supporting the other layers (i.e. messaging…)

This Framework (figure 2) helps users submit their health complaints and questions. The real purpose of the chatbot is to help people by giving them advice on how to live healthy. The way the system works is as follows:

- **Asking Questions and getting details:** It is possible to ask some health care questions and get more details about symptoms.
- **Interactive mode:** Questions are related text-to-text. It is also related to voice-to-text and text-to-voice conversations. For example, children who cannot write and send text, they can send a vocal message.
- **Google API and Chatbot API:** Using Google APIs for voice-to-text and text-to-voice conversions. The Chatbot API sends requests to chatbots, receives corresponding responses, and references those responses.
- **Disease Prediction:** Depending on the disease symptoms, the NLP algorithm can predict a disease.

4. HYBRID RECOMMENDATION ALGORITHM FOR INTELLIGENT KINECP FRAMEWORK

Matrix factorization allows the system to represent its data structure in a more concise and relevant way, in order to achieve much more competitive processing times and storage space savings. Moreover, it is used to generate an output in the form of recommendations. The scalar product of the patient matrix and the item matrix can produce a rating matrix, while the patient matrix has the form k(patient)*f(feature) and the item matrix has the form j(item)*f(feature). From patient's and item's matrices, features of the videos can be its spasticity, treatment, etc. After obtaining the best factors to approximate the ratings we have, we then perform dot product of the factor matrices to fill in the missing entries in the rating matrix. These filled in ratings are then used to provide recommendations to the users.

Algorithm1: Matrix factorization for recommendation

```
Input: R: rating matrix, P: |U|*k (user features matrix), Q:|D|*k (item features matrix), k: latent features, step: iteration, α: learning rate, β: regularization parameter
Output: P, Q
Begin
For (step=0, step<=STEP, step++)
    For (i=0, i<=long(R), i++)
        For (j=0, j<=long(R[i]), j++)
            If R[i][j] > 0
                eij = R[i][j] – P[i]Q[j]
            end if
            For (k=0, k<=K, k++) # calculate gradient with α and β parameter
                P[i][k] = P[i][k] + α * (2 * eij * Q[k][j] – β * P[i][k])
                Q[k][j] = Q[k][j] + α * (2 * eij * P[i][K] – β * Q[k][j])
    eR = P*Q
    e=0

    For (i=0, i<=long(R), i++)
        For (j=0, j<=long(R[i]), j++)
            If R[i][j] > 0
                e = e + (R[i][j])^(P[i]Q[j])
            End if
            For (k=0, k<=K, k++)
                e = e + (β/2) * (P[i][k])^2 + (Q[k][j])^2
    If e<0.001 # 0.001: local minimum
        Exit
    End if
    Return P, Q
End
```

Cosine similarity is used to measure similarities between two vectors, regardless of their size. It is most used in information retrieval, image recognition, text similarity, bioinformatics, and recommender systems.

$$\text{Similarity} = cos(\theta) = \frac{A \cdot B}{\|A\|\|B\|} = \frac{\sum_{i=1}^{n} A_i B_i}{\sqrt{\sum_{i=1}^{n} A_i^{21}} \cdot \sqrt{\sum_{i=1}^{n} B_i^2}}$$

An advantage of the cosine similarity is that it preserves the sparsity of the data matrix. It gives the similarity of two n-dimensional vectors, P and Q, by determining the cosine of their angle. This score is frequently used in text mining. If we consider the cosine function, its value at 0 degrees is 1 and -1 at 80 degrees. This means that for two overlapping vectors, the value of the cosine will be maximum and minimum for two exactly opposite vectors. The spatial.distance.cosinus(o) function in the scipy module calculates the distance instead of the cosine similarity, but to achieve this, we can subtract the distance value from 1.

Algorithm2: Calculating the similarity using CosineSimilarity

```
Input: P, Q, R, K
Output: MatrixSimilarity
Begin
For (i=0, i<=long(R), i++)
    For (k=0, k<=K, k++)
        MatrixSimilarity[i][k] = SimilarityCosine(i, k)
    End for
End for
For (k=0, k<=K, k++)
    For (j=0, j<=long(R[k]), j++)
        MatrixSimilarity[k][j] = SimilarityCosine(k, j)
    End for
End for
Return (1 − spatial.distance.cosinus((P[i][k]), (Q[k][j]))
End
```

5. FRAMEWORK ONTOLOGICAL MODELS

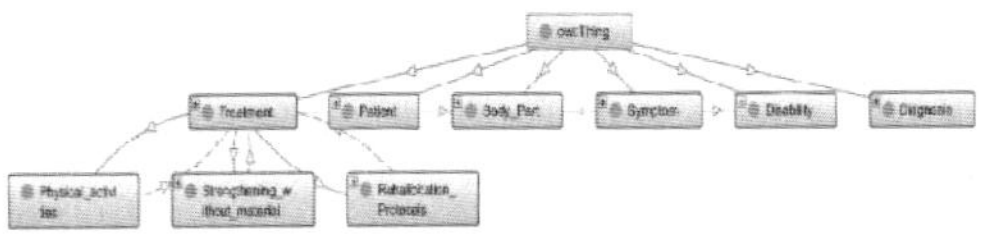

Figure 3. OntoGraph of the personalization model

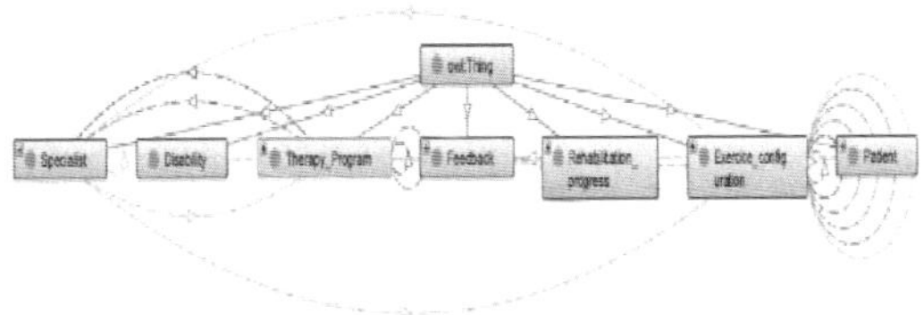

Figure 4. OntoGraph of the learner model

We started with the idea of building an ontology representing only the concepts constituting medicine physical. The figure 3 shows the different classes implemented in our system and individuals for each class. We take an example the class 'treatment' and its individuals which are medical care given to a patient for a spasticity to deal.

We propose a learner ontology that contains the required knowledge about the user's preferences (figure 4). It is created from the learner's data, typically collected by intelligent tutoring systems through interactions between the learner and the learner's tutoring system. We have seen that the proposed OWL is about generally 6 terms which are: disability, exercise configuration, patient, rehabilitation progress, specialist, and therapy program. Those terms represent a model to describe health domains for personalization the patient. Thus, it indicates a patient behavior.

6. SWRL RULES FOR THE INTELLIGENT CP FRAMEWORK

SWRL allows the application of production and inference rules within the Semantic Web. The proposed rule takes the form of an implication between an antecedent (body) and a consequent (head) (Zhai 2018).

SWRL rules provide a mechanism for discovering a lifestyle pattern. The rule R1 classifies a child(patient) according to its treatment: If a child attends symptom, then he must have treatment.

- **R1:** Child(?c) V Symptom(?s) V Attend(?c, ?s) → Treatment(?c)

The next step consisted of to introduce in the ontology an object property called has disability and classifying a person's degree of illness, as it's shown in R2, if a patient has a special disability, then he must has exercise training refer to his disability.

- **R2:** Patient(?p) V has disability(?p, Disability) → Exercise training(?p))

The next rule defines a type of strengthening without material (planks) and it presents a type of treatment.

- **R3:** Strengthening without material(?s) V is a(?s, ?t) V Treatment(?t) → Planks(?s)

7. INTELLIGENT FRAMEWORK DEVELOPMENT

Figure 5 presents the patient's chatbot interface where he can contact it in any time by taping "send" and he will receive a message at the same time. It shows a dialog between a chatbot and a patient in our platform. The patient asks about a solution for his problem and the chatbot gives him the right exercises that he must practice. These questions are in form of data.json where we have used nltk (Natural Language Toolkit) to mesure the similarity by applying stemming.

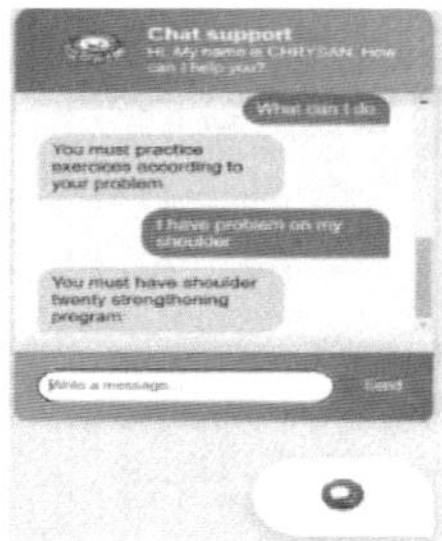

Figure 5. Interface of chatbot

8. CONCLUSION AND FUTURE WORK

This research aims to help children with CP by providing them a platform that contains different exercise videos to select the adapted one to their profile and handicap. It puts also a medical chatbot to be in contact with them and provides answer their questions. As a future work, we aim to develop further our solution to be better adapted to various learners' contexts, enhance our platform to be, also, a mobile application and the chatbot by adding the phase voice-to-voice and edit the data for further personalization of the rehabilitation.

REFERENCES

Alabdulqader, Ebtisam and Stockwell, Katy and Montague, Kyle and Jackson, Dan and Monk, Andrew and Pennington, Lindsay and McNaney, Roisin and Lindsay, Stephen and Wu, Ling and Olivier, Patrick. (2022). Understanding the Therapeutic Coaching Needs of Mothers of Children with Cerebral Palsy. *In Designing Interactive Systems Conference.*

Algehyne, Ebrahem A and Jibril, Muhammad Lawan and Algehainy, Naseh A and Alamri, Osama Abdulaziz and Alzahrani, Abdullah K. (2022). Fuzzy neural network expert system with an improved Gini index random forest-based feature importance measure algorithm for early diagnosis of breast cancer in Saudi Arabia. *Big Data and Cognitive Computing* (MDPI), 6(1): 13.

Berdina, Olga N and Bairova, Tatyana A and Rychkova, Lyubov V and Sheptunov, Sergey A. (2017). The pediatric robotic-assisted rehabilitation complex for children and adolescents with cerebral palsy: Background and product design. In *2017 International Conference Quality Management, Transport and Information Security, Information Technologies* (IT\&QM\&IS), 360--363.

Cooney, Nicholas J and Minhas, Atul S. (2021). Humanoid Robot Based Platform to Evaluate the Efficacy of Using Inertial Sensors for Spasticity Assessment in Cerebral Palsy. *IEEE Journal of Biomedical and Health Informatics* (IEEE) 26 (1): 254--263.

El-Sappagh, Shaker and Alonso, Jose M and Ali, Farman and Ali, Amjad and Jang, Jun-Hyeog and Kwak, Kyung-Sup. (2018). An ontology-based interpretable fuzzy decision support system for diabetes diagnosis. *IEEE Access 6:* 37371-37394.

Essa, Youssef M and Hemdan, Ezz El-Din and El-Mahalawy, Ahmed and Attiya, Gamal and El-Sayed, Ayman. (2019). IFHDS: intelligent framework for securing healthcare BigData. *Journal of medical systems* 43 (5): 1-13.

Gong, Chen and Wu, Guang. (2021). Design of Cerebral Palsy Rehabilitation Training System Based on Human-Computer Interaction. In *2021 International Wireless Communications and Mobile Computing* (IWCMC), 621--625.

Huo, Yunliang and Liu, Junbo and Xiong, Ji and Xiao, Wenjun and Zhao, Jianfeng. (2022). Machine learning and CBR integrated mechanical product design approach. *Advanced Engineering Informatics* (Elsevier) 52: 101611.

Pham, Thanh-Tu and Le, Minh-Binh and Le, Lawrence H and Andersen, John and Lou, Edmond. (2021). Assessment of hip displacement in children with cerebral palsy using machine learning approach. *Medical \& Biological Engineering \& Computing* (Springer) 59 (9): 1877--1887.

Sermet, Yusuf and Demir, Ibrahim. (2021). A Semantic Web Framework for Automated Smart Assistants: A Case Study for Public Health. *Big Data and Cognitive Computing* 5 (4): 57.

Vengatesh, G and Rajesh, R and Naveenkumar, T. (2020). An Intelligent Computer Vision for Children Affected with Cerebral Palsy. In *2020 International Conference on System, Computation, Automation and Networking* (ICSCAN).

Zhai, Zhaoyu and Martínez Ortega, José-Fernán and Lucas Martínez, Néstor and Castillejo, Pedro. (2018). A rule-based reasoner for underwater robots using OWL and SWRL. *Sensors* 18 (10): 3481.

EXCHANGING PERSONAL DATA THROUGH BLOCKCHAIN TECHNOLOGY TO FULFIL INCREASING PRIVACY NEEDS

Petrus J. Roos and Henri E. van Rensburg
North-West University, Potchefstroom, South Africa

ABSTRACT

The risk of privacy intrusion is a developing concern due to the advancement in data mining techniques and the increased value of data. This study focuses on developing a system that implements blockchain technology to allow the exchange of personal data while ensuring the authenticity and privacy of the exchanged data are preserved. The privacy of data is ensured using encryption while the authenticity is intuitively built into blockchain technology with the consensus algorithm and cryptographic signatures. The blockchain interaction was enhanced by developing a companion application that simplifies exchanging data over the blockchain using QR codes. The expectation is to create awareness of the potential for using blockchain technology for secure-, private-, but verifiable data exchange, the possible implementations for future systems, and to reduce negative sentiments in regards to data sharing.

KEYWORDS

Blockchain, Privacy, Secure, Cryptography, Personal, Data

1. INTRODUCTION AND BACKGROUND

The risk of privacy intrusion is a developing concern due to the advancement in data mining techniques and the increased value of data. Blockchain technology can be used to prevent this issue. Blockchain technology is a distributed ledger where each record is encapsulated in a block, each block is connected to a previous block forming a chain (Heister & Yuthas, 2020:2).

The focus of this paper is to develop and implement a system where the capability of blockchain technology is tested by securely exchanging personal data. The main focal point is ensuring the authenticity of data stored in the blockchain, along with preserving the privacy of data exchanged to third parties. The proposed blockchain system enables a fast and effective exchange of personal data through the use of QR codes to authenticate trustworthy third-parties and consent to share personal data with.

Facebook disclosed the data of 87 million users to Cambridge Analytica for user profiling, which they used on various social media platforms to persuade voters in the United States elections (Isaak & Hanna, 2018:56-58). With more than 87 million people affected through the action of two companies, it indicates that personal data is not protected. Identity theft is when personal information is used to impersonate an individual such as to open a credit account leaving the victim many times unknowingly with debt (Holvast, 2007:23). Moreover, identity theft affects up to 7% of the United States population with the amount of money embezzled reaching figures up to 16 billion US dollars (Graves & Sexton, 2017:217). The Centre for International Governance Innovation (CIGI-Ipsos, 2019) conducted a survey which stated that 75% of participants claimed that social media are the main cause for skepticism in internet privacy with 45% of participant claiming that this skepticism prevented them from disclosing personal information online. In retrospect, the intrusion of personal data poses a great threat to the trustworthiness of respectable businesses in the Information Technology (IT) sector. Legislations are put in place for a reason however, as demonstrated, powerful companies does not follow these legislations, thus alternative measures must be taken. Blockchain technology can perhaps prevent the intrusion of privacy, encouraging better trust in IT businesses and professionals.

The key features of blockchain technology comprise out of immutable blocks and a decentralized network (Haughwout, 2017). This means that, once a block is added to the blockchain and distributed across the network it cannot be removed. Haughwout (2017) also stated that with each addition to the chain, a timestamp is added to the block as well as a cryptographic signature known as a hash which is then used to verify the validity of the chain. Figure 1 illustrates three blocks in a blockchain. The blocks are connected by storing the previous hash in the block similar to a linked list. Suppose that a block is manipulated, the hash is then recalculated and will not correspond to the next block anymore declaring the whole blockchain null and void. Figure 1 also demonstrate that each block has a timestamp represented in epoch Unix time and is calculated once a block is added to the chain. Moreover, in Figure 1 the cryptographic signature is calculated using the participant's public key to encrypt the hash forming a digital signature to enhance the authenticity of each block added to the chain. Blocks are added to the blockchain in a process called mining (Bashir, 2018:167). The last observation from Figure 1 is a simple example of personal data to be stored in the blockchain.

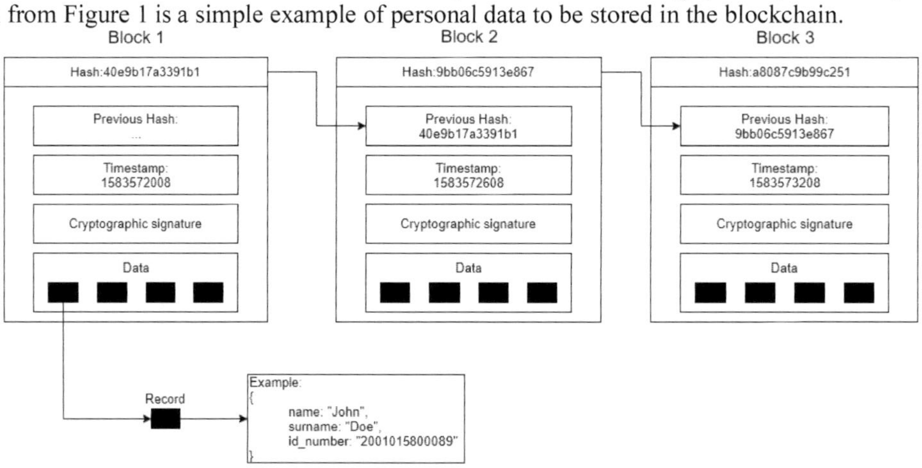

Figure 1. A graphical representation of blocks in a blockchain containing personal data

By utilizing blockchain technology, data stored in the blocks are immutable and authentic. However, there is an issue storing data in a general blockchain since data is publicly available. Hence a lightweight algorithm should be implemented to encrypt and decrypt data asymmetrically allowing only the participating users to provide access to their data. Therefore the proposed system implements blockchain technology for data exchange to allow participants to exchange personal data while ensuring that the authenticity and privacy of exchanged data are preserved.

1.1 Data Privacy and Protection

The data-driven world which emerged in the last few decades created platforms which saw a rise in privacy issues. These issues range from the illegal selling of personal data to big corporate companies and direct crimes such as identity theft and fraud. In the last decade, Facebook was one of the biggest culprits where they sold the data of millions of users (Isaak & Hanna, 2018:56-58).

The most prominent implementation of privacy protection is to implement legislation to penalize companies after infringing these laws. The European Union enforced legislation called the General Data Protection Regulation (GDPR) which protects the privacy of citizen in the European Union (Herrle & Hirsh, 2019). According to Wolford (2020), there are seven principles when processing data which include the essential principle of ensuring the confidentiality and integrity of the data being processed. The penalty of not being GDPR compliant are fines that reach a value of 20 million euros and these fines could also apply to offenders outside of the European Union (Wolford, 2020). Although this is the case for the European Union, not all regions of the world have concrete legislation to protect the privacy of citizens.

According to van den Hoven and Warnier (2020), privacy intrusion might be caused by IT systems, but IT can also help to improve privacy protection. Moreover, development methodologies should cater to privacy protection needs along with implementing tools to enhance privacy such as cryptography to encrypt personal data (van den Hoven & Warnier, 2020).

The legislation enforced to enhance privacy protection will only prevent privacy violations from happening to some extent since companies could still infringe these laws and pay the fines. In contrary, the implementation of a technical solution to enhance privacy protection will provide the required preventative measures to stop it from happening at all.

1.2 Blockchain Technology for Privacy

The research proposes the utilization of blockchain technology to fulfil increasing privacy needs to ensure the privacy and authenticity when exchanging personal data. The key features of blockchain technology, as discussed previously, comprise out of immutable blocks that are distributed across the network to ensure the authenticity of the data (Haughwout, 2017); however, it does not ensure the privacy of the data exchanged.

Since the blockchain is distributed, data stored in the blocks should be encrypted to ensure it is kept private. The RSA encryption algorithm is an appropriate light weight encryption algorithm to implement for the blockchain based private data transmission. According to Singh and Chauhan (2017), there are three steps to follow when implementing RSA encryption which includes generating a public and private key, encrypting data using the public key and decrypting using the private key. When a public key is used to encrypt data and a private key is used to decrypt data, it is classified as asymmetric cryptography (Bashir, 2018:80).

RSA encryption is commonly used in blockchain solutions due to it being relatively computationally inexpensive; however, encryption will increase the size of the data (Singh & Chauhan, 2017). According to Bashir (2018:50), the largest downside to blockchain technology is that it can only store a small amount of data; therefore to reduce the amount of data to be stored on the blockchain, it is necessary to apply a compression algorithm to the encrypted data.

2. ARTEFACT IMPLEMENTATION

A blockchain based solution is developed to exchange personal data while retaining privacy and authenticity. The key aspects that enable the proposed blockchain implementation to be a viable solution is shortly discussed below.

A. Blockchain implementation

The fundamental components of a blockchain was developed as a starting reference. The object-oriented class structure includes the transaction, the block, and the blockchain. The transaction object stores the sender and receiver's public keys along with a digital signature and in this case, the personal data to be exchanged. The block object stores an index, the previous hash, a timestamp and a list of transactions. This previous hash is a reference to the hash of the previous block, and the timestamp is the date and time of when the block was added to the chain. The blockchain object stores a list of blocks, the open transactions which should still be added to the chain and the public key of the participant.

Additional classes include; the repository, the hash utility, and the verification class. The repository class has two fields; the public- and private keys of a participant. The repository class provides functions to generate, save, and load public- and private keys as well as to sign- and verify transactions. The hash utility class has two functions; the hash string and hash block. The hash string function applies a SHA-256 hash function to a string. The hash block function uses the hash string method to hash a block by serializing the block as a string. Finally, the verification class receives a list of transactions and the previous hash to validate the chain of transactions and to verify the new transaction received from the repository to be added to the blockchain.

B. Personal data dictionary

In the transaction class, instead of representing a single value, a data field is included to use a dictionary as a data type. The dictionary data type stores values as a collection of key-value pairs. Using a dictionary to store personal data provides flexibility when it comes to data storage and exchange. Depending on the purpose of each data exchange, various personal data fields may, or may not be included in the data dictionary of the transaction. The data dictionary provides flexibility of data that can be exchanged over the blockchain such as biographical, address, and medical information.

C. Privacy and Encryption

To ensure privacy of the exchanged data, an encryption algorithm to encrypt the data dictionary was added to each transaction using the public key of the recipient. The recipient will then be able to decrypt the data using their private key. This was achieved by using the asymmetric keys generated by the *Repository* class to encrypt and decrypt the data dictionary.

The RSA asymmetric encryption displayed a limitation that can only encrypt a fixed size of characters based on the byte size of each character. This limitation was overcome by splitting the data dictionary into a list of strings that can be encrypted and stored on the blockchain. This enabled the recipient to decrypt the list of strings, concatenating these strings-, and converting it back to a data dictionary for the personal data to be viewed.

D. Compression

The literature review asserted that once data is encrypted the size of data increases. Thus a compression algorithm is necessary to reduce the size of the data exchanged on the blockchain. The Python compression module was used to seamlessly implement compression on the serialized data dictionaries. Compression was implemented on the personal data where the serialized dictionaries were compressed before it was passed on to the encryption functions and then decompressed after it was decrypted.

E. Network – (consensus algorithm)

The term consensus refers to the agreement nodes have with each other on what the current state of the blockchain is (Bashir, 2018:35). The implementation of the consensus algorithm therefore ensures that all blocks on the decentralised network are identical. A publish-subscribe pattern was implemented which allowed nodes to communicate seamlessly across the network. Figure 2 displays the working of a publish-subscribe pattern where there are three entities the publisher, the subscriber, and the publish-subscribe server.

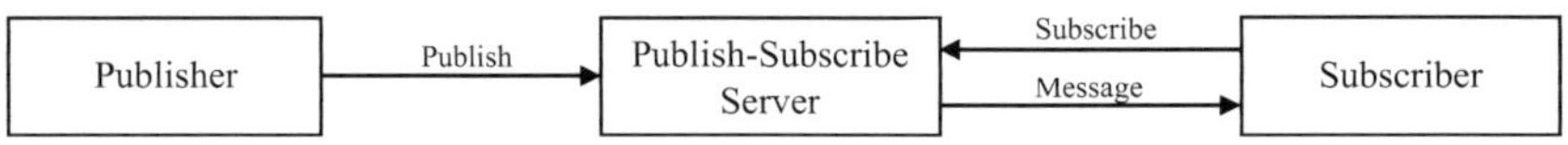

Figure 2. Publish-Subscribe architecture

The publish-subscribe server acts as a mediator between the publisher and the subscriber. The subscriber is a user who subscribes to a certain channel to get specific messages from publishers. The publisher is a user who publishes messages to a channel the publish-subscribe server forwards the message to the subscriber. The blockchain will require all nodes in the network to be publishers and subscribers simultaneously. It is important to add the required test cases to ensure that publishers and subscribers do not echo to each other. In the peer discovery, two test cases is added to verify if the sender is itself or if the node is added to the peer node list yet to prevent an echo loop to occur. The peer node list can now be used to broadcast new transactions, new blocks, and resolve nodes that are not up to date with the main chain.

F. User interaction interface / Companion application development

A web user interface and a companion app is created to facilitate interaction with the blockchain by generating a QR code to represent the public key or scanning the QR code when a transaction is performed. The user is then able to add key-value pairs to a list view (data dictionary) and then send the data to the receiver. Figure 3 demonstrates the simplicity of the transaction process of sending private data over the blockchain using the companion application.

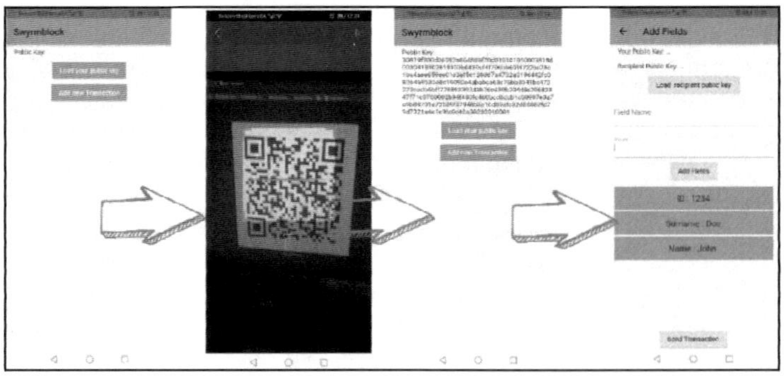

Figure 3. Companion application transaction process

3. SUMMARY AND RESULTS

The resulting system provided the ability to send private data using blockchain technology. The implementation of the blockchain makes it possible to exchange data while ensuring authenticity and privacy. Privacy is ensured by using an encryption algorithm to encrypt the personal data added to the blockchain. Authenticity is intuitively built into blockchain technology by making use of the consensus algorithm to ensure that the blockchain is stored identically across the decentralized network. The use of cryptographic signature is added to each transaction that authenticates the sender and receiver. The implementation of blockchain including the exchanging of personal data was programmed using python.

The user interface allows participants to send and receive transactions using the QR codes. After the transaction is sent to a recipient, the encrypted transaction can be viewed in an open transaction tab before it is added to the chain. The decrypted data can be viewed by the recipient using their private key to decrypt. The web application's front end was developed using HTML5, the backend developed using Flask and an API to communicate with the companion app that was developed using Flutter to enable native features such as accessing the camera to scan the public keys represented as QR codes.

4. CONCLUSION

The study aimed to implement a blockchain system that allows participants to exchange personal data while ensuring that the authenticity and privacy of exchanged data are preserved. The information gathered from the literature review indicated that encryption is required to ensure privacy of the exchanged data. The encryption size expansion issue was resolved by performing a compression algorithm before it is added to the blockchain in order to reduce the overall size of the blockchain. The companion application simplified the usability by providing an easy to use interface, allowing the exchange of customizable data through the use of QR codes.

In conclusion, this study encapsulates the importance of data privacy followed by a technological implementation of the proposed solution in the form of a blockchain based system that enables the exchange of personal data while ensuring the privacy and authenticity of the data is preserved.

REFERENCES

Bashir, I. (2018). *Mastering Blockchain: Distributed ledger technology, decentralization, and smart contracts explained.* Second edition. Packt Publishing Ltd.

CIGI-Ipsos. (2019). CIGI-Ipsos Global Survey on Internet Security and Trust. www.cigionline.org/internet-survey-2019 Date of access: 29 February 2020.

Graves, P.E. & Sexton, R.L. (2017). Optimal Public Policy against Identity Theft. *American Economist,* Vol. 62, No. 2, pp. 217-221.

Haughwout, J. (2017). Blockchain: A Single, Immutable, Serialized Source of Truth: Blockchain technology could help introduce higher levels of security to and confidence in supply chain transactions. *Material Handling & Logistics,* Vol. 72, No. 8, pp. 27-29.

Heister, S. & Yuthas, K. (2020). The blockchain and how it can influence conceptions of the self. *Technology in Society*. Elsevier. Vol. 60, pp.101218.

Herrle, J. & Hirsh, J. (2019). The Peril and Potential of the GDPR. https://www.cigionline.org/articles/peril-and-potential-gdpr/ Date of access: 21 May 2020.

Holvast, J. (2007). History of privacy. *The History of Information Security*. Elsevier Science BV. pp. 737-769.

Isaak, J. & Hanna, M.J. 2018. User Data Privacy: Facebook, Cambridge Analytica, and Privacy Protection. *Computer*, Vol. 51, No. 8, pp. 56-59.

Singh, P. & Chauhan, R.K. (2017). A Survey on Comparisons of Cryptographic Algorithms Using Certain Parameters in WSN. *International Journal of Electrical & Computer Engineering (2088-8708),* Vol. 7, No. 4, pp. 2232-2240.

van den Hoven, J.B.M.P.W. & Warnier, M. (2020). Privacy and Information Technology. (In Zalta, E.N., ed. The Stanford Encyclopedia of Philosophy. Metaphysics Research Lab, Stanford University.

Wolford, B. (2020). What is GDPR, the EU's new data protection law? https://gdpr.eu/what-is-gdpr/ Date of access: 21 May 2020.

PROMOTING CYBERSECURITY AWARENESS UTILIZING A "BUILD YOUR OWN ADVENTURE" SERIOUS GAME

Christo Croucamp, Günther Richard Drevin and Dirk Snyman
School of Computer Science and Information Systems, North-West University, 11 Hoffman Street, Potchefstroom, South Africa

ABSTRACT

Cybersecurity is of critical importance as we continue into the digital era. With technology improving rapidly and the accessibility of such technological devices becoming more prominent globally, the need for proper cybersecurity awareness has drastically increased. This has led to a need for methods to improve cybersecurity awareness. This paper addresses one such method, a "build your own adventure" serious game, where the aspects of cybersecurity awareness are combined with effective gaming principles. A serious game that teaches the users about cybersecurity awareness in a novel way is proposed.

KEYWORDS

Cybersecurity Awareness, Serious Game, Build Your Own Adventure

1. INTRODUCTION

Technological advancement is happening rapidly, and with that, accessibility to devices. Globally, there are estimated to be around 5.31 billion cellular connections. Approximately 4.95 billion internet users, or 62.5 percent of the total population at the start of 2022, have access to the internet (Kemp, 2022). The need for adequate education regarding the internet, cyberspace, and cybersecurity is critically important. In organizations, the employee is one of the biggest threats to information security (Whitman and Mattord, 2022). With rapidly rising cyber-threats associated with the increase of accessibility to devices able to connect to the internet, the user's lack of skills in protecting themselves is a serious vulnerability (Kshetri, 2019).

The high rate of growth in technology and the ease of connecting to the internet, social media, online communications, and the internet of things has led to most people being connected to cyberspace (Allers *et al.*, 2021). With people being connected to cyberspace without realizing it, the threat of unintentionally sharing personal information that can be used in an attack targeted at the user is always present. This vulnerability has led to cybersecurity becoming a necessary aspect relevant to all internet users. To achieve personalized data protection, the users need to be educated on safe practices that provide a solid foundation. Therefore, education on cybersecurity should become a critical component in the education of young people (AlShabibi and Al-Suqri, 2021). Recently, serious games (i.e., games with the intention to teach) have been proposed as a viable method of teaching cybersecurity (Allers *et al.*, 2021). Therefore, the aim of this paper is to expand on this idea and propose a serious game for promoting cybersecurity awareness among the youth.

2. THREATS OF CYBERSPACE

With cyberspace being a vast virtual environment, the threat of malicious entities using this platform to perform malicious actions on unsuspecting persons is growing daily. In this section the aim is to provide a cursory overview on the most common threats found in cyberspace, and how these threats function.

2.1 Types of Threats

Cyber threats are mostly experienced as an attack that is initiated by another human. This section will review different types of attack vectors that are commonly used. Although that natural threats also exist, these are not relevant to the study as they occur in the physical world and are therefore not discussed here. Table 1 categorizes the different threats related to cybersecurity.

Table 1. Twelve categories of threats to information security (Whitman and Mattord, 2022)

Category of Threat	Attack Examples
Compromises to intellectual property	Piracy, copyright infringement
Deviation in quality of service	Internet and power outages
Espionage or trespass	Unauthorized access and/or data collection
Forces of nature	Fire, floods, lightning
Human Error or failure	Accidents, employee mistakes
Information extortion	Blackmail, information disclosure
Sabotage or vandalism	Destruction of systems or information
Technical hardware failures or errors	Equipment failures
Technical software failure or errors	Bugs, code problems, unknown loopholes
Software attacks	Viruses, worms, macros, denial of service
Technological obsolescence	Antiquated or outdated technologies
Theft	Illegal confiscation of equipment or information

2.2 Types of Attacks

The nature of cyberspace creates opportunities for malicious entities to execute attacks on assets without leaving the comfort of home or their workspace. With the ease of executing these attacks becoming increasingly accessible and how the global state of things in 2020 to 2022 is, the number of cybercrimes has increased (Vojinovic, 2022). One of the core defence strategies against any form of cyber-attack is having knowledge about the types of attacks, how they are executed and what kind of danger these attacks pose (Allers *et al.*, 2021). Some of these possible attacks include:

Privacy Attacks: These attacks are designed to compromise data privacy and information on a system. These attacks are considered passive in nature because privacy attacks do not attempt to inflict any damage to a system or to compromise the integrity of the system. This form of attack hides in the system and gathers information anonymously (Padmavathi and Shanmugapriya, 2009).

Denial-of-Service attacks: With a denial-of-Service attack the attacker send a large number of connections or information requests to a target. The number of requests eventually becomes too much to handle not allowing the service to provide for the legitimate request. This could lead to a server crash or just loosing functionality (Whitman and Mattord, 2022).

Back Door attacks : By using a known or newly discovered access gateway, malicious entities can access a system or network through a back door (Whitman and Mattord, 2022). These back doors are sometimes designed by programmers that need to access the system and then not removed when the software is shipped. These access gateways can be used to further infiltrate the system or place malicious software that perform actions on the system or network.

Malware Attacks : Malware or Malicious software is designed with the intent to be malicious. These intentions could be from affecting a browser pushing advertising to a full system infiltration and disruption (Whitman and Mattord, 2022).

Password Attacks: falls under the term espionage or trespassing as the malicious entity is trying to gain access to information that does not belong to them. Trying to reverse engineer or guess a password is often referred to as cracking and various methods are used to try and find a person password these are (Whitman and Mattord, 2022):

Phishing : This is a method or using various strategies to trick a user into disclosing sensitive information, compromising online accounts, compromising computer systems, and/or other personal or organizational information technology resources (Abroshan *et al.*, 2021). These are mainly executed using emails to catch users that are not fully aware of the danger.

These threats are just some of the common instances and there are daily updates to antivirus services that help with protecting people from these kinds of threats. By being aware of them a person can further protect themself.

3. CYBERSECURITY AWARENESS THROUGH SERIOUS GAMES

The process of creating awareness with regards to cybersecurity refers to any activities designed to focus on cybersecurity issues and inform an individual about these issues. (Allers *et al.*, 2021) An awareness program is designed to keep information security at the forefront of a user's mind. (Whitman and Mattord, 2022). If this is accomplished, users will be aware of any issues that might be encountered and if the users knows what is to be expected they can counteract the attempt by the malicious entities without further intervention. There are various methods used from posters to videos to class sessions that promote cybersecurity awareness (Whitman and Mattord, 2022). An important aspect of security awareness is that it should be simplistic but also address the correct dangers that are encountered by the users. An awareness campaign should be actively implemented to ensure that the information is always being revised and addressed as new issues arise (Whitman and Mattord, 2022). One way of providing structured material designed around cybersecurity is to incorporate the learning material into a serious game that provides a fun and interactive experience.

3.1 Serious Games

A serious game can be defined as:

> "[a] *computer application, for which the original intention is to combine with consistency, both serious (Serious) aspects such as non-exhaustive and non-exclusive, teaching, learning, communication or the information, with playful springs from the video game (Game).*" (Alvarez and Djaouti, 2011).

By incorporating an education aspect to a game, we can provide a fun learning experience where users can learn about threats when using devices with access to the internet. This game can provide a safe environment that allows for mistakes to be made and, in turn, encourages learning from the mistakes. The game should also contain aspects to make the user want to play it again. These include originality, replayability, surprise, and creative control (Kramer, 2000).

Another aspect of gaming that can be implemented into a serious game is to allow the user to choose how the adventure will unfold by giving the user choices that impact the gameplay and story. These scenarios could emulate real-life threats and will enable the user to experience these threats in a safe environment before encountering them in the real-world context. By incorporating interactive storytelling based on threats readily available on the internet, users can learn to reduce their online self-disclosure footprint (Dincelli and Chengalur-Smith, 2020). By including "build your own adventure" aspects into a serious game, it is possible to create a gaming experience that contributes to the goal of spreading awareness about cybersecurity among young people, while retaining enjoyability and replayability without reducing the impact of the learning material.

3.2 Characteristics of a "Build Your Own Adventure" Game

The artefact will be designed using a "build your own adventure" model where actions in the game will provide the player with choices that will alter the game and provide an experience based on the choices made. These choices can change the path taken through the story or affect the character's abilities. Figure 1 shows possible routes through a stage in the game until eventually reaching the stage's final boss.

Another aspect that can be implemented into the game to promote replayability and fun is a roguelike aspect. Roguelikes are dungeon-exploration games in randomly generated environments with randomly generated events and equipment to create a unique experience every time the game is played. (Harris, 2020). These randomly generated events can be designed to implement common cybersecurity vulnerabilities experienced; using this, the player can learn about how these events occur and how to counteract them when encountered on personal devices.

The user will start at the staging area indicated by the start node in Figure 1.

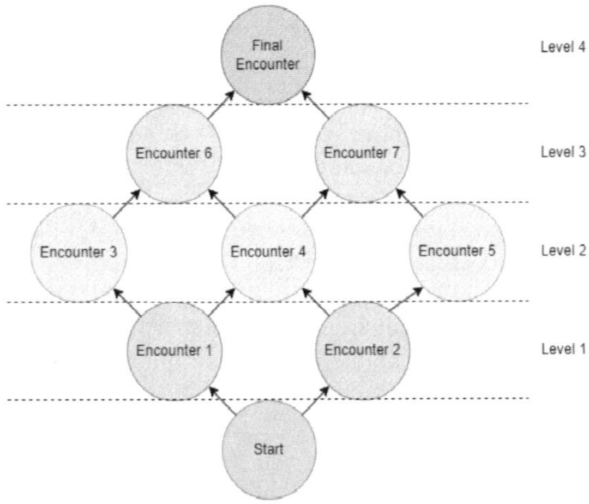

Figure 1. Possible paths of a character

This is where the user will make a choice on which character to play. Each character has their own strength and weaknesses. A choice on which room to progress to will also be made. This will then trigger the start of the adventure. Each room (node) will have a different event that occurs, and the difficulty of these events will scale with the level as indicated in Figure 1. This will create unique encounters as the user progresses through the stages, these unique encounters will also promote replayability will have to play the game multiple times to experience all the possible combinations of encounters.

Figure 2. Start Menu

Figure 3. Character Select

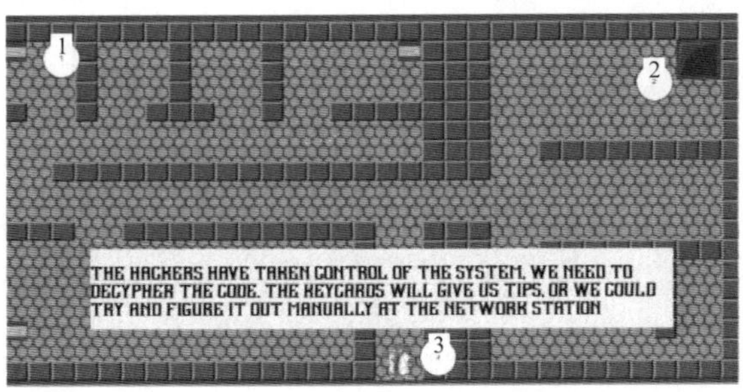

Figure 4. Stage 1

4. CYBER CRASH GAME

The game will start like a normal game with a menu page as shown in Figure 2. This will serve as the gateway to the rest of the game. This screen consists of a background, a label that displays the games name, and four buttons that will navigate to separate sections of the game. *New Game* (1) leads to a new instance of the adventure, *Load Game* (2) leads to an already active instance of the adventure, *Settings* (3) allows the user to adjust game volume and other aspect of the game like difficulty and graphical adjustments. *Quit Game* (4) exits the program. Figure 3 shows the different characters and future characters than can be selected by the player, these characters each have different benefits, like the elephant having a larger memory capacity that can be used to store more information clues found in the adventure. This is the first choice made that affect the way the game will be played, and interesting characters will provide for a better experience. Figure 4 shows the layout of the first stage that implement a simple puzzle to decipher the system that has been infiltrated. This can be done in different ways by choosing to take the longer route and first go for the clue tokens (Figure 4 (1)) or go straight to the console and try to determine whether the system has been compromised (Figure 4 (2)). The goal is to finish the stage with the lowest number of actions possible. Allowing the user to choose the risk reward levels they are willing to take. Failed attempts at the cipher will lead to penalties being applied. That will affect the rest of the stages.

5. SUMMARY AND CONCLUSION

In this article, a youth-focussed cybersecurity awareness serious game, based on the characteristics of a "build your own adventure" approach, was proposed. This was achieved by identifying common cybersecurity threats and attacks and highlighting how serious games can be used to promote awareness of these threats. A brief overview of serious games, and how they can be developed to incorporate the principles of "build your own adventure" was presented. Finally, the resulting cybersecurity awareness game, *Cyber Crash*, was highlighted. By incorporating effective gaming strategies found in commercial games the goal of creating an effective cybersecurity game can be reached, by adding the "build your own adventure" aspect to promote better immersion when playing the game. By adding real world attack paths into the gaming environment, the user can learn about how malicious entities are attacking and learn how to counter these attacks.

REFERENCES

Abroshan, H., Devos, J., Poels, G. and Laermans, E. (2021), "COVID-19 and Phishing: Effects of Human Emotions, Behavior, and Demographics on the Success of Phishing Attempts During the Pandemic", *IEEE Access,* Vol. 9, pp. 121916-121929.

Allers, J., Drevin, G.R., Snyman, D.P., Kruger, H.A. and Drevin, L. (2021), "A mobile serious game to promote digital wellness among pre-school children".

Alshabibi, A. and Al-Suqri, M. (2021), "Cybersecurity Awareness and Its Impact on Protecting Children in Cyberspace", IEEE, pp. 1-6.

Alvarez, J. and Djaouti, D. (2011), "An introduction to Serious game Definitions and concepts", *Serious Games & Simulation for Risks Management,* Vol. 11, No. 1, pp. 11-15.

Dincelli, E. and Chengalur-Smith, I. (2020), "Choose your own training adventure: designing a gamified SETA artefact for improving information security and privacy through interactive storytelling", *European Journal of Information Systems,* Vol. 29, No. 6, pp. 669-687.

Harris, J. (2020), "Exploring Roguelike Games", *CRC Press.*

Kemp, S. 2022. *Digital 2022: Global Overview report* [Online]. DATAREPORTAL. Available: https://datareportal.com/reports/digital-2022-global-overview-report [Accessed 10/05 2022].

Kramer, W. 2000. *What makes a game good* [Online]. The Games Journal, A Magazine about Boardgames. Available: http://www.thegamesjournal.com/articles/WhatMakesaGame.shtml [Accessed 01/05 2022].

Kshetri, N. (2019), "Cybercrime and Cybersecurity in Africa", *Journal of Global Information Technology Management,* Vol. 22, No. 2, pp. 77-81.

Padmavathi, D.G. and Shanmugapriya, M. (2009), "A survey of attacks, security mechanisms and challenges in wireless sensor networks", *arXiv preprint arXiv:0909.0576.*

Vojinovic, I. 2022. *More than 70 Cybercrime Statistics - A \$6 Trillion Problem* [Online]. dataprot. Available: https://dataprot.net/statistics/cybercrime-statistics/ [Accessed 20/07 2022].

Whitman, M.E. and Mattord, H.J. (2022), "Principles of information security", *Cengage.*

USE OF YOLOV5 OBJECT DETECTION ALGORITHMS FOR INSECT DETECTION

Lino Oliveira[1], Margarida Victoriano[1], Adilia Alves[2] and José Pereira[2]
[1]*INESC TEC, Campus da FEUP, R. Dr. Roberto Frias, 4200-465 Porto, Portugal*
[2]*CIMO – IPB, Campus de Santa Apolónia, 5300-253 Bragança, Portugal*

ABSTRACT

Climate change affects global temperature and precipitation patterns that influence the intensity and, in some cases, the frequency of extreme environmental events, such as forest fires, hurricanes and storms. These events can be particularly conducive to the increase of plant pests and diseases, which causes significant production losses. So, the early detection of pests is of the main importance to reduce pest losses and implement more safe control management strategies protecting the crop, human health, and the environment (e.g., precision in the pesticide application). Nowadays, pests' detection and prediction are mainly based on counting insects on attacked organs or in traps by experts, but this is a costly and time-consuming task for extensive and geographically dispersed olive groves. Machine learning algorithms, using image analysis, can be used for autonomous pests' detection and counting. In the present practical work, YOLOv5 was chosen to detect and count the olive fly adults (*Bactrocera oleae* Rossi), a key pest of olives. YOLOv5s architecture of YOLO's algorithm was used to test its efficiency in olive fly detection on a mobile deployment solution. The results obtained were quite satisfactory, and the experimental results obtained have been analyzed and presented, encompassing a set of metrics such as precision, recall, and the mean average precision. This study will be extended for other pests and disease detection in future work. Also, this solution will be integrated into a web-based information and management service (with sensors and e-traps) that remotely detect the presence and severity of pest attacks.

KEYWORDS

Object Detection, YOLOv5, Machine Learning, Sustainable Agriculture, CIMO-IPB Dataset

1. INTRODUCTION

Climate change affects global temperature and precipitation patterns. These conditions, in turn, influence the intensity and, in some cases, the frequency of extreme environmental events. In general, these events can be particularly conducive to the increase of plant pests and diseases. The attack of pests and diseases is one of the main causes of crop losses, causing an average 30% decrease in potential crop production. And, in severe cases, it can destroy all the crops. Agricultural ecosystems are known to be complex, multivariable, and unpredictable. To protect crops, it is important to anticipate the attack of pests and diseases to improve its control by more ecological and economical methods (e.g., precision in pesticide application). In this frame, it is urgent to look for real-time detection methods and prediction models for pests. In the olive crop, the olive fly, *Bactrocera oleae* Rossi, is a key pest of olives, causing significant losses in quantity and quality. Quantity losses result from the direct pulp consumption by the olive fly larvae, and quality losses result from the failure of positive attributes for olive oil and table olives.

Identification and localization of objects in photos or video frame's is a computer vision task called 'object detection'. Several algorithms have emerged in the past few years to tackle this task. Nowadays, one of the most popular algorithms for real-time object detection is YOLO (You Only Look Once) because of its speed and accuracy. YOLOv5 (Glenn Jocher, 2022) was used for olive fly detection and counting, from image analysis, in olive grows - essential data to predict future pests' occurrence and severity. For YOLO's algorithm train, a yellow sticky trapped insects' dataset and a McPhail trapped insects' dataset were used previously and manually tagged with labelImg (Tzutalin, 2015). The unique tagged class identified on the dataset was adults of the 'olive fly', one of the most dangerous olive pests in the Mediterranean basin.

2. STATE OF THE ART

Object detection aims to recognize one or more objects in media, drawing bounding boxes around these objects. There are two main methods for object detection, it can be either a neural network-based or non-neural network approach. For non-neural approaches, it is necessary to identify features using a certain method (e.g., scale-invariant feature transform) and then to do classification using another method (e.g., support vector machine). On the other hand, neural network-based techniques usually do not need to specify features and are able to perform end-to-end object detection. This approach is typically based on convolutional neural networks. Examples of that approach are YOLO and R-CNN. YOLO family was first described by Joseph Redmond (Redmond et al, 2015), and it analyses the whole image during training and testing, so it considers contextual information about classes and object's appearance. After inputting the images into the convolutional network, YOLO completes the prediction of the object's classification and location information according to the calculation of the loss function. YOLOv5 is one of the successors of YOLO that aims to detect objects with high performance and is a PyTorch based version (Nelson & Solawetz, 2020), that supports mobile and web deployment.

2.1 YOLO Architecture

The YOLO model was the first object detector to associate the bounding box prediction procedure with class labels in an end-to-end differentiable network. The network is divided in the input, the backbone, the neck, and the head (Solawetz, 2020). The input terminal is responsible for preprocessing the incoming data, comprising the mosaic data augmentation and adaptative image filling. After inputting the images, the algorithm finishes the prediction of the classification and object location, according to the calculation of the loss function, thus transforming this into a regression problem. The adaptative anchor frame computation that YOLOv5 includes, allows it to automatically set the original anchor frame size whenever the dataset changes, enabling it to adjust to different datasets (Li, et al., 2022). The backbone network is used for pre-training and mainly uses a cross-stage partial network (CSP) to reduce the number of calculations and increase the speed of inference. It also uses spatial pyramid pooling (SPP) to extract feature maps from the input image by splitting the significant features, which helps improve detection accuracy. The backbone can be executed either on GPU or CPU platforms. The feature pyramid structures of FPN and PAN are used in the neck network. PAN aggregates parameters from different backbone levels (Liu, 2018). The neck is composed of a set of layers to blend and combine image features and send them forward to prediction. The head receives the features from the neck and moves on to the bounding box and class prediction phase. The YOLOv5 consists of four models with several architectures. The main difference between them lies in the number of feature extraction modules and convolution kernels at specific locations on the network, so the training time and obtained results will be different. The YOLOv5s model was chosen since it was the most adequate to use, because, in the next steps, the model will be exported to a web/mobile application. The training task is essential to the success of an object detection system. Two techniques are available of special relevance during the training phase: data augmentation and loss calculations. Data augmentation aims to perform transformations to the base training data to expose the model to a larger set of semantic variations relative to the original training set and the images are sent through a data loader to be augmented. On the other hand, it also performs a total loss calculation from constituent loss functions to maximize the mean average precision. The detection task is accomplished by dividing an image into a grid system, and each grid detects objects contained. To predict bounding boxes, the model learns the anchor boxes based on the distribution of bounding boxes in the given dataset, with K-means and genetic learning algorithms.

3. PROBLEM DEFINITION AND PROPOSED SOLUTION

The attack of pests and diseases is the main reason for crop losses. Therefore, it is crucial to anticipate the occurrence of crop pests and diseases to improve and implement control strategies. Detecting pests in real time and applying prediction models are important tools to achieve this. In this context, the proposed technological solution implemented a computer vision module that aims to identify olive flies (the most dangerous fruit pests of olives the Mediterranean basin), allowing to increase the sustainability of the olive operation. The model was trained using YOLOv5 algorithm with a yellow sticky trapped insects' dataset (images collected on Portuguese olive grove) (Pereira, J. A., 2022) together with a McPhail trapped insects' dataset (images collected on Greek olive groves) (Kalamatianos R., 2018).

3.1 Specifying the Dataset

Initially, images referring to the pest under study were collected. Then the image identification task for training was performed using the labelImg tool, where the objects present in the images were properly identified with a bounding box and tagged. The dataset collected was composed of 341 images, collected in various olive groves locations located in Trás-os-Montes, Portugal, from 2021 September to 2021 October. A Greek dataset, consisting of 848 labelled images collected from 2015 to 2017 in Corfu (Greece), was also used. To reduce false positives, the original dataset was augmented with background images (yellow sticky traps without olive fly specimens) acquired from Portuguese traps (45 images) and from a public dataset (164 images) (Tellez, 2019). The dataset used for YOLO's training was obtained by merging these datasets. After this task, it was necessary to standardize the provided dataset since it was obtained by merging different sources, and it's expectable to have some inconsistencies. Having a consistent and clean dataset is essential, as this is necessary for the success of the detection task. Note that just one class of objects was identified. The annotation files provided were on the pascal VOC format but since the algorithm only accepts the YOLO format, it was developed a Python3 script to handle the conversion between these two formats. In YOLO format, each image has a correspondent text file which contains one line per object. Each line starts with the class number, indexed to zero, followed by the coordinates and width and height of the object's bounding box.

3.2 YOLOv5 Training

The training category contains 80% of the dataset images, and both the validation and test categories correspond to 10% of the dataset images. After the physical organization of the input images and labels, the dataset.yaml file was created to specify the dataset settings: the dataset root directory, the relative paths to the training, validation and test folders, the number of classes to be detected and, finally, their names. After, collecting and standardizing the dataset and building the dataset.yaml file, it is possible to start training. Training was started using the smallest model available (YOLOv5s), all layers, and pre-trained weights. Although the pre-trained weights were used, the model was fine-tuned to the loaded dataset. So, the training process accepts as inputs the dataset.yaml file and the corresponding weights. The image size was chosen to be 640 pixels, as stated previously. The batch size corresponds to a hyperparameter that defines the number of samples to process before updating the internal model parameters. This value can be defined according to the available GPU memory. On the other hand, an epoch is a hyperparameter that indicates the number of times that the algorithm will parse through the entire training dataset. Datasets are usually grouped into batches, and an epoch consists of one or more batches.

4. CASE STUDY AND EXPERIMENTAL RESULTS

The implementation targets of this practical work are the autonomous detection and count of olive flies in olive groves. Images were collected and annotated in the olive groves of Trás-os-Montes, Portugal, and used in conjunction with the Greek dataset to train a network that detects a pest from images, to be applied in images collected there. After training, the YOLO algorithm produced the following graphs, regarding losses and some metrics. The YOLOv5 loss function is composed of *box_loss* that refers to the bounding box regression loss, obtained by the mean squared error, the *obj_loss* that refers to the confidence of object presence is the objectness loss, obtained by the binary cross entropy and *cls_loss* that that is the classification loss, obtained by the cross entropy. Since YOLOv5 algorithm is being used for the detection of a single class, there are no class misidentifications, and the classification error is always zero, so the graphs regarding the train and validation class loss are constantly represented by zero. The precision metric measures how much of the bounding box predictions are correct and the recall metric measures how much of the true bounding box predictions are actually correct. The mAP_0.5 is the mean average precision at the intersection over union (IoU) threshold of 0.5. The mAP_0.5:0.95 is the average mAP over different IoU thresholds, ranging from 0.5 to 0.95. The following image shows the obtained results in training and validation steps, and it describes the metrics presented above.

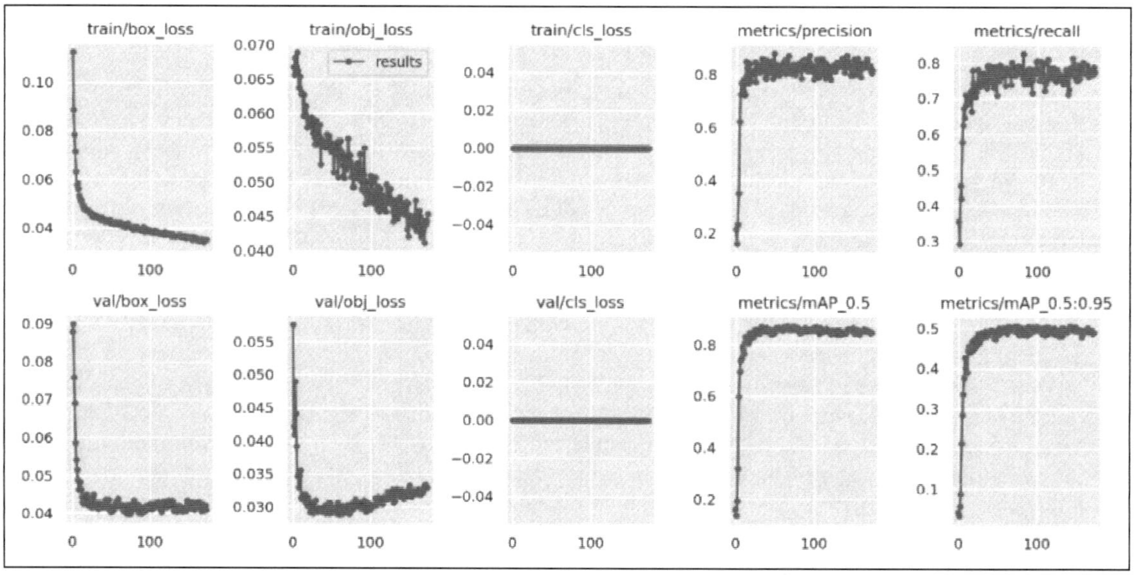

Figure 1. Experimental results

Finally, the inference was performed on a set of four unannotated images and 44 background images from the captures on Portuguese olive groves, using the weights obtained in the training phase.

This process resulted and showed a good performance and excellent detection results. The boxes are around the detected objects with associated confidence, and, as we can see, in the four images below, most of the pests were correctly identified with good confidence.

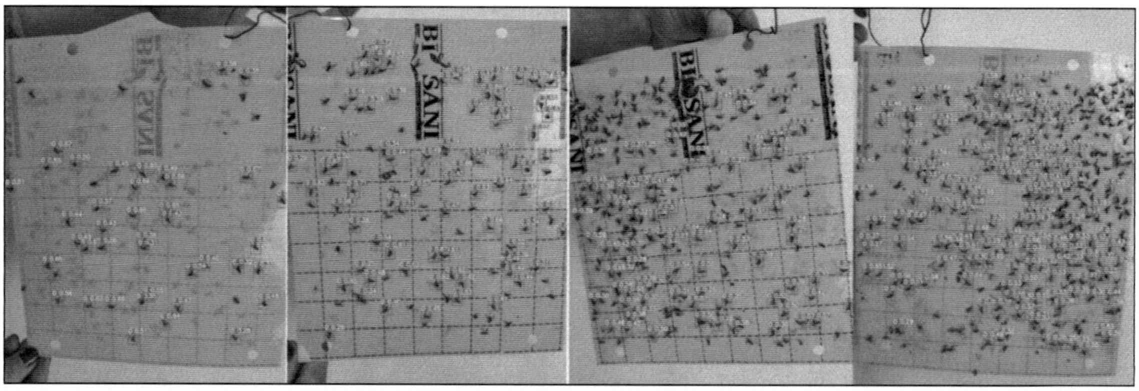

Figure 2. Inference results

5. CONCLUSION AND FUTURE WORK

This work presents the application of YOLOv5, more precisely of its YOLOv5s architecture, to autonomous olive fly, the most important pest of olives. For YOLOv5 algorithm training, it was used a dataset of trapped insects collected both in Portuguese and Greek olive groves. YOLOv5 algorithm has shown good results and performance. The training of the algorithm will be extended for different pests and disease detection by expanding the input dataset. YOLOv5 training is being improved with dataset's image preprocessing and with hyper-parameters configuration (e.g., using weighted boxes fusion). In the next phase, robotic traps with sensors will be developed and placed in Trás-os-Montes region, which will automatically collect images of pests in the field. For future work, a web-based information and management system will be developed, integrating this computer vision module, which will receive the images collected from the field by a robotic smart trap, and return the image with the detection results. Since the algorithm was developed in PyTorch, it will be easier to export to mobile and web platforms.

ACKNOWLEDGEMENT

This work is financed by National Funds through the Portuguese funding agency, FCT - Fundação para a Ciência e a Tecnologia, within project LA/P/0063/2020.

REFERENCES

Glenn Jocher, e. a., 2022. *ultralytics/yolov5: v6.1 - TensorRT, TensorFlow Edge TPU and OpenVINO Export and Inference.* [Online] Available at: https://zenodo.org/record/6222936 [Accessed 1 May 2022].

Kalamatianos R., K. I. D. D. a. A. M., 2018. DIRT: The Dacus Image Recognition Toolkit.

Liu, S. a. Q. L. a. Q. H. a. S. J. a. J. J., 2018. *Path Aggregation Network for Instance Segmentation.* [Online] Available at: https://arxiv.org/abs/1803.01534 [Accessed 5 July 2022].

Li, Z., Tian, X., Liu, X. & Liu, 2022. A Two-Stage Industrial Defect Detection Framework Based on Improved-YOLOv5 and Optimized-Inception-ResnetV2 Models. *Applied Science,* 12(2), p. 834.

Nelson, J. & Solawetz, J., 2020. *YOLOv5 is Here: State-of-the-Art Object Detection at 140 FPS.* [Online] Available at: https://blog.roboflow.com/yolov5-is-here/ [Accessed 18 May 2022].

Redmond, J. e. a., 2015. You Only Look Once: Unified, Real-Time Object Detection. *arXiv.*

Solawetz, J., 2020. *Roboflow.* [Online] Available at: https://blog.roboflow.com/yolov5-improvements-and-evaluation/ [Accessed 18 May 2022].

Tellez, A. (. N. a. J. (. H. a. D. (. J. a. H. (. S. a. L. (. B. a. V. (. S. a. N. (. B. a. E. (. R. a. M. (. d. M., 2019. *Raw data from Yellow Sticky Traps with insects for training of deep learning Convolutional Neural Network for object detection.* [Online] Available at: https://data.4tu.nl/articles/dataset/Raw_data_from_Yellow_Sticky_Traps_with_insects_for_training_of_deep_learning_Convolutional_Neural_Network_for_object_detection/12707066 [Accessed 11 July 2022].

Tzutalin, 2015. *LabelImg Git code.* [Online] Available at: https://github.com/tzutalin/labelImg [Accessed 16 May 2022].

STATE-OF-THE-ART ANALYSIS OF ARTIFICIAL INTELLIGENCE APPROACHES IN THE MARITIME INDUSTRY

Christos Kontzinos[1], Ioanna Kanellou[2], Vasilis Michalakopoulos[1], Spiros Mouzakitis[2], Giannis Tsapelas[1], Panagiotis Kapsalis[2], Giorgos Kormpakis[2] and Dimitris Askounis[3]

[1]*Electrical & Computer Engineering, Decision Support Systems Lab, National Technical University of Athens, Greece*

[2]*Energy Processing Unit, National Technical University of Athens, Greece*

[3]*School of Electrical and Computer Engineering, National Technical University of Athens, Greece*

ABSTRACT

The beginning of 2020 finds Artificial Intelligence and Big Data in the forefront of digital transformation. The maritime industry is embracing them wholeheartedly due to their true potential to meet the ever-increasing and complex traffic and shipping demand for safety, performance, energy efficiency, automation, and environmental impact. The implementation of AI approaches in maritime stems from the need to effectively process and analyse the extremely large amounts of data that are being generated by maritime vessels. The key to addressing these challenges lies in research and innovation, especially in novel algorithms, tools, and platforms within the areas of AI and Big Data to unlock the new possibilities of a diverse range of current maritime applications. Under this context, the current publication aims at showcasing AI approaches and research initiatives in the maritime industry by performing an indicative landscape analysis of research publications in the aforementioned domains, between the period 2016-2022. The various AI initiatives uncovered from the research are grouped and presented in three representative categories to provide a clear picture of the research effort of integrating AI in maritime processes.

KEYWORDS

Artificial Intelligence, Landscape Analysis, Maritime Industry, Operation Monitoring, Fuel Consumption, Canal Passage

1. INTRODUCTION

The beginning of 2020 finds Artificial Intelligence and Big Data in the forefront of digital transformation. The maritime industry is embracing them wholeheartedly due to their true potential to meet the ever-increasing and complex traffic and shipping demand for safety, performance, energy efficiency, automation, and environmental impact. The implementation of AI approaches in maritime stems from the need to effectively process and analyse the extremely large amounts of data that are being generated by maritime vessels. The key to addressing these challenges lies in research and innovation, especially in novel algorithms, tools, and platforms within the areas of AI and Big Data to unlock the new possibilities of a diverse range of current maritime applications for vessel traffic monitoring and management, ship energy system design and operation, autonomous shipping, fleet intelligence and route optimisation, and so on. While digital transformation is progressing rapidly in all aspects of the society, it is now the right time to unlock the potential of extreme-scale data and advanced technologies to address the high computational, modelling and data processing demands required for accurate modelling, estimation and optimization of design and operation of ships and fleets under various dynamic conditions in a timely manner. Under this context, the current publication aims at showcasing AI approaches and research initiatives in the maritime industry by performing an indicative landscape analysis of research publications in the aforementioned domains, between the period of 2016-2022. This specific time period was chosen to assess the latest AI initiatives that are being developed in the maritime industry. All in all, 18 distinct AI initiatives were uncovered from the analysis, which were in turn grouped and presented in three representative categories to provide a clear picture of the research effort of integrating AI in maritime processes, while also identifying shortcomings, challenges, and future directions. This paper was written under the context of the EU funded project, VesselAI that aims to develop, validate and demonstrate a novel holistic framework based on a combination of the state-of-the-art HPC, Big Data and AI technologies, capable of performing extreme-scale and distributed analytics for fuelling the next generation digital twins in maritime applications and beyond, including vessel motion and behaviour modelling, analysis and prediction, ship energy system design and optimisation, unmanned vessels, route optimisation and fleet intelligence.

2. ANALYSIS OF ARTIFICIAL INTELLIGENCE APPROACHES IN THE MARITIME INDUSTRY

This section consists of the main body of research of this paper and breaks down the identified research papers in three main groups based on the area of implementation of the research approach: operations monitoring, fuel consumption and canal passage. While other papers were also found in categories such as crew management, maritime policy and quality management, the volume of papers was not enough to generate solid conclusions.

2.1 Operations Monitoring

Managing vessels and ensuring their smooth operation is a decisive factor for the successful transport of any cargo and thus for maximizing the profit of the ship-owner/company. Trajectory prediction is one of the kernel problems that must be addressed to realize proactive information service. Qi and Zheng (Qi and Zheng 2016) proposed an intelligent model to solve the issue of the trajectory prediction of vessels based on data mining and machine learning methods. The spatial clustering algorithm of data mining is used to cluster the historical trajectories of vessels, and the cluster results represent the distribution patterns of these historical trajectories. The support vector machine algorithm of machine learning is used to train the classifiers and the classifiers define the pattern of the new trajectory of the vessel, which must be predicted. De Arijit (De Arijit et al. 2017) presented a mixed integer non-linear programming model considering various scheduling and routing constraints, loading/unloading constraints and vessel capacity constraints. Several time window constraints are inculcated in the mathematical model to enhance the service level at each port. Owing to the inherent complexity of the aforementioned problem, an effective search heuristic named Particle Swarm Optimization for Composite Particle (PSO-CP) is employed. Another research paper (Fadilah et al. 2021), created a website-based management system by using the programming language PHP with MySQL database and CodeIgniter framework. The result of this research was that the Cilacap Nusantara Maritime Academy's administrative system can increase the efficiency of time for filing permits and writing letters. Furthermore, Chen et al. (Chen et al. 2022), tested synthetic data to classify boat activities into three categories: random walk, following and chasing, and the proposed AI-based system evaluated an efficient method of detecting boat activities and maritime threats. Hongchu Yu et al. (Yu et al. 2022), wrote a paper, in which they aimed to integrate ship movement behaviour, geographical features, and the International Regulations for Avoiding Collisions at Sea. The proposed methods sought to reduce the human error associated with maritime accidents. The proposed AI method was a path optimisation model which evaluated economic efficiency and safety-driven unmanned ship path planning that will promote the future growth of intelligent port development. Miguel A. Salido (Salido, Rodriguez-Mollins and Barber 2022), tested two AI based techniques; the first was a planning technique in order to solve the container tracking problem and the second was an optimised algorithm to solve the berth allocation problem. The result was that a terminal operator was conducted and could decide which algorithm was the most appropriate to solve both problems together. Giovanni Soldi (Soldi et al. 2021), reviewed space-based technologies for Maritime Surveillance. The used methodology was a combination of Bayesian and statistical fusion techniques with AIS data, and the results showed that to track multiple targets, heterogeneous space-based and terrestrial sensors had to be used. Rizk (Rizk, Khater and Abdelwahab, 2011) wrote a paper, in which he described the use of Neural Networks for object classification using collected RCS real data from radar system in order to classify vessels according to RCS signals that are important for many maritime applications. The study indicated that the NN based classification scheme provides excellent performance in targets classification, especially when 72 equally distributed RCS values from the whole RCS polar plot are used by model NN1 for classification. Masoud Abedi (Abedi and Pourkiani 2020), proposed an artificial intelligence-based task distribution algorithm (AITDA) which aimed to reduce the response time and the internet traffic by distribution of the tasks between fog and cloud services. The result of the AITDA algorithm shows that this method reduces the response time and internet traffic compared to the cloud-fog-based approaches. In another paper (Theodoropoulos et al. 2021), the examined methodology is based on 1 D Convolutional Neural Network (CNN) using time series data in order to harmonise data collected by sensors onboard, and to implement an artificial intelligent framework to recognise patterns that indicate early signs of defective behaviour in the operational state of the vessel. (Liu et al. 2021), proposed the development of a Convolutional Neural Network to improve ship detection under different weather conditions. The proposed methodology is capable to create CNN-based detection results, which are more reliable and robust under adverse weather conditions. This learning method shows superior performance in terms of accuracy and efficiency than the other methods (SSD, Faster R-CNN, YOLOv2 and YOLOv3).

2.2 Fuel Consumption

Fuel and energy in general make up the highest cost in every journey. As diesel prices continue to rise, plenty of research has been conducted to find a more efficient way to predict fuel consumption and asset health during sea voyages. Wenshuo Tang (Tang, Flynn and Valentin, 2016), explored the feasibility of data-driven methods to evaluate Remaining Useful Life (RUL) of the system assets to inform a preventative and cost-efficient management system. The paper's resulting model is based on a state-of-the-art machine learning technique, Relevance Vector Machine (RVM), which is a powerful tool for resolving uncertainty in large data sets, and more specifically in a public battery life cycle testing dataset, provided from NASA Ames Research Centre. Ugo Campora (Campora, Cravero and Zaccone 2018) described a simulation based monitoring and diagnostic method to overcome the lack of data. A MATLAB-SIMULINK® model of the frigate propulsion system was used to generate a database of different faulty conditions of the plant. A monitoring and diagnostic system, based on Mahalanobis distance and artificial neural networks have been developed. Experimental data measured during the sea trials have been used for model calibration and validation. Finally, Zhe Xiao (Xiao et al. 2020), proposed machine learning methods to improve the quality of data passed to emission models in order to be applied not only to improve emission consumption but also to other GPS and time-series problems. The results showed that the methodology can improve the default methods proposed to cover missing data. Also, the proposed methodology can boost the detection otherwise undetectable emissions.

2.3 Port Canal – Canal Passage

Movement in ports or canals can lead to great delays in a naval journey and thus increase the travel cost and lower efficiency. In this category, Enrico Alderini (Anderlini, Parker and Thomas 2019) used reinforcement learning strategies to control the docking of an AUV onto a fixed platform in a simulation environment. Two reinforcement learning schemes were investigated: one with continuous state and action spaces, deep deterministic policy gradient (DDPG), and one with continuous state but discrete action spaces, deep Q network (DQN). Adding to this, Shaoning Pang (Pang et al. 2016) proposed a cognitive background modelling method for land and water composition scenes (CBM-lw) to interpret the traffic of boats passing across boat ramps. An adaptive learning rate was computed to account for changes on land and water composition scenes, in which a geometrical model is integrated with pixel classification to determine the portion of water changes caused by tidal dynamics and other environmental influences. Experimental comparative tests and quantitative performance evaluations of real-world boat-flow monitoring traffic sequences demonstrated the benefits of the proposed algorithm. As Beatriz Molina Serrano mentions in (Serrano et al. 2017), Bayesian networks are a useful tool to make an efficient planning because they facilitate the knowledge of relationships between variables, even when there is a large number of them. Finally, Maria Inês Pereira (Pereira et al. 2021), proposed a lightweight volumetric Convolutional Neural Network (vCNN) which can recognise different docking-based structures using 3D data in real time. The used methodology demonstrated a 90% accuracy in the recognition of different docking structures using low resolution sensors. Results were obtained by using a real autonomous surface vehicle trained on vCNN, which showed that the synthetic-to-real domain adaptation approach was suitable for maritime mobile robots.

3. CONCLUSION

The scope of this publication was to perform a landscape analysis to assess the most popular categories of maritime processes, in which AI applications are being implemented according to the research bibliography. The analysis showed that in recent years, operations monitoring, fuel consumption and canal passage are three categories that gather the interest of the research community. Operations monitoring is an umbrella term that includes various maritime processes. Fuel consumption optimisation is a category of growing interest although there are challenges that are being reported and concern the willingness of maritime companies to share the data produced from naval journeys. Such data is integral for any AI model training and this challenge concerns the entirety of maritime research. Finally, canal passage is a very specific challenge for naval journeys that requires very specific solutions that consider the parameters of a given vessel, journey, body of water etc. Other categories that were uncovered include crew safety and management, maritime policy, and quality assurance but could not be reported in this paper due to space limitations. Future steps of the current research would focus in extending the results of the landscape analysis and identifying more categories of AI research in maritime.

ACKNOWLEDGEMENT

This work has been co-funded by the European Union's Horizon 2020 Research and Innovation programme under the VesselAI project, Grant Agreement No 822404.

REFERENCES

Abedi, M. and Pourkiani, M., (2020). Resource Allocation in Combined Fog-Cloud Scenarios by Using Artificial Intelligence. *2020 Fifth International Conference on Fog and Mobile Edge Computing (FMEC)*, pp. 218-222.

Anderlini, E., Parker, G. G., and Thomas, G., (2019). Docking control of an autonomous underwater vehicle using reinforcement learning. *Applied Sciences*, Vol. 9(17), 3456.

Campora, U., Cravero, C., and Zaccone, R., (2018). Marine gas turbine monitoring and diagnostics by simulation and pattern recognition. *International journal of naval architecture and ocean engineering*, Vol. 10(5), pp. 617-628.

Chen, I. et al, (2022). Combining Perception Considerations with Artificial Intelligence in Maritime Threat Detection Systems. *2022 17th Annual System of Systems Engineering Conference (SOSE)*, pp. 417-422.

De, Arijit, et al, (2017). Sustainable maritime inventory routing problem with time window constraints. *Engineering Applications of Artificial Intelligence*, Vol. 61, pp. 77-95.

Fadilah, A. U. et al, (2021). Design of Cadets Administration System for Nusantara Cilacap Maritime Academy Based on Website. *2021 1st International Conference on Computer Science and Artificial Intelligence (ICCSAI),* Vol. 1, pp. 142-147

H. Yu et al, (2022). Ship Path Optimization That Accounts for Geographical Traffic Characteristics to Increase Maritime Port Safety. *IEEE Transactions on Intelligent Transportation Systems*, Vol. 23, no. 6, pp. 5765-5776.

Liu, R. W. et al, (2021). An enhanced CNN-enabled learning method for promoting ship detection in maritime surveillance system. *Ocean Engineering*, 235: 109435.

Pang, S. et al, (2016). Modelling land water composition scene for maritime traffic surveillance. *International Journal of Applied Pattern Recognition.*

Pereira, M. I. et al, (2021). Advancing Autonomous Surface Vehicles: A 3D Perception System for the Recognition and Assessment of Docking-Based Structures, *IEEE Access*, vol. 9, pp. 53030-53045.

Qi, L. and Zheng, Z., (2016). Trajectory prediction of vessels based on data mining and machine learning. *J. Digit. Inf. Manage*, Vol. 14(1), pp. 33-40.

Rizk, M. R. M., Khater, H. A., and Abdelwahab, M. M., (2011). Application of Artificial Intelligence in Classification of Maritime Targets. *Proceedings on the International Conference on Artificial Intelligence (ICAI) (p. 1).* The Steering Committee of The World Congress in Computer Science, Computer Engineering and Applied Computing (WorldComp).

Salido, M. A., Rodriguez-Molins, M., and Barber, F., (2011). Integrated intelligent techniques for remarshaling and berthing in maritime terminals. *Advanced Engineering Informatics*, Vol. 25(3), pp. 435-451.

Serrano, B. M. et al, (2017). Looking for an efficient port planning: analysis of Spanish Port System through artificial intelligence. *World Scientific News*, Vol. 83, pp. 75-91.

Soldi, G. et al, (2021). Space-based global maritime surveillance. *Part II: Artificial intelligence and data fusion techniques. IEEE Aerospace and Electronic Systems Magazine,* Vol. 36(9), pp. 30-42.

Tang, W., Flynn, D., and Valentin, R., (2016). Applying machine learning to predict asset health in hybrid maritime vessels. *13th International Conference on Condition Monitoring and Machinery Failure Prevention Technologies, CM 2016/MFPT.* Paris, France.

Theodoropoulos, P. et al, (2021). A Deep Learning-Based Fault Detection Model for Optimization of Shipping Operations and Enhancement of Maritime Safety. *Sensors*, Vol. 21(16), 5658.

Xiao, Z., et al, (2020). Traffic Pattern Mining and Forecasting Technologies in Maritime Traffic Service Networks: A Comprehensive Survey. *IEEE Transactions on Intelligent Transportation Systems*, Vol. 21, pp. 1796-1825.

ESTABLISHING CYBERSECURITY AWARENESS OF TECHNICAL SECURITY MEASURES THROUGH A SERIOUS GAME

Jaden Harding, Dirk Snyman and Gunther Richard Drevin
School of Computer Science and Information Systems, North-West University, 11 Hoffman Street, Potchefstroom, South Africa

ABSTRACT

Cybersecurity is broadly considered an important concept for the protection of individuals and families, and also governments and organizations from online threats. This importance notwithstanding, there is a lack of understanding regarding cybersecurity globally, not only within the working class but within the general public. It can therefore be deduced, that there must also exist a lack of understanding regarding the technical principles of cybersecurity, such as how an individual's computer keeps them safe within an online environment using techniques such as firewalls and cryptography. This paper addresses this lack of understanding by means of a serious game.

KEYWORDS

Serious Games, Information Security Awareness, Cybersecurity

1. INTRODUCTION

Cybersecurity is broadly considered a very important concept for the protection of individuals and families, as well as government and organizations from online threats (Goutam, 2015). This importance notwithstanding, there is a lack of awareness regarding good cybersecurity practices, not only within the working class but also within the general public (Aldawood & Skinner, 2018). It further stands to reason that, given this lack of awareness, there should exist a lack of understanding regarding the technical principles of cybersecurity measures, e.g., how an individual's computer keeps them safe within an online environment using techniques such as firewalls and cryptography. This global phenomenon is further exacerbated in developing countries, such as South Africa. Technology is commonly used by many, but there is a lack of formal digital literacy which is a result of high levels of unemployment and lower levels of education (Sutherland, 2017). A possible modern solution to addressing the lack of digital literacy, is the use of serious games (Laamarti et al., 2014).

Serious games can be defined as an approach to active learning in which pedagogy is incorporated into a game with the purpose of providing organised education and training (Greitzer et al., 2007). These games involve activities that instruct and educate, yielding results such as skills and knowledge. The twofold goal behind a serious game is therefore: to be educational; and to be enjoyable and entertaining. Considering the immense growth and the expected future growth, as well as its current application in numerous areas (Laamarti et al., 2014), there is a consensus that serious games are a valid method for education and awareness.

Therefore, the aim of this paper is *to describe the initial development of a proof-of-concept serious game aimed at raising awareness and understanding of these cybersecurity techniques and practices.*

The remainder of the paper is structured as follows: **Section 2** provides a summary of the literature pertaining to cybersecurity awareness, and serious games. Literature on the combination of Serious games for teaching cybersecurity principles is discussed in **Section 3**, while **Section 4** is used to illustrate the proof-of-concept game that is proposed in this research. Finally, **Section 5** summarises the findings and possible future work.

2. RELATED LITERATURE

In this section, a brief overview of related literature is presented in a two-fold manner, i.e., literature about cybersecurity and related concepts is summarised, and a cursory overview of serious games is provided.

2.1 Cybersecurity Awareness

Cybersecurity and its awareness are the core themes of the given problem description; however, cybersecurity is a commonly used term, and its definition often varies depending on the context and interpretation. A definition which suits the purpose of this research is:

"Cybersecurity is the collection of tools, policies, security concepts, security safeguards, guidelines, risk management approaches, actions, training, best practices, assurance and technologies that can be used to protect the cyber environment and organization and user's assets" (ITU, 2009:2).

Cybersecurity produces defensive procedures, which conserve the integrity, availability and confidentiality of devices and data by protecting them against malware, vulnerabilities, and threats (Jang-Jaccard & Nepal, 2014). Malware refers to a large class of threats, which are loaded onto a system, compromising the integrity, availability, and confidentiality of data, without the knowledge of the user. Examples include viruses, spyware, trojan horses and bot executables (Jang-Jaccard & Nepal, 2014). A vulnerability is a weakness in a system's functionality or design, which allows an outside threat to execute code, gain access to private information and launch denial-of-service attacks. A threat refers to an activity that exploits a system's security flaws and consequently endangers it (Abomhara & Køien, 2015). Once present on a user's system, malware targets hardware, software flaws, and network infrastructure and protocol weaknesses (Jang-Jaccard & Nepal, 2014).

With the increasing use of network devices among the public, cyberattacks are becoming more common, and the security precautions against them are a vital part of Information Technology governance (Ben-Asher & Gonzalez, 2015). Reports of cyberespionage, cybercrimes, and the exploitation of data breaches emerge daily, as organisations and government agencies are compromised, and sensitive information is stolen. Essential infrastructure such as financial markets, communication systems, and electric power grids are vulnerable to cyberattacks (Spidalieri & Kern, 2014). Furthermore, a need for education and awareness of cybersecurity is essential. Society cannot expect modern security technologies, which are crucial components of cybersecurity, to secure an organisation's information and operations alone, nor should cybersecurity experts be the only ones with the responsibility of preventing and suppressing cyber threats, but all members of organisations share responsibility (Spidalieri & Kern, 2014) which can only be facilitated through a keen awareness of cyber threats.

Cyber risk in an organisation can be attributed to two types of employees: malicious or negligent: Malicious insiders are employees who intentionally endanger or harm an organisation, in order to benefit themselves or an outside entity. They might do so by stealing or distributing sensitive information, damaging networks and network devices, or committing fraud for financial gain. Negligent or error-prone insiders unintentionally harm or endanger an organisation through carelessness or a lack of knowledge. This can occur by an employee sharing too much personal information online, falling victim to phishing attempts, losing hardware with sensitive information, or accidentally creating a vulnerability when configuring software (Bailey et al., 2018).

2.2 Serious Games

Serious games are the method by which this research paper plans to attempt to increase awareness of cybersecurity. Suitable definitions for serious games are:

"Serious games are designed to have an impact on the target audience, which is beyond the pure entertainment aspect. One of the most important application domains is in the field of education given the acknowledged potential of serious games to meet the current need for educational enhancement" (Bellotti et al., 2013:1).

Considering the significant growth in the field of serious games within the 21st century, it is a consensus that serious games are a valid form of education and learning (Laamarti et al., 2014). Blunt (2009), conducted three studies in an attempt to confirm the validity of serious games. The first study was conducted at a university to analyse the impact of the implementation of a simulation game into an Introduction to Business and Technology course. One-fifth (227) of the total students (1028) played the game, and the results indicated that students who did not play the game averaged just under 80%, and those who did, averaged just over 90% for the course test. The second study evaluated the addition of another simulation game, on university economic course students, to better understand the application of various concepts. 322 of the total 556 students played the game, and the results indicated, similarly to the first study, that the average of students who did not play the game was just below 80%, and those who did average above 90%. The aim of the final study was to compare the effectiveness of the implementation of a serious game, by means of various variables such as test score, gender, ethnicity, and age, on third-year management students. Half of the class was given the game to play. The final results indicated that the average test scores of students who had not played the game were below 70%, and those who did play the game averaged just below 90%. From these three studies on a variety of students, it is seen that serious games are effective and viable forms of learning and education.

Serious games are applicable in a number of areas such as education and training, wherein games are used in classrooms for education, as the study by Blunt (2009) confirms; well-being, wherein serious games are used to increase the physical activity of its players, through motivation and reward systems; advertisement, where specific brands and products are promoted to players while playing the game; cultural heritage, which allows players to interact with reconstructed scenes from virtual representations of history and ancient sites, and interpersonal communication, with games that allow players to speak in the game and improve their communication skills and in some games, learn culturally appropriate expressions and gestures (Laamarti et al., 2014).

Examples of successful serious games are Supercharged!, a game created with the goal of improving physics education, focusing on electromagnetism (Jenkins et al., 2003); Biohazard, a component of the training program for firefighters to perform effectively in terrorist situations (Carnegie Mellon Entertainment Technology Center & Scientists, 2004); Re-Mission, which was used to improve the knowledge and understanding of cancer patients, on how various treatments such as chemotherapy work, which in turn improved their well-being (Tate et al., 2009); and SnowWorld, used to lessen pain and distract patients who suffered burns during daily wound cleaning and physical therapy (Hoffman, 2004).

The main goal of serious games, and therefore the greatest challenge, is twofold. Firstly, and most importantly, serious games must be educational. Secondly, the game must be entertaining and captivating (Bellotti et al., 2013). Some challenges such as those from the social, educational, and technological dimensions should also be considered. The social dimension involves the negative view games have from society, as they have been associated with addiction, violence, and sexism in extreme cases (Griffiths, 2010). Games also seem a more playful and less serious activity for the education system. The educational dimension is connected to concerns about the educational value of games, their effectiveness when compared to traditional methods, and the issues that arise when assessments are considered. The technological dimension consists of issues such as the cost of creating and implementing the game, and the tools necessary to facilitate the game (Fernández-Manjón et al., 2015).

2.3 Cybersecurity Awareness Through Serious Games

From the literature regarding cybersecurity awareness and serious games respectively, we can now deduce that there is a lack of, and need for, awareness of cybersecurity and that serious games are capable of being more effective than traditional methods for educating and increasing awareness, due to their interactive nature.

There is a need to properly inform and teach users how to protect themselves from cyber risks, considering how often cyberattacks are successful. It has been suggested that serious games can be used for cybersecurity training and awareness and that the use of such training and awareness programs has the potential to attract more individuals to the field, which in turn can help close the cybersecurity workforce gap (VanSteenburg, 2017).

Le Compte et al. (2015) state that it will be advantageous to gamify cyber security education and training. While serious games have shown pedagogic value in this field, they have only been applied in a small number of contexts, and some limitations have been identified. Le Compte et al. (2015) propose that serious games could be utilised in more informal settings, and still produce comparable pedagogical outcomes. Using serious games in this manner has the potential to reach a wider audience than more formal serious games, and still adhere to national cyber strategies.

There has been an increase in the use of serious games for cybersecurity training and education over recent years, however, VanSteenburg (2017:56) remarks that *"Research is still limited, and additional studies must be conducted to better understand the specific elements of serious games that are effective"*

Therefore, serious games are an appropriate and effective way of increasing awareness and educating learners and the general public of cybersecurity and its principles. The next section shows the proof-of-concept cybersecurity game that is developed to raise awareness of technical cybersecurity measures.

3. CYBERSCENE GAME

CyberScene is a proof-of-concept single-player mobile serious game, which aims to educate the public about technical cybersecurity principles by means of various mini-games. These mini-games will cover a number of topics and increase awareness and educate the player, while they play. An example of one of these mini-games is a *cryptography cipher-solving game*. The game will consist of various phases wherein the user will learn more about and then solve a specific cipher:

Cipher information – After selecting a difficulty, the user will be given information regarding a specific cipher. As can be seen in Figure 1, the user receives a theoretical explanation of the Caesar cipher, as well as an image to further help them understand.

Cipher testing – To further improve understanding, the user is given a screen wherein they are allowed to test the cipher previously discussed. In Figure 2, the user is able to enter any sentence or arrangement of letters, as well as the numeric value that the sentence should shift left, to personally test the cipher and learn by these means.

Cipher solving – Finally, the user will be prompted with a series of questions, which ask them to apply the previously learnt cipher to a given input. In Figure 3, the user is asked to apply the Caesar cipher to a simple sentence. When the user enters their solution, a simple message will alert them whether they are correct, or whether they need to try again. When they solve the cipher, they can return to the difficulty selection screen, or continue questions of the previously chosen difficulty.

The paper is concluded in the following section where future work is also discussed.

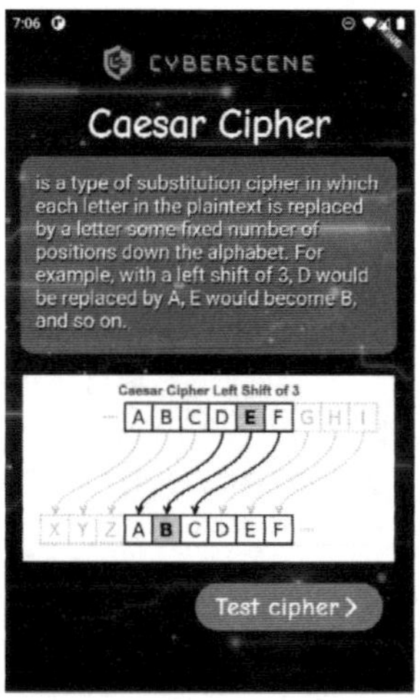

Figure 1. Layout of cipher information screen

Figure 2. Layout of cipher testing screen

Figure 3. Layout of cipher solving screen

4. CONCLUSION AND FUTURE WORK

Given that the current version of Cyberscene is a proof-of-concept, there are various limitations which cannot be addressed at the given time. Incentives are an important concept within serious games, to improve enjoyability, and will be implemented in future research. CyberScene has a variety of advantages which will allow it to be a successful game. The game is mobile-accessible and user-friendly, allowing a large portion of the general population to access it. The difficulty is scalable and therefore allows for a larger player base. Given the mini-games style of the game, it is easy to provide future updates with new games providing previously unknown information in the field of cybersecurity, which provides endless applications to inform and educate users. Future work includes expanding the mini-game to provide the user with incentives, and competitively driven rewards. With the implementation of a user login, gamification elements such as achievements and badges can be incorporated. These include timed achievements, to measure how quickly they are able to solve ciphers. Users could also receive a CyberScene currency, which would allow them to redeem in-game items or purchase locked mini-games that address further security awareness concepts.

REFERENCES

Abomhara, M. and Køien, G. M. (2015). Cyber security and the internet of things: vulnerabilities, threats, intruders and attacks. *Journal of Cyber Security and Mobility:65–88.*

Aldawood, H. and Skinner, G., (2018). December. Educating and raising awareness on cyber security social engineering: A literature review. In 2018 *IEEE International Conference on Teaching, Assessment, and Learning for Engineering (TALE)*. IEEE, pp. 62-68.

Bellotti, F., Kapralos, B., Lee, K., Moreno-Ger, P. and Berta, R. (2013). Assessment in and of Serious Games: An Overview. *Advances in Human-Computer Interaction, 2013:136864.*

Ben-Asher, N. and Gonzalez, C. (2015). Effects of cyber security knowledge on attack detection. *Computers in Human Behavior, 48:51-61.*

Blunt, R. (2009). Do Serious Games Work? Results from Three Studies. *eLearn, 2009(12):Article 1.*

Carnegie Mellon Entertainment Technology Center and Scientists, M. C. F. o. A. 2004. Team Hazmat.

Fernández-Manjón, B., Moreno-Ger, P., Martinez-Ortiz, I. and Freire, M. (2015). Challenges of serious games. *EAI Endorsed Transactions on Serious Games, 2(6).*

Goutam, R.K., (2015). Importance of cyber security. *International Journal of Computer Applications*, *111*(7).

Greitzer, F.L., Kuchar, O.A. and Huston, K., (2007). Cognitive science implications for enhancing training effectiveness in a serious gaming context. *Journal on Educational Resources in Computing (JERIC)*, *7*(3): 2:1-2:16.

Griffiths, M. (2010). Adolescent video game addiction: Issues for the classroom. *Education Today, 60(4):32-34.*

Hoffman, H. G. (2004). Virtual-reality therapy. *Scientific American, 291(2):58-65.*

ITU (2009) 'Overview of Cybersecurity', *Recommendation ITU-T X.1205.* Available at: http://www.itu.int/rec/T-REC-X.1205-200804-I/en.

Jang-Jaccard, J. and Nepal, S. (2014). A survey of emerging threats in cybersecurity. *Journal of Computer and System Sciences, 80(5):973-993.*

Jenkins, H., Klopfer, E., Squire, K. and Tan, P. (2003). Entering the education arcade. *Computers in Entertainment (CiE), 1(1):1-11.*

Laamarti, F., Eid, M. and El Saddik, A. (2014). An Overview of Serious Games. *International Journal of Computer Games Technology, 2014:358152.*

Le Compte, A., Elizondo, D. and Watson, T. (2015). A renewed approach to serious games for cyber security. *Proceedings of the 2015 7th International Conference on Cyber Conflict: Architectures in Cyberspace: IEEE, pp. 203-216.*

Spidalieri, F. and Kern, S. (2014). Professionalizing cybersecurity: A path to universal standards and status. *Newport, RI: Pell Center for International Relations and Public Policy, Salve Regina University.*

Sutherland, E., 2017. Governance of cybersecurity-the case of South Africa. *The African Journal of Information and Communication, 20:83-112.*

Tate, R., Haritatos, J. and Cole, S. (2009). HopeLab's approach to Re-Mission. *International journal of Learning and Media, 1(1):29-35.*

VanSteenburg, M. (2017). Applications of serious gaming to cybersecurity training and awareness. Master's Thesis, *Utica College.*

A QUALITATIVE STUDY ON THE PERCEIVED DRIVERS OF THE DIGITAL DIVIDE IN A DEVELOPING COUNTRY

Ayanda Magida and Brian Armstrong
University of Witwatersrand, Wits Business School, 1 Jan Smuts Ave, Braamfontein, Johannesburg, 2000, South Africa

ABSTRACT

The study aimed to assess the perceived drivers of the digital divide in developing countries. In-depth interviews were collected with the public members to understand their perceptions and drivers of the digital divide. A total of 12 qualitative in-depth interviews were conducted for the study. The participants believed that the internet and data costs were exorbitant and made it difficult for those living below the poverty line to afford data. The participant also highlighted the infrastructure challenges, such as spectrum availability and load shedding, as potentially driving the digital divide. Most participants believed that the digital divide challenges are deeply embedded in the societal and economic challenges that continue to affect the country. Although studies support that the access divide has been bridged in other countries, in South Africa, access issues continue to be challenging and are driven by the above factors. The study provided some insights into digital divide perceptions.

KEYWORDS

Drivers of the Digital Divide, Internet Access, Developing Country, Qualitative Study

1. INTRODUCTION

The divide can be broadly defined as a gap between the haves and have concerning access to information and communication technologies. Over the years and most recently in the last two years, the digital divide issue was spotlighted. The past two years (2019-2022) have been characterised by remote working and online education. During the hard lockdowns, there were a lot of physical restraints on movement, resulting in most learning and working activities taking place online. This meant that individuals needed resources such as mobile phones, computers and internet access to continue with year work and school activities. This study aimed to assess the perceptions and drivers of the digital divide. The literature on the digital divide tended to use secondary data from the world bank, International Telecommunication Union (ITU) and OECD (ITU, 2019; OECD, 2001). Most of the studies also employed quantitative means using web-based surveys to collect data associated with the digital divide (Cruz-Jesus et al., 2012). A few studies have explored the digital divide with an interpretivism methodological orientation (Mumporeze & Prieler, 2017). The qualitative study aimed to assess the perceived drivers of the digital divide in a developing country. In particular, the following research questions informed the study:

- What are the perceptions of the digital divide?
- What are the drivers of the digital divide?

2. LITERATURE REVIEW

2.1.1 Levels of the Digital Divide

Literature on the digital divide broadly distinguishes between the three levels of the digital divide (Van Deursen & van Dijk, 2019). The first level is concerned with access (Van Deursen & van Dijk, 2019), the second level emphasises skills and usage (Hargittai, 2002), and the third level of the digital divide is based on the tangible outcomes associated with being online (Van Deursen & Helsper, 2015). Internet penetration and access are high in developing countries compared to developing countries. In some developing countries, mobile devices are shared within households (Burrell, 2010), and there exist disparities concerning the internet and mobile phone access (Blumenstock, 2012).

Earlier work on the digital divide focused on the first level of the digital divide, or what others call the first level digital divide, which was more prevalent from 2000-to 2010. The first level of the digital divide focused on the schism between the have and have regarding mobile device ownership and internet access. The first level of the digital divide is also known as the access divide. The literature research from 2010 to date has shifted slightly to focus on usage and skills or the second-level digital divide (Haight et al., 2014; Helsper & Van Deursen, 2015). From 2015 onwards, the literature has progressed to focus on the third-level digital divide (Helsper et al., 2016; Van Deursen et al., 2014). The third level of the digital divide is characterised by the tangible outcomes associated with being online.

2.1.2 Drivers of the Digital Divide

The literature distinguishes between the micro and macro drivers of the digital divide. These will be discussed briefly. The micro drivers include social, economic, income, social status, age, gender, and ethnicity. Age is one of the widely measured drivers of research on the digital divide. Several studies have examined differences between age and the digital divide. Van Deursen and van Dijk (2019) found that younger people between 18 and 36 were more likely to use tablets than older people between 36 and 65. Some studies suggest that women are more likely to be digitally underdeveloped and thus less likely to access and use ITC products (Kalmus et al., 2013; Mesch et al., 2013) than their male counterparts. A study conducted in Latin America has further exacerbated disparities in the internet usage of women compared to men (Gray et al., 2017). Ethnic minority groups are less likely to access and use the Internet (Mesch & Talmud, 2011). Research suggests that the levels of education are associated with more significant internet usage (Szeles, 2018).

In addition to the personal or individual drivers of the digital divide, there are country-level macro drivers linked to the infrastructure, economy, GDP, poverty and policies (Shenglin, Simonelli, Ruidong, Bosc, & Wenwei, 2017; Ben, Bosc, Jiao, Li, Simonelli, & Zhang, 2017). Some of the infrastructure challenges, such as electricity, play a pivotal role in driving the digital divide. Against this context, the study aimed to understand the drivers of the digital divide.

3. METHODS

The study employed an interpretive approach through qualitative interviews. Data were collected using in-depth interviews with the public members to understand their perceptions of the digital divide. A non-probability sampling using a purposive sampling frame was adopted in the study. The research followed an inductive method, allowing for the emergence of themes from the data (Fereday & Muir-Cochrane, 2006). A six-step thematic analysis approach by Braun and Clarke (2012) was adopted, and the following steps were followed: familiarising with the data *(1)*, which involved reading the transcripts. The second stage was the generation of the initial codes from the data *(2)*, followed by searching for the potential themes based on the initial codes developed (3). The initial themes were reviewed *(4)* and then defined *(5),* and an analysis report was produced *(6)*.

The study received ethical clearance from the University of the Witwatersrand Human Ethics Committee (Non-Medical). In addition to the ethics approval, the study followed the ethical principles applicable in qualitative studies or research involving human subjects. Informed consent was obtained from the participants. Pseudo-names were used instead of their real names to protect the real identity of the participants.

A total of 12 interviews were conducted with individuals between the ages of 18-45 years. There was an equal split of gender; six participants were female, and another six were male. All the interviews were conducted between the period of November to December 2022. Data saturation was reached in the 12 interviews (Fusch & Ness, 2015). All the interviews were conducted in English and transcribed verbatim.

The following themes emerged from the data: *The perceptions of the digital divide, Infrastructure challenges, Data costs and affordability, The lack of digital literacy skills, and Poverty levels*

3.1.1 The Perceptions of the Digital Divide

The participants have expressed different views on what informs the digital divide. Their views and understanding were centred on internet access. Across the board, the participants believe that the digital divide is the gap between those with access to the internet, mobile phones, or computers.

"My understanding of the digital divide is around the accessibility to a digital environment, so it speaks to the infrastructure of the digital to which you so, for instance, if we look at something like data, is data easily available to you in terms of affordability and the infrastructure giving the data itself? So, if we look at fibre, do you have easy access to fibre" - ***Participant 3***

3.1.2 Infrastructure Challenges

Across the board, the participants have expressed the infrastructure issue as one of the key drivers of the digital divide. They believe that infrastructure plays a crucial role in enabling internet access and is one of the leading causes of the digital divide. The infrastructure issue further perpetuates the divide. The participants have also mentioned that although one can have or own a mobile phone, without the necessary infrastructure, they may not be able to access the internet. The issue of infrastructure enabling internet access is a challenge in the country.

"If you think about someone who has a cell phone but does not have access to the internet, if I stay in sixth -a pack, for example, didn't you know the western part of South Africa not only infrastructure challenge but also. Therefore, the ability to fight that's daily also a challenge – ***Participant 2***

3.1.3 Data Costs and Affordability

Second to the issue of infrastructure was the issue of affordability. Most participants believed that the cost of data to access the internet is one of the factors driving the digital divide; they have expressed that most people cannot afford to buy data due to the high data costs. In contrast, those on contract may be able to get data at a cheaper rate. Most individuals cannot afford contracts and use prepaid; purchasing data or internet on prepaid can be hefty. The participants seem to agree that the issue of affordability is fundamental in the debate on the digital divide. They believed that the higher cost of the data plays a critical role in enabling internet access, which results in fewer people being able to afford the data. Most people are unemployed, and therefore, the affordability of data is an issue.

"And then some of the key so many some of the communities, first, data is costly. I mean, it's expensive, and the gadget, you know, is costly, and the government of ours is trying to rid some of them have some intervention, you know, try to have. - ***Participant 12***

3.1.4 Lack of Digital Literacy Skills

Some participants believed that literacy levels could potentially drive the digital divide. They have argued that some people do not have the digital literacy skills to participate online. Even though they may have access to fancy devices and the internet, most people may not be able to know what benefits are associated with being online and having a mobile phone due to their level of digital literacy. Therefore, the lack of digital literacy plays a significant role in perpetuating the digital divide.

" So even when someone might have a cell phone, they might not be able or allowed to use it instead to receive calls and make calls. And so many people are not trained enough to use these gadgets. – ***Participant 2***

3.1.5 Poverty and Inequality

Some participants believed poverty and inequality are crucial in driving this country's digital divide. The levels of poverty and inequality are high, impacting some of the issues highlighted above. Because people are poor, they cannot afford data to access the internet. The participants have expressed that in the current times, most people need the internet to access everything, search for jobs and education and communicate via social media. Therefore, those without any means must debate between buying food or the internet.

"If you look at the huge inequalities of this country where you know, people are living below, you know, one day. And so, people must constantly choose between buying food and having access to some, you know, but because people are unemployed, they don't have the resources to buy a cell phone or a laptop. So that creates that space and that gap within our society "– ***participant 2***

4. CONCLUSION

The study sought to understand the perceptions and drivers of the digital divide. Over the years, the digital divide has declined in developed countries due to the availability of infrastructure and increased levels in the number of individuals with internet access (Myovella, Karacuka & Haucap, 2021). The first level of the digital divide, concerned with access, has not been entirely reduced in developing countries. However, many countries have shown some increase in the number of people accessing the internet (Haight, 2014; Várallyai, 2015). Some significant issues still impede individuals from accessing the internet in developing countries. The current study explored the perceptions and drivers of the digital divide in a developing country. The study findings have shown that participants have different perceptions and understanding of the digital divide. This is consistent with previous literature on the variations in understanding what informs the digital divide (Srinuan & Bohlin, 2011). The lack of a consensus and clear understanding of the digital divide creates challenges for digital inclusion.

The study has identified four possible factors that drive the digital divide: namely, infrastructure, data costs and affordability, lack of digital literacy skills, literacy levels, and Poverty and inequality. This is consistent with other findings from other countries. All 12 participants in the study highlighted the issue of affordability as one of the key drivers of the digital divide. In most developing countries, the availability of infrastructure and spectrum remains the biggest challenge. People in rural communities have network challenges which impact internet access. The affordability issue as a driver of the digital divide is consistent with a study conducted in Nigeria by Tayo et al. (2016) and other studies (Drake, 2019; Velaga, 2012). The availability of infrastructure is necessary and crucial in enabling digital inclusion in developing countries. The participants highlighted that the lack of digital literacy could drive the digital divide. Digital literacy includes the cognitive and emotional ability to use the internet and operate a digital device (Reddy, Sharma, & Chaudhary, 2020). The lack of digital skills plays a significant role in digital inclusion (Martínez-Cantos, 2017;). Individuals who lack digital skills are limited in what they can do on the internet and how they can use their devices optimally. Most people are not digitally literate, making it difficult for them to effectively utilise the internet and thus further exacerbating the digital divide (Nishijima et al., 2017). A link between literacy levels and the digital divide has been established in the literature (Correa et al., 2020; Ferro et al., 2011).

In addition to the three factors mentioned above, the participants also highlighted the levels of poverty and inequality as contributing to the digital divide. Weiss et al. (2015) found a link between income inequality and the digital divide. The participants also highlighted the plight of poverty as a potential driver of the digital divide. Internet access can assist in tackling poverty in developing counties (Mora-Rivera & García-Mora, 2021). The levels of poverty play a significant role in perpetuating the digital divide in developing countries (Henry, 2019; Mecinas Montiel, 2016). Reducing the data costs and enabling the availability of infrastructure to facilitate internet resources in rural areas can assist in bridging the digital divide. There is also a greater need for integrating digital literacy programmes into traditional basic education to equip learners with the necessary digital skills at an early age needed to compete in the digital world. Unless the poverty and inequality levels are addressed, some of the socioeconomic issues associated with the digital divide will continue to perpetuate in developing countries. There is a greater need for free access to the internet to enable digital inclusion and facilitate access for all. Internet access is fast becoming a need; without internet access, people cannot socialise, communicate, transact, or access education. Therefore, the government in developing countries needs to consider freeing internet access for all to benefit.

ACKNOWLEDGEMENT

This work would not have been possible without the financial support of the Female Academic Leadership Fellowship (FALF).

REFERENCES

Ben, S., Bosc, R., Jiao, J., Li, W., Simonelli, F., & Zhang, R. (2017). Digital infrastructure: overcoming the Digital divide in China and the European Union. *Centre for European Policy Studies*.

Blumenstock, J.E. and Eagle, N., (2012). Divided, we call disparities in access and use of mobile phones in Rwanda. Information Technologies & International Development, 8(2), pp. pp-1.

Braun, V. and Clarke, V., 2012. Thematic analysis. American Psychological Association.

Burrell, J., 2010. Evaluating Shared Access: social equality and the circulation of mobile phones in rural Uganda. Journal of computer-mediated communication, 15(2), pp.230-250.

Correa, T., Pavez, I. and Contreras, J., (2020). Digital inclusion through mobile phones?: A comparison between mobile-only and computer users in internet access, skills and use. *Information, Communication & Society*, *23*(7), pp.1074-1091.

Cruz-Jesus, F., Oliveira, T. and Bacao, F., (2012). Digital divide across the European Union. *Information & Management*, *49*(6), pp.278-291.

Drake, C., Zhang, Y., Chaiyachati, K.H. and Polsky, D., (2019). An observational study of the limitations of poor broadband internet access for telemedicine in rural America. *Annals of internal medicine*, *171*(5), pp.382-384.

Fereday, J. and Muir-Cochrane, E., (2006). Demonstrating rigour using thematic analysis: A hybrid approach of inductive and deductive coding and theme development. International journal of qualitative methods, 5(1), pp.80-92.

Ferro, E., Helbig, N.C. and Gil-Garcia, J.R., (2011). The role of IT literacy in defining digital divide policy needs. *Government Information Quarterly*, *28*(1), pp.3-10.

Fusch, P.I. and Ness, L.R., (2015). Are we there yet? Data saturation in qualitative research. *The qualitative report*, *20*(9), p.1408.

Haight, M., Quan-Haase, A. and Corbett, B.A., (2014). Revisiting the digital divide in Canada: The impact of demographic factors on access to the internet, level of online activity, and social networking site usage. *Information, Communication & Society*, *17*(4), pp.503-519.

Hargittai, E. (2002). Second-level digital divide: Differences in people's online skills. First monday, 7(4).

Henry, L. (2019). Bridging the urban-rural digital divide and mobilizing technology for poverty eradication: challenges and gaps. *GSM Association. URL: https://www. un. org/development/desa/dspd/wp-content/uploads/sites/22/2019/03/Henry-Bridging-the-Digital-Divide-2019. pdf [accessed 2021-12-19].*

Helsper, E.J. and Van Deursen, A.J.A.M., (2015). Digital skills in Europe: Research and policy. *Digital divides: The new challenges and opportunities of e-inclusion*, *195*, p.125.

Helsper, E.J., Van Deursen, A.J.A.M. and Eynon, R., (2016). Measuring types of Internet use. *From digital skills to tangible outcomes project report*.

ITU. (2019). ITU Core Indicators on access to and use of ICT by households and individuals.

Mora-Rivera, J. and García-Mora, F., (2021). Internet access and poverty reduction: Evidence from rural and urban Mexico. *Telecommunications Policy*, *45*(2), p.102076.

Mumporeze, N. and Prieler, M., (2017). Gender digital divide in Rwanda: A qualitative analysis of socioeconomic factors. Telematics and Informatics, 34(7), pp.1285-1293.

Myovella, G., Karacuka, M., & Haucap, J. (2021). Determinants of digitalization and digital divide in Sub-Saharan African economies: A spatial Durbin analysis. Telecommunications Policy, 45(10), 102224.

Nishijima, M., Ivanauskas, T.M. and Sarti, F.M., (2017). Evolution and determinants of digital divide in Brazil (2005–2013). *Telecommunications policy*, *41*(1), pp.12-24.

Organisation for Economic Co-operation and Development, (2011). OECD guide to measuring the information society 2011. OECD.

Reddy, P., Sharma, B., & Chaudhary, K. (2020). Digital literacy: A review of the literature. International Journal of Technoethics (IJT), 11(2), 65-94.

Shenglin, B., Simonelli, F., Ruidong, Z., Bosc, R., & Wenwei, L. (2017). Digital infrastructure: Overcoming the digital divide in emerging economies. G20 Insights, 3, 1-36.

Tayo, O., Thompson, R. and Thompson, E., (2016). Impact of the digital divide on computer use and internet access on the poor in Nigeria. Journal of Education and Learning, 5(1), pp.1-6.

Van Deursen, A.J., Helsper, E.J. and Eynon, R., (2014). Measuring digital skills. From digital skills to tangible outcomes project report.

Van Deursen, A.J. and Helsper, E.J., (2015). The third-level digital divide: Who benefits most from being online?. In *Communication and information technologies annual*. Emerald Group Publishing Limited.

Weiss, J.W., Gulati, G.J., Yates, D.J. and Yates, L.E., (2015), January. Mobile broadband affordability and the global digital divide--an information ethics perspective. In *2015 48th Hawaii International Conference on System Sciences* (pp. 2177-2186). IEEE.

A PROOF OF CONCEPT: CYBERSECURITY LEARNING CONTENT IN LTI BASED, EDUCATIONAL SYSTEMS

Ehm Kannegieser, Sergius Dyck and Daniel Atorf
Fraunhofer Institute of Optronics, System Technologies and Image Interpretation, IOSB, Fraunhoferstr.1, 76131 Karlsruhe, Germany

ABSTRACT

Serious Games are an important part of technology aided learning. Since the learning outcome of intrinsically motivated learners is generally higher, a learning system should support the learner in achieving this state. Serious Games utilize the natural intrinsic motivation of playing a game by incorporating learning objectives. Concepts such as Digital Game Based Learning (DGBL) and Immersive Didactics achieve this by creating a learning environment that feels like an entertainment game by aligning learning and gaming goals. This puts players in a state of peaked intrinsic motivation which allows them to achieve increased levels of learning success - even while enjoying the game itself. Learning content for Serious Games is usually taken from existing courses or other materials. This work in progress explores the implementation of the interoperability standard LTI for integration purposes of third-party learning content into a Serious Game context.

KEYWORDS

LTI, Interoperability, DGBL, Learning Content Creation

1. INTRODUCTION

In the domain of Cybersecurity being addressed here, traditional education courses exist that offer subject-specific spotlights but few cross-topic learning opportunities. The presented concept allows to recombine existing learning content into case-specific tailored learning arrangements. The additional integration of the learning content in a game context leads to an intensified engagement of the learner with the subject matter, high intrinsic motivation and thus ensures a sustainable build-up of knowledge (Krapp et al. 2009; Prensky, 2007; Bopp, 2006).

In our previous paper (Atorf et al., 2021), a methodological and technical concept was developed with the primary goal to extend a Serious Game with a feature that allows learning content, available in third-party learning systems to be included with the lowest possible integration cost for authors. It is proposed to use the interoperability standard "Learning Tools Interoperability" (LTI) version 1.3 (IMS LTI, 2022) which links the individual systems involved in the project. The LTI standard makes a fundamental distinction between two system components: LTI-Tools provide the learning content which is consumed by the LTI platforms. The learning content considered is based on the thematic domain of cybersecurity. The content focus can be broadened to any content domain with the concept presented.

2. PROOF OF CONCEPT

Figure 1 shows the system architecture of the pre-developed concept, implemented during the proof-of-concept. Thereby, LTI layers are used to integrate different learning content providers into the serious game context. The dotnet reference implementation (LTI Advantage Platform, 2022) serves as the platform layer. For the implementation of the tool layer, two different libraries are used: a .Net-based (LTI Advantage Tool, 2022) and a JavaScript-based (ltijs, 2022) library.

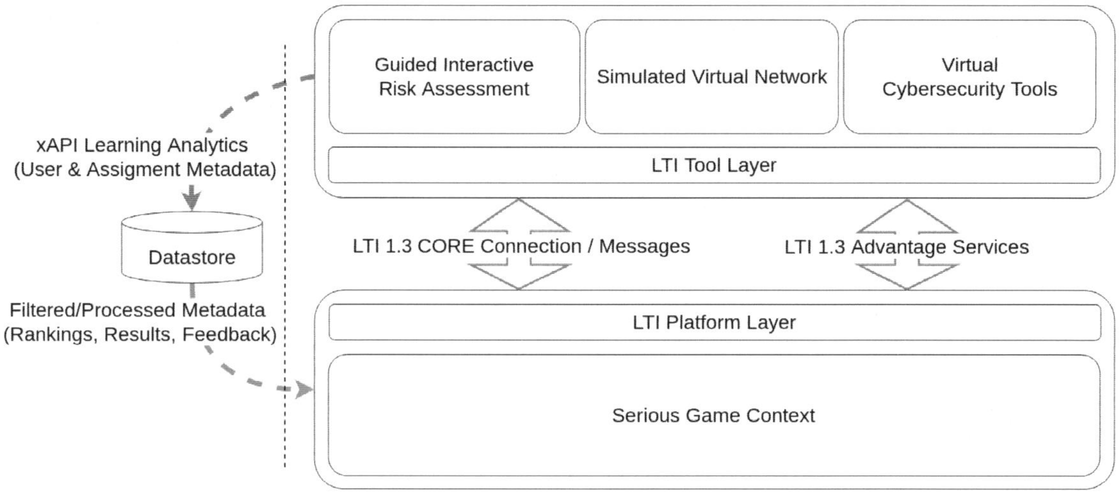

Figure 1. System architecture: LTI Tools integrated in the Serious Game Context via LTI Layers

The concept further provides for a learning record store that enables learning analytics and adaptivity response based on learner interaction using xAPI. This will be addressed in later work. Below is a brief description of the individual components shown in the figure 1.

2.1 Serious Game Platform

Serious games, and especially those that follow the digital game-based learning concept, are time-consuming to create. For each part of the development, such as the development of the story, the creation of graphic assets, sound, music, GUIs, etc., a separate expert is usually needed, to whom the idea of the game must be explained anew. This makes communication time-consuming and these experts are also subject to the fluctuations of the market. Once a Serious Game is developed, it seldom can be reused in other contexts; each application and learning purpose usually requires its own, new game. This is also true for existing learning content originating from training systems, learning platforms or simulators in schools or companies, which cannot be easily integrated, but must be reproduced in the game at great expense.

To further the required domain-specific adaptation and development of the Serious Game Platform, e.g. background story, missions, characters as well as tasks from the Cybersecurity domain, an experimental game development framework utilizing a modular concept is used. The framework provides finished game mechanics like resource management cycles, missions, story chapter structure etc. Depending on the requirements, elements can be added, adapted and extended, greatly reducing complexity of creation and improving the "recreatability" of Serious Games. Its central element is the so-called Game-Loop, which defines the general game play and game mechanics and essentially remains the same for each use case. The other elements Storytelling (if needed, a story is told in the chosen setting to give more context for the execution of missions), Setting (defining the game world), Missions (tasks from the application domain to achieve the learning goals) and Gamification (achievements and rewards for further motivational support) are only adapted or used where it becomes necessary for the use case. These customizations represent an instantiation of the framework using round-based and resource cycle approach (see Figure 2). The framework uses WebGL (WebGL, 2022) as deploy target, allowing the game to completely run in a web browser, platform independent and easily accessible. A full introduction of the framework instantiation features like core game mechanics and storyline would go beyond the scope of this work in progress paper and will be addressed in future publications.

Figure 2. Instance implementation of the used framework

Existing learning systems (Learning Management Systems, simulators, etc.) are integrated for the execution of missions. This integration is done via interoperability standards like LTI, integrating even external learning content seamlessly, making it "part of the game". The technical integration of the learning content can also be achieved with any other LTI-capable system without the possibility of using the benefits of the framework described above.

2.2 LTI Platform Layer

The dotnet reference implementation is chosen as Platform Layer (Atorf et al., 2021) and deployed on Ubuntu 20.10. The LTI platform is configured to forward content of connected LTI-Tools via LTI 1.3 Core functionality (deep linking). Additionally, LTI 1.3 Advantage Services (i.e. grading service) were implemented (see Figure 1).

2.3 LTI Tool Layer

LTI 1.3 Tool implementation is added to multiple existing learning courses, which then would be made available in the Serious Game Context via the LTI 1.3 Platform reference implementation (or any other LTI 1.3 compatible platform) mentioned before. Those courses are:

2.3.1 Guided Interactive Risk Assessment

Guided Interactive Risk Assessment (GIRA) is used to assess the risk of a particular industrial automation and control system (IACS), to identify and apply security countermeasures to reduce that risk to tolerable levels, according to the relevant IEC standard (IEC 62443-3-2, 2022). The learner is made familiar with this process by completing the risk assessment for a given system.

2.3.2 Simulated Virtual Network

The Simulated Virtual Network (SVN) is a development of a virtualized training platform in the Industry 4.0 context (Rösch et al., 2021). Its primary goal is to provide availability of a virtual platform instead of the physical platform itself. This enables learners to conduct training content themselves as a preparation or follow-up to classical classroom training without the need of physical access to the real hardware. The SVN allows the learner to observe an energy process of voltage regulation from an attacker's (blackhat) perspective by manipulating it with various simple attack techniques.

The SVN is based on a virtualization of host systems and a network for data exchange. The hosts are virtualized by implementing containerization using Docker. These hosts contain simplified functionality of the real components and provide real user and communication interfaces. The virtual network is implemented using the Containernet framework and allows the flexible construction of different network infrastructures. The learning scenario includes the use of the Nmap tool and introduces the learners to the topic of network scans, by providing a Kali-Linux container which serves as a user interface.

2.3.3 Virtual Cybersecurity Tools

A set of network and security tools (i.e. wireshark, tcpdump) are made available through a virtual Linux desktop. The tools can be used to monitor simulated (see SVN) or real networks which are connected to the Linux box.

3. CONCLUSION AND FUTURE WORK

To leverage a learner's intrinsic motivation, this paper concerned itself with a proof-of-concept of integrating external educational resources in a Serious Game context using the interoperability standard LTI. It is shown that the LTI platform reference implementation can be used to access third-party learning content. The main take-away is, that the more open standards are followed during implementation of learning content the easier the process of integration into new learning environments.

In a next step, this proof-of-concept work will be used to demonstrate the implementation of a learning record store for enabling learning analytics and adaptivity response based upon learner interaction using xAPI statements (see Fig.2). Additionally, it is planned to integrate into the overarching CLM Learning Environment (Krauss & Hauswirth, 2020).

REFERENCES

Atorf, D., Dyck, S., Kannegieser, E. (2021). Integrating System-independent Learning Content with the Benefits of Digital Game Based Learning. In: Human Systems Engineering and Design (IHSED2021): Future Trends and Applications. AHFE (2021) International Conference. AHFE Open Access, vol 21. AHFE International, USA.http://doi.org/10.54941/ahfe1001149#

Bopp, M. (2006): Immersive Didaktik und Framingprozesse in Computerspielen. In Neitzel, B. and Nohr, R.F. Das Spiel mit dem Medium. Partizipation-Immersion-Interaktion. Zur Teilhabe an den Medien von Kunst bis Computerspiel, pp. 170-186, Schüren, Marburg.

IEC 62443-3-2, Security for industrial automation and control systems – Part 3-2: Security risk assessment for system design, https://webstore.iec.ch/preview/info_iec62443-3-2{ed1.0}en.pdf (accessed 22.06.2022)

IMS LTI® 1.3 and LTI Advantage, http://www.imsglobal.org/activity/learning-tools-interoperability (accessed on 22.07.2022)

ltijs, https://github.com/Cvmcosta/ltijs (accessed on 22.06.2022)

Krapp, A., Schiefele, U., and Schreyer, (2009) I.: Metaanalyse des Zusammenhangs von Interesse und schulischer Leistung. In: Zeitschrift für Entwicklungspsychologie und Pädagogische Psychologie. 25. pp. 120-148

Krauss, C. and Hauswirth, M. (2020). Interoperable education infrastructures: a middleware that brings together adaptive, social and virtual learning technologies. In: The European Research Consortium for Informatics and Mathematics (ed) ERCIM NEWS: Special Theme: Educational Technology, pp. 9–10 (2020). ISSN 0926-4981. https://ercim-news.ercim.eu/images/stories/EN120/EN120-web.pdf. (accessed 20.06.2022)

LTI Advantage Platform, https://github.com/LtiLibrary/LtiAdvantagePlatform (accessed on 22.06.2022)

LTI Advantage Tool, https://github.com/LtiLibrary/LtiAdvantageTool (accessed on 22.06.2022)

Prensky, M. (2007) : Digital Game-Based Learning. Paragon House, St. Paul

Rösch, D., Nicolai, S. and Bretschneider, P. (2021). Combined simulation and virtualization approach for interconnected substation automation. In: 6th International Conference on Smart and Sustainable Technologies (SpliTech), 2021, pp. 1-6, doi: 10.23919/SpliTech52315.2021.9566380.

WebGL: 2D and 3D graphics for the web, https://developer.mozilla.org/en-US/docs/Web/API/WebGL_API (accessed on 22.07.2022)

A CASE STUDY FOR ANALYSIS AND PREDICTION IN LEARNING USING A PEER LEARNING SYSTEM

Adelina Aleksieva-Petrova[1] and Milen Petrov[2]
[1]*Technical University of Sofia, Faculty of Computer Systems and Technologies, Bulgaria*
[2]*Sofia University, Faculty of Mathematics and Informatics, Bulgaria*

ABSTRACT

Using data from different learning systems and tools to analyze and predict student achievements and behaviors is a method to increase learning effectiveness. In this paper, the peer learning system is presented and used to simulate analysis and prediction processes in a learning environment. The aggregation and sorting methods enforce the analysis process. The Decision Tree classification method is applied and evaluated to predict the result.

KEYWORDS

Learning Environment, Prediction, Student Behavior, Technology-Enhanced Learning

1. INTRODUCTION

The COVID-19 pandemic has significantly changed the world and influenced every sector of society. Technology Enhanced Learning (TEL) became extremely popular during the global epidemic as different platforms and tools must be used to transform all learning activities to remote or mixed mode. Using learning management systems (LMS), tools for videoconference, systems for assessments, and many others help to support the learning process and to deliver learning content to students in an effective way. These systems define the learning environment as a technology model which could be used by both students and teachers.

Most of the systems and tools are web-based, leading to the challenge of web browsers used by students and teachers. On the other hand, some tools are desktop applications, that require installation and configuration depending on the operating system. Therefore, knowing the preferences of learners in using OS or browsers is a challenge to setting up an appropriate learning environment.

Those systems also generate and collect data that could use for different analyses of student achievements or problems and predict student needs and behaviors which teachers could be used to improve the learning process and outcomes. This process is known as Educational Data Mining which "converts raw data coming from educational systems into useful information that could potentially have a great impact on educational research and practice" (Kaur, 2015). This data could give information about learner achievements and results and also help with selecting and configuring the learning environment.

All these challenges the APTITUDE project tries to resolve, specifically to propose a framework based on learning analytics for improving adaptation and recommendation of the learning process. The project has designed and developed the platform which is a middleware layer between different learning systems and tools to deploy the learning environment. Using data for student behaviors from external systems and tools the APTITUDE platform has analyzed and predicted the learning process and content.

This research aims to investigate the possibility of using systems learning data to be used in two directions as regards the analysis of learner preferences of different things and to predict different outcomes which could be used in the learning environment. To address the research goal, we investigate the data provided by a web-based peer learning system in the Web Technologies course at Sofia University.

This paper is organized as follows. After the introduction, Section 2 reviews the literature regarding related work. A brief conceptual description of the APTITUDE framework, main components, systems, subsystems, and its relations are given in Section 3. Section 4 presents the case study for an internal peer learning system. The analysis and prediction process using system data are described in Section 5 and the results are reported and interpreted. Section 6 concludes the paper.

2. RELATED WORKS

Different approaches are used to analyze learning data to predict student achievements and behavior. For example, the approach based on Bayesian Networks for modeling the behavior of the students is proposed in cases where the assessment or prediction should take into consideration very large amounts of data from a variety of sources. The results are promising as regards both predict of student behaviors, based on modeled past experience, and assessment (Xenos, 2004).

Using classification-based algorithms, such as multi-layer perception, Naïve Bayes, SMO, J48, and REPTree supported by the WEKA tool, the slow learners among students are identified and predicted. The results show that multi-layer perception performs best with 75% accuracy and proves to be a potentially effective and efficient classifier algorithm (Kaur, 2015). Machine learning algorithm Nave Bayes is also investigated to concentrate student efforts in a specific area to improve their academic achievement (Pallathadka, 2021). It is compared with the other three algorithms such as ID3, C4.5, and SVM. In this research SVM is the most accurate technique for classifying a data set of student performance.

A combination of Random Matrix Theory, a Community Detection algorithm, and statistical hypothesis tests is proposed to detect groups of students who have similar learning behaviors and outcomes (Mai, 2022). The experiments show that the higher performing groups are more active in practical-related activities throughout the course rather than groups that engage more with lecture notes.

The next research point is to investigate the learning environment and the use of different approaches to providing effective learning to students. For example, the introduction of educational games (gaming) and related virtual reality significantly improves the perception of educational material and the results obtained in all studied disciplines in the field of engineering and IT sciences (Getova, 2021). For that reason, several software instruments are created for analyzing and evaluating both the learning and playing outcomes of the player with different knowledge, learning goals, preferences, and learning styles (Dankov, 2021). In other research implementation of automated testing and evaluation is present which is involved in a learning environment (Chenchev, 2018).

The technology-enriched classrooms including videoconferences and video streaming lessons are investigated using a neuro-fuzzy model of Quality of Experience prediction for students. The results show that the perceived Quality of Experience is mostly influenced by the person's personality traits and learning style (Vasileva-Stojanovska, 2015).

3. A BRIEF INTRODUCTION TO THE APTITUDE PROJECT

The Aptitude project proposes a flexible framework aimed to recommend and adapt learning content and activities from/to different learning platforms, systems, and tools based on learning analytics (figure 1). For the conceptual system design of the framework, the main software components, systems, subsystems, tools, and its relations are given here. For the components on the diagram, we use a similar notation to the UML class diagram, but instead of classes, we represent software components. As the proposed overview is at a high level, UML component diagrams are not appropriate, as they represent too many specifics on the implementation of the components. The central system component here is the Aptitude server.

The Publisher and Consumer Registers components contain a list of systems and tools which are registered into the Aptitude platform. The Publisher Register is where the source of the data from systems log files and event streams is used in learning analytics. When considering the learning content and activities in different learning systems, we define the micro and macro level of the adaptation and the recommendation processes. The micro-level is related to learning resources and activities inside the system itself, while the macro level is related to learning resources and activities that are outside the system. Conversely, the Consumer Register is a component that has a role as external consumers of services offered by the Aptitude framework.

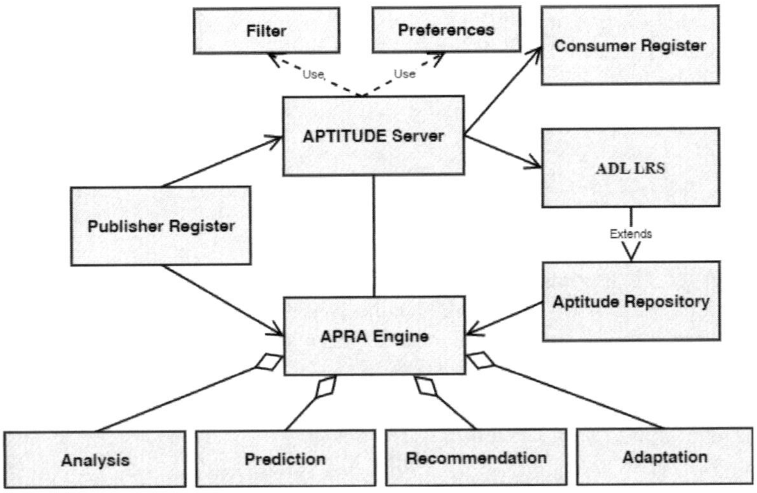

Figure 1. Meta model of Aptitude framework

Filter and Preferences components help to set the configurations and to establish a connection between the registered learning system or tools and the APTITUDE Server. The students are identified through ADL Learning Record Store based on the xAPI standard and stored in Aptitude Repository. Also, reference to learning content and activities is collected into the repository too. APRA engine is a core component, working behind the scenes, and is a complex component, that aggregates four subsystems for Analysis, Prediction, Recommendation, and Adaptation. It is outside the scope of the current paper, but in general, it manages its sub-components and has bi-directional interaction with the APTITUDE server: from one side it collects data from the server and its state, feeding four subcomponents, and from the other, it supports the work of the server for adaptation and recommendation processes.

4. CASE STUDY DESCRIPTION

The presented framework was applied in the last semester of the academic year 2021/2022 in the Web technologies course at Sofia University for a bachelor's degree in Software Engineering. Publisher Register is an internal peer learning system that is deployed and set up. The system is a web-based application that provides peer review and peer assessment as a subset of the peer learning process (Petrov, 2022). The students can see and choose a topic in the subject of Web technologies and they should write an essay based on paper bibliographies which provide a flexible and non-invasive, in which one can quantify actual student behavior involving library products and resources (Hovde, 2000). In such a way they would need to locate appropriate resources for the assigned research paper.

When the student essay is uploaded into the system the peer review process is started. The students could anonymously comment on individual parts of a submitted essay or write a general comment and assign a grade (peer assignment). All students see the comments and grades, but without knowing which peer student wrote the comment.

To create a model of analysis of learning data and prediction, we have simulated two components from the aforementioned APRA Engine using the system log file in two directions:

- Analysis process – learning preferences analysis according to learning content, and according to used browsers;
- Prediction process – here prediction is defined conceptually, as most of the information about students in the current study is confidential, so we use only prediction of operating system usage. Even though this didn't give much insight into the learning it positions the prediction system component as a viable one in the whole process.

The system log file with a total of 21767 data instances and 9 variables are taken for the analysis of this research. The log file includes information for the type of learner activity, started date of activity, learner device type, operating system, browser, description, anonymized ID (identifier), and IP address of the user.

In this paper, the selected potential variables are id, browser, device_type, os, type, IP_ANON, and ANON_ID. The variables started_at and description are used as meta attributes.

5. RESULTS

5.1 Analysis Process

For data processing, in this section, we use Talend Open Studio, which is open source and allows us to "execute simple extract, transform and load (ETL) and data integration tasks of data, and manage files"[1]. The workflow in the Talend software tool is implemented to create data analysis (figure 2). To identify the most interesting essay topics and most using OS and browser data aggregation and sorting are provided.

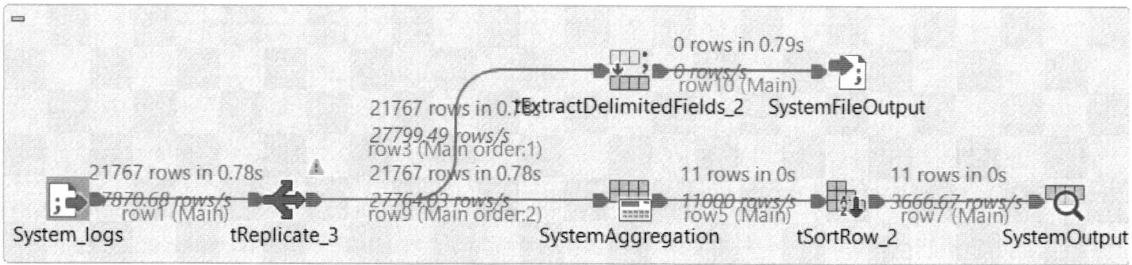

Figure 2. Workflow for the Analysis process

Figure 3 shows the statistics for the most used browsers and most reading essays. The results show that most students use Chrome browser, followed by Firefox, Opera, Edge, and Safari. There is a significant number of users, browsing the system via Facebook mobile application.

```
.                                        .
|            SystemOutput                |
|=----------------------+------------=|
|description            |StudentCount|
|=----------------------+------------=|
|Chrome                 |16353       |
|Firefox                |2091        |
|Opera                  |1406        |
|Edge                   |1113        |
|Safari                 |415         |
|Facebook App           |344         |
|Mobile Safari UIWebView|25          |
|Ecosia                 |11          |
|IE                     |3           |
|Miui Browser           |3           |
|Samsung Browser        |3           |
'-----------------------+------------'
```

```
Starting job SystemReferats at 11:11 28/06/2022
[statistics] connecting to socket on port 3718
[statistics] connected
welcome|4803
history|2863
system|2760
referat/81762_1_3       |381
referat/81760_2_4       |234
referat/81868_1_68      |229
referat/81842_1_79      |157
referat/9999_1_0        |154
referat/81805_7_140     |153
referat/81932_2_174     |148
referat/81883_2_38      |138
referat/81862_1_115     |137
referat/81933_2_5       |128
referat/81850_1_141     |125
referat/81848_2_58      |124
referat/81360_11_46     |116
```

Figure 3. Experimental data results on left, and top reading results on the right

The statistics for the most visited pages are the welcome page (landing page of the system, after successful authentication); history page (with the last results of the submitted works), system pages, and follows (anonymously) ranking on the reading results. The ranking on the reading results shows which essay is most browsed and read. A test account (with id 9999_1_0) has published an example of an essay for students which is first published in the system, and it ranks in the top 5 readings of the students. The results can help in ranking the essays as content and quality, ranking the authors of the essays, as the most credible reviewers, and using the results as input for classifications. It can be used as pointing out good practices, and a good example for other students.

[1] https://www.talend.com/products/talend-open-studio/

5.2 Prediction Process

To elevate student satisfaction with a given technology-enhanced educational setup, we used the classification technique as a Decision Tree to predict which OS is used by students. First, we used a random sample with 75 % of the data to create a model based on the given training data. This model is used to predict the response for the remaining 5441 instances.

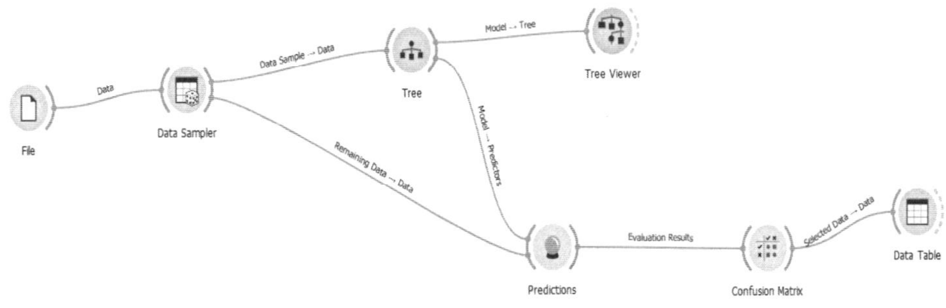

Figure 4. Workflow for the Prediction process

To measure the effectiveness of our model confusion matrix is used (figure 5). The Precision, Recall, and F1 of the model are 0.987 which means the high accuracy of the model. F1-score combines two competing metrics: precision and recall. The best results in prediction are achieved for mobile OS, such as Android, iPad, and iPhone.

The next important measurement is AUC (Area Under the Curve) ROC (Receiver Operating Characteristics) curve which is an important evaluation metric for checking any classification model's performance. The AUC value in our case is 0.992 which is considered outstanding and means better performance of the model.

Predicted

Actual	Android	Linux	Mac OS X	Ubuntu	Windows 7	Windows 8.1	Windows 10	iPad	iPhone	Σ
Android	205	0	0	0	0	0	0	0	0	205
Linux	0	492	1	0	3	0	23	0	0	519
Mac OS X	0	3	617	1	0	0	20	0	0	641
Ubuntu	0	0	0	160	0	0	0	0	0	160
Windows 7	0	0	0	0	101	0	4	0	0	105
Windows 8.1	0	0	0	0	0	25	7	0	0	32
Windows 10	0	2	4	1	0	0	3724	0	0	3731
iPad	0	0	1	0	0	0	0	6	0	7
iPhone	0	0	0	0	0	0	0	0	41	41
Σ	205	497	623	162	104	25	3778	6	41	5441

Figure 5. Confusion matrix

6. CONCLUSION

The APTITUDE project has the main role in learning analytics for adaptation and recommendation of learning contents and activities. Four components are the core of the platform which deliver the main processes: Analysis, Prediction, Recommendation, and Adaptation.

The current case study focuses on the validation of the Analysis and Prediction components. The data from the peer learning system is investigated to create a model for prediction. The results are promising with the high values of AUC and F1.

The limitation of the work is that the collected parameters (variables) for every log record are too limited to provide a more meaningful conclusion. According to Winne (2020) it is important to decide what trace data should be gathered and how trace data can contribute to recommendations for improving learning. Better prediction can be dependent on popularity, according to the subject, type of essay (scientific, overview, with more practical examples, or literacy), and level of essay (easy, intermediate, advanced). To produce such results, it needs external labeling of the essays.

Therefore, our future work will be to enrich the number of parameters and make colorations between them.

ACKNOWLEDGEMENT

The research reported here was funded under a project entitled "An innovative software platform for big data learning and gaming analytics for a user-centric adaptation of technology enhanced learning (APTITUDE)" by the Bulgarian National Science Fund with contract №: KP-06OPR03/1 from 13.12.2018.

REFERENCES

Chenchev, I., (2018). MySQL Scripts Evaluation with Moodle and Virtual Programming Lab. *Journal "CAx technologies*, issue 6, ISSN 1314-9628, pp.83-87

Dankov, Y. et al, (2021). Designing software instruments for analysis and visualization of data relevant to playing educational video games. International Conference on Human Interaction and Emerging Technologies. Springer, Cham.

Getova, I., et al. (2021). "Results and trends in e-learning of students, conducted during a lockdown. *ICERI2021 Proceedings. RATED*

Hovde, Karen. (2000). Check the citation: library instruction and student paper bibliographies. *Research Strategies* 17.1 3-9

Kaur, P. et al, (2015). Classification and prediction-based data mining algorithms to predict slow learners in education sector. *Procedia Computer Science*, 57, 500-508.

Mai, Tai Tan, et al, (2022). Learning behaviours data in programming education: Community analysis and outcome prediction with cleaned data. *Future Generation Computer Systems* 127 (2022): 42-55

Pallathadka, Harikumar, et al, (2021). Classification and prediction of student performance data using various machine learning algorithms. *Materials today: proceedings*.

Petrov, M. Y. (2022). Design and implementation of a configurable software architecture for peer learning. Paper presented at the *2022 57th International Scientific Conference on Information, Communication and Energy Systems and Technologies, ICEST 2022,* doi:10.1109/ICEST55168.2022.9828640

Vasileva-Stojanovska, Tatjana, et al. 2015. An ANFIS model of quality of experience prediction in education. *Applied Soft Computing* 34 (2015): 129-138

Winne, Philip H. (2020) Construct and consequential validity for learning analytics based on trace data. *Computers in Human Behavior* 112 106457

Xenos, Michalis, (2004). Prediction and assessment of student behaviour in open and distance education in computers using Bayesian networks. *Computers & Education* 43.4 (2004): 345-359.

CO-CREATING ICT SOLUTIONS TO AID MIGRANT INTEGRATION: LESSONS LEARNED FROM THE H2020 MIICT[1] PROJECT

Karen Latricia Hough and Babak Akhgar
CENTRIC, Sheffield Hallam University, 20 Furnival Street, Sheffield S1 2NU, UK

ABSTRACT

This paper presents the results of the prestigious Horizon 2020 MIICT: ICT-enabled services for migration innovation project. The project was conducted by a multidisciplinary team of technical developers, social scientists, lawyers, practitioners, and migration experts in three pilot countries of Cyprus, Spain, and Italy. The project focused on deepening societal understanding of the factors that impact upon refugee and migrant populations' ability to access key public services and subsequently created an ICT solution to solve these problems. The project deployed a co-creation methodology, which proved essential when designing ICT solutions to aid migrant integration, enabling researchers to involve both the migrants and those assisting them in their migration journeys, namely NGOs and service providers in the study as co-researchers. The researchers, together with the participants co-designed a multilingual, intuitive, inclusive, interactive platform called IMMERSE that catered for the *real* needs of migrants, asylum seekers and refugees. The innovative co-creation methodology deployed empowered migrants to be proactive and independent in their migration journeys and the resulting interactive platform created provides vital access to information and services like health, language, housing, employment, education, and legal assistance in a one-stop-shop design. This paper further highlights the lessons learned from the research, concerning the need for digital training courses to be implemented to overcome the digital divide and the inclusion of extensive legal and ethical protocols in migrant languages, to be integrated into the platform to counteract migrants' fears of digital surveillance and create confidence and wider usage of the ICT platform.

KEYWORDS

Co-creation, IMMERSE Platform, MIICT Project, Migrants, Refugees, Integration

1. INTRODUCTION

Immigration to the EU from non-member countries was 1.9 million in 2020 (Eurostat, 2020). The current refugee crisis in the Ukraine highlights the need for states to harmonise their responses to ensure refugees receive vital assistance.[2] The problems of integration, discrimination, unemployment, and education are particularly prevalent among migrants, asylum seekers and refugees from different demographic characteristics. Current research shows that migrants experience poverty, discrimination and marginalization whilst living in the EU (Kuschminder, 2018; Patterson & Leurs, 2019; Sawert, 2020). This has been exacerbated by the COVID-19 pandemic (Le Louvier & Hough, 2021).

Technological solutions can prove vital in aiding migrant integration, solving the above-mentioned problems, since migrants rely heavily on technology to aid their migration journeys (Bakewell & Jolivet, 2015; Borkert et al., 2018; Crawley & Hagen-Zanker, 2018; Dekker, & Engbersen; Dekker et al., 2016; Dhoest, 2020; Fiedler, 2019; Gillespie, et al, 2018; Frouws, 2016). ICTs have been proven useful in helping migrants to interact with public administrations or participate in public life (Osorio & Rodríguez, 2014) and can facilitate administrations in achieving the Sustainable Development Goals of leaving no-one behind,[3] including migrants.

[1] The MIICT project was funded under the Horizon 2020 scheme. See https://www.miict.eu/ for more information
[2] This is because some states on the frontline like Poland are under great pressure with higher numbers of refugees. https://data2.unhcr.org/en/situations/ukraine
[3] See IOM & GMDAC Leave no migrant behind, the 2030 agenda and data disaggregation. https://publications.iom.int/system/files/pdf/Migrants-in-the-SDGs.pdf

In recent years, there has been a proliferation in the creation of several high-tech tools designed to support refugees' integration in their host States.[4] However, not all technologies address the ethical and legal problems derived from the misuse of new technologies and the potential breach of basic human rights. Furthermore, many of these have taken a top-down approach, meaning that they often do not fulfil the real needs of migrants, and as a consequence are sometimes not taken up by many users (Dekker et al., 2018) risking becoming digital litter (Benton, 2019).

The MIICT project responds to this gap by using an innovative co-creative methodology to successfully customize the interfaces used to access key public services so that they better address the requirements of migrants and refugees. This human centred, bottom-up grassroots approach is essential in ensuring that the ICT solution caters for the needs of the beneficiaries, including vulnerable groups like LGBTQ+ refugees, unaccompanied minors, and pregnant women, whilst at the same time underlying certain risk factors regarding the uptake amongst certain populations. The innovative co-creative methodology ensures migrants are empowered and aware of their rights, boosting their socio-economic integration into the host country. The MIICT project thus contributes to developing inclusive societies that respond to upcoming challenges by providing migrants with up-to-date information via ICT tools in a cost-effective way, ensuring their integration into the labour market via a job matching tool, thereby leading to the creation of more positive narratives surrounding migration. This helps reduce social inequality and decrease the current xenophobia pervading in many EU states.

2. METHODOLOGY

In the MIICT project a human centred design approach was taken in which the end users were deeply ingrained within the participatory design process throughout three phases of research. The first phase, the *inspiration phase*, focused on identifying the main services essential for migrant integration to the host society, which included status, social integration, health care, housing, employment, language, education and training, transport, and social security. A variety of methods were used, to elicit these challenges, including an extensive literature review, in-depth interviews, online surveys, and co-creation workshops using mind-maps and storyboards in the three pilot locations of Cyprus, Italy, and Spain. The researchers used visual methods to avoid the re-traumatisation of migrants, asylum seekers and refugees, as they have often undergone traumatic journeys. The co-creation workshops were essential as they enabled "marginalised" participants to exercise greater control over the data production and direct the research project itself (Strokosch & Osborne, 2016). Using mind-maps as a research method further enriched the data collection process by breaking down communication obstacles through facilitating the visualisation of key concepts and their related sub-concepts (Mahmud et al, 2011).

The second phase, *ideation phase*, consisted of conducting a series of co-design and co-creation workshops in each of the three pilot locations of Cyprus, Italy, and Spain in order to co-design and co-create solutions to the challenges identified in the *inspiration phase* with the project's stakeholders. Researchers used visual methods once more to enable the participants to design the platform and landing page. Researchers also used a synthesis methodology in this phase to interpret the co-creation data and create personas representing migrant profiles to enable easier engagement with the platform. In keeping with the co-creative and participatory approach of the MIICT project, periodic conjunction points were inserted so that all key stakeholders could provide their feedback to the technical development.

In the final phase, *implementation phase*, two testing phases were undertaken – namely the live prototyping phase which was conducted in each of the three pilot locations for a period of one week and the sustained service delivery testing phase, which lasted six months and was undertaken in-situ in a real-world environment with live data. Each testing per pilot was designed to enable feedback to be incorporated into the next location by the technical team developing the platform in order to enhance the creation of the platform. Feedback was gathered via questionnaires, focus groups and interviews with all stakeholders. The researchers further adopted a Privacy-by-Design approach to ensure full inclusivity and protection.

[4] Among these, Germany stands out with the introduction of various Apps that accompany refugees and asylum seekers like Welcome App Germany and Integreat and the IOM MIGRAPP is also very successful. https://www.iom.int/migapp.

3. RESULTS

3.1 The Immerse Platform

The IMMERSE platform (Integration of Migrants MatchER Service) provides a series of sustained and improved inclusion services that capture the specific socio-cultural, economic, and legal contexts of migrants and foster them to overcome key challenges they encounter when they arrive in the destination country, namely regarding social security, language, transportation, housing, education and training, social integration, healthcare, employment status. The IMMERSE platform also acts as a firewall, reducing the potential for discrimination and bias, via a job matching tool to aid the integration of migrants into the labour market. It is also available in a mobile-friendly version in several languages including English, Italian, Spanish, Greek, Arabic and French. It provides a one-stop-shop solution helping migrants to create their CV and register for jobs and training courses via both transactional and informational services. Its innovative advantage consists in an adaptive "plug in and play" integration framework, that allows for the incorporation of new ICT modules depending on the needs of users, also enabling an easy integration of IMMERSE into existing IT infrastructures. Video tutorials were incorporated to help illiterate users and those with special needs use the platform more easily.

The IMMERSE platform is built using state of the art architecture with different layers including the user interface, application, semantic, data management and security layers (Ntioudis, 2022). The User Interface (UI) is developed to enable stakeholders such as service providers and migrants to interact with the system as well as with each other. Another feature is the IMMERSE domain ontology, a lightweight knowledge representation model in the semantic layer, responsible for the storage and retrieval of the information that is available in the Knowledge Base Repository (KBR). It acts as a *matchmaking* service that dynamically enriches user profiles of migrant users, that have previously registered to the IMMERSE platform, with personalized recommendations for jobs, training courses, houses and volunteering offers that are offered in the platform by service providers. Another innovative feature is the Data management system (DMS) running on the MIICT backend with a twofold responsibility including the central storage of device profiles and the correlation of existing information with newly acquired data from other repositories and sources (for patch and firmware updates as well as manufacturer use documentation).

The platform has been entirely conceived and built using evidence-based research. It is user-friendly giving solutions to reduce cumbersome administrative practices. Through a pathway of customisation, the platform increases migrant´s interest and motivation. It is transparent and easy to operate and navigate, enabling migrants to mark their favourite posts. All legal and ethical protocols have been followed to ensure adherence to the GDPR, thereby safeguarding migrants. An outline of the system architecture is provided in figure 1.

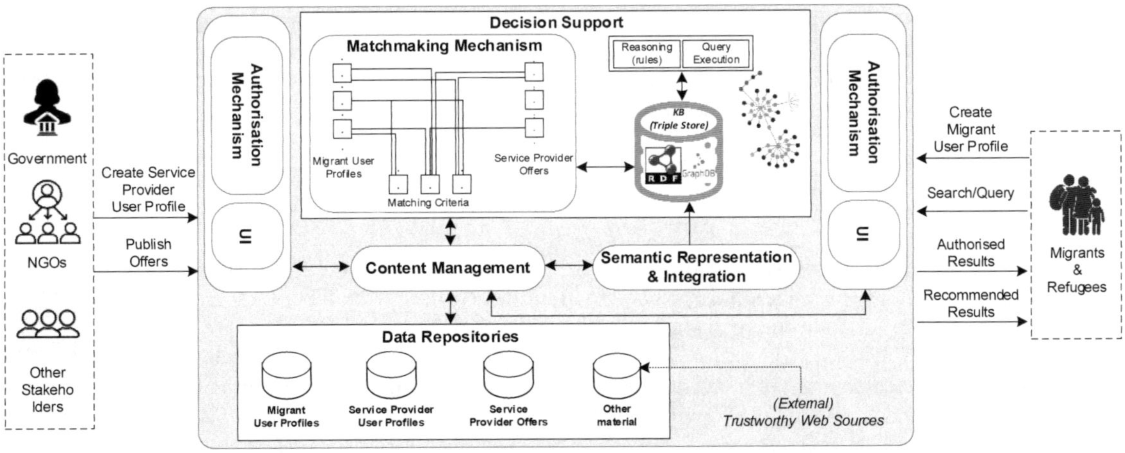

Figure 1. IMMERSE system architecture

3.2 Testing

One crucial, and innovative element of the MIICT project consisted in its live testing of the proposed ICT solution in two phases by all target groups in the three pilot locations to ensure stress testing, and the feasibility of the platform. The first phase, a live prototyping phase consisted of one week to evaluate the functionality of the offered services against the actual users' requirements as well as the performance of the IMMERSE platform. The technical team gathered feedback via questionnaires and were also able to fix any bugs at this stage.

The second testing phase, the sustained service delivery was conducted over a six-month period in a live environment, in each pilot location, testing the utility, desirability, scalability and other important factors pertinent to the success of the platform. Several feedback sessions were conducted with the participants via focus groups and questionnaires resulting in a positive overall view of the platforms' impact in tackling their problems. Over 50% of migrants, reported that just by taking part in the research itself, their confidence in public service providers has improved, thus showing the impact of participatory methods. A further 80% of participants reported being satisfied with the platforms ability to save time and effort in the communication between service providers and migrants. The service providers further pointed out that around 90% of the demands of the migrants to their organisations is related to employment and as such, they consider the job matching tool on the IMMERSE platform to be valuable.

3.3 Lessons Learned

During the research several challenges were raised concerning the successful deployment of the IMMERSE platform with researchers outlining the need to be sensitive to issues of cultural diversity, digital positioning, researcher bias, eurocentrism, and inclusivity. One challenge raised concerns the fact that not all individuals have equal access to technology and usage depends on several factors including, but not exclusive to, age, socio-economic status, and gender, known in the literature as the digital divide (Alam & Imran, 2015; Adam, & Alhassan, 2020). To overcome this hindrance, researchers in the project suggest state run digital training courses for all migrants and service providers, as well as inbuilt courses on the ICT solution itself. This issue is linked to inclusivity, and researchers suggest the added need for the creation of hubs in open spaces, like libraries with free Wi-Fi and devices to ensure migrants can access the ICT solution easily.

Another issue that arose from the research concerned migrants' fears of digital surveillance (Dekker et al., 2016; Gillespie et al., 2018). Some migrants were reluctant to give their personal emails to register on the platform due to their insecure status, and the persecution they had suffered in their countries of origin. To overcome this effective information campaigns, need to run alongside the deployment of any ICT solution, and the inclusion of privacy protocols need to be provided on the platform itself using simple terminology, that is translated into several migrant languages. These should be included on the landing page of the platform to reinforce migrants' sense of trust and confidence in uploading their personal details.[5] Another challenge is the continued safeguarding of migrants, and any future administrator needs to deploy a privacy by default and by design approach to vet all contacts and links and keep them up to date to protect migrants, demonstrating the need for increased funding in the sustainability period.

4. CONCLUSION

This paper has presented some of the main results from the H2020 MIICT: ICT–enabled public services for migration project. It has evidenced how the co-creation and co-design methodology adopted in the MIICT project was crucial to eliciting the relevant key stakeholder driven requirements for the development of the IMMERSE platform. The MIICT project has designed a one-stop-shop multi-lingual, interactive platform called IMMERSE that aids migrant integration via transactional and informational services. The design is user friendly and intuitive culminating in a mobile friendly version. It enables migrants to get access to employment via a job matching tool, as well as access to education and training courses and offers help with creating a CV.

[5] Researchers deployed a privacy by design approach and carried out extensive DPIA, Fundamental Risk assessment and ensured all research was carried out in relation to Article 35 of the General Data Protection Regulation (GDPR) - Regulation (EU) 2016/679.

However, the paper highlights that certain challenges surround the deployment of such ICT solutions in real life situations.

Technological innovation does not exist in a vacuum, so whilst co-created ICT solutions go a long way in aiding migrant integration, the deployment of such tools need to be accompanied by several *enabling conditions* for them to have real impact. These include the creation of hubs with free Wi-Fi, built in digital training courses for both service providers and migrants, and the inclusion of legal and ethical protocols in migrant friendly languages to build trust amongst migrants. Continued funding needs to be obtained to ensure the successful administration of the platform for long-term use to enable the administrator to vet all applications and monitor all external links are accurate and trustworthy to ensure migrants' protection.

ACKNOWLEDGEMENT

This project has received funding from the European Union's Horizon 2020 Research and Innovation Programme under Grant Agreement No 822380. However, the opinions expressed herewith are solely of the authors and do not necessarily reflect the point of view of any EU agency.

The authors would like to thank the entire MIICT consortium for their contributions to the research.

REFERENCES

Alam, K., & Imran, S. (2015). The digital divide and social inclusion amongst refugee migrants: A case in regional Australia. *Information Technology & People, 28*(2) 344-365.

Adam, I.O., & Alhassan, M.D. (2020). Bridging the global digital divide through digital inclusion: the role of ICT access and ICT use. *Transforming government, people process, and policy. Emerald Publishing limited* vol 15 (4) pp. 1-18.

Bakewell, O., & Jolivet, D. (2015). Broadcast feedback as causal mechanisms for migration. *International Migration Institute working papers, Oxford university, paper 113*, retrieved from Migration Institute website: https://www.migrationinstitute.org/publications/wp- 113-15. Accessed 24, August 2021.

Benton, M. (2019). Digital Litter: the downside to using technology to help refugees. *Migration Policy Institute.* https://www.migrationpolicy.org/article/digital-litter-downside-using-technology-help-refugees.

Borkert, M., Fisher, K.E., & Yafi, E. (2018). The Best, the Worst, and the Hardest to Find: How People, Mobiles, and Social Media Connect Migrants In(to) Europe. *Social Media + Society* pp. 1-11.

Crawley, H., & Hagen-Zanker, J. (2018). Deciding Where to go: Policies, People and Perceptions Shaping Destination Preferences. *International Migration,* Vol 57 (1) pp. 20-35.

Dekker, R., Engbersen, G., Klaver, J., & Vonk, H. (2018). Smart Refugees: How Syrian Asylum Migrants Use Social Media Information in Migration Decision-Making. *Social Media and Society,* Vol 4 (1) pp. 1-11.

Dekker, R., Engbersen, G., & Faber, M. (2016). The use of online media in migration networks. *Population, Place and Space,* Vol 22 (6) pp. 539–551.

Dekker, R., & Engbersen, G. (2014). How social media transform migrant networks and facilitate migration. *Global Networks, a journal of transnational affairs* Vol 14 (4) pp. 401-418.

Dhoest, A. (2019). Digital (dis)connectivity in fraught contexts: The case of gay refugees in Belgium. *European Journal of Cultural Studies* Vol 23 (5) pp. 1 –17.

Eurostat, (2020) https://ec.europa.eu/eurostat/data/database

Fiedler, A. (2019). The gap between here and there: Communication and information processes in the migration context of Syrian and Iraqi refugees on their way to Germany. *The International Communication Gazette,* Vol 81(4) pp. 327–345.

Frouws, B., Phillips, M., Hassan., A. & Twigt, M. (2016). Getting to Europe the 'Whatsapp way'. The use of ICT in contemporary mixed migration flows to Europe. *Danish Refugee Council. RMMS Briefing paper No2.* Accessed 20, August 2021.

Gillespie, M., Osseiran, S., & Cheesman, M. (2018). Syrian Refugees and the Digital Passage to Europe: Smartphone Infrastructures and Affordances. *Social Media & Society* pp. 1-12.

Kuschminder, K. (2018). Afghan Refugee Journeys: Onwards Migration Decision-Making in Greece and Turkey. Journal of Refugee Studies, Vol, 31 (4) pp. 566-587.

Le Louvier, K. & Hough, K.L. (2021) Migration management and the conflicting imaginaries of the UK border. World Conference on Humanitarian Studies (IHSA). Paris.

Mahmud, I, Rawshon, S., & Rahman, M.J. (2011). Mind-map for academic writing: A tool to facilitate university level students. *Educational Journal of Educational Science and Research,* Vol 1 (1) pp. 21-30.

Mosler Vidal., E (2021) *Leave no migrant behind, the 2030 agenda and data disaggregation.* IOM & GMDAC , Geneva. https://publications.iom.int/system/files/pdf/Migrants-in-the-SDGs.pdf

Ntioudis, D., Karakostas, A., Vrochidis, S., & Kompatsiaris, I. (2022) IMMERSE: A matching service addressing the challenges of migrant integration. In Akhgar, B., Hough., K.L., Abdel-Samad, A., Bayerl., S & Karakostas, T. (Eds) (2022) *Information and Communications Technology in Support of Migration.* Springer: Geneva: Switzerland.

Osorio, M., & Rodríguez, R. (2014). La integración de los inmigrantes medianteInternet en la Comunidad de Madrid. *Comunicación y Hombre: Revista interdisciplinar de ciencias de la comunicación y humanidades*, Vol (12), pp. 135–151.

Patterson, J., & Leurs, K. (2019). 'We Live Here, and We Are Queer!' Young Adult Gay Connected Migrants' Transnational Ties and Integration in the Netherlands. Media and Communication, Vol 7 (1) pp. 90-101.

Sawert, T. (2020). Understanding the mechanisms of ethnic discrimination: a field experiment on discrimination against Turks, Syrians, and Americans in the Berlin shared housing market. Journal of Ethnic and Migration Studies, Vol 46 (19), pp. 3937-3954.

Strokosch, K., & Osborne, S. (2016). Asylum seekers and the co-production of public services: understanding the implications for social inclusion and citizenship. *Journal of Social Policy. Cambridge University Press,* Vol 45(4), pp. 673-690.

THE LEGAL UNCERTAINTY ASPECT OF THE REGULATORY APPROACH REGARDING ONLINE CONTENT MODERATION

Eduardo Helfer de Farias and Gabriel Rached
Fluminense Federal University, Niterói/RJ, Brazil

ABSTRACT

Since the creation of the internet, online content moderation has been facing uncertainty regarding its lawful application even in situations where there is a specific law addressing the issue. Internet users around the world have been dealing with the struggle to define the boundaries of lawful disagreement and unlawful speech. In this sense, this research aims to identify how the State's regulatory approach may influence the legal uncertainty regarding online content moderation. For this purpose, there were selected specific countries representing three different regulatory models for the internet: the USA (self-regulation); Brazil (command and control regulation); and Germany (standard-based regulation). The research intends to compare the laws and precedents of each selected legal system and contrast how they address: (i) the moderator's identity; (ii) the criteria for moderation; (iii) the moderation tools; (iv) the "the checks and balances" over the decision-making of the moderator; and (v) the liability to be applied against wrongful decision. The level of legal uncertainty in each of these five aspects shall be measured exclusively by the extent of the law's ambiguity and the discretion of the decision-makers in interpreting it. So, it will not address the "subjective uncertainty". In this discretion, given the legislation may vary according to the subject matter presented for content moderation, three main topics were taken into consideration: privacy, fake news, and hate speech. These topics have been selected for being sensitive issues in all countries, including the three selected for this study. The preliminary results indicate that the command and control regulation as presented in the Brazilian version might be the one with the highest legal uncertainty while the self-regulation as presented in the US version appears as the one with the lower legal uncertainty. In the conclusion, these results would be summarized indicating how the law's ambiguity and decision-maker's discretionary reflects on the cyber environment.

KEYWORDS

Online Content Moderation, Legal Uncertainty, Regulation, Decision-Making, Liability, Cyberspace

1. INTRODUCTION

This research intends to identify how the legal uncertainty regarding online content moderation is influenced (lower or higher) by the regulatory approach of the internet adopted by the State agents, such as self-regulation, command and control regulation; and standard-based regulation. Specifically, the intent is to find out to which degree the regulatory approach adopted for online content moderation increases or decreases the legal uncertainty in the cyber environment, reflecting on the decision-maker's choice.

By "legal uncertainty" refers to the law's ambiguity and the decision-makers discretion in interpreting it (CALFEE & CRASWELL, 1986; SEGAL & STEIN, 2006). It is not considered in this study the so-called "subjective uncertainty", which means people's perception of the law (DAVIS, 2011), because it would require a different methodological approach.

US Supreme Court Judge Oliver Wendell Holmes understood the law as a "prediction of how the courts behave" (HOLMES, 1897), which means the law offers a degree of certainty about public administration behavior. Therefore, most scholars sustain that the uncertainty of the law may frustrate the law's goal of deterring antisocial behavior and even undermine the rule of law (KERHUEL & RAYNOUARD 2010). Also, it cannot be presumed that legal uncertainty reduces naturally over time giving the bias of judges and legal scholars in "upsetting expectations" and the "economic incentives" in favoring those "disadvantaged by legal rules" (D'AMATO, 1983). So, the issue is a problem requiring action to be solved. Assuming these premises, the regulatory approach which succeeds in minimizing uncertainty contributes also to minimizing antisocial behavior and preserving the rule of law.

Unfortunately, most academic research about the legal uncertainty arousing from content moderation restricts themselves to the social media environment (HELDT & DREYER, 2021; CHEN, 2007; FAUST. 2017). These references give insights into how content moderation should be handled, but they are restricted to an environment controlled by a single agent. Besides, platforms such as social media are just the most visible level of the internet. There are other four internet categories capable of content moderation: internet service providers, domain registers, payment services, antivirus providers, cloud storage services, and platforms.

To narrow the scope, the analysis is restricted to the online content moderation exercised through the five levels of the internet under the labels of "privacy", "fake news" and "hate speech" in countries representatives of the three different internet regulatory approaches: USA (self-regulation); Brazil (command and control regulation); and Germany (standard-based regulation). These countries have been selected as representatives for their regulatory approach because of the maturity of their legal systems. For all purposes, "Content moderation" refers to all actions taken to suppress, restrict or promote a specific speech.

The methodological approach consists of analyzing the law and precedents of these three countries regarding the answers they provide to these five questions: 1) who is the moderator (the one who decides about the content to be promoted or restricted); 2) which contents are moderated; 3) which tools are applied for this purpose; 4) which "checks and balances" should be applied to the moderation decisions, and 5) which liability process should be enforced to correct or minimize the consequences of wrongful decisions.

Considering this is part of a thesis ongoing research, the content to be shown in the final remarks could be considered preliminary results.

2. A THEORY OF CONTENT MODERATION: CASE STUDIES

The legal uncertainty regarding online content moderation is detrimental to the exchange of ideas necessary for preserving basic human rights, such as free speech. To evaluate how the State's regulatory approach to the internet influences this uncertainty, this research shall analyze the sources of objective legal uncertainty (law's ambiguity and decision-makers discretionary) in the regulatory approaches of the USA (self-regulation), Brazil (command and control regulation) and Germany (standard-based regulation): (i) establish the moderator's identity; (ii) chose the criteria for moderation; (iii) addresses the moderation tools; (iv) impose "checks and balances" over the moderator's decision-making; and (v) take measure to correct wrongful decisions.

For the first question, it is hypothesized three possible moderators: government, internet infrastructure owner, or the general public. "Government" means any state structure, may it be the executive, legislative, or judiciary. "Internet infrastructure owner" means any holder of the technologies that sustain the internet. "General public" means any internet user that does not fit the two first categories.

In all countries selected for study, one of the three possible moderators assumes as a protagonist over the other two, without eliminating them. The USA's First Amendment and Section 230 of the Communications Decency Act turns protagonist the general public. In opposition, Brazil nominates its Judiciary as the main moderator regarding speeches (arts. 9 § 1, 18 and 19 of Internet Civil Regulation). Germany delegated the moderation responsibility to the internet infrastructure owners, setting boundaries for them to act under government supervision (Netzwerkdurchsetzungsgesetz of 2017). Therefore, the study of each one of them gives a glimpse of a different approach to dealing with the issue.

For the second question, it has been selected three categories under which a speech may deem to be vetoed or restricted: privacy, misinformation, and hate speech. "Privacy" refers to any identifiable information regarding a natural person, such as name, social security number, health status, and behavior. "Misinformation" means any false statement, intentional or not. "Hate speech" means any speech that intends for the audience to take violent actions against an identifiable group of persons. These choices were made to have a comparison standard between these three countries, given that all of them are dealing with these issues.

The internet infrastructure owners – all based in the USA – have vowed to moderate the online content to prevent the spread of misinformation. On the other hand, the Brazilian top Judiciary Court started a confidential investigation by itself (Inquérito 4.781/2020) to arrest and reprimand those whom the Court deemed to be part of an online criminal organization to discredit the Judiciary. In Germany, the Gesetz Zur Verbesserung der

Rechtsdurchsetzung in sozialen Netzwerken imposed on the internet infrastructure owners the duty to remove "clearly illegal content" on their behalf. Therefore, all three countries are taking action on the issue.

In the third question, the main moderator's tools are identified as fear, friction, and flooding (ROBERTS, 2017). "Fear" is the result of widespread awareness that one specific speech will be sanctioned by moderators if publicized. "Friction" means any imposition of restrictions to access or promote a specific speech, such as filtering or demanding conditions for accessing, such as confirming age or payment. "Flooding" means the widespread promotion of a specific speech through the internet to make it harder for internet users to be aware of the existence of opposing speech.

Internet infrastructure owners are taking the responsibility to moderate online content by themselves or being forced to take it by the government in all three jurisdictions. Moderation is always as visible as restriction of accesses. It may also be as subtle as promoting one view disproportionality disregarding the other or imposing barriers for one specific content to be known. This research shall see which techniques are being deployed by each jurisdiction.

For the fourth question, it is evaluated if there are clear boundaries for a moderator to make his/her decision, if these boundaries are enforced by a third party beyond the moderator and if the subject target of the moderation may present defense on his/her behalf.

This question investigates how each country set boundaries to avoid bias or mistaken decisions among moderators. Assuming there is no foolproof moderation system, it's important to check how this risk is minimized.

For the fifth question, we evaluate if there is any legal remedy the subject targeted by moderators may seek reparation in case it is proven it was not according to law for his speech to be restricted or banned. Even with fail safes in place, it is inevitable for "false positives" to happen. The final question would be how each of these three jurisdictions shall deal with the aftermath of a failed moderation.

3. CONCLUSION

Online content moderation is a sensitive issue for any regulatory approach on the internet.

In the current research status, the observed preliminary results point out that the self-regulation of the internet in its USA approach seems to be the one with the least legal uncertainty, and the command and control regulation in the Brazilian approach seems to be the one with the highest legal uncertainty, standard-based regulation of Germany being in between regarding its certainty.

It's important to note that certainty does not refer to concepts of fairness or equity, being a topic related to predictability. Therefore, this research does not address the morality surrounding the regulatory approaches, which is a topic that may be explored in future research.

It may be impossible to eliminate the legal uncertainty surrounding online content moderation, but it's reasonable to search for ways of minimizing it. This research's goal is to contribute to settling some degree of predictability over law enforcements and business behavior regarding the boundaries of speech to avoid the escalation of conflicts.

REFERENCES

Calfee, J. E. & Craswell, R. (1984). Some Effects of Uncertainty on Compliance with Legal Standards. In Virginia Law Review, Vol. 70 pp. 965-1003.

Chen, P. J. (2013). *Australian Politics in the Digital Age.* Anu Press, Canberra, Australia.

D'Amato, A. (1983). Legal Uncertainty. In California Law Review, Vol. 71 pp.1-53

Davis, K. E. 2011. The Concept of Legal Uncertainty: Definition and Measurement. Available at SSRN: https://ssrn.com/abstract=1884664 or http://dx.doi.org/10.2139/ssrn.1884664.

Faust, G. (2017). Hair, Blood, and the Nipple: Instagram Censorship and the Female Body. In: Urte Undine Frömming et al. Digital Environments: Ethnographic Perspectives Across Global Online and Offline Spaces. Bielefeld, Germany, pp. 159–170.

Heldt, A., & Dreyer, S. (2021). Competent third parties and content moderation on platforms: Potentials of Independent Decision-Making Bodies from a Governance Structure Perspective. In: Journal of Information Policy, Vol. 11, pp. 266-300.

Holmes, O. W. (1897). The path of the law. In: Harvard Law Review, Vol. 10, pp. 457-478.

Kerhuel, A. et. al. (2011). Measuring the Law: Legal Certainty as a Watermark (In French). International Journal of Disclosure and Governance, Vol. 8, 4, pp. 360–379.

Roberts, M. E. (2018). Censored: distraction and diversion inside China's Great Firewall. Princeton University Press, New Jersey, USA.

Segal, U. & Stein, A. (2006). Ambiguity Aversion and the Criminal Process. In Notre Dame Law Review Vol. 86, pp. 1495-1551

EXPLORING CLOUD COMPUTING PREVALENCE FOR COMPETITIVE ADVANTAGE IN ONLINE PUBLICATION PLATFORMS

Tendani J. Lavhengwa
Tshwane University of Technology (TUT), 2 Aubrey Matlala Road, Soshanguve South Campus, Tshwane, South Africa

ABSTRACT

The use of Online Publication Platforms (OPPs) by individuals and organizations has overtaken reliance on print media. The paper investigated the prevalent cloud computing themes towards competitive advantage. A cross-sectional study using a content analysis approach was followed with data collected from selected OPPs between the years 2015 and 2020. Seven hundred and ninety-three OPPs articles were purposefully selected, then thematically analysed. OPPs used for establishing prevalence and current issues pertaining to disruptive technologies. Six prevalent cloud computing themes are proposed that can be used as guidelines were uncovered and conceptualized for practitioners and the research community.

KEYWORDS

Cloud Computing, Competitive Advantage, Online Publication Platforms (OPPs)

1. INTRODUCTION

(Sharma & Husain, 2017) indicates that the concept of cloud computing is becoming popular, this supporting that it has become a technology that cannot be ignored for individuals and enterprises. Cloud technologies are highlighted as a technology to aid in the digital disruption (Prevost et al., 2018). Studying and exploring cloud computing prevalence is important for organisations to maintain or gain competitive advantage in the markets. Cloud computing as an emerging technology that attracts attention towards business benefit (Truong, 2010). While studying Universities in Jordanian, (Moh et al., 2015) asserted that cloud computing adoption is essential as part of a strategy and to achieve competitive goals. In support of costs, a South African study (Mvelase et al., 2016) asserts that the pricing model for public cloud services offered by providers is not affordable and economical for Small, Medium and Micro Enterprises (SMME). The use of Websites by organisations is also noted as a source for competitive intelligence (Pellissier & Kruger, 2010). Subsequent sections feature: problem outline; literature; methods; results; conclusion and recommendations.

2. THE PROBLEM OUTLINE AND RESEARCH QUESTIONS

Print media publications have provided data, content, information and knowledge to multiple users, readers, and contributors over the years. The use of OPPs by individuals and organisations has overtaken their reliance on print media. In a study on organisational strategic alliances, (Pellissier & Kruger, 2010) list Websites as one of the most important sources for the collection of competitive intelligence. Other sources are competitor's products, annual reports, and research reports. The stories and notes contained in the OPPs can also impact markets trends. Various stakeholders such as service providers, managers, administrators, developers, and users rely on this content on a regular basis. (Suo, 2013) identified recurrent themes in a study on cloud implementations in organisations. The objective of the article was to investigate cloud computing prevalent themes as presented on the SA OPPs towards competitive advantage for individuals and enterprises between 2015-2020. The gap and novelty for this article is in looking at sourcing data from OPPs using content analysis.

3. CLOUD COMPUTING AND OPPs

The literature presented a foundations for the cloud computing, SA, collection from OPPs and theory.

3.1 Computing, Cloud Computing Defined and Previous Studies

While analysing the difference in computing concepts, (Sharma & Husain, 2017) lists: Cluster, Grid, Utility and Cloud. They further state that cloud computing will become the main technology in our information life. The National Institute of Standards and Technology (NIST) definition of cloud computing (Mell & Grance, 2011) identified three focus areas in defining cloud computing: ***Essential Characteristics, Service Models and Deployment Models***. In a study on cloud implementation in organizations, (Suo, 2013) identified '*full migration program of infrastructure and applications*' as one of the themes and '*Data migration*' as a challenge confirming for cloud computing. Various cloud computing studies conducted within SA context for the period investigated by the study of 2015 to 2020.

Goldstuck (2017) reported SA's Internet penetration growth reaching 40% in 2017. This is important since cloud computing is dependent on Internet infrastructure. Statista (2021) further supported this in a recent report indicating Internet user penetration in South Africa having reached 57.8% in 2021 and a projection of 62.3% in 2025. An early study by (Mohlameane & Ruxwana, 2014) indicate a lack of cloud computing awareness leading to limited knowledge on the benefits and services. It is important to understand and address this challenge for SA organisations to realise the opportunities presented by cloud computing. While that study used interviews, expert reviews, literature, and questionnaires this current study unobstructively collected its data from media publications. The levels of cloud computing adoption are noted from a different data sources.

While focusing on healthcare providers, (Sadoughi et al., 2020) highlighted security towards the cloud as an important concern. A cloud computing study by (Mosweu et al., 2019) focused on '*records management in Africa*', this supports the feasibility for OPPs in SA. The study indicated that there are good tools that can bring business efficiency and improvement. Identifying cloud computing as an '*achilles heel of the digital era*' also presented an opportunity for this study to investigate further while focusing on the SA context.

3.2 Cloud Computing Evolution

An early investigation comparing and contrasting Cloud and Grid computing, (Foster et al., 2008) indicate the intricate connection between cloud computing and the Grid computing paradigm which is linked to utility and cluster computing technologies. (Voas & Zhang, 2009) further outline 6 computing paradigms as mainframe computing, PC computing, network computing, Internet computing, grid computing, and cloud computing.

In discussing modern computing paradigms, (De Donno et al., 2019) identified Cloud, Internet-of-Things (IoT), Edge, and Fog. The rapid deployment of smart devices and IoT systems and the need for real time services has led to the emergence of Fog Computing (Choudhari et al., 2018). (Yi et al., 2015), terms Fog Computing the same as Edge Computing towards providing elastic resources and services to end users at the edge of network. (Syed et al., 2016) asserts that Fog Computing brings virtualized cloud services to the edge of the network to control the IoT devices. Malik et al (2018) outlines various technologies functioning behind the platform of cloud computing technologies: virtualization, Service-Oriented Architecture (SOA), grid computing and utility computing.

3.3 The South Africa Cloud Computing Context

This context was selected because SA is one of the front runners in the technology industry on the African continent. The Industrial Development Corporation (Industrial Development Corporation, 2020) demonstrated interest in cloud computing by conducting research under the following title: "*An overview of the global cloud computing industry and the SA perspective for the formulation for IDC Strategies as a funder and a user' [2013/4]*". This project is a motivation for further work on the mission of bringing benefits for SA and Africa on industrial development and innovation.

(Foster et al., 2008) list cloud industries: Amazon, Google, Yahoo, Microsoft, and IBM. The top cloud providers in SA on a 2019 publication were (MyBroadBand, 2019) were: Google Cloud (39.19%); Microsoft

Azure (32.16%); AWS (12.97%); VMWare Cloud (5.41%); IBM Cloud (3.51%); Oracle Cloud (2.70%) and Others (12.43%). In 2020 (ZDNet, 2020) lists the top three service providers in the world as AWS, Azure and GCP. The sources presented have common service providers indicating shared results across the two years 2019 and 2020. None of these cloud service providers are based in SA or the African continent that propelled this study to investigate and understand what is happening in this part of the world. (Mvelase et al., 2014) proposed a Virtual Enterprise Model for cloud computing to assist SMME in acquiring or subscribing to Public Cloud infrastructure. (Mohlameane & Ruxwana, 2014) found the use of Websites as part of the Internet as a business enabler for entering new local and international markets.

3.4 OPPs as a Source of Information

The use of Websites as a source was motivated by reflecting on (Crossland & Chigona, 2010) when investigating the functionality and delivery of Websites of political parties in SA. Earlier studies investigating media and democracy cited the weakness of African Websites highlighting poor search and archive capabilities and the journalists not being independent (Kreutzer & Berger, 2002). The Websites selected for this study addressed all these by introducing new functionality. Organisation's content is generated by users based on their projects which is converted into interactive Website for dissemination and public use (Jessee et al., 2011).

3.5 Theoretical Perspectives in Support of the Study

Diffusion of Innovation (DOI) theory as defined by (Rogers, 1983) focusing on the five categories of individual innovativeness was used as a guide. (Sadoughi et al., 2020) notes the use of DOI and adopted constructs for cloud technology. The prevalence of cloud computing in OPPs is an indicator of technology adoption.

4. MATERIALS AND METHODS

This study followed a content analysis approach motivated by its use in an investigation on the implications of cloud computing services in archives and records management (Mosweu et al., 2019). Studies have cited the interest in qualitative research increase during the latter half of the 20th century investigating issues while iterative and flexible (Physiopedia contributors, 2020). OPPs articles were published between 2015 and 2020.

NIST (Mell & Grance, 2011) defines cloud computing as a model for enabling ubiquitous, convenient, on-demand network access to a shared pool of configurable computing resources. The preliminary focus areas from the definition are as follows (number of items in bracket): *cloud computing characteristics (5), cloud computing service models (3) and cloud computing deployment models (4)*. The first phase being deductive, twelve codes were loaded from the preliminary focus areas into Atlas.Ti; Qualitative Data Analysis Software (QDAS). Secondly, the inductive phase featured reading the articles, using coding to identify emerging codes. (Physiopedia contributors, 2020) indicated that thematic analysis reviews all of the data to identify common ideas which reoccur. (Krippendorff, 2004) introduced the five step research design of content analysis. (Herring, 2004) further describes these steps as the traditional approach while discussing Content Analysis for New Media. The adapted content analysis stages were in four stages. a) Research Question development; b) Define complete texts to for the articles from the OPPs as data sources; a sample was purposively selected; c) Identification and loading of preliminary codes from literature; d) Coding and analysis using a QDAS.

5. CONTENT ANALYSIS: PURPOSIVE SAMPLING FROM TEXTS

In addressing stage two of the content analysis process, the data collection were conducted by searching for studies that investigated ICT OPPs in SA. Websites were visited, the search function was located and used to extract the data using keywords "*cloud computing*".

Firstly, (King, 2020) produced the "*Top South African news publications revealed*" as indicated with the Website name and their unique browser records in brackets: MyBroadband (2,588,359), Techcentral (217,090), ITWeb (202,301), Engineering News (97,698) and Memeburn (73,180). Secondly, the above list was also supported by (Du, 2020) when they published "*10 best South African technology websites*", listing: *My BroadBand, TechCentral, Bandwidth Blog, Memeburn, Mail & Guardian, News24 Technology, Gearburn, ITWeb, Stuff, and ITNewsAfrica*. Further, (CommunikaySA, 2020) published a list of "*Technology publications in South Africa*", these are: ITWeb, TechCentral, MyBroadband, Brainstorm Magazine, Futurewave BusinessIT, IT-Online, BusinessTech.co.za, Gadget, Channelwise, Bandwidth Blog, EngineerIT, The Margin, Stuff and htxt.africa. All three publications MyBroadband (King, 2020), WebAfrica (Du, 2020) and CommunikaySA CommunikaySA (CommunikaySA, 2020) featured these Websites amongst the top in SA. The top three selected for data collection Websites were: *ITWeb, MyBroadband* and *Techcentral*. The '*Brainstorm Magazine*' is a business technology magazine, this was also included since it presented an overlap between printed and digital publications. The printed version is sold at retail stores and featured at ICT events and conferences. This article only considered the online version of the magazine. (Zhang, 2005) concluded that random sampling is widely applied with a Websites as a data source after studying thirty-nine cases. The adapted steps used with purposive sampling incorporated:

Population: All ICT OPPs Websites in SA; **Sample Frame**: All ICT OPPs Websites represented in the four OPPs; **Sampling Method:** "*cloud computing*" was used for searching then a document was generated with all results. Next, three articles were purposively selected per OPPs; **Sample Size**: twelve articles; plus, four documents for the period. Sixteen sources (documents); **Unit of analysis**: Websites of the selected OPPs.

6. RESULTS, OUTPUT AND ANALYSIS

This section starts by outlining OPPs where the data collected followed by theme development for analysis.

6.1 Participants' Websites and OPPs Context

OPPs were inspected to provide a context for this study. (Qi et al., 2010) proposed a Website evaluation framework featuring three main dimensions: Usefulness, Service Quality and Website Physical Accessibility. The 'Usefulness' dimension was applied which addresses the *Functionality* and *Usability*. The OPPs consulted for data collection was inspected and met all seven requirements, indicated as **functionality**: Context of Website, Flexibility and Accessibility. **Usability**: Navigability, Layout and design, Ease of use and Playfulness.

6.2 Data Extracted from OPPs (Documents and Articles) Overview

The overview of data extracted from OPPs (Articles) as indicated in Table 1 below:

Table 1. Data extracted from OPPs

OPPs	***Articles sampled***	***Number of pages extracted***	***Number of articles***
Brainstorm	86	22	221
Techcentral	84	28	120
ITWeb	108	82	164
MyBroadband	35	47	288
Totals	**313**	**179**	**793**

The *number of pages extracted* differ since some of the returned results were primarily text based while others included images which take up space hence the higher numbers. Word clouds were used as a familiarization tactic to visualize frequent words. Highlighted at the centre were phrases: "*cloud*" and "*computing*".

6.3 Presenting Prevalent Cloud Computing Themes

Twelve codes were identified from literature and twenty-eight codes from data, consolidated into six themes:

a) **People – human capital:** Leadership, people and skills, cloud user and growth and maturity. Various people are part of the cloud computing community. This is from leaders in organizations to the end users. They all require various skills to develop in order to benefit from this technology. Growth and maturity for all is essential for the future of cloud computing.

b) **Economic and finance:** Finance represented by the need for funding is central to the discussion cloud. The human resources, hardware and software infrastructure must be funded for the cloud projects to be successful. These funds are sourced from various locations and structures.

c) **Technical and technologies:** Deployment, power - electricity challenges, big data, Edge Computing, cloud challenges-concerns, digitally transform. Big data and edge computing are underlying technologies. 'Fog Computing' was not identified in the data. This may indicate that there may be delays in evolution on themes within the SA context. There is an on-going transformation leading to environmental concerns noted through the data centres needing to adapt to new requirements of energy saving and electricity savings.

d) **Cloud Service Provider - products and services:** These needs to be understood for wide usage.

e) **Geographical location:** Cloud computing bypasses geographical boundaries. This promotes opportunities and changes that need to be understood and addressed. Business and operating models must be updated with services located in other parts of the world. Accessibility and regulations may be a challenge with the physical location of data and services not known to the end consumer.

f) **Information access and platforms:** These are presented by publications, news and media. OPPs have become an important source of information for cloud computing in a rapidly changing operating environment.

The themes demonstrate opportunities and challenges for competitive advantage as supported by (Truong, 2010). Each theme can be a contribution towards the prevalence and understanding of cloud computing.

7. CONCLUSION AND RECOMMENDATIONS

Studying cloud computing using OPPs can present a competitive advantage for individuals and enterprises with the range of discourse that can be generated and analysed in short period. Organisations can benefit from assessing themselves on the adopter category that they belong to as indicated by (Rogers, 1983). The '*Late Majority*' and '*Laggards*' needs to work harder not to miss the benefits of cloud computing. OPPs can be used for establishing prevalence and current issues pertaining to disruptive technologies such as cloud computing, artificial intelligence and data mining. Second, the cloud computing focus areas must be considered as a lens when studying an organisation's adoption and use of cloud computing. While '*Fog Computing*' did not return data entries alongside the theme on '*Edge Computing*', these needs further investigation.

REFERENCES

Choudhari, T., Moh, M., & Moh, T. S. (2018). Prioritized task scheduling in fog computing. *Proceedings of the ACMSE 2018 Conference, 2018-Janua*. https://doi.org/10.1145/3190645.3190699

CommunikaySA. (2020). *PUBLIC RELATIONS SEARCH ... SEARCH ...*. https://communikaysa.wordpress.com/tech-publications/

Crossland, M., & Chigona, W. (2010). An evaluation of the functionality and delivery of websites of political parties in South Africa. *SA Journal of Information Management*, *12*(1), 1–5. https://doi.org/10.4102/sajim.v12i1.453

De Donno, M., Tange, K., & Dragoni, N. (2019). Foundations and Evolution of Modern Computing Paradigms: Cloud, IoT, Edge, and Fog. *IEEE Access*, *7*, 150936–150948. https://doi.org/10.1109/ACCESS.2019.2947652

Du, S. (2020). *Top 10 South African technology websites*. https://www.webafrica.co.za/blog/websites/top-10-technology-websites-in-south-africa/

Foster, I., Zhao, Y., Raicu, I., & Lu, S. (2008). Cloud Computing and Grid Computing 360-degree compared. *Grid Computing Environments Workshop, GCE 2008*. https://doi.org/10.1109/GCE.2008.4738445

Herring, S. C. (2004). Content Analysis for New Media : Rethinking the Paradigm. *New Research for New Media: Innovative Research Methodologies Symposium Working Papers and Reading, March 2016*, 47–66. https://doi.org/10.1177/1461444804039906

Industrial Development Corporation. (2020). *News filter*. https://www.idc.co.za/research-reports/industry-sector-research-2/

Jessee, E., Zembrzycki, S., & High, S. (2011). Stories matter: Conceptual challenges in the development of oral history database building software. *Forum Qualitative Sozialforschung*, *12*(1). https://doi.org/10.17169/fqs-12.1.1465

King, B. (2020). *Top South African news publications revealed.* https://mybroadband.co.za/news/internet/326225-top-south-african-news-publications-revealed.html

Kreutzer, T., & Berger, G. (2002). Generation Mobile: Online and Digital Media Usage on Mobile Phones among Low-Income Urban Youth in South Africa. *Gazette*, *64*(January 2009), 21–45. https://doi.org/10.1177/1748048502064001020l

Krippendorff, K. (2004). Reliability in content analysis: Some common misconceptions and recommendations. *Human Communication Research*, *30*(3), 411–433. https://doi.org/10.1093/hcr/30.3.411

Mell, P., & Grance, T. (2011). The NIST-National Institute of Standars and Technology- Definition of Cloud Computing. *NIST Special Publication 800-145*, 7.

Moh, E., Masa, T., Al-Lozi, M., & Rateb Mahmoud Darawsheh, S. (2015). Cloud Computing Adoption in Jordanian Universities. *Journal of Business & Management Prof. Musa; Darawsheh, Dr. Saddam Rateb Mahmoud Journal of Business & Management (COES&RJ-JBM)*, *33*(44), 2306–7179. https://doi.org/10.17632/t839whwkz2.1

Mohlameane, M., & Ruxwana, N. (2014). The Awareness of Cloud Computing: A Case Study of South African SMEs. *International Journal of Trade, Economics and Finance*, *5*(1), 6–11. https://doi.org/10.7763/ijtef.2014.v5.332

Mosweu, T., Luthuli, L., & Mosweu, O. (2019). Implications of cloud-computing services in records management in Africa: Achilles heels of the digital era? *SA Journal of Information Management*, *21*(1), 1–12. https://doi.org/10.4102/sajim.v21i1.1069

Mvelase, P., Dlamini, Z., Macleod, D., Dlodlo, N., & Sithole, H. (2014). A business model for a South African government public cloud platform. *2014 IST-Africa Conference and Exhibition, IST-Africa 2014*, 1–10. https://doi.org/10.1109/ISTAFRICA.2014.6880662

Mvelase, P., Dlodlo, N., Sithole, H., & Adigun, M. (2016). *Depiction of experimental findings for a cloud enterprise architecture*. 1–10. https://doi.org/10.1109/cccs.2015.7374185

MyBroadBand. (2019). *Cloud services in South African companies – Here are the latest stats*. 1–4. https://mybroadband.co.za/news/cloud-hosting/306766-cloud-services-in-south-african-companies-here-are-the-latest-stats.html

Pellissier, R., & Kruger, J. P. (2010). A study of strategic intelligence as a strategic management tool in the long-term insurance industry in South Africa. *WMSCI 2010 - The 14th World Multi-Conference on Systemics, Cybernetics and Informatics, Proceedings*, *3*, 72–77. https://doi.org/10.4102/sajim.v13i1.426

Physiopedia contributors. (2020). *Qualitative Research*. https://www.physio-pedia.com/Qualitative_Research

Prevost, M., Johnston Prof, K. A., & Tanner, M. (2018). Awareness and Preparedness of IT managers to digital disruption: A South African Exploratory Case Study. *The African Journal of Information Systems*, *10*(4), 2.

Qi, S., Ip, C., Leung, R., & Law, R. (2010). A new framework on website evaluation. *Proceedings of the International Conference on E-Business and E-Government, ICEE 2010*, 78–81. https://doi.org/10.1109/ICEE.2010.27

Rogers, E. M. (1983). *Diffusion of innovations* (3rd ed.). The Free Press - A Division of Macmillan Publishing Co., Inc. https://doi.org/10.4324/9780203710753-35

Sadoughi, F., Ali, O., & Erfannia, L. (2020). Evaluating the factors that influence cloud technology adoption—comparative case analysis of health and non-health sectors: A systematic review. *Health Informatics Journal*, *26*(2), 1363–1391. https://doi.org/10.1177/1460458219879340

Sharma, M., & Husain, S. (2017). Analyzing the Difference of Cluster, Grid, Utility & Cloud Computing. *IOSR Journal of Computer Engineering*, *19*(01), 55–60. https://doi.org/10.9790/0661-1901045560

Suo, S. (2013). Cloud implementation in organizations: Critical success factors, challenges, and impacts on the it function. *ProQuest Dissertations and Theses*, *August*, 192. http://search.proquest.com/docview/1467505085?accountid=28547

Syed, M. H., Fernandez, E. B., & Ilyas, M. (2016). A pattern for Fog Computing. *ACM International Conference Proceeding Series*, 1–10. https://doi.org/10.1145/3022636.3022649

Truong, D. (2010). How Cloud Computing Enhances Competitive Advantages: A Research Model. *The Business Review, Cambridge*, *15*(1), 59–66. http://works.bepress.com/dtruong/12/

Voas, J., & Zhang, J. (2009). Cloud computing: New wine or just a new bottle? *IT Professional*, *11*(2), 15–17. https://doi.org/10.1109/MITP.2009.23

Yi, S., Li, C., & Li, Q. (2015). A survey of fog computing: Concepts, applications and issues. *Proceedings of the International Symposium on Mobile Ad Hoc Networking and Computing (MobiHoc)*, *2015-June*, 37–42. https://doi.org/10.1145/2757384.2757397

ZDNet. (2020). *Top cloud providers in 2020 : AWS , Microsoft Azure , and Google Cloud , hybrid , SaaS players The cloud computing race in 2020 will have a definite multi-cloud spin . Here ' s a look at how the cloud leaders stack up , the hybrid market , and the SaaS pl.* https://www.zdnet.com/article/the-top-cloud-providers-of-2020-aws-microsoft-azure-google-cloud-hybrid-saas/

Zhang, J. (2005). Content analysis of web sites from 2000 to 2004: a thematic meta-analysis. *Sites The Journal Of 20Th Century Contemporary French Studies*, *August*, 105.

REFLECTIONS

INFORMATION SYSTEMS INFRASTRUCTURE DEVELOPMENT – ROAD AHEAD

Seppo J. Sirkemaa
University of Turku, P.O. Box 170, 20101 Pori, Finland

ABSTRACT

Information systems is the basis of business activities and processes in organizations. Technology has an increasingly critical role and therefore the reliability of information systems becomes a key element in successful operations. In this article we look at information systems infrastructure development. It is the mortar and basis for any other systems and operations in modern organization. Therefore, it needs to be reliable and robust. However, as environment, needs and requirements can change rapidly, the infrastructure should also be flexible. Infrastructure development is about making incremental changes to existing infrastructure. It is rare that technology can be chosen freely, new systems become part of existing infrastructure rather than replace it. Compatibility and standards are essential elements in development of a reliable, smoothly operating infrastructure. They make interoperability of different systems and technologies possible, increasing the flexibility of infrastructure.

KEYWORDS

Development, Information Systems, Infrastructure, Reliability

1. INTRODUCTION

In this article we look at development of information systems in organization (Xu & Quaddus, 2013). The emphasis is on information systems infrastructure. It consists of systems and technologies, which need to be compatible with existing systems, and at the same time robust and open for future changes.

Information systems infrastructure is here considered as the basis of processes and activities in companies and organizations. Infrastructure functions as a mortar for a wide variety of operations, such as manufacturing and sales activities. Therefore, reliability is one of the most important requirements for infrastructure. Infrastructure should be robust and functionable, even in situations when there are lot of users and processes going on simultaneously. This is referred to as trustworthiness of infrastructure (Sirkemaa, 2018).

Reliability, robustness and trustworthiness are not the only elements that are needed in information systems. Information systems infrastructures should also provide flexibility. In any organization there are constantly changes within the organization and goals, and in the outside environment. For example, rapid changes can be necessary in business when there are changes in competitive environment.

Information systems development is not a purely technical process that could be carried out in isolation from other organizational functions and processes (Laudon & Laudon, 2015). There are several perspectives and goals that should be considered in the process. Strategic information systems planning is about identifying potential areas and opportunities so that information systems can provide greater competitiveness (Doherty et al., 1999; Peppard & Ward, 2004).

2. SUCCESSFULNESS

Generally, development is a process where a development area is identified, and thereafter a plan to is being prepared so that the issues or development needs could be solved. Information systems are often critical for organizational processes and functions, therefore they should be developed and managed as resources (Kearns, 2006; Johnson & Lederer, 2010). Implementing the plan is a vital part of successful development process. (Checkland & Scholes, 1999; Cram & Brohman, 2013).

It is often noted that management support is important for projects. Clearly, management support is a critical element also in information systems infrastructure development (Gibson et al., 1984). Development activities need to be accepted, understood and supported by managers, otherwise the odds of success will be low. Managers play an important role in organizing resources, and therefore their role is important. Furthermore, management can encourage developers in the development work. Management also helps in implementing technology and new systems.

Information systems and infrastructure development is not only a technological challenge, as understanding organization, organizational processes, and people in the organization are needed as well. Information systems and infrastructures have a wide impact on the organization; therefore technologies and infrastructures should fit to the organization (Schein, 1986; Markus, 1991, Pearlson et al., 2016). Here management's role is very important, as managers facilitate change and make new organizational practices possible. In information systems development, the question is how to use technology to bring added value to operations and activities. This involves also mapping the future potential of information systems and technologies, as solutions should be feasible, robust and flexible in the long run (Sirkemaa, 2019).

Information systems development involves several persons from different organizations. There are plenty of skills and expertise needed in the process. It is evident that technology and systems are complex. They change, partly because of technological change, but also because they may be used differently, and for purposes they were not originally designed. People involved in infrastructure development should have expertise in technologies, but also understand needs of users and business so that technology enables processes and brings added value to operations and business. Having a combination of experts in different technologies and systems, together with key persons with business understanding and experience is an important success factor. Often development relies on systems providers and their expertise in planning and developing infrastructure. They have best expertise in technologies and systems, but they may not know the organization, the processes and goals where this are being planned. It is therefore vital to have business knowledge and experience so that technologies can be chosen not because of technological sophistication, but in a way, they provide business value and make it possible to pursuit new businesses. They also need to fit existing systems, run reliably and remain flexible for possible changes in the future (Sirkemaa, 2019).

The developers of information systems infrastructure have a major impact on the successfulness of development work (Markus, 1991). The involvement of key persons, especially from management, IT department and information systems users are a critical factor in information systems infrastructure development (Schein, 1986; Henderson, 1990; Sirkemaa, 2019). Successful development is not about having extensive technical expertise available or most sophisticated technology. There is also need for persons who understand organizational processes and who can recognize processes and needs in a way that developers can provide solutions to these needs on both strategic and operative level (Dos Santos & Sussman, 2000). Understanding development goals is important, so that it would be possible to provide resources for the development process. Furthermore, development methods and timeline for development work need to be mutually agreed.

It is important to pay attention to key elements of project management. These include managing the development process with (Railing & Housel, 1990).

- Understanding requirements and keeping them in mind throughout the process.
- Managing changes during the project and at the same time adherence to plans.
- Assigning responsibilities clearly at each stage of the development work.
- Having different experts in the development team and using external expertise when needed.
- Managing and integrating external partners during the process (such as systems providers).

Information systems development calls for project management. The role of project management is critical. Furthermore, interaction in the development team, between experts and key persons from has a vital impact on the successfulness of the development work. The results rely also on technology and it's fit to organization. (Orlikowski & Robey, 1991; Orlikowski, 1992)

Interaction is a key element in any project. In information systems development everything relies on communication between people involved in the project, IT-people and users of technology, as well as internal and external experts coming from different companies. Interaction is recognized as one of the most important elements of successful projects, implementation and change process (King, 1978; Cram et al., 2016). It should still be noticed that even though interaction and discussion are important, but they will not automatically ensure desired results (King, 1978). Successful information systems development depends ultimately on "the human factor" (Orlikowski, 1992; Laudon, 1995; Sirkemaa 2019). As a result, managing interaction is a critical part of successful information systems development.

3. CONCLUSION

Information systems infrastructure is referred to as the basic information infrastructure which is a backbone for other business systems and processes. The role of infrastructure is critical as all other systems rely on it. Therefore, reliability and robustness are important elements in infrastructure. However, infrastructure should also be open for changes. Developing an infrastructure that operates as a robust backbone for daily operations and can be changed should there be changes in business needs, is a challenge for the developers of information systems infrastructure. It is important to develop a system that can be modified if there are needs to make changes. This is referred to as flexibility, which is needed in creating an information systems infrastructure.

Information systems infrastructure development involves various stages and careful project management. Information systems developers need to provide technical solutions, but also understand feasibility of the systems. The lifecycle of systems and technologies in infrastructure is long, making choices that are optimal on short-term are not necessarily best in longer run. Planned technologies and systems need to be implemented to the organization. Here we also highlight the importance of changes. Timetables, technical factors and similar factors require changes during the development process. Changes are also needed later when for example, there are changes in business environment. Technological changes impact also organizational culture, individuals and groups. In this process the role of management is important (Schein, 1986). Information systems development impacts organization in many ways, bringing also results that may not be directly measurable (Segars & Grover, 1998).

REFERENCES

Checkland, P. & Scholes, J. (1999) Soft Systems Methodology in Action. John Wiley & Sons Ltd.

Cram, W.A. & Brohman, M.K. (2013) Controlling information systems development: a new typology for an evolving field. *Information Systems Journal*, Vol 23, Issue 2, pp.137-154.

Cram, W.A., Brohman, M.K. & Gallupe, R.B. (2016) Hitting a moving target: a process model of information systems control change. *Information Systems Journal*, Vol 26, Issue 3, pp. 195-226.

Doherty, N., Marples, C., & Suhaimi, A. (1999) The relative success of alternative approaches to strategic information systems planning: An empirical analysis. *The Journal of Strategic Information Systems*, 8(3), pp. 263–283. doi:10.1016/S0963-8687(99)00024-4

Dos Santos, B. & Sussman, L. (2000) Improving the return on IT investment: the productivity paradox. *International Journal of Information Management* 20, pp. 429-440.

Gibson, Cyrus F., Singer, Charles J,.Schnidman, Ava A. & Davenport, Thomas H. (1984) Strategies for Making an Information System Fit Your Organization. *Management Review*, January, pp. 8-14.

Henderson, J.C. (1990) Plugging into Strategic Partnerships: The Critical IS Connection. *Sloan Management Review*, Vol 31, No 3, pp. 7-18.

Johnson, A. M., & Lederer, A. L. (2010) CEO/CIO mutual understanding, strategic alignment, and the contribution of IS to the organization. *Information & Management*, 47(3), pp. 138–149. doi:10.1016/j.im.2010.01.002

Kearns, G. S. (2006) The effect of top management support of SISP on strategic IS management: Insights from the US electric power industry. *Omega*, 34(3), pp. 236–253. doi:10.1016/j.omega.2004.10.008

King, W.R. (1978) Strategic planning for management information systems. *MIS Quarterly*, Vol 2, No 1, pp. 27-37.

Laudon, Kenneth C. (1995) Ethical Concepts and Information Technology. *Communications of the ACM*, Vol 38, pp. 33-39.

Laudon, K. C. & Laudon, J.P. (2015) *Management Information Systems: Managing the Digital Firm Plus Mymislab with Pearson Etext -- Access Card Package* (14th ed.). Prentice Hall Press, Upper Saddle River, NJ, USA.

Markus, M. L. (1991) *Systems in Organizations*. Cambridge.

Orlikowski, W.J. & Robey, D. (1991) Information Technology and the Structuring of Organizations. *Information Systems Research*, Vol 2, No 2, pp. 143-169.

Orlikowski, W.J. (1992) The Duality of Technology: Rethinking the Concept of Technology in Organizations. *Organization Science*, Vol 3, No 3, pp. 398-427.

Pearlson, K.E., Saunders, C.S. & Galletta, D.F. (2016) *Managing and Using Information Systems: A Strategic Approach*, Sixth Edition. John Wiley & Sons, USA.

Peppard, J. & Ward, J., (2004) Beyond strategic information systems: towards an IS capability. *Journal of Strategic Information Systems*, Vol. 13, No. 2, pp. 167-194.

Railing, L. & Housel, T. (1990) A network infrastructure to contain costs and enable fast response: The TRW process. *MIS Quarterly*, Vol 14, No 4, pp. 405-420.

Schein, E.H. (1986) *Organizational Culture and Leadership*. Jossey-Bass Publishers.

Segars, A. H., & Grover, V. (1998) Strategic information systems planning success: An investigation of the construct and its measurement. *MIS Quarterly*, 22(2), pp. 139–163.

Sirkemaa, S. (2018) Towards Understanding the Role of Trust in Electronic Business. *International Journal of Economics and Management Systems*, Volume 3, pp. 151-154.

Sirkemaa, S. (2019) Key Perspectives in Information Technology Infrastructure Management. *Journal of Advances in Information Technology* Vol. 10, No. 3, August, pp. 100-103.

Xu J., Quaddus M. (2013) Managing Infrastructure for Information Systems. In: *Managing Information Systems*. Atlantis Press, Paris

AI ADOPTION IN HEALTHCARE: TRUST AND PRIVACY CONCERNS

Mousa Albashrawi
King Fahd University of Petroleum and Minerals
Academic Belt Road, Dhahran, Saudi Arabia

ABSTRACT

This study aims to provide an empirical investigation of different factors that could affect AI adoption in healthcare. Since prior research has overlooked AI adoption in healthcare, especially in the Arab context, this research in progress can fill this untapped gap and develop a theoretical framework to evaluate the customer-concerned factors (i.e., trust and privacy concerns) across different healthcare services. Due to its good generalizability, a theory of planned behavior can fit well to the healthcare context and hence can provide an adequate theoretical lens to understand the phenomenon of AI adoption. This study can expand our knowledge of AI and highlight the importance of its role to reinforce the provided healthcare services as well as meet the pressing patients' needs for better quality.

KEYWORDS

AI, Theory of Planned Behavior, Adoption, Healthcare, Trust, Privacy

1. INTRODUCTION

Artificial intelligence (AI), with its ability to transform global economy and identify strategic necessities, is one of the most rapidly developing fields across various sectors. Prior research of AI has been conducted across various contexts such as identifying fault types and locations of power transmission lines (Hassan et al. 2017), detecting the consequences of cancer diseases (Kuboń et al. 2017), and increasing the efficiency of oil drilling (Hegde & Gray, 2017). AI, in essence, can effectively help in executing various human tasks, such as decision making, speech recognition, visual perception, and translation of languages (Dande & Samant, 2018).

As per McKinsey's report (2017), AI is composed of five technological areas; autonomous vehicles, natural language processing, computer vision, virtual agents, machine learning, and smart robotics. Machine learning is reported to receive the most investment among AI's areas with around 5-7 billion. This survey report, spanning 10 countries and 14 sectors, indicates that only 20% of the firms really adopt AI affiliated technologies in their business processes and 31% partially adopt, while 10% of these companies experiment and 40% contemplate. The firms of high tech, telecom, automotive, and financial sectors appear to be on a high AI adoption curve, whereas their counterparts of healthcare, education, travel sectors seem to be on a low AI adoption curve. Although AI in healthcare has become an essential tool, especially in diseases diagnosis, image recognition and interpretation, therapy recommendation, patient management, and telemedicine (Gorunescu, 2015), its adoption as indicated in McKinsey's report is lacking and needs further investigation to help understand its promising role across different healthcare services. This has been supported by Secinaro et al. (2021) who highlighted how emerging the use of AI in healthcare, which gives us a higher motivation to disclose to what extent AI can play a role in affecting health services, considering the patients' privacy and trust.

Healthcare organizations produce an enormous amount of data, which resides in different and uncoordinated repositories sources such as lab and imaging systems, electronic medical records, health-insurance claims, and physicians' notes. Besides this, the nature of such data makes it highly sensitive for access and disclosure and hence brings privacy with its regulatory issues to scene as well as trust. With such hurdles, AI has been less adopted in the healthcare industry. Accordingly, in this study, we incorporate privacy concerns (a cognitive factor) and trust (an emotional factor) into theory of planned behavior to explain healthcare's behavioral intention to adopt AI. By doing so, we aim to extend the explanatory power of theory planned behavior from a privacy perspective, while addressing its limited consideration of emotional factors. Hence, we would address the following research question; how trust and privacy concerns affect AI adoption in healthcare?

This paper contributes to theory and practice. Theoretically, this study would provide a better understanding for AI adoption and use in the healthcare sector and so could evaluate the market readiness and maturity especially in the Arab context. Second, it would to expand theoretical boundaries of theory of planned behavior by complementing it with privacy concerns and trust to provide more predictive power. Practically, the healthcare companies might be hesitant to move faster on adopting AI as they look for clear benefits of using this emerging technology. Therefore, this study can help those companies further understand the AI market and obtain different indications on how stable, profitable, and more importantly valuable to provide better services to their customers.

2. THEORETICAL BACKGROUND

2.1 Theory of Planned Behavior

Ajzen (1991) first introduced TPB that proposes the three elements of attitude, subjective norms, and perceived behavioral control and their impact on an individual's behavioral intention. Attitude refers to the extent to which an individual evaluates a specific behavior positively or negatively (Bergevoet et al. 2004). Subjective norms refer to the extent to which an individual performs or avoids a particular behavior according to the pressure of social circle. Perceived behavioral control refers to the extent to which an individual determines the level of difficulty to perform a specific behavior (Gird and Bagraim 2008).

Theory of planned behavior has been widely used in IS research. It has been regarded a very popular model because; 1) its capacity to provide a good explanation to people's social behavior (Ajzen 2011); and 2) its reliable generalizability across different disciplines, for instance, in education (Iakovleva et al. 2011; Pihie and Bagheri 2013), healthcare (Rashidian & Russell 2011; Sivell et al. 2013), consumer behaviors (Weisheng et al. 2014), mobile commerce (Mishra 2014), and entrepreneurship (Albashrawi and Alashoor, 2020).

Nevertheless, of its wide use in literature, theory of planned behavior has been criticized for its limited capacity of explaining individuals' behavioral intention (Conner and Armitage 1998) as well as its deficiency to include an emotional factor (Rapaport and Orbell 2000). On the other hand, Sunarti et al. (2021) highlight how serious privacy concerns among patients when applying AI. In the same vein, Schwalbe and Wahl (2020) underline that the current research hasn't focused much on the ethical consideration (i.e., privacy) when using and deploying AI applications in healthcare. Hence, this study can expand the theoretical boundary of theory of planned behavior and provide further comprehension for AI adoption and use in healthcare.

2.2 Related Work and Potential Hypotheses

In the context of artificial intelligence and its affiliated areas, several scholars have investigated its adoption and usage in various industries. For instance, Rana et al. (2014) have developed a case study to show that providing accurate predictions and insights from data can significantly lead to adoption of machine learning for software defect predications. Moták et al. (2017) have used technology acceptance model and theory of planned behavior to examine the adoption of autonomous shuttle among college students. They have found that perceived usefulness, group norm, and experience significantly predict college students' intention toward the use of autonomous shuttle. Riek (2017) with her descriptive study of healthcare robotics has identified five major elements that stakeholders consider when deploying robotic agents in healthcare; safety and reliability, usability and accessibility, cost effectiveness, clinical effectiveness, and capability and function. Buckley et al. (2018) have investigated the intended use of automated vehicles using both technology acceptance model and theory of planned behavior through a simulated experimental drive and survey, and shown that theory of planned behavior's three pillars, perceived usefulness, and trust significantly determine the intention to use automated vehicles among US participants. Burlina et al. (2017) have used machine learning and deep learning to evaluate ultrasound for classification of myositis and illustrated their high accuracy in such classification. Machin et al. (2018) have described the use of AI's techniques like genetic algorithm and fuzzy logic in intelligent transportation systems especially across vehicle control, traffic control and predication, and road safety and accident prediction. Cosmin (2011) has described expert systems, special sensors, and robots and automatic systems as intelligent agents and their adoption in agriculture. Tan and Shao (2015) have predicted student potential dropout in e-learning using machine learning by examining personal characteristics and academic performance for students. Hassan et al. (2017) have employed machine learning to detect fault types and locations of power transmission lines to help in increasing reliability. Boyko et al. (2018) have suggested that machine learning especially survivalNet can be effective in detecting the consequences of cancer diseases.

Many other studies have used artificial intelligence techniques across different contexts, for example, in predicating consumers' preferences with organic food (Kuboń et al. 2017), shortening the behavioral diagnosis of autism (Wall et al. 2012), predicting pressure drops in rough pipes (Sahai et al. 2017), and increasing the efficiency of oil drilling for nearby wells (Hegde and Gray, 2017). It appears that many studies have been conducted in the domain of AI, though the literature lacks to reveal the big role of AI on healthcare and especially it further lacks to understand the AI adoption and use in the Arab context. Accordingly, we would develop hypotheses that evaluate the relationships between the three elements of theory of planned behavior, besides privacy concerns and trust, and AI adoption.

In the next research progress, we will develop a research model that provides underlying theoretical lens used to investigate the adoption of AI in healthcare and rationalizes the following hypotheses:

H1: Attitude is positively related to the adoption of AI
H2: Subjective norm is positively related to the adoption of AI
H3: Perceived behavioral control is positively related to the adoption of AI
H4: Trust is positively related to the adoption of AI
H5: Privacy concern is negatively related to the adoption of AI

3. RESEARCH METHOD AND CONCLUSION

In the next phase of our research, we will include a field survey to collect the study data and test the postulated relationships. All study variables will be adapted from well-established indicators from prior research to ensure better reliability, while will be measured using a 7-Point Likert Scale to ensure greater variance with 7 (strongly agree) and 1 (strongly disagree). By such, we can ensure better alignment of both construct and internal validity, though external validity may not be satisfied due to cross-sectional data of the survey. Although the study research design can establish a further empirical evidence of how TPB's factors are associated with AI adoption besides trust and privacy, future research should use a longitudinal research design to tackle the external validity. However, demographic variables will be collected to understand the study sample and control for their effect on the hypothesized relationships.

This research-in-progress work will use TPB as a theoretical lens and focus on revealing the influencing factors, in particular privacy concerns and trust, to streamline AI adoption in the healthcare sector. As such area has received a little attention in IS literature, this study can expand the existing knowledge of AI adoption and provide a ground where future studies can build on. Investigating the AI adoption in the Arab region can add a more layer of understating for this under-investigated context. In summary, this work will add a theoretical and practical value through extending the boundaries of TPB and addressing the market need by providing a better comprehension of this emerging phenomenon.

REFERENCES

Albashrawi M. and Alashoor, T., 2020. Entrepreneurial Intention: The Impact of General Computer Self-Efficacy and Computer Anxiety. *Interacting with Computers*, Vol. 32, No. 2, pp118-131.

Ajzen I., 1991. The Theory of Planned Behavior. *Organizational Behavior and Human Decision Processes,* Vol. 50, No. 2, pp. 179-211.

Ajzen I., 2011. The Theory of Planned Behavior: Reactions and Reflections. *Psychology and Health,* Vol. 26, No. 9, pp 113-1127.

Bergevoet R. et al, 2004. Entrepreneurial Behaviour of Dutch Dairy Farmers under A Milk Quota System: Goals, Objectives and Attitudes. *Agricultural Systems,* Vol. 80, No. 1, pp 1-21.

Boyko N. et al, 2018. Use of Machine Learning in the Forecast of Clinical Consequences of Cancer Diseases. *Proceedings of* 7th Mediterranean Conference on Embedded Computing (MECO), Budva, Montenegro, pp. 1-6.

Buckley L. et al, 2018. Psychosocial Factors Associated with Intended Use of Automated Vehicles: A Simulated Driving Study. *Accident Analysis & Prevention,* Vol. 115, pp 202-208.

Burlina P. et al, 2017. Automated Diagnosis of Myositis from Muscle Ultrasound: Exploring the Use of Machine Learning and Deep Learning Methods. *PloS one*, Vol. 12, No. 8.

Conner M. et al, 1998. Extending the Theory of Planned Behavior: A Review and Avenues for Future Research. *Journal of Applied Social Psychology,* Vol. 28, pp 1429-1464.

Cosmin P. et al, 2011. Adoption of Artificial Intelligence in Agriculture. *Bulletin UASVM Agriculture*, Vol. 68, No. 1.

Dande P. et al, 2018. Acquaintance to Artificial Neural Networks and Use of Artificial Intelligence as a Diagnostic Tool for Tuberculosis: A Review. *Tuberculosis*, Vol. 108, pp 1-9.

Hasan A. et al, 2017. The Use of Machine Learning Techniques to Classify Power Transmission Line Fault Types and Locations. *Proceedings of Optimization of Electrical and Electronic Equipment (OPTIM) & Intl Aegean Conference on Electrical Machines and Power Electronics (ACEMP)*, Brasov, Romania, pp. 221-226.

Hegde, C. and Gray, K. E., 2017. Use of Machine Learning and Data Analytics to Increase Drilling Efficiency for Nearby Wells. *Journal of Natural Gas Science and Engineering*, Vol. 40, pp 327-335.

Kubon M. et al, 2017. Use of Artificial Intelligence Methods for Investigating Purchase Preferences of Clients of Organic Farms. *Proceedings of 17th International Multidisciplinary Scientific GeoConference SGEM 2017*, Vienna, Austria, pp. 1099-1106.

Gorunescu F., 2015. Intelligent Decision Systems in Medicine: A Short Survey on Medical Diagnosis and Patient Management. *Proceedings of E-Health and Bioengineering Conference (EHB)*, Iasi, Romania, pp. 1-9.

Gird, A. and Bagraim, J. J., 2008. The Theory of Planned Behaviour as Predictor of Rntrepreneurial Intent Amongst Final-Year University Students. *South African Journal of Psychology,* Vol. 38, No. 4, pp 711-724.

Iakovleva T. et al, 2011. Entrepreneurial Intentions in Developing and Developed Countries. *Education and Training,* Vol. 53, No. 5, pp 353-370.

Machin M. et al, 2018. On the Use of Artificial Intelligence Techniques in Intelligent Transportation Systems. *Proceedings of Wireless Communications and Networking Conference Workshops (WCNCW)*, Barcelona, Spain, pp. 332-337.

Mishra S., 2014. Adoption of M-Commerce in India: Applying Theory of Planned Behaviour Model. *Journal of Internet Banking and Commerce,* Vol. 19, No. 1, pp 1-17.

Moták L. et al, 2017. Antecedent Variables of Intentions to Use An Autonomous Shuttle: Moving beyond TAM and TPB?. *European Review of Applied Psychology,* Vol. 67, No. 5, pp 269-278.

Pihie Z. A. L. and Bagheri, A., 2013. Students' Entrepreneurial Regulation and Intention to Become an Entrepreneur: A Comparison between Public and Private Universities. *South African Journal of Business Management,* Vol. 44, No. 4, pp 25-32.

Rana R. et al, 2014. The Adoption of Machine Learning Techniques for Software Defect Prediction: An Initial Industrial Validation. *Proceedings of Conference on Knowledge-Based Software Engineering,* Volgograd, Russia, pp. 270-285.

Rapaport P. and Orbell, S., 2000. Augmenting the Theory of Planned Behaviour: Motivation to Provide Practical Assistance and Emotional Support to Parents. *Psychology and Health,* Vol. 15, pp 309-324.

Rashidian A. and Russell, I., 2011. Intentions and Statins Prescribing: Can the Theory of Planned Behaviour Explain Physician Behaviour in Following Guideline Recommendations? *Journal of Evaluation in Clinical Practice,* Vol. 17, No. 4, pp 749-757.

Riek L., 2017. Healthcare Robotics. *Communications of the ACM*, Vol. 60, No. 11, pp 68-78.

Sahai S. et al, 2017. Use of Artificial Neural Network to Predict Pressure Drop in Rough Pipes. Proceedings of Computing Methodologies and Communications (ICCMC), Erode, India, pp. 452-455.

Schwalbe, N., and Wahl, B. 2020. Artificial Intelligence and the Future of Global Health. *The Lancet*, Vol. 395, No. 10236, pp 1579-1586.

Secinaro, S. et al, 2021. The Role of Artificial Intelligence in Healthcare: A Structured Literature Review. *BMC Medical Informatics and Decision Making*, Vol. 21, No. 1, pp 1-23.

Sivell S. et al., 2013. Factors Influencing the Surgery Intentions and Choices of Women with Early Breast Cancer: The Predictive Utility of An Extended Theory of Planned Behaviour. *BMC Medical Informatics and Decision Making,* Vol. 13, No. 1, pp 1-8.

Sunarti, S. et al, 2021. Artificial Intelligence in Healthcare: Opportunities and Risk for Future. *Gaceta Sanitaria*, Vol. 35, pp 67-70.

Tan M. and Shao, P., 2015. Prediction of Student Dropout in E-Learning Program through the Use of Machine Learning Method. *International Journal of Emerging Technologies in Learning*, Vol. 10, No. 1, pp 11-17.

Wall D. P. et al, 2012. Use of Artificial Intelligence to Shorten the Behavioral Diagnosis of Autism. *PloS one*, Vol. 7, No. 8.

Weisheng C. et al, 2014. Consumer Behavior toward Counterfeit Sporting Goods. *Social Behavior and Personality,* Vol. 42, No. 4, pp 615-624.